# Baby Stats!

## An Introduction to Statistics in Social Sciences

**2nd Edition Updated**

**Rachel A. Vannatta**
Bowling Green State University
http://www.babystatsbook.com

ISBN- 978-1-716-42068-9
Paperback

# Brief Contents


## Module

### 1 Introductory Concepts
Part 1. The Concepts....................................... 1
Part 2. The Learning Guide ............................ 8

### 2 Descriptive Statistics: Counting
Part 1. The Concepts..................................... 15
Part 2. The Learning Guide ........................... 23

### 3 Descriptive Statistics: Measures
Part 1. The Concepts..................................... 39
Part 2. The Learning Guide ........................... 46

### 4 Probability and z-scores
Part 1. The Concepts..................................... 57
Part 2. The Learning Guide ........................... 63

### 5 Distribution of Sample Means
Part 1. The Concepts..................................... 73
Part 2. The Learning Guide ........................... 79

### 6 Hypothesis Testing
Part 1. The Concepts..................................... 89
Part 2. The Learning Guide ........................ 102

### 7 The t Statistic
Part 1. The Concepts.................................. 121
Part 2. The Learning Guide ........................ 127

### 8 t-Test of Independent Samples
Part 1. The Concepts.................................. 147
Part 2. The Learning Guide ........................ 155

## Module

### 9 t-Test of Related Samples
Part 1. The Concepts .................................. 173
Part 2. The Learning Guide........................ 180

### 10 ANOVA: Analysis of Variance
Part 1. The Concepts ..................................197
Part 2. The Learning Guide.........................204

### 11 Correlation & Regression
Part 1. The Concepts ..................................219
Part 2. The Learning Guide.........................228

### 12 Chi-Square
Part 1. The Concepts ..................................245
Part 2. The Learning Guide.........................253

### 13 All Together Now!
The Concepts & Learning Guide ..............271

## Appendices
A. The *z* Distribution...............................279
B. Power Table for *z*-Test.......................283
C. The *t* Distribution ...............................284
D1. Power: *t* Single and *t* Related.............285
D2. Power: *t* independent..........................286
E. The *F* Distribution..............................287
F. Pearson Correlation.............................289
G. Chi-Square .........................................290
H. Baby Stats! Answer Key ......................291

# Table of Contents

(V sections are addressed in Module Videos)


**Module 1: Introductory Concepts........................1**

**Part 1: The Concepts**

1.11 Where do data come from? ................................ 1
1.12 Types of Statistics: Descriptive and Inferential...... 3
1.13 Types of Variables: Categorical/Quantitative, Independent/Dependent..................................... 3
1.14 Types of Relationships Explored through Statistics: Causal and Mutual ............................................. 4
1.15 Types of Research Designs ................................ 5
Inclusivity: The Limitations of Statistics .............. 7
1.16 Module Summary ............................................. 8

**Part 2: The Learning Guide**

1.21V Where do data come from? ................................ 9
1.22V Types of Statistics: Descriptive and Inferential...... 9
1.23V Types of Variables: Categorical/Quantitative, Independent/Dependent..................................... 9
1.24V Types of Relationships Explored through Statistics: Causal and Mutual ........................................... 10
1.25V Types of Research Designs ............................... 11
1.26V Examples....................................................... 11
1.27V Additional Practice ......................................... 12
1.28 Exercises
Reviewing the Concepts ............................... 13
Applying the Concepts ................................ 13

**Module 2: Descriptive Statistics: Counting.... 15**

**Part 1: The Concepts**

2.11 Intro to Frequency Distributions: Definition, Proportion, Percentages.................................... 16
2.12 Types of Frequency Distribution Graphs ............. 17
2.13 Creating a Grouped Frequency Distribution......... 18
2.14 Shapes of Frequency Distributions: Normal, Positive, Negative........................................... 19
2.15 Misuse of Statistical Graphs.............................. 19
2.16 Module Summary ............................................ 22

**Part 2: The Learning Guide**

2.21V Intro to Frequency Distributions: Definition, Proportion, Percentages.................................... 23
2.22V Types of Frequency Distribution Graphs ............. 24
2.23V Creating a Grouped Frequency Distribution......... 24
2.24V Shapes of Frequency Distribution: Normal, Positive, Negative........................................... 25
2.25V Misuse of Statistical Graphs ............................. 26
2.26V Examples....................................................... 28
2.27V Additional Practice ......................................... 29
2.28 Activity ........................................................ 30
2.29V In the Literature.............................................. 31
2.30 Using the Computer......................................... 32
2.31 Exercises
Reviewing the Concepts .............................. 35
Interpreting Results...................................... 36
Conducting the Analysis ............................... 38

**Module 3: Descriptive Statistics: Measures ....39**

**Part 1: The Concepts**

3.11 Measures of Central Tendency: Mean, Median, Mode ............................................................40
3.12 Measures of Central Tendency and Distributions ..40
3.13 Measures of Variability: Range and Standard Deviation........................................................42
3.14 Standard Deviation for a Sample........................43
3.15 Standard Deviation and the Normal Distribution...44
3.16 Module Summary............................................45

**Part 2: The Learning Guide**

3.21V Measures of Central Tendency: Mean, Median, Mode ............................................................46
3.22V Measures of Central Tendency and Distributions ..46
3.23V Measures of Variability: Range and Standard Deviation........................................................47
3.24V Standard Deviation for a Sample........................48
3.25V Standard Deviation and the Normal Distribution...48
3.26V Examples........................................................49
3.27V Additional Practice ..........................................50
3.28V Hands-on Activity: The Impact of Standard Deviation........................................................51
3.29V In the Literature ..............................................52
3.30 Using the Computer..........................................53
3.31 Exercises
Reviewing the Concepts ...............................54
Interpreting Results.......................................55
Conducting the Analysis ...............................57

**Module 4: Probability and *z*-scores................. 59**

**Part 1: The Concepts**

4.11 Introduction to Probability................................60
4.12 Definition and Calculation of a *z*-score ...............60
4.13 The Unit Normal Table .....................................61
4.14 Probability and *z*-scores ...................................62
4.15 Using a *z*-Score to Make Comparisons to Other Distributions...................................................63
4.16 Module Summary............................................64

**Part 2: The Learning Guide**

4.21V Introduction to Probability................................65
4.22V Definition and Calculation of a *z*-Score...............65
4.23V The Unit Normal Table .....................................66
4.24V Probability and *z*-scores ...................................67
4.25V Using a *z*-Score to Make Comparisons to Other Distributions.................................................. 68
4.26V Examples........................................................68
4.27V Additional Practice ..........................................69
4.28V Applet Activity: Normal Distribution ..................70
4.29 Exercises
Reviewing the Concepts ...............................71

**Module 5: Distribution of Sample Means** ........ 73
**Part 1: The Concepts**
5.11 Distribution of Sample Means ........ 74
5.12 Definition and Calculation of Standard Error ....... 75
5.13 Probability and the Distribution of Sample Means 75
5.14 Module Summary ........ 78
**Part 2: The Learning Guide**
5.21V Distribution of Sample Means ........ 79
5.22V Definition and Calculation of Standard Error ....... 80
5.23V Probability and the Distribution of Sample Means 80
5.24V A Complete Example ........ 82
5.25V Additional Practice ........ 82
5.26V Activity: Sampling Distribution Applet ........ 83
5.27V In the Literature ........ 84
5.28 Exercises
Reviewing the Concepts ........ 85

**Module 6: Hypothesis Testing** ........ 89
**Part 1: The Concepts**
6.11 Purpose and Steps of Hypothesis Testing ........ 90
6.12 Step 1: State the Hypotheses ........ 90
6.13 Step 2: Establish Significance Criteria ........ 92
6.14 Step 3: Collect and Analyze Data ........ 93
6.15 Step 4: Evaluate Null Hypothesis and Draw Conclusion ........ 93
6.16 Errors in Hypothesis Testing ........ 94
6.17 Assumptions of a *z*-Test ........ 95
6.18 Issues with Hypothesis Testing ........ 95
6.19 Effect Size ........ 96
6.20 Estimation with Confidence Intervals ........ 96
6.21 Power ........ 97
6.22 Directional (One-tailed) Hypothesis Tests ........ 98
6.23 Module Summary ........ 100
**Part 2: The Learning Guide**
6.21V Purpose and Steps of Hypothesis Testing ........ 102
6.22V Step 1: State the Hypotheses ........ 102
6.23V Step 2: Establish Significance Criteria ........ 103
6.24V Step 3: Collect and Analyze Data ........ 104
6.25V Step 4: Evaluate Null Hypothesis and Draw Conclusion ........ 105
6.26V Errors in Hypothesis Testing ........ 106
6.27V Assumptions of a *z*-Test ........ 106
6.28V Issues with Hypothesis Testing ........ 106
6.29V Effect Size ........ 106
6.30V Estimation with Confidence Intervals ........ 106
6.31V Power ........ 107
6.32V Directional (One-tailed) Hypothesis Tests ........ 107
6.33V A Complete Example ........ 110
6.34V Additional Practice ........ 111
6.35V Activity: *p* and *z* Applet ........ 113
6.36 Using the Computer ........ 114
6.37 Exercises
Reviewing the Concepts ........ 115
Interpreting Results ........ 116
Conducting Analysis ........ 118

**Module 7: The *t* Statistic** ........ 121
**Part 1: The Concepts**
7.11 Distribution of Sample Means ........ 122
7.12 Estimation with *t*-Test of Single Sample ........ 125
7.13 Effect Size and Power ........ 125
7.14 Reporting Results ........ 126
7.15 Module Summary ........ 127
**Part 2: The Learning Guide**
7.21V The *t* Statistic ........ 127
7.22V Estimation with *t*-Test of Single Sample ........ 130
7.23V Effect Size and Power ........ 131
7.24V Reporting Results ........ 131
7.25V A Complete Example ........ 132
7.26V Additional Practice ........ 133
7.27 Activity: Chips Ahoy ........ 135
7.28V In the Literature ........ 136
7.29 Using the Computer ........ 138
7.30 Exercises
Reviewing the Concepts ........ 139
Interpreting Results ........ 140
Conducting Analysis ........ 144

**Module 8: *t*-Test of Independent Samples** ..... 147
**Part 1: The Concepts**
8.11 *t*-Test of Independent Samples ........ 148
8.12 Estimation with *t*-Test of Independent Samples .. 150
8.13 Effect Size ........ 151
8.14 Power ........ 152
8.15 Reporting Results ........ 152
8.16 Directional (One-tailed) Hypothesis Tests ........ 153
8.17 Module Summary ........ 154
**Part 2: The Learning Guide**
8.21V *t*-Test of Independent Samples ........ 155
8.22V Estimation with *t*-Test of Independent Samples .. 156
8.23V Effect Size ........ 156
8.24V Power ........ 157
8.25V Reporting Results ........ 157
8.26V Directional (One-tailed) Hypothesis Tests ........ 157
8.27V Additional Practice ........ 159
8.28 Hands-on Activity: Coke vs Pepsi Experiment... 161
8.29V In the Literature ........ 163
8.30 Using the Computer ........ 164
8.31 Exercises
Reviewing the Concepts ........ 166
Interpreting Results ........ 167
Conducting Analysis ........ 171

**Module 9: *t*-Test of Related Samples** ........ 173
**Part 1: The Concepts**
9.11 *t*-Test of Related Samples ........ 174
9.12 Estimation with *t*-Test of Related Samples ........ 176
9.13 Effect Size and Power ........ 176
9.14 Reporting Results ........ 177
9.15 Directional (One-tailed) Hypothesis Test ........ 177
9.16 Module Summary ........ 179
**Part 2: The Learning Guide**
9.21V *t*-Test of Related Samples ........ 180
9.22V Estimation with *t*-Test of Related Samples ........ 181
9.23V Effect Size and Power ........ 182
9.24V Reporting Results ........ 182
9.25V Directional (One-tailed) Hypothesis Test ........ 182
9.26V Additional Practice ........ 184
9.27 Hands-on Activity: Coke vs Pepsi Experiment Continued ........ 186
9.28V In the Literature ........ 187
9.29 Using the Computer ........ 188
9.30 Exercises
Reviewing the Concepts ........ 189
Interpreting Results ........ 190
Conducting Analysis ........ 194

**Module 10: Analysis of Variance (ANOVA)...197**

**Part 1: The Concepts**

10.11 ANOVA: Purpose and Hypothesis Notation ...... 198
10.12 The Concepts in Calculating ANOVA *F*-ratio.... 198
10.13 The *F* Distribution & Determining Significance. 199
Calculating the F-Ratio (F-bomb—Ugh!) ......... 200
10.14 Effect Size and Power .................................... 202
10.15 Post Hoc Tests................................................ 202
10.16 Reporting the Results ..................................... 203
10.17 Module Summary ........................................... 203

**Part 2: The Learning Guide**

10.21V ANOVA: Purpose and Hypothesis Notation ...... 204
10.22V The Concepts in Calculating ANOVA *F*-ratio.... 204
10.23V The *F* Distribution & Determining Significance. 204
10.24V Effect Size and Power .................................... 205
10.25V Post Hoc Tests................................................ 205
10.26V Reporting the Results ..................................... 206
10.27V A Complete Example ..................................... 207
10.28V Additional Practice ........................................ 208
10.29V Hands-on Activity: *F*-Ratio Applet................... 209
10.30V In the Literature.............................................. 210
10.31 Using the Computer ....................................... 211
10.32 Exercises
Reviewing the Concepts ............................. 212
Interpreting Results .................................... 213
Conducting Analysis .................................. 217

**Module 11: Correlation & Regression...........219**

**Part 1: The Concepts**

11.11 Characteristics of Correlation: Direction, Form, Degree.......................................................... 220
11.12 Calculation and Interpretation of the Pearson Correlation Coefficient.................................. 221
11.13 Coefficient of Determination ........................... 223
11.14 Hypotheses Notation with Pearson Correlation .. 223
11.15 Reporting the Results ..................................... 224
11.16 Regression .................................................... 224
11.17 Module Summary ........................................... 226

**Part 2: The Learning Guide**

11.21V Characteristics of Correlation: Direction, Form, Degree.......................................................... 228
11.22V Calculation and Interpretation of the Pearson Correlation Coefficient.................................. 229
11.23V Coefficient of Determination ........................... 229
11.24V Hypotheses Notation with Pearson Correlation .. 230
11.25V Reporting the Results ..................................... 230
11.26V Regression .................................................... 230
11.27V Additional Practice ........................................ 232
11.28 Hands-on Activities ........................................ 233
11.29V In the Literature.............................................. 234
11.30 Using the Computer ....................................... 235
11.31 Exercises
Reviewing the Concepts ............................. 237
Interpreting Results .................................... 238
Conducting Analysis .................................. 242

**Module 12: Chi Square Tests...........................245**

**Part 1: The Concepts**

12.11 Chi Square Goodness of Fit..............................246
12.12 Chi Square Test of Independence......................248
12.13 Effect Size.....................................................250
12.14 Assumptions..................................................251
12.15 Reporting the Results......................................251
12.16 Module Summary...........................................251

**Part 2: The Learning Guide**

12.21V Chi Square Goodness of Fit..............................253
12.22V Chi Square Test of Independence......................255
12.23V Effect Size.....................................................257
12.24V Assumptions..................................................257
12.25V Reporting the Results......................................257
12.26V A Complete Example: Chi Square Goodness of Fit .......................................................................258
A Complete Example: Chi Square Test of Independence.................................................259
12.27 Hands-on Activity ..........................................260
12.28V In the Literature: Test of Independence.............261
12.29 Using the Computer: Chi Square Goodness of Fit .......................................................................262
12.30 Using the Computer: Chi Square Test of Independence.................................................263
12.31 Exercises
Reviewing the Concepts ..............................265
Interpreting Results.....................................266
Conducting Analysis ...................................269

**Module 13: All Together Now! .......................271**

**The Concepts & Learning Guide**

13.11V Overview of Statistical Tests ...........................272
13.12V Determining the Appropriate Statistical Test ......273
13.13V Effect Sizes...................................................275
13.14V The Power of Statistics ..................................276
13.15 Additional Practice.........................................276
13.16 Activity ........................................................277
13.17 Exercises ......................................................277

**Appendices**

A. The *z* Distribution...............................................279
B. Power Table for *z*-Test.........................................283
C. The *t* Distribution ...............................................284
D1. Power: *t* Single and *t* Related ...............................285
D2. Power: *t* Independent ..........................................286
E. The *F* Distribution ...............................................287
F. Pearson Correlation...............................................289
G. Chi-Square.........................................................290
H. Baby Stats! Answer Key.......................................291

# About the Author

Dr. Rachel Vannatta is a Professor at Bowling Green State University (Ohio). In her 25 years of teaching in higher education, she has focused on creating more accessible and relatable statistics content. Since 2004, she has been teaching statistics in an online environment with videos and course packets. *Baby Stats!* is the product of fourteen years of experimenting with various instructional methods to better engage students in the learning process. Although she is a self-proclaimed numbers geek, numbers and statistics didn't always come easy. As a result, she is always thinking of ways in which she can improve her instruction to guide student understanding and facilitate a love of statistics!

Dr. Vannatta lives in Ohio with her five children, three grandchildren, and a great dog named Ole!

# About Baby Stats!

Specifically designed for an online or hybrid learning environment, *Baby Stats!* provides three distinct resources to support student learning.

- The Concepts is text-based and comparable to a traditional textbook but focuses on key concepts to keep the length down to 6-7 pages for each module.
- The Learning Guide is a workbook that guides the student through the module videos. The Learning Guide presents: notes for the video lecture; examples; activities; step-by-step instruction for using SPSS and StatCrunch; and exercises that facilitate conceptual understanding, interpretation of output and literature results, and application of analysis. **A paper version of the Learning Guide is essential while viewing the videos.**
- Each module video simulates face-to-face classes in which content is presented by the author and facilitates interaction with the content through reinforcing activities, practice problems. Videos typically run 30-45 minutes in length and are available for free at

http://www.babystatsbook.com

The name *Baby Stats!* came from my doctoral students, who always referred to the prerequisite introductory course as "Baby Stats." After adopting this title, I decided to utilize my children's art work to support the theme. All module cover drawings were created by my children (when they were 3 or 4-year-old) with the exception of the *F*-bomb of course! Please know that the title is not meant to be derogatory in that you the students are "babies." Rather the title just plays off the idea that such an introductory course provides all the foundational concepts necessary for more advanced study in statistics.

# Module 1

## Introductory Concepts

### Learning Targets

After completing Module 1, you should be able to:

- Comprehend and utilize basic statistical terms in the research process: population ($N$), sample ($n$), raw data, random sampling methods, parameter, statistic, descriptive statistics, inferential statistics, sampling error, data, variable, measurement scale, categorical (nominal) variable, quantitative (ordinal, interval, ratio) variable, independent variable, dependent variable, confounding variable, causal relationship, mutual relationship
- Analyze and identify the various components in research questions/scenarios: measurement scale of variables, roles of relationship (independent and dependent variables), and types of relationship (mutual or causal).
- Identify the type of research design being utilized in research questions/scenarios: causal (experimental, quasi-experimental, causal-comparative), and mutual (correlational).

# Part 1: The Concepts

Statistics are everywhere! The use of numbers in the form of statistics has become a mandatory means of supporting an argument for some kind of action. Whether it is a company's decision to create a new flavor of toothpaste or a university's decision to change its admissions criteria, the use of data and statistics has become the NORM in the decision-making. This book will attempt to arm you with some basic skills for conducting simple statistical analyses and critically examining statistical results. This module will lay the foundation of statistical concepts and terminology so that we can delve a bit deeper in into ***Baby Stats!***

### 1.11 Where do data come from?

Statistics are numbers that attempt to summarize and describe data. Data typically come from a sample of individuals, since it is usually too difficult to gather data from the entire population. While gathering data from the population may be more accurate, it is extremely costly and labor-intensive and sometimes nearly impossible. Even the U.S. government recognizes the challenges in gathering data from the population as it conducts the U.S. census only every 10 years. In order to create more timely and up-to-date snapshots of the country's economic well-being, the Current Population Survey is used to collect data from a sample of about 72,000 U.S. households every month. Keep in mind, the population is not always "everyone who lives in the country or world," rather the ***population*** is the bigger group of people we want to study and hope to generalize our results to. The ***sample*** is the smaller group of individuals we actually study—the group that provides the actual ***raw data***. Characteristics of the sample often determine who the population is. Researchers will use notation to indicate the population and sample size. Typically, ***N*** refers to the size of the population and ***n*** represents the sample size. There are times when *N* is used to represent the total sample.

Suppose that Dr. Burns wants to study binge drinking among college freshmen at small liberal arts colleges. Since it is impossible for Dr. Burns to study every single college freshman enrolled in small liberal arts colleges in the U.S., Dr. Burn's studies freshmen enrolled at two nearby Midwest liberal arts colleges with undergraduate enrollments of 800-1,500 students. A total of 700 freshmen are invited to complete an online survey; 425 participate. So can Dr. Burns generalize his findings to all college freshmen in the U.S.? NO, quite the contrary! The sample of 425 students was generated from the population of 700 freshmen at two small liberal arts colleges. The true population is the 700 freshmen at the two specific liberal arts colleges. The broader population could possibly be freshmen at small Midwest liberal arts colleges. However, a closer look reveals that the sample is quite homogeneous in race with less than 5% minority. So who can Dr. Burns cautiously generalize his results to? Freshmen enrolled in small, Midwest liberal arts colleges with predominantly Caucasian students.

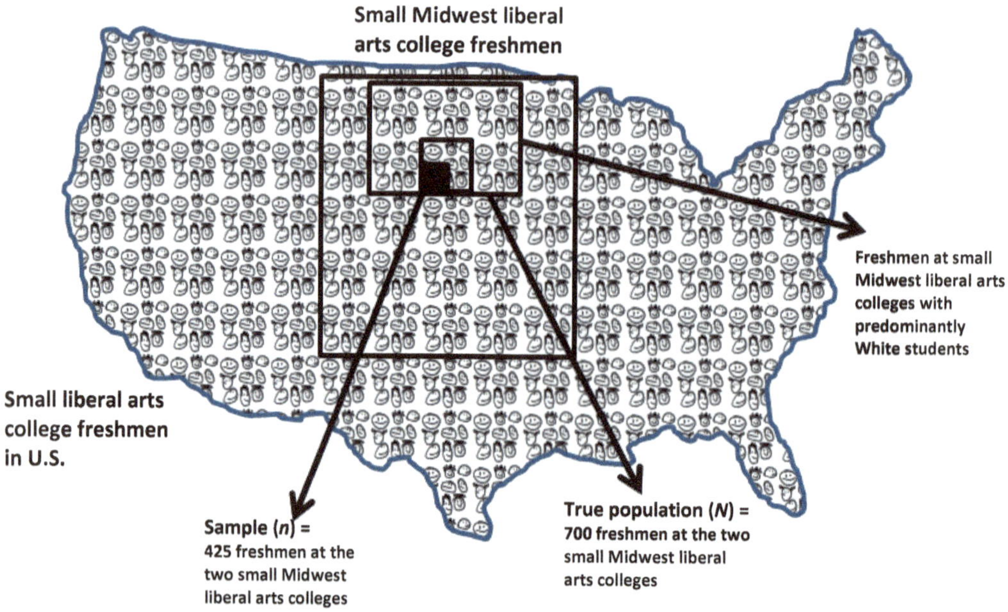


**Figure 1.1**
*Relationship between Populations and Sample*

Since the sample data and results are used to create a picture of the population, ensuring that the studied sample is representative of the population is of utmost importance. Most researchers attempt to use some type of ***random sampling method*** in which individuals within the population have an equal chance of being selected. Random selection helps ensure that the individuals represent the diverse characteristics across the population. As we later learn about the inferential techniques in this book, most of the tests assume that a random sample is used to generate the data. Unfortunately, random sampling is often difficult in social sciences. While non-random samples have never stopped most studies from proceeding, researchers must be extremely cautious in generalizing to the broader population when examining data from non-random samples.

A number that describes an aspect of the population a ***parameter***. Most assume that statistics are numbers that can be used to describe any set of individuals, whether a sample or a population, however, a ***statistic*** is a number that describes a sample and is used to estimate the population parameter.

**Margin of Error**

Likely you have seen a common method of reporting sampling error in how the media presents survey results—the margin of error. Typically, the media uses a 95% confidence level when calculating the margin of error.

In a December 2014, GPA Strategies conducted a telephone poll of 1,000 likely 2016 Oregon voters to determine support for increasing the minimum wage. Results indicate that 54% supported the increase of minimum wage, from $9.25 to $15 per hour. Margin of Error: +/- 3.5%.

This means that we can be 95% confident that 50.5% -57.5% of the Oregon voters would support the increase in minimum wage.

### 1.12 Types of Statistics: Descriptive and Inferential

A variety of statistics is used to organize, summarize, and interpret data. These statistical procedures may be classified into two types: descriptive and inferential. ***Descriptive statistics*** use procedures that organize and summarize raw data so that the consumer can get a quick picture of the sample. Such procedures include percentages, frequencies, means, tables, graphs, and charts. ***Inferential statistics*** are techniques that allow us to examine relationships between variables and generalize our results to the population by studying a sample. Inferential statistics are very important since we rarely ever study the entire population. However, it is impossible to select a sample that perfectly represents the population. As a result, there will always be some amount of error or difference between the sample and the population—this is called ***sampling error***. Researchers work hard to minimize sampling error by using random sampling and having an adequate sample size. In general, a larger sample helps to ensure adequate representation of the population, therefore decreasing error. The concept of error is huge in statistics and will be discussed in future modules.

### 1.13 Types of Variables: Categorical/Quantitative, Independent/Dependent

The task of research involves the collection of data—the gathering of information by making observations and recording measurements. Quantitative ***data*** (plural) are measurements or observations that have been converted to numbers. These data contain information about individuals— information that represents variables. A ***variable*** is a characteristic or condition that can vary or change across individuals. It can have different values for different individuals, such as eye color, weight, IQ, reading ability, personality type. A condition can change as well, such as location, treatment, or type of reinforcement. A variable can be characterized two ways as a result of its: 1) measurement scale, and 2) role in relationship. These variable aspects will help in determining the appropriate type of statistical analyses that is necessary.

#### Measurement Scale: Categorical or Quantitative?

Based upon a variable's numerical properties, it may be typed as either categorical or quantitative. A ***categorical variable*** uses a number that only represents a group or category, such as gender, race, religion, college major. The number does not have any numerical value. For example, gender may use three categories: 1=male, 2=female, 3=transgender. The number 1 only represents the male gender and does not have numerical value in that 1 would indicate male as the "lowest" gender. In addition, an individual can only fall into one of the three categories; a score of 2.5 is not possible. In contrast, a ***quantitative variable*** uses numbers with numerical value. For example, the variables of height, time, and IQ can be divided into infinite fractional parts. So for the variable of height, a low value of 18" is pretty small, while a high value of 78" is quite tall. In addition, it is possible for an individual to have a height of 55.28". Keep in mind, a quantitative variable can be transformed into a categorical variable. For example based upon heights of individuals, we can categorize them into short, average, and tall groups.

Researchers may also describe the measurement scale with more specificity using the four descriptors of: nominal, ordinal, interval, and ratio. Although we will not apply these scale descriptors in Baby Stats!, you need to be familiar with them as you may encounter these terms in manuscripts. ***Nominal*** is just another term for categorical. The word nominal actually means "having to do with names," hence the notion that numbers only represent a name of a group or category. The next scale is ***ordinal***, where numbers do have numerical value but only in terms of rank, which is usually based upon some other measure. Think of the winners of the 2016 Olympic Men's 100 m finals. Obviously, Usain Bolt came in first with the fastest time of 9.81 seconds. Second place had a time of 9.89, while third place crossed the line with a time of 9.91. Notice that Bolt beat second place by .08 seconds, while the gap between second and third place was .03 seconds. The interval or gap in times between two places is not consistent. In addition, the numerical value is typically reversed, where 1 (first) is the best. Another common scenario that applies to an ordinal scale is the use of a Likert scale, where level of agreement is measured using a four to five point scale in which one represents "strongly disagree" and four/five represents "strongly agree." Although the numerical value is now parallel with amount of agreement, meaning the higher the value the greater the agreement, the interval between agree and strongly agree is truly unknown and based upon an individual's thoughts and feelings since we forced the respondent to choose between these discrete levels. There is no option for 3.5. Because of the limitations associated with ordinal data, we will discuss some possible options in a bit.

The next measurement scale is ***interval***, where numbers have real value and true intervals that may divided into fractional parts. However, an interval scale does not have a <u>real</u> zero, where zero is truly "nothing" or complete absence of the variable. An interval variable has an arbitrary zero for the sake of convenience. For example, most tests would fall under an interval scale, since a zero doesn't necessarily mean a complete absence of reading or math ability. Rather the zero may mean the student didn't complete the test, didn't turn it in, or turned it in late. The zero is only the convenient starting place for scoring. The final measurement scale is ***ratio***, which has all the characteristics of interval scale but has a real zero. Money, time, height, weight are all examples of ratio variables. Because the notion of a "real zero" can get rather philosophical, many researchers just refer to quantitative variables as ***interval/ratio***. Another important point regarding these specific measurement scales is the handling of ordinal variables. While there are several statistical techniques to analyze ordinal variables, researchers will often choose to <u>treat</u> an ordinal variable as categorical OR interval/ratio for the sake of analysis. For example, many will treat an ordinal Likert-style variable as interval/ratio. Figure 1.2 presents the relationship between categorical and quantitative variables with the scales of nominal, ordinal, interval/ratio. Again, as we progress we will focus on the scale distinctions of categorical and quantitative.

**Figure 1.2**
*Measurement Scales*

| Scale | | Role of Numbers |
|---|---|---|
| Categorical | Nominal | No value; they only represent groups/categories. |
| | Ordinal | Numerical value but in terms of rank. |
| Quantitative | Interval | Actual value with equal intervals but has not "real" zero |
| | Ratio | Actual value with equal intervals AND has a "real" zero |

**Role of Relationship: Independent or Dependent?**

Research questions (RQs) typically examine relationships between or among variables. In each relationship being posed, variables play different roles. The two main roles we are focusing on at this point are: 1) explaining and 2) responding. The explaining role is played by the ***independent variable (IV)***, which explains or influences the change in the outcome variable, known as the dependent variable. Therefore, the ***dependent variable (DV)*** plays the responding role and measures the outcome or response. While independent and dependent variables can be categorical or quantitative, most of the analysis in this text will utilize a dependent variable that is quantitative. A quantitative dependent variable has many advantages that will be explained later and is essential for conducting most basic statistical techniques. So for now, assume that the RQs and scenarios presented will utilize a quantitative dependent variable. Since social sciences examine human behavior, it is impossible to statistically isolate the impact of the independent variable on the dependent variable. In other words, all sorts of other variables (some measured and some not) can change the outcome of the dependent variable. These "other" variables are referred to as ***confounding variables***.

## 1.14 Types of Relationships Explored through Statistics: Causal and Mutual

Most research questions pose one of two relationships: causal or mutual. The types of variables presented in a research question and how they work together determines the type of relationship being examined. The only way to examine cause and effect or causation is by comparing groups, which creates a categorical variable. When examining a ***causal relationship***, we are attempting to show that a change in the IV caused the DV to change. Often treatment and control groups are studied to show causation. Since most of our study in this textbook will utilize basic statistical techniques that require a quantitative dependent variable, when we examine a RQ and identify a variable as categorical, then it is likely the independent variable. And remember, if the IV is categorical, then a causal relationship is being examined. So the basic cause-effect scenario has an IV that is categorical and a DV that is quantitative. A causal RQ will often use key words such as cause, effect, increase, or decrease, to indicate that cause and effect is being examined.

**Causal Example**

**RQ:** Does the treatment of a <u>new curriculum on phonics</u> increase <u>reading achievement</u> among 1st grade students?

**Who?** 1st grade students

**Key Word?** Increase. Indicating a causal relationship so the IV needs to be categorical.

**Variables?**

- <u>New curriculum on phonics</u>—this is a treatment→ categorical.
- <u>Reading achievement</u>—represented by some test score→quantitative.

**IV?** New curriculum since it is the treatment and is categorical.

**DV?** Reading achievement—this is the outcome that we hope will change.

When both variables are quantitative, a ***mutual relationship*** is being examined. We cannot show that the IV caused a change in the DV, rather we can only show that as one variable increases, the other variable increases (or decreases). When one of the variables chronologically occurs before the other, this earlier variable is the IV as it can explain the change in DV.

**Mutual Example**

**RQ:** Does the number of books read at home during the school year positively relate to end of year reading achievement among 1st grade students?

**Who?** 1st grade students
**Key Word?** Relate. Indicating a mutual relationship so the IV will be quantitative
**Variables?**

- Number of books read at home—→ quantitative.
- Reading achievement—represented by some test score→quantitative.

**IV?** Number of books read at home occurs throughout the year, before reading achievement is measured.
**DV?** Reading achievement is measured at the end of the year and is the outcome that we hope will change.

In the mutual example, the relationship between number of books read at home and end of the year reading achievement was examined. While one understands that the more one reads the more reading skills a person has, the relational direction could easily change if the timing for measuring reading achievement was changed to the beginning of the year. This would flip the variables (IV/DV) so that reading achievement explains the number of books that one reads at home, indicating that the better readers read more books. In either case, the IV does not cause the increase in the DV; it can only explain. So the basic mutual relationship scenario has an IV that is quantitative and a DV that is quantitative. Often a mutual RQ will use key words such as relate, relationship, predict, and associate to indicate that a mutual relationship is being explored. Figure 1.3 shows how variable types and key words may vary by the relationship being examined.

**Figure 1.3**
*Differences in Relationship Type*

| | Causal | Mutual |
|---|---|---|
| Independent Variable | Categorical | Quantitative |
| Dependent Variable | Quantitative | Quantitative |
| Key Words | Cause<br>Effect<br>Increase/Decrease<br>Difference | Relate<br>Relationship<br>Predict<br>Associate |
| Research Design | Experimental<br>Quasi-Experimental<br>Causal-Comparative | Correlational |

## 1.15 Types of Research Designs

A researcher will use a variety of research designs to examine research questions—which design depends upon the relationship being explored, the variables being measured, and the sample being selected. We will take a very brief look at the four primary designs employed in social science research.

### Exploring Causation

Three research designs allow for the examination of cause and effect—experimental, quasi-experimental, and causal-comparative. Recall that groups must be compared (IV is categorical) in order to examine causation, thus these three designs will have a categorical independent variable. The most rigorous of these designs is experimental.

1) The ***experimental design*** follows the scientific method of implementing a treatment in one group (the treatment group) and withholding it from another (the control group). Therefore the IV (the treatment) is manipulated and controlled. The impact of the treatment is measured on some quantitative dependent variable. An important characteristic of experimental research is the creation of the groups, in that individuals must be randomly assigned to groups. The sample does not have to be randomly selected, but random assignment to groups must occur. The experimental design is often difficult to conduct in social sciences due to the requirement of random assignment, however it is quite common in medical research.

**Experimental Example**

**RQ:** Does the new drug, alirocumab, significantly decrease LDL (bad) cholesterol among high risk heart patients?

**Scenario:** 314 high risk heart patients were randomly assigned to two groups. Group 1 took the new drug; Group 2 took the statin, Zetia.

2) The ***quasi-experimental design*** is similar to experimental, BUT it does not utilize random assignment and therefore uses existing groups. The IV (treatment) is still being manipulated and being compared, using either a control group or a pre/post situation. The effect of the treatment is measured on the quantitative dependent variable. This type of design is quite common in education, since it is much easier to implement a treatment with existing groups such as classrooms, schools, and districts.

3) ***Causal-comparative design*** allows for group comparison, but often the categorical independent variable is not a result of a treatment but rather an innate characteristic, such as gender, race, religion, hair color. Since these types of characteristics rarely cause a change in a dependent variable, the exploration of causality is difficult. As such, the researcher must be extremely cautious in inferring cause and effect when comparing groups based upon participant traits. In such an instance, it is best to avoid causal wording and focus on group differences.

### Examining Mutual Relationship

Only one research design, ***correlational***, allows for the exploration of a mutual relationship between quantitative variables. A treatment is not implemented; groups are NOT being compared. Often researchers are interested in establishing a mutual relationship between two variables to use one variable to predict the other.

**Quasi-Experimental Example**

**RQ:** Does instructional format (flipped vs. traditional) significantly affect course grades among 11th grade English students?

**Scenario:** Ms. Johnson teaches four sections of 11th grade English. Two sections receive flipped instruction, where all content is presented outside of class and class time is used for practice and reinforcement. Semester course grades are compared.

**Causal-Comparative Example**

**RQ:** Does math achievement differ by gender among 8th grade students?

**Scenario:** Research continues to explore gender differences in mathematics, but notice that the focus is on gender differences not on gender causing differences in math achievement. Research has shown that many socio-cultural variables within the gender experience are at play.

**Correlational Example**

**RQ:** Does amount of exercise (minutes per week) significantly relate to Body Mass Index (BMI) among young adults?

**Scenario:** 100 young adults track their minutes exercising for one month. A weekly average is calculated for each participant. BMI is measured at the end of the month.

# Inclusivity: The Limitations of Statistics

When quantitative research and statistics in the social sciences emerged over 100 years ago, the socio-political culture of the United States was very different. Most research was conducted by white males, which provided a limited perspective. As our culture has evolved, the norms of gender, sexuality, race, and ethnicity have also changed. Today, gender identification is not limited to the binary choices of male and female but may include "Transgender," "Non-binary Gender," "Gender Non-conforming," and "Other" as well as additional response options. The measurement of race and ethnicity has continued to create confusion. While ethnicity refers to the cultural background of a person (nationality, customs, ancestry), race indicates physical characteristics (skin color, bone structure, etc.). Even the U.S. Census Bureau has struggled with ways to measure these characteristics. In 2010, the Census first posed a question regarding ethnicity (specifically Hispanic, Latino, or Spanish) and then asked about race (White, Black, Asian, Native-American/Alaskan Native, Native Hawaiian/Other Pacific Islander, and Other). Many individuals selected "Other," which unfortunately, did not present a clean description of the population. As a result, the 2020 Census is considering an item that combines race and ethnicity and provides numerous options for multiple selection.

While including more options to describe our samples is extremely helpful in understanding our participants, the actual numbers in these marginalized groups are often very small, which may lead to exclusion from further inferential analysis (due to a violation of test assumptions, which we will learn about later in this text). Therefore, the use of statistics has its limitations. Past research typically presents traditional binary gender and limited race/ethnic options. Even current research may have similar demographic limitations due to a variety of reasons: characteristics of the target population, the nature of the research, and the size of marginalized groups being too small to include in inferential analysis. By definition, quantitative research is designed to be generalizable to the population. Inferential statistics require a critical mass of responses to generate accurate and useful results. As such when conducting inferential analysis, you may need to merge groups or possibly omit groups from analysis, due to limited responses of marginalized groups.

Therefore as a consumer of research, you should be aware that the research community is struggling with ways to be inclusive, and as such past and current studies may not reflect the current views of inclusivity. Many studies in this text present traditional measures of gender and race. As our culture evolves and the identification with marginalized groups becomes less stigmatized, the integration and measurement of marginalized groups in quantitative research will hopefully increase. However, I acknowledge that there may be both conscious and unconscious bias in some of the examples used in this text, even though the material is primarily of a scientific nature.

As a potential researcher, you should be aware of the context and sensitivity of posing inclusive demographic questions. You may need to explain WHY such information is important to your study. Whenever possible, inclusive language and the acknowledgement of all people and their identities should be used to collect accurate data. However, the use of more sensitive and inclusive demographics should be appropriate to your study's:

- Target population (Are inclusive demographics integral to understanding your sample? Will respondents understand the options? Will questions or options be perceived as offensive?)
- Research questions (Are inclusive demographics integral to your research question?)
- Specific culture in which your research is being conducted (Are inclusive demographics appropriate to the studied culture?)

Finally, since the pace of change is ever-increasing, it is important to stay up to date on best practices for socially conscious research.

Special thanks to my Advanced Quantitative Methods class—Andrea Hauser, Kristin Hidinger, Brittany House, Jody Kunk, Travis Sheaffer, Yan Xiong, and Jeremy Zilmer—for inspiring me to address a sensitive but very important topic in statistics. Your assistance in crafting this section was a gift to my growth as a teacher and a writer. Thank you!

## 1.16 Module Summary

- Statistics are numbers that summarize and describe data.
- Data typically come for a sample of individuals.
  - Sample (*n*) is the smaller group of individuals that we actually study; selected from population, intended to represent the population
    - Statistic is a value that describes the sample; often used to estimate the population parameter
  - Population (*N*) is the bigger group of individuals that the researcher WISHES to study and hopes to generalize their results to.
    - Parameter is a value that describes the population
  - Random Sampling Method provides each individual in the population an equal chance of being selected.
    - Used to ensure representation of the population

**Types of Statistics**

- Descriptive Statistics organize and summarize raw data to create a quick picture of the sample.
- Inferential Statistics examine relationships between /among variables and study a sample and generalize results to a population.

- Variable is a characteristic/condition that can vary or change across individuals (gender, height, test scores, eye color, weight, IQ, reading ability); can be characterized in two ways as a result of its:
  1. Measurement properties
     - Categorical variable uses numbers to represent groups/categories (gender, major, ethnicity); number has no numerical value.
     - Quantitative variable uses numbers that have numerical value (height, test score, age).
  2. Role of relationship
     - Independent Variable (IV) <u>explains</u> or influences the change in the outcome variable (DV)
     - Dependent Variable (DV) plays the <u>responding</u> role and measures the outcome or response

**Types of Relationships**

- Causal compares groups (IV is categorical); examines how a change in the IV caused the DV to change
- Mutual examines relationship between quantitative variables; shows that as one variable increases the other variable increases (or decreases)

- The Research Design used in a study depends upon the relationship being explored, the variables being measured, and the sample being selected.
  - Exploring Causation—Three designs; all compare groups (IV is categorical)
    - Experimental—compares treatment and control groups, uses random assignment to groups.
    - Quasi-Experimental—examines effect of treatment; uses existing groups.
    - Causal Comparative— compares groups created by some categorical characteristic.
  - Exploring Mutual Relationship—one design
    - Correlational—studies relationships among 2 or more variables to explain for predict behaviors.

# Part 2: Learning Guide

## 1.21V Where do data come from?

Statistics are numbers that summarize and describe data.

- Data typically come from a sample of individuals.

Population (*N*)—the bigger group of individuals that the researcher WISHES to study and hopes to generalize their results to.

Sample (*n*)—the smaller group of individuals that we actually study; selected from population, intended to represent the population

- Random Sampling Method—each individual in the population has an equal chance of being selected
    - Used to ensure representation of the population

Parameter—value that describes the population

Statistic—value that describes the sample; often used to estimate the population parameter

## 1.22V Types of Statistics: Descriptive and Inferential

Descriptive Statistics—organize and summarize raw data to create a quick picture of the sample
Inferential Statistics—1) examine relationship between /among variables; 2) study a sample and generalize results to a population

- Sampling Error—amount of error between the sample statistic and the population
    - Random sampling and having adequate sample size are methods used to minimize sampling error.
    - Margin of Error is a common method of reporting sampling error.
        - Media will often report a 95% confidence level
        - **Example:** In December 2014, GPA Strategies conducted a telephone poll of 1,000 likely 2016 Oregon voters to determine support for increasing the minimum wage. Results indicate that 54% supported the increase of minimum wage, from $9.25 to $15 per hour. Margin of Error: +/- 3.5%. This means that we can be 95% confident that 50.5% -57.5% of the Oregon voters would support the increase in minimum wage.

## 1.23V Types of Variables: Categorical/Quantitative, Independent/Dependent

Quantitative data—measurements or observations converted to numbers

Variable—characteristic/condition that can vary or change across individuals (gender, height, test score, eye color, weight, IQ, reading ability); can be characterized two ways as a result of its:

1. Measurement properties
2. Role of relationship

### Measurement: Categorical or Quantitative?

Based upon a variable's measurement or numerical properties, a variable may be typed as either:

- Categorical Variable—uses numbers to represent groups or categories (e.g., gender, religion, classification of personality)
    - Number has no numerical value; number only represents a group
- Quantitative Variable—uses numbers with numerical value; can be divided into an infinite number of fractional parts (e.g., height, time, age)
    - Can be converted to categorical. Height: short, average, tall

Researchers may also use more specific measures scales: nominal, ordinal, interval, ratio.

| Scale | | Role of Numbers |
|---|---|---|
| Categorical | Nominal | No value; they only represent groups/categories. |
| | Ordinal | Numerical value but in terms of rank. |
| Quantitative | Interval | Actual value with equal intervals but has not "real" zero |
| | Ratio | Actual value with equal intervals AND has a "real" zero |

**Role of Relationship: Independent or Dependent?**
Research questions (RQs) typically examine relationships between or among variables.

Variables play different roles; the two main roles are:

- Independent Variable (IV)— explains or influences the change in the outcome variable, known as the dependent variable

> **Causal Example**
> **RQ:** Does the treatment of a new curriculum on phonics increase reading achievement among 1st grade students?
>
> **Who?** 1st grade students
> **Key Word?** Increase. Indicating a causal relationship so the IV needs to be categorical.
> **Variables?**
> - New curriculum on phonics—this is a treatment→ categorical.
> - Reading achievement—represented by some test score→quantitative.
>
> **IV?** New curriculum since it is the treatment and is categorical.
> **DV?** Reading achievement—this is the outcome that we hope will change.

- Dependent Variable (DV)— plays the responding role and measures the outcome or response; it's advantageous having a quantitative DV

Confounding Variable—a variable can change the outcome of the DV

**1.24V Types of Relationships Explored through Statistics: Mutual and Causal**
The types of variables presented in a research question and how they work together determines the type of relationship being examined.

Causal relationship attempts to show that a change in the IV caused the DV to change.

- Groups must be compared to examine cause and effect→ groups are created by a categorical variable

Mutual relationship attempts to show that as one variable increases the other variable increases (or decreases).

- Both variables are quantitative; cannot show cause and effect.
- When one of the variables chronologically occurs before the other, this earlier variable is the IV as it can explain the change in DV.

> **Mutual Example**
> **RQ:** Does the number of books read at home during the school year positively relate to end of year reading achievement among 1st grade students?
>
> **Who?** 1st grade students
> **Key Word?** Relate. Indicating a mutual relationship so the IV will be quantitative
> **Variables?**
> - Number of books read at home—→ quantitative.
> - Reading achievement—represented by some test score→quantitative.
>
> **IV?** Number of books read at home occurs throughout the year, before reading achievement is measured.
> **DV?** Reading achievement is measured at the end of the year and is the outcome that we hope will change.

Key words are often used in the research question to reflect the type of relationship being examined.

| | Causal | Mutual |
|---|---|---|
| **Independent Variable** | Categorical | Quantitative |
| **Dependent Variable** | Quantitative | Quantitative |
| **Key Words** | Cause<br>Effect<br>Increase/Decrease<br>Difference | Relate<br>Relationship<br>Predict<br>Associate |
| **Research Design** | Experimental<br>Quasi-Experimental<br>Causal-Comparative | Correlational |

**1.25V Types of Research Designs**

A variety of research designs are used to examine research questions—which design depends upon the relationship being explored, the variables being measured, and the sample being selected.

**Exploring Causation**

Three research designs explore causation—all have an IV that is categorical and a DV that is quantitative.

- **Experimental**—examines cause and effect; manipulates a treatment and tests the outcome; compares the experimental and control groups (groups are randomly created)
  - IV=categorical; DV= quantitative
    - **RQ:** Does the new drug, alirocumab, significantly decrease LDL (bad) cholesterol among high risk heart patients?
    - **Scenario:** 314 high risk heart patients were randomly assigned to two groups. Group 1 took the new drug; Group 2 took the statin, Zetia.

- **Quasi-Experimental**—examines cause and effect; indirectly manipulates a treatment and tests the outcome; compares the experimental and control groups (uses existing groups)
  - IV=categorical; DV= quantitative
    - **RQ:** Does instructional format (flipped vs. traditional) significantly affect course grades among 11th grade English students?
    - **Scenario:** Ms. Johnson teaches four sections of 11th grade English. Two sections receive flipped instruction, where all content is presented outside of class and class time is used for practice and reinforcement. Semester course grades are compared.

- **Causal Comparative**—examines cause and effect (cautiously); compares groups created by some categorical characteristic (gender, religion, ethnicity)
  - IV=categorical; DV= quantitative
    - **RQ:** Does math achievement differ by gender among 8th grade students?
    - **Scenario:** Research continues to explore gender differences in mathematics, but notice that the focus is on gender differences not on gender causing differences in math achievement. Research has shown that many socio-cultural variables within the gender experience are at play.

**Exploring Mutual Relationship**

Only one research design explores mutual relationship.

- **Correlational**—studies relationships among two or more variables to explain for predict behaviors
  - IV and DV are usually quantitative
    - **RQ:** Does amount of exercise (minutes per week) significantly relate to Body Mass Index (BMI) among young adults?
    - **Scenario:** 100 young adults track their minutes exercising for one month. A weekly average is calculated for each participant. BMI is measured at the end of the month.

**1.26V Examples**

In the following research questions, identify the independent and dependent variables and indicate if they are categorical or quantitative. Based upon the variables and relationship being examined, identify the research design.

1. Is there a significant relationship between college GPA and SAT scores among college freshmen?

   independent variable—

   dependent variable—

   research design—

2. Does receiving a special diet of oat bran significantly decrease cholesterol levels among middle-age adults? Note: Researcher compared a treatment group to a control group. Groups were created using random selection and assignment.

   independent variable—

   dependent variable—

   research design—

3. Does amount of extracurricular activity differ by major among college juniors?
   independent variable—

   dependent variable—

   research design—

4. Does receiving whole-language reading instruction increase reading achievement among elementary students? Note: Research compared treatment group (whole-language) to control group (traditional). Existing groups were used.
   independent variable—

   dependent variable—

   research design—

**1.27V Additional Practice**

In the following research questions, identify the independent and dependent variables and indicate if they are categorical or quantitative. Based upon the type of variables and relationship being examined, identify the research design.

1. Does writing ability differ by gender among 8th graders?
   independent variable—

   dependent variable—

   research design—

2. Does amount of physical flexibility significantly relate to one's body mass index among baby boomers?
   independent variable—

   dependent variable—

   research design—

3. Does a one-to-one laptop program significantly increase reading achievement among middle school students? Note: Researcher compared treatment group (laptop) to control group (no laptop). Existing groups were used.
   independent variable—

   dependent variable—

   research design—

4. Does a new extended student orientation program significantly increase student satisfaction with the university experience in the first semester among entering freshmen? Note: Researcher compared treatment group (extended orientation) to control group (limited orientation). Individuals were randomly assigned to groups.
   independent variable—

   dependent variable—

   research design—

5. Does political affiliation (Democrat, Republican, Independent) impact the number of hours that millennials volunteer in the community?
   independent variable—

   dependent variable—

   research design—

## 1.28 Exercises

### Reviewing Concepts

1. In Figure 1.1, the relationship between the sample and the population is presented. Explain why Dr. Burns is unable to generalize his results to the liberal arts college freshmen across the U.S.

2. Why is random sampling important in research that strives to generalize results to the population?

3. Explain the difference between descriptive and inferential statistics.

4. The variable of political affiliation is categorical (1=Democrat, 2=Republican, 3=Independent). Based upon these numerical assignments, can you conclude that the Independent Party is better since it has the highest value?

5. What is the main difference between experimental and quasi-experimental research designs?

6. Which research design does not examine cause and effect? Why is this design unable to do so?

### Applying Concepts

1. Identify the variables in the research scenarios. Obviously, the research design is identified as a hint.

   a. Does the new drug, alirocumab, significantly decrease LDL (bad) cholesterol among high risk heart patients? 314 high risk heart patients were randomly assigned to two groups. Group 1 took the new drug; Group 2 took the statin, Zetia.

      independent variable—

      dependent variable—

      research design—experimental

   b. Does instructional format (flipped vs. traditional) significantly affect course grades among 11th grade English students? Ms. Johnson teaches four sections of 11th grade English. Two sections receive flipped instruction, where all content is presented outside of class and class time is used for practice and reinforcement. Semester course grades are compared.

      independent variable—

      dependent variable—

      research design—quasi-experimental

c. Does math achievement differ by gender among 8th grade students?
   independent variable—

   dependent variable—

   research design—causal-comparative

d. Does amount of exercise (minutes per week) significantly relate to Body Mass Index (BMI) among young adults? 100 young adults track their minutes exercising for one month. A weekly average is calculated for each participant. BMI is measured at the end of the month.
   independent variable—

   dependent variable—

   research design—correlational

In the following research questions, identify the independent and dependent variables and indicate if they are categorical or quantitative. Based upon the type of variables and relationship being examined, identify the research design.

2. Do 30-year-olds with a bachelor's degree have higher income than those who do not?
   independent variable—

   dependent variable—

   research design—

3. Does the number of hours of work per week significantly relate to GPA among full-time college seniors?
   independent variable—

   dependent variable—

   research design—

4. Which teaching method (direct instruction, feedback using rubric, or combination of both methods) significantly improves critical thinking skills among college freshmen? Researcher randomly assigned students into the three treatment groups.
   independent variable—

   dependent variable—

   research design—

5. Does the amount of alcohol use at Our University significantly differ from the national campus norm among college freshmen?
   independent variable—

   dependent variable—

   research design—

6. Do gamblers (gamble at least once a month) have more optimism than non-gamblers?
   independent variable—

   dependent variable—

   research design—

7. Do college students who complete financial-aid counseling through an online module have significantly more federal loan debt than students who complete the counseling through a face-to-face session? Students select the type of counseling they prefer to complete prior to loan disbursement.
   independent variable—

   dependent variable—

   research design—

# Module 2

## Descriptive Statistics: Counting

### Learning Targets

After completing Module 2, you should be able to:

- Comprehend and utilize basic statistical terms in the research process: frequencies, frequency distribution, proportion, percentage, bar graph, *Y*-axis, *X*-axis, pie chart, histogram, frequency polygon, interval, normal distribution, skewed (positive, negative) distributions,
- Calculate proportions and percentages based upon a data set.
- Construct bar graphs and pie charts for categorical data.
- Construct frequency distribution tables and graphs for quantitative data.
- Identify distribution shapes (normal, positive, negative).
- Analyze statistical graphs for possible misuse.

# Part 1: The Concepts

Organizing raw data is always the first step in the analysis process. Today's technology has simplified this organizational step. Whether you are downloading data from an online survey or manually entering data, most likely the raw data will be organized in some kind of spreadsheet format. Spreadsheets utilize columns for variables and rows for individuals.

Figure 2.1 displays a portion of a data set in SPSS from an evaluation of a one-to-one laptop pilot program with 8th graders. A district piloted a one-to-one (1:1) laptop program with half of its 8th graders—half received laptops, the other half didn't. Students completed several instruments regarding their technology use and skill before and after the pilot. This example only presents data for 40 1:1 participants, seen in the rows, and three variables (Device, Use, and Skill) seen in the columns. So what do these numbers mean for each variable? The 1:1 Data Guide below the data grid, defines the variables and their values. You can see that for the categorical variable of Device, students were asked to identify their preferred device using four options (1=basic cellphone, 2=Smartphone, 3=tablet, 4=computer). Two variables, Use and Skill, are quantitative, since numerical value is applied. Use is actually Technology Use and is a variable that combines responses from several survey items. In this case, five items were used to measure Tech Use. The five items used a 4-point frequency scale, where 1=I don't use!; 2=I use maybe once a month, 3=I use weekly; 4=I use every day! To calculate the overall Tech Use score, the sum of all five item responses were computed. Therefore, scores can only range from 5 to 20. The variable of Skill, represents Technology Skill and is the score from a 50-point technology skill test. Notice that participant #4 prefers a smartphone (1), has a Use score of 17, and a Skill score of 23.

**Figure 2.1**
*1:1 Data and Data Guide*

| | device | use | skill |
|---|---|---|---|
| 1 | 1.00 | 10.00 | 31.00 |
| 2 | 1.00 | 13.00 | 20.00 |
| 3 | 1.00 | 19.00 | 19.00 |
| 4 | 1.00 | 17.00 | 23.00 |
| 5 | 1.00 | 15.00 | 33.00 |
| 6 | 1.00 | 11.00 | 46.00 |
| 7 | 1.00 | 16.00 | 41.00 |
| 8 | 2.00 | 10.00 | 39.00 |
| 9 | 2.00 | 17.00 | 50.00 |
| 10 | 2.00 | 17.00 | 9.00 |
| 11 | 2.00 | 16.00 | 42.00 |
| 12 | 2.00 | 15.00 | 50.00 |
| 13 | 2.00 | 15.00 | 39.00 |
| 14 | 2.00 | 20.00 | 11.00 |
| 15 | 2.00 | 19.00 | 21.00 |
| 16 | 2.00 | 15.00 | 27.00 |
| 17 | 2.00 | 15.00 | 42.00 |
| 18 | 2.00 | 15.00 | 47.00 |
| 19 | 2.00 | 14.00 | 27.00 |
| 20 | 2.00 | 13.00 | 50.00 |
| 21 | 2.00 | 13.00 | 44.00 |
| 22 | 2.00 | 13.00 | 44.00 |
| 23 | 2.00 | 10.00 | 29.00 |
| 24 | 2.00 | 11.00 | 41.00 |
| 25 | 2.00 | 11.00 | 36.00 |
| 26 | 2.00 | 11.00 | 25.00 |
| 27 | 2.00 | 11.00 | 30.00 |
| 28 | 2.00 | 11.00 | 31.00 |
| 29 | 2.00 | 12.00 | 36.00 |
| 30 | 2.00 | 12.00 | 12.00 |
| 31 | 2.00 | 12.00 | 35.00 |
| 32 | 2.00 | 12.00 | 41.00 |
| 33 | 3.00 | 13.00 | 32.00 |
| 34 | 3.00 | 14.00 | 47.00 |
| 35 | 3.00 | 15.00 | 29.00 |
| 36 | 3.00 | 20.00 | 18.00 |
| 37 | 3.00 | 17.00 | 42.00 |
| 38 | 4.00 | 20.00 | 48.00 |
| 39 | 4.00 | 19.00 | 46.00 |
| 40 | 4.00 | 19.00 | 47.00 |

**Data Guide**

**Device:** Survey Item #2. Identify your preferred device. 1=basic cell phone, 2=Smartphone, 3=tablet, 4=computer

**Tech Use:** Subscale sum of 5 items (4-point frequency scale: 1=don't use; 4= use all the time).

**Skill Score:** Score from 50 point technology test.

## 2.11 Frequency Distributions: Definition, Proportion, Percentages

Understanding a sample is rather difficult if we are attempting to read 40 lines of data. The typical first step in gleaning information from a sample is to count the different responses—this works with both categorical and quantitative variables. These counts are known as ***frequencies***. Using frequencies will allow us to summarize our 1:1 data for all three variables. Describing variables with few categories or values can be done within a sentence or two. For our example, the preferred device for the majority of our sample was a smartphone ($n$=25), followed by basic cellphone ($n$=7), tablet ($n$=5), and computer ($n$=3).

When variables have a large range of values, in that it is a quantitative variable or has many categories, frequency distributions are used. A ***frequency distribution*** organizes the data by presenting the reported values and the number of individuals at each value. A frequency distribution may be presented in a table or graphic; in either format, a frequency distribution organizes data to give the reader a quick picture of how the data is distributed across the measurement scale.

**Figure 2.2**
*Frequency Distribution Table for Preferred Device*

| Preferred Device | |
|---|---|
| $X$ | $f$ |
| 1 | 7 |
| 2 | 25 |
| 3 | 5 |
| 4 | 3 |

Let's first take a look at creating a frequency distribution table, which consists of two columns (see Figure 2.2). The first column presents the possible scores of the variable, while the second column presents the frequencies, denoted by $f$. For the variable of Preferred Device, the individual values ($X$) are organized from low (1) to high (4) in column one. Then the number of individuals that selected each device is indicated in column 2.

The frequency distribution table for the variable of Tech Use is a little more complex since the values range from 10-20 (see Figure 2.3). Although an individual could score as low as 5, the lowest score is 10, which will be the starting value for the distribution. All the possible scores within the range are listed, even if a score has 0 frequency. While it is helpful to see the number of individuals for each score, typically reporting the portion of the total sample that have each score is more meaningful—this is done through proportion and percentage.

***Proportion*** **(*p*)** measures the fraction (in decimal form) of the total sample for each score. For the 1:1 example, we were given data for 40 students ($N$=40). For the Tech Use score of 10, the proportion of individuals is 3 out 40 ($f/N$=3/40=.075). Most researchers will convert the proportion to a ***percentage*** **(%)** by multiplying $p$ times 100.

Figure 2.3
*Frequency Distribution for Tech Use*

| Tech Use | | | |
|---|---|---|---|
| *X* | *f* | *p* | % |
| 10 | 3 | .075 | 7.5 |
| 11 | 6 | .150 | 15.0 |
| 12 | 4 | .100 | 10.0 |
| 13 | 5 | .125 | 12.5 |
| 14 | 2 | .050 | 5.0 |
| 15 | 7 | .175 | 17.5 |
| 16 | 2 | .050 | 5.0 |
| 17 | 4 | .100 | 10.0 |
| 18 | 0 | .000 | 0.0 |
| 19 | 4 | .100 | 10.0 |
| 20 | 3 | .075 | 7.5 |
| | $N=\Sigma f$ | | |

$$\text{Proportion} = p = \frac{f}{N}$$

$$\text{Percentage} = p(100) = \frac{f}{N}(100)$$

If you need to determine the size of the total sample from a frequency distribution table, just add up the frequencies. The Greek letter, sigma ($\Sigma$) represents summation or sum of.

$$\text{Total sample } N = \Sigma f$$

## 2.12 Types of Frequency Distribution Graphs

Converting a frequency distribution table to a graph can be very helpful to the consumer. While we will look at several different types of graphs, most will utilize two perpendicular lines, called axes. The horizontal line is the ***X*-axis** and displays the measurement scale of the variable in increasing value from left to right. The vertical line is the ***Y*-axis** and displays the frequencies in increasing value from bottom to top.

### Graphs for Categorical Variables

Two common ways to display categorical data are through a bar graph and a pie chart. The ***bar graph*** displays the frequencies ($Y$-axis) for each category, which is represented by a bar ($X$-axis). Figure 2.4 presents a bar graph and pie chart for the variable of Preferred Device. Notice the bar graph (Graph A) displays bars that are not touching—this indicates that each bar represents a distinct category. The ***pie chart*** (Graph B) also presents frequencies for categories, but does so using a circle that represents the whole (total sample) and divides the circle into wedges that represent the relative frequency or proportion for that category. We can see that over half of the sample prefers a smartphone.

Figure 2.4
*Bar Graphs and Pie Chart of Preferred Device*

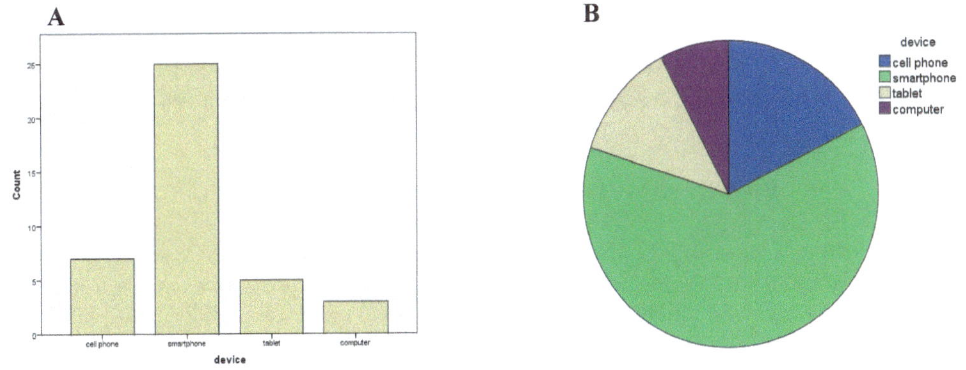


### Graphs for Quantitative Variables

Similar to a bar graph, a ***histogram*** uses bars to display the frequencies for each score of a quantitative variable. However, the bars in a histogram touch to show the continuous nature of the quantitative score. Figure 2.5 presents a histogram and line graph for Tech Use. The histogram for Tech Use (Graph A) presents the same data as in the frequency distribution table but provides a visual comparison of scores and their relative frequency. The line graph or ***frequency polygon*** doesn't use bars to indicate the frequency of scores, rather a continuous line shows frequency of each score. Both graphs use the $X$-axis for the quantitative variable and the $Y$-axis to represent frequencies. Both graphs are very helpful in examining the distribution of scores, but the frequency polygon is more effective when comparing the distributions of groups.

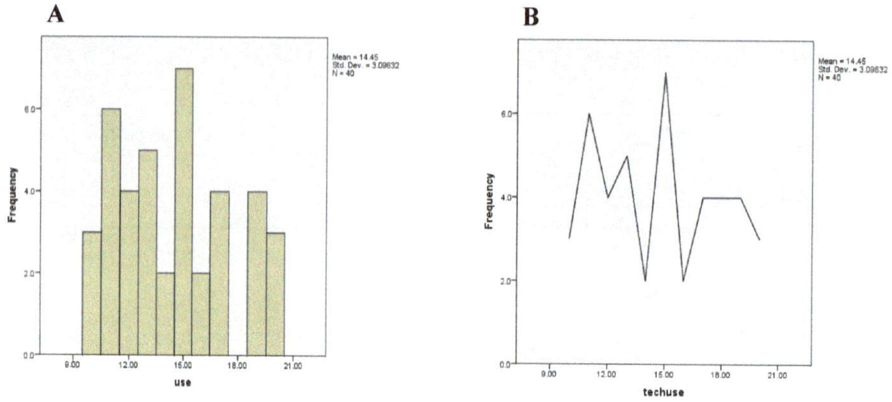


**Figure 2.5**
*Graphs of Tech Use*

## 2.13 Creating a Grouped Frequency Distribution

In most of the previous examples, the range of data has been relatively small, which allowed us to list the entire range of scores in the frequency distributions. The ***range*** of scores is the difference between the highest and lowest scores (range = $X_{max} - X_{min}$). However, when a set of data presents a wide range of scores, typically greater than 20, it is unreasonable to list all of these scores. This is the case for the last 1:1 variable of Technology Skill, which was based upon a 50-point test. Grouping scores into consistent intervals will help to effectively and efficiently summarize the data. An ***interval***, also referred to as a class interval, is way to divide the range of scores into groups. Identifying the appropriate interval is critical in presenting an accurate picture of the data. We will follow a set of rules to guide the creation of grouped frequency distributions. But keep in mind, these rules are only applicable if you have a sample size of at least 20 and a range of scores 20 or greater.

**Rule 1** **Utilize the appropriate number of intervals (ideally 10, but 8-12 is acceptable).** This step is crucial! If you have too many intervals, the data will be too spread out; too few, the data are bunched up. While 8-12 intervals are ideal, the number of intervals really depends on the range of data and sample size. If the sample size was in the 100s and the range of data was rather large, it may be acceptable to use 20 intervals.

**Rule 2** **Select an interval width that supports the appropriate number of intervals.** If possible, try to use a width of 2, 5, 10, etc. Notice that Rule 1 and 2 go hand in hand. You may have to increase the number of intervals to use a better width, or vice versa.

**Rule 3** **The start or end of each interval should be a multiple of the width.** This really depends on the range of your scores. Remember the first interval needs to include the lowest score and the last interval needs to include the highest score.

**Rule 4** **All intervals must be the same width.** Make sure there are no overlaps or gaps.

For the Technology Skill variable the range is: highest (50) – lowest (9) = 41. To account for rounding and the need to include all our scores in our distribution, we are going to calculate a statistical range by adding one; this is also known as an **inclusive range** ($X_{max} - X_{min} + 1$). For Technology Skill, the statistical range is 42 (50 – 9 + 1). To determine the appropriate number of intervals and the interval width, divide the statistical range by a good interval width. Knowing the statistical range is 42, an interval width of 5 is a good place to start.

$$\frac{X_{max} - X_{min} + 1}{\text{interval width}} = \text{\# of intervals}$$

$$\frac{42}{5} = 8.4\ (round\ up\ to\ 9)$$

Using an interval width of 5 generates 8.4 intervals, but it is impossible to have 8.4 intervals. We can't round down, since we would be excluding some data, so we must round up to 9. When calculating the number of intervals, ALWAYS round up. The next step is to determine the starting point for the first interval. Since the highest score is 50, it makes sense to have the end of the intervals be the multiple of the width (5). So the last interval will be 46-50, which takes us to the very first interval of 6-10. Figure 2.6 shows the grouped frequency table (A) and histogram (B) for Tech Skill. The grouped frequency distribution table for our Tech Skill scores shows the 9 intervals with each specific interval range. Although the histogram applies the exact same intervals for the bars, the labels on the $X$-axis just indicate end points of each interval. This is often done to accommodate limited space.

**Figure 2.6**
*Grouped Frequency Distribution Table and Histogram*

**A**

| Tech Skill | *f* |
|---|---|
| 6-10 | 1 |
| 11-15 | 2 |
| 16-20 | 3 |
| 21-25 | 3 |
| 26-30 | 5 |
| 31-35 | 5 |
| 36-40 | 4 |
| 41-45 | 8 |
| 46-50 | 9 |

**B**

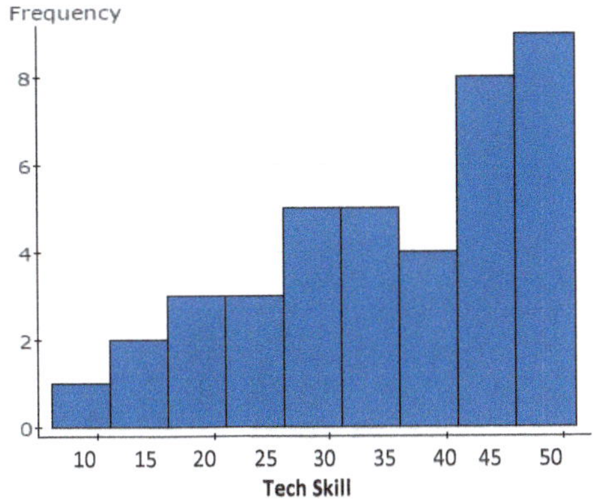


## 2.14 Shapes of Frequency Distributions: Normal, Positive, Negative

Creating a frequency distribution graph is very helpful in examining and identifying the shape of the distribution. The shape of a distribution tells us a lot about how and where the scores are clustered. We will focus on three types of shapes: normal, positive skew, and negative skew (see Figure 2.7).

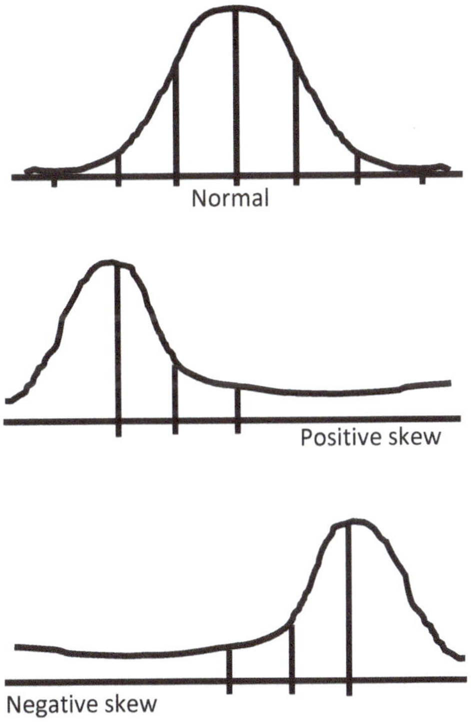


**Figure 2.7**
*Distribution Types*

A ***normal distribution*** is the most well-known distribution, since it has been the basis of the testing industry for decades. Also known as the bell curve, the normal distribution is symmetrical with the majority of scores falling in the middle and the least frequent scores on the two ends.

A ***skewed distribution*** has scores clustered on one end and very few scores on the other end. When identifying the direction of skewness, you should focus on the end that has outliers or the few extreme scores—this is also known as the tail. A ***positively skewed*** distribution has the tail of a few outliers on the high end of the distribution. The majority of scores are on the low end of the distribution. A very difficult exam creates a positive distribution.

In contrast, a ***negatively skewed distribution*** has the tail of a few outliers on the low end of the distribution. The majority of scores are on the high end of the distribution. This is the kind of distribution most students would prefer, where the majority of students score very high and only a few score low. The distribution of Tech Skill (Figure 2.4) is a great example of a negative skew.

## 2.15 Misuse of Statistical Graphs

Unfortunately, the eye is easily tricked into making such spatial comparisons. Some statistical abuses are intentional to sway the consumer, and other mistakes are just made out of ignorance. As a consumer of statistics, you should be aware of some of the tricks used to obtain your support. First and foremost, you need to be mindful of the information source and its political bias and/or agenda. Most media outlets have some political tilt, either to the right or to the left; very few give a balanced perspective. In addition, most businesses and organizations have a clear agenda—whether it is trying to sell you a product or an idea. As a result, media and organizations take advantage of the consumer by exaggerating the graphics, scales, and numbers of statistical charts and graphs to communicate a message. Remember, the goal of a statistical graph is to efficiently communicate numerical comparisons. The following examples attempt to review some common methods used to twist the conclusion one may draw from the graphic.

1. **Not starting the *Y*-axis at zero (0)** is one of the easiest ways to exaggerate change. Notice the two bar graphs in Figure 2.8. Graph A truncates the *Y*-axis by starting it at 94,000,000 and not 0 in order to exaggerate the change in bars. Graph B applies the appropriate starting point showing that the change isn't so extreme.

A B

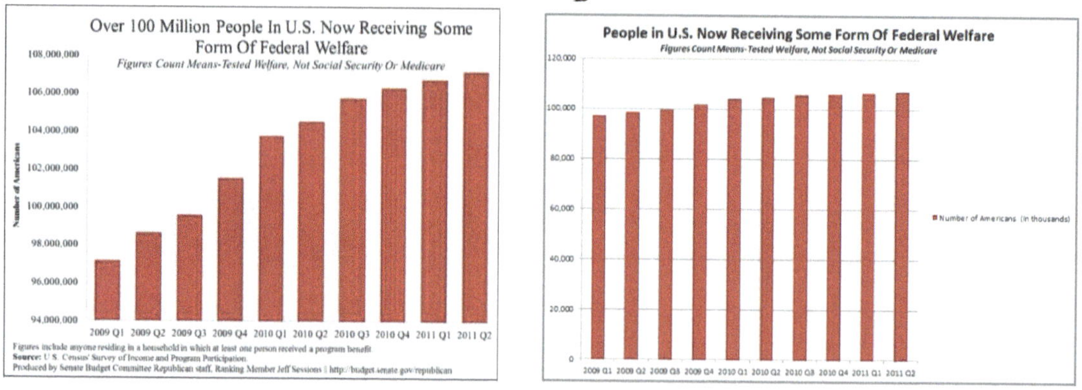


**Figure 2.8** *Bar Graphs of People Receiving Federal Welfare*

2. Exaggerating graphics
   - **Exaggerating graphics to convince.** Figure 2.9 compares the sales of major fast food restaurants in 2002 by using logos to represent each restaurant. Although the scale of the *Y*-axis is correct, logos are enlarged along the *X*-axis as well. This gives McDonalds a huge visual advantage. Figure 2.10 presents two line graphs that present the U.S. unemployment rate for 2011. Graph A exaggerates tick marks that are inconsistent with the numerical values, giving the illusion that the unemployment rate has been stagnant. Graph B is a corrected version and presents a more accurate picture of the fluctuation in rates. Keep in mind the *Y*-axis still does not begin at 0.

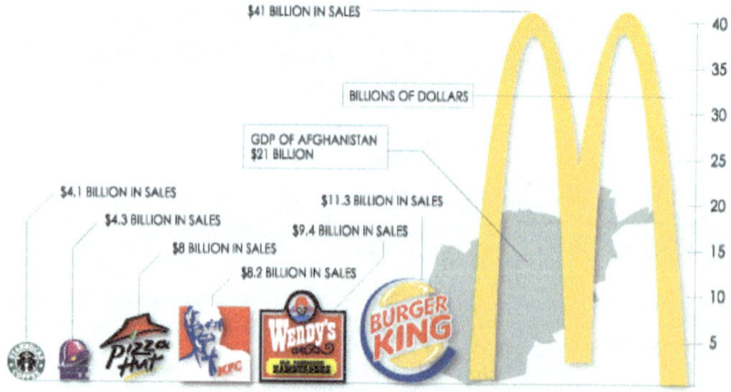


**Figure 2.9** *Graph Comparing Restaurant Sales for 2002*

https://i1.wp.com/ticktockmaths.co.uk/wp-content/uploads/2017/10/bad-graphs-3.png

A B

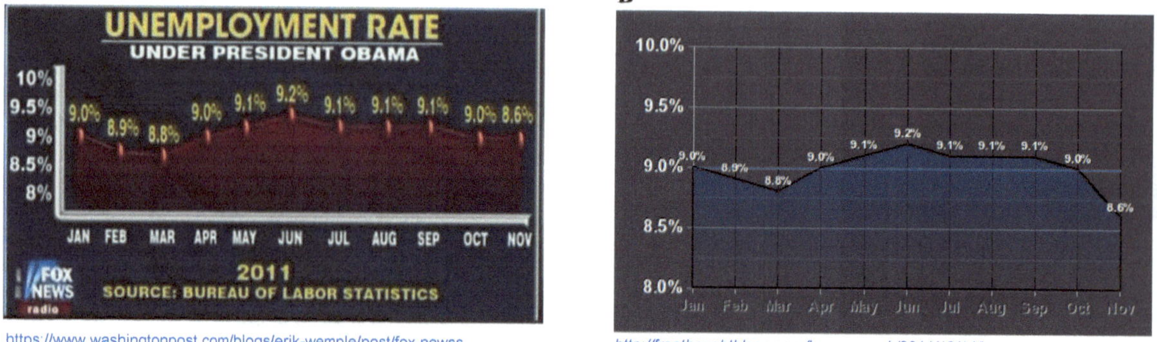


**Figure 2.10** *Line Graphs of 2011 U.S. Unemployment Rate*

https://www.washingtonpost.com/blogs/erik-wemple/post/fox-newss-unemployment-chart-bettergraphics/2011/12/12/gIQAUVgNqO_blog.html

http://freethoughtblogs.com/lousycanuck/2011/12/14/im-better-at-graphs-than-fox-news/

- **Exaggerating graphics to confuse.** Graphs should quickly communicate a message. The next two examples apply visual overload that create confusion. Figure 2.11 presents a pie chart of how often people share recommendations online. Although the percentages add up to 100%, the visual effects (color, texture, dimension) used have distorted the proportions such that the viewer must read the numbers to understand the results.

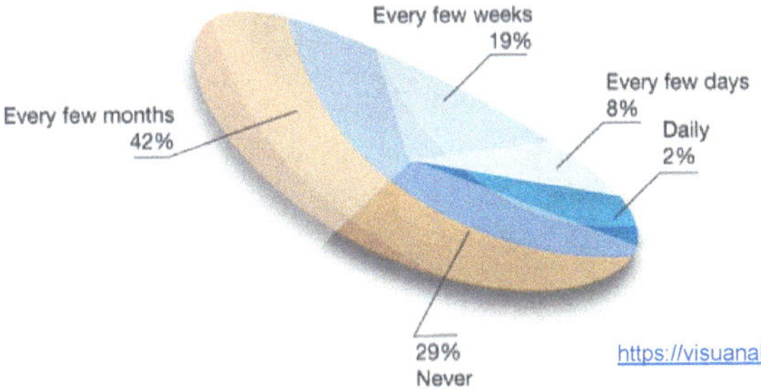


https://visuanalyze.wordpress.com/2013/02/05/bad_piecharts/

**Figure 2.11**
*Pie Chart of Frequency of Sharing Recommendations Online*

Figure 2.12 presents a bar chart that compares how people travel to work in large U.S. cities. The use of city abbreviations with the colored proportions embedded makes it difficult to understand. In addition, a *Y*-axis isn't labeled.

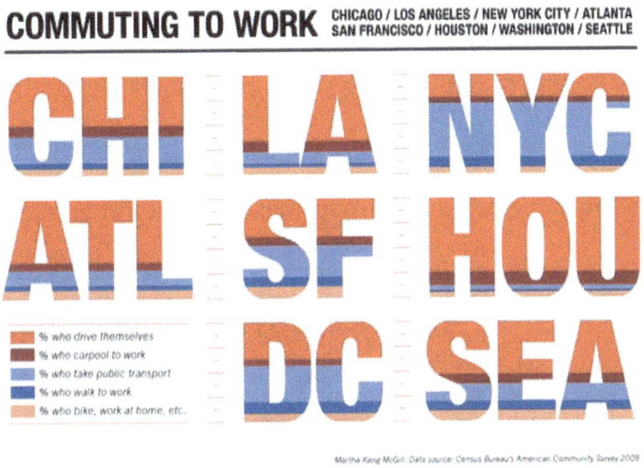


**Figure 2.12**
*Bar Chart Comparing Cities and Methods of Work Commute*

3. **Absent or inappropriate labels or titles.** Figure 2.13 presents a bar graph comparing Lanacane to hydrocortisone. Although the title indicates itch relief and the graphic indicates 1 minute and 60 minutes, neither axes are labeled so it is hard to tell what is being measured.

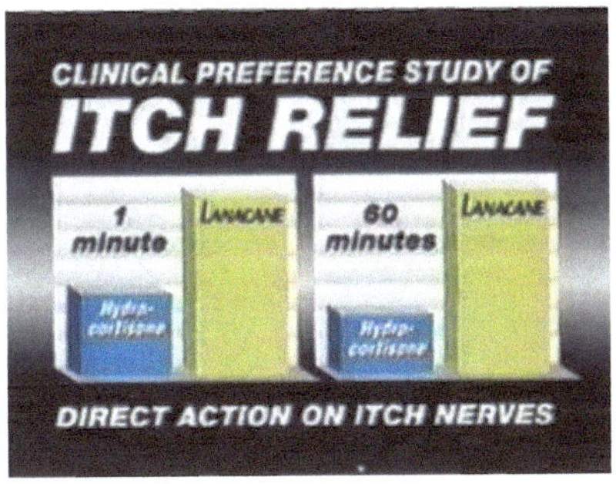


www.statisticshowto.com

**Figure 2.13**
*Bar Chart Comparing Lanacane and Hydrocortisone*

Figure 2.14 presents a line graph titled, Job Loss by Quarter; however, the dates on the *X*-axis are not aligned with quarters. In addition, the *Y*-axis isn't labeled. And finally, the line points do not accurately display the numerical values reported.

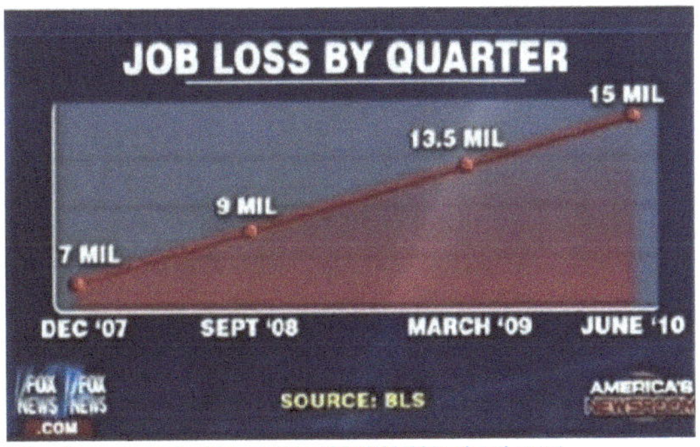


https://www.mediamatters.org/blog/2010/06/28/updated-worst-chart-ive-seen-all-day/166862

**Figure 2.14**
*Job Loss by Quarter*

4. **Presenting numbers that don't add up.** Pie charts are an abused graphic! While they should present how 100% of the pie is divided, many pie chart creators add too many ingredients. Figure 2.15 presents two bad pie charts. Chart A, A Real Pie Chart, attempts to present results for the top three favorite pies. Although the chart indicates that percentages do not add up to 100% since people voted on their top 3 favorite pies, it still doesn't help in understanding it. Chart B somehow attempts to present a distribution of energy-related federal subsidies. However, the layers, colors, and quadrants presented make this pie a mess.

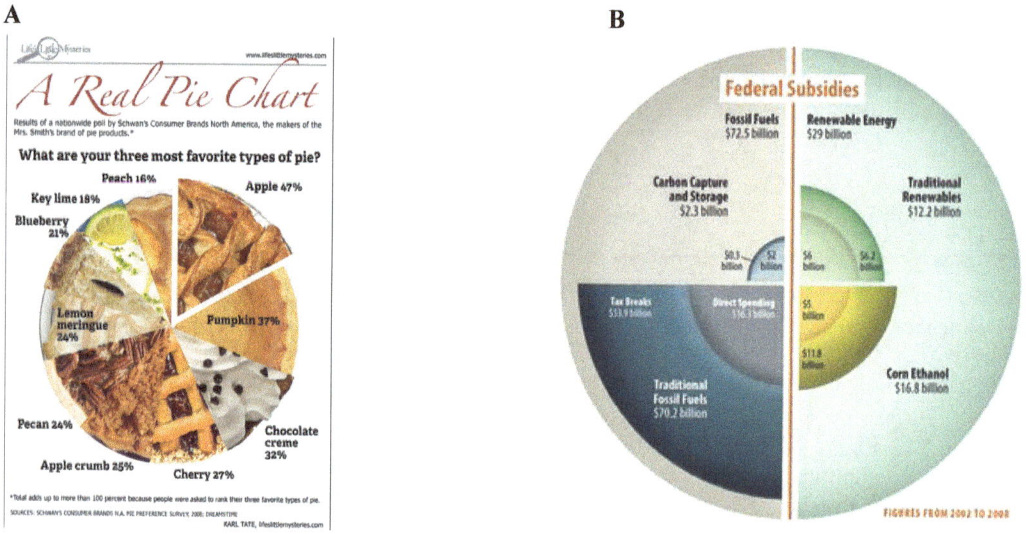


https://www.livescience.com/33111-favorite-pie-america.html

http://straightstatistics.fullfact.org/article/who-ate-all-pies

**Figure 2.15**
*Bad Pie Charts*

## 2.16 Module Summary

- Raw data are usually organized into a spreadsheet format. Columns are variables, and rows are individuals.
- ***Frequencies***—the number (count) of responses for each value
- ***Frequency distributions*** organize data by presenting the reported values and the number of individuals at each value.
  - Can be a table or graph and will often present:
  - ***Proportion*** (***p=f/N***) measures the fraction (in decimal form) of the total sample for each score. Most researchers will convert the proportion to a ***percentage*** **(%)** by multiplying $p$ times 100.
- Graphs for categorical variables
  - ***Bar graph***—displays the frequencies ($Y$-axis) for each category, which is represented by a bar ($X$-axis). Bars do not touch
  - ***Pie Chart***—uses a circle that represents the whole (total sample) and divides the circle into wedges that represent the relative frequency or proportion for that category
- Graphs for quantitative variables
  - ***Histogram***—uses bars to display the frequencies ($Y$-axis) for each score of a quantitative variable ($X$-axis). Bars touch to show the continuous nature of the quantitative score.
  - ***Line graph*** (frequency polygon)—similar to histogram but uses a line instead of bars.
- Grouped Frequency Distributions are appropriate when range of scores AND sample size are 20 or greater.
  - Rules for creating grouped frequency distribution:
    1. Try to have 8-12 intervals.
    2. Select an interval width that supports appropriate number of intervals. Widths of 2, 5, 10, etc. are good. Use the following equation to determine appropriate width and number:
       $$\frac{X_{max} - X_{min} + 1}{\text{interval width}} = \text{\# of intervals}$$
    3. The start or end of each interval should be a multiple of the width.
    4. All intervals must be the same width.
- Shapes of frequency distributions
  - ***Normal***—bell curve, symmetrical, majority of scores in the middle
  - ***Skewed***—A few extreme scores (outliers) create lopsided distributions
    - ***Positive skew*** has the tail of a few outliers on the high end of the distribution. The majority of scores are on the low end of the distribution.
    - ***Negative skew*** has the tail of a few outliers on the low end of the distribution. The majority of scores are on the high end of the distribution.
- Misuse of statistical graphs occur out of ignorance and/or the intention to sway the consumer toward an idea. Four commons techniques are used:
  1. Not starting the $Y$-axis at zero (0)
  2. Exaggerating graphics
  3. Absent or inappropriate labels or titles
  4. Presenting numbers that don't add up.

# Part 2: Learning Guide

Typically the first step in the analysis process is to organize raw data into some kind of statistical program—all of which will utilize a spreadsheet format. Columns are variables, and rows are individuals.

## Example

A district piloted a one-to-one laptop program with half of its 8th graders—half received laptops, the other half didn't. Students completed several instruments regarding their technology use and skill. The full example presents data for 40 1:1 participants, seen in the rows, and three variables (Device, Use, and Skill) seen in the columns.

**Data Guide**

**Device:** Survey Item #2. Identify your preferred device. 1= basic cell phone, 2= Smartphone, 3=tablet, 4=computer

**Tech Use:** Subscale sum of 5 items (4-point frequency scale: 1=don't use; 4= use all the time).

**Skill Score:** Score from 50 point technology test.

| | device | use | skill |
|---|---|---|---|
| 1 | 1.00 | 10.00 | 31.00 |
| 2 | 1.00 | 13.00 | 20.00 |
| 3 | 1.00 | 19.00 | 19.00 |
| 4 | 1.00 | 17.00 | 23.00 |
| 5 | 1.00 | 15.00 | 33.00 |
| 6 | 1.00 | 11.00 | 46.00 |
| 7 | 1.00 | 16.00 | 41.00 |
| 8 | 2.00 | 10.00 | 39.00 |
| 9 | 2.00 | 17.00 | 50.00 |
| 10 | 2.00 | 17.00 | 9.00 |
| 11 | 2.00 | 16.00 | 42.00 |
| 12 | 2.00 | 15.00 | 50.00 |
| 13 | 2.00 | 15.00 | 39.00 |
| 14 | 2.00 | 20.00 | 11.00 |

### 2.21V Intro to Frequency Distributions: Definition, Proportion, Percentages

- **Frequencies** count responses; can be used for categorical and quantitative variables.
  - Frequencies easily summarize categorical variables.
  - Frequency distribution presents data for quantitative variables.
- **Frequency Distribution** organizes data by presenting the reported values and the number of individuals at each value.
  - May be table or graphic format

**Figure 2.2**

*Frequency Distribution for Preferred Device*

| Preferred Device | |
|---|---|
| *X* | *f* |
| 1 | 7 |
| 2 | 25 |
| 3 | 5 |
| 4 | 3 |

**Figure 2.3**

*Frequency Distribution for Tech Use*

| Tech Use | | | |
|---|---|---|---|
| *X* | *f* | *p* | % |
| 10 | 3 | .075 | 7.5 |
| 11 | 6 | .150 | 15.0 |
| 12 | 4 | .100 | 10.0 |
| 13 | 5 | .125 | 12.5 |
| 14 | 2 | .050 | 5.0 |
| 15 | 7 | .175 | 17.5 |
| 16 | 2 | .050 | 5.0 |
| 17 | 4 | .100 | 10.0 |
| 18 | 0 | .000 | 0.0 |
| 19 | 4 | .100 | 10.0 |
| 20 | 3 | .075 | 7.5 |
| | $N=\Sigma f$ | | |

- **Proportion** (*p*) measures the fraction (in decimal form) of the total sample for each score.

$$\text{Proportion} = p = \frac{f}{N} \qquad \text{Percentage} = p(100) = \frac{f}{N}(100)$$

- If you need to determine the size of the total sample from a frequency distribution table, just add up the frequencies. The Greek letter, sigma ($\Sigma$) represents summation or sum of.

Total sample $N = \Sigma f$

## 2.22V Types of Frequency Distribution Graphs

Presenting frequency distributions in graphic form can be an efficient strategy.
Many graphs will utilize axes—two perpendicular lines.

- *X*-axis is the horizontal line and displays the measurement scale of the variable in increasing value from left to right.
- *Y*-axis is the vertical line and displays the frequencies in increasing value from bottom to top.

**Graphs for Categorical Variables.**

- **Bar Graph** presents the frequencies (*Y*-axis) for each category, which is represented by a bar (*X*-axis).
  - Bars do not touch; they represent distinct categories.
- **Pie Chart** uses a circle to present frequencies for categories.
  - Circle represents the whole (total sample), which is divided into wedges that represent the relative frequency or proportion for that category.

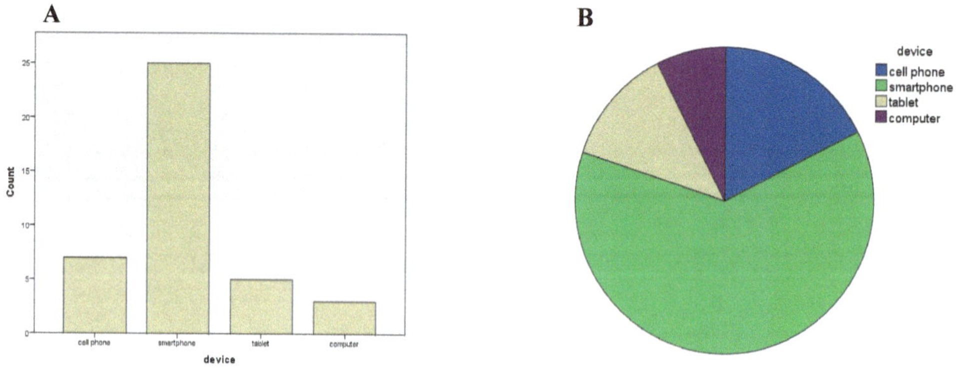


**Figure 2.4**
*Bar Graphs and Pie Chart of Preferred Device*

**Graphs for Quantitative Variables**

- Histograms and line graphs display frequency distributions where the X-axis displays the variable values and the Y-axis presents the frequencies for each value.
- Histogram has bars that touch to show the continuous nature of the data.
- Frequency polygon is more effective when comparing the distributions of groups.

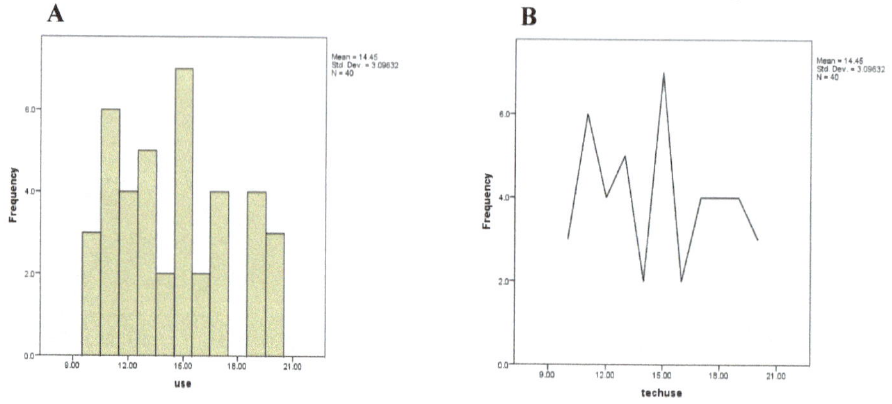


**Figure 2.5**
*Graphs of Tech Use*

## 2.23V Creating a Grouped Frequency Distribution

When data presents a wide range of scores (20+) and the sample is somewhat large ($n$>20), grouped frequency distributions can effectively and efficiently summarize the data.

- ***Range*** of scores is the difference between the highest and lowest scores.
- Identifying the appropriate interval is critical in presenting an accurate picture of the data.

- **Rules for Creating a Grouped Frequency Distribution**

  **Rule 1** Utilize the appropriate number of intervals (ideally 10, but 8-12 is acceptable).

  **Rule 2** Select an interval width that supports the appropriate number of intervals. If possible, try to use a width of 2, 5, 10, etc.

$$\frac{X_{max} - X_{min} + 1}{\text{interval width}} = \text{\# of intervals}$$

  **Rule 3** The start <u>or</u> end of each interval should be a multiple of the width.

  **Rule 4** All intervals must be the same width.

- **Example** with Technology Skill
  - **Determine statistical range**
    - Range = $X_{max} - X_{min}$
      - Range for Tech Skill is highest (50) – lowest (9) = 41.
    - Statistical range adds 1; ($X_{max} - X_{min} + 1$).
      - Accounts for rounding and the inclusion of all scores
      - Also known as inclusive range
      - Statistical range for Tech Skill = highest (50) – lowest (9) +1 = 42

  - **Determine interval width and # of intervals**

$$\frac{X_{max} - X_{min} + 1}{\text{interval width}} = \text{\# of intervals}$$

$$\frac{42}{5} = 8.4\ (round\ up\ to\ 9)$$

    - **Tech Skill:** An interval width of 5 generates 9 intervals—super!
    - Always round up!
    - Try different widths to obtain appropriate # of intervals (8-12).

  - **Determine starting point or end point.**
    - Start or end of interval must be an interval of the width.
    - **Tech Skill:** For the low score of 9, high score of 50 and a width of 5, let's have the end point be a multiple of 5.

**A**

| Tech Skill | *f* |
|---|---|
| 6-10 | 1 |
| 11-15 | 2 |
| 16-20 | 3 |
| 21-25 | 3 |
| 26-30 | 5 |
| 31-35 | 5 |
| 36-40 | 4 |
| 41-45 | 8 |
| 46-50 | 9 |

**B**

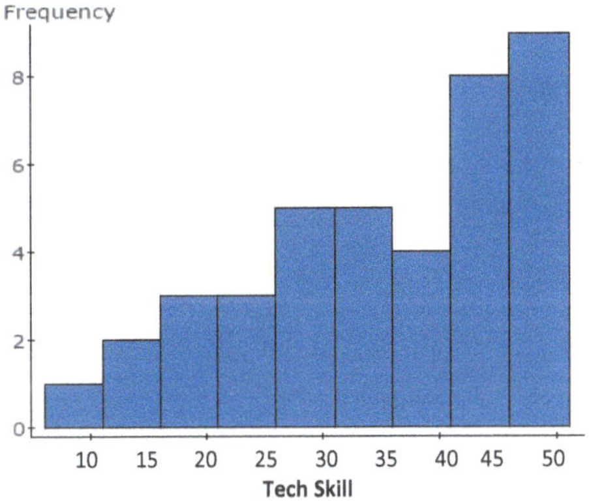


**Figure 2.6**
*Grouped Frequency Distribution Table and Histogram*

## 2.24V Shapes of Frequency Distribution: Normal, Positive, Negative

Frequency distribution graphs are helpful in examining the shape of the distribution. The shape tells us how scores are clustered.

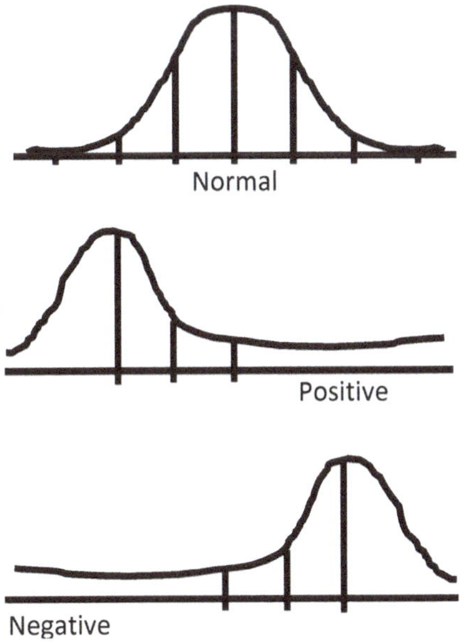


**Figure 2.7**
*Distribution Types*

- **Normal**—typical bell curve; symmetrical; majority of scores in the middle
- **Skewed**—scores are clustered on one end with outliers on the other; focus on the outliers in identifying direction of skew
  - **Positive**—the tail of a few outliers are in the high end of the distribution. The majority of scores are on the low end of the distribution. A very difficult exam creates a positive distribution.
  - **Negative**—the tail of a few outliers on the low end of the distribution. The majority of scores are on the high end of the distribution.

## 2.25V Misuse of Statistical Graphs

Some media outlets and organizations intentionally or accidently misrepresent data in graphs in order to communicate a message. Several techniques used to trick the eye.

1. *Y*-axis doesn't start at 0 (Figure 2.8)
2. Exaggerating graphics (Figures 2.9, 2.10, 2.11, 2.12)
3. Absent or inappropriate labels or titles (Figures 2.13 and 2.14)
4. Presenting numbers that don't add up (Figure 2.15)

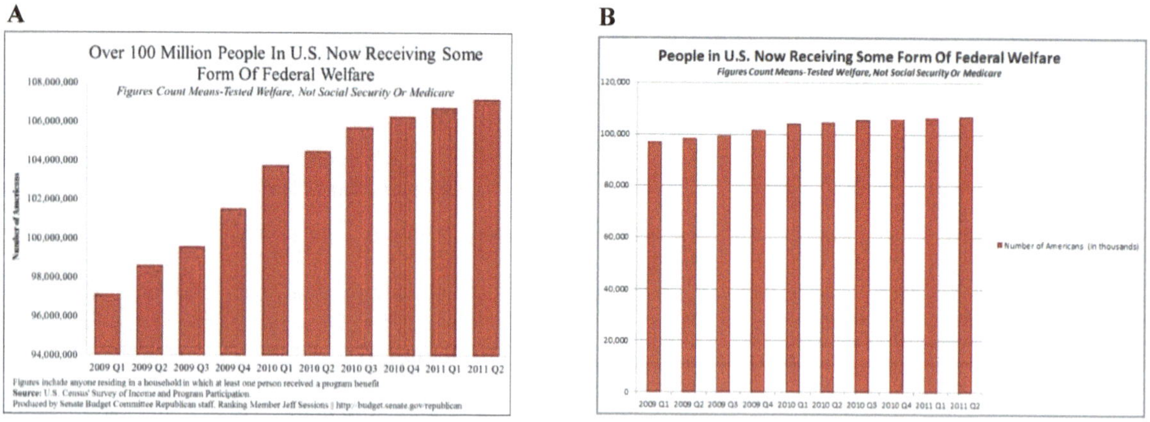


**Figure 2.8**
*Bar Graphs of People Receiving Federal Welfare*

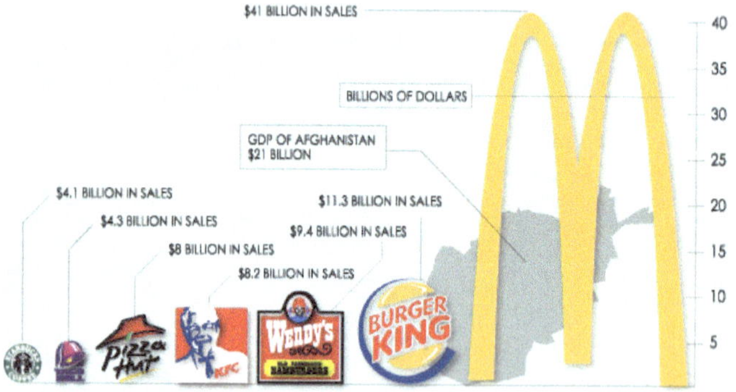


**Figure 2.9**
*Graph Comparing Restaurant Sales for 2002*

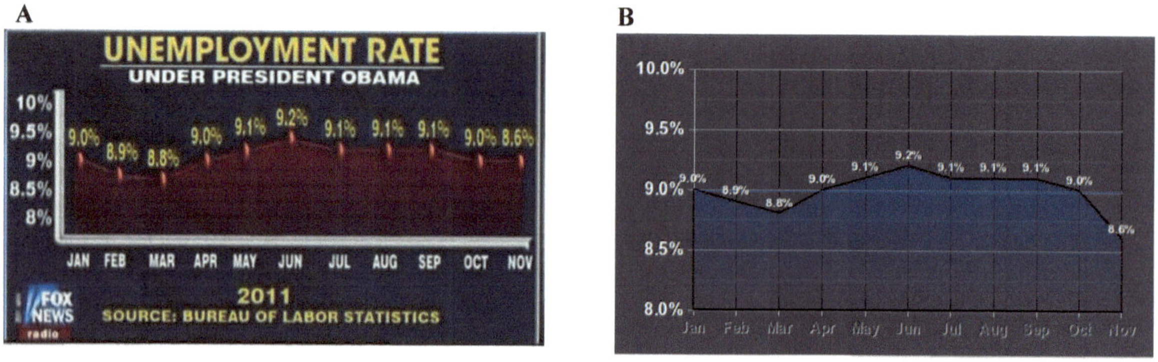


**Figure 2.10**
*Line Graphs of 2011 U.S. Unemployment Rate*

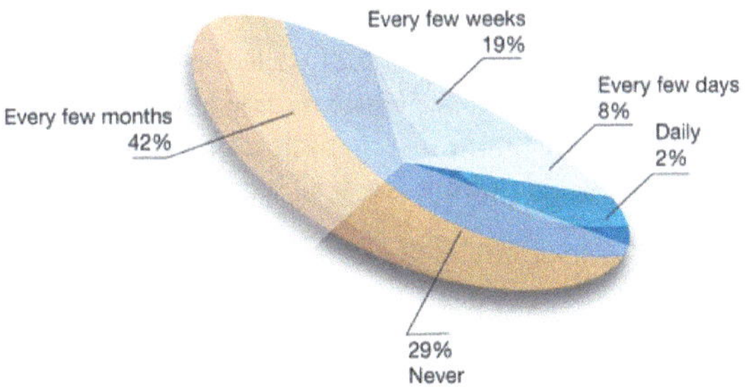


**Figure 2.11**
*Pie Chart of Frequency of Sharing Recommendations Online*

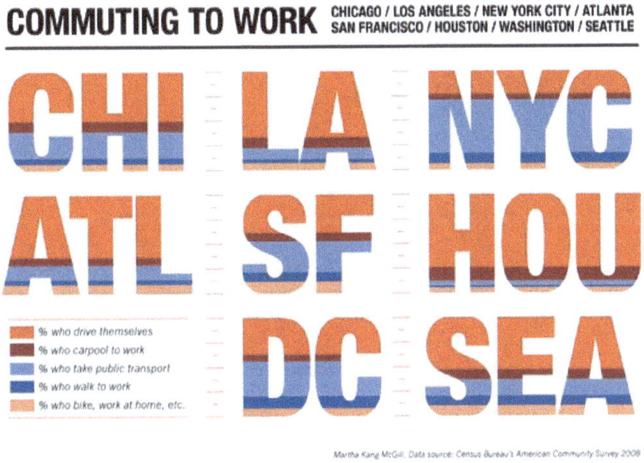


**Figure 2.12**
*Bar Chart Comparing Cities and Methods of Work Commute*

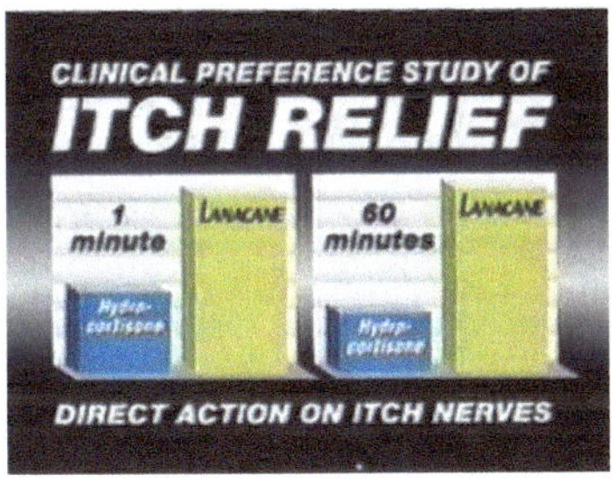

**Figure 2.13**
*Bar Chart Comparing Lanacane and Hydrocortisone*

**Figure 2.14**
*Job Loss by Quarter*

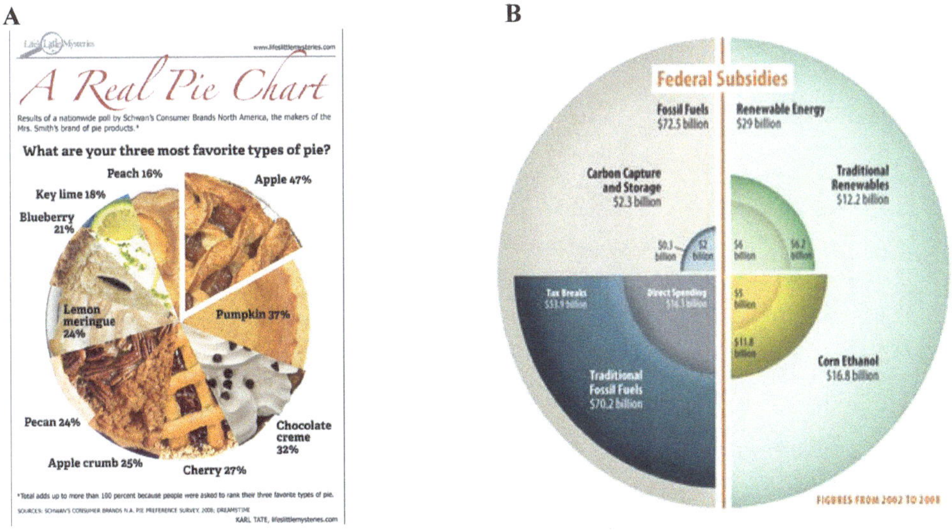


**Figure 2.15**
*Bad Pie Charts*

## 2.26V Examples

1. A recent study examined cell phone use among college students. Roberts et. al. (2014) found that women spend an average of 10 hours per day on their cell phone, while men spend about 8 hours. The following data is from 40 college students reporting daily cell phone use separated by gender. Create separate frequency distributions graphs for females and males. Based upon your distributions, are the sample participants similar to those that Roberts studied in 2014?

   Females: 4, 6, 7, 8, 8, 9, 9, 9, 9, 10, 10, 10, 11, 11, 11, 11, 11, 12, 12, 12

   Males: 4, 5, 5, 6, 6, 7, 7, 8, 8, 8, 8, 8, 9, 9, 9, 9, 10, 10, 11, 12

2. You just completed a 100 point Statistics exam. The scores of 30 classmates are below. Construct a grouped frequency histogram.

   54, 55, 55, 59, 62, 65, 65, 73, 73, 73, 76, 79, 79, 87, 87, 88, 88, 88, 88, 89, 89, 89, 93, 93, 95, 99, 99, 100, 100, 100

   Interval width =

   # of intervals

   Starting interval =

   Approximate shape=

## 2.27V Additional Practice

**A cup of energy!** The intake of caffeinated drinks continues to be a cultural norm in the U.S. Many individuals rely on caffeine to provide the boost they need to get through the day. The National Coffee Association reports in the *National Coffee Drinking Trends 2010* that Americans drink an average of 3.1 cups of coffee per day with 65% drinking coffee with breakfast, 30% drinking coffee between meals, and 5% drinking coffee with meals other than breakfast.

1. Create a statistical chart/graph that is appropriate for reporting data on WHEN Americans drink coffee.

2. The following data represents the number of cups of coffee consumed per day for 35 college students. Construct a frequency distribution table and histogram for the data.

   0, 0, 1, 1, 2, 2, 2, 2, 2, 2, 3, 3, 3, 3, 3, 4, 4, 4, 4, 4, 4, 4, 4, 5, 5, 5, 5, 6, 6, 6, 6, 7, 8, 10, 10

   a. Based upon the histogram, what shape is the distribution?

   b. Does it look like college students drink more coffee than the American average of 3.1 cups per day? Less? Or about the same?

3. HealthResearchFunding.org indicates that teenagers and young adults consume approximately 100 mg. of caffeine per day. The data below is the average daily caffeine intake for 30 freshmen college students who monitored caffeine intake for a week. Use the data to create a grouped frequency histogram.

   0, 0, 42, 45, 54, 59, 66, 78, 88, 88, 90, 95, 100, 110, 110, 116, 120, 122, 126, 133, 136, 140, 144, 160, 178, 180, 199, 206, 215, 222

   Interval width =

   # of intervals

   Starting interval =

   Approximate shape=

**2.28 Activity**

This applet allows you to utilize several different data sets (College SAT-Math scores, NBA team payrolls, horsepower of cars, male body fat %, school spending per student, and gas mileage) to create histograms by manipulating interval width and starting points (for *X* and *Y*). Use the link below to get started.

http://www.shodor.org/interactivate/activities/Histogram/

Select a data set. Note the original interval size, starting points for X and Y, then indicate the number of bars presented and the general shape of the distribution. Go about increasing or decreasing the interval width, noting the change in the number of bars and distribution shape.

| | **Interval Width** | **Y Starting Point** | **X Starting Point** | **# of Bars** | **Distribution Shape** |
|---|---|---|---|---|---|
| Original | | | | | |
| Increase width | | | | | |
| Double increase width (from above) | | | | | |
| Decrease width from original | | | | | |
| Double decrease width from above | | | | | |

Based upon your results, what interval width do you think provides the best picture of the dataset? Why?

## 2.29V In the Literature

Often frequencies and proportions are reported across multiple variables. That is the case in this example on college student credit card debt. Also notice that only percentages are reported.

Excerpt from Jassim, A.A. & Taylor, J. C. (2010). College students'credit card usage and debt. *Competition Forum, 8*(1), 101-110.

> The increasing levels of college students' credit card debt are raising alarm among parents, educators, news outlets, and various government agencies. The purpose of this study is to explore credit card debt and use by undergraduate students and examine whether gender and household income have an effect on that use. The credit card debt questionnaire was given to students attending various classes at the Craig School of Business (CSB) at California State University (CSUF) during the spring 2009 semester. Of the 648 participants, 53% were male; 44% were Caucasian, 24% were Hispanic or Latino, 16% were Asian, 5% were African American, and 11% classified themselves as others. In terms of class standing, 5% of respondents were freshmen, 8% were sophomores, 36% were juniors, and 51% were seniors. Finally, 89% of respondents were business majors and 11% were non- business majors taking introductory business classes as elective classes within their General Education course requirements. Table 1 compares levels of credit card debt by gender and household income.

**Table 1.** Balances Carried on Students' Credit Cards by Gender and Income Reported in Percentages

| | Under $1,000 | $1,000-$5,000 | $5,000-10,000 | Over $10,000 |
|---|---|---|---|---|
| **Gender** | | | | |
| Male (*n*=343) | 66 | 23 | 8 | 3 |
| Female (*n*=305) | 64 | 24 | 8 | 4 |
| **Household Income** | | | | |
| Less than $40,000 | 59 | 27 | 10 | 3 |
| $40,000-$80,000 | 63 | 26 | 8 | 3 |
| Over $80,000 | 72 | 19 | 7 | 2 |

Use the Jassim & Taylor excerpt to complete the following questions.

1. The values reported in Table 1 are percentages. Based upon the female sample size of 305, how many female participants have over $10,000 in credit card debt?

2. Based upon the percentages presented, can you conclude any gender differences in credit card debt?

3. Based upon household income, which group has the most credit card debt?

4. Based upon household income, which group has the least credit card debt?

5. The authors indicate that 51% of the sample were seniors and 36% were juniors. How does a sample that consists of a majority of upper classmen impact the results?

## 2.30 Using the Computer

Frequency distributions can be in table or graphic form. The following instructions will provide guidance on how to generate: frequency tables, bar graphs, pie charts, and histograms. First, steps for SPSS will be presented, then StatCrunch. Whichever program you use, you do need to keep a few things in mind when deciding what type output to generate.

1. Variable type is everything!
   - Categorical variables are great for bar graph and pie charts.
   - Quantitative variables are appropriate for histograms.
2. Frequency tables
   - Programs cannot generate grouped frequency tables.
   - Frequency tables for variables with a wide range of values will be really long!
3. SPSS and StatCrunch differences
   - SPSS `Frequencies` allows for the generation of other descriptive statistics and charts in addition to frequencies.
   - StatCrunch requires separate analyses.

### SPSS Step by Step Instructions

Generate `Frequencies` (with statistics and charts)

1. 👆 the `Analyze` menu.
2. Select `Descriptive Statistics`, then `Frequencies`.
3. 👆 variable(s) to be analyzed and move under `Variable(s)`.
4. 👆 Statistics; check appropriate options. Typical selections include: Mean, Median, Mode, Std. deviation, and Range. 👆 Continue.
5. 👆 Charts. Select appropriate options.

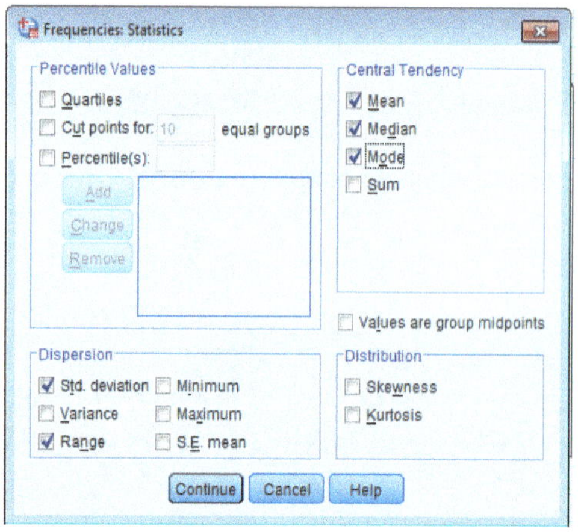


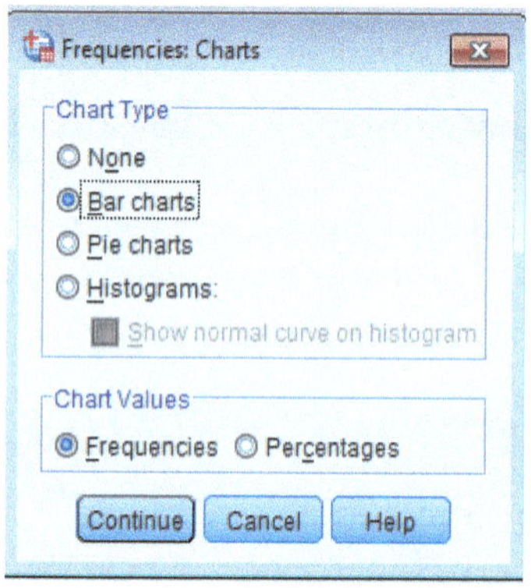


Create `Bar Graph`

1. 👆 `Graph`, 👆 `Chart Builder`
2. Under Gallery and Choose from, 👆 `Bar`.
3. Drag the picture of the simple bar graph to the chart preview area.
4. Under Variables, 👆 the categorical variable and drag it to the *X*-axis? box in the preview area.
5. 👆 `OK`.

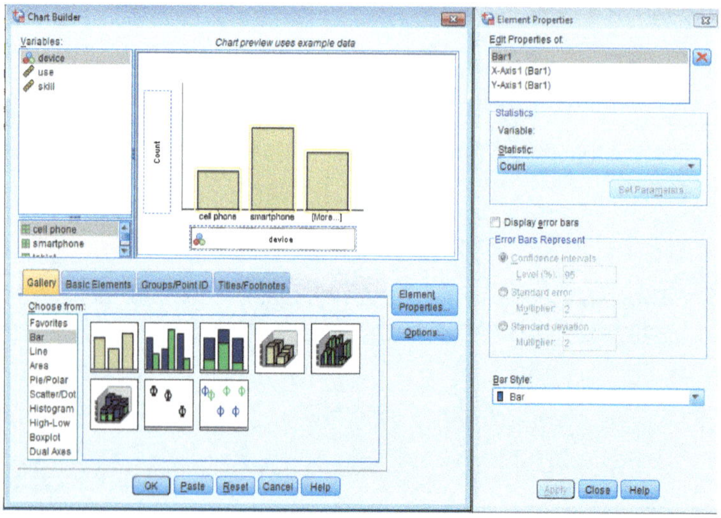

Create **`Pie Chart`** that represents the breakdown of frequencies by category.

1. **`Graph`**, **`Chart Builder`**
2. Under Gallery and Choose from **`Pie/Polar`**.
3. Drag the picture of the pie to the chart preview area.
4. Under Variables, select the categorical variable and drag to the Slice By? box.
5. **`OK.`**

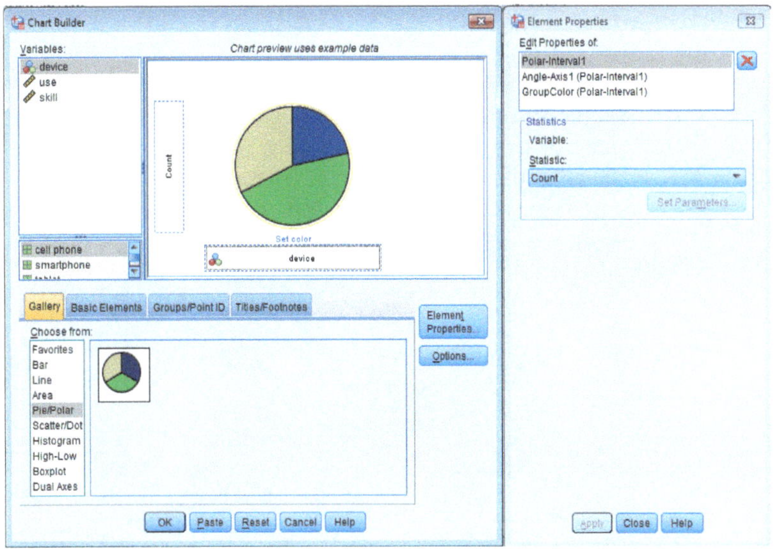


Create **`Histogram`**

1. **`Graph`**, **`Chart Builder`**
2. Under Gallery and Choose from **`Histogram`**.
3. Drag the picture of the simple histogram to the chart preview area.
4. Under **`Variables`**, select the quantitative variable and drag to the *X*-axis? box.
5. If you want to create a histogram for specific groups,
   - **`Groups/Point ID`** table and check Grouping/Stacking variable.
   - Drag your categorical variable to the **`Stack: set color`** box.
6. **`OK.`**

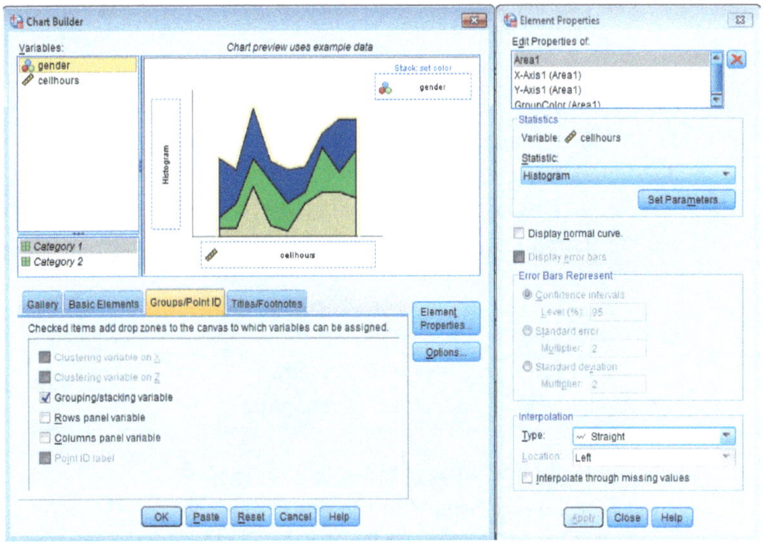

## **Stat**Crunch Step by Step Instructions

Generate **Frequencies**

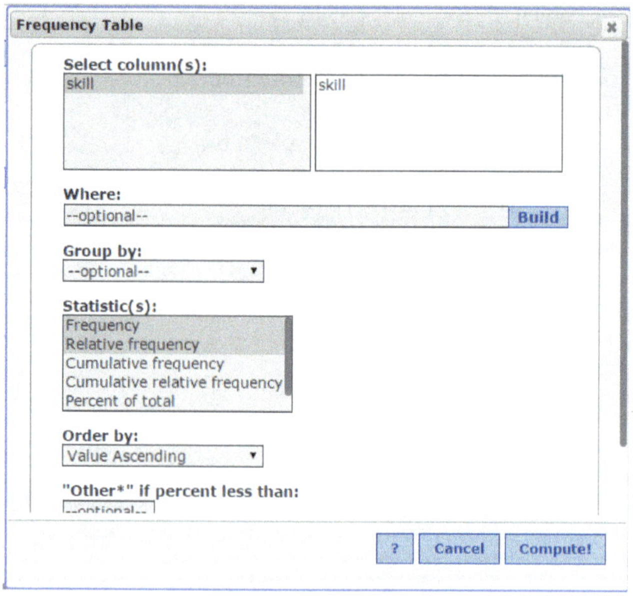


1. the **Stat** menu, select **Tables, >Frequency**
2. Under Select column(s), your variable.
3. Under Statistics, choose option. Typical selections will be Frequency, Relative frequency, and Percent of total.

Create **Bar Graph.**

1. **Graph** menu, select **Bar Plot >With Data.**
2. Under Select Column(s), categorical variable.
3. **Compute.**

Create **Pie Chart.**

1. **Graph** menu, select **Pie Chart >With Data.**
2. Under Select Column(s), categorical variable.
3. Under Display, choose Count or Percent of Total.
4. **Compute.**

Create **Histogram.**

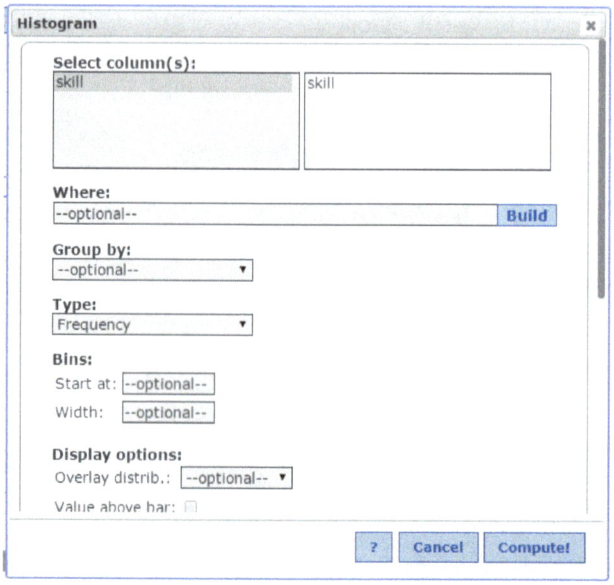


1. **Graph** menu, select **Histogram.**
2. Under Select Column(s), quantitative variable.
3. If you want to create a histogram for specific groups, under Group by: --optional-- and select the categorical variable that will create the groups.
4. If you want to create a grouped frequency histogram based upon a specific interval, under **Bins,**
   - Indicate a starting point for **Starts at:**
   - Indicate the interval width for **Width:**
5. **Compute**

## 2.31 Exercises
### Reviewing Concepts

1. Why do the bars touch in a histogram and do not touch in a bar graph?

2. Why is it helpful to report the percentage of respondents for specific values in a frequency distribution table?

3. What is the appropriate situation to utilize a pie chart?

4. When is it appropriate to utilize a grouped frequency distribution?

5. Describe the differences in shape between normal, positively skewed, and negatively skewed distributions?

6. Why is the manipulation of statistical graphs such an easy method to trick the consumer?

7. Go to https://youtu.be/0Rnq1NpHdmw to view *Last Week Tonight* with John Oliver in which he discuss the media and scientific research. What role does media play in informing and/or misinforming society on new research? How can you as a consumer avoid falling for these tricks? **Warning:** John uses the “F” word quite a bit.

## Interpreting Results

8. Utilize the excerpt and table to complete the questions.

A 2014 study conducted by the Pew Research Center examined social media use among U.S. adults. Data were collected through phone surveys (land and cell) with 1,597 individuals who identified themselves as Internet users. Results show that Facebook continues to be the most popular social media site. While its growth has slowed, the level of user engagement with the platform has increased. Other platforms like Twitter, Instagram, Pinterest, and LinkedIn saw significant increases over the past year in the proportion of online adults who now use their sites. Table 1 compares adult use of the various social media sites between 2012 and 2014.

**Table 1**

**Social media sites, 2012-2014**

*% of online adults who use the following social media websites, by year*

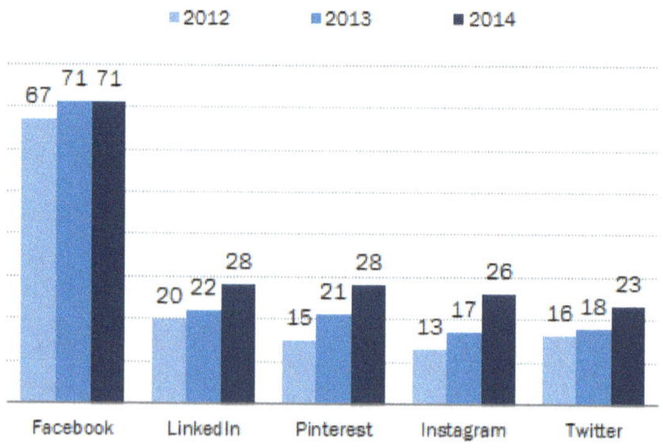


Pew Research Center's Internet Project Surveys, 2012-2014. 2014 data collected September 11-14 & September 18-21, 2014. N=1,597 internet users ages 18+.

PEW RESEARCH CENTER

http://www.pewinternet.org/2015/01/09/social-media-update-2014/

a. Which social media site had the fewest users in 2012?

b. Which social media site saw the greatest growth in use from 2012 to 2014?

c. Which social media site saw the greatest growth in use from 2013 to 2014?

d. Based upon the trends reported, what would you estimate to be the 2015 use for Facebook?

e. The report indicates the margin of sampling error is ±2.9% with 95% confidence. Based upon the margin of error, what is the range of 2014 Facebook users?

9. In an article titled, "These Two Charts Prove that a College Education Just Isn't Worth the Money Anymore" for *Degreed* and the *Business Insider*, David Blake presents two charts and ideas to support his argument. Using Figure 1, Blake asserts that the cost of education now far outweighs the earnings of a college graduate. With Figure 2, he indicates that the majority of unemployed are college graduates.

Figure 1

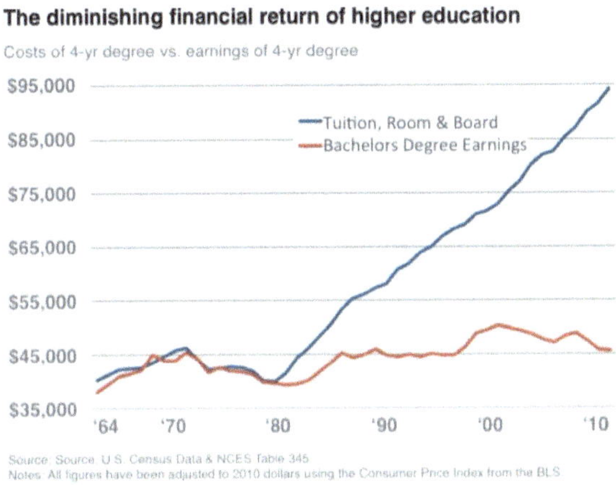


Figure 2

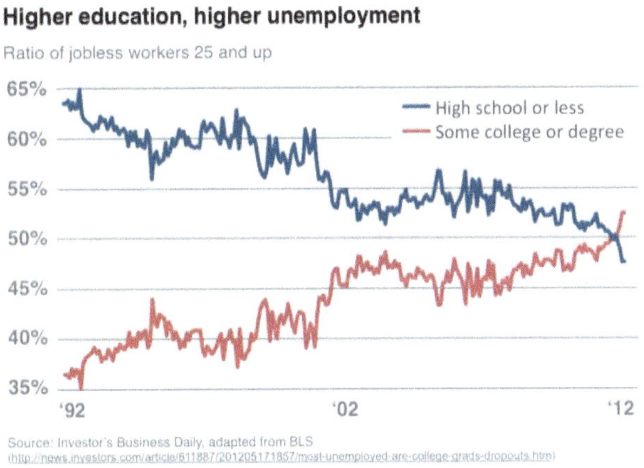


However, statisticshowto.com disagrees with Blake. The instructional website indicates that Figure 1 utilizes appropriate scales but asserts that its interpretation has been twisted. First, Figure 1 lacks a critical piece of information—the cost of not going to college in that the prospective earnings of a high school graduate are much less than a college graduate. Second, the chart itself provides annual income of $45,000 in 2010. If a college graduate works till the age of 65 and continued to earn $45,000 every year, the lifetime income would be $1,935,000. Subtracting the college expense of $95,000, one's net earnings would be $1,840,000. However, the U.S. Department of Education considered raises and cost of living increases and estimates that the college graduate will earn $2.9 million in a lifetime. Compared to a high school graduate who will only earn $1.3 million in a lifetime, the college graduate will certainly earn more.

a. What do you think? Technically, Blake's Figure 1 is accurate, yet statisticshowto.com says it lacks information. So how could Blake have included this critical information in Figure 1?

b. Interestingly, statisticshowto.com didn't mention any disagreement with Figure 2. If college graduates are experiencing more unemployment, how does that impact the lifetime earnings argument?

## Conducting the Analysis

Utilize SPSS or StatCrunch to conduct the following analyses.

10. In Example 1, we explored cell phone use between gender. The data below is the same data that you used to construct frequency distributions for males and females. Enter this data in SPSS or StatCrunch—remember to create two columns; one for gender and another for cell phone hours—so that you have 40 lines of data. Save your data set for later use.

| Row | gender | cellhours |
|---|---|---|
| 1 | 1 | 4 |
| 2 | 1 | 6 |
| 3 | 1 | 7 |
| 4 | 1 | 8 |
| 5 | 1 | 8 |
| 6 | 1 | 9 |
| 7 | 1 | 9 |
| 8 | 1 | 9 |
| 9 | 1 | 10 |
| 10 | 1 | 10 |

Females: 4, 6, 7, 8, 8, 9, 9, 9, 9, 10, 10, 10, 11, 11, 11, 11, 11, 12, 12, 12

Males: 4, 5, 5, 6, 6, 7, 7, 8, 8, 8, 8, 8, 9, 9, 9, 9, 10, 10, 11, 12

a. Create histogram(s) for cell phone hours that differentiate gender. How do these histograms differ from the ones you created by hand? Note: StatCrunch will create a separate histogram for each group; however, SPSS will stack groups within one histogram.

b. Create a pie chart for gender. What would be the most effective method to report gender for this study?

c. Create a pie chart for cell phone hours. Why isn't this an appropriate method for this variable?

11. Additional Practice #3 explored amount of caffeine consumed daily among college students. Enter the data (also presented below) in StatCrunch or SPSS and generate a histogram. The program will automatically create grouped intervals.
0, 0, 42, 45, 54, 59, 66, 78, 88, 88, 90, 95, 100, 110, 110, 116, 120, 122, 126, 133, 136, 140, 144, 160, 178, 180, 199, 206, 215, 222

a. How many intervals were used? What is the interval width?

b. How does the computer generated histogram compare to the one you created by hand?

c. Which is more accurate?

# Module 3

## Descriptive Statistics: Measures

### Learning Targets

After completing Module 3, you should be able to:

- Calculate and interpret measures of central tendency and variability,
- Identify distribution shapes and the typical placement of mean, median, and mode for each shape.
- Explain the role of degrees of freedom when calculating standard deviation for a sample.
- Apply the properties of a normal distribution when interpreting sample descriptive measures.

# Part 1: The Concepts

Presenting the frequencies and frequency distributions for variables is extremely helpful in understanding the data; however, several measures can summarize data using a single value. These are the measures we explore in this chapter, more specifically, we examine measures of central tendency and variability.

## 3.11 Measures of Central Tendency: Mean, Median, Mode

You are likely very familiar with measures of central tendency. You learned about them in school and are regularly exposed to them in the media. ***Measures of central tendency*** use a single value to represent the entire distribution by defining the center of the distribution. Three methods for defining the center of the distribution are: mean, median, and mode.

**Population Mean**

$$\mu = \frac{\Sigma X}{N}$$

**Sample Mean**

$$\bar{X} \text{ or } M = \frac{\Sigma X}{n}$$

The ***mean*** is the most common measure of central tendency and is the arithmetic average of scores or the sum of scores divided by the number of scores. In terms of notation, the population mean is indicated by the Greek letter mu ($\mu$). You will soon notice that the statistical notation for any population value will use a Greek letter. The notation for the sample mean is $\bar{X}$ or $M$. $M$ is used in publications and reports, so that is the notation applied in this text. For a sample ($n$=7) of seven scores—1, 2, 3, 3, 3, 4, 5—the mean is

$$M = \frac{\Sigma X}{n} = \frac{21}{7} = 3$$

**Median**

*Odd # of scores:*
- Find middle score.

*Even # of scores:*
- Calculate the average of the two middle scores.

The ***median*** is the midpoint of the distribution. So if all the scores are in order from low to high, the median is the very middle score such that half the scores are below this value and the other half are above. This measure has no special notation or abbreviation, in addition, the median is calculated the same for a population and a sample. The first step in determining the median is to arrange scores from lowest to highest. If a data set has an odd number of scores, then the score in the middle is the median. In our previous example of 7 scores—1, 2, 3, 3, 3, 4, 5—the median is 3. If a data set has an even number of scores, the median is the average of the two middle scores. Suppose we added one more value to our set of seven scores. Now the sample has eight scores—1, 2, 3, 3, 3, 4, 4, 5. The median is the average of the two middle scores: $(3 + 3)/2 = 3$.

If you have a large distribution of scores and don't want to count all the way to the middle, identifying the location of the middle score can be quite helpful. Suppose you have a sample ($n$=153) of 153 scores, which have been arranged in numerical order such that the lowest score is the first score and the highest score is the last, or #153. The location of the median is ($n$+1)/2. For our example of 153 scores,

$$\textbf{location of median} = \frac{n+1}{2} = \frac{153+1}{2} = 77th\ score$$

This equation can work for odd and even numbered data sets. If the sample has an even number of scores ($n$=154), the location will include a half (location=77.5), meaning that the location of the median is between the 77$^{th}$ and 78$^{th}$ scores. You would still need to calculate the average between those two scores.

The last measure of central tendency is mode. ***Mode*** is the score with the greatest frequency or the most common score. When examining a histogram, the tallest bar would indicate the mode since that score has the greatest frequency. In our previous example of 7 scores—1, 2, 3, 3, 3, 4, 5—the mode is 3. Mode is also an appropriate measure to report when describing a categorical variable.

## 3.12 Measures of Central Tendency and Distributions

Although these three measures all represent central tendency, each measures a different aspect. As such, these measures can display differently depending upon the shape of the distribution. Researchers can examine the measures of central tendency to determine the shape of the distribution. So far we have learned about three types of distributions--normal, positively skewed, and negatively skewed—however, our discussion will focus around symmetrical and skewed distributions.

### Symmetrical Distributions

The normal distribution is symmetrical, meaning that the left side of the distribution is a mirror image of the right side. Symmetrical distributions consistently apply measures of central tendency. When a distribution is symmetrical, we know that the median and mean are equal because:

1) The median is at the very center of the distribution, since it divides the distribution in half.
2) The mean is also at the very center of the distribution, since it averages all the scores.

Therefore, the median and mean are equal and in the center for symmetrical distributions. However, a symmetrical distribution can have a variety of shapes, as long as the left and right sides are mirror images of each other. In the three symmetrical distributions (Figure 3.1), notice that the mean and median are the same value and at the center of every distribution. Recall that the mode is the most frequent score, so in a frequency distribution the highest point represents the mode. For the normal distribution (A), the mode, the highest point of the curve, is also at the center. The normal distribution is the only distribution where the mean, median, and mode are the same. Distribution B has two modes and is called bimodal, while Distribution C has no mode, meaning that the same number of individuals reported each possible score.

**Figure 3.1**
*Symmetrical Distributions*

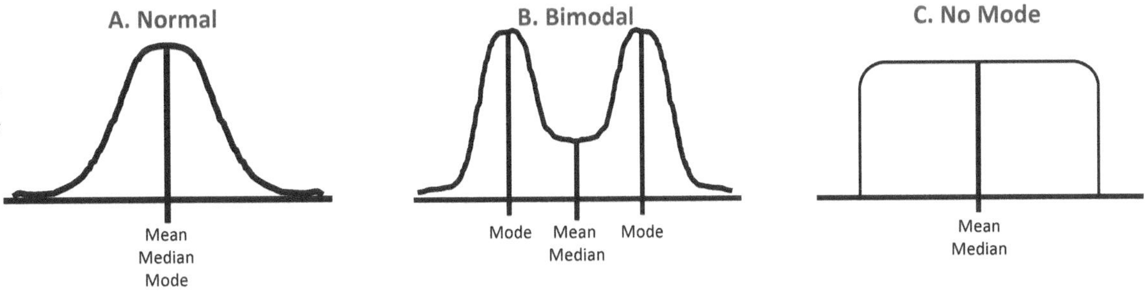


### Skewed Distributions

Much of the time, a distribution will not be symmetrical, rather it will be skewed or lopsided. Previously you were introduced to two types of skewed distributions: positive and negative. A positively skewed distribution has the extreme scores (the tail) on the high end of the distribution (see Figure 3.2). It is called positively skewed because the high extreme scores are skewing or distorting the shape of distribution as well as the measures of central tendency. A negatively skewed distribution has some low scoring outliers, which creates the tail on the low end of the distribution. Outliers generally influence the mean the most, so the mean is always pushed furthest out in the tail. The mode is the most frequent score and easily identified by the peak of the distribution. The median cuts the distribution so that 50% of the scores are below and 50% above. In terms of placement relative to mode and mean, median will be between these two values.

**Figure 3.2**
*Skewed Distributions*

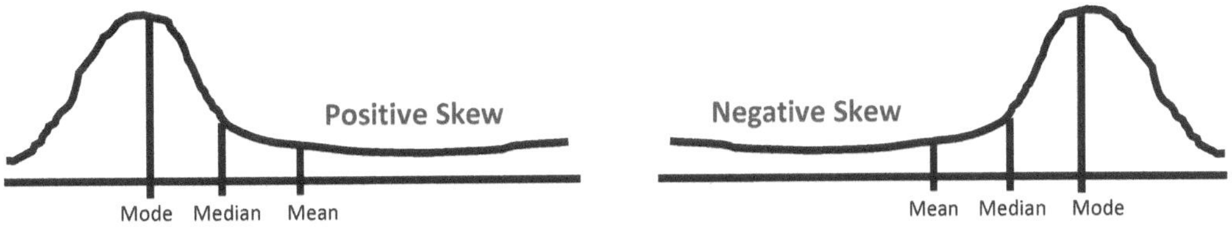


Understanding how the measures of central tendency are located in various distribution types can help you determine the distribution shape just by examining these measures. Based upon the values of mean, median, and mode and their order (from low to high), we can draw the following conclusions in Figure 3.3.

**Figure 3.3**
*Measures of Central Tendency by Distribution Shape*

| Measures of Central Tendencies | Conclusion about Distribution Shape |
|---|---|
| Mean = median | Symmetrical |
| Mean = median = mode | Normal |
| Mode (lowest), median, mean (highest) | Positive skew |
| Mean (lowest), median, mode (highest) | Negative skew |

### Choosing Measures of Central Tendency

While you should examine all three measures of central tendency for a quantitative variable, you may not want to report all three. In addition, some measures may not be appropriate to report depending upon the variable and/or distribution. Here are some guidelines to consider when analyzing and reporting descriptive results (see Figure 3.4). When examining a quantitative variable, you definitely should generate all three measures of central tendency in order to determine the distribution shape and if outliers are present. For distributions that are fairly normal, the mean is the best measure to report. However, for distributions that are skewed, the median is best since the mean is very sensitive to outliers. Finally, when summarizing categorical variables, the mode is the best measure of central tendency.

**Figure 3.4**
*Distribution Shapes and Measures by Variable Type*

| Variable Type | Distribution Shape | Measure to Report |
|---|---|---|
| Quantitative | Fairly Normal | Mean |
| | Skewed | Median |
| Categorical | | Mode |

## 3.13 Measures of Variability: Range and Standard Deviation

Measures of central tendency are extremely helpful in understanding how most of the sample score, but such measures only give us a partial picture of the distribution. We still don't know how spread out the distribution is. A ***measure of variability*** indicates how spread out the scores are in the distribution. The most basic measure of variability is the ***range***, which if you recall, is the difference between the highest and lowest scores of a distribution.

$$\textbf{Range} = X_{\max} - X_{\min}$$

This easy calculation gives a quick measure of spread. However, comparing the three very different distributions of reading scores in Figure 3.5, we see that mean, median, and range are all equal. Since the lowest and highest scores were identical across all three distributions, the range is the same. Obviously, a lot more is happening between the lowest and highest scores to create such different shapes.

**Figure 3.5**
*Comparison of Symmetrical Distributions*

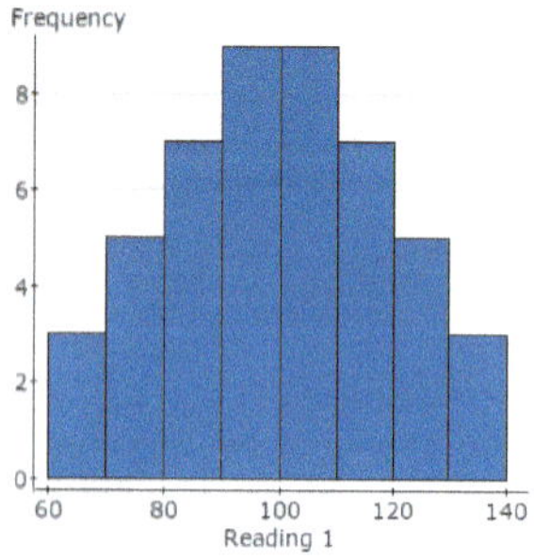


1. μ=100
   Median=100
   Mode=100
   Range=79

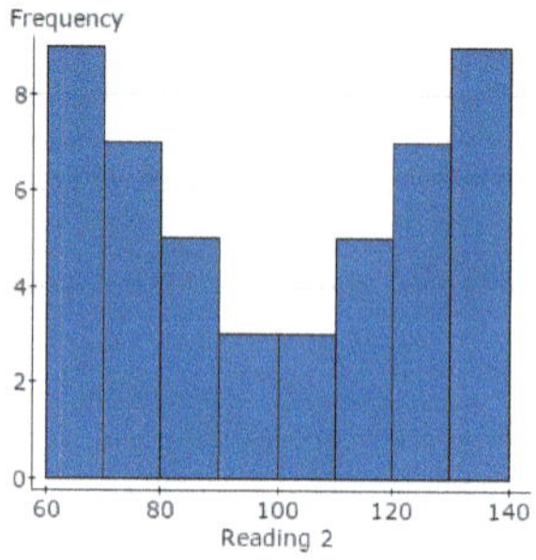


2. μ =100
   Median=100
   Bimodal
   Range=79

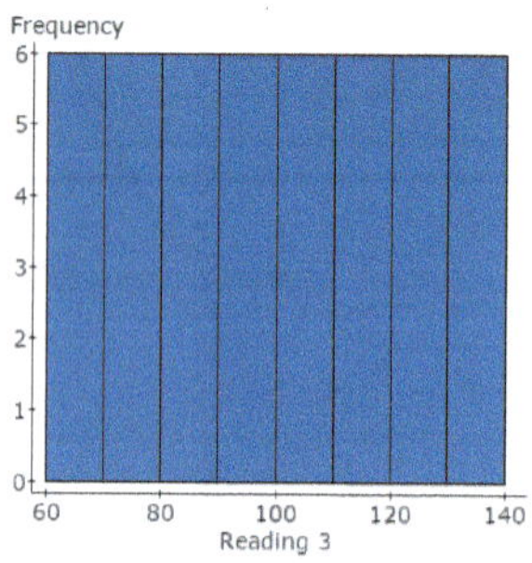


3. μ =100
   Median=100
   No mode
   Range=79

### Standard Deviation

Since the range only relies upon the two extreme scores of a distribution, it often does not provide an accurate description of the distribution's spread. Therefore, a more accurate and common measure of variability is the standard deviation. ***Standard deviation*** uses the mean as a reference point or standard to calculate the distance between each score and the mean. Basically, the standard deviation represents the average distance of each score from the mean. Notation for standard deviation for the population is the Greek letter sigma (lower case), σ. For a sample, the standard deviation is represented by *s* or *SD*. Since *SD* is commonly used in publications, this is the symbol utilized in this text. Calculating standard deviation seems a bit complex at first so we will break it down into steps with a set of scores for a population ($N$=16). The data is organized in Figure 3.6 where Column A displays the scores ($X$) and Column B shows the mean (μ) of the scores.

**Figure 3.6**
*Calculation of Standard Deviation*

| A | B | C | D |
|---|---|---|---|
| Score | Mean | Difference | Squared Difference |
| **X** | μ | **(X - μ)** | **(X - μ)²** |
| 2 | 5 | -3 | 9 |
| 3 | 5 | -2 | 4 |
| 3 | 5 | -2 | 4 |
| 4 | 5 | -1 | 1 |
| 4 | 5 | -1 | 1 |
| 4 | 5 | -1 | 1 |
| 5 | 5 | 0 | 0 |
| 5 | 5 | 0 | 0 |
| 5 | 5 | 0 | 0 |
| 5 | 5 | 0 | 0 |
| 6 | 5 | 1 | 1 |
| 6 | 5 | 1 | 1 |
| 6 | 5 | 1 | 1 |
| 7 | 5 | 2 | 4 |
| 7 | 5 | 2 | 4 |
| 8 | 5 | 3 | 9 |

Recall that standard deviation compares each score to the mean, so **Step #1** is to calculate the difference of each score from the mean ($X$ - μ), see Column C. Notice that these differences are negative and positive, since we are comparing to the mean which averages all the scores. If we were to truly compute the average of differences, we would calculate the sum of differences and divide by the number of scores. However, these differences will always add up to zero.

To eliminate these negative values, **Step #2** squares each difference, $(X - \mu)^2$, see Column D. The next two steps create the average of these squared differences.

**Step #3** calculates the sum of the squared differences [$\Sigma(X - \mu)^2$], also known as the **sum of squares (SS)**. For our example, sum of squares is 40.

**Step #4** divides this sum by the number of scores ($N$). So far, we have calculated the average of squared differences, known as **variance**. However, since we squared the differences, this value is difficult to interpret.

Our last step, **Step #5** removes the effect of squaring, by taking the square root of the variance. Putting this altogether, creates the following equation:

$$\sigma = \sqrt{\frac{\Sigma(X-\mu)^2}{N}} = \sqrt{\frac{40}{16}} = \sqrt{2.5} = 1.58$$

**Summary of Steps to Calculate Standard Deviation**

1. Compute each difference from mean ($X - \mu$)
2. Square each difference $(X - \mu)^2$
3. Sum the squared differences, $\Sigma(X - \mu)^2$
4. Divide sum of squares by $N$
5. Take the square root

Let's take a look at what standard deviation means in relation to our previous set of distributions that visually look very different but have the same mean, median and range (see Figure 3.7). Standard deviation will give us a better idea of where the scores are within each distribution. Remember standard deviation represents the average distance of scores from the mean, so you always need to think of the scores in relation to the mean. Since the three distributions are symmetrical, the mean is the middle of each distribution. For Distribution #1, the standard deviation ($\sigma$=18.80) is the lowest of the three distributions, meaning that most of the scores are clustered around the mean. Distribution #2 has the highest standard deviation ($\sigma$ =26.5), meaning the scores are further away from the mean, clustered toward the tails—therefore the scores are more spread out. Distribution #3 has a standard deviation of 23 ($\sigma$ =23), so it has more scores away from the mean in comparison to Distribution #1, but less than Distribution #2.

**Figure 3.7**
*Comparison of Symmetrical Distributions with Standard Deviation*

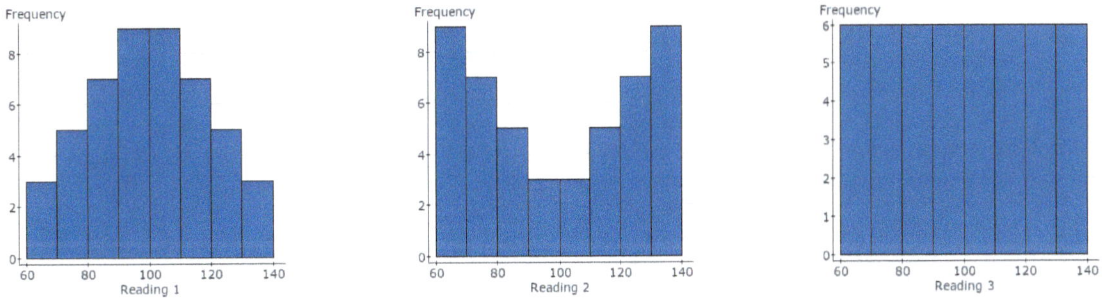


1. $\mu$=100
   Median=100
   Range=79
   **$\sigma$=18.8**
2. $\mu$ =100
   Median=100
   Range=79
   **$\sigma$ =26.5**
3. $\mu$ =100
   Median=100
   Range=79
   **$\sigma$ =23.0**

In summary, standard deviation represents the average distance of scores from the mean. A larger standard deviation indicates that scores are further away from the mean and thus more spread out. A smaller standard deviation indicates that scores are closer to the mean and less spread out.

## 3.14 Standard Deviation for a Sample

Since we are usually studying a sample instead of a population, we need to be able to calculate the standard deviation for a sample. The calculations are quite similar except for one minor difference. When calculating the average of squared differences for the population, we divide by N, the number of scores. In contrast, for the sample, we divide by $n$-1 to compute the average of squared differences. This difference in using $n$-1 is an adjustment for sample bias. Remember, we are studying a sample that is hopefully representative of the population so that we can generalize our results to the population. Since there is always sampling error, the sample is less variable than its population. Therefore, the sample standard deviation underestimates the population standard deviation. To adjust for the bias, the sample standard deviation divides by $n$-1 instead of $N$. This adjustment is also known as ***degrees of freedom*** ($df = n$-1). Dividing by a smaller number ($n$-1) produces a larger value and makes the sample standard deviation more accurate in estimating the population standard deviation.

**Population Standard Deviation**

$$\sigma = \sqrt{\frac{\Sigma(X-\mu)^2}{N}}$$

**Sample Standard Deviation**

$$SD = \sqrt{\frac{\Sigma(X-M)^2}{n-1}}$$

### Degrees of Freedom

Using $n$-1 for calculating sample standard deviation is not only to obtain a smaller denominator, but also to account for a restriction in the calculation. To calculate the population standard deviation, we are able to use the population mean (μ); however, when calculating the sample *SD* we don't know the population mean. So the sample mean is used to estimate the population mean. Therefore, before you even begin computing the differences, you have to compute the sample mean. Identifying the sample mean places a restriction on the sample variability. For example, suppose we have an unknown sample of three scores ($n$=3) that produce a mean of 6 ($M$=6). The different combinations of three values that create a mean of 6 are extensive; the only limit is that the sum of the three scores is 18 (since 18/3=6). Therefore the values must be between 0 and 18. In the five different data sets (A-E), we can identify the first two values without any restriction; but once they are identified, the third score must be a certain value to generate a sum of 18 and a mean of 6. This means that of our sample values, $n$-1 has the freedom to vary, but the last score's variability is restricted. Thus the term ***degrees of freedom*** ($n$-1) is an adjustment for sample bias and accounts for the restriction of variability on the final score in the sample. Degrees of freedom will continue to be used with many sample statistics.

| | A | B | C | D | E |
|---|---|---|---|---|---|
| 1st score | 1 | 5 | 7 | 10 | 12 |
| 2nd score | 11 | 8 | 3 | 2 | 6 |
| 3rd score must be: | 6 | 5 | 8 | 6 | 0 |

### 3.15 Standard Deviation and the Normal Distribution

Since numerous psychological, social, and biological variables are normally distributed in the population, the normal curve is the foundation for many inferential calculations. Remember, the normal curve: 1) is a frequency distribution of individual scores for some quantitative variable; 2) is symmetrical; and 3) has equal central measures (mean, median, and mode). The area under the curve, which represents these individual scores, can be divided into segments based upon the standard deviation. Standard deviation plays a unique role in the normal distribution in that it controls the spread of the distribution. Since standard deviation is the average distance of scores from the mean, we know that the spread of a normal distribution will typically hold six standard deviations. The segments or standard deviations above the mean are considered positive (+1, +2, +3) and the standard deviations below the mean are considered negative (-1, -2, -3). While normal distributions may vary in size and scale, all normal distributions follow two basic rules (See Figure 3.8).

**Figure 3.8**
*Normal Distribution with Percentages and SAT-Math Norms.*

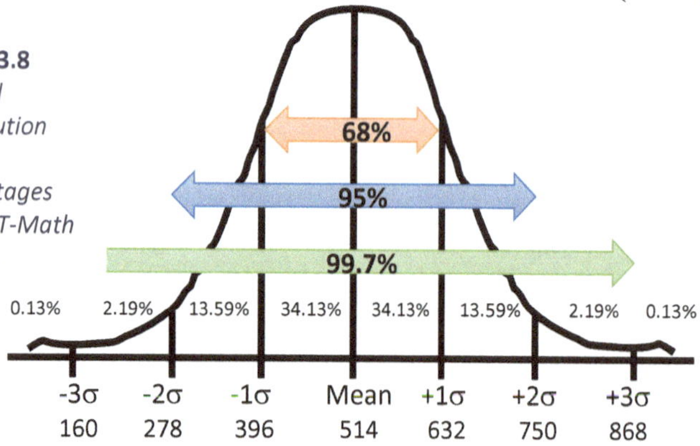


**Rule #1:** Three standard deviations fall on each side of the mean and equally divide the X-axis.

**Rule #2:** ***68-95-99.7***
The area between standard deviations differs. Approximately 68% of the scores fall within one standard deviation of the mean, 95% fall between two standard deviations, and 99.7% of scores fall between three standard deviations.

Let's apply this to a real-life example—the SAT exam—an exam most of you completed in preparation for college. SAT scores follow a normal distribution, also presented in Figure 3.5. In 2013, SAT reported the following norms for the mathematics exam (μ=514, σ=118). To apply these values to a distribution, we place the mean in the very middle. The value of the standard deviation is added at each segment (each standard deviation) above the mean, and subtracted at each segment below the mean. Notice that at +1σ, you need to add one standard deviation of 118 to the mean of 514. The value of 632 is the score represented at one standard deviation above the mean. Based upon the distribution for the 2013 SAT-Math, we can conclude that approximately:

- 68% of the population scored between 396 and 632;
- 95% scored between 278 and 750; and
- 99.7% scored between 160 and 868.

The concepts around normal distribution will be applied in the next chapter and allow us to glean more information about a population or sample.

## 3.16 Module Summary

- ***Measures of central tendency*** use a single value to represent the entire distribution by defining the center of the distribution.
    - ***Mean*** is the arithmetic average of scores or the sum of scores divided by the number of scores.
        - population mean ($\mu$)
        - sample mean ($\overline{X}$ or $M$)
    - ***Median*** is the midpoint of the distribution; 50% of scores below, 50% of scores above
    - ***Mode*** is the score with the greatest frequency or the most common score. Mode is the highest point in a histogram
- Measures of central tendency can display differently depending upon the shape of the distribution.
    - ***Symmetrical distributions*** have equivalent, mirror sides; mean and median are equal.
        - ***Normal distribution*** (A) is symmetrical
            - Mean, median, and mode are equal in the middle.
    - ***Skewed distributions*** are not symmetrical, rather they are lopsided due to some outliers in a tail.
        - ***Positively skewed*** distribution has the extreme scores (the tail) on the high end of the distribution. Order: Mode (lowest), median, mean (highest)
        - ***Negatively skewed*** distribution has some low scoring outliers, which creates the tail on the low end of the distribution. Order: Mean (lowest), median, mode (highest)
- Choosing a measure of central tendency:
    - Quantitative variable
        - Normally distributed→mean
        - Skew distribution→median
    - Categorical variable→mode

- ***Measures of variability*** indicate how spread out the scores are in the distribution.
    - ***Range*** is the most basic measure of variability; the difference between the highest and lowest scores of a distribution.
        - **Range** = $X_{max} - X_{min}$
        - Since range only uses the two extreme scores of data set, it usually doesn't provide an accurate picture of a distribution's spread.
    - ***Standard deviation*** represents the average distance of each score from the mean.
        - The mean is the reference point (standard) to calculate the distance between each score and the mean.
        - Larger standard deviation means scores are further away from the mean and more spread out;
        - Smaller standard deviation indicates that scores are closer to the mean and less spread out.
        - Population standard deviation ($\sigma$)

$$\sigma = \sqrt{\frac{\Sigma(X-\mu)^2}{N}}$$

        - Sample standard deviation ($s$ or $SD$)

$$SD = \sqrt{\frac{\Sigma(X-M)^2}{n-1}}$$

    - Sample standard deviation uses degrees of freedom in its calculation.
        - ***Degrees of freedom*** ($df = n$-1) is an adjustment for sample bias since the sample is typically less variable than the population. It is also used because of a restriction in calculation.
        - Dividing by a smaller number ($n$-1) produces a larger value and makes the sample standard deviation more accurate in estimating the population standard deviation.
    - Because the normal curve is a frequency distribution of some quantitative variable, is symmetrical, and has equal central measures (mean, median, mode), the area under the curve represents 100% of scores and can be divided into segments using the standard deviation.
        - Standard deviation controls the spread of the distribution.
        - Normal distribution will typically hold six standard deviations.
        - Normal distribution will vary in size and scale but will always follow two basic rules:
            - **Rule #1:** Three standard deviations fall on each side of the mean and equally divide the $X$-axis.
            - **Rule #2:** ***68-95-99.7*** Approximately 68% of the scores fall within one standard deviation of the mean, 95% fall between two standard deviations, and 99.7% of scores fall between three standard deviations.

# Part 2: Learning Guide

## 3.21V Measures of Central Tendency: Mean, Median, Mode

***Measures of central tendency*** use a single value to represent the entire distribution by defining the center of the distribution.

- ***Mean*** is the arithmetic average of scores or the sum of scores divided by the number of scores.
  - population mean is indicated by the Greek letter mu (μ)
    - $\mu = \frac{\Sigma X}{N}$
  - sample mean is $\bar{X}$ or $M$
    - $\bar{X}$ or $M = \frac{\Sigma X}{n}$
- ***Median*** is the midpoint of the distribution; 50% of scores below, 50% of scores above.
  - Steps to find the median:
    1. Arrange scores from low to high.
    2. Find middle:
       - For odd # scores; find the middle.
       - For even # scores, calculate the average of the two middle scores.
  - If you have a large number of scores, locate the median by using:
    - **location of median** $= \frac{n+1}{2}$
- ***Mode*** is the score with the greatest frequency or the most common score. Mode is the highest point in a histogram.

## 3.22V Measures of Central Tendency and Distributions

Measures of central tendency can display differently depending upon the shape of the distribution.

- Symmetrical distributions have equivalent sides, meaning that the left side of the distribution is a mirror image of the right side.
  - Median and mean are equal.
  - Can have a variety of shapes, as long as the left and right sides are mirror images of each other.

**Figure 3.1**
*Symmetrical Distributions*

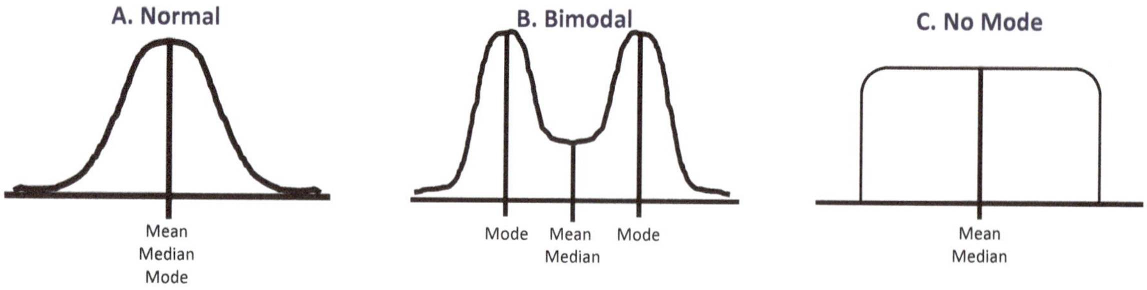


- ***Normal distribution*** (A) is symmetrical
  - Mean, median, and mode are equal in the middle.
- ***Skewed distributions*** are not symmetrical, rather they are lopsided due to some outliers in a tail.
  - Outliers influence the mean the most, so the mean is always pushed out into the tail the most.
  - Mode is always the highest point in the distribution.
  - Median is positioned between mode and mean.
  - ***Positively skewed*** distribution has the extreme scores (the tail) on the high end of the distribution.
  - ***Negatively skewed*** distribution has some low scoring outliers, which creates the tail on the low end of the distribution

**Figure 3.2**
*Measures of Central Tendency by Distribution Shape*

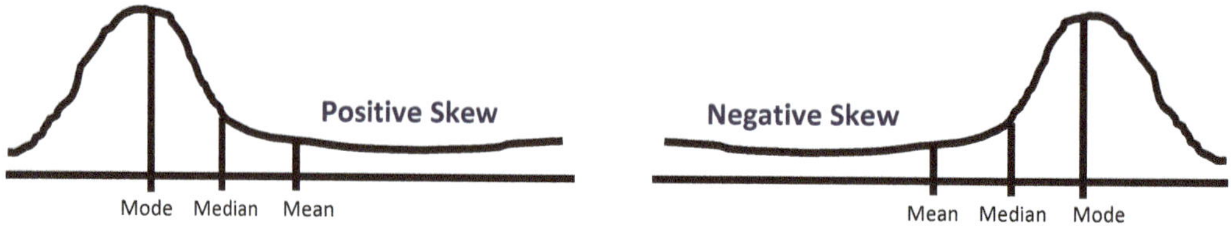

- Choosing the appropriate measure of central tendency to report is dependent upon the variable type and distribution shape.

**Figure 3.3**
*Distribution Shape and Measure of Central Tendency by Variable Type*

| Variable Type | Distribution Shape | Measure to Report |
|---|---|---|
| Quantitative | Fairly Normal | Mean |
| | Skewed | Median |
| Categorical | | Mode |

### 3.23V Measures of Variability: Range and Standard Deviation

***Measure of variability*** indicates how spread out the scores are in the distribution.

- ***Range*** is the most basic measure of variability; the difference between the highest and lowest scores of a distribution.
  - **Range** = $X_{max} - X_{min}$
  - Since range only uses the two extreme scores of data set, it usually doesn't provide an accurate picture of a distribution's spread.

**Figure 3.7**
*Comparison of Symmetrical Distributions*

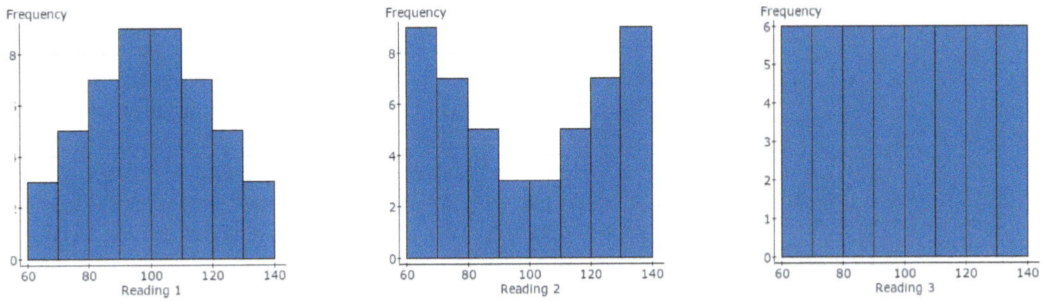


1. μ=100
   Median=100
   Mode=100
   Range=79
   **σ=18.8**
2. μ =100
   Median=100
   Bimodal
   Range=79
   **σ =26.5**
3. μ =100
   Median=100
   No mode
   Range=79
   **σ =23.0**

- ***Standard deviation*** represents the average distance of each score from the mean.
  - Uses the mean as a reference point or standard to calculate the distance between each score and the mean.
  - Population standard deviation uses Greek letter sigma (lower case), σ.
  - **Steps to calculate population standard deviation:**
    1. Compute each difference from the mean ($X$- μ)
    2. Square each difference $(X-\mu)^2$
    3. Sum the squared differences $\Sigma(X-\mu)^2$
    4. Divide the sum of squares by $N$
    5. Take the square root

$$\sigma = \sqrt{\frac{\Sigma(X-\mu)^2}{N}} = \sqrt{\frac{40}{16}} = \sqrt{2.5} = 1.58$$

  - Since standard deviation represents the average distance of scores from the mean,
    - a larger standard deviation means scores are further away from the mean and thus more spread out;
    - a smaller standard deviation indicates that scores are closer to the mean and less spread out.

| A | B | C | D |
|---|---|---|---|
| Score | Mean | Difference | Squared Difference |
| $X$ | μ | ($X$ - μ ) | $(X-\mu)^2$ |
| 2 | 5 | -3 | 9 |
| 3 | 5 | -2 | 4 |
| 3 | 5 | -2 | 4 |
| 4 | 5 | -1 | 1 |
| 4 | 5 | -1 | 1 |
| 4 | 5 | -1 | 1 |
| 5 | 5 | 0 | 0 |
| 5 | 5 | 0 | 0 |
| 5 | 5 | 0 | 0 |
| 5 | 5 | 0 | 0 |
| 6 | 5 | 1 | 1 |
| 6 | 5 | 1 | 1 |
| 6 | 5 | 1 | 1 |
| 7 | 5 | 2 | 4 |
| 7 | 5 | 2 | 4 |
| 8 | 5 | 3 | 9 |
| | | 0 | SS = 40 |

### 3.24V Standard Deviation for a Sample

- Sample standard deviation is represented by *s* or *SD*.
- Calculation of sample standard deviation is similar to that of population, except for one minor difference.
  - Divide by *n*-1 not *N*.
  - *n*-1 is degrees of freedom (*df*)
- ***Degrees of freedom*** (*df* = *n*-1) is an adjustment for sample bias since the sample is typically less variable than the population.
  - Dividing by a smaller number (*n*-1) produces a larger value and makes the sample standard deviation more accurate in estimating the population standard deviation.

**Population Standard Deviation**

$$\sigma = \sqrt{\frac{\Sigma(X-\mu)^2}{N}}$$

**Sample Standard Deviation**

$$SD = \sqrt{\frac{\Sigma(X-M)^2}{n-1}}$$

#### Degrees of Freedom

Is used not only to obtain a smaller denominator, but also to account for a restriction in the calculation.

- **Restriction**
  - Calculating sample standard deviation requires the sample mean, since we don't know the population mean.
  - Identifying the sample mean places a restriction on the sample variability.
  - Suppose we have an unknown sample of three scores (*n*=3) that produce a mean of 6 (*M*=6).
    - The different combinations of three values with a mean of 6 are extensive; the only limit is that the sum of the three scores is 18 (since 18/3=6). Values must be between 0 and 18.
    - In the five different data sets (A-E), we can identify the first two values without any restriction; but once they are identified, the third score must be a certain value to generate a sum of 18 and a mean of 6. This means that of our sample values, *n*-1 has the freedom to vary, but the last score's variability is restricted.

| | A | B | C | D | E |
|---|---|---|---|---|---|
| 1st score | 1 | 5 | 7 | 10 | 12 |
| 2nd score | 11 | 8 | 3 | 2 | 6 |
| 3rd score must be: | 6 | 5 | 8 | 6 | 0 |

### 3.25V Standard Deviation and the Normal Distribution

- The normal curve:
  1) is a frequency distribution of individual scores for some quantitative variable;
  2) is symmetrical; and
  3) has equal central measures (mean, median, and mode).
- Area under curve represents individual scores and can be divided into segments based upon the standard deviation.
  - Standard deviation controls the spread of the distribution.
  - Normal distribution will typically hold six standard deviations.
  - Normal distribution will vary in size and scale but will always follow two basic rules:
    - **Rule #1:** Three standard deviations fall on each side of the mean and equally divide the *X*-axis.
    - **Rule #2:** ***68-95-99.7*** The area between standard deviations differs. Approximately 68% of the scores fall within one standard deviation of the mean, 95% fall between two standard deviations, and 99.7% of scores fall between three standard deviations.

**Example**

The SAT exam follows a normal distribution. In 2013, SAT reported the following norms for the mathematics exam (μ=514, σ=118). Based upon this distribution, we can conclude that approximately:

- 68% of the population scored between 396 and 632;
- 95% scored between 278 and 750; and
- 99.7% scored between 160 and 868.

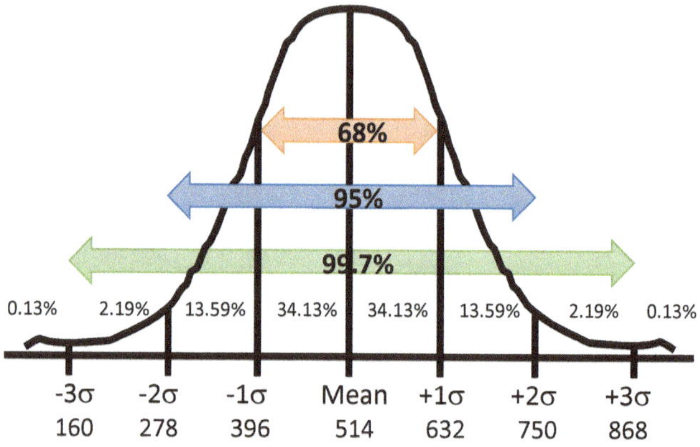

### 3.26V Examples

1. Most people know that drinking under the influence is illegal, but many do not realize how few drinks it really takes to reach legal toxicity (.08). Understanding how alcohol affects an individual can mean the difference between life and death. For a 200 pound male, four drinks in an hour will generate legal intoxication. Fourteen ($n$ =14) 200 lb. men were asked how many drinks it would take for them to be legally intoxicated.

   a. Use the data to calculate the following.

   Mean =

   Range =

   Median =

   Degrees of freedom =

   Mode =

   Standard deviation =

| $X$ | $M$ | $X$-$M$ | $(X\text{-}M)^2$ |
|---|---|---|---|
| 3 | | | |
| 4 | | | |
| 4 | | | |
| 4 | | | |
| 5 | | | |
| 5 | | | |
| 5 | | | |
| 5 | | | |
| 5 | | | |
| 5 | | | |
| 6 | | | |
| 6 | | | |
| 6 | | | |
| 7 | | | |

   b. Based upon the measures of central tendency, what distribution shape does this data create?

   c. What percent of the sample would likely be arrested for driving while intoxicated if pulled over after drinking?

2. The SAT is an important admission criteria for college admissions. A high school is interested in examining Critical Reading exam results for students enrolled in honors courses. Specifically, the school wants to compare students who have taken honors courses and college classes to those who have only take honors courses The following SPSS output is compares these two groups.

   a. Use the output to complete the table.

| | Honors Only | College Courses |
|---|---|---|
| Mean | | |
| Median | | |
| Range | | |
| *SD* | | |

**Descriptives**

| | HSgroup | | | Statistic | Std. Error |
|---|---|---|---|---|---|
| SAT | honors only | Mean | | 621.7500 | 15.66976 |
| | | 95% Confidence Interval for Mean | Lower Bound | 588.9528 | |
| | | | Upper Bound | 654.5472 | |
| | | 5% Trimmed Mean | | 620.2778 | |
| | | Median | | 610.0000 | |
| | | Variance | | 4910.829 | |
| | | Std. Deviation | | 70.07731 | |
| | | Minimum | | 510.00 | |
| | | Maximum | | 760.00 | |
| | | Range | | 250.00 | |
| | | Interquartile Range | | 108.25 | |
| | | Skewness | | .286 | .512 |
| | | Kurtosis | | -.585 | .992 |
| | college courses too | Mean | | 666.7500 | 15.36621 |
| | | 95% Confidence Interval for Mean | Lower Bound | 634.5882 | |
| | | | Upper Bound | 698.9118 | |
| | | 5% Trimmed Mean | | 666.3889 | |
| | | Median | | 663.0000 | |
| | | Variance | | 4722.408 | |
| | | Std. Deviation | | 68.71978 | |
| | | Minimum | | 550.00 | |
| | | Maximum | | 790.00 | |
| | | Range | | 240.00 | |
| | | Interquartile Range | | 89.75 | |
| | | Skewness | | .293 | .512 |
| | | Kurtosis | | -.560 | .992 |

   b. Which group had the highest average?

   c. Which group had the least variability?

3. The previous problem utilized results from the SAT Critical Reading exam with a mean of 496 and a standard deviation of 115 ($\mu$=496, $\sigma$=115). Use these norms to complete the normal distribution below.

   a. What percentage of the population will typically score between 381 and 611?

   b. What percentage of the population will typically score between 266 and 726?

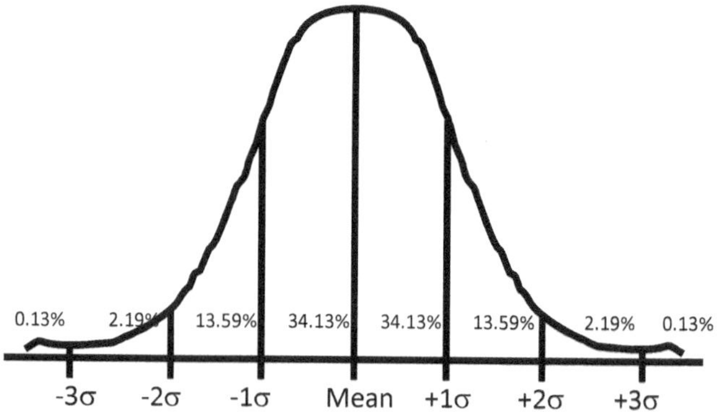


**3.27V Additional Practice**

1. An absolutely amazing statistics professor had her class of fifteen students ($n$=15) evaluate her teaching using a 10-point scale, with 1 being Dreadful, and 10 being Fabulous. Her class generated the data in the table.

   a. Use the data to calculate the following.

   Mean =

   Range =

   Median =

   Degrees of freedom =

   Mode =

   Standard deviation =

   b. Based upon the measures of central tendency, what distribution shape does this data create?

| $X$ | $M$ | $X$-$M$ | $(X\text{-}M)^2$ |
|---|---|---|---|
| 2 | | | |
| 5 | | | |
| 7 | | | |
| 7 | | | |
| 8 | | | |
| 8 | | | |
| 8 | | | |
| 9 | | | |
| 9 | | | |
| 9 | | | |
| 9 | | | |
| 9 | | | |
| 10 | | | |
| 10 | | | |
| 10 | | | |

**3.28V Hands-on Activity: The Impact of Standard Deviation**

- You need 16 pieces of candy (M-n-M's, Skittles, or chocolate chips.)
- You must use all 16 pieces for each distribution.
- Use graphs below.

1. For distribution A, create a **<u>normal</u>** distribution with the mean at 5. Trace the outline of the distribution.

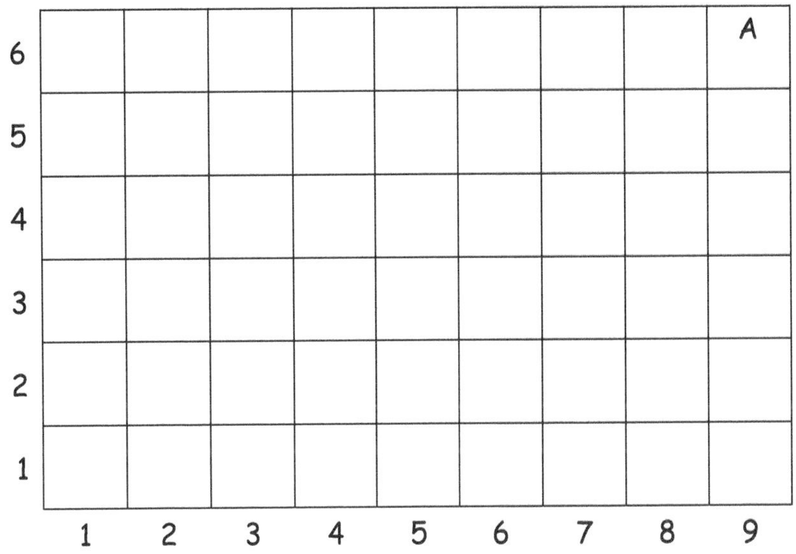


2. For distribution B, move candy around to create a distribution that has **<u>greater variability than A</u>**. Trace outline of distribution.

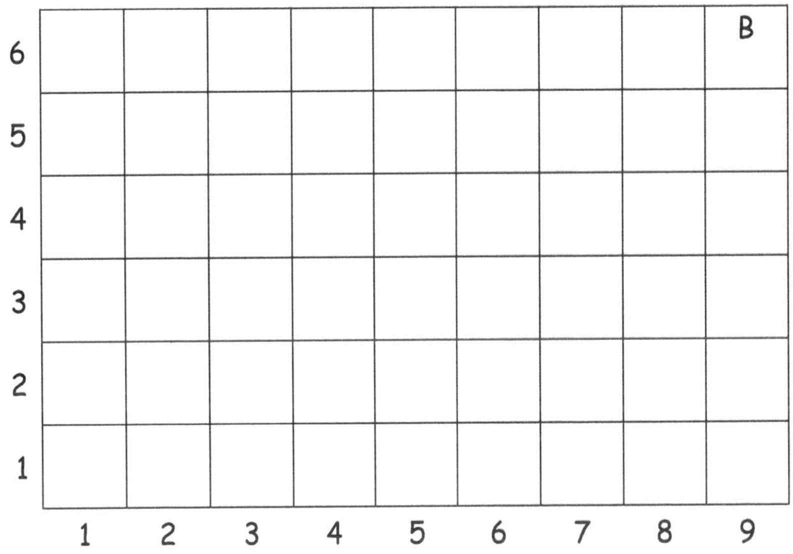


3. For distribution C, move candy around to create a distribution that has **<u>less variability than A</u>**. Trace outline of distribution.

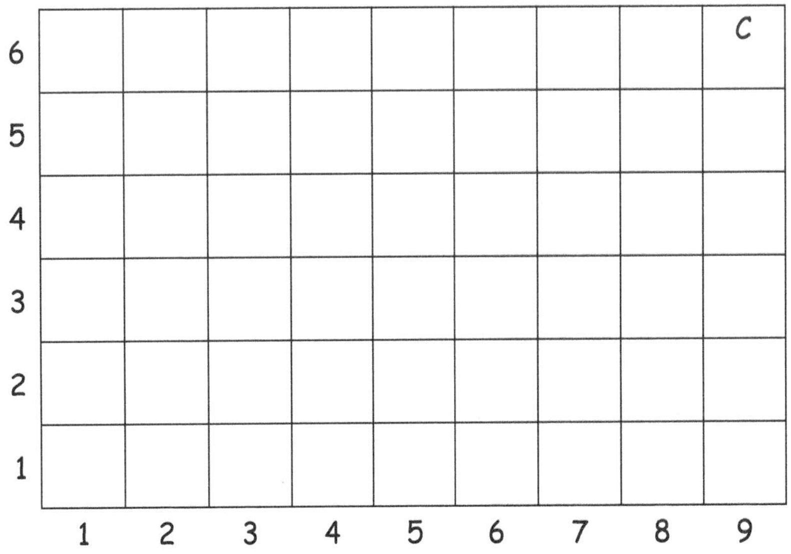

**3.29V In the Literature**

**Excerpt from:** Roberts, J. A., Yaya, L.H.P., & Manolis, C. (2014). The invisible addiction: Cell phone activities and addiction among male and female college students. *Journal of Behavioral Addictions*, *3*(4), 254-265.

Researchers conducted a study of 164 Baylor University students to examine their cell phone use and addiction. Students completed an online questionnaire that asked how much time they spend on 24 cell phone activities. The researchers were specifically interested in examining gender differences in these activities. Previous research indicates that females use technology as social and communication tools; whereas, males use technology for entertainment and informational purposes. Table 1 presents the means and standard deviations for the 24 activities between males and females.

**Table 1.** Gender Differences in the Number of Minutes per Day for Various Cell Phone Uses

| | Males | | Females | |
|---|---|---|---|---|
| | *M* | *SD* | *M* | *SD* |
| Calls | 29.3 | 34.5 | 37.1 | 38.3 |
| Texting | 84.4 | 59.1 | 105.4 | 69.9 |
| E-mails | 40.1 | 36.1 | 57.3 | 55.2 |
| Banking | 9.3 | 13.6 | 10.8 | 12.9 |
| Pictures | 13.0 | 16.2 | 21.3 | 28.8 |
| Games | 24.0 | 30.1 | 13.4 | 27.6 |
| Calendar | 11.0 | 16.0 | 23.8 | 43.5 |
| Clock | 19.3 | 27.6 | 30.5 | 44.7 |
| Books | 6.3 | 16.6 | 6.0 | 14.6 |
| Bible | 6.9 | 18.3 | 7.8 | 20.4 |
| Facebook | 31.4 | 40.3 | 46.2 | 46.0 |
| Twitter | 22.0 | 41.2 | 30.1 | 48.1 |
| Pinterest | 1.0 | 5.7 | 26.1 | 39.8 |
| Instagram | 8.3 | 23.7 | 25.6 | 37.3 |
| YouTube | 14.3 | 23.0 | 10.4 | 17.6 |
| iTunes | 10.0 | 21.2 | 9.1 | 20.1 |
| iPod | 26.3 | 45.9 | 27.5 | 43.7 |
| Pandora | 28.0 | 44.3 | 28.0 | 43.2 |
| Internet | 33.1 | 31.6 | 35.8 | 42.8 |
| eBay | 3.0 | 9.8 | 3.1 | 9.3 |
| Amazon | 3.1 | 10.8 | 6.1 | 21.8 |
| CouponApps | 1.1 | 5.4 | 5.1 | 15.1 |
| GoogleMaps | 8.5 | 18.2 | 11.3 | 20.3 |
| Other Apps | 24.8 | 38.5 | 22.4 | 34.5 |
| Total | 458.5 | 344.2 | 600.1 | 392.3 |

1. Which gender had the greatest number of total minutes of cell phone use?

2. Compare the means between males and females and complete the table by indicating which group was higher for each use. If groups are within one minute, consider them to be similar.

| Males Higher | Females Higher | About the Same |
|---|---|---|
| | | |

   a. How many cell phone uses did women report more minutes for than men?

   b. Are there any surprises in terms of uses between genders?

3. What are the top two cell phone uses for women? For men?

4. Which cell phone use presents the greatest difference between men and women?

5. Which cell phone use (other than Total) has the largest standard deviation? Why do you think the SD is so large?

6. Which cell phone use has the smallest standard deviation for males? Based upon the mean for this use, would the distribution shape likely be skewed? Explain.

7. Do these results support the findings of previous research—that females use technology for social/communication purposes while men use technology for entertainment and information?

## 3.30 Using the Computer

### SPSS Step by Step Instructions

Although running **Descriptives** within SPSS can generate measures of central tendency and variability, we will focus on the use of **Explore**. **Explore** not only generates many descriptive statistics and graphs (at the same time) but allows you to compare groups. Within Plots, we will only utilize a histogram. The Boxplots and Stem-and-leaf graphs are very helpful in detecting outliers, which is not in the scope of this course.

Conduct **Explore** (with statistics and plots)

1. the **Analyze** menu.
2. Select **Descriptive Statistics**, then **Explore**.
3. quantitative variable(s) to be analyzed and move under **Dependent List**.
4. categorical variable(s) to be analyzed and move under **Factor List.** If you don't have any categorical variables to include—that's OK. Just leave this blank.
5. Within the Explore dialogue menu, **Plots**.

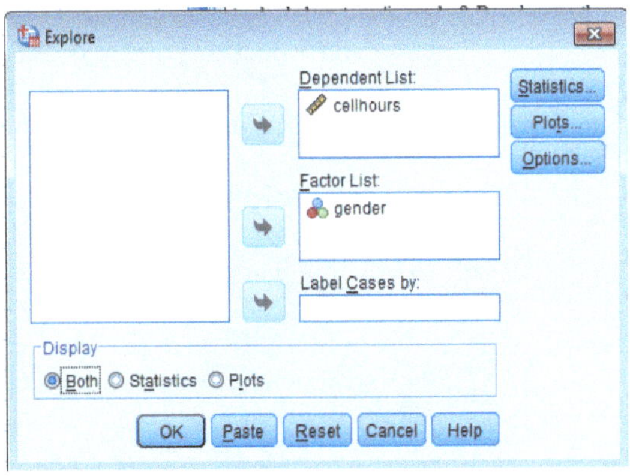


6. Within **Explore:Plots** dialogue box,
   - Under **Boxplots**, None.
   - Under **Descriptives**, uncheck Stem-and-Leaf, check Histogram.
   - **Continue**.
7. **OK**.

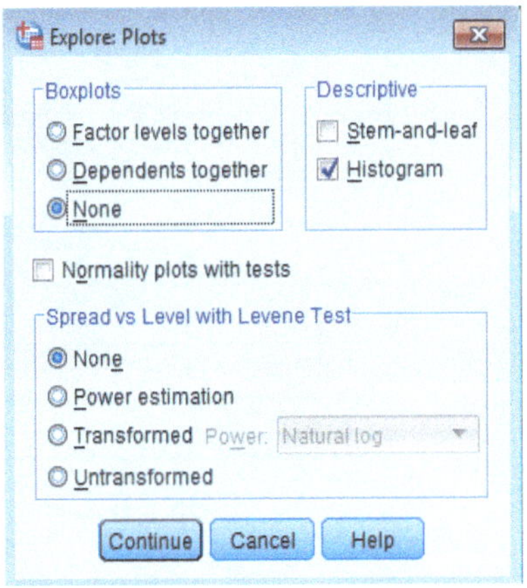


### StatCrunch Step by Step Instructions

Generate **Summary Statistics**

1. the **Stat** menu, select **Summary Stat, >Columns**
2. Under Select column(s), the quantitative variables to be examined.
3. Under Group by:, select the categorical variable. You don't have to compare groups, you may leave this blank.
4. **Compute.**

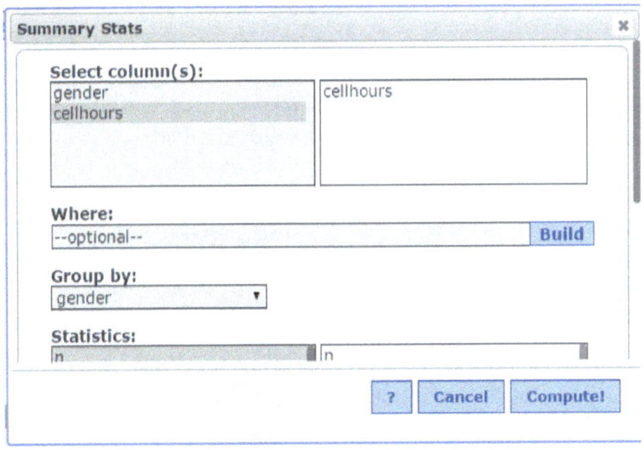

## 3.31 Exercises
### Reviewing Concepts

1. Explain when (the type of variables and distributions) the different measures of central tendency should be used.

2. Suppose you have a 10-point quiz. Based upon the measures of central tendency, identify the distribution shape.

   a. Mean=2, Median =4, Mode=6.

   b. Mode=2, Median=4, Mean=6.

   c. Mean, median, mode all equal 7.

3. Explain why standard deviation is a more accurate measure of variability than range.

4. Calculate standard deviation for the following data sets. Both have a mean of 6. Notice that dataset A has many scores away from the mean of 6, whereas B has 3 data points right at the mean. How does having more scores at or close to the mean change the standard deviation?

**A**

| *X* | *M* | *X-M* | $(X-M)^2$ |
|---|---|---|---|
| 2 | 6 | | |
| 2 | 6 | | |
| 8 | 6 | | |
| 8 | 6 | | |
| 10 | 6 | | |
| | | SS = $(X-M)^2$ = | |

**B**

| *X* | *M* | *X-M* | $(X-M)^2$ |
|---|---|---|---|
| 2 | 6 | | |
| 6 | 6 | | |
| 6 | 6 | | |
| 6 | 6 | | |
| 10 | 6 | | |
| | | SS = $(X-M)^2$ = | |

5. IQ tests are typically normed with a mean of 100 and a standard deviation of 15 ($\mu$=100, $\sigma$=15). Use these norms to complete the normal distribution below.

   a. What percentage of the population will typically score between 85 and 115?

   b. What percentage of the population will typically score between 70 and 130?

   c. Between what two scores will 99.7% of the population score?

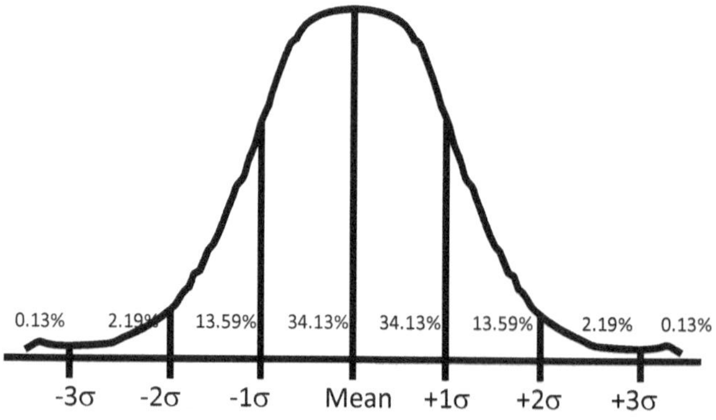

## Interpreting Results

6. Barry Bonds holds the current career record for home runs (HRs) with 762. The previous two record holders were Hank Aaron (755) and Babe Ruth (714). Barry Bonds and Babe Ruth played for 22 seasons, while Hank Aaron played 23. The number of home runs per season were entered into StatCrunch for these three leaders. Descriptive statistics were generated using Summary Statistics.

**Summary statistics for Home Runs:**
Group by: Player

| Player | n | Mean | Variance | Std. dev. | Std. err. | Median | Range | Min | Max | Q1 | Q3 |
|---|---|---|---|---|---|---|---|---|---|---|---|
| Bonds | 22 | 34.636364 | 197.09957 | 14.039215 | 2.9931708 | 34 | 68 | 5 | 73 | 25 | 45 |
| Aaron | 23 | 32.826087 | 125.05929 | 11.182991 | 2.3318148 | 34 | 37 | 10 | 47 | 26 | 44 |
| Ruth | 22 | 32.454545 | 408.45022 | 20.210151 | 4.3088187 | 38 | 60 | 0 | 60 | 11 | 47 |

a. Compare the mean and median for these three players. Who had the greatest season HR average? Which measure of central tendency did you choose and why?

b. Who had the fewest HRs in a season?

c. Who had the greatest HRs in a season?

d. Who had the greatest variability (*SD*) in HRs across one's career? Who had the least variability (*SD*) in HRs across one's career? What can you conclude about the consistency in hitting home runs of these two players?

7. Remember the 1:1 pilot conducted with 8th graders. Approximately half the students received laptops (Group 1, *n*=336) and the other half did not (Group 2, *n*=300). Basically one 8th grade team received laptops and the other team did not. Technology Use is compared between the two groups at the end of the school year. Technology Use is a sum of five items and ranges from 5 to 20. Based upon the SPSS output, complete the following.

**Descriptives**

| | group | | | Statistic | Std. Error |
|---|---|---|---|---|---|
| techuse | 1.00 | Mean | | 17.1908 | .10643 |
| | | 95% Confidence Interval for Mean | Lower Bound | 16.9814 | |
| | | | Upper Bound | 17.4001 | |
| | | 5% Trimmed Mean | | 17.2753 | |
| | | Median | | 17.4000 | |
| | | Variance | | 3.806 | |
| | | Std. Deviation | | 1.95081 | |
| | | Minimum | | 9.80 | |
| | | Maximum | | 20.00 | |
| | | Range | | 10.20 | |
| | | Interquartile Range | | 2.78 | |
| | | Skewness | | -.515 | .133 |
| | | Kurtosis | | .079 | .265 |
| | 2.00 | Mean | | 14.1633 | .11512 |
| | | 95% Confidence Interval for Mean | Lower Bound | 13.9368 | |
| | | | Upper Bound | 14.3899 | |
| | | 5% Trimmed Mean | | 14.1577 | |
| | | Median | | 14.2350 | |
| | | Variance | | 3.975 | |
| | | Std. Deviation | | 1.99386 | |
| | | Minimum | | 9.53 | |
| | | Maximum | | 19.68 | |
| | | Range | | 10.15 | |
| | | Interquartile Range | | 2.70 | |
| | | Skewness | | .025 | .141 |
| | | Kurtosis | | -.150 | .281 |

a. Which group had greater Tech Use? Which measure of central tendency did you use and why?

b. Is the variability similar between the two groups? What does this mean?

8. **Excerpt from:** Robb, K.A., Simon, A.E., & Wardle, J. (2009), Socioeconomic disparities in optimism and pessimism. *International Journal of Behavioral Medicine, 16*(4), 331-338.

A group of researchers examined socio-economic differences in optimism and pessimism among Scottish (*n*=10,650) and English (*n*=5,099) adults aged 55-64 years. Participants completed the Life Orientation Test Revised (LOT-R), which measures optimism and pessimism separately and not as one continuum. A 5-point Likert scale is used with 0=strongly disagree and 4=strongly agree. The LOT-R generates three scores:

- Optimism (expecting good events to occur)-subscale score that indicates agreement with three positively worded items such that a high score indicates high optimism.
- Pessimism (expecting bad events to occur)-subscale score that indicates agreement with three negatively worded items such that a high score indicates high pessimism.
- Total Optimism-the total score of the instrument, however Pessimism items are reverse scored such that a high Total score represent high Optimism and low Pessimism.

Since many participants were retired, income was not the determining factor for SES, rather a socio-deprivation index that took into account, education level, housing, car ownership, etc. was utilized. Four SES groups were created. Table 1 presents the LOT-R scores for the various SES groups by Scottish and English samples. In addition, Figure 1 displays the relationship between SES and Optimism and Pessimism.

**Table 1.** LOT-R Scores by SES for Scottish and English Samples

| | Scottish | | | | English | | | |
|---|---|---|---|---|---|---|---|---|
| | **Low** | **Low-Middle** | **High-Middle** | **High** | **Low** | **Low-Middle** | **High-Middle** | **High** |
| | *n*=840 | *n* =1891 | *n* =1846 | *n* =1,293 | *n* =216 | *n* =523 | *n* =1,409 | *n* =1,326 |
| Total | 18.10 (4.36) | 18.80 (4.53) | 20.20 (4.45) | 21.00 (4.52) | 17.30 (4.55) | 18.20 (4.64) | 19.20 (4.52) | 20.60 (4.66) |
| Pessimism | 8.60 (2.93) | 8.03 (3.01) | 6.73 (2.82) | 5.96 (2.67) | 9.09 (3.10) | 8.46 (3.12) | 7.40 (2.97) | 6.23 (2.89) |
| Optimism | 9.68 (2.62) | 9.80 (2.63) | 9.99 (2.52) | 10.00 (2.60) | 9.36 (2.78) | 9.65 (2.72) | 9.56 (2.52) | 9.81 (2.58) |

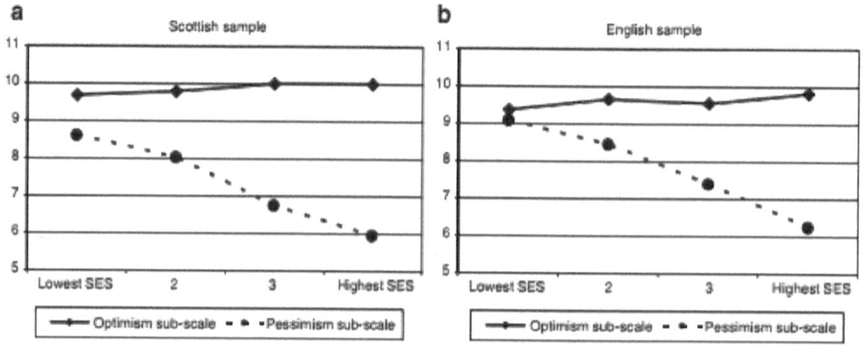


**Fig. 1** Relationship between SES and optimism and pessimism subscales

a. Which SES group (for both Scottish and English) had the highest Pessimism score?

b. Which SES group (for both Scottish and English) had the highest Total and Optimism scores?

c. Based upon the line graphs, can you conclude a relationship between:
   - SES and Optimism?
   - SES and Pessimism?

d. Which sample is more Optimistic and less Pessimistic?

## Conducting the Analysis

9. U.S. News & World Report ranks nearly everything in our world today. Here are their top 10 Luxury Sports Cars for 2015. A luxury sports car is priced above $35,000. Enter the data in SPSS or StatCrunch. Calculate the mean, median and standard deviation for starting price, city mpg, and highway mpg.

| **Rank** | **Model** | **Starting Price** (in thousands) | **City MPG** | **Hwy MPG** |
|---|---|---|---|---|
| 1 | Porsche Boxster | 50.1 | 20 | 30 |
| 2 | Corvette Stingray | 53.9 | 17 | 29 |
| 3 | Porsche Cayman | 51.7 | 20 | 30 |
| 4 | Porsche 911 | 84.1 | 19 | 27 |
| 5 | BMW 4-Series | 38.9 | 22 | 32 |
| 6 | Jaguar F-Type | 63.8 | 20 | 28 |
| 7 | Audi R8 | 112.3 | 11 | 20 |
| 8 | Nissan GT-R | 99.4 | 16 | 23 |
| 9 | BMW Z4 | 47.3 | 17 | 24 |
| 10 | Audi TT | 40.4 | 22 | 31 |

a. Use your output to complete the following.

| | *M* | **Median** | ***SD*** |
|---|---|---|---|
| Starting Price | | | |
| City MPG | | | |
| Highway MPG | | | |

b. Which measure of central tendency is most appropriate to report for Starting Price data? Why?

c. Which measure of central tendency is most appropriate to report for City MPG data? Why?

d. If you could afford a luxury sports car but were also environmentally conscious, which sports car would you select? Why?

10. In our last chapter, we created a frequency distribution table and histogram for the number of cups of coffee consumed per day among college students ($n$=35). Enter the data into SPSS or StatCrunch and generate descriptive statistics

0, 0, 0, 1, 1, 2, 2, 2, 2, 2, 2, 2, 2, 3, 3, 3, 3, 3, 4, 4, 4, 4, 4, 5, 5, 5, 5, 6, 6, 6, 7, 8, 8, 10, 10

a. Use the data above to calculate the following.

Mean = Range =

Median = Degrees of freedom =

Mode = Standard deviation =

b. Based upon the measures of central tendency, what distribution shape does this data create?

c. Previous research found that Americans drink an average of 3.1 cups of coffee per day. How does this sample of college students compare to the national norm?

11. In the last chapter, we explored cell phone use between genders. Enter this data in SPSS or StatCrunch—remember to create two columns; one for gender and another for cell phone hours—so that you have 40 lines of data. Generate descriptive statistics for each group.

| Row | gender | cellhours |
|---|---|---|
| 1 | 1 | 4 |
| 2 | 1 | 6 |
| 3 | 1 | 7 |
| 4 | 1 | 8 |
| 5 | 1 | 8 |
| 6 | 1 | 9 |
| 7 | 1 | 9 |
| 8 | 1 | 9 |
| 9 | 1 | 10 |
| 10 | 1 | 10 |

Females: 4, 6, 7, 8, 8, 9, 9, 9, 9, 10, 10, 10, 11, 11, 11, 11, 11, 12, 12, 12

Males: 4, 5, 5, 6, 6, 7, 7, 8, 8, 8, 8, 8, 9, 9, 9, 9, 10, 10, 11, 12

a. Use the output to complete the following table that summarizes cell phone hours for males and females.

| | Females | Males |
|---|---|---|
| *N* | | |
| *M* | | |
| Median | | |
| Mode | | |
| *SD* | | |
| Range | | |

b. Which group had greater cell phone use?

c. Based upon your results, are the sample participants similar to those that Roberts studied in 2014 that found women's use at 10 hours and men's use at 8?

# Module 4

## Probability and z-scores

### Learning Targets

After completing Module 4, you should be able to:

- Apply the concepts of probability and *z*-scores in a normal distribution.
- Calculate a *z*-score when given a raw score and population distribution parameters.
- Use the Unit Normal Table to identify probability and/or percentile rank for a given *z*-score.
- Use *z*-scores to make comparisons to other population distributions.

# Part 1: The Concepts

## 4.11 Introduction to Probability

Many people believe that statistics and research is about proving something, like a hypothesis. However, that is not the case when studying a sample. In actuality, we cannot prove anything! Rather we can only draw conclusions about the sample with some degree of confidence that it is applicable to the population. Remember, with inferential statistics, we are studying a sample with the goal of generalizing the results to the population. So how can we be confident in generalizing our results to the population? The concept of probability allows us to calculate the degree to which sample results are due to error or chance and therefore the likelihood that the result would occur in the population. Although probability is a huge topic, one that far exceeds the confines of this text, we will examine the basics of probability as it applies to an introduction to statistics.

***Probability*** is the fraction or proportion of selecting a specific outcome out of the total number of possible selections. So to calculate the probability of the event (A) occurring, we would need to determine the number of As and divide by the total number of possible outcomes.

$$\text{Probability of } A = \frac{\text{number of outcomes for } A}{\text{total number of possible outcomes}}$$

Let's apply this to a deck of cards, which has 52 total cards. The probability of selecting a heart (♥) is

$$p(♥) = \frac{13}{52} = \frac{1}{4} = .25 = 25\%$$

Probability can be expressed as a fraction, decimal, or percentage. So the probability of selecting a heart from a complete deck of cards is one out of four (1/4) or 25%. If we think of the deck of cards as a population, we can easily apply the concept of probability to our normal distribution. Recall, under the normal curve is 100% of individuals in the population. Because the normal distribution is symmetrical with the mean, median, and mode in the center, that 100% can divided into six sections using the standard deviation. Three standard deviations divide each side of the distribution. So we can count the number of standard deviations a score or individual is away from the mean. Instead of referring to the number of standard deviations away from the mean, statisticians often refer to a *z*-score.

## 4.12 Definition and Calculation of a *z*-Score

A ***z-score*** is used to identify the exact location of a score within a distribution. It represents the number of standard deviations a raw score is from the mean. Since the mean is used as the reference point, the negative sign indicates that the *z*-score is below the mean and a positive sign indicates that the *z*-score is above the mean. To convert a raw score to a *z*-score, the following equation is used:

$$z = \frac{X - \mu}{\sigma}$$

**Figure 4.1**
*Normal Distribution with z-scores and Percentages*

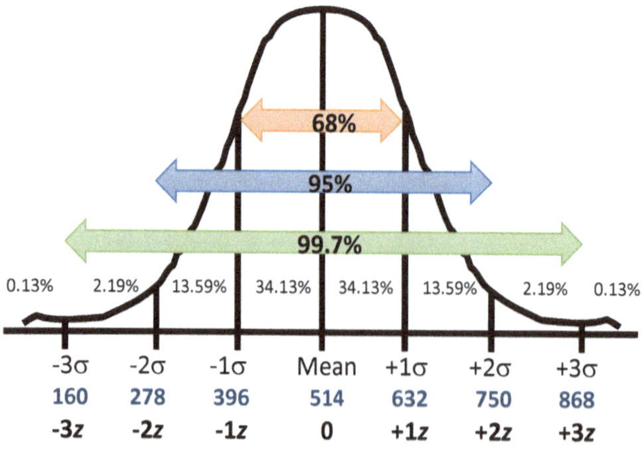


**z-Score Examples**

In the previous chapter, we learned that the 2013 SAT math exam generated the following norms ($\mu$=514, $\sigma$=118). Sara reported a score of 632. What is Sara's *z*-score? Sara has a *z*-score of 1, meaning that she scored 1 standard deviations above the mean.

$$z = \frac{X - \mu}{\sigma} = \frac{632 - 514}{118} = \frac{118}{118} = 1z$$

On the same exam, Sam scored 412. What is Sam's *z*-score? Sam's *z*-score is -.86, meaning that Sam scored .86 standard deviations below the mean. Because Sam scored below the mean, his *z*-score is negative.

$$z = \frac{X - \mu}{\sigma} = \frac{412 - 514}{118} = \frac{-102}{118} = -.86z$$

Recall that the area (100% of the population) in the normal distribution can be divided into six sections. Because the distribution is bell shaped, each section of the distribution contains a different proportion of the population, however, these proportions are standard and can be applied to all normal distributions. This means that the proportion or percent between any two *z*-scores is consistent. So the percent between -3*z* and -2*z* (or 3*z* and 2*z*) is always 2.19%; just as the percent between the mean and 1*z* (or mean and -1*z*) is always 34.13%. These standard divisions of proportion allow us to use the *z*-score to not only determine placement within the distribution, but also: 1) identify the percentile rank of a raw score; 2) determine the probability of obtaining such a score; and 3) compare to other distributions.

The most common application of the *z*-score is percentile rank. ***Percentile rank*** represents the percent of the population or sample that falls below the raw score. For example, scoring at the 92^th^ percentile indicates that 92% of the population or sample scored below you, which is quite a good score! The bottom two rows in Figure 4.2 presents how the proportion (and percentage) of the distribution cumulates from left to right. Percentile rank is typically rounded to a whole percentage, except when dealing with percentiles less than 1% or greater than 99%. A person can never fall at the 100^th^ percentile, since her score is a part of the population. Therefore, the lowest percentile ever reported is .1% and the highest is 99.9%.

**Figure 4.2**
*SAT-Math Distribution*

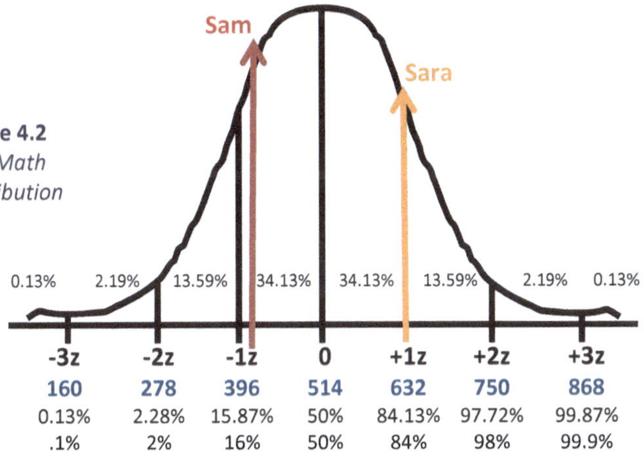


**Percentile Rank Example**

Continuing the SAT-Math exam (μ=514, σ=118) example for Sara and Sam, we learned that Sara's raw score of 632 corresponds to a *z*-score of +1*z*. The cumulative percentages indicate that Sara falls at 84.13%, rounded to 84%. This means that 84% of the population falls below Sara's score of 632. Sara's score was easy to place in the distribution since it converts to a whole *z*-score.

Sam's score is not as easy to find the percentile rank. Previously, we determined that Sam's raw score of 412 converts to -.86 *z*. Since Sam's score is negative, it falls below the mean. We can place it in the distribution and estimate that his percentile rank will be a little above 16%. To determine Sam's exact percentile rank will require the use of the Unit Normal Table.

## 4.13 The Unit Normal Table

The ***unit normal table*** provides a detailed listing of all possible *z*-scores with their corresponding proportions. A complete unit normal table is presented in Appendix A. Notice that this table only presents positive *z*-scores ranging from 0 to 4.0. Since the normal distribution is symmetrical, the proportions are the same. However, this does require special attention to the *z*-score sign (+ or -) and which proportion is in question. Figure 4.3 presents an excerpt from the unit normal table that we will apply to several examples. The unit normal table is organized into four columns. Column A lists the *z*-scores. The remaining columns list different proportions: Column B (body), Column C (tail), and Column D (between mean and *z*).

Let's continue our example with Sara, who has a *z*-score of +1*z*. Using the unit normal table to determine her percentile rank, we first need to find her *z*-score of 1. Since percentile rank is the percentage of individuals that scored below Sara, the proportion in the body (Column B) is the pertinent value, which is .8413 or 84%.

**Figure 4.3**
*Excerpt of Unit Normal Table with Sara's and Sam's Percentile Rank*

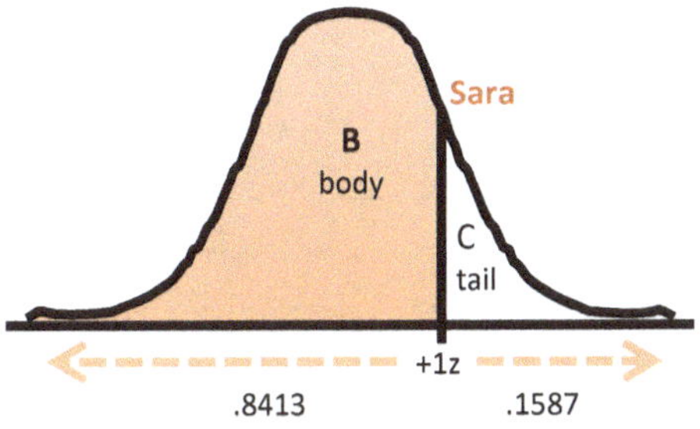


If we were asked the percent of individuals that scored above Sara, the proportion in the tail (Column C) is .1587 or 16%.

| (A) z | (B) *Proportion in body* | (C) *Proportion in tail* | (D) *Proportion between M & z* |
|---|---|---|---|
| 0.85 | .8023 | .1977 | .3023 |
| 0.86 | .8051 | .1949 | .3051 |
| 0.87 | .8078 | .1922 | .3078 |
| 0.88 | .8106 | .1894 | .3106 |
| 0.89 | .8133 | .1867 | .3133 |
| 0.90 | .8159 | .1841 | .3159 |
| 0.91 | .8186 | .1814 | .3186 |
| 0.92 | .8212 | .1788 | .3212 |
| 0.93 | .8238 | .1762 | .3238 |
| 0.94 | .8264 | .1736 | .3264 |
| 0.95 | .8289 | .1711 | .3289 |
| 0.96 | .8315 | .1685 | .3315 |
| 0.97 | .8340 | .1660 | .3340 |
| 0.98 | .8365 | .1635 | .3365 |
| 0.99 | .8389 | .1611 | .3389 |
| 1.00 | .8413 | .1587 | .3413 |
| 1.01 | .8438 | .1562 | .3438 |
| 1.02 | .8461 | .1539 | .3485 |

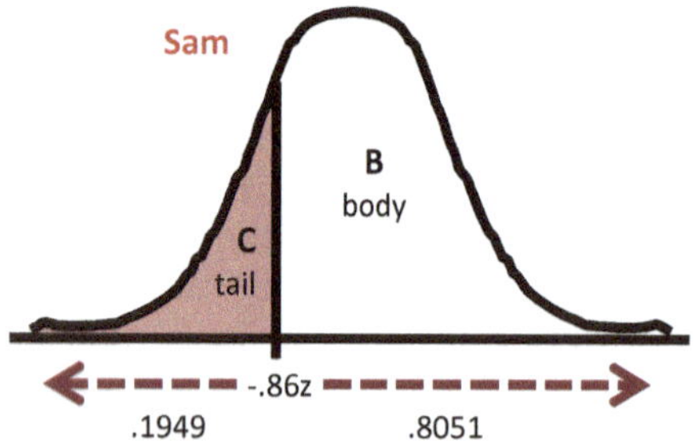


**Figure 4.4** *Sam's Percentile Rank*

Let's get back to Sam, who has a raw score of 412 and a -.86*z*. Since Sam has a negative *z*-score, we have to be careful as to which proportion is appropriate. Again, we want his percentile rank, the percent that score below Sam. But since Sam has a negative *z*, the proportion in the tail is appropriate (Column C), which in this case is .1949 or 19%. If we wanted to determine the proportion of individuals that scored above Sam, then we would look in the body (Column B) and find .8051or 81%.

## 4.14 Probability and *z*-Scores

So far, we have only used *z*-scores and the unit normal table to identify proportions of a population that fall above or below a certain score. We can also think of these proportions as probabilities in order to determine the probability of obtaining a score above or below a certain value. For example, the probability of scoring higher than Sam is quite large—82% chance. However, the probability of scoring higher than Sara is pretty low—only 16% chance. Probability or proportion can only be determine for an area above or below a certain value—the unit normal table cannot be used to identify the probability of obtaining an exact score.

**Steps to Determine Proportion or Probability (*p*) for an Individual Score**

1. Convert raw score to z-score: $z = \frac{X-\mu}{\sigma}$
2. Use unit normal table to determine *p* associated with *z*-score.
   - For positive *z*-score (+*z*), determining:
     - Percentile rank (amount below)→Look in body.
     - Amount above→Look in tail.
   - For negative *z*-score (-*z*), determining:
     - Percentile rank (amount below)→Look in tail.
     - Amount above→Look in body.

Let's apply all of these concepts to several problems that utilize results from the American College Testing (ACT) math exam, which is normally distributed (μ=18, σ=6). Figure 4.X shows the ACT distribution and the placement of scores for three students: Abby (*X*=26), Austin (*X*=21), and Avery (*X*=16).

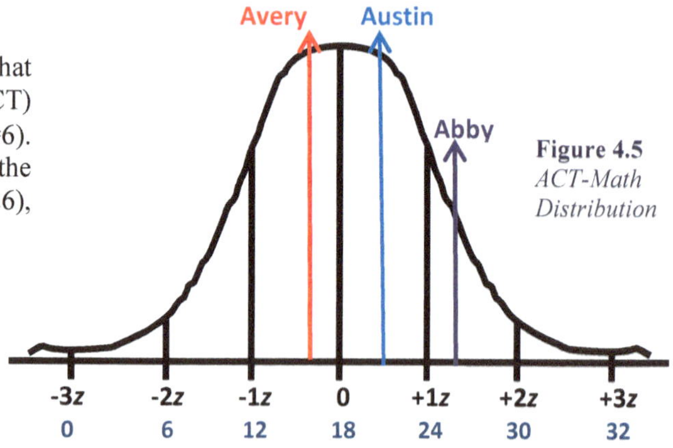


**Figure 4.5** *ACT-Math Distribution*

A. Abby scored 26. What is her percentile rank?
   1. Convert raw score to a *z*-score.

      $z = \frac{X-\mu}{\sigma} = \frac{26-18}{6} = \frac{8}{6} = +1.33z$

   2. Use unit normal table to find *p*.
      - Since *z* is positive and percentile rank is the proportion below, we need to look in the body (Column B).
      - *p*=.9082, round up to 91st percentile

| (A) *z* | (B) *Proportion in body* | (C) *Proportion in tail* | (D) *Proportion between M & z* |
|---|---|---|---|
| 1.30 | .9032 | .0968 | .4032 |
| 1.31 | .9049 | .0951 | .4049 |
| 1.32 | .9066 | .0934 | .4066 |
| 1.33 | .9082 | .0918 | .4082 |
| 1.34 | .9099 | .0901 | .4099 |

B. Austin scored 21. What is the probability of scoring above Austin?
   1. Convert raw score to a *z*-score.

      $z = \frac{X-\mu}{\sigma} = \frac{21-18}{6} = \frac{3}{6} = +.5z$

   2. Use unit normal table to find *p*.
      - Since *z* is positive and probability is above, we need to look in the tail (Column C).
      - *p*=.3085 or 30.85% chance

| (A) *z* | (B) *Proportion in body* | (C) *Proportion in tail* | (D) *Proportion between M & z* |
|---|---|---|---|
| 0.50 | .6915 | .3085 | .1915 |
| 0.51 | .6950 | .3050 | .1950 |
| 0.52 | .6985 | .3015 | .1985 |
| 0.53 | .7019 | .2981 | .2019 |
| 0.54 | .7054 | .2946 | .2054 |

C. Avery scored 16. What is her percentile rank?
   1. Convert raw score to a *z*-score.

      $z = \frac{X-\mu}{\sigma} = \frac{16-18}{6} = \frac{-2}{6} = -.33z$

   2. Use unit normal table to find *p*.
      - Since *z* is negative and percentile rank is the proportion below, we need to look in the tail (Column C).
      - *p*=.3707, round down to 37th percentile

| (A) *z* | (B) *Proportion in body* | (C) *Proportion in tail* | (D) *Proportion between M & z* |
|---|---|---|---|
| 0.30 | .6179 | .3821 | .1179 |
| 0.31 | .6217 | .3783 | .1217 |
| 0.32 | .6255 | .3745 | .1255 |
| 0.33 | .6293 | .3707 | .1293 |
| 0.34 | .6331 | .3669 | .1331 |

## 4.15 Using a $z$-Score to Make Comparisons to Other Distributions

Since a $z$-score score is a measure of relative position, we can use $z$-scores to compare scores from different distributions. For example, our chapter problems have dealt with scores from the SAT-math and the ACT-math. Both of these exams are used to for college admissions as a means of predicting college success. Most high school students complete either the SAT or ACT. We have learned that these exams have very different distributions. And likely if you and your friend took different exams, it is difficult to compare scores. That is the case for Sara and Abby. Recall that Sara took the SAT-math and achieved a score of 632, while Abby scored a 26 on the ACT-math. These two are good friends but pretty competitive and wondering who scored better. However, such a comparison cannot be made without knowing the mean and standard deviation of each exam. Knowing the norms for the SAT and ACT allow us create the distributions and make the comparison. We can actually compare these scores three ways: 1) placement, 2) $z$-score, and 3) percentile rank. By creating the distributions (see Figure 4) and placing each student by her raw score, we can visualize that Abby definitely had a higher score than Sara. However, drawing out the distribution every time a comparison is required is cumbersome. An easier way is to compare $z$-scores. Earlier, we determined that Sara has a $z$-score of $+1z$ and Abby has a $z$-score of $+1.33z$, which indicates that Abby has the higher score. Finally, we could also compare percentile rank, which is based upon the $z$-score. Often, percentile rank is indicated on a test report, but if not it can be generated using the unit normal table. Earlier, we determined their percentile ranks as: Sara (84%) and Abby (91%). So again, percentile ranks indicate that Abby has the higher score.

**Figure 4.6**
*SAT and ACT Comparison*

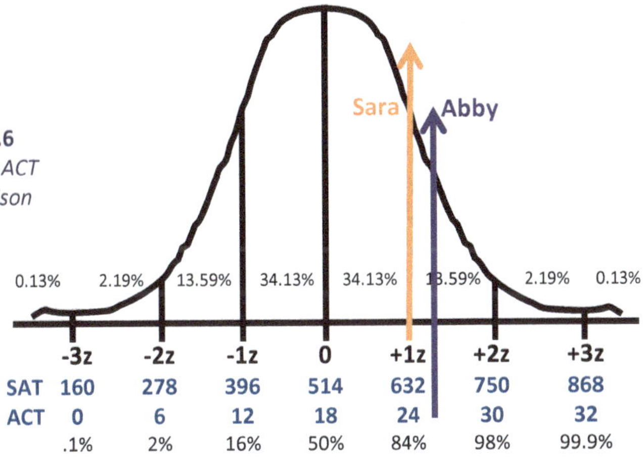


Suppose Sara just couldn't accept losing to Abby based upon location, $z$-score, and percentile rank. Well, we could also calculate what Sara would likely score on the ACT based upon her SAT achievement. So we will use Sara's SAT-math score to calculate a new raw score, in this case an ACT-math score. To calculate a new raw score, we use the following equation:

$$new\ raw\ score = \mu + z\sigma$$

Notice that you must have the mean and standard deviation of the new distribution and the SAT-math score must be converted to a $z$-score. Using the ACT norms ($\mu$=18, $\sigma$=6) and knowing that Sara's $z$-score is $+1z$, we can calculate:

$$Sara's\ ACT\ raw\ score = \mu + z\sigma = 18 + 1(6) = 18 + 6 = 24$$

Based upon Sara's SAT-math score, we can determine that she would likely generate a score of 24 on the ACT-math, which is obviously lower than Abby's score of 26.

## 4.16 Module Summary

- Probability allows us to calculate the degree to which sample results <u>are due to error or chance</u> and therefore the likelihood that the result would occur in the population.
    - ***Probability*** is the fraction or proportion of selecting a specific outcome out of the total number of possible selections. The probability of A occurring:

$$\text{Probability of } A = \frac{\text{number of outcomes for } A}{\text{total number of possible outcomes}}$$

    - Probability applies to the normal distribution since it: represents 100% of the individuals; is symmetrical; has equal mean, median, and mode; and can be divided into six sections using standard deviation.
        - Instead of referring to the number of standard deviations away from the mean, statisticians often refer to a *z*-score.

- A ***z-score*** represents the number of standard deviations a raw score is from the mean.
    - Used to identify the exact location of a score within a distribution
    - Since the mean is the reference point (or standard), the negative sign indicates that the *z*-score is below the mean and a positive sign indicates that the *z*-score is above the mean.
    - To convert a raw score to a *z*-score, use: $z = \frac{X-\mu}{\sigma}$
    - The standard divisions (6 standard deviations) in a normal distribution allow us to use the *z*-score to not only determine placement within the distribution, but also: 1) identify the percentile rank of a raw score; 2) determine the probability of obtaining such a score; and 3) compare to other distributions.
- ***Percentile rank*** represents the percent of the population or sample that falls <u>below</u> the raw score.
    - Rounded to a whole percentage. Lowest percentile ever reported is .1% and the highest is 99.9%.
- ***Unit normal table*** provides a detailed listing of all possible *z*-scores with their corresponding proportions.
    - Since normal distribution is symmetrical, *z* table only presents positive z-scores ranging from 0 to 4.0.
    - Need to pay close attention to the *z*-score sign (+ or -) and which proportion is in question (above or below)
    - Organized into four columns: Column A lists the z-scores, Column B (proportions in body), Column C (proportions in tail), and Column D (proportions between mean and *z*).
    - Proportions can also be used as probabilities in obtaining a score above or below a certain value.

- **Steps to Determine Proportion or Probability (*p*) for an Individual Score**
    1. Convert raw score to *z*-score: $z = \frac{X-\mu}{\sigma}$
    2. Use unit normal table to determine *p* associated with *z*-score.
        - For positive *z*-score (+*z*), determining:
            - Percentile rank (amount below)→Look in body.
            - Amount above→Look in tail.
        - For negative *z*-score (-*z*), determining:
            - Percentile rank (amount below)→Look in tail.
            - Amount above→Look in body.

- *z*-scores can be used to make comparisons to other distributions.
    - As along as the norms are known from the two compared distributions, we can use *z*-scores to compare distribution placement.
    - $new\ raw\ score = \mu + z\sigma$

# Part 2: Learning Guide

## 4.21V Introduction to Probability

Many think that statistics and research is about using data to PROVE something, when in actuality we cannot prove anything!

- Our goal is to be able to draw conclusions about our sample with some degree of confidence that the conclusion is generalizable to the population.
- Probability allows us to calculate the degree to which sample results are due to error or chance and therefore, the likelihood that the result would occur in the population.
- ***Probability*** is the fraction or proportion of selecting a specific outcome out of the total number of possible selections.
  - The probability of A occurring:

$$\text{Probability of } A = \frac{\text{number of outcomes for } A}{\text{total number of possible outcomes}}$$

  - Applied to a deck of cards, the probability of selecting a heart (♡) is:

$$p(\heartsuit) = \frac{13}{52} = \frac{1}{4} = .25 = 25\%$$

  - Probability can be expressed as a fraction, decimal, or percentage.
- Probability applies to the normal distribution since it represents 100% of the individuals; is symmetrical; has equal mean, median, and mode; and can be divided into 6 sections using standard deviation.
  - Instead of referring to the number of standard deviations away from the mean, statisticians often refer to a *z*-score.

## 4.22V Definition and Calculation of a *z*-Score

- A ***z-score*** represents the number of standard deviations a raw score is from the mean.
  - Used to identify the exact location of a score within a distribution
  - Since the mean is the reference point (or standard), the negative sign indicates that the *z*-score is below the mean and a positive sign indicates that the *z*-score is above the mean.
  - To convert a raw score to a *z*-score, use: $z = \frac{X-\mu}{\sigma}$

**_z_-Score Examples**

In the previous chapter, we learned that the 2013 SAT math exam generated the following norms ($\mu$=514, $\sigma$=118). Sara reported a score of 632. What is Sara's *z*-score? Sara has a *z*-score of 1.0, meaning that she scored 1 standard deviations above the mean.

$$z = \frac{X-\mu}{\sigma} = \frac{632-514}{118} = \frac{118}{118} = 1z$$

On the same exam, Sam scored 412. What is Sam's *z*-score? Sam's *z*-score is -.90, meaning that Sam scored .9 standard deviations below the mean. Because Sam scored below the mean, his *z*-score is negative.

$$z = \frac{X-\mu}{\sigma} = \frac{412-514}{118} = \frac{-102}{118} = -.86z$$

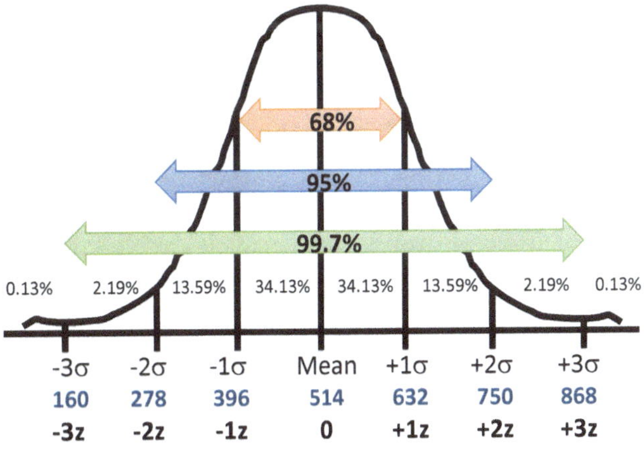


- Since the area under the normal curve (100% of population) can be divided into six section, each section contains a different proportion of the population.
  - The proportions are standard and can be applied to all normal distributions.
  - These standard divisions allow us to use the z-score to not only determine placement within the distribution, but also: 1) identify the percentile rank of a raw score; 2) determine the probability of obtaining such a score; and 3) compare to other distributions.
- ***Percentile rank*** represents the percent of the population or sample that falls below the raw score.
  - Most common application of a z-score.
  - Typically rounded to a whole percentage.
  - Lowest percentile ever reported is .1% and the highest is 99.9%.

**Percentile Rank-Example**

SAT-Math exam ($\mu$=514, $\sigma$=118)

Sara's raw score= 632 = +1z. = 84%

Sam's raw = 412 = -.86z.

- Sam's z-score is negative, it falls below the mean.
- We can estimate that his percentile rank will be a little above 19%,
- Require the use of the Unit Normal Table.

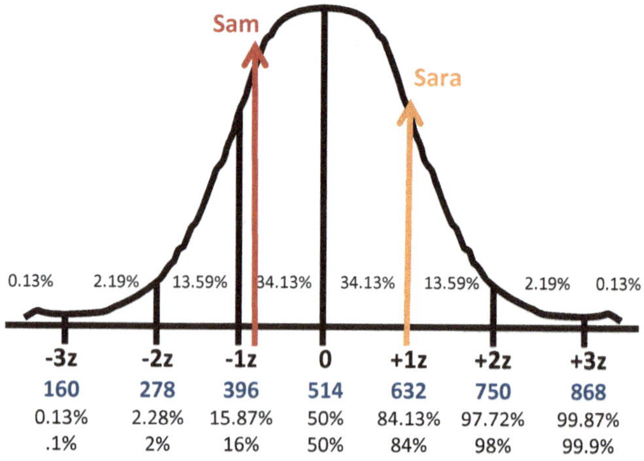


## 4.23V The Unit Normal Table

- The ***Unit normal table*** provides a detailed listing of all possible *z*-scores with their corresponding proportions.
  - Since normal distribution is symmetrical, a *z* table (or Unit Normal table) only presents positive z-scores ranging from 0 to 4.0.
  - Need to pay close attention to the z-score sign (+ or -) and which proportion is in question (above or below)
  - Organized into four columns: Column A lists the z-scores, Column B (proportions in body), Column C (proportions in tail), and Column D (proportions between mean and z).

**Using the Unit Normal Table-Example**

SAT-Math exam ($\mu$=514, $\sigma$=118)

Sara's raw score= 632 = +1*z*

- z-score is positive; we want to find percentile rank or proportion in body (Column B).
- +1z corresponds to .8413 or 84%.

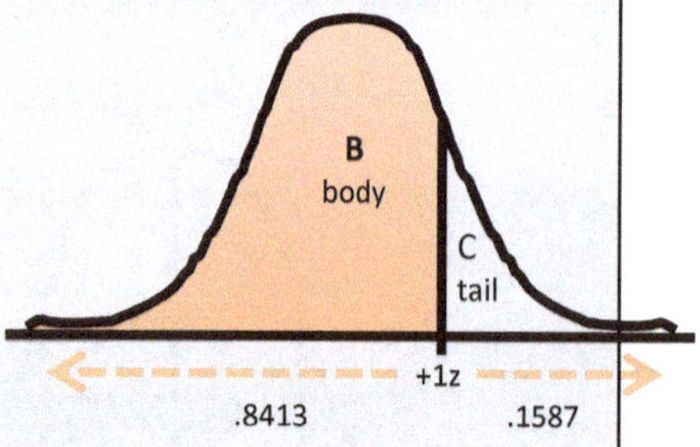


Sam's raw = 412 = -.86*z*.

- Sam's z-score is negative (below the mean). We want to find his percentile rank or proportion in tail (Column C)
- .86z (9n tail) corresponds to .1949 or 19%.

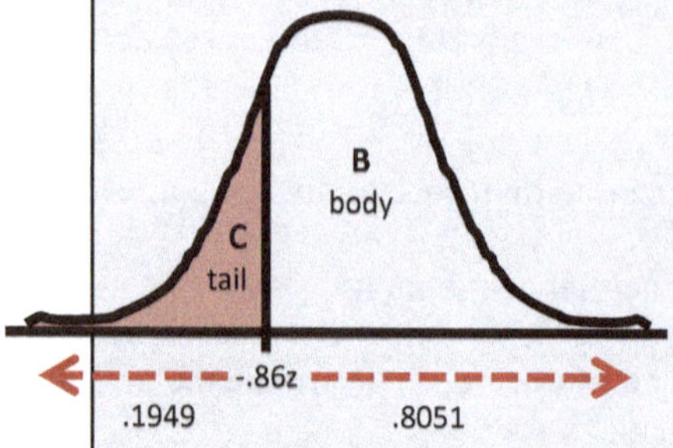


| (A) *z* | (B) *Proportion in body* | (C) *Proportion in tail* | (D) *Proportion between M & z* |
|---|---|---|---|
| 0.85 | .8023 | .1977 | .3023 |
| 0.86 | .8051 | .1949 | .3051 |
| 0.87 | .8078 | .1922 | .3078 |
| 0.88 | .8106 | .1894 | .3106 |
| 0.89 | .8133 | .1867 | .3133 |
| 0.90 | .8159 | .1841 | .3159 |
| 0.91 | .8186 | .1814 | .3186 |
| 0.92 | .8212 | .1788 | .3212 |
| 0.93 | .8238 | .1762 | .3238 |
| 0.94 | .8264 | .1736 | .3264 |
| 0.95 | .8289 | .1711 | .3289 |
| 0.96 | .8315 | .1685 | .3315 |
| 0.97 | .8340 | .1660 | .3340 |
| 0.98 | .8365 | .1635 | .3365 |
| 0.99 | .8389 | .1611 | .3389 |
| 1.00 | .8413 | .1587 | .3413 |
| 1.01 | .8438 | .1562 | .3438 |
| 1.02 | .8461 | .1539 | .3485 |

**Steps to Determine Proportion or Probability (*p*) for an Individual Score**

1. Convert raw score to z-score: $z = \frac{X-\mu}{\sigma}$
2. Use unit normal table to determine *p* associated with *z*-score.
   - For positive *z*-score (+*z*), determining:
     - Percentile rank (amount below)→Look in body.
     - Amount above→Look in tail.
   - For negative *z*-score (-*z*), determining:
     - Percentile rank (amount below)→Look in tail.
     - Amount above→Look in body.

## 4.24V Probability and z-scores

We can also think of these proportions as probabilities.

- We can determine the probability of obtaining a score above or below a certain value.
- The probability of scoring higher than Sam is quite large—82% chance.
- The probability of scoring higher than Sara is pretty slim—only 16% chance.

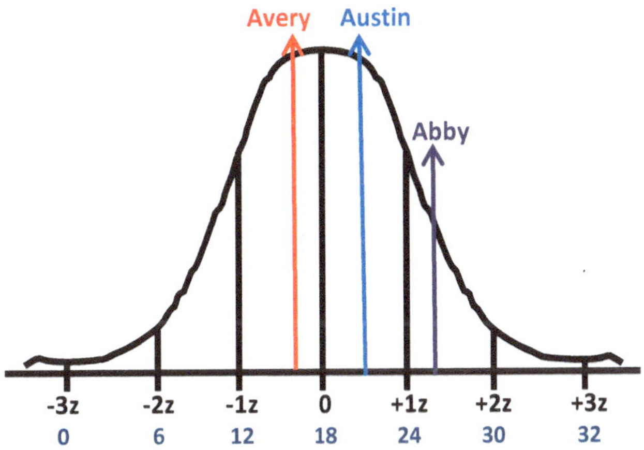


> **Example**
>
> American College Testing (ACT) math exam is normally distributed ($\mu$=18, $\sigma$=6). Figure 4.5 shows the ACT distribution and the placement of scores for three students: Abby ($X$=26), Austin ($X$=21), and Avery ($X$=16).

A. Abby scored 26. What is her percentile rank?

1. Convert raw score to a z-score.

$$z = \frac{X-\mu}{\sigma} = \frac{26-18}{6} = \frac{8}{6} = +1.33z$$

2. Use unit normal table to find $p$.
   - Since $z$ is positive and percentile rank is the proportion below, we need to look in the <u>body</u> (Column B).
   - $p$=.9082, round up to 91st percentile

| (A) $z$ | (B) *Proportion in body* | (C) *Proportion in tail* | (D) *Proportion between M & z* |
|---|---|---|---|
| 1.30 | .9032 | .0968 | .4032 |
| 1.31 | .9049 | .0951 | .4049 |
| 1.32 | .9066 | .0934 | .4066 |
| 1.33 | .9082 | .0918 | .4082 |
| 1.34 | .9099 | .0901 | .4099 |

B. Austin scored 21. What is the probability of scoring above Austin?

1. Convert raw score to a z-score.

$$z = \frac{X-\mu}{\sigma} = \frac{21-18}{6} = \frac{3}{6} = +.5z$$

2. Use unit normal table to find $p$.
   - Since $z$ is positive and probability is above, we need to look in the <u>tail</u> (Column C).
   - $p$=.3085 or 30.85% chance

| (A) $z$ | (B) *Proportion in body* | (C) *Proportion in tail* | (D) *Proportion between M & z* |
|---|---|---|---|
| 0.50 | .6915 | .3085 | .1915 |
| 0.51 | .6950 | .3050 | .1950 |
| 0.52 | .6985 | .3015 | .1985 |
| 0.53 | .7019 | .2981 | .2019 |
| 0.54 | .7054 | .2946 | .2054 |

C. Avery scored 16. What is her percentile rank?

1. Convert raw score to a z-score.

$$z = \frac{X-\mu}{\sigma} = \frac{16-18}{6} = \frac{-2}{6} = -.33z$$

2. Use unit normal table to find $p$.
   - Since $z$ is negative and percentile rank is the proportion below, we need to look in the <u>tail</u> (Column C).
   - $p$=.3707, round down to 37th percentile

| (A) $z$ | (B) *Proportion in body* | (C) *Proportion in tail* | (D) *Proportion between M & z* |
|---|---|---|---|
| 0.30 | .6179 | .3821 | .1179 |
| 0.31 | .6217 | .3783 | .1217 |
| 0.32 | .6255 | .3745 | .1255 |
| 0.33 | .6293 | .3707 | .1293 |
| 0.34 | .6331 | .3669 | .1331 |

## 4.25V Using a z-score to Make Comparisons to Other Distributions

- z-score score is a measure of relative position, so we can use z-scores to compare scores from different distributions.
- As long as the norms are known from the two compared distributions, we can use z-scores to compare distribution placement.
  - $new\ raw\ score = \mu + z\sigma$

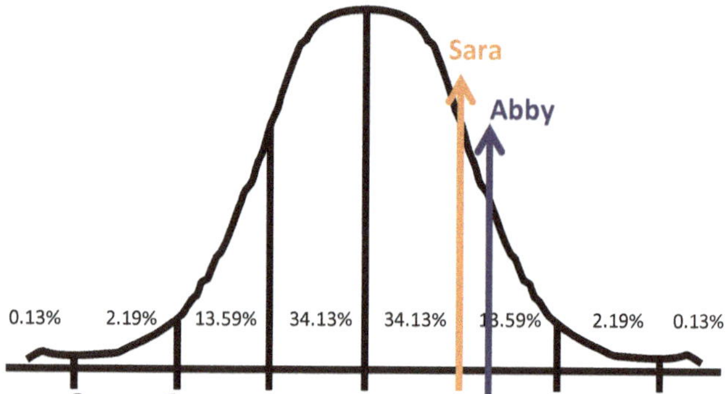


| | -3z | -2z | -1z | 0 | +1z | +2z | +3z |
|---|---|---|---|---|---|---|---|
| SAT | 160 | 278 | 396 | 514 | 632 | 750 | 868 |
| ACT | 0 | 6 | 12 | 18 | 24 | 30 | 32 |
| | .1% | 2% | 16% | 50% | 84% | 98% | 99.9% |

> **Example**
>
> Sara took the SAT-math and achieved a score of 632, while Abby scored a 26 on the ACT-math. Who scored better?
> - ACT-math ($\mu$=18, $\sigma$=6)
> - SAT-math ($\mu$=514, $\sigma$=118)
>
> Abby's ACT score of 26→+1.33z→91st%
> Sara's SAT score of 632→+1z→84th%
> Sara's ACT = $\mu + z\sigma = 18 + 1(6) = 18 + 6 = 24$

## 4.26V Examples

The Graduate Record Exam (GRE) is used by many universities as admission criteria for graduate programs. The exam has three sections--verbal reasoning, quantitative reasoning, and analytical writing—each of which is separately scored. The Verbal section applies the score scale of 130-170 with $\mu$=150 and $\sigma$=8.5.

Another norm-referenced exam used for graduate school admissions is the Miller Analogies Test (MAT), which follows the norms of $\mu$=400, $\sigma$=25. The MAT scores are often compared to the GRE-Verbal. Apply these distributions to complete the following items.

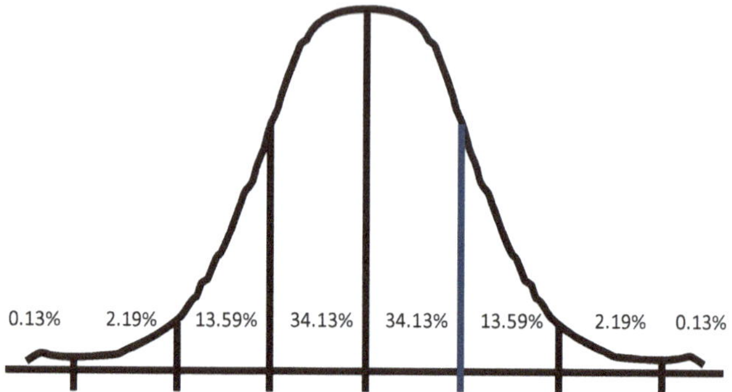


| | -3z | -2z | -1z | 0 | +1z | +2z | +3z |
|---|---|---|---|---|---|---|---|
| GRE-V | 124.5 | 133 | 141.5 | 150 | 158.5 | 167 | 175.5 |
| MAT | 325 | 350 | 374 | 400 | 425 | 450 | 475 |
| | .1% | 2% | 16% | 50% | 84% | 98% | 99.9% |

1. Bridget has a score of 155 on the GRE-Verbal. What is her z-score and percentile rank?

2. Bobby has a score of 137 on the GRE-Verbal. What is his z-score and percentile rank?

3. Blake has a score of 459 on the MAT. What is his z-score and percentile rank?

4. What is the probability of scoring above Blake on the MAT?

5. Billie has a score of 381 on the MAT. What is her z-score and percentile rank?

6. Billie is wondering how she would do on the GRE-Verbal. Use her MAT performance to determine a likely GRE-verbal score.

## 4.27V Additional Practice

The heights of adults are normally distributed: Men ($\mu$=70", $\sigma$=4"), Women ($\mu$=65", $\sigma$=3.5"). Use these norms to complete the Men's and Women's distributions below. Then proceed to problems 1 and 2.

1. Brad and Belle are both 6' (72") tall. What are their percentile ranks? Why is Belle's percentile rank so much higher than Brad's?

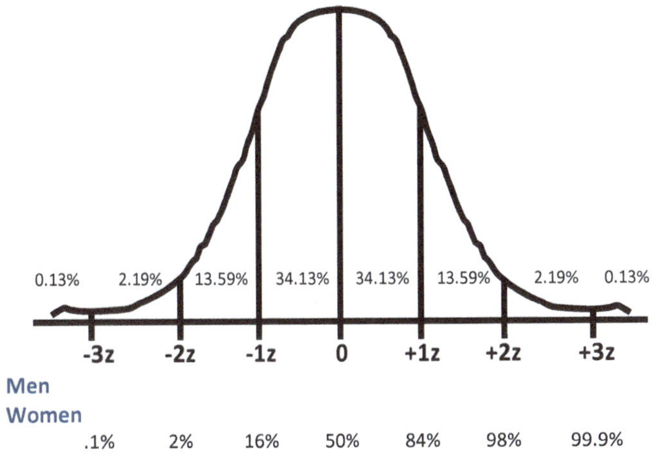


2. Alayna is only 5' (60") tall. What is her percentile rank?

## 4.28 Applet Activity: Normal Distribution

Go to the Interactive Normal Probability Distribution Graph at:

http://www.intmath.com/counting-probability/normal-distribution-graph-interactive.php

Scroll down to the normal distribution graph. You will notice two red dots and two green dots—all of which can be moved. The first red dot is the distribution mean. The second red dot is the standard deviation. The green dots represent two possible scores, $x_1$ and $x_2$. First try dragging/moving these dots/values around. Notice that the values are presented and change as the dot is moved. The values presented for $x_1$ and $x_2$ are the raw scores based upon the distribution scale.

1. Move the red dots so that $\mu$=4.0 and $\sigma$=1.0. Move the green dots so that $x_1$=3.0 and $x_2$=5. Below the distribution, check (✓): Show standard normal curve; Show z-score calculations; and Show probability calculation. What are the z-scores for $x_1$ and $x_2$? What is the probability between $x_1$ and $x_2$?

2. Now drag the standard deviation dot to increase it to 1.5. What happens to the shape of the distribution? What are the z-scores for $x_1$ and $x_2$? What is the probability between $x_1$ and $x_2$? Why did these values change when you changed the standard deviation?

3. Now drag the standard deviation dot to decrease it to 0.5. What happens to the shape of the distribution? What are the z-scores for $x_1$ and $x_2$? What is the probability between $x_1$ and $x_2$?

4. Why did the probability between for $x_1$ and $x_2$ increase when the standard deviation decreased?

5. Did the amount of area (or proportion) under the curve change when the shape of the distribution changed?

## 4.29 Exercises

### Reviewing Concepts

1. What is the probability of drawing the king of hearts from a deck of cards?

2. A *z*-score is a standard score. What standard is being applied?

3. Describe the difference between percentile rank and percentage correct on a test.

4. Why are only positive *z*-scores presented in the Unit Normal Table?

5. The 2014 SAT-Critical Reading exam norms are $\mu$=497 and $\sigma$=115. The ACT-Reading has norms of $\mu$=21 and $\sigma$=6. Use these norms to complete the following.

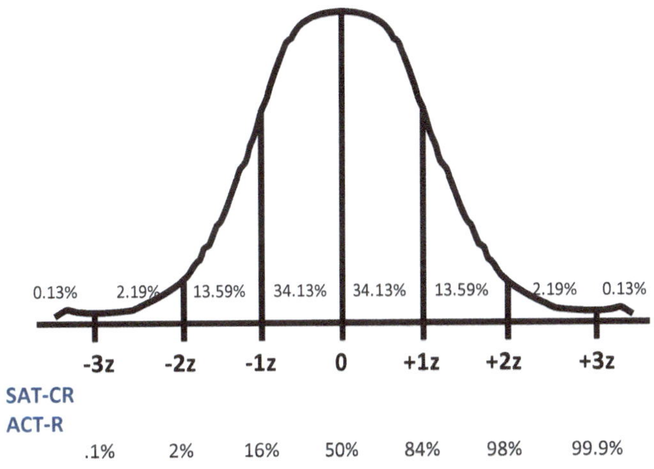


   a. Ella scored 426 on the SAT. What is her percentile rank?

   b. Kade scored 538 on the SAT. What is his percentile rank?

   c. Nelson can only remember his SAT percentile rank, which was the 78$^{th}$. What was Nelson's SAT raw score?

   d. What would Kade's score be if he completed the ACT-reading exam?

   e. Kellen received a score of 14 on the ACT. What is the probability of score higher than Kellen?

6. Birth weights in the U.S. are normally distributed ($\mu$=7.5 lbs., $\sigma$=1.25 lbs.). Based upon this distribution, complete the distribution and the following items.

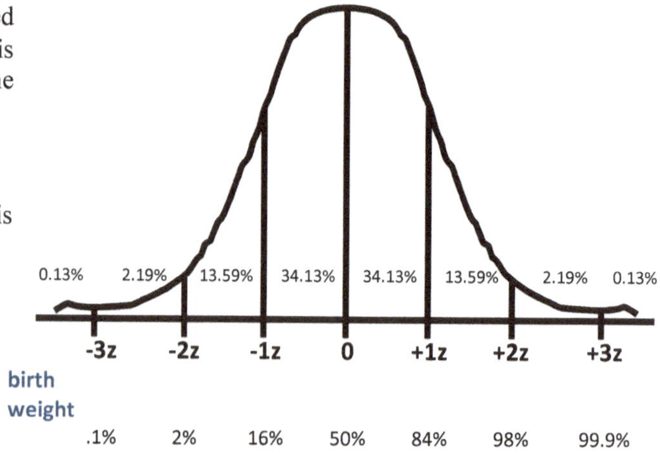


a. Baby Ian was born at 6.5 lbs. What is his percentile rank?

b. The medical community indicates that birth weight below 5.5 lbs. is classified as "low birth weight." What percent of babies are born with low birth weight?

c. Between what two weights does 95% of the population fall?

d. A newborn classified as "large for gestational age" must be greater than the 90th percentile. What weight is the benchmark for this classification? In other words, what weight is associated with the 90th percentile?

e. What was your birth weight? What was your percentile rank based upon today's distribution of U.S. birth weight?

# Module 5

## Distribution of Sample Means

### Learning Targets

After completing Module 5, you should be able to:

- Apply the concepts of the Central Limit Theorem to transform a population distribution of individuals to a population distribution of sample means.
- Use population parameters to calculate the expected value of *M* (mean of sample means) and standard error of the mean ($\sigma_M$).
- Calculate a certain probability of a sample mean using the distribution of sample means.

# Part 1: The Concepts

## 5.11 Distribution of Sample Means

In the last chapter, we learned how to compare an individual score to a population of individual scores. Applying the concepts of a normal distribution, we were able to use a *z*-score to determine exactly where that individual falls in the distribution, since that *z*-score corresponds to a proportion or probability (*p*). We could make this comparison since an individual raw score was being compared to a population of individual scores. However, most researchers are studying a sample and trying to generalize those sample results to the population. This generalization requires that we compare the studied sample to the population. This creates a couple of issues:

1) *We can't compare a sample (a group) to a population of individuals.* This is not a parallel comparison. So the population of individuals needs to be transformed into a population of samples, but not just any samples, similarly sized samples. For example, we can only compare a sample of 25 to a population of samples, each with 25 individuals.
2) While we hope that our studied sample is representative of the population, we know that it is impossible to create a sample that is perfectly representative of the population. In addition, every sample selected will likely be different since it contains a different set of individuals. So there will always be some difference between the sample and the population, called ***sampling error***. *How can we study a sample, that we know is different from the population, yet still generalize the results to the population?*

**Figure 5.1**
*Distribution of IQ*

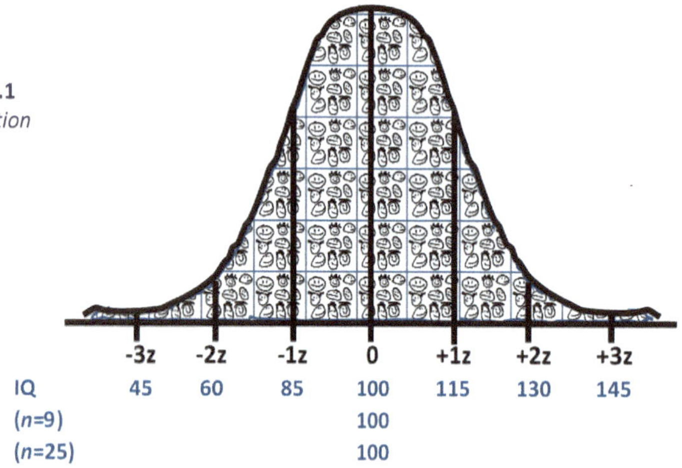


When we compared an individual score to the population, that population was a normal distribution of all the possible individual scores. Figure 5.1 presents a population distribution of all possible individual IQ scores, which are normally distributed ($\mu$=100, $\sigma$=15). However, if we randomly grouped individuals into similar sized samples (*n*=9), then calculated the means of all these samples, the means of those samples would also be normally distributed. This is called the ***distribution of sample means***—the distribution of sample means for all the possible random samples of a specific size, obtained from a population. Any distribution that is based upon sample statistics and NOT individual scores is referred to as a ***sampling distribution***. The distribution of sample means is the basis for many statistical tests, so let's take a closer look.

### Properties of the Distribution of Sample Means

Notice in Figure 5.1, the population mean of individual scores is 100. In the distribution of sample means, the overall mean (the mean of sample means) will also be 100. That's because the distribution still includes the same individuals, but we have randomly grouped them into samples of the same size. So whether we divide the population of individuals into samples of 9 or 25, the mean of sample means will always equal the population mean of individual scores. This is referred to as the ***expected value of M (mean of sample means)***.

Although the means of the distributions will stay the same, the variability of the sampling distributions will differ based upon sample size. In our example, samples of 9 were created—so 9 individual scores were averaged into the sample mean. As a result, the variability of these sample means would be less than the original distribution, since we have combined 9 scores into each sample mean. Suppose we were to create samples of 25, instead of 9 people. Now 25 individual scores are contributing to each sample mean, thus decreasing variability even more. Two conclusions can be drawn: 1) sample means are less variable than individual scores, and 2) results of larger samples are less variable than those of smaller samples. We can also think of these concepts of variability and sample size within the context of generalizing sample results to the population. Recall that with inferential statistics, we are studying a sample in order to generalize to the population; therefore a larger sample helps ensure that it is more representative of the population. Since the larger sample is a better estimate of the population, there is less error and less variability. Thus a new standard deviation has to be calculated for our new distribution of sample means. This new standard deviation is called the standard error of the mean since it is a function of sample size and error.

These characteristics of the distribution of sample means are derived from the ***Central Limit Theorem***, which states that for <u>any</u> population (with a mean μ and standard deviation σ), the following is true:

- The mean of the sampling distribution equals the mean of the population of individual scores;
- The distribution of sample means approximates a normal distribution;
- The larger the sample size ($n \geq 30$), the less error, hence the better the distribution approximately normality.
- The standard deviation of a sampling distribution, known as ***standard error of the mean*** ($\sigma_M$), is:

$$\sigma_M = \frac{\sigma}{\sqrt{n}}$$

In the IQ example, individual scores are normally distributed, so it is fairly easy to understand why the sample means of these same scores would be normally distributed. However, the Central Limit Theorem indicates that ANY population will have a sampling distribution that approximates normality. This is a pretty important finding for inferential statistics, as it indicates that no matter what the shape, mean, or standard deviation of the original population, its sampling distribution will approximate normality. Another important finding from the Central Limit Theorem is guidance on sample size, since we now know that a sampling distribution will have near perfect normality when the sample size is 30 or greater.

## 5.12 Definition and Calculation of Standard Error

In order to transform the population distribution of individuals into the distribution of sample means, a new standard deviation, called ***standard error of the mean***, must be calculated. Standard error is the standard amount of difference between the *M* (mean of sample means) and μ of the original population. Although we "expect" the mean of sample means to equal the population mean, a sample mean is not a perfect estimate of the population mean. We know there is always some degree of sampling error. Standard error is used to estimate sampling error. You can see from the equation, standard error is based upon two values—the population standard deviation and sample size. As such, standard error is an inverse function of sample size—meaning that as sample size increases, error decreases; and as sample size decrease, error increases.

**Standard Error of *M***

Standard amount of difference between *M* and μ

$$\sigma_M = \frac{\sigma}{\sqrt{n}}$$

**Figure 5.2**
*IQ Distribution of Sample Means for (n=9) and (n=25)*

| | -3z | -2z | -1z | 0 | +1z | +2z | +3z |
|---|---|---|---|---|---|---|---|
| IQ | 45 | 60 | 85 | 100 | 115 | 130 | 145 |
| (*n*=9) | 85 | 90 | 95 | 100 | 105 | 110 | 115 |
| (*n*=25) | 91 | 94 | 97 | 100 | 103 | 106 | 109 |

Let's take another look at the IQ (μ=100, σ=15) example and the two different sample sizes of 9 and 25. We have already established that the mean of all the distributions is 100. We now need to calculate standard error for our sample distribution of *n*=9.

$$\sigma_M = \frac{\sigma}{\sqrt{n}} = \frac{15}{\sqrt{9}} = \frac{15}{3} = 5$$

The standard deviation of the distribution of samples means (*n*=9) is 5. You can see that when the distribution was of individual scores, values ranged from 45 to 145; but for samples of 9, means range between 85 and 115. The standard deviation went from 15 to 5. That's because each sample mean eliminates the variability among 9 scores, so the standard deviation decreased quite a bit. Now let's look at the distribution for samples of 25. This distribution of sample means still has a mean of 100, but the new standard deviation needs to account for sample sizes of 25.

$$\sigma_M = \frac{\sigma}{\sqrt{n}} = \frac{15}{\sqrt{25}} = \frac{15}{5} = 3$$

Since the sample size increased, standard error decreased to 3. Now sample means range between 91 and 109. Again, since each mean eliminates the variability of 100 individuals, standard error decreased. In addition, larger sample means are more representative of the population so there is less error.

## 5.13 Probability and the Distribution of Sample Means

Since the distribution of sample means creates a normal bell-curve and is based upon all (100% of) possible scores, we can apply the concepts we have learned about normal distributions, probability and *z*-scores. Just as we converted an individual raw score to a *z*-score to compare the individual score to the population of individuals, we can also convert a specific sample mean to a $z$-score to compare the sample mean to the population of sample means. However, in order to do so, the distribution of individuals must be transformed to the distribution of samples by calculating the standard error ($\sigma_M$). This transformation is what allows us to compare a sample mean to the population (of similarly sized samples) and thus generalize our results to the population. We will utilize a three step process in determining proportion/probability for a sample mean: 1) calculate standard error; 2) convert sample mean to a $z$-score by comparing the sample mean to the population mean; and 3) use unit normal table to determine $p$ associated with $z$.

**Steps to Determine Proportion or Probability ($p$) for a Sample Mean**

1. Create distribution of sample means by calculating standard error ($\sigma_M$): $\sigma_M = \frac{\sigma}{\sqrt{n}}$
2. Convert sample mean to $z$-score: $z = \frac{M-\mu}{\sigma_M}$
3. Use unit normal table to determine $p$ associated with $z$-score.
   - For positive $z$-score (+$z$), determining:
     - Percentile rank (amount below)→Look in body.
     - Amount above→Look in tail.
   - For negative $z$-score (-$z$), determining:
     - Percentile rank (amount below)→Look in tail.
     - Amount above→Look in body.

Let's apply this process to two different samples, both of which were derived from the IQ test we have been discussing. Recall that this IQ exam is normally distributed ($\mu$=100, $\sigma$=15).

A. This first sample of 9 students has a mean ($M$=108). What is the probability of obtaining a sample mean above this group?

1. Calculate standard error. $\sigma_M = \frac{\sigma}{\sqrt{n}} = \frac{15}{\sqrt{9}} = \frac{15}{3} = 5$
2. Convert sample mean to a $z$-score.

$$z = \frac{X-\mu}{\sigma_M} = \frac{108-100}{5} = \frac{8}{5} = +1.6\ z$$

| (A) $z$ | (B) Proportion in body | (C) Proportion in tail | (D) Proportion between M & z |
|---|---|---|---|
| 1.60 | .9452 | .0548 | .4452 |
| 1.61 | .9463 | .0537 | .4463 |
| 1.62 | .9474 | .0526 | .4474 |
| 1.63 | .9484 | .0516 | .4484 |
| 1.64 | .9495 | .0505 | .4495 |

3. Use unit normal table to find $p$.
   - Since $z$ is positive and we are examining probability above, we need to look in the tail (Column C).
   - $p$=.0548
   - Other samples of 9 have less than a 6% chance of scoring a mean higher than 108 on this IQ test—that is pretty small.

B. Our second sample of 25 students also has a mean of 108. What is the probability of obtaining a sample mean above this group?

1. Calculate standard error. $\sigma_M = \frac{\sigma}{\sqrt{n}} = \frac{15}{\sqrt{25}} = \frac{15}{5} = 3$
2. Convert raw score to a $z$-score. $z = \frac{X-\mu}{\sigma_M} = \frac{108-100}{3} = \frac{8}{3} = +2.67z$
3. Use unit normal table to find $p$.
   - Since $z$ is positive and we are examining probability above, we need to look in the tail (Column C). In this case, a $z$ of 2.67, which corresponds to .0038.
   - $p$=.0038

| (A) $z$ | (B) Proportion in body | (C) Proportion in tail | (D) Proportion between M & z |
|---|---|---|---|
| 2.65 | .9960 | .0040 | .4960 |
| 2.66 | .9961 | .0039 | .4961 |
| 2.67 | .9962 | .0038 | .4962 |
| 2.68 | .9963 | .0037 | .4963 |
| 2.69 | .9964 | .0036 | .4964 |

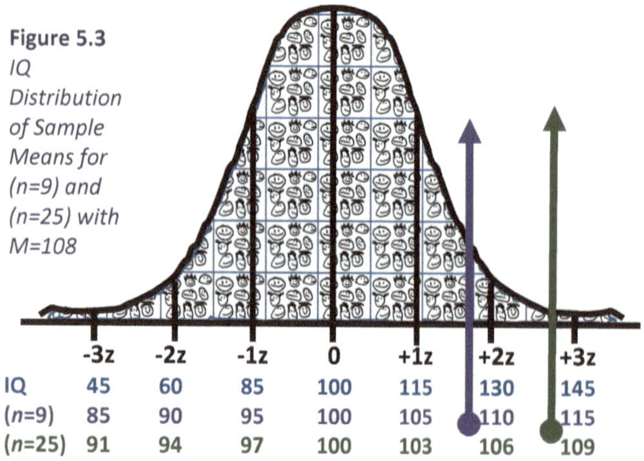


**Figure 5.3** *IQ Distribution of Sample Means for (n=9) and (n=25) with M=108*

- This means that other samples of 25 have less than .4% chance of scoring above a mean of 108. Wow, that probability is super small. How is it that a sample of 9 has about a 5% chance of obtaining a mean higher than 108, while a sample of 25 has a miniscule (.4%) chance? Recall that the distribution mean is 100. A score of 108 is obviously above the mean, so randomly selecting 9 individuals who generate mean of 108 is going to be difficult but not impossible. However, randomly selecting 25 individuals who score high enough to create a mean of 108 would be nearly impossible.

In the last two examples, we identified a proportion or probability associated with a specific sample mean. However, there are times when we need to identify a sample mean based upon a certain proportion or probability. For example, suppose we need to identify the range of means that would contain 95% of the sample. This task requires us to apply the process somewhat in reverse. Of course, we are still needing to transform the distribution of individuals to the distribution of sample means and therefore must first calculate standard error ($\sigma_M$). The next steps utilize $p$ to obtain a $z$-score, which is then used to calculate the sample mean.

**Steps to Determine a Sample Mean For a Proportion or Probability ($p$)**

1. Create distribution of sample means by calculating standard error ($\sigma_M$):
$$\sigma_M = \frac{\sigma}{\sqrt{n}}$$
2. Determine $p$. For boundaries of a proportion or %, divide in half.
3. Use unit normal table to determine $z$-score associated with $p$.
4. Determine $M$ value using z-score. $M = \mu \pm z(\sigma_M)$

C. Utilizing the distribution of sample means for $n$=100, determine the range of scores that contain 95% of sample means.

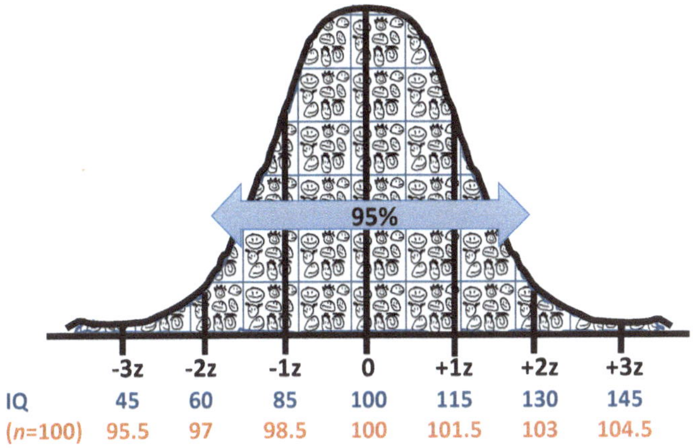


1. Calculate standard error.
$$\sigma_M = \frac{\sigma}{\sqrt{n}} = \frac{15}{\sqrt{100}} = \frac{15}{10} = 1.5$$

2. Determine $p$. The $z$-table only presents half of the distribution. Since the 95% (.9500) we are examining is in the middle of the distribution, we need to split this in half (.9500/2 = .4750), such that 47.5% is right of the mean and 47.5% is left of the mean. $p$=.4750

3. Use $z$-table to find corresponding $z$-score. Look in Column D to determine the proportion between the mean and $z$. $z$ = 1.96. This means that 95% of sample means fall between -1.96$z$ and +1.96$z$. However, these are the $z$-score boundaries, not the actual test score boundaries.

| (A) $z$ | (B) *Proportion in body* | (C) *Proportion in tail* | (D) *Proportion between M & z* |
|---|---|---|---|
| 1.95 | .9744 | .0256 | .4744 |
| 1.96 | .9750 | .0250 | .4750 |
| 1.97 | .9756 | .0244 | .4756 |
| 1.98 | .9761 | .0239 | .4761 |
| 1.99 | .9767 | .0233 | .4767 |

4. Use $z$-score to determine sample mean boundaries. Remember, a $z$-score represents the number of standard deviations (or standard errors) away from the mean. To convert this to test values, we use a similar equation to calculate a new raw score, but this time we are calculating the specific sample means:

$$M = \mu \pm z(\sigma_M)$$

Therefore, we plug in the population mean of 100 and add that to the product of $z$-score multiplied by $SE$ (1.96*1.5 = 2.94). So 95% of sample means will fall between 100 ± 2.94 (or 97.06 and 102.94).

## 5.14 Module Summary

- In Module 4, we learned how to compare an individual score to a population of individual scores. In Module 5, we learned how to compare a sample mean to the population of sample means.
- Inferential statistics typically utilize sample data in an attempt to generalize the results to the population.
  - The ability to generalize requires that we compare the studied sample to the population.
  - Since we can't compare a sample to a population of individuals, the population distribution of individuals must be transformed into a population distribution of similarly sized samples.
- The ***distribution of sample means***—the distribution of sample means for all the possible random samples of a specific size obtained from a population.
- The ***Central Limit Theorem*** states that for <u>any</u> population (with a mean μ and standard deviation σ), the following is true:
  - The mean of the sampling distribution equals the mean of the population of individual scores;
  - The distribution of sample means approximates a normal distribution;
  - The larger the sample size ($n \geq 30$), the less error, hence the better the distribution approximates normality.
  - The standard deviation of a sampling distribution, known as ***standard error of the mean*** ($\sigma_M$), is:

$$\sigma_M = \frac{\sigma}{\sqrt{n}}$$

- Standard error is the standard amount of difference between the $M$ (mean of sample means) and μ of the original population.
  - Since standard error is based upon two values (population standard deviation and sample size), standard error is an inverse function of sample size. In that, as sample size increases, error decreases; and as sample size decreases, error increases.

- **Steps to Determine Proportion or Probability (*p*) for a Sample Mean**
  1. Create distribution of sample means by calculating standard error ($\sigma_M$): $\sigma_M = \frac{\sigma}{\sqrt{n}}$
  2. Convert sample mean to *z*-score: $z = \frac{M-\mu}{\sigma_M}$
  3. Use unit normal table to determine *p* associated with *z*-score.
     - For positive *z*-score (+*z*), determining:
       - Percentile rank (amount below)→Look in body.
       - Amount above→Look in tail.
     - For negative *z*-score (-*z*), determining:
       - Percentile rank (amount below)→Look in tail.
       - Amount above→Look in body.

- **Steps to Determine a Sample Mean for a Proportion or Probability (*p*)**
  1. Create distribution of sample means by calculating standard error ($\sigma_M$): $\sigma_M = \frac{\sigma}{\sqrt{n}}$
  2. Determine *p*. For boundaries of a proportion or %, divide in half.
  3. Use unit normal table to determine *z*-score associated with *p*.
  4. Determine *M* value using z-score. $M = \mu \pm z(\sigma_M)$

# Part 2: Learning Guide

## 5.21V Distribution of Sample Means

- In Chapter 4, we learned how to compare an individual score to a population of individual scores.
- Inferential statistics typically utilize sample data in an attempt to generalize the results to the population.
- The ability to generalize requires that we compare the studied sample to the population. This raises a couple of issues:
  1. Comparing a sample (a group) to a population of individuals is not a parallel comparison. We must compare a sample to a population of similarly sized samples.
  2. How can we study a sample that we know is different from the population, yet still generalize the results to the population?
- Since we can't compare a sample to a population of individuals, the population distribution of individuals must be transformed into a population distribution of similarly sized samples.
  - The ***distribution of sample means***—the distribution of means for all the possible random samples of a specific size obtained from a population.
  - Any distribution that is based upon sample statistics and NOT individual scores is referred to as a ***sampling distribution***.

**Example**

Most IQ tests are normed with $\mu$=100 and $\sigma$=15. As a result the distribution ranges between 45 and 130.

If we randomly grouped individuals into similar sized samples ($n$=9), then calculated the means of all these samples, the means of those samples would also be normally distributed.

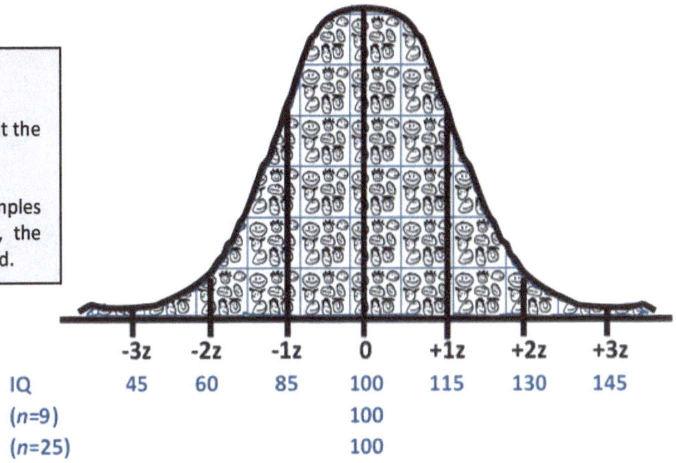


### Properties of the Distribution of Sample Means

- Since the distribution of sample means still includes the population (just divided into samples), the overall mean (of sample means) will be the same as the population mean of individuals. This overall mean of sample means is referred to as the ***expected value of M (mean of sample means).***
- Although the means of the distributions will stay the same, the variability of the sampling distributions will differ based upon sample size.
  - When individuals scores are averaged in a sample, the variability of all those individuals has been lost into that one sample mean score.
  - Two conclusions can be drawn: 1) sample means are less variable than individual scores, and 2) results of larger samples are less variable than those of smaller samples.
  - A larger sample helps ensure that it is more representative of the population and is a better estimate of the population since there is less error and less variability.
  - Since variability is dependent upon sample size, a new standard deviation (called standard error of the mean) has to be calculated for our new distribution of sample means.
- The ***Central Limit Theorem*** states that for <u>any</u> population (with a mean $\mu$ and standard deviation $\sigma$), the following is true:
  - The mean of the sampling distribution equals the mean of the population of individual scores;
  - The distribution of sample means (for any population) approximates a normal distribution;
  - The larger the sample size ($n \geq 30$), the less error, hence the better the distribution approximates normality.
  - The standard deviation of a sampling distribution, known as ***standard error of the mean*** ($\sigma_M$), is:

$$\sigma_M = \frac{\sigma}{\sqrt{n}}$$

## 5.22V Definition and Calculation of Standard Error

- Standard error is the standard amount of difference between the $M$ (mean of sample means) and $\mu$ of the original population.
- Since standard error is based upon two values (population standard deviation and sample size), standard error is an inverse function of sample size. In that, as sample size increases, error decreases; and as sample size decreases, error increases.

> **Example**
>
> **Creating a Distribution of Sample Means**
>
> Most IQ tests are normed with $\mu$=100 and $\sigma$=15. As a result the distribution ranges between 45 and 130.
>
> **Sample #1 (*n*=9),** $\mu$=100
> Calculate standard error
>
> $$\sigma_M = \frac{\sigma}{\sqrt{n}} = \frac{15}{\sqrt{9}} = \frac{15}{3} = 5$$
>
> Now population distribution of samples of 9 ranges from 85 to 115.
>
> **Sample #2 (*n*=25),** $\mu$=100
> Calculate standard error
>
> $$\sigma_M = \frac{\sigma}{\sqrt{n}} = \frac{15}{\sqrt{25}} = \frac{15}{5} = 3$$
>
> Now population distribution of samples of 100 ranges from 91 to 109.

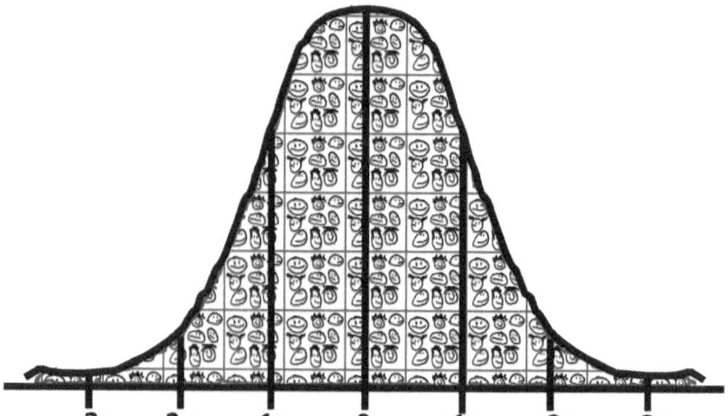

| | -3z | -2z | -1z | 0 | +1z | +2z | +3z |
|---|---|---|---|---|---|---|---|
| IQ | 45 | 60 | 85 | 100 | 115 | 130 | 145 |
| (*n*=9) | 85 | 90 | 95 | 100 | 105 | 110 | 115 |
| (*n*=25) | 91 | 94 | 97 | 100 | 103 | 106 | 109 |

## 5.23V Probability and the Distribution of Sample Means

- Previously we compared an individual score to a population of individuals by using a *z*-score. Now we can compare a specific sample mean to a population sample means also using a *z*-score. Just as we converted an individual raw score to a *z*-score, we can also convert a specific sample mean to a *z*-score.
- The distribution of individuals must be transformed to the distribution of samples by calculating the standard error ($\sigma_M$).
- This transformation is what allows us to compare a sample mean to the population (of similarly sized samples) and thus generalize our results to the population.

**Steps to Determine Proportion or Probability (*p*) for a Sample Mean**

1. Create distribution of sample means by calculating standard error ($\sigma_M$): $\sigma_M = \frac{\sigma}{\sqrt{n}}$
2. Convert sample mean to *z*-score: $z = \frac{M-\mu}{\sigma_M}$
3. Use unit normal table to determine *p* associated with *z*-score.
   - For positive *z*-score (+*z*), determining:
     - Percentile rank (amount below)→Look in body.
     - Amount above→Look in tail.
   - For negative *z*-score (-*z*), determining:
     - Percentile rank (amount below)→Look in tail.
     - Amount above→Look in body.

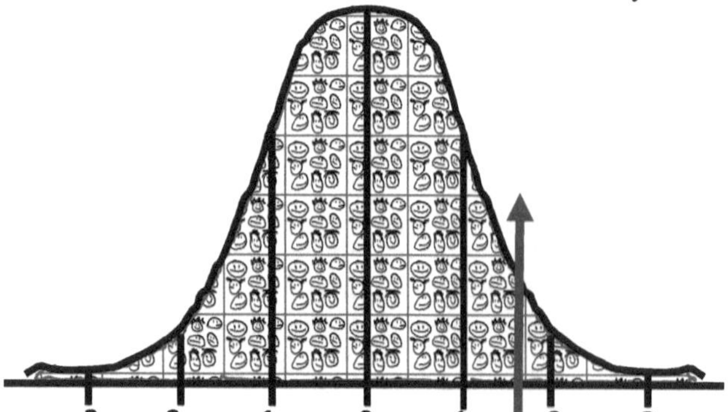

| | -3z | -2z | -1z | 0 | +1z | +2z | +3z |
|---|---|---|---|---|---|---|---|
| IQ | 45 | 60 | 85 | 100 | 115 | 130 | 145 |
| (*n*=9) | 85 | 90 | 95 | 100 | 105 | 110 | 115 |
| (*n*=25) | 91 | 94 | 97 | 100 | 103 | 106 | 109 |

> **Example**
>
> **Determining Probability of Sample Means**
>
> IQ test distribution of individuals ($\mu$=100, $\sigma$=15).
>
> **Sample #1 (*n*=9)** has a mean of 108. What is the probability of obtaining a sample of 9 with a mean greater than 108?
>
> Calculate standard error.
>
> $$\sigma_M = \frac{\sigma}{\sqrt{n}} = \frac{15}{\sqrt{9}} = \frac{15}{3} = 5$$
>
> Convert sample mean to a *z*-score.
>
> $$z = \frac{X-\mu}{\sigma_M} = \frac{108-100}{5} = \frac{8}{5} = +1.6z$$
>
> Use unit normal table to find *p*. Since *z* is positive and we are examining probability above, we need to look in the tail (Column C). *p*=.0548

| (A) *z* | (B) Proportion in body | (C) Proportion in tail | (D) Proportion between M & z |
|---|---|---|---|
| 1.60 | .9452 | .0548 | .4452 |
| 1.61 | .9463 | .0537 | .4463 |
| 1.62 | .9474 | .0526 | .4474 |
| 1.63 | .9484 | .0516 | .4484 |
| 1.64 | .9495 | .0505 | .4495 |

# Example

**Determining Probability of a Sample Mean**

IQ test distribution of individuals (μ=100, σ=15).

**Sample #2 (*n*=25)** also has a mean of 108. What is the probability of obtaining a sample of 100 greater than a mean of 108?

Calculate standard error $\sigma_M = \frac{\sigma}{\sqrt{n}} = \frac{15}{\sqrt{25}} = \frac{15}{5} = 3$

Convert sample mean to a *z*-score.

$$z = \frac{M - \mu}{\sigma_M} = \frac{108 - 100}{3} = \frac{8}{3} = +2.67z$$

Use unit normal table to find *p*.
Since *z* is positive and we are examining probability above, we need to look in the tail (Column C). ***p*=.0038**

| (A) *z* | (B) *Proportion in body* | (C) *Proportion in tail* | (D) *Proportion between M & z* |
|---|---|---|---|
| 2.65 | .9960 | .0040 | .4960 |
| 2.66 | .9961 | .0039 | .4961 |
| 2.67 | .9962 | .0038 | .4962 |
| 2.68 | .9963 | .0037 | .4963 |
| 2.69 | .9964 | .0036 | .4964 |

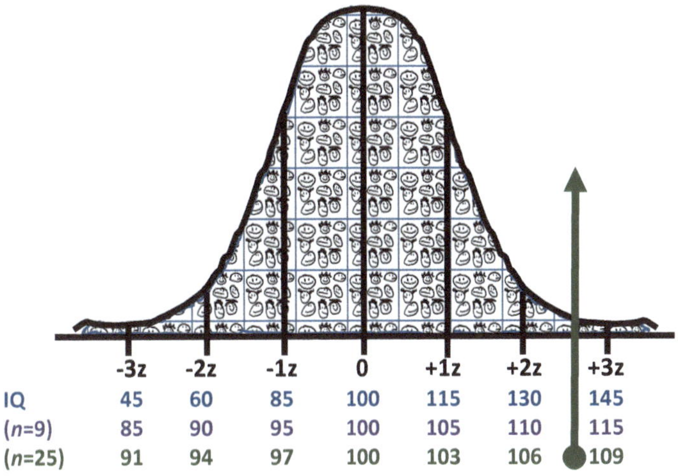


**Steps to Determine a Sample Mean for a Proportion or Probability (*p*)**

1. Create distribution of sample means by calculating standard error ($\sigma_M$): $\sigma_M = \frac{\sigma}{\sqrt{n}}$
2. Determine *p*. For boundaries of a proportion or %, divide in half.
3. Use unit normal table to determine *z*-score associated with *p*.
4. Determine *M* value using z-score. $M = \mu \pm z(\sigma_M)$

# Example

**Determining a Sample Mean Based upon Probability**

Based upon the previous distribution of sample means (μ=100, σ=15, *n*=100, *SE*=1.5), **determine the range of values that contain 95% of sample means?**

- This 95% is from the center of the distribution, the mean.
- The *z*-table only presents *p* for half of the distribution, 95% needs to be divided in half (95/2=47.5→.475

- Use *z*-table; look in Column D for *p* of .475.
  - *z*=1.96
  - This means that 95% of sample means fall between -1.96z and +1.96.

| (A) *z* | (B) *Proportion in body* | (C) *Proportion in tail* | (D) *Proportion between M & z* |
|---|---|---|---|
| 1.95 | .9744 | .0256 | .4744 |
| 1.96 | .9750 | .0250 | .4750 |
| 1.97 | .9756 | .0244 | .4756 |
| 1.98 | .9761 | .0239 | .4761 |
| 1.99 | .9767 | .0233 | .4767 |

- Calculate sample mean. To convert this to test values, just multiply the *z*-score by SE (1.96*1.5 = 2.94). So 95% of sample means will 100 ± 2.94. The lower boundary is 100-2.94 =97.06. The upper boundary is 100+2.94=102.94

  $M = \mu \pm z(\sigma_M)$
- So 95% of sample means will fall between 97.06 and 102.94.

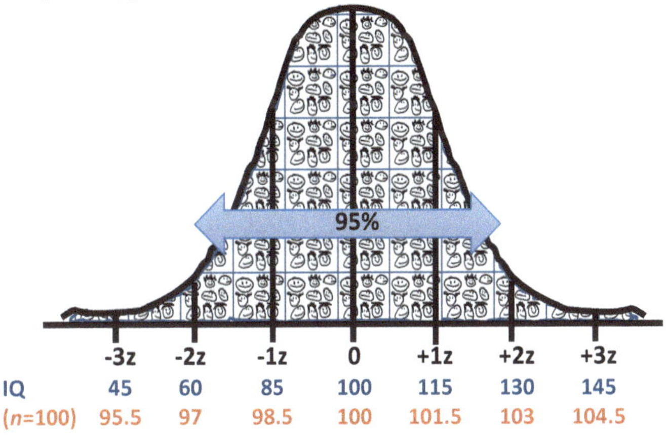

## 5.24V A Complete Example

If you recall, the ACT-Math exam is normally distributed ($\mu$=18, $\sigma$=6). A school district wants to compare two different groups to the population.

1. The first group ($n$=36, $M$=20)) consists of students who completed Trigonometry before they took the ACT. What is the probability of scoring below this group? What is the probability of scoring above this group?

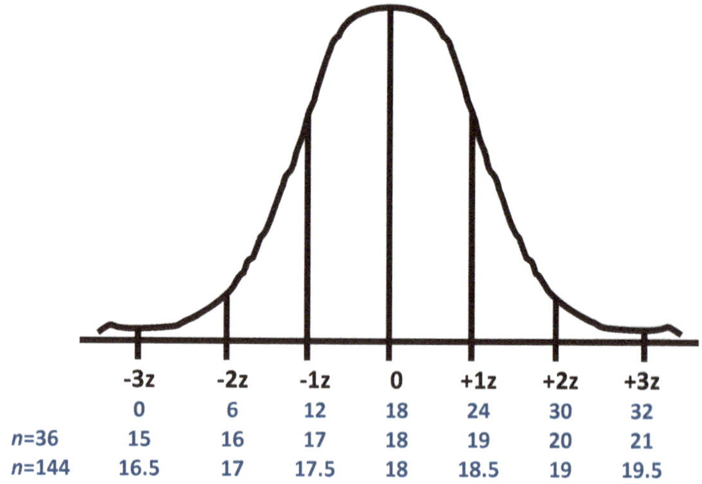


2. The second group ($n$=144, $M$=17.5) consists of students who had only completed Algebra I by the time they took the ACT. What is the probability of scoring above this group? Between what values will 95% of the sample means fall?

## 5.25V Additional Practice

1. The Critical Thinking Assessment Test (CAT) measures one's ability to evaluate and interpret information, problem solve, think creatively, and effectively communicate. The overall test score is normally distributed with a mean of $\mu$=19 and standard deviation of $\sigma$=6.

   a. For a sample of $n$=9, what is the probability of scoring below $M$=22?

   b. For a sample of $n$=36, what is the probability of scoring higher than $M$=20? Between what values will 99% of the sample means fall?

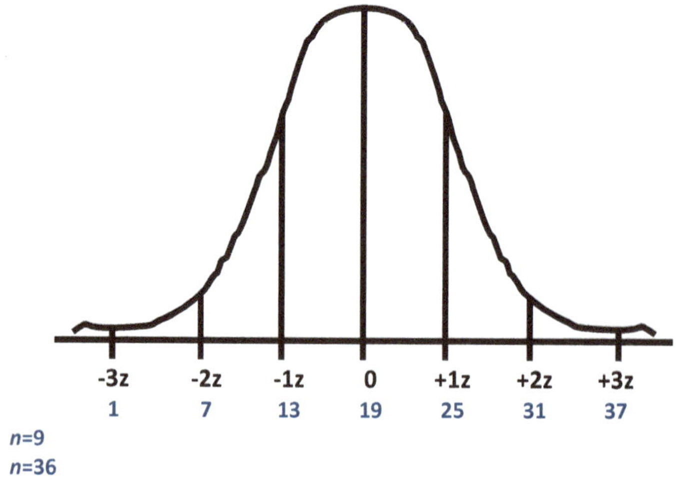

## 5.26 Activity: Sampling Distribution Applet

This activity will allow you to manipulate a population distribution to generate different distributions of sample means. Go to the Sampling Distribution of the Sample Mean applet at:

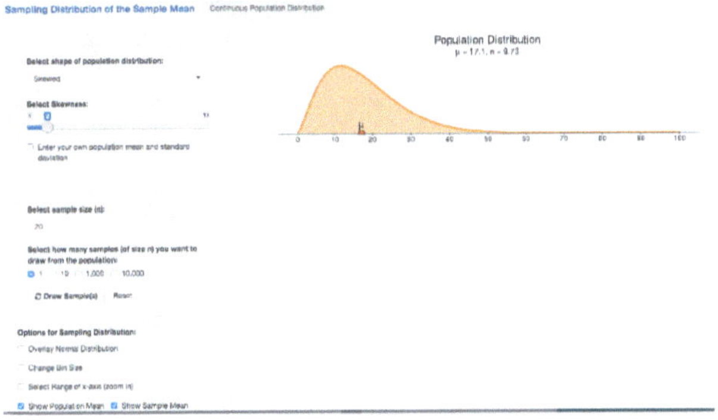

https://istats.shinyapps.io/sampdist_cont/

To the left of the Population Distribution is a drop-down menu; click and select **Bell-shaped**. You will not need to change this setting for the rest of the activity. The distribution is based upon the population mean, standard deviation and sample size you select. Changing the population mean (μ) using the slider below will create a new distribution, as will the population standard deviation (σ) slider.

Clicking the box below the SD slider will allow you to manually enter the population means and standard deviations in the table below. You may use either the sliders or manual entry to complete the activity. Set the population mean (μ) at 50 and the standard deviation (σ) at 10. The text entry box below the mean and standard deviation allows you to choose a sample size (*n*). The radial buttons below sample size allow you to choose the number of samples you want to draw from the population (*N*). Select **10,000**. You will not need to change this setting for the rest of the activity.

We will mainly be focusing our attention on the sampling distribution of sample means that will appear below the histogram after each sample is drawn. Once you have indicated Bell shaped, set the mean and standard deviation for the population, and have chosen 10,000 as the number of samples you will draw, you will be changing the sample size (*n*). Remember, each time you change the sample size (*n*), you will need to click the Draw Sample(s) button to generate the distributions.

1. Run the applet with sample sizes of 5, 10, 100, and 1000 to complete the table.

| **Sample Size (*n*)** | ***M*** | ***SD*** (aka, standard error) |
|---|---|---|
| 5 | | |
| 10 | | |
| 100 | | |
| 1000 | | |

2. What happened to the standard deviation (standard error) as sample size increased?

3. Although all of the distributions followed a normal shape, how did the shape change as the sample size increased?

4. Based upon your observations, summarize the relationship between sample size and standard error.

## 5.27V In the Literature

Research articles will often report standard error for a sample rather than the standard deviation, especially when generalization to the population is priority. While the standard deviation is helpful in understanding the variability across the sample, the standard error (*SE*) will give us a better picture of the error in the sample and therefore how the value would likely playout in the population.

**Excerpt from:** Cunningham, B.C., Hoyer, K. M. & Sparks, D. (2015). Gender Differences in Science, Technology, Engineering, and Mathematics (STEM) Interest, Credit Earned and NAEP Performance in the 12th Grade. *Stats in Brief.* NCES 2015-075. ERIC ED 554303.

A sample of over 41,000 graduating seniors participated in the 2009 National Assessment of Education Progress (NAEP) program, representing approximately 3 million high school graduates. Participants completed NAEP exams on mathematics and science as well as the 2009 NAEP Grade 12 Mathematics and Science Student Questionnaire, which elicited information regarding student's classroom experiences and educational support. Interest in mathematics and science was measured with four items that utilized a 4-point Likert scale ranging from strongly disagree to strongly agree. Students who indicated agree or strongly agree were considered to respond positively to the statement. Table 1 presents the percentages of males and females that reported agreement with interest statements. In addition, standard error is reported for each item.

**Table 1. Percent of High School Graduates Who Reported Interest in Mathematics and Science by Gender**

| Reported Interest | Male | | Female | |
|---|---|---|---|---|
| | % | *SE* | % | *SE* |
| Like mathematics | 58.7 | 0.66 | 53.2 | 0.58 |
| Mathematics is one of my favorite subjects | 50.4 | 0.76 | 42.6 | 0.62 |
| Like science | 69.9 | 1.28 | 59.4 | 1.08 |
| Science is one of my favorite subjects | 47.6 | 1.39 | 34.2 | 1.07 |

SOURCE: U.S. Department of Education, Institute of Education Sciences, National Center for Education Statistics, High School Transcript Study (HSTS), 2009; National Assessment of Educational Progress (NAEP), 2009 Mathematics and Science Assessments.

1. More males report positive interest toward mathematics and science; however, which item presents the greatest gender difference? How would you explain this difference?

2. Which item presents the smallest difference between males and females? This item also has the smallest standard error. Why do you think this item has the least amount of error?

3. Standard error is relatively high for "Science is one of my favorite subjects" for both males and females. Why is it nearly double than "Like mathematics?" Keep in mind the sample size is fairly stable across these items.

## 5.28 Exercises

### Reviewing the Concepts

1. Explain why a distribution of individuals must be transformed to a distribution of sample means in order to compare a sample mean to the population.

2. When transforming a population distribution of individuals to a distribution of sample means, why does the mean stay the same but the standard deviation change?

3. Define standard error.

   a. How is standard error calculated?

   b. What happens to standard error as sample size increases?

4. Why is a sample size of 30 or greater a good thing in statistics?

5. For the following items, apply the population parameters ($\mu$=80, $\sigma$=10).
   a. For a sample of *n*=25, what is the expected value of *M*? What is the standard error?

   b. For a sample of *n*=100, what is the expected value of *M*? What is the standard error?

6. West (2004) used the Spiritual Well-Being Scale to measure existential well-being among college students, who generated the norms ($\mu$=50, $\sigma$=5). The subscale of existential well-being represents the "individual's sense of meaning and purpose in life;" subscale scores can range from 10 to 60. Use these norms to compare the various samples.

   a. A Catholic college randomly selects 100 graduates to complete the Spiritual Well-Being Scale. This sample produces a mean of 53. What is the probability of scoring higher than this sample?

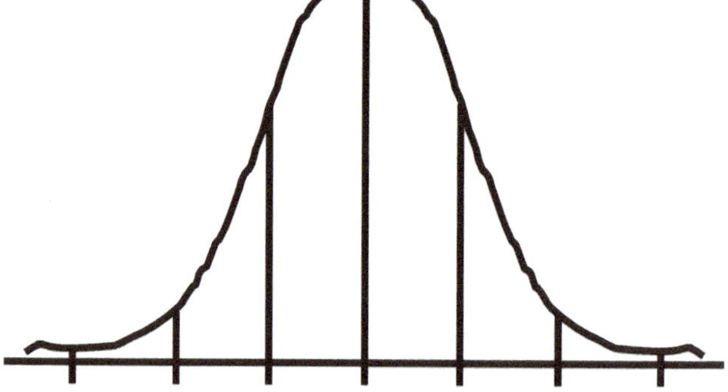

| | -3z | -2z | -1z | 0 | +1z | +2z | +3z |
|---|---|---|---|---|---|---|---|
| | 35 | 40 | 45 | 50 | 55 | 60 | 65 |
| *n*=100 | 48.8 | 49 | 49.5 | 50 | 50.5 | 51 | 51.5 |
| *n*=25 | 47 | 48 | 49 | 50 | 51 | 52 | 53 |
| n=400 | 49.25 | 49.5 | 49.75 | 50 | 50.25 | 50.5 | 50.75 |

   b. This same Catholic college randomly selects 25 freshman students. This sample produces a mean of 49 on the existential well-being subscale. What is the probability of scoring below this sample? What is the probability of scoring higher than this sample?

   c. A public university randomly selects 400 undergraduate students (*M*=51) who are participating in some kind of service-learning activity. What is the probability of scoring higher than this sample? Between what two values will 95% of the sample means fall?

West, K. F. (2004) Spiritual well-being: Assessment and intervention in a college population. Dissertation. Xavier University, ProQuest, UMI Dissertations Publishing, 2004. DP20189

7. Excerpt from Goodman, M., Finnegan, R., Mohadjer, L., Krenzke, T., & Hogan, J. (2013). *Literacy, Numeracy, and Problem Solving in Technology-Rich Environments Among U.S. Adults: Results from the Program for the International Assessment of Adult Competencies 2012: First Look* (NCES 2014-008). U.S. Department of Education. Washington, DC: National Center for Education Statistics. Retrieved [04/03/2015] from http://nces.ed.gov/pubsearch

The Program for the International Assessment of Adult Competencies (PIAAC) is a cyclical, large-scale study of adult skills and life experience focusing on education and employment. PIAAC was developed and organized by the Organization for Economic Cooperation and Development (OECD). In the United States, the study was conducted in 2011–12 with a nationally representative sample of 5,000 adults between the ages of 16 and 65. Similar nationally representative samples of adults were surveyed in each of the 22 other participating countries. The goal of PIAAC is to assess and compare the basic skills and the broad range of competencies of adults around the world. The assessment focuses on cognitive and workplace skills necessary for successful participation in 21st-century society and the global economy. Specifically, PIAAC measures relationships between individuals' educational background, workplace experiences and skills, occupational attainment, use of information and communication technology, and cognitive skills in the areas of literacy, numeracy, and problem solving in technology-rich environments.

The numeracy area evaluates basic mathematical and computational skills that are considered fundamental for functioning in everyday work and social life. Numeracy in the PIAAC framework is defined as "the ability to access, use, interpret, and communicate mathematical information and ideas, to engage in and manage mathematical demands of a range of situations in adult life" (Organization for Economic Cooperation and Development [OECD], 2012). Table 1 presents the numeracy means and standard errors for the participating countries. The international average was 269.

**Table 1.** Average score on the PIAAC Numeracy Scale for Adults Age 16-65 by Country

| | *M* | *SE* |
|---|---|---|
| International | 269 | 0.2 |
| Australia | 268 | 0.9 |
| Austria | 275 | 0.9 |
| Flanders-Belgium | 280 | 0.8 |
| Canada | 265 | 0.7 |
| Cyprus | 265 | 0.8 |
| Czech Republic | 276 | 0.9 |
| Denmark | 278 | 0.7 |
| Estonia | 273 | 0.5 |
| Finland | 282 | 0.7 |
| France | 254 | 0.6 |
| Germany | 272 | 1.0 |
| Ireland | 256 | 1.0 |
| Italy | 247 | 1.1 |
| Japan | 288 | 0.7 |
| Korea | 263 | 0.7 |
| Netherlands | 280 | 0.7 |
| Norway | 278 | 0.8 |
| Poland | 260 | 0.8 |
| Slovak Republic | 276 | 0.8 |
| Spain | 246 | 0.6 |
| Sweden | 279 | 0.8 |
| United Kingdom | 262 | 1.1 |
| United States | 253 | 1.2 |
| Italy | 247 | 1.1 |

a. The United States has a mean of 253. How many countries scored above the U.S.?

b. How many countries score below the U.S.?

c. Which country scored the highest? The lowest?

d. The international standard error is only 0.2, while standard error for individual countries range between 0.5 and 1.2. Why is the international standard error so much lower?

e. Why does the U.S. have such a larger standard error than Estonia?

# Module 6

## Hypothesis Testing

### Learning Targets

After completing Module 6, you should be able to:

- Apply the steps to conduct a hypothesis test for a *z*-test of single sample to compare a sample mean to a population mean (with a known population standard deviation); and determine statistical significance.
    1. State the hypotheses (identify variables, identify variables; determine number of tails (one-tailed or two-tailed); write hypotheses (alternative and null) in sentence form; develop hypotheses notation.
    2. Establish significance criteria
    3. Collect and analyze data
    4. Evaluate null hypothesis and draw conclusion
- Interpret *z*-test results (hand calculations, StatCrunch output) to determine statistical significance and confidence intervals and draw appropriate conclusions.
- Utilize *z*-test results to calculate appropriate effect size and power.
- Write appropriate conclusions with statistical results notation.

# Part 1: The Concepts

The primary goal of most quantitative research is to study a sample and generalize those results to the population. In the last module, we compared a sample means to the population of sample means. And while we were able to determine where the sample mean fell within the distribution of sample means, we weren't able to generalize anything to the population. This module introduces the concepts and process of hypothesis testing, the most commonly used inferential technique. Hypothesis testing will be applied throughout the remainder of this resource, so a step by step process will be outlined.

## 6.11 Purpose and Steps of Hypothesis Testing

Likely you are familiar with hypothesis testing from any science classes you took in high school or college. In most of your labs, you conducted an experiment to test the hypothesis or prediction. A part of the experiment was collecting and analyzing data in order to draw a conclusion. Hypothesis testing within social sciences will apply a similar process, however, as you know, research in social sciences is dealing with people. As we have already established, it is usually impossible to study a population. Therefore, ***hypothesis testing*** in social sciences involves studying a sample to evaluate a hypothesis about the population so that we can generalize the results to the population.

In Module 1, you learned about causal and mutual relationships. Hypothesis testing will typically predict that a mutual or causal relationship will occur in the population, when it occurs in the sample. In Module 5, we learned that many measures create normal sampling distributions in populations. We can now use these population norms as a baseline that represents the population before any treatment has occurred. When the treatment is implemented with the sample, we predict that the treatment will affect the sample mean so that the sample mean will be significantly different from the population mean (norm). We can compare the sample mean to the population distribution of sample means. If the treatment does have a significant effect, the treatment (sample) mean should be very different from the population mean and therefore be out in the tails with the extreme means, where the probability is very low. Hypothesis testing applies a formal process that follows these four steps:

1. State the hypotheses
2. Establish significance criteria
3. Collect and analyze data
4. Evaluate null hypothesis and draw conclusion

These four steps will be described in the following sections and applied throughout this resource.

## 6.12 Step 1: State the Hypotheses

### Alternative and Null

Statistics are all about testing a hypothesis; however, we aren't testing the hypothesis you think. In most research, one is predicting a mutual or causal relationship in the population. This actual prediction of a relationship is called the ***alternative hypothesis*** and is represented by $H_A$ or $H_1$. Most believe that research sets out to "prove a hypothesis." However, it is impossible to prove the alternative hypothesis true since it would require examination of the entire population to show 100% support. Consequently, inferential statistics set out to disprove the null hypothesis in order to provide support for the alternative. The ***null hypothesis*** states that a relationship is NOT present in the population. The null hypothesis is abbreviated as $H_0$ and can be read as "H-nought" or "H-oh." Testing the null eliminates the need to study the population and allows us to examine a sample and generalize the result to the population.

Hypothesis testing is about contradictions. The language of opposites and multiple negatives can get pretty confusing, so let's look at an example. Suppose I make the prediction that all introductory statistics books will have a chapter on statistical power. For this prediction, the hypotheses would be written as:

**Alternative hypothesis ($H_1$)**—All introductory statistics textbooks will have a chapter on statistical power.
**Null hypothesis ($H_0$)**—All introductory statistics textbooks will NOT have a chapter on statistical power.

Notice that the null hypothesis has identical wording of the alternative, but with a NOT inserted. Proving the alternative would require that I examine all introductory stats texts and that all of them have a chapter on statistical power. This process would take forever and is pretty much impossible. Even if I found 100 textbooks that have a chapter on statistical power, it still does not prove the hypothesis. So let's focus on the null. The null states that all stats texts will NOT have a chapter on statistical power. Disproving the null only requires that I find one textbook that HAS a chapter on statistical power. The process of disproving the null is a heck of a lot easier to conduct. However, disproving the null still does not prove the alternative; rather, disproving the null only provides support for the alternative.

### Directional and Non-directional

While every hypothesis will have an alternative and a null hypothesis, these hypotheses will be either ***directional*** or ***non-directional***. Often a researcher has a specific prediction about the treatment effect in that the treatment will increase or decrease performance—this type of prediction utilizes a directional hypothesis. Since a directional hypothesis is examining a change in a specific direction, this type of hypothesis applies a one-tailed test. In contrast, a non-directional hypothesis just examines some relationship, effect, or difference—it isn't specific. For our critical thinking example, the alternative hypothesis is:

***H*₁**: College freshman who participant in a treatment of critical thinking feedback have significantly <u>different</u> critical thinking skills than the norm ($\mu$=19).

The word "different" indicates a non-directional or two-tailed hypothesis, since the sample mean could be lower or higher than the population mean. If our hypothesis stated that the treatment would significantly increase critical thinking skills so that the participants would have a "higher" mean than the population norm, the hypothesis would be directional or one-tailed, since we would be searching for only an increase.

## Example

Suppose a researcher conducts a study to determine if a semester-long treatment significantly effects critical thinking scores as measured by the Critical Thinking Assessment Test ($\mu$=19, $\sigma$=6). The treatment consists of providing consistent feedback using a critical thinking rubric for all writing assignments in an Introduction to Business course. The researcher randomly selects 144 freshman students enrolled in the class. The researcher will examine this effect on critical thinking skills by comparing the sample mean to the population norm.

**RQ:** Will college freshman who participant in a <u>treatment of critical thinking feedback</u> have significantly different <u>critical thinking skills</u> than the norm ($\mu$=19)?

**Step 1: State the Hypotheses**

**IV:** Treatment of critical thinking feedback
**DV:** Critical thinking skills
**Key Word:** different→two-tailed

**Alternative Hypothesis:** College freshman who participant in a treatment of critical thinking feedback have significantly different critical thinking skills than the norm ($\mu$=19).

$$H_1: \mu_{feedback} \neq 19$$

**Null Hypothesis:** College freshman who participant in a treatment of critical thinking feedback do NOT have significantly different critical thinking skills than the norm ($\mu$=19).

$$H_0: \mu_{feedback} = 19$$

### Hypothesis Notation

Hypotheses are expressed in sentence form as well as in notation. The sentence hypotheses provide the details about the variables, relationship, and population. Hypothesis notation presents the mathematical proposition being tested and clarifies the comparisons and values used to make a decision regarding the hypothesis. Applying the critical thinking example, where we predict that: College freshman who participant in a treatment of critical thinking feedback have significantly <u>different</u> critical thinking skills than the norm ($\mu$=19), the hypotheses notation for the alternative and null are:

$$H_1: \mu_{feedback} \neq 19 \qquad H_0: \mu_{feedback} = 19$$

Remember, hypotheses are predictions about the population, so the population mean symbol ($\mu$) is used. But notice that the subscript of *feedback* is used to define this particular subgroup within the population. Since we are predicting that our treatment mean will be different than the population norm of 19, the not equal ($\neq$) symbol is used in the alternative hypothesis. The null hypothesis indicates that the treatment mean will equal (=) the population norm. Figure 6.1 presents keywords that indicate direction or non-direction as well the various hypotheses for the critical thinking example using both directional and non-directional tests.

**Figure 6.1** Comparison of Directional and Non-Directional Hypotheses

| | Directional | Non-Directional |
|---|---|---|
| Key Words | Increase, decrease, higher, lower, positive, negative | Effect, difference, change, impact, relationship |
| Alternative | ***H*₁**: College freshman who participate in a treatment of critical thinking feedback have significantly <u>higher</u> critical thinking skills than the norm ($\mu$=19).<br><br>$H_1$: $\mu_{feedback} > 19$ | ***H*₁**: College freshman who participate in a treatment of critical thinking feedback have significantly <u>different</u> critical thinking skills than the norm ($\mu$=19).<br><br>$H_1$: $\mu_{feedback} \neq 19$ |
| Null | ***H*₀**: College freshman who participate in a treatment of critical thinking feedback do NOT have significantly <u>higher</u> critical thinking skills than the norm ($\mu$=19).<br><br>$H_0$: $\mu_{feedback} \leq 19$ | ***H*₀**: College freshman who participate in a treatment of critical thinking feedback do NOT have significantly <u>different</u> critical thinking skills than the norm ($\mu$=19).<br><br>$H_0$: $\mu_{feedback} = 19$ |

As you can see, the process of stating the hypotheses applies several concepts. To guide you in this process, ***Baby Stats!*** will always have you complete the following:

- Identify variables;
- Determine number of tails—one-tailed or two-tailed;
- Write hypotheses (alternative and null) in sentence form;
- Develop hypotheses notation.

## 6.13 Step 2: Establish Significance Criteria

Remember our goal for hypothesis testing is to disprove the null hypothesis in order to support the alternative hypothesis. Falsifying the null requires that the treatment did have an effect and therefore the treatment mean will be different than the population norm. But if the treatment mean is just slightly greater than the population norm is that enough of a difference? Not likely. Instead, hypothesis testing requires <u>adequate</u> evidence to disprove the null; and adequate is all about probability.

Let's consider our critical thinking example ($\mu$=19, $\sigma$=6) and the distribution of sample means for $n$=144. Standard error for this distribution is $\sigma_M = 6/\sqrt{144} = 6/12 = .5$. The majority of sample means will be clustered around the population mean of 19 (see Figure 6.2). However, to disprove the null and show a "significant" difference, we will require that the sample mean be very different from the population norm. To be very different, the sample mean would be out in a tail of our sampling distribution, such that the probability of obtaining such a mean would be very low. This is accomplished by selecting an acceptable probability value, known as the level of significance or alpha level. The ***alpha level*** ($\alpha$) creates a cut-off that defines the low probability or significant samples that are not consistent with the null. Typical alpha levels applied are $\alpha$=.05 (5%) and $\alpha$=.01 (1%). If an alpha of .05 is used for a non-directional test (like our example), then the sample mean must fall within the outer 5% (white areas) and differ from 95% of the middle sample means (blue area) in order for us to disprove the null and support the alternative. In Figure 6.2, the white areas are the 5% divided between the two tails and represents the ***critical region*** in which our sample mean falls. The critical region is composed of those extreme sample means that have a very low probability of being obtained. The alpha level determines the boundaries for the critical region.

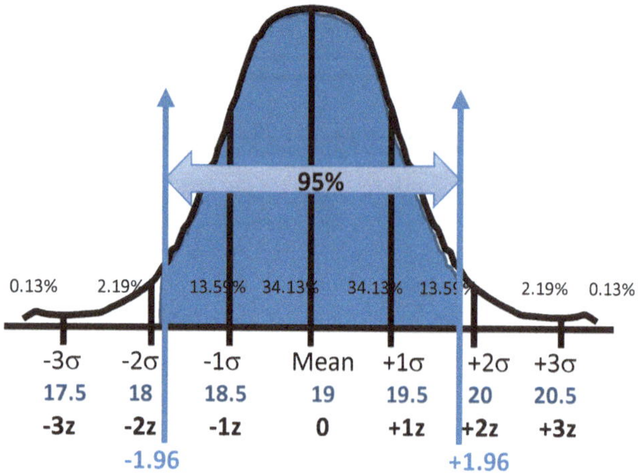


**Figure 6.2**
Two-tailed test with $\alpha$=.05

| (A) $z$ | (B) Proportion in body | (C) Proportion in tail | (D) Proportion between M & z |
|---|---|---|---|
| 1.95 | .9744 | .0256 | .4744 |
| 1.96 | .9750 | .0250 | .4750 |
| 1.97 | .9756 | .0244 | .4756 |
| 1.98 | .9761 | .0239 | .4761 |
| 1.99 | .9767 | .0233 | .4767 |

So how do we determine if our sample mean falls within the critical region and therefore significantly differs from the population norm? Using $z$-scores, of course! In the last chapter, we learned to use a $z$-score to determine the probability of obtaining a specific sample mean. In this process we will use the alpha level to determine the $z$-scores that define the critical region. With an alpha of .05 for a non-directional test, that 5% is divided between the two tails so that 2.5% (.025) is in each tail. Using the unit normal table, we can look up the proportion of .025 in Column C and identify a $z$-score of 1.96. This means that for any normal distribution, the critical region for an alpha of .05 falls beyond $z$ = +1.96 and $z$ = -1.96. Therefore, for our sample mean to be considered significantly different, it must fall beyond $\pm 1.96z$.

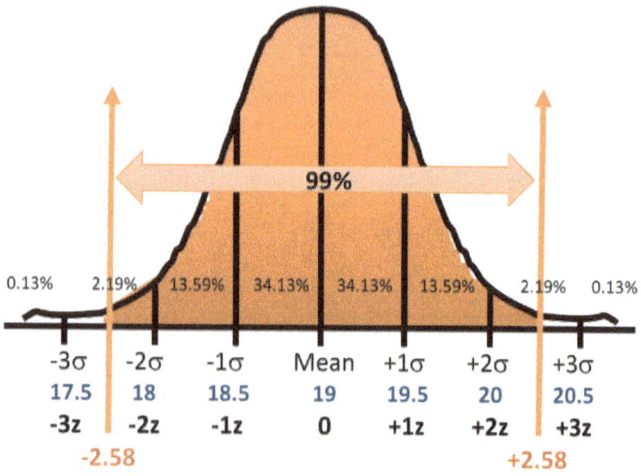


**Figure 6.3**
Two-tailed test with $\alpha$=.01

If an alpha of .01 were used for a non-directional (two-tailed) hypothesis, the critical region of 1% is divided between the two tails so that .005 is in each tail. The corresponding $z$-score for .005 is 2.58 (See Figure 6.3). Therefore, to significantly differ from the population norm (and 99% of the sample means), our sample mean must fall beyond $\pm 2.58z$. The $z$ values that represent the critical boundaries are often referred to as $z_{critical}$. However, identifying critical boundaries is only necessary when conducting the calculations by hand. If you are using a computer, the exact $p$-value or probability will be calculated for the $z$ statistic. This simplifies the process of determining significance quite a bit since all you have to do is compare the $p$-value to the alpha level. In order to be significant, the $p$-value must be less than the alpha level.

## 6.14 Step 3: Collect and Analyze Data

This next step is to collect and analyze data from our random sample ($n$=144). In our example, the sample mean is calculated ($M$=20). Now we need to compare the sample mean to the population norm ($\mu$=19, $\sigma$=6) within the distribution of sample means by calculating the $z$-score for our sample mean. The standard error has been calculated, $\sigma_M$=.5. Using the same equation from the previous module, a sample mean of 20 (for samples $n$=144) converts to $2z$. The $z$ value that is based upon a sample mean is called $z_{calculated}$.

$$z_{\text{calculated}} = \frac{M - \mu}{\sigma_M} = \frac{20 - 19}{.5} = 2$$

Most hypothesis testing and data analysis is conducted using a computer. However, a $z$-test isn't that common, so SPSS doesn't even provide this function. Fortunately, StatCrunch is able to conduct a $z$-test and for our example produced the following output. Notice that the $z$ statistic is calculated along with the exact probability for that $z$-score, $p$=.0455. The probability calculated for a test statistic is called a ***p-value***. This will really help us when we get to the decision-making step.

**StatCrunch Output**

**Hypothesis test results:**
μ : Mean of population
H0 : μ = 19
HA : μ ≠ 19
Standard deviation = 6

| Mean | n | Sample Mean | Std. Err. | Z-Stat | P-value |
|---|---|---|---|---|---|
| μ | 144 | 20 | 0.5 | 2.0 | 0.0455 |

Because we are using $z$ as an inferential statistic, it is considered a test statistic in this application. A ***test statistic*** is any value that is based upon sample data and used to test a hypothesis. We will be learning about many more test statistics throughout this resource. In general, a test statistic helps determine if the treatment created a difference more than would be expected by chance. Notice in calculating z, we divide the observed difference (between the sample and population) by the error between the sample and population (or the difference to error). When we apply an alpha level of .05 or .01, this means that the observed difference needs to be substantially more than chance (2-3 times bigger).

### Example

Will college freshman ($n$=144) who participate in a treatment of critical thinking feedback have significantly different critical thinking skills than the norm ($\mu$=19, $\sigma$=6)? Test at $\alpha$=.05.

***Step 1: State Hypotheses***

**$H_1$:** College freshman who participate in a treatment of critical thinking feedback have significantly different critical thinking skills than the norm ($\mu$=19).

**$H_0$:** College freshman who participate in a treatment of critical thinking feedback do NOT have significantly different critical thinking skills than the norm ($\mu$=19).

**$H_1$:** $\mu_{feedback} \neq 19$     **$H_0$:** $\mu_{feedback} = 19$

***Step 2: Establish Significance Criteria***

An alpha of .05 is used for a two-tailed test.

***Step 3: Collect and Analyze Data***

StatCrunch results: $z$=2.0, $p$=.045

***Step 4: Evaluate Null and Draw Conclusion***

*p of .045* is less than .05, therefore sample mean is significantly different from population norm.

- Significance→Reject the null→Restate alternative
- College freshman who participate in a treatment of critical thinking feedback ($n$=144, $M$=20) have significantly different critical thinking skills than the norm ($\mu$=19, $\sigma$=6); $z$=2.0, $p$=.045, two-tailed.

$$z_{\text{calculated}} = \frac{M - \mu}{\sigma_M} = \frac{\text{observed difference}}{\text{difference due to error}}$$

## 6.15 Step 4: Evaluate Null Hypothesis and Draw Conclusion

In Step 2, we identified criteria to determine significance and disprove the null. Two decisions are possible, both of which focus on the null hypothesis. The first decision is to ***reject the null hypothesis***; this occurs when the sample mean is significantly different from the population and therefore falls into the critical region. Rejecting the null is the same as disproving the null—the goal of hypothesis testing. This means that the sample mean differs from the majority of the other means within the population and the probability of obtaining such a sample mean is extremely low and is unlikely to occur if the null were true. When the null is rejected, the evidence supports (not proves) the alternative hypothesis so that we conclude that the treatment did have an effect on the sample and therefore, would likely occur in the population.

The second possible decision occurs when sample data do not fall within the critical region and therefore are not significantly different from the population norm. In this case, the treatment did NOT significantly affect the sample so the decision is to ***fail to reject the null hypothesis***. Now just because there isn't enough evidence to disprove the null doesn't mean that we can prove the null, rather there is just a lack of evidence against the null. When the decision is fail to reject the null hypothesis, the researcher concludes that the treatment does not appear to have an effect.

To make a decision regarding the null, one must compare the sample statistic to the criteria determined in Step 2. If you are using your hand calculations, then you need to compare $z_{calculated}$ to $z_{critical}$.. When considering our critical thinking example in which the sample mean converted to $z$=2, we can see that the sample mean falls beyond ±1.96z and therefore falls within the critical region. Essentially, $z_{calculated}$ needs to fall beyond $z_{critical}$ to be significant. This means that the treatment had a significant effect on the sample. For this conclusion, we can essentially restate the alternative hypothesis and conclude: *College freshman who participate in a treatment of critical thinking feedback have significantly different critical thinking skills than the norm.*

Another way to make our comparison and decision is to use the $p$-value that was generated in the StatCrunch output. Since the exact $p$-value was calculated for the specific test statistic, we can compare the $p$-value of .045 to the alpha level of .05. Basically, in order for the sample mean to be considered significantly different, $p$ must be less than alpha. In our example, $p$ of .045 is less than alpha of .05, therefore a significant difference is present. Comparing $p$ to alpha is much easier since it does not require that we find the critical boundaries in terms of $z$. For the most part, we will be using the computer in our analyses and so will be comparing $p$ to alpha to make our decision about the null. Figure 6.4 presents the comparisons and subsequent decisions and conclusions. In summary, when $p$ is less than alpha, statistical significance is present, so we reject the null and restate the alternative hypothesis.

**Figure 6.4** Decision-Making Process in Determining Significance and Conclusion

| | Comparison → | Significance → | Decision → | Conclusion |
|---|---|---|---|---|
| Hand Calculations | $z_{calculated} > z_{critical}$ | Significance! | Reject Null | Restate Alternative |
| | $z_{calculated} \leq z_{critical}$ | Not! | Fail to Reject Null | Restate Null |
| Computer | $p <$ alpha | Significance! | Reject Null | Restate Alternative |
| | $p \geq$ alpha | Not! | Fail to Reject Null | Restate Null |

### Results Notation

In addition to providing a concluding statement, we must also report the statistical results as evidence for the conclusion. These results utilize a special notation and have several parts. Since we are comparing a sample mean to a population norm, these values should be reported along with the sample size, all of which can be embedded within the conclusion. In addition, the specific $z$ results are written at the end of the sentence. The critical thinking example is applied to each of these parts seen in **bold**.

- Sample size and mean ($n$=144, $M$=20)
- Population norm ($\mu$=19, $\sigma$=6)
- $z$ results: $z$ value, $p$-value (or alpha level), and number of tails; $z$=2.0, $p$=.045, two-tailed

College freshman who participate in a treatment of critical thinking feedback **($n$=144, $M$=20)** have significantly different critical thinking skills than the norm **($\mu$=19, $\sigma$=6); $z$=2.0, $p$=.045, two-tailed.**

Notice in the example that parentheses are used to offset the statistics embedded within the sentence. The results notation at the end of the sentence begins with a semi-colon. All statistical letters ($z$, $p$, $M$, etc.) are italicized. Finally, if you have utilized computer output, report the exact $p$-value. This gives the reader additional information regarding the exact probability of the result.

## 6.16 Errors in Hypothesis Testing

Since there are two possible decisions that we can make about the null (reject the null or fail to reject the null), there are two possible errors that can occur in hypothesis testing. Remember, there is always some degree of error in statistics, since we are typically studying a sample and trying to generalize the results to the population. Our sample provides limited information and may or may not be representative of the population.

### Type I Error

One possible error occurs when we reject the null and conclude that the treatment had an effect, when in fact the sample was already significantly different from the norm. In this case, we found significance when we really shouldn't have—we found significance and rejected the null out of error. This is called a ***Type I error***, which occurs when a researcher rejects the null that is actually true. The consequences of Type I error can be quite serious. When significant results are found (indicating that a treatment had an effect), leaders are quick to respond in an effort to improve practice and performance. As such, resources in time and money are typically invested in the implementation of the treatment. In addition, other researchers may attempt to build upon the study, which is based upon false results.

Fortunately, type I errors are controlled through the alpha level one selects. We are only at risk of a Type I error when significance is found. So if we select an alpha level that makes it difficult to determine significance, then we also minimize the risk of committing a Type I error. For example, an alpha level of .05 means that our sample mean must differ from 95% of the population in order to be consider significant. Only 5% of the sample means in the population have a chance of being significant; and those 5% must be in the extreme tails. As such, the chance of committing a Type I error is also 5%. If we decrease the alpha level to .01, then only 1% of the sample means have a chance of being significant so the chance of committing a Type I error is also 1%. So what does this mean for data analysis? Most researchers will utilize an alpha level of .05 and live with the 5% chance of a Type I error. However, if one is conducting many (20+) statistical tests in a study, the researcher may apply a more conservative alpha like .01.

### Type II Error

The second type of error coincides with the other possible hypothesis decision (fail to reject the null). In this case, the researcher did not find a significant treatment effect, when in fact there was a real effect. A ***Type II error*** occurs whenever one has failed to reject the null that is really false. This can happen when the treatment does effect the sample, but the size of the effect is not enough to move the sample mean to the extreme tails of the distribution. The consequences of a Type II error are usually not as serious as a Type I error, since resources are not invested in the new treatment. However, many individuals in need may miss out on a promising new treatment just because it was falsely insignificant. Unfortunately, the probability of committing a Type II error depends upon many factors and cannot be calculated into one specific number. However, the probability of Type II error is represented by the symbol $\beta$, the Greek letter beta.

## 6.17 Assumptions of a *z*-test

The computations utilized in hypothesis testing are based upon a set of assumptions. In order to be confident in the results, these assumptions should be fulfilled. If they are not fulfilled, the hypothesis test and subsequent results may be compromised. The specific assumptions associated with a *z*-test are:

- **Random Sampling**—Since the distribution of sample means is based upon random samples, it is assumed that the studied sample was generated through random selection. In addition, random sampling helps ensure that the sample is representative of the population. However, random sampling is a difficult assumption to fulfill in social sciences, and as such it is often violated.
- **Normal Distribution in the Population**—The dependent variable, which is quantitative, should be normally distributed in the population. The Central Limit Theorem tells us that if our sample is large ($n$>30), the distribution of sample means will be normal even if the sample distribution is not. This means that the *z*-test is fairly tolerant of violations of normality.

At this point you might be thinking, why have test assumptions when it doesn't matter if they are fulfilled or not. Well, it does matter! Fulfilling test assumptions helps to minimize error and increase generalizability—both very important characteristics of quality research.

## 6.18 Issues with Hypothesis Testing

Although hypothesis testing is the most common statistical technique for evaluating sample data, there are several limitations within the hypothesis testing process that cause concern among researchers. Recall, that the goal of hypothesis testing is to disprove or reject the null hypothesis and determine that the treatment did have a significant effect on the sample and thus the population. A significant effect requires that the sample mean is very different (due to the treatment) from the population norm by differing from at least 95% or 99% of the sample means. That significance level (or *p*-value) of .05 only means that there is less than a 5% chance of finding significance out of error; it in no way indicates the size or magnitude of the effect. In addition, the calculation of the $z$ statistic is dependent upon standard error and thus sample size. Therefore, statistical significance is easier to achieve when a large sample size is utilized. For example, let's go back to the scenario on critical thinking, in which it was hypothesized that college freshmen who participate in a treatment of critical thinking feedback have significantly different critical thinking skills than the norm ($\mu$=19, $\sigma$=6). A sample of 144 students generated a mean of 20. Using $\alpha$=.05, it was concluded that: College freshman who participate in a treatment of critical thinking feedback ($n$=144, $M$=20) have significantly different critical thinking skills than the norm ($\mu$=19, $\sigma$=6); $z$=2.0, $p$=.045, two-tailed. Notice the sample differed from the population by only one point! One point isn't much of an increase, yet it was statistically significant. Suppose instead, we had a sample of 25 students who achieved a mean of 21. Our calculations ($\sigma_M$=$6/\sqrt{25}$ =1.2; $z$= $(21-19)/1.2 = 1.67$) do not generate a significant result at .05 even though the effect was two times as great than with the sample of 144. So you can see that in studies with small samples, statistical significance is more difficult to achieve significance and often miss important effects that are actually present in the population. Therefore, this module will examine methods used to provide additional information about the effect in the population and ultimately aid in our ability to generalize results to the population.

## 6.19 Effect Size

Since tests of significance do not provide information regarding the size of a treatment effect, the research community recommends the reporting of an effect size whenever a significant effect is reported. However, even when you have failed to reject the null you many still want to calculate an effect size especially if you have a small sample size. There are several indices of ***effect size*** that provide a measure of the size of the treatment effect. Therefore, as we continue to learn about additional inferential techniques more effect sizes will be introduced. The most basic measure of effect size is Cohen's $d$, which measures the mean difference in terms of the original standard deviation. Notice sample size has nothing to do with effect size; rather effect size indicates how large the difference is based upon the standard deviation. So a Cohen's $d$ of .75 means that the treatment created a change in scores by ¾ of a standard deviation. Let's take a look at our samples of 25 and 144.

$n$=144 Cohen's $d = \frac{20-19}{6} = \frac{1}{6} = .167$

$n$=25 Cohen's $d = \frac{21-19}{6} = \frac{2}{6} = .33$

Cohen suggests criteria to use in evaluating the size of the effect. Applying this criteria, we can see that the significant result with $n$=144 produced a small effect while the statistically insignificant result with $n$=25 has a medium effect.

| Cohen's $d$ | Size |
|---|---|
| < 0.2 | Small |
| 0.2 – 0.8 | Medium |
| > 0.8 | Large |

**Effect Size for z**

Cohen's $d = \frac{M-\mu}{\sigma}$

For our original sample of $n$=144, we have already determined that:

- $\mu$ = 20
- $\sigma$ = 6
- $M$ = 19

Using these values, we calculate Cohen's $d$ as follows:

Cohen's $d = \frac{20-19}{6} = .167$

This value indicates a small effect.

## 6.20 Estimation with Confidence Intervals

Although hypothesis testing attempts to provide support for the presence of the treatment effect in the population, a significant result really only indicates that there is enough evidence to indicate that the null is false. Granted the $p$-value does provide a probability of finding significance out of error; however that $p$-value is so sensitive to sample size that interpreting hypothesis test results can be tricky. So again, the research community recommends the reporting of confidence intervals when an effect has been found or when estimating the treatment effect on the population. A ***confidence interval (CI)*** estimates the population parameter by providing an interval (range) of values that will include a percent of the population. A confidence interval isn't used to disprove the null rather it is used to estimate the treatment effect in the population.

**Figure 6.5**
Comparison of 95% and 99% Confidence Intervals

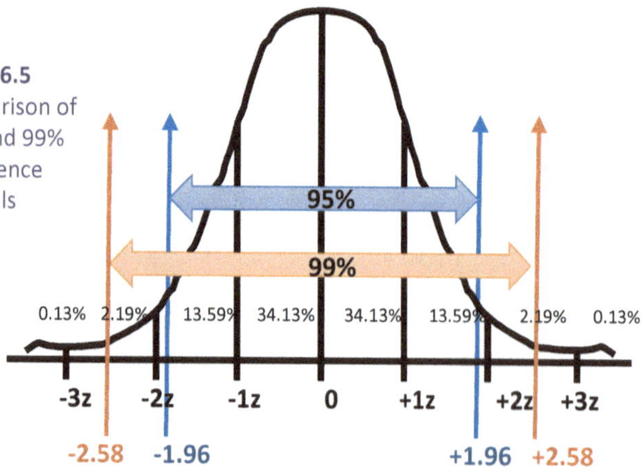


We can use the distribution of sample means to estimate the population mean (after the treatment). Remember in Module 5 when we calculated the boundaries that contained a certain percentage of means within our distribution of sample means? We used this equation: $M = \mu \pm z(\sigma_M)$. We can apply the same process using the sample mean to estimate the population mean (after the treatment). Instead, we will use: $\mu = M \pm z(\sigma_M)$. All that we have done is switch the sample and population means. Notice the range is built around the sample mean. The $z$ value used in the equation is based upon the confidence you desire. If you want to include 95% of the population, then $z$ is based upon $p$=.025 (.05 divided in two tails) and $z$=1.96 (See Figure 6.5). If 99% is desired, then $p$=.01 is divided between the two tails so that z is based upon $p$=.005 and $z$=2.58. This means that as our confidence (or percent of population) increases, so does the interval. Since an interval includes two boundaries, the probability is always divided between the two tails.

Let's apply this to our critical thinking example ($M$=20, $n$=144) in order to calculate the 95% confidence interval for the population mean after the treatment of feedback. Recall the population parameters before the treatment are μ=19, σ=6. To calculate a 95% interval, $z$=1.96. Standard error is computed ($\sigma_M = 6/\sqrt{144} = .5$). Applying these values to the confidence interval equation generates:

$$\mu = M \pm z(\sigma_M)$$

$$\mu = 20 \pm 1.96(.5) = 20 \pm .98$$

**Confidence Interval for Estimating μ after Treatment**

$$\mu = M \pm z(\sigma_M)$$

We have already determined that:

- $M$ = 19, σ = 6

Previous we also determined that $z_{critical}$ for a one-tailed test at .05 was 1.697. However, a confidence interval is always two-tailed, so we need to utilize the $t$ Distribution Table to identify a two-tailed $t_{critical}$ at .05.

This means that we are 95% confident that the treatment of critical thinking feedback will produce an effect in the population such that the mean will range between 19.02 and 20.98. Again, considering that the population norm (before the treatment) was 19, you can see that the treatment effect is not that great. Keep in mind, confidence intervals can also be calculated within statistical software. As you can see, StatCrunch produced the same lower and upper limits.

**StatCrunch Output**

**95% confidence interval results:**
μ : Mean of population
Standard deviation = 6

| Mean | n | Sample Mean | Std. Err. | L. Limit | U. Limit |
|---|---|---|---|---|---|
| μ | 144 | 20 | 0.5 | 19.020018 | 20.979982 |

## Reporting the Results

Both effect size and confidence intervals are often used in conjunction with hypothesis testing and are then included in the results and conclusions. As such, effect size and the confidence interval are typically tacked on at the end of the results notation.

> College freshman who participate in a treatment of critical thinking feedback **($n$=144, $M$=20)** have significantly different critical thinking skills than the norm **(μ=19, σ=6); $z$=2.0, $p$=.045, two-tailed, Cohen's $d$=.167, 95% CI [19.02, 20.98].**

Note that reporting a confidence interval includes the percentage of confidence (usually 90%, 95%, or 99%) and then the range (lower end and upper end) of scores in square parentheses.

## 6.21 Power

If you recall, two errors are possible in hypothesis testing: Type I and Type II. The probability of a Type I error (finding significance in error) is represented by alpha (α). The probability of a Type II error (not finding significance when we should have) is represented by beta (β). Statistical ***power*** of a study is the probability that the study accurately determines significance. It's the likelihood that the test is correctly rejecting the null hypothesis (i.e. "supporting" your hypothesis). Therefore, power is related to Type II error in that (power = 1 – β). Obviously, correctly finding statistical significance is a primary goal of hypothesis testing, so power is quite important. Cohen suggests that an appropriate level of power is .80 or 80%, which would mean that a study has an 80% chance having a true significant result. High statistical power means that the test results are likely valid. However, as the power increases, so does the possibility of a Type II error, so there is somewhat of a balancing act that occurs. We want power to be high, but we don't want the risk of a Type II error to be that great. The calculation of power is differs by the statistical test. However, power is typically based upon three parameters: sample size, effect size or test statistic, and alpha level. Analysis of power may be conducted:

- **retrospectively** (post hoc), which computes the statistical power of a test given sample size studied, the alpha level used, test results.
- **prospectively** (a priori), which is used to determine a required sample size to achieve target statistical power. To identify a minimum sample size for a study using a particular statistical test, you will need to enter the alpha level you plan to use, the effect size you hope to find (typically the medium level of .5), and the recommended power of .80.

Although power is not calculated in most statistical programs, several power calculators are available online. Since power is associated with a specific inferential test, be sure you select the appropriate calculator.

For our example study on critical thinking feedback, we will use the online site powerandsamplesize.com/Calculators/ to calculate retrospective power. This calculator is specific to a *z*-test and requires the following values: $\mu$=19, $\sigma$=6, *M*=20, *n*=144, $\alpha$=.05, two-tailed (See Figure 6.6). The results generate a power of .52, which means we have a 52% chance of finding accurate significance—not quite the recommended .80. We can also use the Power Table for *z* (see Appendix B). Figure 6.6 also presents an excerpt for power table related to *z*. Since the two-tailed test with an alpha of .05 generated *z*=2.0, the associated power is .516.

**Figure 6.6**
Power Table and Calculator for z

| z | α=.05 | | α=.01 | |
|---|---|---|---|---|
| | 2-tail | 1-tail | 2-tail | 1-tail |
| 2.0 | .516 | .639 | .282 | .372 |
| 2.1 | .556 | .675 | .317 | .410 |
| 2.2 | .595 | .711 | .354 | .450 |
| 2.3 | .633 | .744 | .391 | .489 |
| 2.4 | .670 | .775 | .430 | .529 |
| 2.5 | .705 | .804 | .470 | .569 |

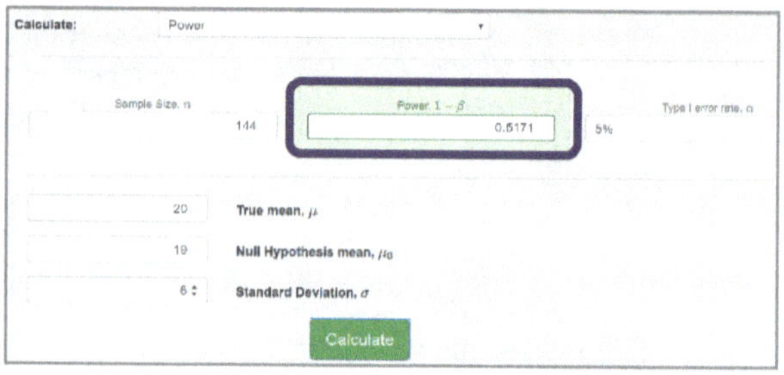


## 6.22 Directional (One-tailed) Hypothesis Tests

Our critical thinking example utilized a non-directional or two-tailed hypothesis since we were examining an effect that could result in either an increase or decrease. The alpha level of .05 was divided into two tails. However, much of the time a researcher has a specific prediction regarding treatment effect. Let's apply the hypothesis process with effect size, confidence intervals, and power to a directional scenario.

Suppose a public university implements a Spiritual Living-Learning (SLL) Community, in which students are housed together and regularly participate in activities that facilitate spiritual exploration. After two years, the university wants to examine if SLL participation increases spiritual well-being as measured by West's (2004) Spiritual Well-Being Scale ($\mu$=50, $\sigma$=5). The university randomly selects 25 participants (*M*= 50.75) to complete the scale. Does participation in the Spiritual Living-Learning (SLL) Community significantly increase spiritual well-being when compared to the norm? Test at .05 level.

**Step 1: State Hypotheses**

- Identify variables: IV=participation in SLL; DV=spiritual well-being
- Determine # of tails. Key word is increase→one-tailed.
- State **alternative hypothesis**: Participation in the Spiritual Living-Learning (SLL) Community significantly increases spiritual well-being when compared to the college student norm.
- State **null hypothesis**: Participation in the Spiritual Living-Learning (SLL) Community does NOT significantly increase spiritual well-being when compared to the college student norm.
- Develop hypotheses notation:

$H_1$: $\mu_{SLL} > 50$ $H_0$: $\mu_{SLL} \leq 50$

**Example**

A public university implements a Spiritual Living-Learning (SLL) Community, in which students are housed together and regularly participate in activities that facilitate spiritual exploration. After two years, the university wants to examine if SLL participation increases spiritual well-being as measured by West's (2004) Spiritual Well-Being Scale ($\mu$=50, $\sigma$=5). The university randomly selects 25 participants (*M*= 50.75) to complete the scale. Does participation in the Spiritual Living-Learning (SLL) Community significantly increase spiritual well-being when compared to the norm? Test at .05 level.

**RQ:** Does participation in the Spiritual Living-Learning (SLL) Community significantly increase spiritual well-being when compared to the norm?

**Step 1: State the Hypotheses**

**IV:** participation in SLL
**DV:** spiritual well-being
**Keyword:** increase→one-tailed

**Alternative Hypothesis:** Participation in the Spiritual Living-Learning (SLL) Community significantly increases spiritual well-being when compared to the college student norm.

**$H_1$:** $\mu > 50$

**Null Hypothesis:** Participation in the Spiritual Living-Learning (SLL) Community does NOT significantly increase spiritual well-being when compared to the college student norm.

**$H_0$:** $\mu \leq 50$

**Step 2: Establish Significance Criteria**

Because we are predicting that the SLL sample will have a higher mean than the population, this is a directional or one-tailed hypothesis. An alpha of .05 is being utilized. If we are utilizing a computer to conduct the analysis, all we need to know is that alpha level. However to conduct the hypothesis test by hand, we need to determine the critical value for $z$ that defines the critical region. For a one-tailed test, the entire 5% goes in the upper tail of our distribution. Using the unit normal table, we can look up where $p$=.05 and determine that $z_{critical}$ = +1.65. This means that $z_{calculated}$ must be greater than $z_{critical}$ of +1.65 to be significantly different from the norm. If the alpha level was .01, then the sample mean would need to differ from 99% of the population and fall within the upper most 1%. Using the unit normal table, an alpha of .01 corresponds with $z_{critical}$ = +2.33. Figure 6.7. displays the alpha levels of .05 and .01 for a one-tailed test.

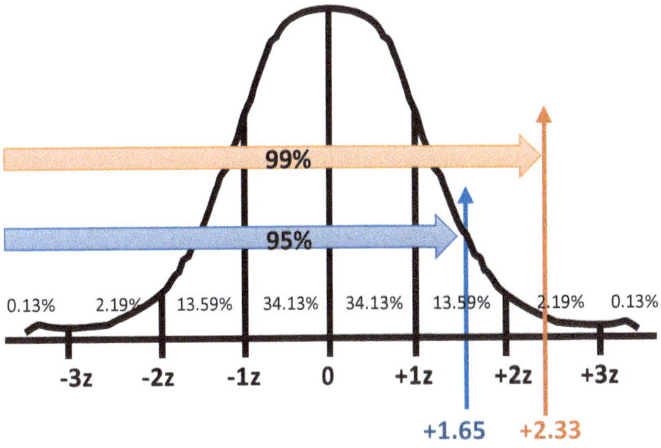


| (A) z | (B) Proportion in body | (C) Proportion in tail | (D) Proportion between M & z |
|---|---|---|---|
| 1.64 | .9495 | .0495 | .4495 |
| 1.65 | .9505 | .0495 | .4505 |
| 1.66 | .9515 | .0485 | .4515 |
| 2.32 | .9898 | .0102 | .4898 |
| 2.33 | .9901 | .0099 | .4901 |
| 2.34 | .9904 | .0096 | .4904 |

**Figure 6.7** One-Tailed Test at .05 and .01 Alpha Levels.

**Step 3: Collect and Analyze Data**

Hand calculations require that we compute the standard error for the sampling distribution ($n$=25); $\sigma_M = 5/\sqrt{25}$ = 5/5 = 1. Using the $\sigma_M$ =1, we can now calculate $z$. Both hand calculations and StatCrunch produce $z$=.75, but StatCrunch also provides the exact $p$-value ($p$=.2266).

$$z_{\text{calculated}} = \frac{M - \mu}{\sigma_M} = \frac{50.75 - 50}{1} = .75$$

**Hypothesis test results:**
μ : Mean of population
H0 : μ = 50
HA : μ > 50
Standard deviation = 5

| Mean | n | Sample Mean | Std. Err. | Z-Stat | P-value |
|---|---|---|---|---|---|
| μ | 25 | 50.75 | 1 | 0.75 | 0.2266 |

**Step 4: Evaluate Null Hypothesis and Draw Conclusion**

To make a decision regarding the null hypothesis, we need to compare our statistic to the criteria we established in Step 2. Hand calculation require that we compare $z_{calculated}$ to $z_{critical}$. In order for our sample mean to be considered significantly different from the population norm, $z_{calculated}$ must be greater than $z_{critical}$ = +1.65. In this case, $z_{calculated}$ = +.75 and is NOT greater than $z_{critical}$ = +1.65. This means we do not have significance, so we fail to reject the null and restate the null for our conclusion.

**Example**

Does participation in the Spiritual Living-Learning (SLL) Community significantly increase spiritual well-being when compared to the norm? Test at .05 level.

***Step 1: State Hypotheses***

$H_1$: $\mu > 50$ $H_0$: $\mu \leq 50$

***Step 2: Establish Significance Criteria***

An alpha of .05 is used for a one-tailed test.

***Step 3: Collect and Analyze Data***

StatCrunch results: $z$=.75, $p$=.2266

***Step 4: Evaluate Null and Draw Conclusion***

*p of .2266* is greater than .05, therefore sample mean is NOT significantly different from population norm.

- NO Significance→Fail to reject the null→Restate null
- Participation in the Spiritual Living-Learning (SLL) Community ($n$=25, $M$=50.75) does NOT significantly increase spiritual well-being when compared to the college norm (μ=50, σ=5); $z$=,75, $p$=.2266, one-tailed.

If we utilize computer output, we compare the $p$-value to the alpha level. In order for our sample mean to be considered significantly different from the population norm, our $p$-value must be less than alpha. For our example, $p$=.2266 and is NOT less than .05. Therefore we do not have significance, so we fail to reject the null and restate the null for our conclusion. To recap, our decision is: Do NOT have significance→Fail to reject the null→Restate null. So our conclusion essentially restates the null and adds the specific results notation.

Participation in the Spiritual Living-Learning (SLL) Community ($n$=25, $M$=50.75) does NOT significantly increase spiritual well-being when compared to the college norm (μ=50, σ=5); $z$=,75, $p$=.2266, one-tailed.

### Effect Size

To calculate Cohen's d, we utilize the sample mean ($M$=50.75), population mean ($\mu$=50), and original population standard deviation ($\sigma$=5). A small effect size of .15 is calculated.

$$\text{Cohen's } d = \frac{50.75-50}{5} = \frac{.75}{5} = .15$$

### Confidence Interval

A confidence interval always has two boundaries. So even if a one-tailed hypothesis test was conducted, two-tailed probability is used for a confidence interval. To calculate a 95% confidence interval, $z$ of 1.96 will be used. Applying the sample mean of 50.75 and standard error ($\sigma_M$=1), we can estimate the population mean after the treatment. The lower end of the interval is 48.79, and the upper end is 52.71. StatCrunch output generates the same limits.

$$\mu = M \pm z(\sigma_M)$$

$$\mu = 50.75 \pm 1.96(1)$$

$$\mu = 50.75 \pm 1.96$$

**95% confidence interval results:**
μ : Mean of population
Standard deviation = 5

| Mean | n | Sample Mean | Std. Err. | L. Limit | U. Limit |
|---|---|---|---|---|---|
| μ | 25 | 50.75 | 1 | 48.790036 | 52.709964 |

**Example**

**Effect Size for z**

$$\text{Cohen's } d = \frac{M-\mu}{\sigma}$$

For our original sample ($n$=25), we know that:

- $\mu = 50$, $\sigma = 5$, $M = 50.75$

$$\text{Cohen's } d = \frac{50.75-50}{5} = \frac{.75}{5} = .15$$

This value indicates a small effect.

**Confidence Interval for Estimating μ after Treatment**

$$\mu = M \pm z(\sigma_M)$$

We have already determined that:

- $M = 50.75$, $\sigma_M = 1$

Since a confidence interval is always two-tailed, we use the $z$ Distribution Table to identify a two-tailed $z_{critical}$ at .05, which is 1.96.

$$\mu = 50.75 \pm 1.96$$

95% CI [48.79, 52.71]

### Power

The power calculator at powerandsamplesize.com/Calculators/ can be used to determine retrospective power. After entering the population mean, population standard deviation, sample mean, number of tails, and alpha, a power of .19 is generated, which is very low.

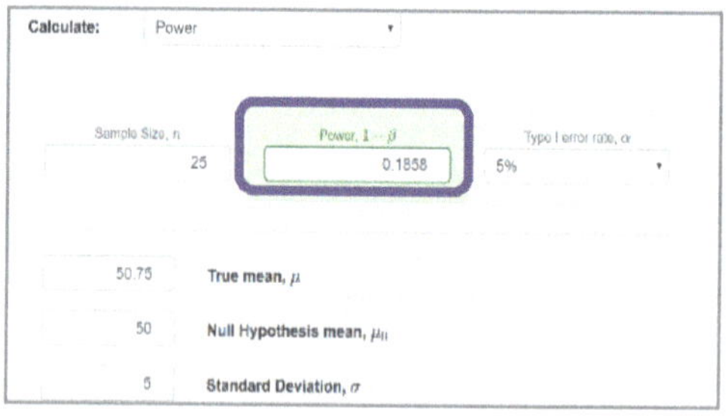


**Figure 6.8**
Power Calculator Results

### Updated Results

The effect size (Cohen's $d$=.15) and confidence interval (95% CI [48.79, 52.71]) results can be easily added to our original results statement at the very end.

> Participation in the Spiritual Living-Learning (SLL) Community ($n$=25, $M$=50.75) does NOT significantly increase spiritual well-being when compared to the college student norm ($\mu$=50, $\sigma$=5); $z$=,75, $p$=.2266, one-tailed, Cohen's $d$=.15, 95% CI [48.79, 52.71].

## 6.23 Module Summary

***Hypothesis testing*** involves studying a sample to evaluate a hypothesis about the population so that we can generalize the results to the population.

- When the treatment is implemented with the sample, we predict that the treatment will affect the sample mean by being significantly different from the population mean (norm)
- Research is not about "proving the hypothesis" since proving requires 100% proof.
- Inferential statistics set out to disprove the null hypothesis in order to provide support for the alternative.

**Step 1: State the Hypotheses**

- Identify variables
- Determine number of tails--one-tailed or two-tailed
  - A ***directional hypothesis*** (one-tailed) examines a change in a specific direction. Key words: increase, decrease, higher, lower, positive, negative
  - A ***non-directional*** (two-tailed) hypothesis just examines some relationship, effect, or difference—it isn't specific. Key words: effect, difference, change, impact, relationship
- Write hypotheses (alternative and null) in sentence form
  - An ***alternative hypothesis*** ($H_1$ or $H_A$) is the actual prediction of a relationship.
  - The ***null hypothesis*** ($H_0$) states that a relationship is NOT present in the population.
- Develop hypotheses notation.
  - Hypothesis notation presents the mathematical proposition being tested and clarifies the comparisons and values used to make a decision regarding the hypothesis.
  - Since hypotheses are predictions about the population, the population mean symbol (μ) is used.

**Step 2: Establish Significance Criteria**

- Falsifying the null requires that the treatment had an effect so that the sample mean is different from the norm.
- Selecting an appropriate ***alpha level*** **(α)** creates a cut-off that defines the low probability or significant samples that are not consistent with the null. Typical alpha levels applied are α=.05 (5%) and α=.01 (1%).
- Hand calculations require that we identify the critical boundaries in terms of z.
  - Two-tailed test: α=.05→$z_{\text{critical}} = \pm 1.96$; α=.01→$z_{\text{critical}} = \pm 2.58$
  - One-tailed test: α=.05→$z_{\text{critical}} = 1.65$; α=.01→$z_{\text{critical}} = 2.33$

**Step 3: Collect and Analyze Data**

- A ***test statistic*** is any value that is based upon sample data and used to test a hypothesis.
- Hand calculations use: $z_{\text{calculated}} = \frac{M-\mu}{\sigma_M} = \frac{\text{observed difference}}{\text{difference due to error}}$

**Step 4: Evaluate Null Hypothesis and Draw Conclusion**

- Two decisions are possible in hypothesis testing—both of which focus on the null hypothesis.
  - **Decision 1: *Reject the null hypothesis***→restate the alternative hypothesis.
    - Occurs when evidence supports (not proves) the alternative hypothesis so that we conclude that the treatment did have an effect on the sample and therefore would likely occur in the population.
    - Reject the null when: $p <$ alpha or $z_{\text{calculated}} > z_{\text{critical}}$
  - **Decision 2: *Fail to reject the null hypothesis***→restate the null hypothesis.
    - Occurs when sample data do not fall within the critical region and therefore is not significantly different from the population norm.
    - Fail to reject the null when: $p \geq$ alpha or $z_{\text{calculated}} \leq z_{\text{critical}}$
- **Results Notation** should include: sample size, mean, and population norms within the conclusion; *z* results (*z*, *p*-value, and number of tails) at the end of the conclusion.

**Errors in Hypothesis Testing** can occur since there are two possible decisions that we can make about the null.

- **Type I Error** occurs when we rejected the null out of error. Alpha level controls the risk of Type I error.
- **Type II Error** occurs whenever one has failed to reject the null that is really false.

- **Assumptions of a *z*-test** are: 1) random sampling and 2) normal distribution in the population.
- Main **limitations of hypothesis testing** are that achievement of significance is easy with large samples, and that the test statistic and *p*-value doesn't indicate the strength or size of the effect. Effect size and confidence intervals are better indications of the treatment effect in the population.
  - **Effect Size** is measure of the size or magnitude of the treatment effect and should be reported when significance has been found or a small sample has been used.
    - **Cohen's *d*** is the most basic measure of effect size used in conjunction with z.
      - Cohen's $d = \frac{M-\mu}{\sigma}$
  - **A Confidence Interval (CI)** estimates the population parameter (after treatment effect) by providing an interval or range of values that will include a percent of the population.
    - $\mu = M \pm z(\sigma_M)$

# Part 2: Learning Guide

## Example

A researcher conducts a study of college freshmen to determine if a semester-long treatment significantly effects critical thinking scores as measured by the Critical Thinking Assessment Test ($\mu$=19, $\sigma$=6). The treatment consists of providing consistent feedback using a critical thinking rubric for all writing assignments in an Introduction to Business course. The researcher randomly selects 144 freshman students enrolled in the class. The researcher will examine this effect on critical thinking skills by comparing the sample mean to the population norm using an alpha level of .05.

**RQ:** Will college freshmen who participate in a treatment of critical thinking feedback have significantly different critical thinking skills than the norm ($\mu$=19)?

**IV:** treatment of critical thinking feedback

**DV:** critical thinking skills

### 6.21V Purpose and Steps of Hypothesis Testing

***Hypothesis testing*** in social sciences involves studying a sample to evaluate a hypothesis about the population so that we can generalize the results to the population.

- A hypothesis will typically predict that a mutual or causal relationship will occur in the population, when it occurs in the sample.
- When the treatment is implemented with the sample, we predict that the treatment will affect the sample mean by being significantly different from the population mean (norm)
- Hypothesis testing applies a formal process that follows these four steps:
    1. State the hypotheses: Identify variables; Determine number of tails—one-tailed or two-tailed; Write hypotheses (alternative and null) in sentence form; Develop hypotheses notation.
    2. Establish significance criteria
    3. Collect and analyze data
    4. Evaluate null hypothesis and draw conclusion

### 6.22V Step 1: State the Hypothesis

#### Alternative and Null

An ***alternative hypothesis*** ($H_1$ or $H_A$) is the actual prediction of a relationship.

- Research is not about "proving the hypothesis."
- Proving requires 100% proof; it requires all the data from the population!

- Inferential statistics set out to disprove the null hypothesis in order to provide support for the alternative.
- The ***null hypothesis*** ($H_0$) states that a relationship is NOT present in the population.

  **Example:** Suppose I make the prediction that all introductory statistics books will have a chapter on statistical power.

  **Alternative hypothesis ($H_1$)**—All introductory statistics textbooks will have a chapter on statistical power.

  **Null hypothesis ($H_0$)**—All introductory statistics textbooks will NOT have a chapter on statistical power.

  - Proving the alternative would require that I examine all introductory stats texts and that all of them have a chapter on statistical power.
  - Disproving the null only requires that I find one textbook that HAS a chapter on statistical power. Disproving the null does not prove the alternative; rather, disproving the null only provides support for the alternative.

#### Directional and Non-Directional

A hypothesis can be specific in its prediction (as in one group will be higher than the other) or general (as in the groups will be different).

- A ***directional hypothesis*** examines a change in a specific direction and applies a one-tailed test.
    - Key words: increase, decrease, higher, lower, positive, negative
- A ***non-directional*** hypothesis just examines some relationship, effect, or difference—it isn't specific—and applies a two-tailed test.
    - Key words: effect, difference, change, impact, relationship

## Example

**RQ:** Will college freshmen who participate in a treatment of critical thinking feedback have significantly different critical thinking skills than the norm (μ=19)?

**Key Word:** different→two-tailed

***Alternative:*** College freshmen who participate in a treatment of critical thinking feedback have significantly different critical thinking skills than the norm (μ=19).

***Null:*** College freshmen who participate in a treatment of critical thinking feedback do NOT have significantly different critical thinking skills than the norm (μ=19).

### Hypothesis Notation

- Hypothesis notation presents the mathematical proposition being tested and clarifies the comparisons and values used to make a decision regarding the hypothesis.
  - Since hypotheses are predictions about the population, the population mean symbol (μ) is used.
  - Often a subscript is used to define the particular subgroup within the population.

| | Directional | Non-Directional |
|---|---|---|
| Key Words | Increase, decrease, higher, lower, positive, negative | Effect, difference, change, impact, relationship |
| Alternative | ***H*₁:** College freshmen who participate in a treatment of critical thinking feedback have significantly higher critical thinking skills than the norm (μ=19).<br><br>***H*₁:** $\mu_{feedback} > 19$ | ***H*₁:** College freshmen who participate in a treatment of critical thinking feedback have significantly different critical thinking skills than the norm (μ=19).<br><br>***H*₁:** $\mu_{feedback} \neq 19$ |
| Null | ***H*₀:** College freshmen who participate in a treatment of critical thinking feedback do NOT have significantly higher critical thinking skills than the norm (μ=19).<br><br>***H*₀:** $\mu_{feedback} \leq 19$ | ***H*₀:** College freshmen who participate in a treatment of critical thinking feedback do NOT have significantly different critical thinking skills than the norm (μ=19).<br><br>***H*₀:** $\mu_{feedback} = 19$ |

**Expansion of Step 1**

To guide you in Step 1, ***Baby Stats!*** will always have you complete the following:

- Identify variables;
- Determine number of tails—one-tailed or two-tailed;
- Write hypotheses (alternative and null) in sentence form;
- Develop hypotheses notation.

### 6.23V Step 2: Establish Significance Criteria

- Falsifying the null requires that the treatment did have an effect and therefore the treatment mean will be different than the population norm
  - Hypothesis testing requires adequate evidence to disprove the null or in other words the sample mean must be very different from the population norm.
  - This means the sample mean would be out in a tail of our sampling distribution so that the probability of obtaining such a mean would be very low.
  - Selecting an acceptable probability value, known as the level of significance or ***alpha level* (α)** creates a cut-off that defines the low probability or significant samples that are not consistent with the null.
  - Typical alpha levels applied are α=.05 (5%) and α=.01 (1%).
  - If an alpha of .05 is used for a non-directional test, 5% is divided between the outer two tails.
  - This extreme 5% is the ***critical region***—the area where our sample mean must fall to be significantly different from the population norm.
  - When the sample mean differs from 95% of the other sample means and falls within the critical region, we disprove the null and support the alternative.
  - Hand calculations require that we identify the critical boundaries of $z$, also known as $z_{critical}$, so that we can compare $z_{calculated}$ to $z_{critical}$ to determine significance, which is found when $z_{calculated}$ exceeds $z_{critical}$.

Identifying $z_{critical}$ for ***Hand Calculations***

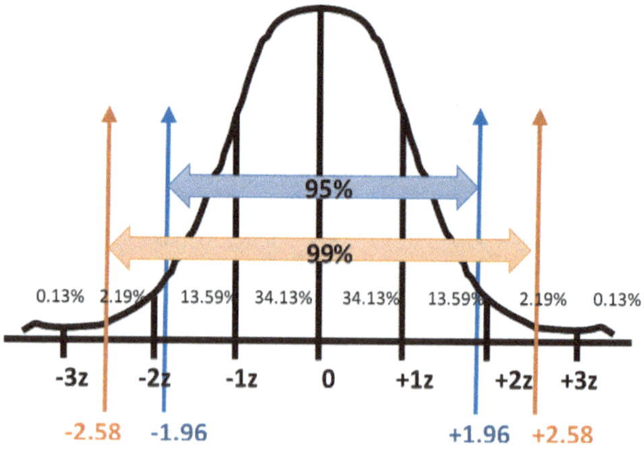


- Because the $z$ distribution is constant, we can identify the critical boundaries for the region of signficance.
- **For a non-directional (two-tailed test) hypothesis**, the alpha is divided into two-tails.
- **When α=.05,** the critical region of 5% is divided between the two tails so that .025 is in each tail.
  - The corresponding $z$-score for .025 is 1.96.
  - Therefore, to significantly differ from the population norm (and 95% of the sample means), our sample mean must fall beyond $\pm 1.96z$
- **When α=.01,** the critical region of 1% is divided between the two tails so that .005 is in each tail.
  - The corresponding $z$-score for .005 is 2.58.
  - Therefore, to significantly differ from the population norm (and 99% of the sample means), our sample mean must fall beyond $\pm 2.58z$.

- **For a directional (one-tailed test),** the alpha is located in ONE tail. So if we were testing for the sample mean to be higher than the population mean, we would look in the upper tail.
  - When $\alpha$=.05, $z_{critical} = +1.65$
  - When $\alpha$=.01, $z_{critical} = +2.33$

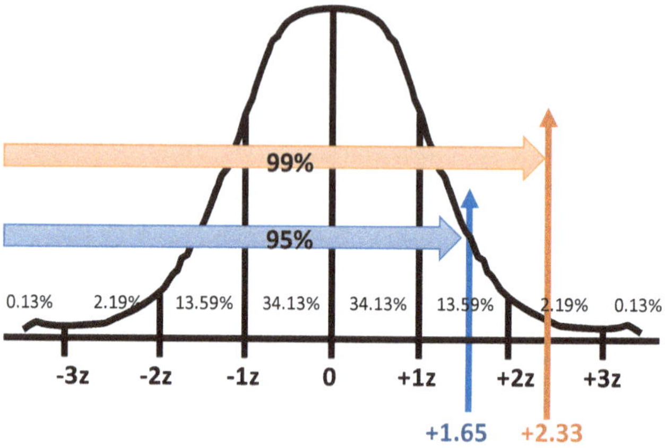


## Example

Our critical thinking example asks us to apply **the alpha of .05** or 5%; we divide that 5% between the two tails so that 2.5% (.025) is in each tail. Using the unit normal table, we can look up the proportion of .025 in Column C and identify a $z$-score of 1.96. This means that for any normal distribution, **the critical region for an alpha of .05 falls beyond $z$ = 1.96 and $z$ = -1.96.** Therefore, for our sample mean to be considered significantly different, it must fall beyond ±1.96$z$.

| (A) *z* | (B) *Proportion in body* | (C) *Proportion in tail* | (D) *Proportion between M & z* |
|---|---|---|---|
| 1.95 | .9744 | .0256 | .4744 |
| 1.96 | .9750 | .0250 | .4750 |
| 1.97 | .9756 | .0244 | .4756 |
| 1.98 | .9761 | .0239 | .4761 |
| 1.99 | .9767 | .0233 | .4767 |

## 6.24V Step 3: Collect and Analyze Data

- Comparing our sample ($n$=144, $M$=20) to the population norm ($\mu$=19, $\sigma$=6) is done within the distribution of sample means. The standard error has already been calculated as $\sigma_M$=.5.
  - When z is used in a hypothesis test, it is considered a test statistic.
  - A ***test statistic*** is any value that is based upon sample data and used to test a hypothesis.
  - The $z$ value that is based upon a sample mean is called $z_{calculated}$.

## Example

Since we are predicting that the sample mean will significantly differ from the population, this is a two-tailed test. An alpha of .05 is applied. We need to create the distribution of sample means for $n$=144, μ=19, σ=6. The standard error for our distribution of sample means ($n$=144) is .5. Our sample ($M$=20, $n$=144) converts to 2$z$.

**Hand Calculations**

**Standard error:** $\sigma_M = \frac{\sigma}{\sqrt{n}} = \frac{6}{\sqrt{144}} = \frac{6}{12} = .5$ $\quad z_{calculated} = \frac{M-\mu}{\sigma_M} = \frac{20-19}{.5} = 2$

**Computer**

$z = 2.0, p = .0455$

**StatCrunch Output**

μ : Mean of population
H0 : μ = 19
HA : μ ≠ 19
Standard deviation = 6

| Mean | n | Sample Mean | Std. Err. | Z-Stat | P-value |
|---|---|---|---|---|---|
| μ | 144 | 20 | 0.5 | 2 | 0.0455 |

### 6.25V Step 4: Evaluate Null Hypothesis and Draw Conclusion

- Two decisions are possible in hypothesis testing—both of which focus on the null hypothesis.
- **Decision 1: *Reject the null hypothesis*.**
  - This occurs when the sample mean is significantly different from the population and therefore falls into the critical region.
  - The probability of obtaining such a sample mean is extremely low and is unlikely to occur if the null were true.
  - When the null is rejected, the evidence supports (not proves) the alternative hypothesis so that we conclude that the treatment did have an effect on the sample and therefore would likely occur in the population.
  - Reject the null when: $p <$ alpha or $z_{calculated} > z_{critical}$
- **Decision 2: *Fail to reject the null hypothesis***
  - This occurs when sample data do not fall within the critical region and therefore is not significantly different from the population norm.
  - Now just because there isn't enough evidence to disprove the null doesn't mean that we can prove the null, rather there is just a lack of evidence against the null.
  - When the decision is fail to reject the null hypothesis, the researcher concludes that the treatment does not appear to have an effect.
  - Fail to reject the null when: $p \geq$ alpha or $z_{calculated} \leq z_{critical}$

| | Comparison → | Significance → | Decision → | Conclusion |
|---|---|---|---|---|
| Hand Calculations | $z_{calculated} > z_{critical}$ | Significance! | Reject Null | Restate Alternative |
| | $z_{calculated} \leq z_{critical}$ | Not! | Fail to Reject Null | Restate Null |
| Computer | $p <$ alpha | Significance! | Reject Null | Restate Alternative |
| | $p \geq$ alpha | Not! | Fail to Reject Null | Restate Null |

#### Results Notation

- Statistical results are provided as evidence for the conclusion.
- Embed within concluding statement:
  - Sample size and mean
  - Population norm
- Include $z$ results at the end of conclusion: $z$ value, $p$-value (or alpha level), and number of tails.

## Example

**Hand Calculations**

- Compare $z_{calculated}$ ($z$=2) to $z_{critical}$ (±1.96). $z_{calculated}$ of 2 exceeds 1.96.
- Significance→Reject the null→Restate alternative

**Computer**

- Compare $p$-value (.0455) to alpha (.05). $p < \alpha$
- Significance→Reject the null→Restate alternative

**Conclusion:** College freshmen who participate in a treatment of critical thinking feedback have significantly different critical thinking skills than the norm.

**Conclusion with results notation:** College freshmen who participate in a treatment of critical thinking feedback ($n$=144, $M$=20) have significantly different critical thinking skills than the norm (μ=19, σ=6); $z$=2.0, $p$=.045, two-tailed.

## 6.26V Errors in Hypothesis Testing

Since there are two possible decisions that we can make about the null (reject the null or fail to reject the null), there are two possible errors that can occur in hypothesis testing.

- ***Type I Error*** occurs when we reject the null and conclude that the treatment had an effect, when in fact the sample was already significantly different from the norm. In this case, we found significance when we really shouldn't have—we found significance and rejected the null out of error.
    - Consequences can be serious—money and time are invested in a treatment that works!
    - Since we are only at risk of a Type I error when significance is found, we can select an alpha level that makes it difficult to determine significance and thus minimize the risk of a Type I error.
    - Most researchers will utilize an alpha of .05 unless they are conducting many (20+) statistical tests in a study and may apply a more conservative alpha like .01.
- **Type II Error** occurs whenever one has failed to reject the null that is really false. This can happen when the treatment does effect the sample, but the size of the effect is not enough to move the sample mean to the extreme tails of the distribution.
    - Consequences of a Type II error are usually not as serious as a Type I error, since resources are not invested in the new treatment. However, many individuals in need may miss out on a promising new treatment just because it was falsely insignificant.
    - The probability of committing a Type II error (represented by the symbol β, the Greek letter beta) depends upon many factors and cannot be calculated into one specific number.

## 6.27V Assumptions of a *z*-test

The computations utilized in hypothesis testing are based upon a set of assumptions. In order to be confident in the results, these assumptions should be fulfilled.

- **Random Sampling**—Since the distribution of sample means is based upon random samples, it is assumed that the studied sample was generated through random selection.
- **Normal Distribution in the Population**—The quantitative dependent variable should be normally distributed in the population. The Central Limit Theorem tells us that if our sample is large ($n$>30), the distribution of sample means will be normal even if the sample is not. The *z*-test is fairly tolerant to normality violations.

## 6.28V Issues with Hypothesis Testing

- Hypothesis testing has many limitations:
    - Disproving the null doesn't necessarily provide support for the alternative.
    - Achievement of significance is easy with large samples. Likewise, studies with small samples may miss an important effect.
    - Test statistic and *p*-value doesn't indicate the strength or size of the effect. Rather *p*-value only represents the probability of finding significance out of error.
    - The research community believes that effect size and confidence intervals are better indications of the treatment effect in the population.

## 6.29V Effect Size

Effect size is a measure of the size or magnitude of the treatment effect.

- Different effect sizes are used with different test statistics.
- Effect size should be reported when significance has been found or a small sample has been used.
- **Cohen's *d*** is the most basic measure of effect size used in conjunction with z.
    - Cohen's *d* measures the mean difference in terms of the original standard deviation.
    - Cohen's $d = \frac{M-\mu}{\sigma}$
    - Cohen suggests that effect sizes should be evaluated as follows:
        - < 0.2 are small
        - 0.2 – 0.8 are medium
        - > 0.8 are large

## 6.30V Estimation with Confidence Intervals

A ***confidence interval (CI)*** estimates the population parameter (after treatment effect) by providing an interval or range of values that will include a percent of the population.

- A confidence interval isn't used to disprove the null but used to estimate the treatment effect in the population.
- The percent of confidence is used to determine the alpha level and the appropriate z.
- Common confidence levels are 90%, 95%, 99%.
- A confidence interval will include a lower boundary and an upper boundary: $\mu = M \pm z(\sigma_M)$

## 6.31V Power

Statistical ***power*** of a study is the probability that the study accurately determines significance and is related to Type II error in that (power = 1 – β).

- Cohen suggests that an appropriate level of power is .80 or 80%, which would mean that a study has an 80% chance having a true significant result.
- As the power increases, so does the possibility of a Type II error, so there is somewhat of a balancing act that occurs.
- Power is typically based upon three parameters: sample size, effect size or test statistic, and alpha level. Analysis of power may be conducted:
  - **retrospectively** (post hoc), which computes the statistical power of a test given sample size studied, the alpha level used, test results.
  - **prospectively** (a priori), used to determine a required sample size to achieve target statistical power (.80).
- Power is calculated for specific inferential test. An online power calculator for *z* is at: powerandsamplesize.com/Calculators/

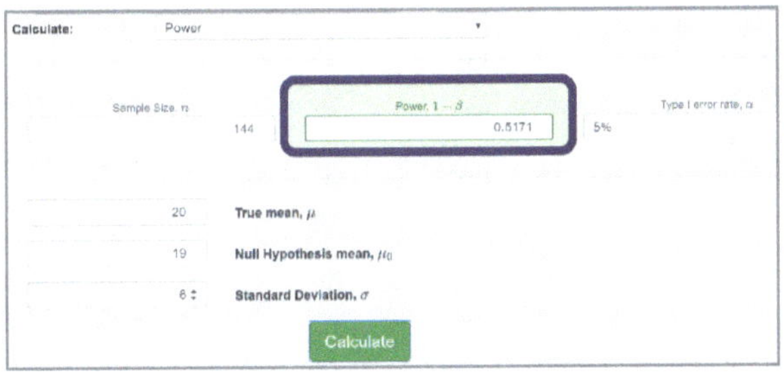


### Example

**Effect Size**

For our sample (n=144, M=20), we determine that the effect size is small (Cohen's *d*=.167).

$$\text{Cohen's } d = \frac{20-19}{6} = \frac{1}{6} = .167$$

**Confidence Interval**

We are 95% confident that the population mean (after the treatment) will range between 19.02 and 20.98.

$$\mu = 20 \pm 1.96(.5) = 20 \pm .98$$

**Power**

To calculate retrospective power. This calculator is specific to a *z*-test and requires the following values: μ=19, σ=6, *M*=20, *n*=144, α=.05, two-tailed. The results generate a power of .52, which means we have a 52% chance of finding accurate significance—not quite the recommended .80.

**Conclusion with results notation:** College freshman who participate in a treatment of critical thinking feedback (*n*=144, *M*=20) have significantly different critical thinking skills than the norm (μ=19, σ=6); *z*=2.0, *p*=.045, two-tailed, Cohen's *d*=.167, 95% CI [19.02, 20.98]. However, the power of the test .52) did not reach Cohen's recommended level of .80.

- A Power Table for *z* is presented in Appendix B (see excerpt below).

| z | α=.05 | | α=.01 | |
|---|---|---|---|---|
| | 2-tail | 1-tail | 2-tail | 1-tail |
| 2.0 | .516 | .639 | .282 | .372 |
| 2.1 | .556 | .675 | .317 | .410 |
| 2.2 | .595 | .711 | .354 | .450 |
| 2.3 | .633 | .744 | .391 | .489 |
| 2.4 | .670 | .775 | .430 | .529 |
| 2.5 | .705 | .804 | .470 | .569 |

## 6.32V Directional (One-tailed) Hypothesis Test

Suppose a public university implements a Spiritual Living-Learning (SLL) Community, in which students are housed together and regularly participate in activities that facilitate spiritual exploration. After two years, the university wants to examine if SLL participation increases spiritual well-being as measured by West's (2004) Spiritual Well-Being Scale (μ=50, σ=5). The university randomly selects 25 participants (*M*= 50.75) to complete the scale. Does college student participation in the Spiritual Living-Learning (SLL) Community significantly increase spiritual well-being when compared to the norm? Test at .05 level.

### Step 1: State Hypotheses

- Identify variables
  - IV=participation in SLL
  - DV=spiritual well-being
- Determine if it is a one-tailed or two-tailed test.
  - One-tailed; keyword→increase
- State **alternative hypothesis**: Participation in the Spiritual Living-Learning (SLL) Community significantly increases spiritual well-being when compared to the college student norm.

- State **null hypothesis**: Participation in the Spiritual Living-Learning (SLL) Community does NOT significantly increase spiritual well-being when compared to the college student norm.
- Develop hypotheses notation: $H_1$: $\mu_{SLL} > 50$ $H_0$: $\mu_{SLL} \leq 50$

## Step 2: Establish Significance Criteria

- Computer analysis requires that we just know the alpha level of .05.
- *Hand Calculations* require the identification of critical boundaries for z.
  - Since this is a one-tailed test, the entire 5% goes in the upper tail of our distribution. Using the unit normal table, we can look up where $p$=.05 and determine that $z_{critical}$ = +1.65. This means that $z_{calculated}$ must be greater than $z_{critical}$ of +1.65 in order to be significantly different from the norm.

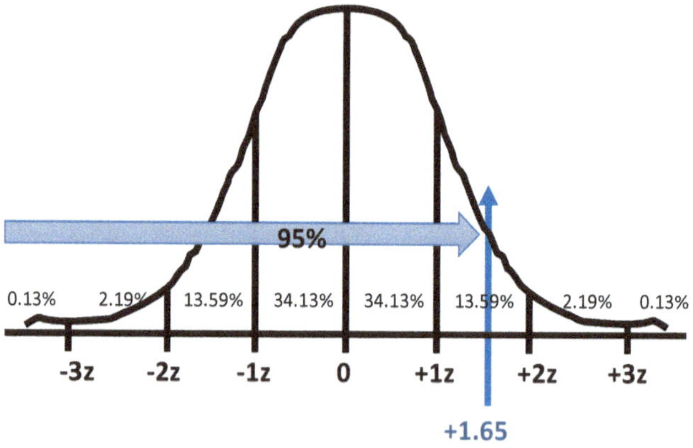


## Step 3: Collect and Analyze Data

*Hand Calculations* require that we first compute standard error for the distribution of samples ($n$=25);

$\sigma_M = 5/\sqrt{25} = 5/5 = 1$. Using the $\sigma_M$=1, we can now calculate $z$.

$$z_{calculated} = \frac{M - \mu}{\sigma_M} = \frac{50.75 - 50}{1} = .75$$

Computer output of **StatCrunch** also produces $z$=.75; however it also provides the exact $p$-value for that z. In this case, $p$=.2266.

**Hypothesis test results:**
μ : Mean of population
$H_0$ : μ = 50
$H_A$ : μ > 50
Standard deviation = 5

| Mean | n | Sample Mean | Std. Err. | Z-Stat | P-value |
|---|---|---|---|---|---|
| μ | 25 | 50.75 | 1 | 0.75 | 0.2266 |

## Step 4: Evaluate Null Hypothesis and Draw Conclusion

- *Hand Calculations* require that we compare $z_{calculated}$ to $z_{critical}$. In order for our sample mean to be considered significantly different from the population norm, $z_{calculated}$ must be greater than $z_{critical}$ = +1.65.
  - $z_{calculated}$ = +.75 and is NOT greater than $z_{critical}$ = +1.65.
  - Do not have significance→fail to reject the null→restate the null for our conclusion.
- `Computer Output` allows us to compare the $p$-value to the alpha level. In order for our sample mean to be considered significantly different from the population norm, our $p$-value must be less than alpha.
  - $p$=.2266 and is NOT less than .05
  - Do NOT have significance→Fail to reject the null→Restate null
- Conclusion essentially restates the null and adds the specific results notation.
  Participation in the Spiritual Living-Learning (SLL) Community ($n$=25, $M$=50.75) does NOT significantly increase spiritual well-being when compared to the college student norm ($\mu$=50, $\sigma$=5); $z$=,75, $p$=.2266, one-tailed.
- Since the results are not significant, you would likely not complete further calculations of effect size, confidence intervals, or power. But for the sake of demonstration, they are included.

### Effect Size

To calculate Cohen's d, we utilize the sample mean ($M$=50.75), population mean ($\mu$=50), and original population standard deviation ($\sigma$=5). A small effect size of .15 is calculated.

$$\text{Cohen's } d = \frac{50.75-50}{5} = \frac{.75}{5} = .15$$

### Confidence Interval

To calculate a 95% confidence interval, $z$ of 1.96 will be used. Applying the sample mean of 50.75 and standard error ($\sigma_M$=1), we can estimate the population mean after the treatment. The lower end of the interval is 48.79, and the upper end is 52.71. StatCrunch output generates the same limits.

$$\mu = M \pm z(\sigma_M)$$

$$\mu = 50.75 \pm 1.96(1)$$

$$\mu = 50.75 \pm 1.96$$

**95% confidence interval results:**
μ : Mean of population
Standard deviation = 5

| Mean | n | Sample Mean | Std. Err. | L. Limit | U. Limit |
|---|---|---|---|---|---|
| μ | 25 | 50.75 | 1 | 48.790036 | 52.709964 |

### Power

Using powerandsamplesize.com/Calculators/, we can determine retrospective power. After entering the population mean, population standard deviation, sample mean, number of tails, and alpha, a power of .19 is generated, which is very low.

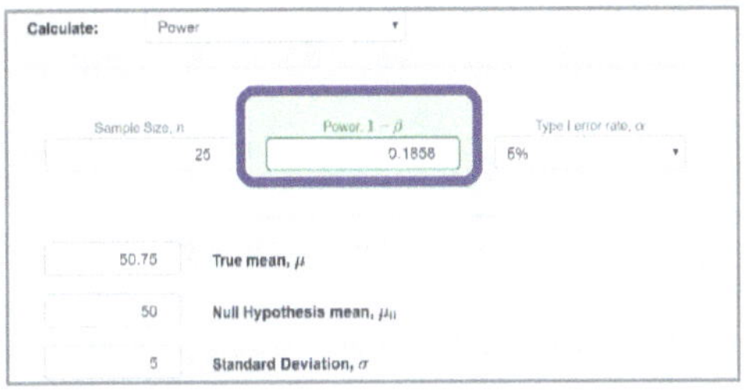


### Updated Results

Participation in the Spiritual Living-Learning (SLL) Community ($n$=25, $M$=50.75) does NOT significantly increase spiritual well-being when compared to the college student norm ($\mu$=50, $\sigma$=5); $z$=,75, $p$=.2266, one-tailed, Cohen's $d$=.15, 95% CI [48.79, 52.71]. Power of the test is quite low at .19.

## 6.33V A Complete Example

In a 2007 national study of children 8-18 years, Gentile (2009) reported that kids are playing video games an average of 13.2 hours per week ($\mu$=13.2, $\sigma$=13.1). Another researcher wants to determine if children's time spent playing video games has significantly increased as a result of the increase in technology and gaming access since 2007. A random sample of 100 kids (age 8-18 years) report a mean of 15.5 hours per week. Use the StatCrunch output to complete the following. Test at $\alpha$=.05.

**Hypothesis test results:**
μ : Mean of population
$H_0$ : μ = 13.2
$H_A$ : μ > 13.2
Standard deviation = 13.1

| Mean | n | Sample Mean | Std. Err. | Z-Stat | P-value |
|---|---|---|---|---|---|
| μ | 100 | 15.5 | 1.31 | 1.7557252 | 0.0396 |

**95% confidence interval results:**
μ : Mean of population
Standard deviation = 13.1

| Mean | n | Sample Mean | Std. Err. | L. Limit | U. Limit |
|---|---|---|---|---|---|
| μ | 100 | 15.5 | 1.31 | 12.932447 | 18.067553 |

**Step 1: Develop Hypotheses:**

a. Independent Variable = Scale: Categorical Quantitative

b. Dependent Variable = Scale: Categorical Quantitative

c. Circle: One-tailed Two-tailed

d. Alternative hypothesis in sentence form.

e. Null hypothesis in sentence form.

f. Write the alternative and null hypotheses using correct notation.

$H_1$: $H_0$:

**Step 2: Establish significance criteria**

g. $\alpha$ =

**Step 3: Calculate test statistic, effect size, confidence interval, and power**

h. $z_{calculated}$ = Level of significance ($p$) =

i. Decision: reject null or fail to reject null

j. Calculate effect size =

k. Determine the 95% confidence interval:

l. Determine the power for this test.

**Step 4: Draw conclusion**

m. Write your conclusion in sentence form including appropriate results notation.

## 6.34V Additional Practice

1. Recall Roberts 2014 study on cell phone use among college students. His research team determined that college students average 528 minutes of cell phone use per week ($\mu$=528, $\sigma$=374)—almost ten hours per week! A psychologist predicts that students majoring in technology related fields (computer science, information technology, etc.) will report different levels of cell phone use than the norm. She collect data from a random sample of 50 computer science majors, who report an average of 567 minutes. Use the StatCrunch output to test at $\alpha$=.05.

**Hypothesis test results:**
μ : Mean of population
$H_0$ : μ = 528
$H_A$ : μ ≠ 528
Standard deviation=374

| Mean | n | Sample Mean | Std. Err. | Z-Stat | P-value |
|---|---|---|---|---|---|
| μ | 50 | 567 | 52.891587 | 0.73735734 | 0.4609 |

**95% confidence interval results:**
μ : Mean of population
Standard deviation = 374

| Mean | n | Sample Mean | Std. Err. | L. Limit | U. Limit |
|---|---|---|---|---|---|
| μ | 50 | 567 | 52.891587 | 463.33439 | 670.66561 |

**Step 1: Develop Hypotheses:**

a. Independent Variable = Scale: Categorical Quantitative

b. Dependent Variable = Scale: Categorical Quantitative

c. Circle: One-tailed Two-tailed

d. Alternative hypothesis in sentence form.

e. Null hypothesis in sentence form.

f. Write the alternative and null hypotheses using correct notation.

$H_1$: $H_0$:

**Step 2: Establish significance criteria**

g. $\alpha$ =

**Step 3: Calculate test statistic, effect size, confidence interval, and power**

h. $z_{calculated}$ = Level of significance ($p$) =

i. Decision: reject null or fail to reject null

j. Calculate effect size =

k. Determine the 95% confidence interval:

**Step 4: Draw conclusion**

l. Write your conclusion in sentence form including appropriate results notation.

2. For the last ten years, a school district has implemented a new math curriculum that not only includes additional intervention for struggling students but also enrichment for advanced students. Two-hundred high school juniors ($n$=200) who have benefited from this curriculum have recently completed the SAT math ($\mu$=514, $\sigma$=118) and generated a sample mean of $M$=530. Does long term implementation (10 years) of a new math curriculum significantly increase SAT math scores among HS juniors? Test at .05.

**Hypothesis test results:**
μ : Mean of population
$H_0$ : μ = 514
$H_A$ : μ > 514
Standard deviation = 118

| Mean | n | Sample Mean | Std. Err. | Z-Stat | P-value |
|---|---|---|---|---|---|
| μ | 200 | 530 | 8.34386 | 1.9175777 | 0.0276 |

**95% confidence interval results:**
μ : Mean of population
Standard deviation = 118

| Mean | n | Sample Mean | Std. Err. | L. Limit | U. Limit |
|---|---|---|---|---|---|
| μ | 200 | 530 | 8.34386 | 513.64633 | 546.35367 |

**Step 1: Develop Hypotheses:**

a. Independent Variable = Scale: Categorical Quantitative

b. Dependent Variable = Scale: Categorical Quantitative

c. Circle: One-tailed Two-tailed

d. Alternative hypothesis in sentence form.

e. Null hypothesis in sentence form.

f. Write the alternative and null hypotheses using correct notation.

$H_1$: $H_0$:

**Step 2: Establish significance criteria**

g. $\alpha$ =

**Step 3: Calculate test statistic, effect size, confidence interval, and power**

h. $z_{calculated}$ = Level of significance ($p$) =

i. Decision: reject null or fail to reject null

j. Calculate effect size =

k. Determine the 95% confidence interval:

l. Calculate the power for this study.

**Step 4: Draw conclusion**

m. Write your conclusion in sentence form including appropriate results notation.

n. How is using the SAT-math as a measure of treatment effect problematic for this study?

## 6.35V Activity: *p* and *z* Applet

This activity will allow you to manipulate the probability/proportion within the *z* distribution. Go to the applet at:

http://wise.cgu.edu/vis/p_z/

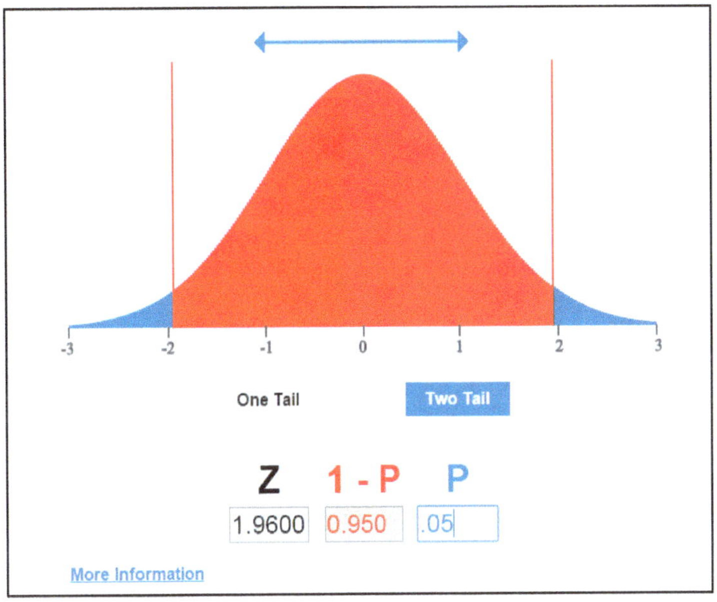


There are two aspects you will manipulate within this applet: *p* and the number of tails. As you adjust these two inputs, the red and blue areas within the distribution will adjust along with z and (1-*p*).

1. Let's start with the basics. Select two-tail and *p*=.05. It should look just like the screen shot to the right. Notice *z*=1.96. Now select one-tail. Notice *z*=1.96 still. Explain what happened to *p*?

2. Still in one-tail, change *p* to .01. What happened to z? Explain.

3. Using an alpha or *p*=.01, which is easier to achieve significance? One-tailed or two-tailed? Explain.

4. Is using an alpha of .05 or .01 easier to achieve significance? Explain.

5. Select two-tail. Notice the red area (1-*p*) is the middle proportion/percent. The red lines in the distribution are the boundaries of the confidence interval. Move the red lines and observe what happens to the red and blue areas, z, 1-*p* and *p*. Why does the interval size increase when the percent of confidence increases for a confidence interval?

## 6.36 Using the Computer

Since using *z* to test a population mean is not very common anymore. SPSS is not capable of conducting such a test. However, StatCrunch can. Not only can StatCrunch use *z* to analyze raw sample data that is entered one by one, but summary statistics can be utilized as well. This means you can just enter the sample mean, sample size, population mean, and population standard deviation to conduct the analysis. Directions will be provided for both scenarios. For these instructions, IQ norms ($\mu$=100, $\sigma$=15) are being used for a one-tailed hypothesis test. When using data summary, sample statistics ($M$=109, $n$=25) were used. You can only conduct a hypothesis test OR confidence interval—they cannot be conducted within the same analysis.

### StatCrunch Step by Step Instructions (with raw data)

1. Enter dependent variable data in first column.
2. Within the data window, 🖱 the **Stat** menu, select ***z* Stats, >One Sample, >with Data**.
3. Within One Sample *z* dialogue box, under **Select Column(s)**, 🖱 your dependent variable.
4. Under **Perform:** select <u>one</u> of the options:

   **Hypothesis Test for μ**
   - By $H_0$ indicate population mean
   - By $H_A$ indicate the direction of test

   **Confidence Interval for μ**
   - Indicate percent of confidence (95% is default)
5. 🖱 **Compute.**

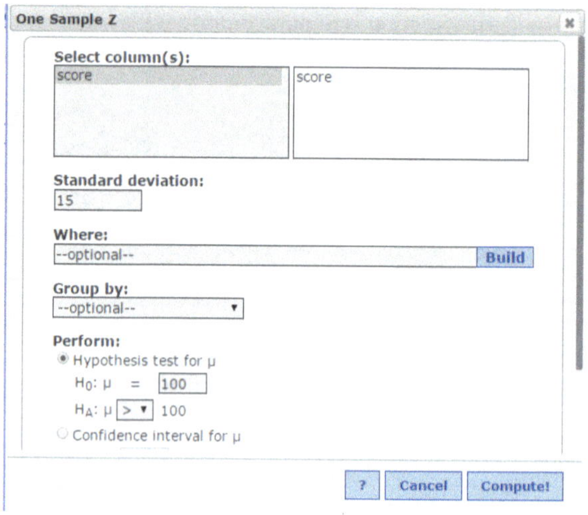


### StatCrunch Step by Step Instructions (with data summary)

1. Open StatCrunch, no need to enter data.
2. Within the data window, 🖱 the **Stat** menu, select ***z* Stats, >One Sample, >with Summary**.
3. Within One Sample *z* Summary dialogue box, enter: sample mean, population standard deviation, sample size.
4. Under **Perform:** select <u>one</u> of the options:

   **Hypothesis Test for μ**
   - By $H_0$ indicate population mean
   - By $H_A$ indicate the direction of test

   **Confidence Interval for μ**
   - Indicate percent of confidence (95% is default)
5. 🖱 **Compute.**

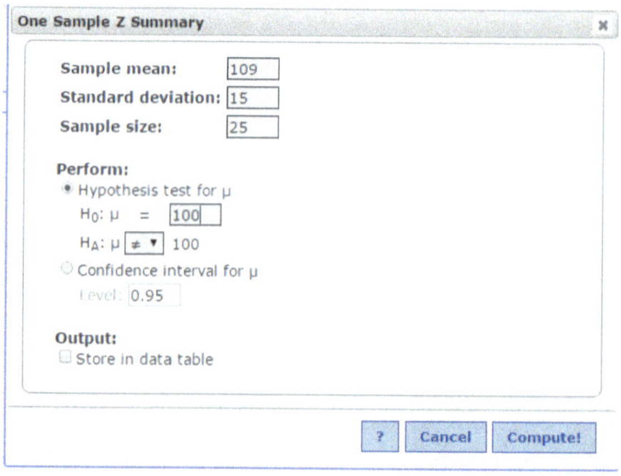


### Power Calculator Step by Step Instructions

1. Go to: [powerandsamplesize.com/Calculators/](powerandsamplesize.com/Calculators/)
2. Under **Test 1 Mean**, select **1-Sample 2-Sided Equality** for a two-tailed test and **1-Sample, 1-Sided** for a one-tailed test. For this example, **1-Sample, 1-Sided** was selected.
3. By Calculate, select **Power**.
4. Enter sample size, sample mean (true mean), population mean (null hypothesis mean), and standard deviation.
5. Press the green **Calculate** button.

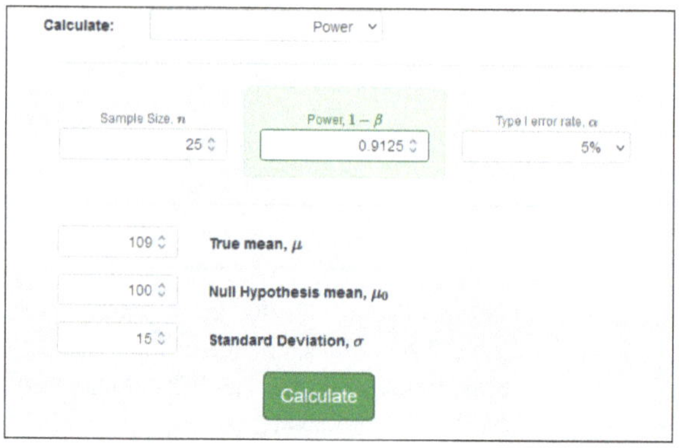

## 6.37 Exercises

### Reviewing the Concepts

1. Why is it impossible to "prove" the alternative hypothesis?

2. Explain the difference between a directional and non-directional hypothesis.

3. Why is the hypothesis notation written using the population mean ($\mu$) when we are really studying the sample mean ($M$)?

4. An alpha level is used to establish the criteria for determining significance. Which alpha level (.05 or .01) is more conservative (more difficult to achieve significance)? Explain.

5. The goal of hypothesis testing is to "reject the null hypothesis." When this decision is made, what does that tell us about the treatment, sample, and population?

6. You are conducting a two-tailed *z* test. Your computer output has generated a *p*-value of .001. If you are using significance criteria of $\alpha$=.05, do you have significance? If you are using $\alpha$=.01, do you have significance? Explain your reasons for both decisions.

7. Although the *p*-value is used to determine significance, what does that *p*-value mean?

8. Explain the difference between a Type I error and Type II error. Why is a Type I error often more serious?

9. Why is the calculation of effect size and confidence intervals recommended when conducting a hypothesis test?

10. Explain the difference between effect size and a confidence interval.

11. Explain the relationship between power and a Type II error.

## Interpreting Results

12. The Mozart Effect touts that listening to classical music can increase IQ performance with greatest impact on visual-spatial processing. A psychologist attempts to examine the Mozart Effect with 30 randomly selected college students. She administers the Stanford-Binet visual-spatial processing subscale that is normally distributed ($\mu$=10, $\sigma$=3). During the testing, Mozart's Sonata in D major for Two Pianos K488 plays. The sample generates a mean of 11. Does listening to Mozart significantly affect visual-spatial processing among college students? Use the output to test at .01.

**Hypothesis test results:**
μ : Mean of population
$H_0 : \mu = 10$
$H_A : \mu \neq 10$
Standard deviation = 3

| Mean | n | Sample Mean | Std. Err. | Z-Stat | P-value |
|---|---|---|---|---|---|
| μ | 30 | 11 | 0.54772256 | 1.8257419 | 0.0679 |

**99% confidence interval results:**
μ : Mean of population
Standard deviation = 3

| Mean | n | Sample Mean | Std. Err. | L. Limit | U. Limit |
|---|---|---|---|---|---|
| μ | 30 | 11 | 0.54772256 | 9.589160 | 12.41084 |

**Step 1: Develop Hypotheses:**

a. Independent Variable = Scale: Categorical Quantitative

b. Dependent Variable = Scale: Categorical Quantitative

c. Circle: One-tailed Two-tailed

d. Alternative hypothesis in sentence form.

e. Null hypothesis in sentence form.

f. Write the alternative and null hypotheses using correct notation.

$H_1$: $H_0$:

**Step 2: Establish significance criteria**

g. $\alpha$ =

**Step 3: Calculate test statistic, effect size, and confidence interval**

h. $z_{calculated}$ = Level of significance ($p$) =

i. Decision: reject null or fail to reject null

j. Calculate effect size =

k. Determine the 99% confidence interval:

**Step 4: Draw conclusion**

l. Write your conclusion in sentence form including appropriate results notation.

13. While one assumes that height is a good indicator of basketball success, what about upper arm length? Upper arm length of U.S. females over 20 years old is normally distributed (μ=35.8 cm, σ=2.1 cm). Twenty players in the WNBA are randomly selected and have an average upper arm length of 39.6 cm. Do professional basketball players have significantly longer upper arms than the norm of U.S. females. Test at .05.

**Hypothesis test results:**
μ : Mean of population
$H_0$ : μ = 35.8
$H_A$ : μ > 35.8
Standard deviation = 2.1

| Mean | n | Sample Mean | Std. Err. | Z-Stat | P-value |
|---|---|---|---|---|---|
| μ | 20 | 39.6 | 0.46957428 | 8.0924365 | <0.0001 |

**99% confidence interval results:**
μ : Mean of population
Standard deviation = 2.1

| Mean | n | Sample Mean | Std. Err. | L. Limit | U. Limit |
|---|---|---|---|---|---|
| μ | 20 | 39.6 | 0.46957428 | 38.67965 | 140.520349 |

**Step 1: Develop Hypotheses:**

a. Independent Variable = Scale: Categorical Quantitative

b. Dependent Variable = Scale: Categorical Quantitative

c. Circle: One-tailed Two-tailed

d. Alternative hypothesis in sentence form.

e. Null hypothesis in sentence form.

f. Write the alternative and null hypotheses using correct notation.

$H_1$: $H_0$:

**Step 2: Establish significance criteria**

g. α =

**Step 3: Calculate test statistic, effect size, and confidence interval**

h. $z_{calculated}$ = Level of significance ($p$) =

i. Decision: reject null or fail to reject null

j. Calculate effect size =

k. Determine the 95% confidence interval:

l. Determine the power for this test.

**Step 4: Draw conclusion**

m. Write your conclusion in sentence form including appropriate results notation.

## Conducting the Analysis

14. The 2009 Census reports that the average commute time is 25.1 minutes ($\mu$=25.1, $\sigma$=10.6) for full-time workers in the U.S. However, highly populated urban areas have been known to require additional commute time. A sociologist randomly samples 100 residents of New York City who are employed full-time. This sample reports an average commute time of 82 minutes. Can the sociologist conclude that NYC residents have significantly longer commute times than the U.S. norm? Test at .01. Conduct the analysis by hand or use StatCrunch (with summary data).

**Step 1: Develop Hypotheses:**

a. Independent Variable = Scale: Categorical Quantitative

b. Dependent Variable = Scale: Categorical Quantitative

c. Circle: One-tailed Two-tailed

d. Alternative hypothesis in sentence form.

e. Null hypothesis in sentence form.

f. Write the alternative and null hypotheses using correct notation.

$H_1$: $H_0$:

**Step 2: Establish significance criteria**

g. $\alpha$ =

**Step 3: Calculate test statistic, effect size, confidence interval, and power**

h. $z_{calculated}$ = Level of significance ($p$) =

i. Decision: reject null or fail to reject null

j. Calculate effect size =

k. Determine the 99% confidence interval:

**Step 4: Draw conclusion**

l. Write your conclusion in sentence form including appropriate results notation.

15. A researcher believes that children who grow up as an only child develop vocabulary skills at a faster rate than children with siblings. To test this, a random sample of $n$ = 10 four-year-old only children are tested on a standardized vocabulary test ($\mu$=60, $\sigma$=10). Can the researcher conclude that children from one child families have greater vocabulary skills than the norm? Test at the .05 level. Use the data below to conduct the analysis.

53, 55, 59, 60, 62, 65, 68, 72, 73, 77

**Step 1: Develop Hypotheses:**

a. Independent Variable = Scale: Categorical Quantitative

b. Dependent Variable = Scale: Categorical Quantitative

c. Circle: One-tailed Two-tailed

d. Alternative hypothesis in sentence form.

e. Null hypothesis in sentence form.

f. Write the alternative and null hypotheses using correct notation.

$H_1$: $H_0$:

**Step 2: Establish significance criteria**

g. $\alpha$ =

**Step 3: Calculate test statistic, effect size, confidence interval, and power**

h. $z_{calculated}$ = Level of significance ($p$) =

i. Decision: reject null or fail to reject null

j. Calculate effect size =

k. Determine the 95% confidence interval:

**Step 4: Draw conclusion**

l. Write your conclusion in sentence form including appropriate results notation.

# Module 7

## The t Statistic

### Learning Targets

After completing Module 7, you should be able to:

- Understand the concepts of the *t* distribution, estimated standard error, and assumptions in conducting a *t*-test of single sample.
- Apply the process of hypothesis testing to conduct *t*-test of single sample to compare a sample mean to a population mean and determine statistical significance.
- Interpret *t*-test results (hand calculations, SPSS/StatCrunch output) to determine statistical significance and confidence intervals and draw appropriate conclusions.
- Utilize *t*-test results to calculate appropriate effect size and power.
- Write appropriate conclusions with statistical results notation.

# Part 1: The Concepts

## 7.11 Distribution of Sample Means

In hypothesis testing we have been able to determine if our sample mean is significantly different from the population mean. This process allows us to test a hypothesis about an unknown population so that we can make conclusions about our population. Since we are comparing a sample mean to the population mean, we have to transform the population distribution of individuals to a population of samples of similar size to the sample we are studying. In transforming the distribution of individual scores to a distribution of sample means, we calculate a new standard deviation—the standard error. Unfortunately, the calculation of standard error requires the population standard, a value that is often not available.

The ***t statistic*** allows us to use the sample standard deviation to *estimate* the standard error while still testing a hypothesis about an unknown population. The $t$ statistic uses a formula very similar to $z$ in that we are still computing the difference between the sample mean and the population mean, but the $t$ statistic divides this difference by the estimated standard error ($s_M$).

$$z = \frac{M - \mu}{\sigma_M} \qquad t = \frac{M - \mu}{s_M}$$

This test is called ***t test of a single sample***, since we are comparing a single sample mean to a population. Although you will likely utilize a statistical program to conduct your analyses, we will demonstrate the calculations so that you understand the meaning behind the numbers.

**Hypothesis Notation.** Since we are generalizing our results to the population, the hypothesis being tested is written in terms of the population. For a $t$ test of single sample, we are comparing our sample mean to a population norm. Therefore, hypothesis notation will predict the relationship between the mean (as written in the form of a population parameter, $\mu$) and the value of the population norm. If we apply a population mean value of 16,000, we generate the following hypotheses. For a two-tailed test, the ***alternative hypothesis*** (**$H_1$**) indicates a difference and so predicts that the mean will not equal the population mean value. In contrast, the ***null hypothesis*** (**$H_0$**) for a two-tailed test predicts (just the opposite of the alternative) that the mean ($\mu$) will equal the population mean value, thus indicating no difference.

$$H_1: \mu \neq 16{,}000 \qquad H_0: \mu = 16{,}000$$

For a one-tailed test in which we predict that the treatment increases performance on our sample, the alternative hypothesis ($H_1$) indicates that the mean will be greater than the population mean value. The null hypothesis ($H_0$) would predict that the treatment will not increase the mean ($\mu$) and therefore the mean will be less than or equal to the population mean value.

$$H_1: \mu > 16{,}000 \qquad H_0: \mu \leq 16{,}000$$

> **Example**
>
> Although media has long supported the notion that women talk more than men, Mehl et. al. (2007) found that both male and female college students speak roughly 16,000 words per day. One researcher believes that personality (extrovert/introvert) may be a factor that creates differences in talking amount. To examine this, the researcher randomly selects 36 college students who identify themselves as extroverts. Just as in Mehl's study, participants wear special devices that record their words for 4 days. The sample generates a mean of 19,227 words per day ($M$=19,227, SD=8,280). Test at the .05 level.
>
> **RQ:** Do extravert college students talk more than the norm of 16,000 words per day?
>
> **IV:** extrovert vs. norm
>
> **DV:** # of words per day
>
> **Alternative Hypothesis:** Extravert college student will talk significantly more word per day than the norm.
>
> **Null Hypothesis:** Extravert college student will NOT talk significantly more word per day than the norm.
>
> **Hypothesis Notation:**
> $H_1$: $\mu > 16{,}000$ $H_0$: $\mu \leq 16{,}000$
>
> **Estimated standard error:**
> $$s_M = \frac{s}{\sqrt{n}} = \frac{8{,}280}{\sqrt{36}} = \frac{8{,}280}{6} = 1{,}380$$
>
> **Calculating *t*:**
> $$t = \frac{M - \sigma}{s_M} = \frac{19{,}227 - 16{,}000}{1{,}380} = 2.34$$

***Estimated standard error*** (**$s_M$**) provides an estimate of the standard distance between the sample mean and the population mean. Since we are unable to use the population standard deviation and must use the sample standard deviation in its place, the value is an estimate. So how can we just estimate standard error and still come up with a fairly accurate result? Recall that with inferential statistics we are studying a sample of individuals that was randomly selected from the population, in the hopes that our sample is representative of the population so that we can then generalize our result to the population. Therefore, our sample should have similar variability to the population. A comparison of how we calculate standard error and estimated standard error, shows the similarities between the two formulas:

$$\text{standard error } (\sigma_M) = \frac{\sigma}{\sqrt{n}} \qquad \text{estimated standard error } (s_M) = \frac{s}{\sqrt{n}}$$

Notice the difference in notation: standard error ($\sigma_M$) uses the population standard deviation ($\sigma$) while estimated standard error ($s_M$) uses sample standard deviation ($s$).

**The *t* Distribution.** All the sample means of similarly sized samples in a population create a normal distribution. The *t* statistics of these samples also create a distribution, called the *t* distribution. Like a *z* distribution, the *t* distribution is bell shaped and symmetrical. However, since the *t* statistic utilizes the estimated standard error ($s_M$), which is based upon the sample standard deviation ($s$) that is calculated using degrees of freedom ($df = n-1$), the *t* distribution is also based on degrees of freedom and not the total sample size. Therefore the *t* distribution only approximates the normal distribution. Recall in Module 3, we learned that degrees of freedom ($df = n-1$) represents the number of scores that are "free to vary."

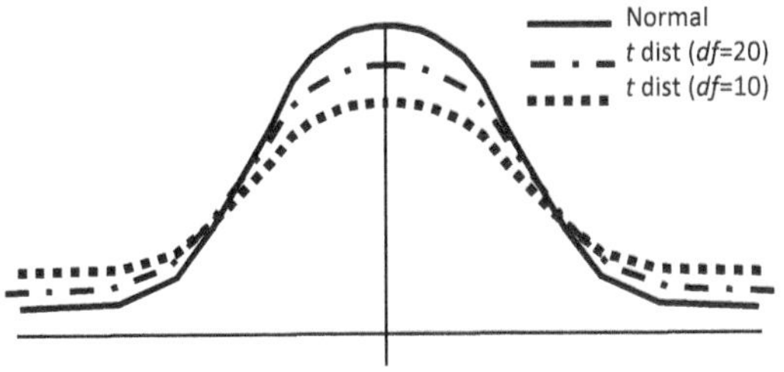


Figure 7.1
*t* Distribution Approximating the Normal Distribution

Because the *t* distribution is based on the estimated standard error, which utilizes degrees of freedom, we have less accurate information regarding our population and therefore more room for error. Although the *t* distribution looks fairly normal in that it follows a bell curve and is symmetrical, it is more spread out and flatter. However, as sample size and degrees of freedom increase, the closer the $s$ represents $\sigma$, and the better the *t* distribution approximates the normal ($z$) distribution. Figure 7.1 shows as the *df* increases, the distribution curve gets closer to the normal distribution.

**Determining Significance with *t*.** Recall that statistical significance indicates that the probability of finding significance out of error or chance is quite low, and therefore the treatment effect is likely to occur in the population. To achieve significance, we require that the probability of error/chance be very low, typically either 5% ($\alpha$=.05) or 1% ($\alpha$=.01). So a result that is significant at $p<.05$ means that we are 95% confident that the significance we found is not due to error/chance. On the flip side, we only have 5% likelihood of obtaining the significant result out of error/chance.

In Module 6 when conducting a *z* test by hand, we compared $z_{calculated}$ to $z_{critical}$. The *z* table was used to identify $z_{critical}$, which was dependent upon the number of tails and the alpha used. Similarly when conducting a *t* test by hand, we will need to compare $t_{calculated}$ to $t_{critical}$, where $t_{critical}$ is identified using the *t* Distribution Table (see Appendix C). Since the *t* statistic is dependent on degrees of freedom, the critical *t* statistics corresponding to levels of significance ($\alpha$) vary with the degrees of freedom, unlike the critical *z* scores (where a two-tailed test at .05 will always corresponds to $z_{critical} = \pm$ 1.96). In Figure 7.2, the normal *z* distribution with its critical (shaded) areas of significance at $\alpha$=.05 (two-tailed) is compared to two *t* distributions; one is a *t* distribution based upon *df*=20 and the other with *df*=10. Notice how the critical regions of significance are further out from $z_{critical}$ of $\pm$1.96 as the degrees of freedom decrease. In contrast, as degrees of freedom increases, the critical regions of significance get closer to the $z_{critical}$. If we had a sample greater than 120, our *t* distribution would be equivalent to the *z* distribution and therefore would have the same critical values of significance ($\pm$1.96). To identify $t_{critical}$, you will need to determine the alpha level being applied, the number of tails for the test (one or two tails), and the degrees of freedom ($df = n-1$). Figure 7.3 presents a portion of the *t* Distribution Table, ranging from *df* of 27 to infinity ($\infty$). Notice that after *df*=30, the table jumps to 40, 60, 120, and infinity. That's because, once a sample is greater than 30, the critical values do not change dramatically.

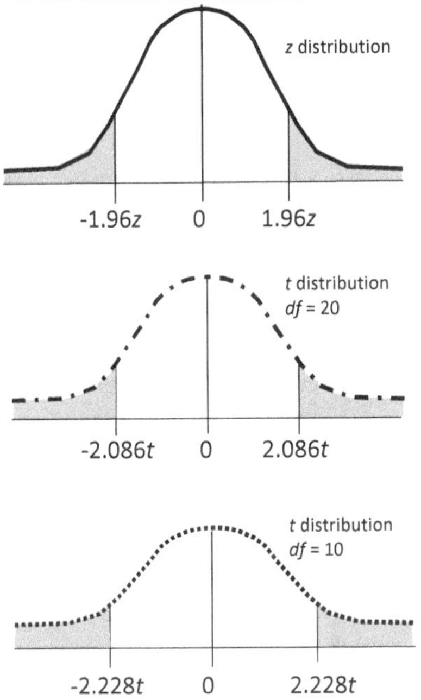


Figure 7.2
Comparison of Critical regions at $\alpha$=.05

Figure 7.3
Excerpt of *t* Distribution Table

| *df* | Proportion in one tail | | | |
|---|---|---|---|---|
| | **0.05** | **0.025** | **0.01** | **0.005** |
| | Proportion in two tails | | | |
| | **0.10** | **0.05** | **0.025** | **0.01** |
| 27 | 1.703 | 2.052 | 2.473 | 2.771 |
| 28 | 1.701 | 2.048 | 2.467 | 2.763 |
| 29 | 1.699 | 2.045 | 2.462 | 2.756 |
| 30 | 1.697 | 2.042 | 2.457 | 2.750 |
| 40 | 1.684 | 2.021 | 2.423 | 2.704 |
| 60 | 1.671 | 2.000 | 2.390 | 2.660 |
| 120 | 1.658 | 1.980 | 2.358 | 2.617 |
| $\infty$ | 1.645 | 1.960 | 2.326 | 2.576 |

**Interpreting Computer Output**. Although computing a single sample $t$ by hand is fairly simple, most of the time you will utilize a statistical analysis program, which will generate the sample mean, standard deviation, and $t$-statistic. In addition, the analysis output will also provide the probability of obtaining that exact $t$ statistic. This makes interpretation a bit different from hand calculations. Recall that for hand calculations, we had to identify $t_{critical}$ for a specific alpha level and compare $t_{critical}$ to $t_{calculated}$ in order to determine significance. In contrast, since the computer output provides the probability of the $t$-statistic, also known as the $p$-value, we don't have to determine a $t_{critical}$. Instead, significance is determined by comparing the $p$-value to the alpha level that has been predetermined. Basically, your $p$-value must be less than the alpha level to be significant. Remember, if we find significance, we reject the null and can restate the alternative hypothesis for our conclusion.

Figure 7.4 presents output generated for our extrovert sample in SPSS and StatCrunch. A couple of things to keep in mind when using these programs. First, SPSS will automatically generate the confidence intervals. Second, SPSS will only calculate a $t$-test (and pretty much any other test statistic) for a two-tailed test. This means that if you are conducting a one-tailed test, you need to adjust the two-tailed $p$-value that SPSS calculates to a one-tailed $p$-value. Fortunately, this is an easy adjustment—just divide the two-tailed $p$-value by 2 to get one-tail! In contrast, StatCrunch will conduct one-tailed tests, however, the generation of confidence intervals is a separate analysis. Steps for conducting these analyses are provided later in the Learning Guide.

**SPSS Output**

**One-Sample Statistics**

| | N | Mean | Std. Deviation | Std. Error Mean |
|---|---|---|---|---|
| words | 36 | 19226.6667 | 8279.98880 | 1379.99813 |

**One-Sample Test**

| | Test Value = 16000 | | | | | |
|---|---|---|---|---|---|---|
| | t | df | Sig. (2-tailed) | Mean Difference | 95% Confidence Interval of the Difference Lower | Upper |
| words | 2.338 | 35 | .025 | 3226.66667 | 425.1215 | 6028.2118 |

**StatCrunch Output**

**Hypothesis test results:**
μ : Mean of variable
$H_0$ : μ = 16000
$H_A$ : μ > 16000

| Variable | Sample Mean | Std. Err. | DF | T-Stat | P-value |
|---|---|---|---|---|---|
| words | 19226.667 | 1379.9981 | 35 | 2.3381674 | 0.0126 |

**95% confidence interval results:**
μ : Mean of variable

| Variable | Sample Mean | Std. Err. | DF | L. Limit | U. Limit |
|---|---|---|---|---|---|
| words | 19226.667 | 1379.9981 | 35 | 16425.122 | 22028.212 |

**Figure 7.4**
SPSS and StatCrunch Output for $t$-test of Single Sample

## Example

**Determining Significance**

***Hand Calculations***

**1. Determine $t_{critical}$:**
For our example,

- α=.05 has already been established;
- The sample is predicted to be higher than the norm, so this is a one-tailed test; and
- $df = 36 - 1 = 35$

Using that information, we can go to our $t$ Distribution Table. Using $df$=30 (since $t$ values for $df$=35 are not provided), $t_{critical}$ is identified as +1.697.

**2. Compare $t_{calculated}$ to $t_{critical}$:**
Since the researcher is predicting that the extrovert's mean will be greater the norm, $t_{calculated}$ needs to be higher than $t_{critical}$ to be significant, which is the case since $t_{calculated} = 2.34$ is higher than 1.697.

**3. Decision?**
Significant→Reject the Null

**Computer Output**

**1. Identify $p$-value**

- If you using SPSS and conducting a one-tailed test, be sure to divide p-value in half (.025/2=.0125)
- $p$=.0125

**2. Compare $p$-value to alpha**
$p$-value must be less than alpha to be significant.

- $p$ of .0125 is less than α of .05.

**3. Decision?**
Significant→Reject the Null

**Assumptions.** As with most parametric tests, two important assumptions must be met in order to conduct a $t$ test of single sample. The first is that sample values or responses are independent observations. Recall that independent observations require that each observation or score is not influenced by any other observation. This is usually satisfied by using a random sample and proper data collection techniques. A random sample helps ensure that the sample is representative of the population and therefore increases our ability to generalize the results to the population. The second assumption is that the sampled population is normal or in other words sample data from the population creates a normal distribution. Again, using a random sample assists in generating a normal distribution since the sample will be more representative of the normally distributed population. Keep in mind the assumption of normality is not especially important if the sample is relatively large.

## 7.12 Estimation with *t* Test of Single Sample

Calculating a confidence interval is another inferential process that allows you determine the size of the treatment effect. This process is called estimation and is often used when you have found significance in the hypothesis test, know there is an effect, or just want some basic information about the unknown population. Recall that a confidence interval allows us to estimate a range of values in which the population mean is likely to fall with a certain degree of confidence. The more confident you want to be in your estimate, the larger the estimated range will be. Since most statistical programs use a default of 95% confidence, we will typically apply that value; however, 99% confidence is also common. When we calculated a confidence interval for a *z* test at 95% confidence, the equation was pretty straight forward since the *z* distribution is not influenced by sample size or degrees of freedom. As a result, the estimated *z* score for a population mean will always fall between -1.96 and +1.96 when using 95% confidence level.

$$\mu = M \pm z\sigma_m \;=\; M \pm 1.96\sigma_m$$

When calculating a confidence interval for a *t* test of single sample, the equation is quite similar in that we use the sample mean ($M$) as the basis of the estimation and then add and subtract the estimated *t* (at 95% or 99% confidence) multiplied by the estimated standard error ($s_m$). Note that the *t* used in this calculation is the $t_{critical}$ and not $t_{calculated}$.

$$\mu = M \pm ts_m$$

Since the *t* distribution is influenced by degrees of freedom, the estimated *t* value will always differ depending upon the sample size. As such, to calculate a 95% confidence interval, you will need to know the sample mean ($M$), the estimated *t* statistic at $\alpha$=.05, and the estimated standard error. Something else to keep in mind when calculating a confidence interval is that we are estimating the lower bound and the upper bound of the population mean, therefore we are looking in both tails of our distribution. Therefore, you will always need to determine $t_{critical}$ for a two-tailed test, even if you are conducting a one-tailed hypothesis test.

> **Example**
>
> **Confidence Interval**
>
> We have already determined that:
>
> - $M$ = 19,227, $s_m$ = 1,380
>
> Previously, we also determined that $t_{critical}$ for a one-tailed test at .05 was 1.697. However, a confidence interval is always two-tailed, so we need to utilize the *t* Distribution Table to identify a two-tailed $t_{critical}$ at .05.
>
> - $t_{critical} = \pm 2.042$
>
> Using this information, our 95% confidence interval is:
>
> $\mu = 19{,}227 \pm 2.042(1{,}380)$
>
> $\mu = 19{,}227 \pm 2{,}818$

**Interpreting Computer Output.** SPSS and StatCrunch calculate the confidence intervals at either 95% or 99% confidence. However, the calculations presented are different. As seen in Figure 7.4, SPSS presents the confidence interval for the difference between the sample mean and the population mean. One option to deal with this is just to report the confidence interval of the difference (i.e., 95% CI Difference [425.12, 6028.21]. The second option is to use the difference to calculate the interval for the population mean. To calculate the lower bound of the population, add the lower difference (425.12) to the population mean ($\mu$=16,000). To calculate the upper bound, add the upper difference (6028.21) to the population mean ($\mu$=16,000).

$$\text{(SPSS) lower bound} = \text{lower difference} + \mu = 425.12 + 16{,}000 = 16{,}425.12$$

$$\text{upper bound} = \text{upper difference} + \mu = 6028.21 + 16{,}000 = 22{,}028.21$$

Notice that SPSS calculates the confidence interval around the population mean; whereas the hand calculations compute the interval around the sample mean. Both methods generate similar results. The only reason the hand calculated confidence interval is slightly lower is because $t_{critical}$ is based upon *df* of 30 and not 35. If our *t* Distribution Table was more detailed, we would get the same interval. StatCrunch results are much easier to interpret, since the lower and upper bounds are presented in the output (see Figure 7.4). Although the generation of confidence intervals is an additional analysis in StatCrunch, it is worth it!

## 7.13 Effect Size and Power

In the previous module, you were introduced to concerns about hypothesis testing. The biggest issue with hypothesis testing is that it is only an indication of "significance"—the likelihood of obtaining the result out of error or chance. A significant effect does not indicate the size of the effect. Since standard error is influenced by sample size, obtaining a significant result is easier if you have a large sample size ($n$>100) or if you are conducting a one-tailed test. As a result many novice researchers may interpret a significant result with a large sample as an indication of a substantial effect, when in actuality the significance is a function of the sample size and not the effect at all. To correct for this issue, the research community recommends the reporting of an effect size whenever a significant effect is reported. However, even when you have failed to reject the null you many still want to calculate an effect size especially if you have a small sample size. There are several indices of effect size that provide a measure of the size of the treatment effect. The most basic measure of effect size associated with a *t* test is Cohen's *d*, which measures the mean difference in terms of the standard deviation. We also used Cohen's *d* when conducting a *z* test, however we used the population standard deviation in its calculation. For a *t* test, we must use the sample standard deviation (*s* or *SD*).

$$\text{Cohen's } d = \frac{M-\mu}{SD}$$

In dividing the mean difference by the standard deviation, we "standardize" the mean difference. StatCrunch users will soon notice that the *t*-test output does not provide the sample standard deviation, which is necessary for computing Cohen's *d*. Rather StatCrunch output reports the estimated standard error (*SE*). Don't make the mistake of just plugging in $s_M$ or *SE*. Instead, you may use *SE* to calculate the sample *SD* (*s*). Recall that to calculate estimated standard error, we divide the sample standard deviation (*s*) by the square root of *n*. Using this equation, we may calculate sample standard deviation by multiplying $s_M$ and the square root of *n*.

$$s_M = \frac{s}{\sqrt{n}} \qquad s = s_M\sqrt{n} \qquad s = 1380\sqrt{36} = 8280$$

> # Example
> **Effect Size**
>
> We have already determined that:
> - *M* = 19,227
> - *SD* = 8,280
> - μ = 16,000
>
> Using these values, we calculate Cohen's *d* as follows:
>
> $$\text{Cohen's } d = \frac{19{,}227-16{,}000}{8{,}280} = .39$$

Notice that effect size does not include any information regarding sample size. However, we can use sample size to evaluate the effect size and determine the ***power*** of our study. Recall that statistical power of a study is the probability that the study will produce a statistically significant result if the hypothesis is true (or we reject the null). The same man who created Cohen's *d* also provides a table to approximate power for studies using a *t* test (Cohen, 1988). Figure 7.5 allows us to evaluate power based upon effect size, the sample size, the number of tails, and a significance level of .05 (StatPages.net, 2007). An expanded version of this table is found in Appendix D1. Determining power in the planning of a study can be very helpful. The researcher can make necessary adjustments in sample size, levels of significance, or number of tails to increase power. We can also use power to evaluate the results of our study, whether our results were statistically significant or not. Typically the more power the better, but Cohen recommends a minimum power of .80 or 80%. Power calculators are also available online, however, most are a-priori for determining a minimum sample size. We will further explore Power and Sample Size calculators in Additional Practice 2.

**Figure 7.5**
*Statistical Power of the t Test of a Single Sample (α=.05)*

| Sample Size | Effect Size | | |
|---|---|---|---|
| | Small (<.20) | Medium (.50) | Large (>.80) |
| Two-tailed test | | | |
| 10 | .08 | .26 | .60 |
| 20 | .13 | .56 | .92 |
| 30 | .18 | .75 | .99 |
| 40 | .23 | .87 | * |
| 50 | .28 | .93 | * |
| 100 | .51 | * | * |
| One-tailed test | | | |
| 10 | .13 | .40 | .75 |
| 20 | .21 | .69 | .96 |
| 30 | .28 | .86 | .99 |
| 40 | .34 | .93 | * |
| 50 | .40 | .97 | * |
| 100 | .63 | * | * |

*Nearly 1

> # Example
> **Power**
>
> For our example, we have determined: *n=36, p<.05, one-tailed, Cohen's d=.39.* Using Figure 7.5, we can approximate statistical power as .86, which indicates that we have a .86 probability of achieving a significant result if the hypothesis is true. This meets Cohen's recommendation for power of .80.

## 7.14 Reporting the Results

The first component of summarizing the results is to provide a statement that indicates the relationship is supported by the results as well as the sample and variables studied. Within this statement, you should integrate the following statistical results:

- Sample mean and standard deviation
- Population mean value
- $t_{calculated}$ with degrees of freedom in parentheses
- Level of significance (*p*)
- Number of tails
- Effect size
- Confidence interval (optional)

Although power results are not typically presented in a results statement, you may want to include this in your discussion as it has implications regarding the practical significance of your results.

> # Example
> **Report Results**
>
> Based upon our results, we can conclude that our sample is significantly different from the norm and state:
>
> Extrovert college students **(*M*=19,227, *SD* = 8,280)** talk significantly more words per day than the population norm of **μ=16,000; *t*(35)=2.34, *p*<.05, one-tailed, Cohen's *d*=.39.** An estimation of the effect in the population with 95% confidence indicates that the population mean (μ) will fall **between 16,409 and 22,045.**

### 7.15 Module Summary

- $t$ test of single sample is used to compare a sample mean to a population norm, when population standard deviation is not available.
- Since we do not know the population standard deviation, we must estimate standard error in order to calculate our $t$ statistic.
- Because standard error is estimated, our $t$ distribution approximates the normal distribution.
- As sample size and degrees of freedom increases, the closer $s_m$ represents $\sigma_M$, therefore error decreases.
- To determine significance, compare $t_{\text{calculated}}$ to $t_{\text{critical}}$ (when doing hand calculations) or compare the $p$-value to the alpha level (when using computer).
- If you found significance or want to know the size of the treatment effect, you should estimate the treatment effect in the population by calculating a confidence interval at 95% or 99% level.
- Since hypothesis testing is only an indication of "significance"—the likelihood of obtaining the result out of error or chance—you should calculate effect size to measure the size of the effect.
- Power of the study is the probability that the study will produce a statistically significant result if the hypothesis is true. You can determine power while planning a study or after conducting a study.

# Part 2: Learning Guide

### 7.21V The *t* statistic

## Example

Although media has long supported the notion that women talk more than men, Mehl et. al. (2007) found that both male and female college students speak roughly 16,000 words per day. One researcher believes that personality (extrovert/introvert) may be a factor that creates differences in talking amount. To examine this, the researcher randomly selects 36 college students who identify themselves as extroverts. Just as in Mehl's study, participants wear special devices that record their words for 4 days. The sample generates a mean of 19,227 words per day ($M$=19,227, $SD$=8,280). Test at the .05 level.

**RQ:** Do extravert college students talk more than the norm of 16,000 words per day?

**IV:** extrovert vs. norm

**DV:** # of words per day

**Alternative Hypothesis**: Extravert college students will talk significantly more words per day than the norm.

**Null Hypothesis**: Extravert college students will NOT talk significantly more words per day than the norm.

### The *t* Statistic

$z$-test requires population standard deviation ($\sigma$) to calculate the standard error of sample means.

- Most of the time we do not know $\sigma$, so what do we do?

$t$-test allows us to compare the sample to the null by using the sample standard deviation to estimate the standard error of sample means.

- ***Estimated standard error* ($s_M$)** provides an estimate of the standard distance between the sample mean and the population mean.

| ***z*-test** | ***t*-test** |
|---|---|
| $z = \dfrac{M - \mu}{\sigma_M}$ | $t = \dfrac{M - \mu}{s_M}$ |
| standard error $(\sigma_M) = \dfrac{\sigma}{\sqrt{n}}$ | estimated standard error $(s_M) = \dfrac{s}{\sqrt{n}}$ |

## Hypotheses Notation

- Hypothesis notation is similar to a *z*-test.
  - Because we will generalize our results to the population, hypothesis notation reflects the population mean (μ) in comparison to the norm. The examples below apply the norm of 16,000 words.

| | Alternative | Null |
|---|---|---|
| One-tailed | $H_1$: $\mu < 16{,}000$ | $H_0$: $\mu \geq 16{,}000$ |
| | $H_1$: $\mu > 16{,}000$ | $H_0$: $\mu \leq 16{,}000$ |
| Two-tailed | $H_1$: $\mu \neq 16{,}000$ | $H_0$: $\mu = 16{,}000$ |

### Example

Since we are predicting that extraverts will talk more than the norm, this is a one-tailed test.

**Hypothesis Notation:** $H_1$: $\mu > 16{,}000$ $H_0$: $\mu \leq 16{,}000$

**Estimated standard error:** $s_M = \frac{s}{\sqrt{n}} = \frac{8{,}280}{\sqrt{36}} = \frac{8{,}280}{6} = 1{,}380$

**Calculating *t*:** $t = \frac{M - \sigma}{s_M} = \frac{19{,}227 - 16{,}000}{1{,}380} = 2.34$

## The *t* Distribution

- Like the *z* distribution, the *t* distribution is also bell shaped and symmetrical (See Figure 7.1).
- The *t* distribution only approximates the normal distribution since:
  - the *t* statistic utilizes the estimated standard error ($s_M$), which is based upon the sample standard deviation ($s$) that is calculated using degrees of freedom ($df = n - 1$), the *t* distribution is also based upon degrees of freedom and not the total sample size.
- The *t* distribution has more variability and is more spread out and flatter.
- As *df* and sample size increase, the closer the *s* represents σ, and the better the *t* distribution approximates the normal (*z*) distribution.
- As *df* increases, the *t* distribution get closer to a normal distribution.
- Use the *t* statistic in a very similar way to *z*, in that we use a *t* distribution table to find the probability of a *t* statistic.
- Note: Since the *t* statistic is dependent on *df*, the critical *t* statistics corresponding to levels of significance (α) vary with *df*, unlike the critical *z* scores (where a two-tailed test at .05 will always corresponds to $z_{critical} = \pm\ 1.96$).

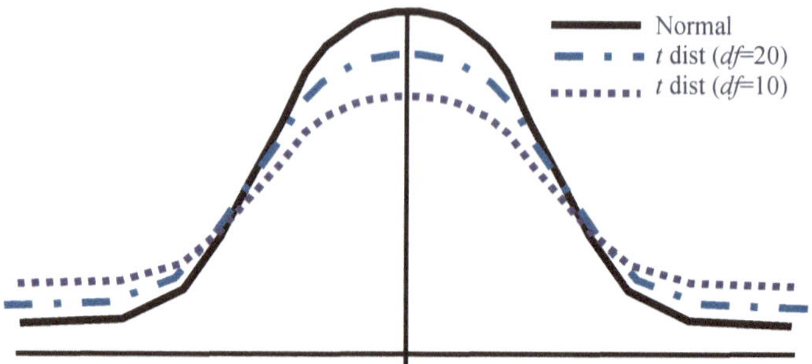


**Figure 7.1**
*The t Distribution Approximating the Normal Distribution*

## Determining Significance with *t*

- Statistical significance indicates that the probability of finding significance out of error or chance is quite low and therefore is likely to occur in the population.
- The process for determining significance is different if you are completing hand calculations or interpreting statistical output.

| | Comparison | Significance? | Decision? | Conclusion |
|---|---|---|---|---|
| Hand Calculations | $t_{calculated} > t_{critical}$ | Significance! | Reject Null | Restate Alternative |
| | $t_{calculated} \leq t_{critical}$ | Not! | Fail to Reject Null | Restate Null |
| Computer | $p <$ alpha | Significance! | Reject Null | Restate Alternative |
| | $p \geq$ alpha | Not! | Fail to Reject Null | Restate Null |

**Note:** $t_{calculated} > t_{critical}$ comparison is using a positive $t_{critical}$. If $t_{critical}$ is negative, then $t_{calculated}$ would need to be less than $t_{critical}$ in order to be significant.

## Hand Calculations

- Determining significance with **Hand Calculations** requires the following steps:
  1. Determine $t_{critical}$—use the $t$ Distribution Table (see Appendix C).
  2. Compare $t_{calculated}$ to $t_{critical}$ to determine significance.
     - $t_{calculated}$ must exceed $t_{critical}$ to be significant.
  3. Make decision regarding null.

### Example

**Determining significance w/Hand Calculations**

**1. Determine $t_{critical}$:** for our example,

- $\alpha$=.05 has already been established;
- The sample is predicted to be higher than the norm, so this is a one-tailed test; and
- $df$ = 36 – 1 = 35

Using that information, we can go to our $t$ Distribution Table. Using $df$=30 (since $t$ values for $df$=35 is not provided), $t_{critical}$ is identified as +1.697.

**2. Compare $t_{calculated}$ to $t_{critical}$:**

Since the researcher is predicting that the extrovert's mean will be greater the norm, $t_{calculated}$ needs to be higher than $t_{critical}$ to be significant, which is the case since $t_{calculated}$ = 2.34 is higher than 1.697.

**3. Decision?**

Significant→Reject the Null

| *df* | Proportion in one tail | | | |
|---|---|---|---|---|
| | 0.05 | 0.025 | 0.01 | 0.005 |
| | Proportion in two tails | | | |
| | 0.10 | 0.05 | 0.02 | 0.01 |
| 27 | 1.703 | 2.052 | 2.473 | 2.771 |
| 28 | 1.701 | 2.048 | 2.467 | 2.763 |
| 29 | 1.699 | 2.045 | 2.462 | 2.756 |
| 30 | 1.697 | 2.042 | 2.457 | 2.750 |
| 40 | 1.684 | 2.021 | 2.423 | 2.704 |
| 60 | 1.671 | 2.000 | 2.390 | 2.660 |
| 120 | 1.658 | 1.980 | 2.358 | 2.617 |
| ∞ | 1.645 | 1.960 | 2.326 | 2.576 |

## Computer Output

- Determining significance with `Computer Output` requires the following steps:
  1. Identify $p$-value in output.
  2. Compare $p$-value to alpha ($\alpha$) to determine significance.
     - $p$-value must be less than the alpha level to be significant.
  3. Make decision regarding null.

- **Output Differences**

**SPSS Output**

- Identifies $p$-value as Sig (2-tailed)
- Only conducts 2-tailed test
  - For 1-tailed test, divide $p$ in half.
- Confidence interval differences are automatically calculated

**One-Sample Statistics**

| | N | Mean | Std. Deviation | Std. Error Mean |
|---|---|---|---|---|
| words | 36 | 19226.6667 | 8279.98880 | 1379.99813 |

**One-Sample Test**

| | Test Value = 16000 | | | | | |
|---|---|---|---|---|---|---|
| | | | | | 95% Confidence Interval of the Difference | |
| | t | df | Sig. (2-tailed) | Mean Difference | Lower | Upper |
| words | 2.338 | 35 | .025 | 3226.66667 | 425.1215 | 6028.2118 |

### Example

**Determining significance w/Computer Output**

**1. Identify p-value in output**

- If you using SPSS and conducting a one-tailed test, be sure to divide p-value in half (.025/2=.0125)
- $p$=.0125

**2. Compare $p$-value to alpha**

$p$-value must be less than or equal to alpha to be significant.

- $p$ of .0125 is less than a of .05.

**3. Decision?**

Significant→Reject the Null

**StatCrunch Output**

- Can conduct both one and two-tailed tests
- Confidence intervals are a separate analysis

**Hypothesis test results:**

μ : Mean of variable

$H_0$ : μ = 16000

$H_A$ : μ > 16000

| Variable | Sample Mean | Std. Err. | DF | T-Stat | P-value |
|---|---|---|---|---|---|
| words | 19226.667 | 1379.9981 | 35 | 2.3381674 | 0.0126 |

**95% confidence interval results:**

μ : Mean of variable

| Variable | Sample Mean | Std. Err. | DF | L. Limit | U. Limit |
|---|---|---|---|---|---|
| words | 19226.667 | 1379.9981 | 35 | 16425.122 | 22028.212 |

**Assumptions of the t test:** independent observations, normal population

## 7.22V Estimation with *t* Test of Single Sample

- A ***confidence interval*** allows us to estimate a range of values in which the population mean is likely to fall with a certain degree of confidence.
- Calculate a confidence interval when you:
  - have found significance in the hypothesis test,
  - know there is an effect, or
  - just want some basic information about the unknown population.
- Recall the equation for calculating a 95% confidence interval for a *z* test.

$$\mu = M \pm z\sigma_m = M \pm 1.96\sigma_m$$

- The equation for calculating a confidence interval for a *t* test is similar.

$$\mu = M \pm ts_m$$

- Since the *t* distribution is influenced by degrees of freedom, the estimated *t* value will always differ depending upon the sample size.

### Hand Calculations

- To calculate a 95% confidence interval, you will need to know:
  - sample mean ($M$),
  - estimated *t* statistic at $\alpha$=.05 (this is $t_{critical}$ for a two-tailed test)
  - estimated standard error.
- To estimate the lower and upper bounds of the population mean, we are looking in both tails of our distribution. Therefore, you will always need to determine $t_{critical}$ for a two-tailed test, even if you are conducting a one-tailed hypothesis test.

### Computer Output

- You can select 95% or 99% confidence intervals.
- SPSS and StatCrunch present confidence intervals differently.

SPSS presents the confidence interval for the difference between the sample mean and the population mean.

- lower bound = lower difference + $\mu$
- upper bound= upper difference + $\mu$
- SPSS calculates the confidence interval around $\mu$; hand calculations compute the interval around $M$.

**One-Sample Test**

| | Test Value = 16000 | | | | | |
|---|---|---|---|---|---|---|
| | | | | | 95% Confidence Interval of the Difference | |
| | t | df | Sig. (2-tailed) | Mean Difference | Lower | Upper |
| words | 2.338 | 35 | .025 | 3226.66667 | 425.1215 | 6028.2118 |

StatCrunch presents the lower and upper bounds in the output—no extra calculation is needed!

**95% confidence interval results:**
μ : Mean of variable

| Variable | Sample Mean | Std. Err. | DF | L. Limit | U. Limit |
|---|---|---|---|---|---|
| words | 19226.667 | 1379.9981 | 35 | 16425.122 | 22028.212 |

## Example

### Confidence Intervals with Hand Calculations

We have already determined that:

- $M$ = 19,227, $s_m$ = 1,380

Previously we also determined that $t_{critical}$ for a one-tailed test at .05 was 1.697. However, a confidence interval is always two-tailed, so we need to utilize the *t* Distribution Table to identify a two-tailed $t_{critical}$ at .05 and $df$=36.

- $t_{critical}$ = ±2.457

Using this information, our 95% confidence interval is:

$\mu$ = 19,227 ± 2.457(1,380)

$\mu$ = 19,227 ± 2,818

- 95% CI: 16,409 to 22,045

### Confidence Intervals w/ SPSS

- Identify the lower and upper differences.
- To calculate lower bound, add the lower difference (425.12) to the population mean ($\mu$=16,000).
  - Lower bound = 425.12 + 16,000 = 16,425.12
- To calculate upper bound, add the upper difference (6028.21) to the population mean ($\mu$=16,000)
  - Upper bound = 6028.21 + 16,000 = 22,028.21
- 95% CI: 16,425.12 to 22,028.21

---

- Notice the difference in hand calculations and computer output. This difference is due to hand calculations using a *df* of 30 for the *t* Distribution Table. The computer output will usually be more accurate since the probability is calculated at the exact percent.
  - Hand calculation: 16,409 to 22,045
  - Computer Output: 16,425.12 to 22,028.21

## 7.23V Effect Size and Power

### Effect Size

- Hypothesis testing is only an indication of "significance"—the likelihood of obtaining the result out of error or chance.
- A significant effect does not indicate the size of the effect.
- Calculate and report an effect size when you:
  - have found significance or
  - know of an effect and want to determine the size of the effect.
- The most basic measure of effect size associated with a *t* test is Cohen's *d*, which measures the mean difference in terms of the standard deviation.

$$\text{Cohen's } d = \frac{M-\mu}{SD}$$

  - If you are using StatCrunch, you will need to convert the estimated standard error (*SE*) to the sample standard deviation ($s = s_M\sqrt{n}$) in order to compute Cohen's *d*.

> **Example**
>
> **Effect Size**
>
> We have already determined:
> *M* = 19,227, *SD* = 8,280, μ = 16,000
>
> Using these values, we calculate Cohen's *d* as follows:
>
> $\text{Cohen's } d = \frac{19{,}227-16{,}000}{8{,}280} = .39$
>
> This value indicates a medium effect.

### Power

- Using effect size, sample size (*n*), alpha level, and number of tails, we can calculate the power of our study.
- Statistical power of a study is the probability that the study will produce statistically significant results if the hypothesis is true (or we reject the null).
- Power may be determined prior to conducting a study so that the study may be improved.
- Power may also be calculated after conducting a study to determine the practical significance of the results, whether we have found significance or not.
- Cohen recommends a minimum power of .80 or 80%.

**Figure 7.5** *Statistical Power of the t Test of a Single Sample (α=.05)*

| Sample Size | Effect Size Small (<.20) | Medium (.50) | Large (>.80) |
|---|---|---|---|
| Two-tailed test | | | |
| 10 | .08 | .26 | .60 |
| 20 | .13 | .56 | .92 |
| 30 | .18 | .75 | .99 |
| 40 | .23 | .87 | * |
| 50 | .28 | .93 | * |
| 100 | .51 | * | * |
| One-tailed test | | | |
| 10 | .13 | .40 | .75 |
| 20 | .21 | .69 | .96 |
| 30 | .28 | .86 | .99 |
| 40 | .34 | .93 | * |
| 50 | .40 | .97 | * |
| 100 | .63 | * | * |

*Nearly 1.

> **Example**
>
> **Power**
>
> We have already determined that:
> - *n=36*
> - *p< .05, one-tailed*
> - *Cohen's d=.39 (medium effect)*
>
> Using Figure 7.5, we can approximate statistical power as .86, which indicates that we have a .86 probability of achieving a significant result if the hypothesis is true.
>
> This meets Cohen's recommendation for power of .80.

## 7.24V Reporting of Results

Results statement for a *t* test combines a concluding sentence and statistical results notation. The following parts are typically included (with example results):

- Conclusion indicating relationship between variables and sample and significance of test
- Sample mean and standard deviation; *M* = 19,227, *SD* = 8,280
- $t_{calculated}$ with the degrees of freedom in parentheses; *t*(35) = 2.75
- Alpha level or *p*-value; *p*< .05 or *p*=.0125
- Indication of direction as in the number of tails (one-tailed)
- Effect size: Cohen's *d* = .39
- 95% CI of population: 95% CI [16,425, 22,028] or of difference: 95% CI of Difference [425, 6028]
- Since computer results are typically used, the actual *p*-value is usually reported.

> **Example**
>
> **Results Statement**
>
> Extrovert college students **(*M*=19,227, *SD* = 8,280)** talk significantly more words per day than the population norm of **μ=16,000; *t*(35)=2.34, *p*=.0125, one-tailed, Cohen's *d*=.39, 95% CI [16,425 and 22,028].**

## 7.25V A Complete Example

Throughout this text, we will be applying the following the steps for hypothesis testing:

**Step 1: Develop hypotheses**
- Identify variables
- Determine if it is a one-tailed or two-tailed test.
- State alternative hypothesis
- State null hypothesis
- Develop hypotheses notation

**Step 2: Establish significance criteria**
**Step 3: Calculate test statistic, confidence interval, effect size, and power**
**Step 4: Draw conclusion**

**Scenario:** A social psychologist is interested in determining if recent unemployment due to being fired impacts one's trait anger, the extent of experiencing angry feelings over time. Fifteen individuals ($n$=15) who have been unemployed in the last six months are randomly selected. Participants complete the State Trait Anger Expression Inventory-2 (Spielberger, 1999) which has a population mean ($\mu$) of 25. Do individuals who have been recently fired from employment significantly differ in trait anger than the norm? Test at the .01.

Data: 32, 25, 35, 28, 40, 23, 45, 19, 28, 17, 30, 50, 28, 39, 31

| | N | Mean | Std. Deviation | Std. Error Mean |
|---|---|---|---|---|
| Anger | 15 | 31.3333 | 9.20145 | 2.37580 |

| | Test Value = 25 | | | | | |
|---|---|---|---|---|---|---|
| | | | | | 99% Confidence Interval of the Difference | |
| | t | df | Sig. (2-tailed) | Mean Difference | Lower | Upper |
| VAR00001 | 2.666 | 14 | .018 | 6.33333 | -.7391 | 13.4057 |

**Step 1: Develop Hypotheses**

a. Independent Variable = Scale: Categorical Quantitative

b. Dependent Variable = Scale: Categorical Quantitative

c. Circle: One-tailed Two-tailed

d. Alternative hypothesis in sentence form.

e. Null hypothesis in sentence form.

f. Write the alternative and null hypotheses using correct notation. $H_1$: $H_0$:

**Step 2: Establish significance criteria** g. $\alpha$ =

**Step 3: Calculate test statistic, effect size, confidence interval, and power**

h. $t_{calculated}$ = Level of significance ($p$) =

i. Decision: reject null or fail to reject null

j. Calculate effect size =

k. Determine the 99% confidence interval:

l. Determine power for the study.

**Step 4: Draw conclusion**

m. Write your conclusion in sentence form including appropriate results notation.

## 7.26V Additional Practice

1. The company of Google has a unique work environment: flexible scheduling, employee lounges, free food, exercise facilities, day care. Does a supportive work environment impact a sense of well-being among its employees? A random sample of Google employees ($n$=14) complete the Friedman Well-Being Scale ($\mu$=50). The sample generated the data below. A $t$-test of single sample was conducted at the .05 level using SPSS.

**Data:** 60, 55, 62, 58, 50, 49, 66, 53, 57, 52, 46, 72, 67, 55

**One-Sample Statistics**

| | N | Mean | Std. Deviation | Std. Error Mean |
|---|---|---|---|---|
| VAR00001 | 14 | 57.2857 | 7.45684 | 1.99292 |

**One-Sample Test**

| | Test Value = 50 | | | | | |
|---|---|---|---|---|---|---|
| | | | | | 95% Confidence Interval of the Difference | |
| | t | df | Sig. (2-tailed) | Mean Difference | Lower | Upper |
| VAR00001 | 3.656 | 13 | .003 | 7.28571 | 2.9803 | 11.5912 |

**Step 1: Develop Hypotheses**

a. Independent Variable = Scale: Categorical Quantitative

b. Dependent Variable = Scale: Categorical Quantitative

c. Circle: One-tailed Two-tailed

d. Alternative hypothesis in sentence form.

e. Null hypothesis in sentence form.

f. Write the alternative and null hypotheses using correct notation.

$H_1$: $H_0$:

**Step 2: Establish significance criteria**

g. $\alpha$ =

**Step 3: Calculate test statistic, effect size, confidence interval, and power**

h. $t_{calculated}$ = Level of significance ($p$) =

i. Decision: reject null or fail to reject null

j. Calculate effect size =

k. Determine the 95% confidence interval:

l. Determine power for the study. Explain what this means for your ability to generalize your results to the population.

**Step 4: Draw conclusion**

m. Write your conclusion in sentence form including appropriate results notation.

2. A college counselor is interested in determining if college students who have reported strong spiritual convictions experience more meaning and purpose in life than the norm. A sample of 20 undergraduate students ($M$=110.85, $SD$=11.5) complete the Purpose in Life Test (Crumbaugh, 1968) that has been standardized for college undergraduate students ($\mu$=109). Conduct a $t$-test of single sample with $\alpha$ = .05.

**Data:** 104, 106, 110, 115, 100, 96, 120, 125, 135, 111, 122, 101, 113, 95, 133, 99, 108, 115, 106, 103

**One sample T hypothesis test:**
μ : Mean of variable
$H_0$ : μ = 109
$H_A$ : μ > 109
**Hypothesis test results:**

| Variable | Sample Mean | Std. Err. | DF | T-Stat | P-value |
|---|---|---|---|---|---|
| purpose | 110.85 | 2.5713758 | 19 | 0.7194592 | 0.2403 |

**One sample T confidence interval:**
μ : Mean of variable
**95% confidence interval results:**

| Variable | Sample Mean | Std. Err. | DF | L. Limit | U. Limit |
|---|---|---|---|---|---|
| purpose | 110.85 | 2.5713758 | 19 | 105.46805 | 116.23195 |

**Power Results**

| Required parameters: | | Enter all but one: | |
|---|---|---|---|
| Alpha: | 0.05 | Difference, μ - μ0: | 1.85 |
| Std. dev.: | 11.5 | Power: | 0.17084184 |
| Alternative: | μ > μ0 | Sample size: | 20 |

**Step 1: Develop Hypotheses**

a. Independent Variable = Scale: Categorical Quantitative

b. Dependent Variable = Scale: Categorical Quantitative

c. Circle: One-tailed Two-tailed

d. Alternative hypothesis in sentence form.

e. Null hypothesis in sentence form.

f. Write the alternative and null hypotheses using correct notation.

$H_1$: $H_0$:

**Step 2: Establish significance criteria**

g. $\alpha$ =

**Step 3: Calculate test statistic, effect size, confidence interval, and power**

h. $t_{calculated}$ = Level of significance ($p$) =

i. Decision: reject null or fail to reject null

j. Calculate effect size =

k. Determine the 95% confidence interval:

l. Determine power for the study. Explain what this means for your ability to generalize your results to the population.

**Step 4: Draw conclusion**

m. Write your conclusion in sentence form including appropriate results notation.

## 7.27 Activity: Chips Ahoy

Answers.com claims that Chips Ahoy cookies average 23 chocolate chips per cookie. This activity seeks to explore the following research question: Does the generic brand of Original Chips Ahoy significantly differ from the Chips Ahoy average of 23 chips per cookie? Test at $\alpha$=.05.

**Directions:**

1. Purchase a package of generic Chips Ahoy Original cookies.
2. Count the number of chips in at least 6 cookies, more would certainly be better. Here are some suggestions:
   - Crush a cookie, then count the number of chips. Record the number of chips in the table.
   - Repeat until you achieve your desired sample size.
   - Ask some friends to help!
3. Enter your data into SPSS or StatCrunch. Use 23 as the population mean.
4. Complete the process below.

| Cookie | # of Chips |
|---|---|
| 1 | |
| 2 | |
| 3 | |
| 4 | |
| 5 | |
| 6 | |
| 7 | |
| 8 | |
| 9 | |
| 10 | |

**Step 1: Develop Hypotheses**

a. Independent Variable = Scale: Categorical Quantitative

b. Dependent Variable = Scale: Categorical Quantitative

c. Circle: One-tailed Two-tailed

d. Alternative hypothesis in sentence form.

e. Null hypothesis in sentence form.

f. Write the alternative and null hypotheses using correct notation.

$H_1$: $H_0$:

**Step 2: Establish significance criteria**

g. $\alpha$ =

**Step 3: Calculate test statistic, effect size, confidence interval, and power**

h. $t_{calculated}$ = Level of significance ($p$) =

i. Decision: reject null or fail to reject null

j. Calculate effect size =

k. Determine the 95% confidence interval:

l. Determine power for the study. Explain what this means for your ability to generalize your results to the population.

**Step 4: Draw conclusion**

m. Write your conclusion in sentence form including appropriate results notation.

## 7.28V In the Literature

Most published research studies are presenting results from multiple hypothesis tests. That is the case for the excerpt presented below. Perry et al. conducted a total of 15 single sample *t*-tests, results of which are presented in a table. The first few lines of Perry's table is presented to demonstrate a few concepts. Notice the column headings identify sample means and standard deviations, the national norms, the *t*-statistic, the *p*-value, degree of freedom, and effect size for each test.

| Skill Area | Institution | | National | | *t* | *p* | *df* | Effect Size |
|---|---|---|---|---|---|---|---|---|
| | *M* | *SD* | μ | σ | | | | |
| Summarize pattern of results. | 0.79 | 0.41 | 0.67 | 0.46 | 2.50 | .02* | 72 | 0.29 |
| Provide alternatives for spurious associations. | 1.59 | 0.74 | 1.56 | 0.86 | 0.31 | .79 | 74 | 0.04 |
| Provide alternatives for results. | 1.31 | 0.85 | 1.35 | 1.04 | -0.44 | .72 | 74 | 0.04 |

- The authors report *p*-values and use asterisks (*) to indicate significance. Most researchers will use *p*-values or asterisks—not both, since the reader knows that a *p*-value of .05 or less is significant. As such, most researchers will report either the *t* statistic with an asterisk (i.e., 2.50*) or the *t* statistic with the *p*-value (no asterisks included).
- The 3rd skill area generates a negative *t* statistic since the sample mean is lower than the population norm.

**Excerpt from:** Perry, D. K., Retallick, M. S., & Paulsen, T. H. (2014). A critical thinking benchmark for a Department of Agricultural Education and Studies. *Journal of Agricultural Education, 55*(5), 207-221.

Critical thinking, problem solving, and communications are skills in high demand for nearly every career in today's job market. The purpose of this study was to examine the critical thinking abilities of students majoring in agricultural education and studies in comparison to national norms. A random sample of 75 senior-level undergraduates majoring in agricultural education completed a Critical Thinking Assessment Test (CAT) during the spring 2013 semester.

The CAT measures four broad domains—evaluate and interpret information, problem solving, creative thinking, and effective communications—and utilizes 14 items that assess specific skill areas. Single sample *t*-tests were conducted to compare sample means to the national norms for each skill area and the CAT total score. Effect size using Cohen's *d* was also calculated. In comparison to the national norm, participants scored statistically higher ($p < .05$) on one skill area and statistically lower ($p < .05$) on four skill areas. In addition, participants scored significantly lower on the CAT total score.

**Table 1.** *t*-Test Results for Critical Thinking Skill Areas

| Skill Area | Institution | | National | | *t* | *p* | *df* | Effect Size |
|---|---|---|---|---|---|---|---|---|
| | *M* | *SD* | μ | σ | | | | |
| Summarize pattern of results. | 0.79 | 0.41 | 0.67 | 0.46 | 2.50 | .02* | 72 | 0.29 |
| Provide alternatives for spurious associations. | 1.59 | 0.74 | 1.56 | 0.86 | 0.31 | .79 | 74 | 0.04 |
| Provide alternatives for results. | 1.31 | 0.85 | 1.35 | 1.04 | -0.44 | .72 | 74 | 0.04 |
| Use basic mathematical skills to solve a problem. | 0.77 | 0.42 | 0.82 | 0.41 | -0.96 | .33 | 74 | 0.12 |
| Separate relevant from irrelevant information. | 3.07 | 1.02 | 3.14 | 0.92 | -0.61 | .50 | 73 | 0.07 |
| Evaluate strength of correlational-type data. | 1.14 | 1.13 | 1.21 | 1.13 | -0.04 | .57 | 73 | 0.06 |
| Evaluate whether information supports a hypothesis. | 0.64 | 0.48 | 0.73 | 0.44 | -1.68 | .07 | 73 | 0.20 |
| Identify solutions for a problem. | 1.07 | 0.85 | 1.18 | 1.03 | -1.14 | .35 | 73 | 0.12 |
| Determine whether an inference is supported by information. | 0.56 | 0.50 | 0.68 | 0.41 | -2.08 | .01* | 74 | 0.26 |
| Use/apply relevant information. | 0.99 | 0.76 | 1.11 | 0.64 | -1.40 | .10 | 74 | 0.17 |
| Explain how changes might affect a solution. | 0.88 | 1.04 | 1.15 | 1.06 | -2.30 | .03* | 74 | 0.26 |
| Identify the best solution. | 1.98 | 1.79 | 2.29 | 1.81 | -1.49 | .14 | 72 | 0.17 |
| Identify additional information. | 0.31 | 0.46 | 0.82 | 0.68 | -9.58 | <.01* | 74 | 0.88 |
| Provide relevant alternative interpretations. | 0.41 | 0.57 | 0.93 | 0.74 | -7.83 | <.01* | 74 | 0.78 |
| CAT total score | 16.42 | 4.15 | 19.04 | 6.04 | -5.48 | <.01* | 74 | 0.51 |

*significant at $p<.05$.

Use the Perry et al. excerpt to complete the following questions.

1. In which skill area did the sample score significantly higher than the norm? What was the $p$-value for this test?

2. In what four skill areas did the sample score significantly lower than the norm?

3. For the hypothesis test for the CAT total score,
   a. What is your decision regarding the null?

   b. Write the concluding statement with results notation.

4. Notice that the authors report the national mean and standard deviation. So if they know the population standard deviation, why didn't they conduct a $z$-test instead of a $t$-test?

5. Which skill area generated the greatest effect size? Based upon this value, is the effect small, moderate, or large?

6. These results are based upon a random sample of seniors majoring in agricultural education. In comparison to national norms, do these students have adequate critical thinking skills?

## 7.29 Using the Computer

**SPSS Step by Step Instructions**

1. Enter dependent variable data in first column.
2. Within the data window, ☝ the **`Analyze`** menu.
3. Select **`Compare Means`** and **`Single Sample t`**
4. ☝ the dependent variable and move under **`Test Variable(s)`** (see Figure 5).
5. Type in population mean in `Test Value:`
6. ☝ `Options` **IF** you want change the confidence interval from 95% to 99%.
7. ☝ `OK.`

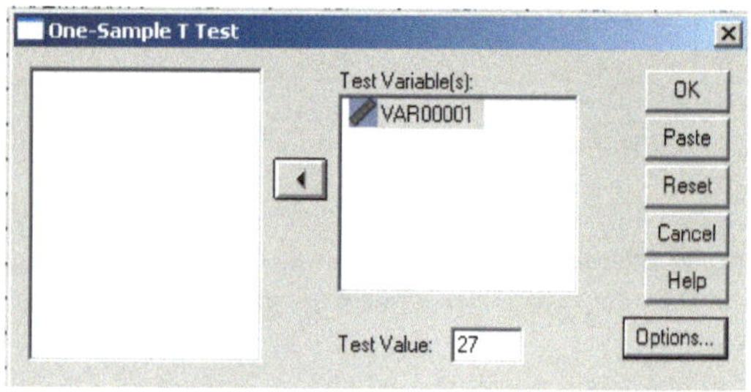


**StatCrunch Step by Step Instructions**

1. Enter dependent variable data in first column.
2. Within the data window, ☝ the **Stat** menu, select **T Stats >One Sample >with Data**.
3. Within One Sample T dialogue box, under **Select Column(s)**, ☝ your dependent variable.
4. Under **Perform:** select <u>one</u> of the options:

   **Hypothesis Test for μ**

   - By $H_0$ indicate population mean
   - By $H_A$ indicate the direction of test

   **Confidence Interval for μ**

   - Indicate percent of confidence (95% is default)

5. ☝ **Compute.**

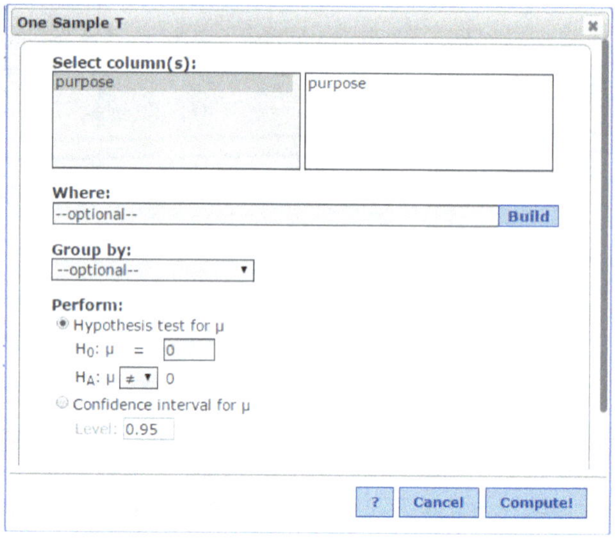


**StatCrunch** also has a power and sample size calculator. Data does not need to be entered in the data columns. To examine **Power** <u>after the fact</u>:

1. Within the data window, ☝ the **Stat** menu, select **T Stats >One Sample> Power/Sample Size**.
2. Under **Required parameters**, enter alpha of .05, the sample *SD*, and the number of tails (>, <, or ≠).
3. Under **Enter all but one:** enter the difference between the μ and *M*, and the sample size. Leave Power blank! ☝ **Compute**.

To determine the **minimum sample** <u>a-priori</u>:

1. Within the data window, ☝ the **Stat** menu, select **T Stats >One Sample> Power/Sample Size.**
4. Under **Required parameters**, enter alpha of .05, the sample *SD*, and the number of tails (>, <, or ≠).
5. Under **Enter all but one:** enter the difference between the μ and *M*, and Power of .80. Leave Sample Size blank! ☝ **Compute**.

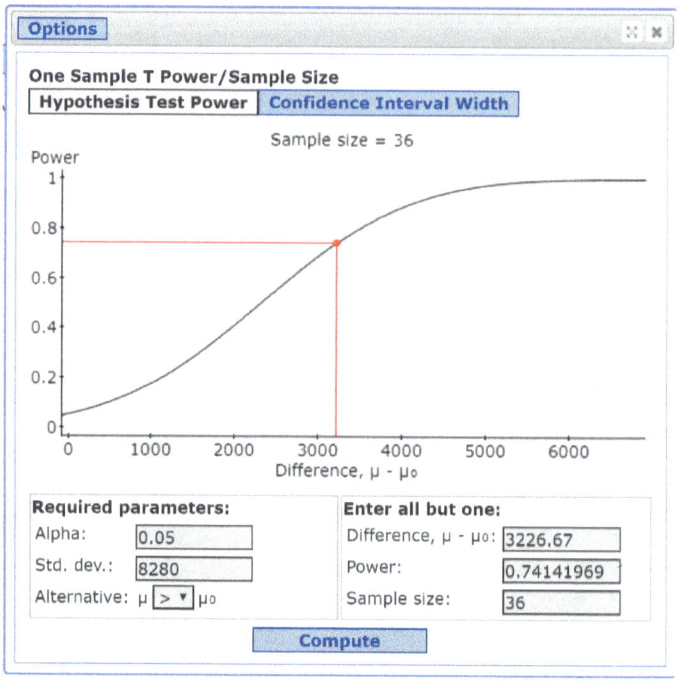

## 7.30 Exercises
### Reviewing Concepts

1. What is the primary difference between a $z$ test and a $t$ test?

2. Why do we have to "estimate" standard error when calculating a $t$ test?

3. If you are conducting a $t$ test of single sample, how large does our sample size need to be in order for the $t$ distribution to normalize and be equivalent to a $z$ distribution?

4. You are conducting a two-tailed $t$ test. Your computer output has generated a $p$-value of .0134. If you are using significance criteria of $\alpha$=.05, do you have significance? If you are using $\alpha$=.01, do you have significance? Explain your reasons for both decisions.

5. You are conducting a one-tailed $t$ test at $\alpha$=.01 by hand in which you are predicting that your sample mean will be significantly <u>less than</u> the population norm. You have generated the following so far: $df$=13, $t$= 3.29. What is $t_{critical}$? Do you have significance? Explain.

6. A confidence interval estimates the treatment effect in the population by calculating an interval in which the population mean is likely to fall. When we increase our confidence from 95% to 99%, what happens to the interval? Explain.

7. How does effect size differ from a $t$ test result?

## Interpreting Results

8. A group of 4th grade students ($n$=49) receive a semester course on test taking skills and reading strategies. At the end of the semester, students complete the statewide 4th grade reading exam ($M$=73, $SD$=6.27). Do course participants significantly outperform the population norm ($\mu$=71) on the statewide 4th grade reading exam? Do students who receive this special curriculum score significantly different from the population norm? Test at the .05 level.

**One-Sample Statistics**

| | N | Mean | Std. Deviation | Std. Error Mean |
|---|---|---|---|---|
| VAR00001 | 49 | 72.9592 | 6.26817 | .89545 |

**One-Sample Test**

| | Test Value = 71 | | | | | |
|---|---|---|---|---|---|---|
| | | | | | 95% Confidence Interval of the Difference | |
| | t | df | Sig. (2-tailed) | Mean Difference | Lower | Upper |
| VAR00001 | 2.188 | 48 | .034 | 1.95918 | .1588 | 3.7596 |

**Step 1: Develop Hypotheses**

a. Independent Variable = Scale: Categorical Quantitative

b. Dependent Variable = Scale: Categorical Quantitative

c. Circle: One-tailed Two-tailed

d. Alternative hypothesis in sentence form.

e. Null hypothesis in sentence form.

f. Write the alternative and null hypotheses using correct notation.

$H_1$: $H_0$:

**Step 2: Establish significance criteria**

g. $\alpha$ =

**Step 3: Calculate test statistic, effect size, confidence interval, and power**

h. $t_{calculated}$ = Level of significance ($p$) =

i. Decision: reject null or fail to reject null

j. Calculate effect size =

k. Determine the 95% confidence interval:

l. Determine power for the study. Explain what this means for your ability to generalize your results to the population.

**Step 4: Draw conclusion**

m. Write your conclusion in sentence form including appropriate results notation.

9. The National Sleep Foundation (sleepfoundation.org) recommends that young adults, age 18-25 years, should sleep at least 7 hours per night. A university dean of students is concerned that his students are sleep deprived. He randomly selects 100 undergraduate students and has them record their sleep times for a week. Can the dean conclude that his college students ($M$=6.15, $SD$=1.25) are sleeping significantly less than the recommended 7 hours? A one-tailed $t$-test of single sample using StatCrunch ($\alpha$=.05) was conducted.

**Hypothesis test results:**
μ : Mean of population
$H_0$: μ = 7
$H_A$: μ ≠ 7

| Mean | Sample Mean | Std. Err. | DF | T-Stat | P-value |
|---|---|---|---|---|---|
| μ | 6.15 | 0.125 | 99 | -6.8 | <0.0001 |

**95% confidence interval results:**
μ : Mean of population

| Mean | Sample Mean | Std. Err. | DF | L. Limit | U. Limit |
|---|---|---|---|---|---|
| μ | 6.15 | 0.125 | 99 | 5.902 | 6.398 |

**Step 1: Develop Hypotheses**

a. Independent Variable = Scale: Categorical Quantitative

b. Dependent Variable = Scale: Categorical Quantitative

c. Circle: One-tailed Two-tailed

d. Alternative hypothesis in sentence form.

e. Null hypothesis in sentence form.

f. Write the alternative and null hypotheses using correct notation.

$H_1$: $H_0$:

**Step 2: Establish significance criteria**

g. $\alpha$ =

**Step 3: Calculate test statistic, effect size, confidence interval, and power**

h. $t_{calculated}$ = Level of significance ($p$) =

i. Decision: reject null or fail to reject null

j. Calculate effect size =

k. Determine the 95% confidence interval:

l. Determine power for the study. Explain what this means for your ability to generalize your results to the population.

**Step 4: Draw conclusion**

m. Write your conclusion in sentence form including appropriate results notation.

10. A dietician performs an experiment to determine if lab rats will eat more than the norm when the temperature is lower. In a 72 degrees Fahrenheit climate, the rats eat an average of 21 grams of food per day. When the temperature is reduced to 50 degrees, the sample of 20 rats eats approximately 28 grams of food per day ($M$=28.1, $SD$ =2.88). Does the change in temperature significantly increase the amount of food that rats eat per day when compared to the norm? Test at the .01 level.

**One-Sample Statistics**

| | N | Mean | Std. Deviation | Std. Error Mean |
|---|---|---|---|---|
| VAR00001 | 20 | 28.1000 | 2.88189 | .64441 |

**One-Sample Test**

| | Test Value = 21 | | | | | |
|---|---|---|---|---|---|---|
| | | | | | 99% Confidence Interval of the Difference | |
| | t | df | Sig. (2-tailed) | Mean Difference | Lower | Upper |
| VAR00001 | 11.018 | 19 | .000 | 7.10000 | 5.2564 | 8.9436 |

**Step 1: Develop Hypotheses**

a. Independent Variable = Scale: Categorical Quantitative

b. Dependent Variable = Scale: Categorical Quantitative

c. Circle: One-tailed Two-tailed

d. Alternative hypothesis in sentence form.

e. Null hypothesis in sentence form.

f. Write the alternative and null hypotheses using correct notation.

$H_1$: $H_0$:

**Step 2: Establish significance criteria**

g. $\alpha$ =

**Step 3: Calculate test statistic, effect size, confidence interval, and power**

h. $t_{\text{calculated}}$ = Level of significance ($p$) =

i. Decision: reject null or fail to reject null

j. Calculate effect size =

k. Determine the 95% confidence interval:

l. Determine power for the study. Explain what this means for your ability to generalize your results to the population.

**Step 4: Draw conclusion**

m. Write your conclusion in sentence form including appropriate results notation.

11. Use the excerpt to complete the questions.

**Research excerpt from:** Kruger, J. & Dunning, D. (1999). Unskilled and unaware of it: How difficulties in recognizing one's own incompetence lead to inflated self-assessments. *Journal of Personality and Social Psychology, 77* (6), 1121-1134.

Incompetent individuals lack the skill of *metacognition* (Everson & Tobias, 1998), the ability to know how well one is performing, when one is likely to be accurate in judgment, and when one is likely to be in error. Incompetent individuals, compared with their more competent peers, will dramatically overestimate their ability and performance relative to objective criteria. This study explores people's perceptions of their competence in a domain of humor that requires sophisticated knowledge and wisdom about the tastes and reactions of other people. To anticipate what is and what others will find funny, one must have subtle and tacit knowledge about other people's tastes.

Sixty-five ($n$=65) undergraduate students were presented with a series of jokes and asked to rate the humor of each one. We then compared their ratings with those provided by a panel of experts, namely, professional comedians who make their living by recognizing what is funny and reporting it to their audiences. By comparing each participant's ratings with those of our expert panel, we could roughly assess participants' ability to spot humor. Participants rated each joke on the same 11-point scale used by the comedians. Afterward, participants compared their "ability to recognize what's funny" with that of the average Cornell student by providing a percentile ranking. In this and in all subsequent studies, we explained that percentile rankings could range from 0 *(I'm at the very bottom)* to 50 *(I'm exactly average)* to 99 *(I'm at the very top).* Our prediction was that participants overall would overestimate their ability to tell what is funny relative to their peers. To find out whether this was the case, we first assigned each participant a percentile rank based on the extent to which his or her joke ratings correlated with the ratings provided by our panel of professionals (with higher correlations corresponding to better performance). On average, participants put their ability to recognize what is funny in the 66th percentile, which exceeded the actual mean percentile (50, by definition) by 16 percentile points, one-sample $t(64) = 7.02$, $p<.0001$.

a. What is the alternative hypothesis that is being tested?

b. Write the hypothesis notation.

c. What is the population norm value that is being compared to the sample mean?

d. Write the concluding statement (including results notation).

e. Based upon the presented results, are you able to calculate effect size? Why or why not?

## Conducting the Analysis

Utilize SPSS or StatCrunch to conduct the following analyses.

12. A psychologist studies 21 individuals (age 40-55 years) who gamble at slot machines at least once per month. She is interested in determining if gamblers have higher levels of positive thinking or optimism than the norm. Participants complete the Attributional Style Questionnaire (Peterson, et al., 1982), which measures positive thinking and has a mean for middle aged adults of $\mu=5$. Test at the .01 level.

    Data: 4, 6, 5, 8, 7, 8, 7, 5, 5, 6, 7, 4, 7, 8, 6, 5, 5, 4, 3, 5, 6

**Step 1: Develop Hypotheses**

a. Independent Variable = Scale: Categorical Quantitative

b. Dependent Variable = Scale: Categorical Quantitative

c. Circle: One-tailed Two-tailed

d. Alternative hypothesis in sentence form.

e. Null hypothesis in sentence form.

f. Write the alternative and null hypotheses using correct notation.

$H_1$: $H_0$:

**Step 2: Establish significance criteria**

g. $\alpha$ =

**Step 3: Calculate test statistic, effect size, confidence interval, and power**

h. $t_{\text{calculated}}$ = Level of significance ($p$) =

i. Decision: reject null or fail to reject null

j. Calculate effect size =

k. Determine the 99% confidence interval:

l. Determine power for the study. Explain what this means for your ability to generalize your results to the population.

**Step 4: Draw conclusion**

m. Write your conclusion in sentence form including appropriate results notation.

13. A fund-raiser for a charitable organization has started to call individuals at home to solicit donations. The average contribution for this organization is $25. This fund-raiser is interested in determining if the phone technique results in larger donations. A random sample of 10 recent phone donations is selected. Do the phone contributions significantly exceed the norm of $25? Test at the .05 level.

Data: 20, 50, 40, 25, 100, 25, 40, 50, 30, 20.

**Step 1: Develop Hypotheses**

a. Independent Variable = Scale: Categorical Quantitative

b. Dependent Variable = Scale: Categorical Quantitative

c. Circle: One-tailed Two-tailed

d. Alternative hypothesis in sentence form.

e. Null hypothesis in sentence form.

f. Write the alternative and null hypotheses using correct notation.

$H_1$: $H_0$:

**Step 2: Establish significance criteria**

g. $\alpha$ =

**Step 3: Calculate test statistic, effect size, confidence interval, and power**

h. $t_{calculated}$ = Level of significance ($p$) =

i. Decision: reject null or fail to reject null

j. Calculate effect size =

k. Determine the 95% confidence interval:

l. Determine power for the study. Explain what this means for your ability to generalize your results to the population.

**Step 4: Draw conclusion**

m. Write your conclusion in sentence form including appropriate results notation.

# Module 8

## t-Test of Independent Samples

### Learning Targets

After completing Module 8, you should be able to:

- Apply the process of hypothesis testing to conduct *t*-test of independent samples to compare two sample group means and determine statistical significance.
- Interpret *t*-test results (hand calculations, SPSS/StatCrunch output) to determine statistical significance and confidence intervals and draw appropriate conclusions
- Utilize *t*-test results to calculate appropriate effect size and power.
- Write appropriate conclusions with statistical results notation.

# Part 1: The Concepts

In the previous two modules, we have learned to examine the treatment effect by comparing a sample mean to the population norm. However, this assumes that the population norm is truly representative of the pre-treatment population. Since this isn't always the case, most researchers will utilize a control group as a comparison to the treatment. This requires the researcher to create two sample groups: 1) control, and 2) treatment. In addition, there are times when the population norm has nothing to do with the comparison. For example, a researcher may want to compare two different groups such as: males and females, Treatment A and Treatment B, republicans and democrats. Comparison of two separate (or independent) samples requires the use of *t*-test of independent samples.

## 8.11 *t*-Test of Independent Samples

The goal of ***t-test of independent samples*** is to evaluate the mean difference between two samples in order to generalize that difference to two populations. To differentiate the two samples, we will use special notation: Sample 1 ($n_1$, $M_1$), Sample 2 ($n_2$, $M_2$). Within hypothesis testing, we will typically predict that the group means will differ or that one group will be higher than the other. For the example applied throughout this module, group differences (in parental limit means) are being predicted between the fighters and non-fighters. This is a non-directional or two-tailed test that would generate the following hypothesis notation.

$H_1$: $\mu_1 - \mu_2 \neq 0$ $\qquad$ $H_0$: $\mu_1 - \mu_2 = 0$

Notice that if group differences are predicted, the difference between sample means will not equal 0 as noted in the alternative hypothesis. Whereas the null indicated that the two sample means will be the same so that the difference between sample means will equal 0. If we predicted that the fighters would have less parental limits, then the hypothesis notation for the one-tailed test would be:

$H_1$: $\mu_1 - \mu_2 < 0$ $\qquad$ $H_0$: $\mu_1 - \mu_2 \geq 0$

Calculating the *t* statistic for independent sample is conceptually similar to t-test of single sample but a little more complex.

| Single Sample *t* | Independent Samples *t* |
|---|---|
| $t = \frac{M - \mu}{s_M}$ | $t = \frac{(M_1 - M_2) - (\mu_1 - \mu_2)}{s_{(M_1 - M_2)}}$ |

Basically for the single sample *t*-test, we calculated the difference between the sample mean and population mean and divided by estimated standard error. The independent samples *t*-test will also calculate the sample mean difference to the population mean difference and divide by estimated standard error. However, we assume that the groups in the population haven't had the treatment and therefore will have a difference of zero—so it really has no bearing on the calculation whatsoever. Estimated standard error for the single sample *t* was pretty simple—take the sample standard deviation ($s$) and divide by the square root of $n$ ($s_M = s/\sqrt{n}$). Recall, standard error measures how accurately the sample statistic represents the population statistics. However, since *t*-test of independent samples has two samples, the estimated standard error estimates how well the sample mean difference ($M_1 - M_2$) represents the population mean difference. That's why the estimated standard error for mean difference is indicated by $s_{(M1-M2)}$.

> **Example**
>
> In the last decade, video games have become prevalent in most teen and young adult lives. Many are concerned about the negative effects violent video games have on children. In a 2004 study, Gentile et. al. examined differences in parental limits of video gaming on adolescents who had or had not been involved in physical fights the previous year. Parental limit was measured by how often parents check the ratings before allowing the purchase or rental of a video game, where 0=never and 5=always. Results are as follows: fighters ($n_1$=179, $M_1$=1.61, $SD_1$=1.38), non-fighters ($n_2$=362, $M_2$=2.21, $SD_2$=1.32). Test at the .05 level.
>
> **RQ:** Does the frequency of parental limits on video gaming differ between adolescents who have been in a physical fight the past year and those who have not?
>
> **Step 1: State the Hypotheses**
>
> **IV:** fighters vs non-fighters
> **DV:** frequency of parental limits
> **Two-tailed:** keyword=differ
>
> **Alternative Hypothesis:** Frequency of parental limits on video gaming will significantly differ between adolescents who have been in a physical fight the past year and those who have not.
>
> **Null Hypothesis:** Frequency of parental limits on video gaming will NOT significantly differ between adolescents who have been in a physical fight the past year and those who have not.
>
> **Hypothesis Notation:**
> $H_1$: $\mu_1 - \mu_2 \neq 0$ $\quad$ $H_0$: $\mu_1 - \mu_2 = 0$

| Estimated Standard Error Single Sample *t* | Estimated Standard Error Independent Samples *t* |
|---|---|
| $s_M = \frac{s}{\sqrt{n}} = \sqrt{\frac{s^2}{n}}$ | $s_{(M_1 - M_2)} = \sqrt{\frac{s_1^2}{n_1} + \frac{s_2^2}{n_2}}$ |

Notice the estimated standard error for independent samples *t* is combining the error from the two sample means. Although this equation is conceptually accurate, this formula is limited to groups of equal sizes, which rarely occurs in research. To correct for the bias of varied sample sizes and variances, pooled variance will replace each sample standard deviation. Pooled variance averages or "pools" the two sample variances (sum of squares, *SS*) and thus gives greater weight to the larger sample. If you recall the calculation of sample standard deviation, the sum of squares (squared differences) was divided by degrees of freedom, which the square root was taken.

$$s = \sqrt{\frac{SS}{df}} \qquad \text{which means that} \qquad SS = s^2(df)$$

Pooled variance is identified by the symbol $s_p^2$ and is computed as

$$s_p^2 = \frac{SS_1 + SS_2}{df_1 + df_2} \text{ or } s_p^2 = \frac{s_1^2(df_1) + s_2^2(df_2)}{df_1 + df_2} \text{ such that } s_{(M_1 - M_2)} = \sqrt{\frac{s_p^2}{n_1} + \frac{s_p^2}{n_2}}$$

As previously mention, the calculation of *t* for independent samples is a bit more complicated, however, we have the wonderful computer programs that will be doing it for us. A couple things to keep in mind. Essentially, the *t* statistic for independent samples calculates the difference between two sample means and divides that by the difference due to error. A large value for *t* indicates that the mean difference between the two samples is larger than expected by chance/error.

$$t = \frac{\text{actual difference between } M_1 \text{ and } M_2}{\text{standard difference (due to error) between } M_1 \text{ and } M_2}$$

**Determining Significance with *t*.** In the last module, we learned that the *t* distribution is normally distributed. But since it is based upon estimated standard error and thus degrees of freedom, the *t* distribution only approximates normality and is dependent upon *df*. Determining significance with *t* of independent samples is identical with *t* single sample, however, we will not bother with doing hand calculations and identifying critical values for *t*. From now on, we will rely upon computer analysis for our statistical results. This means to determine significance, we will always compare the *p*-value reported in the output to the predetermined alpha level. As always, if *p* is less than alpha, significance is found so we reject the null and restate the alternative hypothesis for the conclusion.

For our example, the following output was generated within SPSS and StatCrunch. Just a reminder, SPSS only conducts two-tailed tests. Fortunately our example utilizes a two-tailed test, so no adjustment for the *p*-value is necessary. SPSS first presents a table of group means, standard deviations, and standard errors. The second table presents the *t*-test results and confidence intervals. The first two columns in this table are the Levene's Test, which we will discuss when we get to assumptions. So at this point, skip to the third column (*t*) first row, where $t$ = -4.875. Continuing across this row, $df$ = 539, Sig. (two-tailed) or $p$ = .000. The negative *t* statistic just indicates that the first mean (the fighters) had a lower mean than the second mean (non-fighters) with respect to frequency of parental limits. If $M_2$ was greater than $M_1$, then the t statistic would be positive. The next value is the degrees of freedom (*df*) for the total number of participants. Since there was a total of 541 participants across two groups, the degrees of freedom is 539 ($df=n-2$ = 541-2 = 539). The next value is *p*, but in SPSS is labeled as "Sig." interestingly, the *p*-value reported is .000, which is technically impossible. Remember, the *p*-value represented the probability of finding significance out of error. We have learned that there is ALWAYS error, but in this case the amount of error is so small, that the computer just rounded to the thousandths place. So whenever $p$=.000 is reported in the output, we will report it as $p$<.0001, to indicate the small amount of error. In terms of determining significance, we can see that *p* is certainly less than our alpha of .05, so the group means are significantly different, and we reject the null.

## Example

**Alternative Hypothesis:** Frequency of parental limits on video gaming will significantly differs between adolescents who have been in a physical fight the past year and those who have not.

**Step 2: Establish Significance Criteria**
An alpha of .05 is used for a two-tailed test.

**Step 3: Collect and Analyze Data**
Output indicates: $t$=-4.875, $df$=539, $p$<.0001.

**Step 4: Evaluate Null and Draw Conclusion**
$p$<.0001 is less than alpha of .05, therefore sample means are significantly different.

- Significance→Reject the Null→Restate Alternative
- Frequency of parental limits on video gaming significantly differs between adolescents who have been in a physical fight the past year and those who have not; $t(539)$=-4.875, $p$<.0001, two-tailed.

**SPSS Output**

**Group Statistics**

| | fighter | N | Mean | Std. Deviation | Std. Error Mean |
|---|---|---|---|---|---|
| Parentlimits | 1.00 | 179 | 1.6089 | 1.37927 | .10309 |
| | 2.00 | 362 | 2.2072 | 1.32467 | .06962 |

**Independent Samples Test**

| | | Levene's Test for Equality of Variances | | t-test for Equality of Means | | | | | | |
|---|---|---|---|---|---|---|---|---|---|---|
| | | | | | | | | | 95% Confidence Interval of the Difference | |
| | | F | Sig. | t | df | Sig. (2-tailed) | Mean Difference | Std. Error Difference | Lower | Upper |
| Parentlimits | Equal variances assumed | .741 | .390 | -4.875 | 539 | .000 | -.59824 | .12271 | -.83929 | -.35720 |
| | Equal variances not assumed | | | -4.809 | 342.290 | .000 | -.59824 | .12440 | -.84293 | -.35356 |

The StatCrunch output is a bit different in that it doesn't present the group means and standard deviations—this requires a separate analysis. The *t*-test results present the difference between the sample means, the standard error of the difference, degrees of freedom, and the *p*-value. Notice that StatCrunch automatically reports *p* as $p<.0001$.

**StatCrunch Output**

**Hypothesis test results:**

$\mu_1$ : Mean of Population 1

$\mu_2$ : Mean of Population 2

$\mu_1 - \mu_2$ : Difference between two means

$H_0 : \mu_1 - \mu_2 = 0$

$H_A : \mu_1 - \mu_2 \neq 0$

(with pooled variances)

| Difference | Sample Diff. | Std. Err. | DF | T-Stat | P-value |
|---|---|---|---|---|---|
| $\mu_1 - \mu_2$ | -0.5983 | 0.12270905 | 539 | -4.8754609 | <0.0001 |

**Assumptions.** As we learned in the previous two modules, certain assumptions should be fulfilled when utilizing various hypothesis tests. Like single sample *t*, assumptions for independent samples *t* include normality, which requires that the dependent variable is quantitative and is much more likely when random sampling is used. The other main assumption is equal variances between the two samples and thus between the two populations. Equal variances is also known as homogeneity of variance. Basically, this means that the standard deviations for the two samples should be fairly equivalent. Remember when calculating pooled variance, the average of the two sample variances is computed. If one of these values is out of whack, the estimated standard error of differences is not very accurate, which means our t statistic is not very accurate. Consequently, satisfying this assumption is pretty important! So important that SPSS has automatically included a special test for this assumption within the independent samples *t*-test. This special test is the Levene's Test. Two values are generated with a Levene's Test: *F* and *p*. The Levene's Test is testing the hypothesis that there are unequal variances between the two samples/populations. The hope is that the Levene's Test will NOT be significant such that $p > .05$ so that we can conclude equal variances.

For our example output, the first two columns in the *t*-test results, $F=.741$ and $p=.390$. These results indicate that the Levene's Test is NOT significant since *p* of .390 is greater than alpha of .05, so we can conclude equal variances between the samples and thus populations. Notice that the first line of the SPSS output is for "Equal Variances Assumed," while the second line presents *t*-test results for when "Equal Variances Not Assumed." You would only utilize the second line of results when the Levene's Test is significant. But keep in mind, this doesn't fix the problem of unequal variances; it just calculates *t* a bit differently so that the unequal variances aren't so exaggerated.

## 8.12 Estimation with *t* Test of Independent Samples

Like the hypothesis tests before, limitations plague the hypothesis process and subsequent results. As such, the calculation of confidence intervals and effect size is strongly recommended in conjunction with hypotheses testing. With hypothesis testing, we determined IF there was a significant difference between groups. With a confidence interval, we will examine HOW MUCH of a group difference. If you recall the confidence interval for single sample *t*, we the range of values that the estimated population mean after the treatment. The level of confidence determined the width of the range. The more confident we want to be, the wider the range of values. In contrast, a *t*-test of independent samples focuses on group difference; therefore, the confidence interval will estimate the size of the group difference in the population.

**Single Sample *t* Confidence Interval**

$\mu = M \pm ts_m$

**Independent Samples *t* Confidence Interval**

$\mu_1 - \mu_2 = M_1 - M_2 \pm ts_{(M1\text{-}M2)}$

As the equation indicates, to estimate the group difference in the population, we need to know: 1) sample mean difference; 2) $t_{critical}$ based upon alpha, number of tails, and *df*; and 3) standard error of mean difference. Fortunately, both SPSS and StatCrunch can calculate confidence intervals for us. SPSS automatically calculates the confidence interval with the *t*-test. However, StatCrunch requires a separate analysis. For our example, the following output was generated for a 95% confidence interval. Notice that both outputs calculate the interval of the difference since the analysis is focused on difference between the two groups.

**Independent Samples Test**

| | | Levene's Test for Equality of Variances | | t-test for Equality of Means | | | | | | |
|---|---|---|---|---|---|---|---|---|---|---|
| | | | | | | | | | 95% Confidence Interval of the Difference | |
| | | F | Sig. | t | df | Sig. (2-tailed) | Mean Difference | Std. Error Difference | Lower | Upper |
| Parentlimits | Equal variances assumed | .741 | .390 | -4.875 | 539 | .000 | -.59824 | .12271 | -.83929 | -.35720 |
| | Equal variances not assumed | | | -4.809 | 342.290 | .000 | -.59824 | .12440 | -.84293 | -.35356 |

**95% confidence interval results:**

μ1 : Mean of Population 1

μ2 : Mean of Population 2

μ1 - μ2 : Difference between two means

(with pooled variances)

| Difference | Sample Diff. | Std. Err. | DF | L. Limit | U. Limit |
|---|---|---|---|---|---|
| μ1 - μ2 | -0.5982 | 0.12270905 | 539 | -0.83929 | -0.35720 |

Based upon our output, we are 95% confident that the difference in parental limits between fighters and non-fighters will range between -.83929 and -.35720.

## 8.13 Effect Size

Effect size is another index that indicates the size of the difference or effect. In the last module, Cohen's *d* was used as a standardized measure of the mean difference, where the difference between the sample and populations means was divided by the sample standard deviation.

**General Cohen's *d***

$$d = \frac{\text{mean difference}}{\text{standard deviation}}$$

**Single Sample *t* Cohen's *d***

$$d = \frac{M - \mu}{SD}$$

**Independent Samples *t* Cohen's *d***

$$d = \frac{M_1 - M_2}{\sqrt{s_p^2}}$$

Cohen's *d* for independent samples *t* is similar in that we calculate the difference between the two means, but that difference is divided by pooled variance. This is rather a pain since most effect sizes must be calculated by hand. Because our statistical analysis will primarily use computer output, which does not report pooled variance, we need to be able to compute pooled variance using the output provided. The equation below, allows us to calculate pooled variance knowing the standard deviation and *df* for each sample. Recall the group statistics for our example: Fighters (*M*=1.61, *s*=1.38, *df*=178), Non-Fighters (*M*=2.21, *s*=1.32, *df*=361). Using these values, we calculate pooled variance as 1.80.

$$s_p^2 = \frac{s_1^2(df_1) + s_2^2(df_2)}{df_1 + df_2} \qquad s_p^2 = \frac{1.38^2(178) + 1.32^2(361)}{178 + 361} = \frac{339+629}{539} = \frac{968}{539} = 1.80$$

We can now calculate Cohen's *d*. Typically, the mean difference is entered as a positive number, in this case .598.

$$d = \frac{M_1 - M_2}{\sqrt{s_p^2}} = \frac{.598}{\sqrt{1.8}} = \frac{.598}{1.34} = .45$$

**Effect Size for Independent Samples t**

$$\text{Cohen's } d = \frac{M_1 - M_2}{\sqrt{s_p^2}}$$

**Percentage of Variance**

$$r^2 = \frac{t^2}{t^2 + df}$$

Effect size tables for various *t*-tests are located in Appendix E. In addition, several online effect size calculators are available. Using a calculator at http://www.socscistatistics.com/effectsize/Default3.aspx, Cohen's *d* is calculated based upon group means, standard deviations, and samples sizes. Our hand calculation is confirmed.

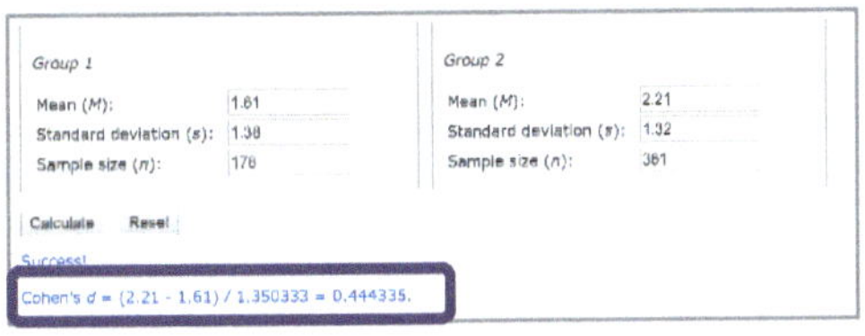

Based upon our evaluation criteria from the previous module, we determine that Cohen's $d$ =.45 is a moderate effect. Another effect size that may be reported instead of Cohen's $d$ is the percentage of variance ($r^2$) accounted for by the independent variable. Calculation of percentage of variance only requires knowledge of $t$ and $df$, so it is quite a bit easier to compute. For our example, $t$ = -4.875 and $df$ = 539 is used.

$$r^2 = \frac{t^2}{t^2 + df} = \frac{-4.875^2}{-4.875^2 + 539} = \frac{23.77}{23.77 + 539} = .042$$

| $r^2$ | Cohen's $d$ | Size of Effect |
|---|---|---|
| < 0.09 | < 0.2 | Small |
| 0.09 – 0.25 | 0.2 – 0.8 | Medium |
| > 0.25 | > 0.8 | Large |

Converting $r^2$ to a percentage allows us to conclude that 4.2% of the variance in the parental limits is explained the group differences in fighting. Cohen also developed criteria for evaluating the size of the effect using $r^2$. You can see that the values of $r^2$ for the various sizes of effect are quite a bit different from those of Cohen's $d$. So be sure that you use apply the correct criteria. The effect size of $r^2$ =.042 indicates a small effect, which differs from Cohen's $d$ that revealed a medium effect. In light of our hypothesis test result, which concluded that the fighting groups significantly differed, the small to moderate effect size indicates that the group differences do not explain a large amount of variance in parental limits. $r^2$ may also be used with $t$-test Single Sample.

## 8.14 Power

In our last module, we were introduced to the concept of power, which represents the probability that the study will produce a statistically significant result if the hypotheses is true (or we reject the null). Determining power in the planning of a study can be very helpful so that the researcher can make necessary adjustments in sample size, levels of significance, or number of tails to increase power. We can also use power to evaluate the results of our study, whether our results were statistically significant or not. Recall that Cohen recommends a minimum power of .80 or 80%. Power calculators and tables are available for a $t$-test of independent samples. Power calculators require Cohen's $d$ for an effect size, which can be a bit monumental if you have to calculate pooled variance. For our example, we used the power table in Appendix D2, which applies a two-tailed test at $\alpha$ = .05. The table required identification of sample size ($n$ = 545, however the largest size is 30), Cohen's $d$=.45 (rounded up to .50)—indicating a power of .48. Since this table is limited to a maximum sample size of 30, it may be used to ***estimate*** power. We will not be focusing on the determination of power for the remaining inferential tests we will learn.

## 8.15 Reporting Results

The first component of summarizing the results is to provide a statement that indicates the relationship supported by the results. This statement should include the sample and variables studied as well as the relationship and is based upon the hypothesis generated. Within this statement, you should integrate the following statistical results:

- Group means and standard deviations
- $t_{calculated}$ with degrees of freedom in parentheses
- Level of significance ($p$)
- Number of tails
- Effect size (Cohen's $d$ or $r^2$)
- Confidence interval (optional)

> **Example**
>
> **Confidence Interval**
>
> Output shows 95% CI Difference [-.84, -.36].
>
> **Effect Size**
>
> Using Cohen's *d*, we generate a medium effect size.
>
> $$d = \frac{M_1 - M_2}{\sqrt{s_p^2}} = \frac{.598}{\sqrt{1.8}} = \frac{.598}{1.34} = .45$$
>
> **Updated Results**
>
> The following conclusion with results notation would be reported.
>
> Frequency of parental limits on video gaming significantly differs between adolescents who have been in a physical fight the past year **(*M*=1.61, *SD*=1.38)** and those who have not **(*M*=2.21, *SD*=1.32); *t*(539)= -4.88, *p*<.0001, two-tailed, Cohen's *d*=.45, 95% CI [-.839, -.357].**

## 8.16 Directional (One-tailed) Hypothesis Tests

Our previous example utilized a non-directional or two-tailed hypothesis since we were examining an effect that could result in <u>either</u> an increase or decrease. Let's apply the hypothesis process with effect size and confidence intervals to a directional scenario.

A District Superintendent examines the impact of a one-to-one iPad program on motivation toward learning among 4th grade students. All 4th grade students at School A (the treatment group, $n$=90) receive an iPad that can be used at school and home. All 4th grade students at School B serve as the control group ($n$=98). After a year of the iPad program, all student participants complete the Learning Motivation Questionnaire. Do 4th graders who participate in the one-to-one iPad program have significantly higher learning motivation than 4th graders who do not participate? Test at the .01 level. Calculate effect size and 99% confidence interval.

**Step 1: State Hypotheses**

- Identify variables: IV=one-to-one iPad; DV=learning motivation
- Determine # of tails. Key word is increase→one-tailed.
- State **alternative hypothesis**: The 4th graders who participate in the one-to-one iPad program will have significantly higher learning motivation than 4th graders who do not participate.
- State **null hypothesis**: The 4th graders who participate in the one-to-one iPad program will NOT have significantly higher learning motivation than 4th graders who do not participate
  - Develop hypotheses notation: $H_1$: $\mu_{iPad} - \mu_{control} > 0$ $H_0$: $\mu_{iPad} - \mu_{control} \leq 0$

**Step 2: Establish Significance Criteria**
The alpha being applied is .01.

**Step 3: Collect and Analyze Data**
The iPad group had a Learning Motivation mean of 49.8 (*M*=49.8, *SD*=4.1), while the control group had a mean of 45.2 (*M*=45.2, *SD*=4.4). StatCrunch output produced $t$=7.40, $p$<.0001.

**Hypothesis test results:**
μ1 : Mean of Population 1
μ2 : Mean of Population 2
μ1 - μ2 : Difference between two means
H0 : μ1 - μ2 = 0
HA : μ1 - μ2 > 0
(with pooled variances)

| Difference | Sample Diff. | Std. Err. | DF | T-Stat | P-value |
|---|---|---|---|---|---|
| μ1 - μ2 | 4.6 | 0.62181521 | 186 | 7.3976961 | <0.0001 |

**Step 4: Evaluate Null Hypothesis and Draw Conclusion**
To determine significance using computer output, we compare the *p*-value to alpha (α=.01). In this case, *p*<.0001 is definitely less than .01, so we have a significant increase in that the iPad group has a significantly higher mean than the control group. With significance, we reject the null and restate the alternative as the conclusion. To recap, our decision is: Significance→Reject the null→Restate alternative. Our conclusion with results notation is:

> The 4th graders who participate in the one-to-one iPad program **(*M*=49.8, *SD*=4.1)** have significantly higher learning motivation than 4th graders who do not participate **(*M*=45.2, *SD*=4.4); *t*(186)=7.40, *p*<.0001, one-tailed.**

## Effect Size

Using the online calculator at http://www.socscistatistics.com/effectsize/Default3.aspx, we generate a Cohen's *d* of 1.08, a very large effect.

| Group 1 | | Group 2 | |
|---|---|---|---|
| Mean (*M*): | 49.8 | Mean (*M*): | 45.2 |
| Standard deviation (*s*): | 4.1 | Standard deviation (*s*): | 4.4 |
| Sample size (*n*): | 90 | Sample size (*n*): | 98 |

Calculate Reset
Success!
Cohen's *d* = (45.2 - 49.8) / 4.252646 = 1.081679.

## Confidence Interval

Since this one-tailed test examined an increase due to the treatment, the confidence interval estimates the increase that occurs in the population due to the iPad treatment. StatCrunch output indicates a lower limit of 2.98 and an upper limit of 6.22 with 99% confidence. This means we are 99% confident that as a result of the iPad treatment, the population increase will range between 2.98 and 6.22.

**99% confidence interval results:**
μ1 : Mean of Population 1
μ2 : Mean of Population 2
μ1 - μ2 : Difference between two means
(with pooled variances)

| Difference | Sample Diff. | Std. Err. | DF | L. Limit | U. Limit |
|---|---|---|---|---|---|
| μ1 - μ2 | 4.6 | 0.62181521 | 186 | 2.9817137 | 6.2182863 |

## Updated Results

The effect size (Cohen's *d* = 1.08) and confidence interval (99% CI [2.98, 6.22]) results can be easily added to our original results statement at the very end.

> The 4th graders who participate in the one-to-one iPad program **(*M*=49.8, *SD*=4.1)** have significantly higher learning motivation than 4th graders who do not participate **(*M*=45.2, *SD*=4.4); *t*(186)=7.40, *p*<.0001, one-tailed, Cohen's *d*=1.08, 99% CI [2.98, 6.22].**

## 8.17 Module Summary

- ***t*-test of independent samples** evaluates the mean difference between two samples in order to generalize that difference to two populations.
  - $t = \frac{M_1 - M_2}{s_{(M_1 - M_2)}}$
- ***Estimated standard error for mean difference*** ($s_{(M1-M2)}$) estimates how well the sample mean difference ($M_1 - M_2$) and represents the population mean difference.
  - $s_{(M_1 - M_2)} = \sqrt{\frac{s_1^2}{n_1} + \frac{s_2^2}{n_2}}$
- This formula is limited to groups of equal sizes. To correct for the bias of varied sample sizes and variances, pooled variance will replace each sample standard deviation.
- ***Pooled variance*** ($s_p^2$) averages or "pools" the two sample variances (sum of squares, *SS*) and gives greater weight to the larger sample.
  - $s_p^2 = \frac{SS_1 + SS_2}{df_1 + df_2}$ or $s_p^2 = \frac{s_1^2(df_1) + s_2^2(df_2)}{df_1 + df_2}$ such that $s_{(M_1 - M_2)} = \sqrt{\frac{s_p^2}{n_1} + \frac{s_p^2}{n_2}}$
- Assumptions include: 1) normality of the dependent variable, and 2) equal variances (homogeneity of variance) between the two samples and thus between the two populations. Levene's Test should not be significant when assumption is fulfilled.
- The confidence interval will estimate the size of the group difference in the population.
  - $\mu_1 - \mu_2 = M_1 - M_2 \pm ts_{(M1-M2)}$
- Two effect sizes can be used to indicate the size of the difference or effect.
  - **Cohen's *d*** requires calculation of pooled variance. **Cohen's *d*** $= \frac{M_1 - M_2}{\sqrt{s_p^2}}$
  - **Percentage of variance ($r^2$)** only requires *t* and *df*. $r^2 = \frac{t^2}{t^2 + df}$
  - **Evaluation of Effect Sizes**

| $r^2$ | Cohen's *d* | Size of Effect |
|---|---|---|
| < 0.09 | < 0.2 | Small |
| 0.09 – 0.25 | 0.2 – 0.8 | Medium |
| > 0.25 | > 0.8 | Large |

- Power may be conducted to examine the probability of obtaining accurate significant results (after the fact) or to determine a minimum sample size (before the study).
- Concluding statement is based upon the hypothesis and should include: the sample, variables, relationship and the following statistical results:
  - Group means and standard deviations
  - $t_{calculated}$ with degrees of freedom in parentheses
  - Level of significance (*p*)
  - Number of tails
  - Effect size (Cohen's *d* or $r^2$)
  - Confidence interval (optional)

# Part 2: Learning Guide

## Example

In the last decade, video games have become prevalent in most teen and young adult lives. Many are concerned about the negative effects violent video games have on children. In a 2004 study, Gentile et. al. examined differences in parental limits of video gaming on adolescents who had or had not been involved in physical fights the previous year. Parental limit was measured by how often parents check the ratings before allowing the purchase or rental of a video game, where 0=never and 5=always. Results are as follows: fighters ($n_1$=179, $M_1$=1.61, $SD_1$=1.38), non-fighters ($n_2$=362, $M_2$=2.21, $SD_2$=1.32). Test at the .01 level.

**RQ:** Does the frequency of parental limits on video gaming differ between adolescents who have been in a physical fight the past year and those who have not?

**Step 1: State the Hypotheses**

**IV:** fighters vs non-fighters
**DV:** frequency of parental limits
**Two-tailed:** keyword=differ

**Alternative Hypothesis:** Frequency of parental limits on video gaming will significantly differ between adolescents who have been in a physical fight the past year and those who have not.

**Null Hypothesis:** Frequency of parental limits on video gaming will NOT significantly differ between adolescents who have been in a physical fight the past year and those who have not.

**Hypothesis Notation:** $H_1: \mu_1 - \mu_2 \neq 0$ $H_0: \mu_1 - \mu_2 = 0$

### 8.21V *t* Test of Independent Samples

***t*-test of independent samples** evaluates the mean difference between two samples in order to generalize that difference to two populations.

- Notation is used to differentiate samples: Sample 1 ($n_1$, $M_1$), Sample 2 ($n_2$, $M_2$).
- Hypothesis notation
  - Two-tailed: $H_1: \mu_1 - \mu_2 \neq 0$ $H_0: \mu_1 - \mu_2 = 0$
  - One-tailed: $H_1: \mu_1 - \mu_2 < 0$ $H_0: \mu_1 - \mu_2 \geq 0$
- Calculating the t statistic for independent sample is conceptually similar to t-test of single sample but a little more complex.

**Single Sample *t***

$$t = \frac{M-\mu}{s_M}$$

**Independent Samples *t***

$$t = \frac{M_1 - M_2}{s_{(M_1 - M_2)}}$$

- Since *t*-test of independent samples has two samples, the estimated standard error estimates how well the sample mean difference ($M_1 - M_2$) represents the population mean difference.
- ***Estimated standard error for mean difference*** is indicated by $s_{(M1-M2)}$ and combines the error from the two sample means.

**Estimated Standard Error Single Sample *t***

$$s_M = \frac{s}{\sqrt{n}} = \sqrt{\frac{s^2}{n}}$$

**Estimated Standard Error Independent Samples *t***

$$s_{(M_1 - M_2)} = \sqrt{\frac{s_1^2}{n_1} + \frac{s_2^2}{n_2}}$$

- This formula is limited to groups of equal sizes. To correct for the bias of varied sample sizes and variances, pooled variance will replace each sample standard deviation.
- ***Pooled variance*** ($s_p^2$) averages or "pools" the two sample variances (sum of squares, *SS*) and gives greater weight to the larger sample.

$$s_p^2 = \frac{SS_1 + SS_2}{df_1 + df_2}$$

- Recall the calculation of sample standard deviation, the sum of squares (squared differences) was divided by degrees of freedom, which the square root was taken.

$$s = \sqrt{\frac{SS}{df}} \quad \text{which means that} \quad SS = s^2(df)$$

- So pooled variance can be calculated as:

$$s_p^2 = \frac{SS_1 + SS_2}{df_1 + df_2} \quad \text{or} \quad s_p^2 = \frac{s_1^2(df_1) + s_2^2(df_2)}{df_1 + df_2} \quad \text{such that} \quad s_{(M_1 - M_2)} = \sqrt{\frac{s_p^2}{n_1} + \frac{s_p^2}{n_2}}$$

### Determining Significance with *t*

- Alpha identified is .01. Compare *p*-value to alpha. If $p < \alpha$, significance is found so we reject the null and restate the alternative hypothesis for the conclusion.
- For our example, $p<.0001$ is less than alpha of .01. Significance→Reject Null→Restate Alternative.

**SPSS Output**

**Group Statistics**

| | fighter | N | Mean | Std. Deviation | Std. Error Mean |
|---|---|---|---|---|---|
| Parentlimits | 1.00 | 179 | 1.6089 | 1.37927 | .10309 |
| | 2.00 | 362 | 2.2072 | 1.32467 | .06962 |

**Independent Samples Test**

| | | Levene's Test for Equality of Variances | | t-test for Equality of Means | | | | | 95% Confidence Interval of the Difference | |
|---|---|---|---|---|---|---|---|---|---|---|
| | | F | Sig. | t | df | Sig. (2-tailed) | Mean Difference | Std. Error Difference | Lower | Upper |
| Parentlimits | Equal variances assumed | .741 | .390 | -4.875 | 539 | .000 | -.59824 | .12271 | -.83929 | -.35720 |
| | Equal variances not assumed | | | -4.809 | 342.290 | .000 | -.59824 | .12440 | -.84293 | -.35356 |

**StatCrunch Output**

**Hypothesis test results:**
$\mu_1$ : Mean of Population 1
$\mu_2$ : Mean of Population 2
$\mu_1 - \mu_2$ : Difference between two means
$H_0 : \mu_1 - \mu_2 = 0$
$H_A : \mu_1 - \mu_2 \neq 0$
(with pooled variances)

| Difference | Sample Diff. | Std. Err. | DF | T-Stat | P-value |
|---|---|---|---|---|---|
| $\mu_1 - \mu_2$ | -0.5983 | 0.12270905 | 539 | -4.8754609 | <0.0001 |

## Example

**Alternative Hypothesis:** Frequency of parental limits on video gaming will significantly differs between adolescents who have been in a physical fight the past year and those who have not.

**Step 2: Establish Significance Criteria**
An alpha of .01 is used for a two-tailed test.

**Step 3: Collect and Analyze Data**
Output indicates: $t= -4.875$, $df=539$, $p<.0001$.

**Step 4: Evaluate Null and Draw Conclusion**
$p<.0001$ is less than alpha of .01, therefore sample means are significantly different.

- Significance→Reject the Null→Restate Alternative
- Frequency of parental limits on video gaming significantly differs between adolescents who have been in a physical fight the past year (*M*=1.61, *SD*=1.38) and those who have not (*M*=2.21, *SD*=1.32); *t*(539)= -4.88, *p*<.0001, two-tailed.

**Effect Size**

Using Cohen's *d*, we generate a medium effect size.

$$d = \frac{M_1 - M_2}{\sqrt{s_p^2}} = \frac{.598}{\sqrt{1.8}} = \frac{.598}{1.34} = .45$$

**Updated Results**

The following conclusion with results notation would be reported.

Frequency of parental limits on video gaming significantly differs between adolescents who have been in a physical fight the past year **(*M*=1.61, *SD*=1.38)** and those who have **not (*M*=2.21, *SD*=1.32); *t*(539)=-4.88, *p*<.0001, two-tailed, Cohen's *d*=.45, 95% CI [-.839, -.357].**

### Assumptions

1. **Normality**, which requires that the dependent variable is quantitative and is much more likely when random sampling is used.
2. **Equal variances** (homogeneity of variance) between the two samples and thus between the two populations. Standard deviations for the two samples should be fairly equivalent.
   - Levene's test is used to examine this. When the assumption is fulfilled, the Levene's test is NOT significant ($p > .05$).

### 8.22V Estimation with *t* Test of Independent Samples

The confidence interval will estimate the size of the group difference in the population.

- To estimate the group difference in the population, we need to know: 1) sample mean difference; 2) $t_{critical}$ based upon alpha, number of tails, and *df*; and 3) standard error of mean difference. $\mu_1 - \mu_2 = M_1 - M_2 \pm ts_{(M1-M2)}$

### 8.23V Effect Size

Two effect sizes may be used to indicate the size of the difference or effect.

- **Cohen's *d*** requires calculation of pooled variance.
  - **Cohen's *d*** $= \frac{M_1 - M_2}{\sqrt{s_p^2}}$
- **Percentage of variance ($r^2$)** only requires *t* and *df* and may be used with all *t*-tests.
  - $r^2 = \frac{t^2}{t^2 + df}$
- **Evaluation of Effect Sizes**

| $r^2$ | Cohen's *d* | Size of Effect |
|---|---|---|
| < 0.09 | < 0.2 | Small |
| 0.09 – 0.25 | 0.2 – 0.8 | Medium |
| > 0.25 | > 0.8 | Large |

## 8.24V Power

Power represents the probability that the study will produce a statistically significant result if the hypotheses is true (or we reject the null). Power may help us in planning to determine a minimum sample size for a study or identify the actual power based upon the results. Recall that Cohen recommends a minimum power of .80 or 80%. Appendix D2 provides a table to determine power for a two-tailed t-test of independent samples with alpha of .05 (Konstantopoulos, 2009).

## 8.25V Reporting Results

Concluding statement is based upon the hypothesis and should include: the sample, variables, relationship and the following statistical results:

- Group means and standard deviations
- $t_{calculated}$ with degrees of freedom in parentheses
- Level of significance ($p$)
- Number of tails
- Effect size (Cohen's $d$ or $r^2$)
- Confidence interval (optional)

## 8.26V Directional (One-tailed) Hypothesis Tests

A District Superintendent examines the impact of a one-to-one iPad program on motivation toward learning among 4th grade students. All 4th grade students at School A (the treatment group, *n*=90, *M*=49.8, *SD*=4.1) receive an iPad that can be used at school and home. All 4th grade students at School B serve as the control group (*n*=98, *M*=45.2, *SD*=4.4). After a year of the iPad program, all student participants complete the Learning Motivation Questionnaire. Do 4th graders who participate in the one-to-one iPad program have significantly higher learning motivation than 4th graders who do not participate? Test at the .01 level. Calculate effect size and 99% confidence interval.

**Step 1: State Hypotheses**

- Identify variables: IV=one-to-one iPad; DV=learning motivation
- Determine # of tails. Key word is increase→one-tailed.
- State **alternative hypothesis**: The 4th graders who participate in the one-to-one iPad program will have significantly higher learning motivation than 4th graders who do not participate.
- State **null hypothesis**: The 4th graders who participate in the one-to-one iPad program will NOT have significantly higher learning motivation than 4th graders who do not participate
- Develop hypotheses notation: $H_1$: $\mu_{iPad} - \mu_{control} > 0$ $H_0$: $\mu_{iPad} - \mu_{control} \leq 0$

**Step 2: Establish Significance Criteria**

The alpha being applied is .01.

**Step 3: Collect and Analyze Data**

The iPad group had a Learning Motivation mean of 49.8 (*M*=49.8, *SD*=4.1), while the control group had a mean of 45.2 (*M*=45.2, *SD*=4.4). StatCrunch output produced *t*=7.40, *p*<.0001.

**Hypothesis test results:**
μ1 : Mean of Population 1
μ2 : Mean of Population 2
μ1 - μ2 : Difference between two means
H0 : μ1 - μ2 = 0
HA : μ1 - μ2 > 0
(with pooled variances)

| Difference | Sample Diff. | Std. Err. | DF | T-Stat | P-value |
|---|---|---|---|---|---|
| μ1 - μ2 | 4.6 | 0.6218152 | 186 | 7.3976961 | <0.0001 |

**Step 4: Evaluate Null Hypothesis and Draw Conclusion**

Significance→Reject the null→Restate alternative.

The 4th graders who participate in the one-to-one iPad program **(*M*=49.8, *SD*=4.1)** have significantly higher learning motivation than 4th graders who do not participate **(*M*=45.2, *SD*=4.4); *t*(186)=7.40, *p*<.0001, one-tailed.**

### Effect Size

Using Cohen's $r^2$ criteria, .38 indicates a large effect and indicates that the iPad treatment accounts for 38% of the variance in the Learning Motivation.

- $r^2 = \frac{t^2}{t^2 + df} = \frac{7.40^2}{7.40^2 + 186} = \frac{54.76}{54.76 + 186} = .38$

## Confidence Interval

StatCrunch output indicates a lower limit of 2.98 and an upper limit of 6.22 with 99% confidence. This means we are 99% confident that as a result of the iPad treatment, the population increase will range between 2.98 and 6.22.

**99% confidence interval results:**

$\mu_1$ : Mean of Population 1

$\mu_2$ : Mean of Population 2

$\mu_1 - \mu_2$ : Difference between two means (with pooled variances)

| Difference | Sample Diff. | Std. Err. | DF | L. Limit | U. Limit |
|---|---|---|---|---|---|
| $\mu_1 - \mu_2$ | 4.6 | 0.62181521 | 18 | 2.9817137 | 6.2182863 |

## Updated Results

The effect size ($r^2$=.38) and confidence interval (99% CI [2.98, 6.22]) results can be easily added to our original results statement at the very end.

> The 4th graders who participate in the one-to-one iPad program **(*M*=49.8, *SD*=4.1)** have significantly higher learning motivation than 4th graders who do not participate **(*M*=45.2, *SD*=4.4); *t*(186)=7.40, *p*<.0001, one-tailed, $r^2$=.38, 99% CI [2.98, 6.22].**

## 8.27V Additional Practice

1. As a high school boys swim coach, you are interested in how off-season training techniques impact swimming performance among short distant swimmers. You randomly assigned your swimmers to two groups. Group 1 was asked to swim intervals of sprints for 45 minutes three times per week. Group 2 swam 3 kilometers three times per week. Treatments are conducted for two months in the off-season. The first day back in practice, you time the swimmers in the 100 m freestyle. Do the training techniques affect swimming performance on the 100 m? Times are listed in seconds for the two groups. Test at the .05 level.

**Group Statistics**

| | treatment | N | Mean | Std. Deviation | Std. Error Mean |
|---|---|---|---|---|---|
| time | 1.00 | 5 | 49.7600 | .50299 | .22494 |
| | 2.00 | 5 | 50.7000 | .86313 | .38601 |

**Independent Samples Test**

| | | Levene's Test for Equality of Variances | | t-test for Equality of Means | | | | | | |
|---|---|---|---|---|---|---|---|---|---|---|
| | | | | | | | | | 95% Confidence Interval of the Difference | |
| | | F | Sig. | t | df | Sig. (2-tailed) | Mean Difference | Std. Error Difference | Lower | Upper |
| time | Equal variances assumed | .968 | .354 | -2.104 | 8 | .069 | -.94000 | .44677 | -1.97024 | .09024 |
| | Equal variances not assumed | | | -2.104 | 6.436 | .077 | -.94000 | .44677 | -2.01550 | .13550 |

**Step 1: Develop Hypotheses:**

a. Independent Variable = Scale: Categorical Quantitative

b. Dependent Variable = Scale: Categorical Quantitative

c. Circle: One-tailed Two-tailed

d. Alternative hypothesis in sentence form.

e. Null hypothesis in sentence form.

f. Write the alternative and null hypotheses using correct notation.

$H_1$: $H_0$:

**Step 2: Establish significance criteria**

g. $\alpha$ =

**Step 3: Calculate test statistic, effect size, and confidence interval**

h. $t_{calculated}$ = Level of significance ($p$) =

i. Decision: reject null or fail to reject null

j. Calculate effect size =

k. Determine the 95% confidence interval:

**Step 4: Draw conclusion**

l. Write your conclusion in sentence form including appropriate results notation.

2. Remember Roberts et. al. (2014) study of cell phone use among college students. His primary research questions focused on gender differences in cell phone use. Another researcher is specifically interested in examining texting among high school students and believes that females text much more than males. Twenty males and twenty females who are juniors or seniors in high school were randomly selected. The number of texts over a week was documented: Females (*M*=676, *SD*=178) and Males (*M*=511, *SD*=189) Do the results indicate that females significantly text more than males among high school students? Test at .05.

**Hypothesis test results:**
$\mu_1$ : Mean of Population 1
$\mu_2$ : Mean of Population 2
$\mu_1 - \mu_2$ : Difference between two means
$H_0 : \mu_1 - \mu_2 = 0$
$H_A : \mu_1 - \mu_2 > 0$
(with pooled variances)

| Difference | Sample Diff. | Std. Err. | DF | T-Stat | P-value |
|---|---|---|---|---|---|
| $\mu_1 - \mu_2$ | 165 | 58.053854 | 38 | 2.8421886 | 0.0036 |

**95% confidence interval results:**

| Difference | Sample Diff. | Std. Err. | DF | L. Limit | U. Limit |
|---|---|---|---|---|---|
| $\mu_1 - \mu_2$ | 165 | 58.053854 | 38 | 47.476116 | 282.52388 |

**Step 1: Develop Hypotheses:**

a. Independent Variable = Scale: Categorical Quantitative

b. Dependent Variable = Scale: Categorical Quantitative

c. Circle: One-tailed Two-tailed

d. Alternative hypothesis in sentence form.

e. Null hypothesis in sentence form.

f. Write the alternative and null hypotheses using correct notation.

$H_1$: $H_0$:

**Step 2: Establish significance criteria**

g. $\alpha$ =

**Step 3: Calculate test statistic, effect size, and confidence interval**

h. $t_{calculated}$ = Level of significance ($p$) =

i. Decision: reject null or fail to reject null

j. Calculate effect size =

k. Determine the 95% confidence interval:

**Step 4: Draw conclusion**

l. Write your conclusion in sentence form including appropriate results notation.

## 8.28 Hands-on Activity: Coke versus Pepsi Experiment

In this activity, you are going to conduct an experiment using the Coke vs. Pepsi Taste Test that investigates two research questions:

1) Are Coke drinkers (when compared to Pepsi drinkers) more accurate in tasting the difference between Coke and Pepsi?

2) When tasting the difference between Coke and Pepsi, is one's prediction of accuracy significantly different from one's actual ability/accuracy?
   - This question will utilize a t-test of related samples, which you will in the next module, but you will collect the data necessary for this question now.

In order to complete this experiment, you need at least one other person to participate. It would be great if you can find 2-4 more individuals. Answer sheets for the Extra Credit are in your Computer Lab Packet.

***Directions:***

1. You will need the following supplies to complete this experiment.
   - 5 small paper cups for each participant
   - Pen or pencil
   - Napkins in case you spill
   - Pretzels or chips for "cleansing one's palate"

2. Once you have your supplies and participants together, record each participant's name in the first column of the data grid below and one's preference (Coke=1, Pepsi=2) in the second column.

| **Data Grid** | | | |
|---|---|---|---|
| **Name** | **Preference** | **Prediction %** | **Actual %** |
| | | | |
| | | | |
| | | | |
| | | | |

3. Have each participant predict how accurate they will be in identifying the pop as Coke or Pepsi. Since each person will be given 5 cups of pop, predict how many times out of 5 chances you will be correct in the identification process (e.g., 3/5). Then, convert that fraction into a percent (e.g., 3/5=60%). Record this percent in the third column (Prediction &) of the grid.

4. Determine who will complete the taste test first. Have that person turn away while another participant fills 5 cups with pop (make sure that some cups have Pepsi and other cups have Coke and that you know which cups have which pop). **Hint:** Don't write the name of the pop on the bottom of the cup; it will show through as the person drinks the pop. Only pour a little bit of pop in each cup.

5. Have the taste tester proceed in identifying the pop in each cup, while another participant records the accuracy. Don't tell the results to the taster until all 5 cups have been tasted. Calculate the number of correct tastes out of five. Convert that fraction into a percent and record the percent in column 4 (Actual %) of the grid.

6. Once you and your fellow participants have finished the taste test, add your results to the spreadsheet below.

| Part ID | Preference | Predict % | Actual % |
|---|---|---|---|
| 1 | 1 | 20 | 20 |
| 2 | 1 | 40 | 60 |
| 3 | 1 | 80 | 20 |
| 4 | 1 | 100 | 100 |
| 5 | 1 | 100 | 60 |
| 6 | 2 | 60 | 80 |
| 7 | 2 | 100 | 80 |
| 8 | 2 | 60 | 20 |
| 9 | 2 | 40 | 0 |
| 10 | 2 | 60 | 40 |
| 11 | | | |
| 12 | | | |
| 13 | | | |
| 14 | | | |
| 15 | | | |
| 16 | | | |
| 17 | | | |

7. Using SPSS or StatCrunch, enter ALL the data from the spreadsheet (including the data provided for 10 individuals). You should have a minimum of $n$=12 for your sample. Conduct a $t$-test of independent samples using $\alpha$=.05 to determine if Coke drinkers are more accurate in tasting the difference between Coke and Pepsi in comparison to Pepsi drinkers. In addition, calculate a 95% confidence interval and effect size. Be sure to save your data as we will use it in the next module!

**T-test of independent samples examined the following research question:**
Are Coke drinkers (when compared to Pepsi drinkers) more accurate in tasting the difference between Coke and Pepsi?

**Use the results to complete the hypothesis process.**

**Step 1: Develop Hypotheses:**

a. Independent Variable = Scale: Categorical Quantitative

b. Dependent Variable = Scale: Categorical Quantitative

c. Circle: One-tailed Two-tailed

d. Alternative hypothesis in sentence form.

e. Null hypothesis in sentence form.

f. Write the alternative and null hypotheses using correct notation.

$H_1$: $H_0$:

**Step 2: Establish significance criteria**

g. $\alpha$ =

**Step 3: Calculate test statistic, effect size, and confidence interval**

h. $z_{calculated}$ = Level of significance ($p$) =

i. Decision: reject null or fail to reject null

j. Calculate effect size =

k. Determine the 95% confidence interval:

**Step 4: Draw conclusion**

l. Write your conclusion in sentence form including appropriate results notation.

## 8.29V In the Literature

This is another example where multiple hypotheses tests are conducted. Group means and standard deviations along with the *t*-test results are presented within the same table. Notice the exact *p*-values are reported for each *t* value.

Excerpt from Bahrami, M. (2011). Investigation of verbal memory and visual perception differences in university students with different personality types. *Procedia - Social and Behavioral Sciences, 30*, 856-861

The personality types of A and B have been explored in a number of studies. Results have documented that Type A individuals are extremely competitive, sensitive to time urgency and tend to feel stressed. In contrast, Type B individuals are able to relax without feeling guilty; they enjoy working steadily and are able to avoid stress. As a result of these difference, researchers hypothesized that information processing would differ between the two personality types such that Type A individuals would perform tasks faster but with less accuracy. To examine this hypothesis, researchers examined 60 randomly selected university students; 30 for each personality type. Three different tests were administered:

- **Test of Reaction Speed** measured response time to a visual stimulus. Less time indicates a faster reaction.
- **Peeron Test of Accuracy** in which participants were asked to cross out shapes similar to the pattern. The number of errors were recorded for each participant. More errors indicates less accuracy.
- **Verbal Memory Test** examined the recall of 20 words presented all at once on a slide. The slide was presented 25 times for .01 second, with 1 second pause between each presentation. Participants were asked to write down the words on paper. More words indicate greater memory.

*T*-tests of independent samples were conducted for the three measures to compare the two personality types. Results are presented in Table 1.

**Table 1.** Personality Comparisons for Reaction Time, Errors, and Memory

| | **Type A** | | **Type B** | | *t* | *p* |
|---|---|---|---|---|---|---|
| | *M* | *SD* | *M* | *SD* | | |
| Reaction Time | 35.20 | 5.12 | 37.5 | 6.61 | -1.51 | 0.068 |
| # of Errors | 3.53 | 3.56 | 1.10 | 3.30 | 3.04 | 0.010 |
| Memory | 9.53 | 1.63 | 7.53 | 1.53 | 4.82 | 0.001 |

1. What is the independent variable being examined?

2. What are the three dependent variables?

3. The excerpt indicates that researchers examined the overall hypothesis-- information processing would differ between the two personality types such that Type A individuals would perform tasks faster but with less accuracy. However, each inferential analysis tests a null hypothesis. Table 1 presents three *t*-test results. Write the three hypotheses being examined.

4. Use the results in Table 1 to complete the questions for each variable.
   a. Reaction Time: Which group is faster? Is this difference significant?

   b. Number of Errors: Which group had more errors? Is this difference significant?

   c. Memory: Which group remembered more words? Is this difference significant?

5. Do these results support the authors overall hypothesis that -- information processing would differ between the two personality types such that Type A individuals would perform tasks faster but with less accuracy. Explain.

## 8.30 Using the Computer

The following instructions will guide you in conducting *t*-test of independent samples in SPSS and StatCrunch. A couple things to keep in mind. SPSS automatically includes group means and standard deviations, the Levine's Test, and confidence intervals with the *t*-test. In contrast, StatCrunch requires separate analyses for each of these. However, with StatCrunch you also have the option of using raw sample data or summary statistics.

### SPSS Step by Step Instructions

1. Enter data.
2. 🖱 the `Analyze` menu.
3. Select `Compare Means` and `Independent Samples t Test`.
4. 🖱 the dependent variable and move under `Test Variable(s)`.
5. 🖱 the independent variable and move to the `Grouping Variable`.
6. 🖱 `Define Groups`... and indicate the values of the groups being compared. Often it is 1 and 2.
7. 🖱 `Options` **IF** you want change the confidence interval from 95% to 99%.
8. 🖱 `OK`.

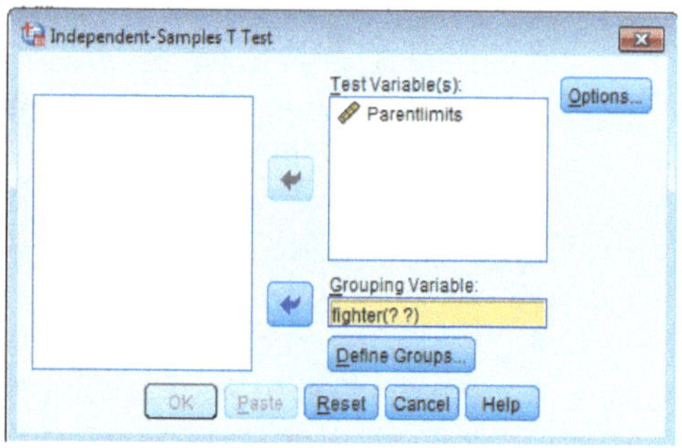


### StatCrunch Step by Step Instructions for Independent Samples *t*-Test (with raw data)

1. Enter data.
2. Within the data window, 🖱 the **Stat** menu, select ***t* Stats**, **>Two Sample, >with Data**.
3. Within Two Sample *t* dialogue box, under **Sample 1:**
   - For **Values in:** select your dependent variable.
   - For **Where:** 🖱 **Build**
     - Within the Expression window, under **Columns:** double click your grouping variable (IV).
     - You should see the variable name in the expression line at the top of this dialogue box. Type (=) and the number that represent the first grouping category. In this example, Group 1 are the fighters, and Group 2 are the non-fighters. So Sample 1 is indicated by **Fighter=1.**
4. Within Two Sample *t* dialogue box, under **Sample 2:**
   - For **Values in:** select your dependent variable.
   - For **Where:** 🖱 **Build**
     - Within the Expression window, under **Columns:** double click your grouping variable (IV).
     - In the expression line indicate the second group. In this example, Group 1 are the fighters, and Group 2 are the non-fighters. So Sample 2 is indicated by **Fighter=2.**
5. Under **Calculation options:** check Pool variances when groups are different sizes.
6. Under **Perform:** select <u>one</u> of the options:
   - **Hypothesis Test for μ**
     - By $H_A$ indicate the direction of test
   - **Confidence Interval for μ**
     - Indicate percent of confidence (95% is default)
7. 🖱 **Compute.**

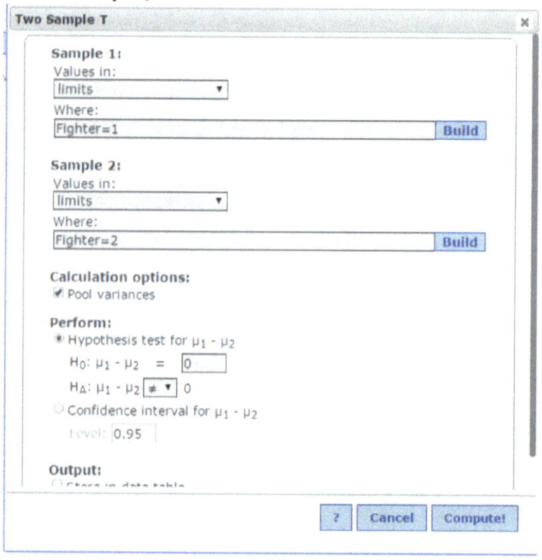


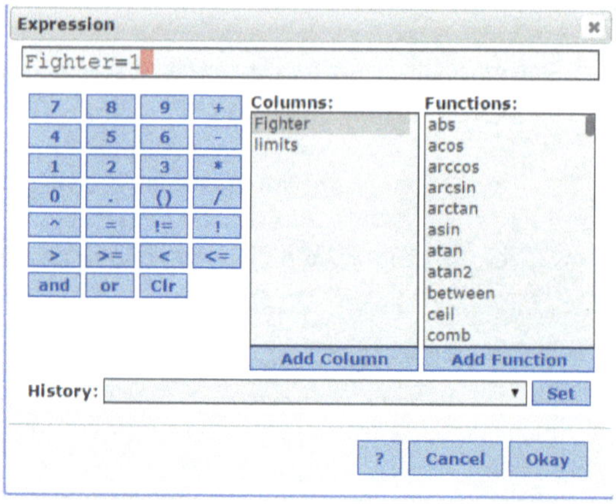

**StatCrunch Step by Step Instructions for Independent Samples *t*-Test (with data summary)**

1. Open StatCrunch, no need to enter data.
2. Within the data window, the **Stat** menu, select ***t* Stats**, **>Two Sample, >with Summary**.
3. Within Two Sample *t* Summary dialogue box, enter: sample mean, sample standard deviation, sample size for Sample 1 and 2.
4. Under **Perform:** select <u>one</u> of the options:
   - **Hypothesis Test for μ**
     - By $H_A$ indicate the direction of test
   - **Confidence Interval for μ**
     - Indicate percent of confidence (95% is default)
5. **Compute.**

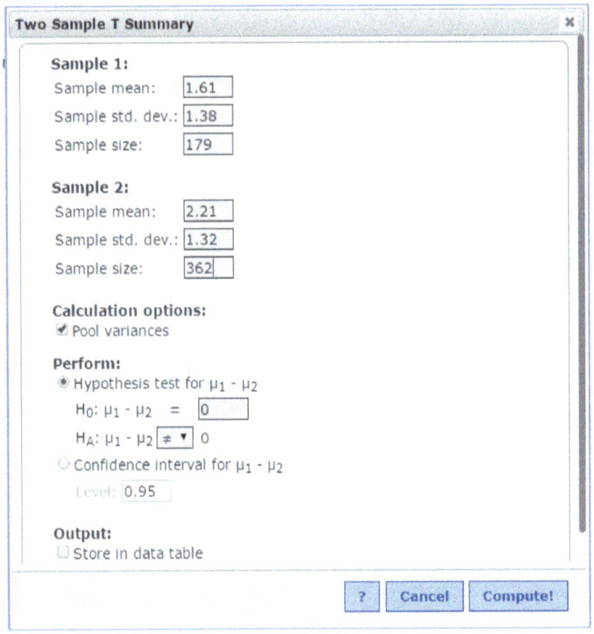


**StatCrunch Step by Step Instructions for Levene's Test**

1. Enter data.
2. Within the data window, the **Stat** menu, select **Variance Stats**, **>Homogeneity**.
3. **Values in a single column:**
   - Under **Samples in:**, select your dependent variable
   - Under **Split by**: select your independent variable.
4. Under **Test:** select Levene's test
5. **Compute.**

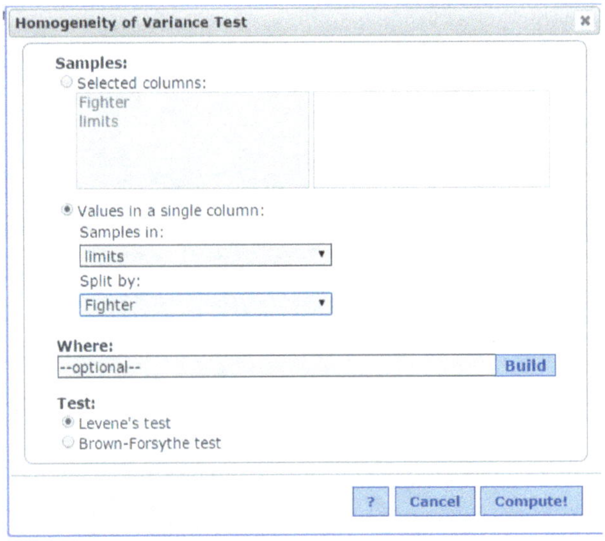

## 8.31 Exercises
### Reviewing the Concepts

1. Explain the difference between Single Sample *t*-test and Independent Samples *t*-test.

2. Why is pooled variance necessary when calculating Independent Samples *t* ?

3. If a Levene's Test result reports $p$=.012, what can you conclude regarding the assumption of equal variances?

4. What does the confidence interval for Independent Samples *t* estimate?

5. Explain the difference between Cohen's *d* and $r^2$. What do they represent? How are the evaluated?

## Interpreting Results

7. Hassan and Malik (2012) studied Pakistani women and the impact of intimate partner violence. The authors found that abused women had significantly greater depression and anxiety and significantly lower self-esteem, life orientation, and psychological well-being. A researchers believes these results can be replicated in U.S.; however, she is specifically interested in university women in abusive relationships. Eight women seeking help at the university counseling center indicate that they have abusive partners. The researcher has these eight women complete the Rosenberg Self-Esteem Scale. In addition, the researcher selects eight other women who are not in abusive relationships; they also complete the self-esteem assessment. SPSS results for the two groups are below. Can the research conclude that college females in abusive relationship have significantly lower self-esteem than non-abused college women? Test at .01.

**Group Statistics**

| | relationship | N | Mean | Std. Deviation | Std. Error Mean |
|---|---|---|---|---|---|
| esteem | abused | 8 | 21.5000 | 2.97610 | 1.05221 |
| | non-abused | 8 | 27.1250 | 4.08613 | 1.44466 |

**Independent Samples Test**

| | | Levene's Test for Equality of Variances | | t-test for Equality of Means | | | | | 95% Confidence Interval of the Difference | |
|---|---|---|---|---|---|---|---|---|---|---|
| | | F | Sig. | t | df | Sig. (2-tailed) | Mean Difference | Std. Error Difference | Lower | Upper |
| esteem | Equal variances assumed | .506 | .489 | -3.147 | 14 | .007 | -5.62500 | 1.78723 | -9.45823 | -1.79177 |
| | Equal variances not assumed | | | -3.147 | 12.796 | .008 | -5.62500 | 1.78723 | -9.49235 | -1.75765 |

**Step 1: Develop Hypotheses:**

a. Independent Variable = Scale: Categorical Quantitative

b. Dependent Variable = Scale: Categorical Quantitative

c. Circle: One-tailed Two-tailed

d. Alternative hypothesis in sentence form.

e. Null hypothesis in sentence form.

f. Write the alternative and null hypotheses using correct notation.

$H_1$: $H_0$:

**Step 2: Establish significance criteria**

g. $\alpha$ =

**Step 3: Calculate test statistic, effect size, and confidence interval**

h. $t_{calculated}$ = Level of significance ($p$) =

i. Decision: reject null or fail to reject null

j. Calculate effect size =

k. Determine the 95% confidence interval:

**Step 4: Draw conclusion**

l. Write your conclusion in sentence form including appropriate results notation.

8. While the internet holds an infinite amount of information and entertainment, some individuals can click away hours on the internet to the point that it negatively affects their social life. Such overuse has been termed "problematic internet use" in which individuals spend excessive time on the internet, experience a state of distress and irritability in situations when internet use is not available, and are compelled to spend even more time on the internet. Since internet use is greatest in the 16-24 age group, Odaci (2011) studied college students and problematic internet use. He compared internet use for college students who owned a computer and those who did not. A sample of 392 college students completed the Problematic Internet Use Scale, which generates scores that range between 33 and 165. The higher the score, the more unhealthy the internet use. His data generated the following results: Computer owners ($n$=273, $M$=92.42, $SD$=40.53), Non-computer owners ($n$=119, $M$=05.95, $SD$=45.90). Can Odaci conclude that computer ownership significantly effects problematic internet use scores among college students? Test at .05.

**Hypothesis test results:**
$\mu_1$ : Mean of Population 1
$\mu_2$ : Mean of Population 2
$\mu_1 - \mu_2$ : Difference between two means
$H_0 : \mu_1 - \mu_2 = 0$
$H_A : \mu_1 - \mu_2 \neq 0$
(with pooled variances)

| Difference | Sample Diff. | Std. Err. | DF | T-Stat | P-value |
|---|---|---|---|---|---|
| $\mu_1 - \mu_2$ | -3.53 | 4.6384968 | 390 | -0.72102241 | 0.470 |

**Two sample T summary confidence interval:**
$\mu_1$ : Mean of Population 1
$\mu_2$ : Mean of Population 2
$\mu_1 - \mu_2$ : Difference between two means
(with pooled variances)

**95% confidence interval results:**

| Difference | Sample Diff. | Std. Err. | DF | L. Limit | U. Limit |
|---|---|---|---|---|---|
| $\mu_1 - \mu_2$ | -3.53 | 4.6384968 | 390 | -12.649588 | 5.5895877 |

**Step 1: Develop Hypotheses:**

a. Independent Variable = Scale: Categorical Quantitative

b. Dependent Variable = Scale: Categorical Quantitative

c. Circle: One-tailed Two-tailed

d. Alternative hypothesis in sentence form.

e. Null hypothesis in sentence form.

f. Write the alternative and null hypotheses using correct notation.

$H_1$: $H_0$:

**Step 2: Establish significance criteria**

g. $\alpha$ =

**Step 3: Calculate test statistic, effect size, and confidence interval**

h. $t_{calculated}$ = Level of significance ($p$) =

i. Decision: reject null or fail to reject null

j. Calculate effect size =

k. Determine the 95% confidence interval:

**Step 4: Draw conclusion**

l. Write your conclusion in sentence form including appropriate results notation.

9. Read the excerpt below to answer the following questions.

**Excerpt from:** Key, S, Popkin, S., Munchus, G., Wech, B, Hill, V., & Tanner, J. (2012). An exploration of leadership experiences among white women and women of color. *Journal of Organizational Change Management, 25* (3), 392-404.

A significant body of research suggests that women of color are treated differently in the workplace from their white peers. Key et. al. (2012) examined factors that influence the success of White and African American female leaders. The researchers invited a regional sample of 738 females identified as leaders in organizations in the public or private sectors. A sample of 371 women completed the survey. One set of questions asked respondents to indicate the degree to which gender and/or race have affected their careers. The questions utilized a 5-point Likert scale. Group (white and Non-White) means for each item were examined using *t*-test of independent samples. These results are presented in Table 1.

**Table 1.** Career Experiences: Impact of Gender and Race

| Likert question/statement | White | | Non-White | | *t*-stat | *p* |
|---|---|---|---|---|---|---|
| | Mean[a] | SD[a] | Mean[a] | SD[a] | | |
| 1. Being a woman has helped me in my career | 3.12 | 1.144 | 2.90 | 1.313 | 1.545 | 0.123 |
| 2. My race has helped me in my career | 3.33 | 1.059 | 2.77 | 1.318 | 4.062 | 0.000* |
| 3. Limits on opportunities at the top of organizations (i.e. the glass ceiling) prevent most women from reaching their full potential | 3.86 | 1.176 | 4.03 | 1.245 | -1.198 | 0.232 |
| 4. Limits on opportunities at the top of organizations (i.e. the glass ceiling) prevent most women of color from reaching their full potential | 3.82 | 1.242 | 4.35 | 1.018 | -3.363 | 0.000* |
| 5. In most situations, women have been helpful to me in my career | 3.94 | 1.026 | 3.49 | 1.213 | 3.434 | 0.001* |
| 6. In most situations, men have been helpful to me in my career | 4.12 | 0.851 | 3.83 | 1.031 | 2.633 | 0.009* |
| 7. I do not think that it is my responsibility to be helpful to other women in their careers | 1.34 | 0.732 | 1.22 | 0.615 | 1.457 | 0.146 |
| 8. I consider myself a leader in my community | 4.05 | 1.018 | 4.24 | 1.141 | -1.462 | 0.145 |

**Notes:** [a] 1 = Strongly disagree; 2 = Slightly disagree; 3 = Neutral; 4 = Slightly agree; 5 = Strongly agree; * significant at $\alpha$ = 0:05

a. Which items showed significant differences? Which group scored higher for each item?

b. Why are some *t* statistics positive and others negative?

c. The *p*-value for item 3 is reported as 0.000. What is the correct way to report this? Explain.

d. Calculate an effect size ($r^2$) for the difference in item 2. Use $df$=369.

e. Which items did <u>not</u> show significant group differences?

f. Based upon these results, what can you conclude regarding race differences among female leaders and their career experiences?

10. In a previous module, you examined group means for the various cell phone uses. The authors used *t*-test of independent samples and Cohen's *d* to examine gender differences.

**Excerpt from:** Roberts, J. A., Yaya, L.H.P, & Manolis, C. (2014). The invisible addiction: Cell phone activities and addiction among male and female college students. *Journal of Behavioral Addictions*, *3*(4), 254-265.

Researchers conducted a study of 164 Baylor University students to examine their cell phone use and addition. Student completed an online questionnaire that asked how much time they spend on 24 cell phone activities. The researchers were specifically interested in examining gender differences in these activities. Previous research indicates that females use technology as social and communication tools; whereas, males use technology for entertainment and informational purposes. Table 1 presents the means and standard deviations for the 24 activities between males and females. *T*-tests of independent samples were conducted to examine gender differences.

**Table 1.** Gender Differences in the Number of Minutes per Day for Various Cell Phone Activities

| | Males *n*=84 | | Females *n*=80 | | *p*-value | Cohen's *d* |
|---|---|---|---|---|---|---|
| | *M* | *SD* | *M* | *SD* | | |
| Calls | 29.3 | 34.5 | 37.1 | 38.3 | 0.18 | -0.2 |
| Texting | 84.4 | 59.1 | 105.4 | 69.9 | **0.04*** | **-0.3** |
| E-mails | 40.1 | 36.1 | 57.3 | 55.2 | **0.02*** | **-0.4** |
| Banking | 9.3 | 13.6 | 10.8 | 12.9 | 0.46 | -0.1 |
| Pictures | 13.0 | 16.2 | 21.3 | 28.8 | **0.02*** | **-0.4** |
| Games | 24.0 | 30.1 | 13.4 | 27.6 | **0.02*** | **-0.4** |
| Calendar | 11.0 | 16.0 | 23.8 | 43.5 | **0.01**** | **-0.4** |
| Clock | 19.3 | 27.6 | 30.5 | 44.7 | **0.05*** | **-0.3** |
| Books | 6.3 | 16.6 | 6.0 | 14.6 | 0.91 | 0.0 |
| Bible | 6.9 | 18.3 | 7.8 | 20.4 | 0.77 | 0.0 |
| Facebook | 31.4 | 40.3 | 46.2 | 46.0 | **0.03*** | **-0.3** |
| Twitter | 22.0 | 41.2 | 30.1 | 48.1 | 0.25 | -0.2 |
| Pinterest | 1.0 | 5.7 | 26.1 | 39.8 | **<.01***** | **-0.9** |
| Instagram | 8.3 | 23.7 | 25.6 | 37.3 | **<.01***** | **-0.5** |
| YouTube | 14.3 | 23.0 | 10.4 | 17.6 | 0.22 | 0.2 |
| iTunes | 10.0 | 21.2 | 9.1 | 20.1 | 0.76 | 0.0 |
| iPod | 26.3 | 45.9 | 27.5 | 43.7 | 0.86 | 0.0 |
| Pandora | 28.0 | 44.3 | 28.0 | 43.2 | 1.00 | 0.0 |
| Internet | 33.1 | 31.6 | 35.8 | 42.8 | 0.66 | -0.1 |
| eBay | 3.0 | 9.8 | 3.1 | 9.3 | 0.91 | 0.0 |
| Amazon | 3.1 | 10.8 | 6.1 | 21.8 | 0.26 | -0.2 |
| GoogleMaps | 8.5 | 18.2 | 11.3 | 20.3 | 0.37 | -0.1 |
| Other Apps | 24.8 | 38.5 | 22.4 | 34.5 | 0.69 | 0.1 |
| Total | 458.5 | 344.2 | 600.1 | 392.3 | **0.02*** | |

**Notes:** Bolded entries designate activities that are significant at two-tails: * $p < 0.05$; ** $p < 0.01$ and *** $p < 0.001$; for Cohen's *d* test results, an effect size of * 0.2 to 0.3 is a "small" effect, ** around 0.5 a "medium" effect and *** equal to 0.8 to infinity is a "large" effect

a. Which cell phone uses have significant gender differences? Which gender has the higher mean for each significant use?

b. The authors use asterisks and bold text to indicate significance. Is it necessary to use both?

c. The authors calculate Cohen's d for each cell phone use. Use Cohen's criteria to evaluate each effect size in bold.

d. The effect size for total cell phone has not been reported. Use the group means and standard deviations to calculate Cohen's *d*. Evaluate the effect.

e. Based upon these results, what is your conclusion about cell phone use among males and females?

## Conducting Analysis

11. A third grade teacher would like to know if her incoming students who participated in the local summer library reading program have higher reading scores than students who did not participate. At the class orientation, she asked parents to report program participation. Within the first week of school, the teacher measured oral reading fluency using DIBELS. Of her class of 25, she determines that 10 students participated in the summer program. Does the summer library reading program significantly increase oral reading fluency (words correct) among third grade students? Use the data to conduct the analysis. Test at the .05 level.

| Group | Reading |
|---|---|
| 1 | 81 |
| 1 | 83 |
| 1 | 70 |
| 1 | 77 |
| 1 | 90 |
| 1 | 100 |
| 1 | 98 |
| 1 | 78 |
| 1 | 130 |
| 1 | 138 |
| 2 | 78 |
| 2 | 88 |
| 2 | 64 |
| 2 | 100 |
| 2 | 109 |
| 2 | 76 |
| 2 | 78 |
| 2 | 66 |
| 2 | 55 |
| 2 | 83 |
| 2 | 99 |
| 2 | 105 |
| 2 | 101 |
| 2 | 72 |
| 2 | 85 |

**Step 1: Develop Hypotheses:**

a. Independent Variable = Scale: Categorical Quantitative

b. Dependent Variable = Scale: Categorical Quantitative

c. Circle: One-tailed Two-tailed

d. Alternative hypothesis in sentence form.

e. Null hypothesis in sentence form.

f. Write the alternative and null hypotheses using correct notation.

$H_1$: $H_0$:

**Step 2: Establish significance criteria**

g. $\alpha =$

**Step 3: Calculate test statistic, effect size, and confidence interval**

h. $t_{calculated} =$ Level of significance ($p$) =

i. Decision: reject null or fail to reject null

j. Calculate effect size =

k. Determine the 95% confidence interval:

**Step 4: Draw conclusion**

m. Write your conclusion in sentence form including appropriate results notation.

12. Researchers have found that child-rearing practice will vary according to different cultural contexts. A human development psychologist conducted research to determine if there is a significant difference in parental control between U.S. and Chinese parents. A sample of 8 Chinese parents and 8 U.S. parents were completed the Parental Control Scale to assess their degree of parental control. The higher the score is, the more controlling the parents are. Conduct a *t*-test of independent samples to determine if a significant difference in the degree of parental control exists between Chinese parents (Group 1) and U.S. parents (Group 2). Test at .05 level.

| Group | Control |
|---|---|
| 1 | 42 |
| 1 | 48 |
| 1 | 45 |
| 1 | 51 |
| 1 | 35 |
| 1 | 44 |
| 1 | 28 |
| 1 | 47 |
| 2 | 25 |
| 2 | 30 |
| 2 | 33 |
| 2 | 31 |
| 2 | 40 |
| 2 | 42 |
| 2 | 44 |
| 2 | 30 |

**Step 1: Develop Hypotheses:**

a. Independent Variable = Scale: Categorical Quantitative

b. Dependent Variable = Scale: Categorical Quantitative

c. Circle: One-tailed Two-tailed

d. Alternative hypothesis in sentence form.

e. Null hypothesis in sentence form.

f. Write the alternative and null hypotheses using correct notation.

$H_1$: $H_0$:

**Step 2: Establish significance criteria**

g. $\alpha$ =

**Step 3: Calculate test statistic, effect size, and confidence interval**

h. $t_{calculated}$ = Level of significance ($p$) =

i. Decision: reject null or fail to reject null

j. Calculate effect size =

k. Determine the 95% confidence interval:

**Step 4: Draw conclusion**

m. Write your conclusion in sentence form including appropriate results notation.

# Module 9

## t-Test of Related Samples

### Learning Targets

After completing Module 9, you should be able to:

- Apply the process of hypothesis testing to conduct *t*-test of related samples to compare paired scores and determine statistical significance.
- Interpret *t*-test results (hand calculations, SPSS/StatCrunch output) to determine statistical significance and confidence intervals and draw appropriate conclusions
- Utilize *t*-test results to calculate appropriate effect size and power.
- Write appropriate conclusions with statistical results notation.
- Differentiate the various *t*-tests (single, independent, and related) in purpose and calculation.

# Part 1: The Concepts

In Module 2, we were introduced to a research example in which a one-to-one laptop pilot program was implement where half of the 8th graders received a laptop and the other half did not. Technology skill and use were measured. While comparing the means between the treatment and control groups is a viable method, these two groups may have been unequal before the treatment even began. As a result, a baseline or a pre-treatment measure is often established so that a comparison between pre and post can be made in order to draw a conclusion about the treatment. In this example, we will examine the effect of the one-to-one laptop program by comparing pre and post technology use for the treatment group. This pre and post comparison will utilize the analysis of a *t*-test of related samples.

> **Example**
>
> One-to-one laptop program is implemented with half of the 8th grade students ($n$=222) in a district. At the beginning of the school year (prior to the program), participating students complete a pre-survey on technology skill and use. At the end of the school year, students complete the post survey. Can the district conclude that the one-to-one laptop program significantly effects technology use? Test at the .05 level.
>
> **RQ:** Does a one-to-one laptop program significantly change technology use among 8th grade participants?

A ***t-test of related samples***, also known as paired samples *t*-test, examines the difference between two measures for one sample group. This type of analysis may be used for two different types of designs. The first is a ***repeated-measures design*** in which a dependent variable is measured at two points in time for the same sample group. This type of design often uses a pre and post test, to measure the dependent variable before and after the treatment is implemented. The 1:1 laptop example utilizes a repeated-measures design a since survey was administered to the 8th grade participants before and after the 1:1 laptop program. Since repeated-measures design uses the same sample to measure the treatment impact, it eliminates the possibility of error due to differences between a treatment group and control group.

Another possible design that utilizes a *t*-test of related samples test is the ***matched-subjects design*** in which individuals from two samples are matched on one or more variables that are especially important to the study. This allows the researcher to take advantage of the benefits of a related samples *t*-test, while still using two separate samples. The matched-subjects design requires that an individual from sample one is matched with an individual from sample two. Suppose we applied the matched-subjects design to our 1:1 example. In this case, we would utilize a treatment and a control group and likely match individuals from the two groups on gender, GPA, and participation in the free/reduced lunch program. These variable may impact technology use and skill. In this scenario, we would not need a pre-survey, rather only a post-survey would be administered with the matched treatment and control group participants. In either design, the data consists of two sets of scores that are directly related. Since matching involves quite a bit of work, matched-subject design is rarely used. As a result, this module will focus on the commonly used repeated-measures design.

## 9.11 *t*-Test of Related Samples

**Calculating *t*.** In the previous *t*-tests, we have examined the difference between two means (sample mean to population mean and sample 1 mean to sample 2 mean). However, with *t*-test of related samples, we have two data sets but from the same sample. In contrast, we want to examine the individual change that has occurred between the two measures (usually as a result of some treatment). This requires that we calculate the difference between every pair of scores. Since we are typically measuring the impact of some treatment, the difference ($D$) will be calculated as Post – Pre or $X_2 - X_1$. Table 9.1 presents an excerpt of pre and post tech use scores for four individuals in our 1:1 data set. For the sake of demonstration, let's assume that the sample is comprised of these four individuals. The difference is calculated for each pair of scores. Both the mean and standard deviation of these differences are computed.

**Figure 9.1** *Excerpt of Pre and Post scores for Tech Use*

| Person | Pre ($X_1$) Tech Use | Post ($X_2$) Tech Use | Difference ($D$) |
|---|---|---|---|
| A | 10 | 15 | 5 |
| B | 15 | 17 | 2 |
| C | 12 | 17 | 5 |
| D | 14 | 16 | 2 |
| | | | $\Sigma D = 14$ |
| $M_D = \Sigma D/n = 14/4 = 3.5$<br>$s_D$=1.73 | | | |

$$\textbf{Difference} = D = X_2 - X_1$$

$$\textbf{Mean of Differences } (M_D) = \frac{\Sigma D}{n}$$

The focus on of *t*-test of related samples is on individual differences, therefore the calculation of related samples $t$ will utilize the mean of differences. Much like our previous test statistics, we will compare the sample to the population and divide by estimated standard error. Once again, the mean difference of the population is assumed to be zero, since the population hasn't experienced the treatment. So essentially to calculate related samples $t$, compute the mean of differences ($M_D$), and divide by the estimated standard error of differences ($S_{M_D}$). Notice that we are NOT calculating the difference between the pre mean and the post mean!

The estimated standard error of differences is based upon the difference scores. Therefore, the standard deviation is calculated for the difference scores, which is then used to compute standard error. Notice that to compute the estimated standard error of differences ($S_{M_D}$), you divide the standard deviation of differences ($s_D$) divide by $\sqrt{n}$.

$$t = \frac{M_D - \mu_D}{S_{M_D}} = \frac{M_D}{S_{M_D}} \qquad where\ S_{M_D} = \frac{s_D}{\sqrt{n}}$$

If we applied these to our sample of four, the estimated standard error of mean differences is .865. To calculate $t$, the mean of difference ($M_D = 3.5$) is divided by the standard error ($S_{M_D}$=.865), so that $t$=4.05. Although calculating a related samples $t$ is fairly easy, we will still rely on computer programs to do our analysis.

$$S_{M_D} = \frac{s_D}{\sqrt{n}} = \frac{1.73}{\sqrt{4}} = .865 \qquad t = \frac{3.5}{.865} = 4.05$$

**Hypothesis Notation.** In terms of hypothesis testing, the prediction focuses on the mean of differences. And since our goal is to generalize to the population, the hypothesis notation is written with the population in mind. For the example applied throughout this module, we predict that the amount of technology use will significantly change after the implementation of a 1:1 laptop program. This is a non-directional or two-tailed test that would generate the following hypothesis notation.

$H_1$: $\mu_D \neq 0$ $\qquad$ $H_0$: $\mu_D = 0$

Notice that if the treatment is predicted to have an effect, then the difference between pre and post scores will not equal 0, as noted in the alternative hypothesis. Whereas the null indicates that the treatment will not have an effect such that the pre/post difference will equal 0. If we predicted that technology use would significantly increase as a result of the treatment, then the hypothesis notation for the one-tailed test would be:

$H_1$: $\mu_D > 0$ $\qquad$ $H_0$: $\mu_D \leq 0$

Remember, the difference is calculated as (post – pre), so an increase from pre to post would create a positive difference that is greater than 0.

**Determining Significance with *t*.** As with the previous *t*-tests, determining significance with the related samples *t* is identical. Since the computer output will generate the exact level of significance (or the probability of error) for the *t* statistic, we just need to compare the *p*-value to the predetermined alpha. For our 1:1 example, an alpha of .05 was applied. The SPSS output provides descriptive statistics for each measure, in this case pre and post. The second table presents the *t*-test results. Notice at the top of the results table is the heading **Paired Differences**. That label emphasizes the analysis of paired differences and NOT mean differences.

## Example

**RQ:** Does a one-to-one laptop program significantly technology use effect among 8th grade participants?

**Step 1: State the Hypotheses**
**IV:** 1:1 laptop program (pre/post)
**DV:** technology use
**Two-tailed:** keyword=change

**Alternative Hypothesis:** Amount of technology use will significantly change after the implementation of a 1:1 laptop program.

**Null Hypothesis:** Amount of technology use will NOT significantly change after the implementation of a 1:1 laptop program.

**Hypothesis Notation:**
$H_1$: $\mu_D \neq 0$ $\qquad$ $H_0$: $\mu_D = 0$

**Step 2: Establish Significance Criteria**
An alpha of .05 is used for a two-tailed test.

**Step 3: Collect and Analyze Data**
Output indicates: $t$=-20.72, $df$=221, $p$<.0001.

**Step 4: Evaluate Null and Draw Conclusion**
$p$<.0001 is less than alpha of .05, therefore the difference between pre and post scores is significant.

- Significance→Reject the Null→Restate Alternative
- Amount of technology use will significantly change after the implementation of a 1:1 laptop program; ***t*(221)=20.72, p<.0001, two-tailed.**

**SPSS Output**

Paired Samples Test

| | | Paired Differences | | | | | t | df | Sig. (2-tailed) |
|---|---|---|---|---|---|---|---|---|---|
| | | | | | 95% Confidence Interval of the Difference | | | | |
| | | Mean | Std. Deviation | Std. Error Mean | Lower | Upper | | | |
| Pair 1 | post - pre | 3.58590 | 2.57850 | .17306 | 3.24485 | 3.92695 | 20.721 | 221 | .000 |

The output indicates that the average difference from pre to post is an increase of 3.59 points ($M_D$=3.59, $s_D$=2.58). The estimated standard error of differences is .173. The $t$ statistic is a large 20.72 with $p$=.000. Notice the degrees of freedom is 221. Since we only have one sample ($n$=222), $df = n$-1 = 221. Since $p$ of .000 is less than the alpha of .05, the difference is significant so we reject the null. StatCrunch output is similar, however does not include the descriptive statistics or the confidence interval.

**StatCrunch Output**

**Hypothesis test results:**

$\mu_D = \mu_1 - \mu_2$ : Mean of the difference between Post and Pre

$H_0 : \mu_D = 0$

$H_A : \mu_D \neq 0$

| Difference | Sample Diff. | Std. Err. | DF | T-Stat | P-value |
|---|---|---|---|---|---|
| Post - Pre | 3.5859009 | 0.17305742 | 221 | 20.720873 | <0.0001 |

**Assumptions.** The only assumption for related samples $t$-test is that the distribution of differences ($D$) should be normal. However, this is only an issue if a small sample is used. Usually, in studies with samples greater than 30 this assumption can be ignored.

## 9.12 Estimation with $t$-Test of Related Samples

Just as the hypothesis test for related samples $t$ focused on the paired differences, so will the confidence interval. A confidence interval will allow us to estimate the treatment effect in the population with a degree of confidence. That estimation involves determining a range of scores in which the majority of the population will fall. The equation to calculate a confidence interval for a t-test of related samples is:

$$\mu_D = M_D \pm t(s_{M_D})$$

SPSS output automatically includes a 95% confidence interval in the $t$-test analysis, whereas, StatCrunch requires a separate analysis. Both results indicate that the 1:1 treatment would generate a change in technology use for 95% of population ranging from 3.25 to 3.93.

**Paired Samples Test**

| | | Paired Differences | | | | | | | |
|---|---|---|---|---|---|---|---|---|---|
| | | | | | 95% Confidence Interval of the Difference | | | | |
| | | Mean | Std. Deviation | Std. Error Mean | Lower | Upper | t | df | Sig. (2-tailed) |
| Pair 1 | post - pre | 3.58590 | 2.57850 | .17306 | 3.24485 | 3.92695 | 20.721 | 221 | .000 |

**95% confidence interval results:**

$\mu_D = \mu_1 - \mu_2$ : Mean of the difference between Post and Pre

| Difference | Sample Diff. | Std. Err. | DF | L. Limit | U. Limit |
|---|---|---|---|---|---|
| Post - Pre | 3.5859009 | 0.17305742 | 221 | 3.2448469 | 3.9269549 |

## 9.13 Effect Size and Power

Effect size is another measure to indicate the size of the treatment effect. Two effect indices are typically used with $t$-test of related samples—Cohen's $d$ and percentage of variance—both of which must be calculated by hand. Cohen's $d$ is much easier to compute for related samples $t$ as it only requires two values: the mean of differences and the standard deviation of differences. In contrast, calculating percentage of variance ($r^2$) is the same as with independent samples $t$ and only requires knowledge of $t$ and $df$. To calculate these effect sizes for our 1:1 example, we identify the following values in the output ($M_D$=3.59, $s_D$=2.58, $t$=20.72, $df$=221).

**Effect Size for Related Samples t**

Cohen's $d = \frac{M_D}{s_D}$

Percentage of Variance

$r^2 = \frac{t^2}{t^2 + df}$

$$\text{Cohen's } d = \frac{M_D}{s_D} = \frac{3.59}{2.58} = 1.39 \qquad r^2 = \frac{t^2}{t^2 + df} = \frac{20.72^2}{20.72^2 + 221} = \frac{429.32}{429.32 + 221} = .66$$

Based upon Cohen's criteria for evaluating these effect sizes, we can see that Cohen's $d$ =1.39 and $r^2$=.66 are both extremely large effect sizes. The percentage of variance indicates that the 1:1 treatment explains 66% of the variance in the pre/post change in technology use.

| $r^2$ | Cohen's $d$ | Size of Effect |
|---|---|---|
| < 0.09 | < 0.2 | Small |
| 0.09 – 0.25 | 0.2 – 0.8 | Medium |
| > 0.25 | > 0.8 | Large |

With most hypothesis tests, power may be calculated as a means of determining the probability that the study will produce an accurate statistically significant result. Determining power in the planning of a study can be very helpful so that the researcher can make necessary adjustments in sample size, levels of significance, or number of tails to increase power. We can also use power to evaluate the results of our study, whether our results were statistically significant or not. Recall that Cohen recommends a minimum power of .80 or 80%. Power tables for a related samples *t*-test may be found in Appendix D1. Utilizing this table for our example—two-tailed test, $\alpha$ = .05, Cohen's $d$ = 1.39, and sample size of 222 (max of 100)—we find ourselves in blank space, which indicates power is 1.0.

## 9.14 Reporting Results

When reporting the results of a related samples *t*-test, you need include a concluding statement with results notation. The concluding statement should identify the sample, the variables, and the relationship studied. Often, this statement is based upon the hypothesis generated. Results notations should be included at the end of this statement:

- Mean of differences, standard error or standard deviation of differences
- $t_{calculated}$ with degrees of freedom in parentheses
- Level of significance ($p$)
- Number of tails
- Effect size (Cohen's $d$ or $r^2$)
- Confidence interval (optional)

> **Example**
>
> **Confidence Interval**
> Output shows 95% CI Difference [3.25, 3.93].
>
> **Effect Size**
> Using Cohen's *d*, we generate a very large effect size.
>
> $$\text{Cohen's } d = \frac{M_D}{s_D} = \frac{3.59}{2.58} = 1.39$$
>
> **Power**
> Using the Power table in Appendix D1, we identify a very high power of 1.0.
>
> **Updated Results**
> Based upon our example, the following conclusion with results notation would be reported.
>
> Amount of technology use significantly changed after the implementation of a 1:1 laptop program among 8th grade participants **($M_D$=3.59, $s_D$=2.58); $t(221)$= 20.72, $p$<.0001, two-tailed, Cohen's $d$=1.39, 95% CI Difference [3.25, 3.93].**

## 9.15 Directional (One-tailed) Hypothesis Tests

In our last example, we examined how technology use changed after the implementation of a 1:1 laptop program. Although, we conducted this as a two-tailed test, the district was certainly predicting an increase. Having a specific prediction (such as an increase or decrease) about the treatment effect is much more common than just an effect. So this next example will utilize a directional (one-tailed) test.

Most of us at some point have felt anxiety when taking a test. However, for some individuals' test anxiety can limit their educational and career prospects. One researcher has created an intervention that addresses the emotional and cognitive aspects of test anxiety. Twenty-five undergraduate students volunteer to participate in three 1-hour class sessions. Prior to the intervention, participants complete the Test Anxiety Inventory. The sessions are implemented within in the first month of a semester. Students are encouraged to apply the strategies throughout the semester. At the end of the semester, participants complete the Test Anxiety Inventory again. *T*-test of related samples ($\alpha$=.05) was conducted to determine if the intervention significantly decreased test anxiety among undergraduate students.

**Step 1: State Hypotheses**

- Identify variables: IV=intervention; DV=Test anxiety
- Determine # of tails. Key word is decrease→one-tailed.
- State **alternative hypothesis**: Test anxiety intervention will significantly decrease test anxiety among undergraduate students.
- State **null hypothesis:** Test anxiety intervention will NOT significantly decrease test anxiety among undergraduate students.
- Develop hypotheses notation: $H_1: \mu_D < 0$ $H_0: \mu_D \geq 0$

**Step 2: Establish Significance Criteria**
The alpha being applied is .05.

**Step 3: Collect and Analyze Data**
The means for pre and post show that test anxiety scores decreased from pre to post. The *t*-test results produced: $t$ = -3.21, $p$=.004.

**Paired Samples Statistics**

| | | Mean | N | Std. Deviation | Std. Error Mean |
|---|---|---|---|---|---|
| Pair 1 | post | 53.5600 | 25 | 13.08014 | 2.61603 |
| | pre | 62.4400 | 25 | 11.36544 | 2.27309 |

**Paired Samples Test**

| | | Paired Differences | | | | | | | |
|---|---|---|---|---|---|---|---|---|---|
| | | | | | 95% Confidence Interval of the Difference | | | | |
| | | Mean | Std. Deviation | Std. Error Mean | Lower | Upper | t | df | Sig. (2-tailed) |
| Pair 1 | post - pre | -8.88000 | 13.84233 | 2.76847 | -14.59383 | -3.16617 | -3.208 | 24 | .004 |

**Step 4: Evaluate Null Hypothesis and Draw Conclusion**

To determine significance using computer output, we compare the $p$-value to alpha ($\alpha$=.05). In this case, $p$=.004 is definitely less than .05, and the negative $t$ value ($t$ = -3.21) shows that there was a decrease in test anxiety from pre to post. With significance, we reject the null and restate the alternative as the conclusion. To recap, our decision is: Significance→Reject the null→Restate alternative.

Our conclusion with results notation is:

The test anxiety intervention significantly decreased test anxiety of undergraduate students **($M_D$= -8.88, $s_D$=13.84); $t$(24) = -3.21, $p$=.004, one-tailed.**

**Effect Size**

To calculate Cohen's $d$, we utilize the $M_D$ and $s_D$ from the SPSS output. Using Cohen's criteria, -.64 indicates a medium negative effect on test anxiety.

$$\text{Cohen's } d = \frac{M_D}{s_D} = \frac{-8.88}{13.84} = -.64$$

**Confidence Interval**

Since this one-tailed test examined a decrease due to the treatment, the confidence interval estimates the decrease that occurs in the population due to the intervention. SPSS output indicates a lower limit of -14.59 and an upper limit of -3.17 with 95% confidence. This means we are 95% confident that due to the intervention, the population decrease will range between -14.59 and -3.17.

**Power**

Using Appendix D1, we obtain an approximate power of .86, where $n$=25, d=.64, one-tailed test at $\alpha$ = .05.

**Updated Results**

The effect size (Cohen's $d$= -.64) and confidence interval (95% CI [-14.59, -3.17]) results can be easily added to our original results statement at the very end.

The test anxiety intervention significantly decreased test anxiety of undergraduate **students ($M_D$= -8.88, $s_D$=13.84); $t$(24)=-3.21, $p$=.004, one-tailed, Cohen's $d$= -.64, 95% CI Difference [-14.59, -3.17].**

## 9.16 Module Summary

A ***t-test of related samples*** (also known as paired samples *t*-test) examines the difference between two measures for one sample group.

- Common designs include pretest/posttest or matched group comparisons.
- The computation of related samples *t* requires the calculation of:
  1. The difference (*D*) between every pair of scores, usually as Post – Pre or $X_2 - X_1$; **Difference = $D = X_2 - X_1$.**
  2. Sum of differences **($\Sigma D$)**
  3. The mean of differences $M_D = \Sigma D/n$
  4. The standard deviation of difference ($s_D$)
  5. The estimated standard error of the mean of differences $s_{M_D} = \frac{s_D}{\sqrt{n}}$
  6. $t = \frac{M_D - \mu_D}{s_{M_D}} = \frac{M_D}{s_{M_D}}$
- Since related samples t is all about the difference between scores, **Hypothesis Notation** is written in terms of the population mean of difference ($\mu_D$)
  - Two-tailed: $H_1$: $\mu_D \neq 0$ $H_0$: $\mu_D = 0$
  - One-tailed: $H_1$: $\mu_D > 0$ $H_0$: $\mu_D \leq 0$
- The primary assumption is that the distribution of differences (*D*) should be normal; however, this is assumption is often ignored in studies with samples greater than 30.
- Effect size or confidence interval should be reported with hypothesis result.
  - The effect size of Cohen's *d* for related *t* focuses on the differences:
    - Cohen's $d = \frac{M_D}{s_D}$
  - A confidence interval allows us to estimate the population difference (between measures) as a result of the treatment with a degree of confidence.
    - $\mu_D = M_D \pm t(s_{M_D})$
- Power may be calculated using an online calculator to determine the power of the study results or identify the minimum sample size prior to the study.
- The concluding statement should identify the sample, the variables, and the relationship studied. Often, this statement is based upon the hypothesis generated. Results notations should be included at the end of this statement:
  - Mean of differences, standard error or standard deviation of differences
  - $t_{calculated}$ with degrees of freedom in parentheses
  - Level of significance (*p*)
  - Number of tails
  - Effect size (Cohen's *d* or $r^2$)
  - Confidence interval (optional)

## Example

One-to-one laptop program is implemented with half of the 8th grade students in a district. At the beginning of the school year (prior to the program), participating students complete a pre-survey on technology skill and use. At the end of the school year, students complete the post survey. Among the participants, only 222 students complete both pre and post surveys. Can the district conclude that the one-to-one laptop program significantly effects technology use? Test at the .05 level.

**RQ:** Does a one-to-one laptop program significantly change technology use among 8th grade participants?

**Step 1: State the Hypotheses**

**IV:** 1:1 laptop program (pre/post)
**DV:** technology use
**Two-tailed:** keyword=change

**Alternative Hypothesis:** Amount of technology use will significantly change after the implementation of a 1:1 laptop program.

**Null Hypothesis:** Amount of technology use will NOT significantly change after the implementation of a 1:1 laptop program.

**Hypothesis Notation:**

$H_1$: $\mu_D \neq 0$ $H_0$: $\mu_D = 0$

### 9.21V *t*-Test of Related Samples

A ***t-test of related samples*** (also known as paired samples *t*-test) examines the difference between two measures for one sample group. This type of analysis may be used for two different types of designs.

- ***Repeated-measures design*** measures a dependent variable at two points in time for the same sample group. This type of design often uses a pre and post test,to measure the dependent variable before and after the treatment is implemented.
- ***Matched-subjects design*** studies individuals from two samples that are matched on one or more variables that are especially important to the study.

#### Calculating *t*

- *t*-test of related samples examines the individual change that has occurred between two measures (usually as a result of some treatment).
- NOT the difference between Pre and Post means!
- Requires the calculation of the difference between every pair of scores. Since we are typically measuring the impact of some treatment, the difference ($D$) will be calculated as Post – Pre or $X_2 - X_1$.
  1. The difference ($D$) between every pair of scores, usually as Post – Pre or $X_2 - X_1$; **Difference = $D = X_2 - X_1$.**
  2. Sum of differences **($\Sigma D$)**
  3. The mean of differences $M_D = \Sigma D/n$
  4. The standard deviation of difference ($s_D$)
  5. The estimated standard error of the mean of differences $S_{M_D} = \frac{S_D}{\sqrt{n}}$
  6. $t = \frac{M_D - \mu_D}{S_{M_D}} = \frac{M_D}{S_{M_D}}$

**Sample Calculation:**

| Person | Pre ($X_1$) Tech Use | Post ($X_2$) Tech Use | Difference ($D$) |
|---|---|---|---|
| A | 10 | 15 | 5 |
| B | 15 | 17 | 2 |
| C | 12 | 17 | 5 |
| D | 14 | 16 | 2 |
| | | | **$\Sigma D$ = 14** |

**Calculation Steps for Sample**

**Sum of Differences** $\Sigma D = 14$

$M_D = \frac{\Sigma D}{n} = \frac{14}{4} = 3.5$

$s_D = 1.73$

$S_{M_D} = \sqrt{\frac{s_D^2}{n}} = \sqrt{\frac{1.73^2}{4}} = \sqrt{\frac{2.99}{4}} = .865$

$t = \frac{M_D}{S_{M_D}} = \frac{3.5}{.865} = 4.05$

#### Hypothesis Notation

- Focus is on the mean of differences ($\mu_D$)
  - Two-tailed: $H_1$: $\mu_D \neq 0$ $H_0$: $\mu_D = 0$
  - One-tailed: $H_1$: $\mu_D > 0$ $H_0$: $\mu_D \leq 0$

### Determining Significance with $t$

- Compare $p$-value to alpha. If $p < \alpha$, significance is found so we reject the null and restate the alternative hypothesis for the conclusion.
- For our example, $p<.0001$ which is less than the alpha of .05. Significance→Reject Null→Restate Alternative.

**SPSS Output**

**Paired Samples Statistics**

| | | Mean | N | Std. Deviation | Std. Error Mean |
|---|---|---|---|---|---|
| Pair 1 | post | 17.6028 | 222 | 1.72539 | .11580 |
| | pre | 14.0169 | 222 | 1.92798 | .12940 |

**Paired Samples Test**

| | | Paired Differences | | | | | t | df | Sig. (2-tailed) |
|---|---|---|---|---|---|---|---|---|---|
| | | | | | 95% Confidence Interval of the Difference | | | | |
| | | Mean | Std. Deviation | Std. Error Mean | Lower | Upper | | | |
| Pair 1 | post - pre | 3.58590 | 2.57850 | .17306 | 3.24485 | 3.92695 | 20.721 | 221 | .000 |

**StatCrunch Output**

**Hypothesis test results:**

$\mu_D = \mu_1 - \mu_2$ : Mean of the difference between Post and Pre

$H_0 : \mu_D = 0$

$H_A : \mu_D \neq 0$

| Difference | Sample Diff. | Std. Err. | DF | T-Stat | P-value |
|---|---|---|---|---|---|
| Post - Pre | 3.5859009 | 0.17305742 | 221 | 20.720873 | <0.0001 |

**Example**

**Step 2: Establish Significance Criteria**
An alpha of .05 is used for a two-tailed test.

**Step 3: Collect and Analyze Data**
Output indicates: $t$=-20.72, $df$=221, $p$<.0001.

**Step 4: Evaluate Null and Draw Conclusion**
$p$<.0001 is less than alpha of .05, therefore the difference between pre and post scores is significant.

- Significance→Reject the Null→Restate Alternative
- Amount of technology use will significantly change after the implementation of a 1:1 laptop program; **$t(221)=20.72$, $p<.0001$, two-tailed.**

### Assumptions

- The distribution of differences ($D$) should be normal; however, this is assumption is often ignored in studies with samples greater than 30.

## 9.22V Estimation with $t$-Test of Related Samples

- A confidence interval allows us to estimate the population difference (between measures) as a result of the treatment with a degree of confidence.
  - $\mu_D = M_D \pm t(s_{M_D})$
  - For our example, results indicate that the 1:1 treatment would generate a change in technology use for 95% of population ranging from 3.25 to 3.93.

**SPSS Output**

**Paired Samples Test**

| | | Paired Differences | | | | | t | df | Sig. (2-tailed) |
|---|---|---|---|---|---|---|---|---|---|
| | | | | | 95% Confidence Interval of the Difference | | | | |
| | | Mean | Std. Deviation | Std. Error Mean | Lower | Upper | | | |
| Pair 1 | post - pre | 3.58590 | 2.57850 | .17306 | 3.24485 | 3.92695 | 20.721 | 221 | .000 |

**StatCrunch Output**

**95% confidence interval results:**

$\mu_D = \mu_1 - \mu_2$ : Mean of the difference between Post and Pre

| Difference | Sample Diff. | Std. Err. | DF | L. Limit | U. Limit |
|---|---|---|---|---|---|
| Post - Pre | 3.5859009 | 0.17305742 | 221 | 3.2448469 | 3.9269549 |

## 9.23V Effect Size and Power

Two effect indices are typically used with $t$-test of related samples—Cohen's $d$ and percentage of variance ($r^2$)—both of which must be calculated by hand.

$$\text{Cohen's } d = \frac{M_D}{s_D} = \frac{3.59}{2.58} = 1.39 \qquad r^2 = \frac{t^2}{t^2 + df} = \frac{20.72^2}{20.72^2 + 221} = \frac{429.32}{429.32 + 221} = .66$$

- Criteria for evaluating effect sizes are the same:

| $r^2$ | Cohen's $d$ | Size of Effect |
|---|---|---|
| < 0.09 | < 0.2 | Small |
| 0.09 – 0.25 | 0.2 – 0.8 | Medium |
| > 0.25 | > 0.8 | Large |

- Based upon Cohen's criteria for evaluating these effect sizes, we can see that Cohen's $d$=1.39 and $r^2$=.66 are both extremely large effect sizes.
- Power may be determined using Appendix D1.

## 9.24V Reporting Results

The concluding statement should identify the sample, the variables, and the relationship studied. Often, this statement is based upon the hypothesis generated. Results notations should be included at the end of this statement:

- Mean of differences, standard error or standard deviation of differences
- $t_{calculated}$ with degrees of freedom in parentheses
- Level of significance ($p$)
- Number of tails
- Effect size (Cohen's $d$ or $r^2$)
- Confidence interval (optional)

### Example

**Confidence Interval**
Output shows 95% CI Difference [3.25, 3.93].

**Effect Size**
Using Cohen's $d$, we generate a very large effect size.

$$\text{Cohen's } d = \frac{M_D}{s_D} = \frac{3.59}{2.58} = 1.39$$

**Power**
Using Appendix D1 (two-tailed, $\alpha$=.05) and applying $n$=222 (max n=100) and Cohen's $d$=1.40, we obtain a power of 1.0.

**Updated Results**
Based upon our example, the following conclusion with results notation would be reported.

Amount of technology use significantly changed after the implementation of a 1:1 laptop program among 8th grade participants **($M_D$=3.59, $s_D$=2.58); $t$(221) = 20.72, $p$<.0001, two-tailed, Cohen's $d$ = 1.39, 95% CI Difference [3.25, 3.93].**

## 9.25V Directional (One-tailed) Hypothesis Tests

A researcher has created an intervention that addresses the emotional and cognitive aspects of test anxiety. Twenty-five undergraduate students volunteer to participate in three 1-hour class sessions. Prior to the intervention, participants complete the Test Anxiety Inventory. The sessions are implemented within in the first month of a semester. Students are encouraged to apply the strategies throughout the semester. At the end of the semester, participants complete the Test Anxiety Inventory again. $T$-test of related samples ($\alpha$=.05) was conducted to determine if the intervention significantly decreased test anxiety among college students.

**Step 1: State Hypotheses**

- Identify variables: IV=intervention; DV=Test anxiety
- Determine # of tails. Key word is increase→one-tailed.
- State **alternative hypothesis**: Test anxiety intervention will significantly decrease test anxiety among college students.
- State **null hypothesis:** Test anxiety intervention will NOT significantly decrease test anxiety among college students.
- Develop hypotheses notation: $H_1$: $\mu_D < 0$ $\qquad$ $H_0$: $\mu_D \geq 0$

**Step 2: Establish Significance Criteria**
The alpha being applied is .05.

**Step 3: Collect and Analyze Data**
The means for pre and post show that test anxiety scores decreased from pre to post. The $t$-test results produced: $t$=-3.21, $p$=.004.

**Paired Samples Statistics**

| | | Mean | N | Std. Deviation | Std. Error Mean |
|---|---|---|---|---|---|
| Pair 1 | post | 53.5600 | 25 | 13.08014 | 2.61603 |
| | pre | 62.4400 | 25 | 11.36544 | 2.27309 |

**Paired Samples Test**

| | | Paired Differences | | | | | t | df | Sig. (2-tailed) |
|---|---|---|---|---|---|---|---|---|---|
| | | | | | 95% Confidence Interval of the Difference | | | | |
| | | Mean | Std. Deviation | Std. Error Mean | Lower | Upper | | | |
| Pair 1 | post - pre | -8.88000 | 13.84233 | 2.76847 | -14.59383 | -3.16617 | -3.208 | 24 | .004 |

**Step 4: Evaluate Null Hypothesis and Draw Conclusion**

To determine significance using computer output, we compare the *p*-value to alpha ($\alpha$=.05). In this case, *p*=.004 is definitely less than .05, and the negative *t* value (*t* = -3.21) shows that there was a decrease in test anxiety from pre to post. With significance, we reject the null and restate the alternative as the conclusion. To recap, our decision is: Significance→Reject the null→Restate alternative.

Our conclusion with results notation is:

> The test anxiety intervention significantly decreased test anxiety of undergraduate students ($M_D$= -8.88, $s_D$=13.84); *t*(24)=-3.21, *p*=.004, one-tailed.

## Effect Size and Power

To calculate Cohen's *d*, we utilize the $M_D$ and $s_D$ from the SPSS output. Cohen's criteria indicates that -.64 is a moderate negative effect on test anxiety.

$$\text{Cohen's } d = \frac{M_D}{s_D} = \frac{-8.88}{13.84} = -.64$$

Using Appendix D1 (one-tailed, $\alpha$ = .05) and applying our example values of *n*=25 and Cohen's d = .64, we obtain a very high power of approximately .92.

## Confidence Interval

Since this one-tailed test examined a decrease due to the treatment, the confidence interval estimates the decrease that occurs in the population due to the intervention. SPSS output indicates a lower limit of -14.59 and an upper limit of -3.17 with 95% confidence. This means we are 95% confident that as a result of the intervention, the population decrease will range between -14.59 and -3.17.

## Updated Results

The effect size (Cohen's *d*= -.64) and confidence interval (95% CI [-14.59, -3.17]) results can be easily added to our original results statement at the very end.

> The test anxiety intervention significantly decreased test anxiety of undergraduate students (**$M_D$= -8.80, $s_D$=13.84); *t*(24)=-3.21, *p*=.004, one-tailed, Cohen's *d* = -.64, 95% CI difference [-14.59, -3.17].**

## 9.26V Additional Practice

1. Fifty years ago, psychologists were convinced that IQ was not inherited. The Minnesota Study of Identical Twins Reared Apart (MISTRA) is a longitudinal study of twins to examine genetic and environmental influences on the development of psychological traits. *T*-test of related samples was conducted to examine if IQ significantly differs for identical twins raised apart, which would suggest that IQ is not genetic but rather a product of one's environment. The results below are for ten sets of twins. Use an alpha of .05.

**Paired Samples Statistics**

| | | Mean | N | Std. Deviation | Std. Error Mean |
|---|---|---|---|---|---|
| Pair 1 | TwinA | 109.5000 | 10 | 10.46953 | 3.31076 |
| | TwinB | 110.1000 | 10 | 14.15352 | 4.47574 |

**Paired Samples Test**

| | Paired Differences | | | | | t | df | Sig. (2-tailed) |
|---|---|---|---|---|---|---|---|---|
| | | | | 95% Confidence Interval of the Difference | | | | |
| | Mean | Std. Deviation | Std. Error Mean | Lower | Upper | | | |
| Pair 1 TwinA - TwinB | -.60000 | 7.66232 | 2.42304 | -6.08129 | 4.88129 | -.248 | 9 | .810 |

**Step 1: Develop Hypotheses:**

a. Independent Variable = Scale: Categorical Quantitative

b. Dependent Variable = Scale: Categorical Quantitative

c. Circle: One-tailed Two-tailed

d. Alternative hypothesis in sentence form.

e. Null hypothesis in sentence form.

f. Write the alternative and null hypotheses using correct notation.
$H_1$: $H_0$:

**Step 2: Establish significance criteria**

g. $\alpha$ =

**Step 3: Calculate test statistic.**

h. $t_{\text{calculated}}$ = Level of significance ($p$) =

i. Decision: reject null or fail to reject null

j. Use the power table to identify a minimum sample size for this study in order to achieve an effect size of .5, power of .8, $\alpha$=.05, two-tailed.

**Step 4: Draw conclusion**

k. Write your conclusion in sentence form including appropriate results notation.

2. Cognitive-behavioral therapy (CBT) is a form of treatment in which patients better understand how their negative thought patterns can lead to negative feelings and behaviors. Patients learn to change their thinking to improve their mood and behaviors. CBT has shown to be very successful in treating a variety of psychological disorders. However, a school counselor is interested in examining the efficacy of CBT in increasing self-esteem among high school students who regularly report feelings of loneliness and mild depression. Eight students agree to participate in a weekly group session that focuses on CBT techniques. The treatment lasts for a semester. Self-esteem was measured before and after the treatment. Can the counselor conclude that cognitive-behavioral therapy significantly increases self-esteem among mildly depressed high school students? Test at the .05 level.

**Paired Samples Statistics**

| | | Mean | N | Std. Deviation | Std. Error Mean |
|---|---|---|---|---|---|
| Pair 1 | SEpost | 18.0000 | 8 | 3.96412 | 1.40153 |
| | SEpre | 16.6250 | 8 | 4.06861 | 1.43847 |

**Paired Samples Test**

| | Paired Differences | | | | | t | df | Sig. (2-tailed) |
|---|---|---|---|---|---|---|---|---|
| | | | | 95% Confidence Interval of the Difference | | | | |
| | Mean | Std. Deviation | Std. Error Mean | Lower | Upper | | | |
| Pair 1 SEpost - SEpre | 1.37500 | 1.40789 | .49776 | .19798 | 2.55202 | 2.762 | 7 | .028 |

**Step 1: Develop Hypotheses:**

a. Independent Variable = Scale: Categorical Quantitative

b. Dependent Variable = Scale: Categorical Quantitative

c. Circle: One-tailed Two-tailed

d. Alternative hypothesis in sentence form.

e. Null hypothesis in sentence form.

f. Write the alternative and null hypotheses using correct notation.

$H_1$: $H_0$:

**Step 2: Establish significance criteria**

g. $\alpha$ =

**Step 3: Calculate test statistic, effect size, and confidence interval**

h. $t_{calculated}$ = Level of significance ($p$) =

i. Decision: reject null or fail to reject null

j. Calculate effect size =

k. Determine the 95% confidence interval:

**Step 4: Draw conclusion**

l. Write your conclusion in sentence form including appropriate results notation.

## 9.27 Hands-on Activity: Coke versus Pepsi Experiment Continued

Recall the Coke versus Pepsi Experiment from Module 8. This activity will also use the data collected from that experiment to examine the second research question:

When tasting the difference between Coke and Pepsi, is one's prediction of accuracy significantly different from one's actual ability/accuracy?

This research question will utilize t-test of related samples for analysis. But keep in mind, we are not comparing the Prediction mean to the Actual mean. The experiment is measuring one's taste ability to differentiate between Coke and Pepsi. Participants first predict their accuracy then complete a test that actually measures their accuracy. Although there isn't a treatment that separate a pre and post measures. The prediction and the actual scores are "related." So think of the independent variable as the prediction versus actual, while the dependent variable is the taste ability.

| Part ID | Preference | Predict % | Actual % |
|---|---|---|---|
| 1 | 1 | 20 | 20 |
| 2 | 1 | 40 | 60 |
| 3 | 1 | 80 | 20 |
| 4 | 1 | 100 | 100 |
| 5 | 1 | 100 | 60 |
| 6 | 2 | 60 | 80 |
| 7 | 2 | 100 | 80 |
| 8 | 2 | 60 | 20 |
| 9 | 2 | 40 | 0 |
| 10 | 2 | 60 | 40 |
| 11 | | | |
| 12 | | | |
| 13 | | | |
| 14 | | | |
| 15 | | | |
| 16 | | | |
| 17 | | | |

Use the Coke/Pepsi dataset that you previously created. Conduct a *t*-test of related samples using $\alpha$=.05. In addition, calculate a 95% confidence interval and effect size. These analyses will require data from the Predict % and Actual % columns.

**Use the results to complete the hypothesis process.**

**Step 1: Develop Hypotheses:**

a. Independent Variable = Scale: Categorical Quantitative

b. Dependent Variable = Scale: Categorical Quantitative

c. Circle: One-tailed Two-tailed

d. Alternative hypothesis in sentence form.

e. Null hypothesis in sentence form.

f. Write the alternative and null hypotheses using correct notation.

$H_1$: $H_0$:

**Step 2: Establish significance criteria**

g. $\alpha$ =

**Step 3: Calculate test statistic, effect size, and confidence interval**

h. $t_{\text{calculated}}$ = Level of significance ($p$) =

i. Decision: reject null or fail to reject null

j. Calculate effect size =

k. Determine the 95% confidence interval:

**Step 4: Draw conclusion**

l. Write your conclusion in sentence form including appropriate results notation.

## 9.28V In the Literature

This example utilizes paired responses in how individuals perceive their safely associated with different categories of graffiti. So this isn't the typical pre/post scenario; however it compares the same individuals' perceptions of safety across four graffiti scenarios. Since *t*-test of related samples can only compare two measures at a time, the various combinations of the four graffiti categories are analyzed. Therefore, six *t*-test of related samples were conducted. Table 1 does not present the category means but instead the difference in category means, since the difference is what is being analyzed. Results include the *t*-statistic and level of significance as well as the 95% confidence interval.

**Excerpt from:** Austin, D. M., & Sanders, C. (2007). Graffiti and perceptions of safety: A pilot study using photographs and survey data. *Journal of Criminal Justice and Popular Culture,* 14 (4), 292-316.

Previous research has shown that incivilities like graffiti relate to individuals' perceptions of safety and crime in the area. Researchers in this pilot study examined how different types of graffiti impact crime-related fear. Ninety-six undergraduate students participated in the study. A total of 24 photographs of graffiti were presented one at a time to the group of participants. After each photograph, respondents answered questions on the Perceptions of Safety Scale, which assessed the level of perceived safety that they would associate with each photograph of graffiti. A four-point Likert scale was used for these items, such that a high score indicates feelings of safety while a low score indicates fear. Graffiti in four categories were presented:

- **Message**- presented a clearly defined message or messages in writing and/or used symbols with little highly stylized graffiti.
- **Positive Mural**- is positive socially sanctioned mural graffiti, which may have been constructed as a result of community groups trying to portray a positive message to onlookers.
- **Hip Hop**-is an expression of the hip hop culture.
- **Gang**-uses gang-related symbols and materials.

Means for each graffiti category indicate that individuals felt most safe when viewing Positive Mural graffiti, followed by Message graffiti. In contrast, Gang related graffiti evoked the lowest level of perceived safety followed by Hip Hop style graffiti. Perceptions of safety were compared for each combination of the graffiti categories using *t*-test of related samples. Results are presented in Table 1. Researchers found that graffiti is not unidimensional, rather the various types create different reactions concerning safety.

**Table 1.** Comparisons of Perceptions of Safety for Graffiti Categories

| Categories Compared | Difference in Means | *SD* | 95% Interval Difference | | *t* | *df* | Sig. 2-tailed |
|---|---|---|---|---|---|---|---|
| | | | Lower | Upper | | | |
| Message—Positive | .19 | 5.02 | -.84 | 1.22 | .37 | 92 | .711 |
| Gang—Positive | 6.22 | 5.73 | 5.04 | 7.40 | 10.46 | 92 | .000 |
| Hip Hop—Positive | 4.52 | 5.64 | 3.37 | 5.66 | 7.84 | 95 | .000 |
| Gang—Message | 5.76 | 5.67 | 4.59 | 6.93 | 9.79 | 92 | .000 |
| Hip Hop—Message | 4.26 | 5.19 | 3.20 | 5.32 | 8.00 | 94 | .000 |
| Gang—Hip Hop | 1.52 | 4.64 | .58 | 2.47 | 3.20 | 94 | .002 |

1. Of the six comparisons analyzed, which one is NOT statistically significant?

2. Of the five significant *t*-tests, which one has the largest *t*-value (or greatest difference)?

3. Four of the comparisons, present levels of significance ($p$) as .000. Is it accurate to report that there is a 0% chance of finding significance out of error? How should the authors report this $p$-value?

4. Explain the confidence interval for comparison between Hip Hop and Positive graffiti.

5. Based upon the *t*-test results, what overall conclusion would you draw regarding perceptions of safety and graffiti categories?

## 9.29 Using the Computer

The following instructions will guide you in conducting *t*-test of related samples in SPSS and StatCrunch. A couple things to keep in mind. SPSS automatically includes group means and standard deviations, and confidence intervals with the *t*-test. In contrast, StatCrunch requires separate analyses for each of these. Also for *t*-test of related samples, StatCrunch does not provide the option of using a data summary for the analysis.

### SPSS

1. Enter data.
2. 🖱 the **Analyze** menu.
3. Select **Compare Means** and **Paired-Samples t Test.**
4. So that the calculated difference is for (post - pre) 🖱 the post variable first and move under Variable 1 in Paired Variables.
5. 🖱 the pre variable and under Variable 2 in Paired Variables
7. 🖱 **Options** IF you want change the confidence interval from 95% to 99%.
8. 🖱 **OK.**

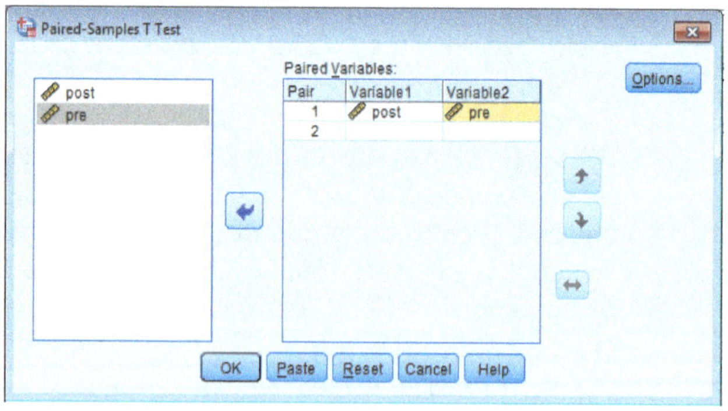


### StatCrunch

1. Enter data.
2. Within the data window, 🖱 the **Stat** menu, select ***t* Stats, >Paired**.
3. Within Paired *t* dialogue box, under **Sample 1 in:**
   - Select Post variable.
4. Under **Sample 2 in:**
   - Select Pre variable.
5. Under **Perform:** select <u>one</u> of the options:
   - **Hypothesis Test for μ**
     - By $H_A$ indicate the direction of test
   - **Confidence Interval for μ**
     - Indicate percent of confidence (95% is default)
6. 🖱 **Compute.**

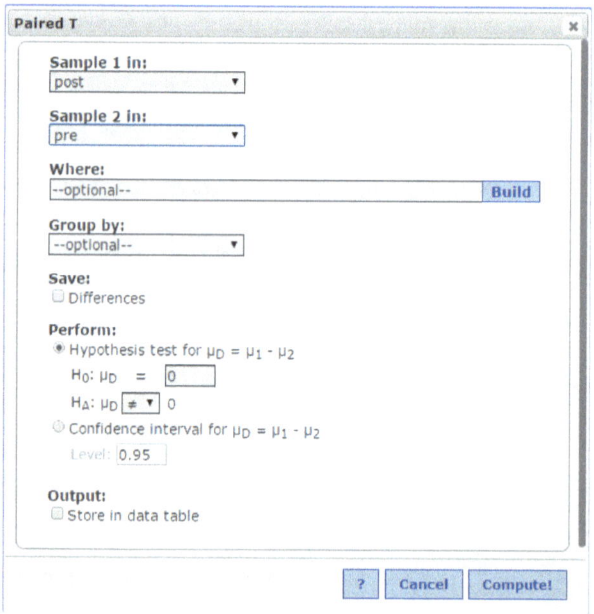

## 9.30 Exercises
### Reviewing the Concepts

1. We have learned about three different *t*-tests. Explain the differences in purpose and calculation.
   - *t*-test of Single Sample

   - *t*-test of Independent Samples

   - *t*-test of Related Samples

2. Why does the hypothesis notation use $\mu_D$?

3. In a pretest/posttest design, are the pretest and posttest means compared when calculating *t*?

## Interpreting Results

4. A middle school counselor is concerned about how her school staff are "dealing" with problem students, with the typical method as a referral to the school counselor. Instead, this counselor would like to empower her staff so that staff may better connect with and support all students. This counselor (Goodwin-Glick, 2017) developed a day-long workshop on Trauma-Informed Care, which recognizes that everyone has experienced some kind of trauma in life, yet the impact of that trauma can be very diverse and devastating. The workshop taught participants about the physiological and emotional impact of trauma, methods of recognizing trauma, skills in demonstrating care and support to students. Participants completed the Trauma-Informed Care Dispositions Survey (TIC-DS) that measured a total of seven subscales, two of which were Trauma-related Knowledge and Empathic Concern. The TIC-DS was only administered at the end of the training, however participants rated both their current and previous knowledge and perceptions. The SPSS output below presents the pre/post comparisons for Trauma-related Knowledge and Empathic Concern. Complete this problem focusing on Trauma-related Knowledge, in which you are examining the impact of the TIC workshop on Trauma-related Knowledge. Use $\alpha$=.05.

**T-Test**

**Paired Samples Statistics**

| | | Mean | N | Std. Deviation | Std. Error Mean |
|---|---|---|---|---|---|
| Pair 1 | postknowledge | 4.2555 | 542 | .51082 | .02194 |
| | preknowledge | 3.8148 | 542 | .68374 | .02937 |
| Pair 2 | postempathetic | 4.4025 | 530 | .53560 | .02326 |
| | preempathetic | 4.3630 | 530 | .51218 | .02225 |

**Paired Samples Test**

| | | Paired Differences | | | | | t | df | Sig. (2-tailed) |
|---|---|---|---|---|---|---|---|---|---|
| | | | | | 95% Confidence Interval of the Difference | | | | |
| | | Mean | Std. Deviation | Std. Error Mean | Lower | Upper | | | |
| Pair 1 | postknowledge - preknowledge | .44063 | .67784 | .02912 | .38344 | .49783 | 15.134 | 541 | .000 |
| Pair 2 | postempathetic - preempathetic | .03950 | .29155 | .01266 | .01462 | .06437 | 3.119 | 529 | .002 |

**Step 1: Develop Hypotheses:**

a. Independent Variable = Scale: Categorical Quantitative

b. Dependent Variable = Scale: Categorical Quantitative

c. Circle: One-tailed Two-tailed

d. Alternative hypothesis in sentence form.

e. Null hypothesis in sentence form.

f. Write the alternative and null hypotheses using correct notation.

*$H_1$:* *$H_0$:*

**Step 2: Establish significance criteria**

g. $\alpha$ =

**Step 3: Calculate test statistic, effect size, and confidence interval**

h. $t_{\text{calculated}}$ = Level of significance ($p$) =

i. Decision: reject null or fail to reject null

j. Calculate effect size =

k. Determine the 95% confidence interval:

**Step 4: Draw conclusion**

l. Write your conclusion in sentence form including appropriate results notation.

5. Use the output from the problem #4, where Goodwin-Glick (2017) examines the impact of Trauma-Informed Care Training on Empathic Concern among her middle school staff. Use $\alpha$=.05.

**Step 1: Develop Hypotheses:**

a. Independent Variable = Scale: Categorical Quantitative

b. Dependent Variable = Scale: Categorical Quantitative

c. Circle: One-tailed Two-tailed

d. Alternative hypothesis in sentence form.

e. Null hypothesis in sentence form.

f. Write the alternative and null hypotheses using correct notation.

$H_1$: $H_0$:

**Step 2: Establish significance criteria**

g. $\alpha$ =

**Step 3: Calculate test statistic, effect size, and confidence interval**

h. $t_{\text{calculated}}$ = Level of significance ($p$) =

ii. Decision: reject null or fail to reject null

j. Calculate effect size =

k. Determine the 95% confidence interval:

**Step 4: Draw conclusion**

l. Write your conclusion in sentence form including appropriate results notation.

Goodwin-Glick, K. (2017). *Impact of Trauma-Informed Care Professional Development on School Personnel Perceptions of Knowledge, Dispsitions, and Behaviors Toward Traumatized Students.* (Electronic Thesis or Dissertation). Retrieved from https://etd.ohiolink.edu/

6. Read the excerpt below to answer the following questions.

**Excerpt from:** Smithson, M. (2012). The positive impact of personal goal setting on assessment. *Canadian Journal of Action Research, 13*(3), 57-73.

Smithson (2012) conducted an action research study on the impact of personal goal setting on academic performance in five areas (reading series, online reading, math, critical thinking/problem-solving, and language arts) among her 3rd grade students (*n*=18). For three weeks, students experiences weekly assessments in the content areas. After which, students were introduced to the concept of goal setting. For the next three weeks, students set personal academic goals for each weekly assessment based upon previous grades and current understanding. Smithson compared student pretreatment (three week average of test scores prior) and post treatment assessment scores (three week average of test scores after). *T*-test of related samples was used to determine if students generated significant increases in assessment scores as a result of the three-week goal setting treatment.

Table 1. *Related Samples t-test Results by Academic Test*

| **Academic Test** | **Pre Mean** | **Post Mean** | ***t*** | ***p*** |
|---|---|---|---|---|
| Reading Series | 88.39 | 89.56 | 0.77 | .22 |
| Online Reading | 71.67 | 69.78 | -1.53 | .07 |
| Math | 75.78 | 75.17 | -0.25 | .40 |
| Critical thinking/Problem-solving | 61.06 | 80.59 | 5.20 | .0001 |
| Language Arts | 84.11 | 90.17 | 2.21 | .02 |

a. Table 1 presents the pre and post means. Are these values actually used in calculating *t*?

b. For the first academic test in the table (Reading Series), what is the null hypothesis being tested? What is your decision regarding the null hypothesis?

c. Explain why two of the five *t*-values in are negative.

d. Which two academic tests produced significant results? What statistical result is necessary to obtain a better understanding of the treatment effect?

e. Is the sample size adequate for this study? What sample size is necessary to generate an effect size of .5, power of .8 using a one-tailed test at .05?

7. Read the excerpt below to answer the following questions.

**Excerpt from:** Goldsberry, J. W. (2015). *Assessing the effects of an STD educational intervention on Greek society college students' knowledge and attitudes toward safe sex behaviors*. Doctoral dissertation. Retrieved from: https://kb.gcsu.edu/cgi/viewcontent.cgi?article=1011&context=dnp

Concerned for the sexual health of college students, Goldsberry (2015) implemented an educational intervention targeting sexually-transmitted diseases (STDs) among Greek society members. She was particularly interested in examining the effect the intervention would have on STD knowledge and attitudes. Prior to the 30-minute session, participants completed instruments that measured knowledge of and attitudes toward STDs. One week after the intervention, participants completed the same measures. A total of 132 Greek society members participated in the training and completed all measures. Results reveal a significant increase in STD knowledge from pre ($M$=13.03, $SD$=6.5) to post ($M$=20.27, $SD$=4.9) $t(131) = -13.53$, $p < .0001$. However, attitudes toward safe sex and STDs did not change from pre ($M$=55.59, $SD$=10.42) to post as a result of the educational session ($M$=55.39, $SD$=12.83) $t(131)=.223$, $p=.948$.

a. Why do the authors report the pre and post means when these values are not used in calculating $t$?

b. Identify the independent variable and the two dependent variables.

c. Which dependent variable significantly changed as a result of the intervention? What statistics support this?

d. Based upon the results, do you believe that there is a relationship between STD knowledge and attitudes?

e. What statistics should the author report to strengthen her results?

## Conducting Analysis

8. The practice of mindfulness—maintaining a moment-by-moment awareness and acceptance of our thoughts, feelings, bodily sensations, and surrounding environment, through a gentle, nurturing lens—has become very popular in recent years as a means of reducing stress, anxiety, and depression. Beauchemin, Hutchins, and Patterson (2008) studied the impact of a mindfulness intervention on self-reported social skills of 34 adolescents with learning disabilities. The intervention consisted of a 45-minute initial session that taught students how to focus their attention on their breathing in an effort to develop calmness and stability. After successfully developing a sense of calm, students were encouraged to note thoughts and feelings as they occur, thereby increasing awareness. For the next five weeks, students practiced mindfulness meditation at the beginning of each class, five days a week. Students completed the Social Skills Rating System before and after the intervention. The follow data is a close representation of their results. Can the researchers conclude that the intervention significantly increases social skills? Use SPSS or StatCrunch to conduct the analysis applying $\alpha$=.05.

| Pre | Post |
|---|---|
| 95 | 101 |
| 98 | 102 |
| 100 | 106 |
| 90 | 92 |
| 92 | 99 |
| 99 | 104 |
| 80 | 85 |
| 103 | 107 |
| 96 | 101 |
| 84 | 92 |
| 99 | 104 |
| 101 | 98 |
| 78 | 85 |
| 104 | 108 |
| 90 | 96 |
| 93 | 99 |
| 94 | 92 |
| 98 | 106 |
| 95 | 99 |
| 99 | 107 |
| 111 | 102 |
| 96 | 103 |
| 94 | 99 |
| 89 | 97 |
| 100 | 106 |
| 94 | 100 |
| 99 | 97 |
| 97 | 104 |
| 101 | 100 |
| 87 | 91 |
| 111 | 105 |
| 92 | 98 |
| 98 | 102 |
| 85 | 92 |

**Step 1: Develop Hypotheses:**

a. Independent Variable = Scale: Categorical Quantitative

b. Dependent Variable = Scale: Categorical Quantitative

c. Circle: One-tailed Two-tailed

d. Alternative hypothesis in sentence form.

e. Null hypothesis in sentence form.

f. Write the alternative and null hypotheses using correct notation.

$H_1$: $H_0$:

**Step 2: Establish significance criteria**

g. $\alpha$ =

**Step 3: Calculate test statistic, effect size, and confidence interval**

h. $t_{\text{calculated}}$ = Level of significance ($p$) =

i. Decision: reject null or fail to reject null

j. Calculate Cohen's $d$ =

k. Determine the 95% confidence interval:

**Step 4: Draw conclusion**

l. Write your conclusion in sentence form including appropriate results notation.

Beauchemin, J., Hutchins, T.L., & Patterson, F. (2008). Mindfulness meditation may lessen anxiety, promote social skills, and improve academic performance among adolescents with learning disabilities. *Journal of Evidence-Based Integrative Medicine, 13*(1), 34-45.

9. The construct of "grit"—the perseverance and passion to complete long-term goals—has become a topic of much research in an effort to develop grittier children (Duckworth et al., 2007) and ultimately more successful adults. A high school counselor has developed a 9-week high school Grit course that focuses on developing a growth mindset through cognitive behavioral techniques. At the beginning and end of the course, students ($n$=20) complete the Grit Scale. Use SPSS or StatCrunch to conduct the analysis applying $\alpha$=.05. Can the counselor conclude that the 9-week Grit course significantly impacts grit among high school students?

| Pre | Post |
|---|---|
| 2.0 | 3.0 |
| 3.0 | 3.9 |
| 4.0 | 4.4 |
| 3.2 | 3.4 |
| 2.8 | 3.2 |
| 3.3 | 4.0 |
| 4.1 | 4.0 |
| 2.2 | 3.0 |
| 2.5 | 2.9 |
| 3.5 | 3.8 |
| 3.7 | 4.3 |
| 2.7 | 3.1 |
| 2.9 | 3.0 |
| 3.6 | 3.8 |
| 3.4 | 3.9 |
| 3.6 | 4.1 |
| 2.6 | 2.8 |
| 2.8 | 3.0 |
| 2.2 | 2.6 |
| 1.9 | 2.8 |

**Step 1: Develop Hypotheses:**

a. Independent Variable = Scale: Categorical Quantitative

b. Dependent Variable = Scale: Categorical Quantitative

c. Circle: One-tailed Two-tailed

d. Alternative hypothesis in sentence form.

e. Null hypothesis in sentence form.

f. Write the alternative and null hypotheses using correct notation.

$H_1$: $H_0$:

**Step 2: Establish significance criteria**

g. $\alpha$ =

**Step 3: Calculate test statistic, effect size, and confidence interval**

h. $t_{calculated}$ = Level of significance ($p$) =

i. Decision: reject null or fail to reject null

j. Calculate effect size =

k. Determine the 95% confidence interval:

**Step 4: Draw conclusion**

l. Write your conclusion in sentence form including appropriate results notation.

Duckworth, A. L., Peterson, C., Matthews, M. D., & Kelly, D. R. (2007). Grit: Perseverance and passion for long-term goals. *Journal of Personality and Social Psychology, 92*(6), 1087-1101.

# Module 10

## ANOVA: Analysis of Variance

### Learning Targets

After completing Module 10, you should be able to:

- Apply the process of hypothesis testing to conduct ANOVA to compare multiple group means and determine statistical significance.
- Interpret ANOVA results (SPSS/StatCrunch output) to determine statistical significance and post hoc tests.
- Utilize ANOVA results to calculate appropriate effect size and power.
- Write appropriate conclusions with statistical results notation.

# Part 1: The Concepts

In the last several modules, we have learned how to compare two groups or two measures using a *t*-test. However, research is not limited to variables with two categories, rather demographic such as race, ethnicity, religion, socio-economic status, and age will likely have many more categories. ***Analysis of Variance*** (referred to as ANOVA) allows us to examine mean differences across two or more groups.

## 10.11 ANOVA: Purpose and Hypothesis Notation

As with all our hypothesis tests, we have been studying samples in order to generalize our result to the population. Since we are typically studying three or more groups, we seek to determine if the mean differences are large enough to conclude that these differences would likely occur in the population. Although we could compare the means of each pair of groups, such testing would only inform us of the difference for each pair and not the differences created by the independent variable as a whole. In addition, statistically examining each pair is not very efficient.

In our example on parent education level differences in adult optimism, ANOVA allows us to examine the mean differences across all three groups in order to draw a conclusion about education level (as a whole) affecting optimism. Essentially, we are predicting that at least one of group means will be significantly different from the rest. In terms of hypothesis notation, the alternative hypothesis would indicate that at least one mean will differ. While the null hypothesis indicates that the group means will not differ:

$H_1$: At least one $M$ will differ $\qquad$ $H_0$: $\mu_1 = \mu_2 = \mu_3$

Notice that the predictions are no longer one-tailed or two-tailed, since we are only looking for a difference across multiple groups.

### Example

The value of a college education has been called into question in light of its increasing cost. A group of researchers examined the how parent education level—

1=no HS diploma ($n$=5),
2= HS diploma ($n$=5),
3=college degree ($n$=5)—

affects optimism among adults (age 20-65). Test at the .05 level.

**RQ:** Does parent education level affect optimism among US adults?

**Step 1: State Hypothesis**
IV: Level of education
DV: Optimism

**Alternative Hypothesis**
Parent education level will significantly affect optimism among US adults.

**Null Hypothesis**
Parent education level will significantly affect optimism among US adults.

**Hypothesis Notation:**
$H_1$: At least one $M$ will differ.
$H_0$: $\mu_1 = \mu_2 = \mu_3$

## 10.12 The Concepts in Calculating ANOVA *F*-ratio

The ANOVA test statistic is similar to the *t* statistic in that we calculate a ratio of mean differences divided by standard error (difference due to chance). Recall that standard error utilizes the standard deviation (the variability within groups) divided by the square root of the group size ($n$).

$$t = \frac{\text{obtained difference between sample means}}{\text{standard error (difference expected due to chance)}}$$

The test statistic for ANOVA is the *F*-ratio and follows a similar structure, however instead of focusing on a single difference, the equation is written in terms of variance, representing the differences across all the groups.

$$F = \frac{\text{variance between group means}}{\text{variance expected due to chance}}$$

The ***F*-ratio** numerator represents the variance (differences) across/between all group means, while the denominator is similar to standard error in that it is a measure of variability within each group. If we think of the sources these specific types of variances, the variance (differences) between sample means may be due to the treatment effect as well as error (differences due to chance). When we divide this value by error (differences due to chance), the treatment effect remains. Therefore, when the variance between groups is small (or close to zero), the treatment did not have an effect. Since the differences due to chance are fairly equivalent, the *F*-value is around 1.0. In contrast, when the treatment has had a significant effect, the variance between groups will be larger than the differences due to chance, generating a larger *F*-ratio.

$$F = \frac{\text{variance between sample means}}{\text{variance expected due to chance}} = \frac{\text{treatment effect + differences due to chance}}{\text{differences due to chance}}$$

The actual calculation of ANOVA is $\quad F = \dfrac{\text{variance between treatments (groups)}}{\text{variance within treatments (groups)}}$

Since sample variance = $s^2 = SS/df$ we need to calculate variance for both between treatments and within treatments. Therefore,

$$F = \frac{SS_{between}/df_{between}}{SS_{within}/df_{within}} = \frac{MS_{between}}{MS_{within}}$$

Since we are calculating the *SS* divided by *df*, this is essentially a mean of squared deviations and is represented my *MS* (Mean Squares). Also, because our *F*-ratio divides the variance between treatments by the variance within, this requires that we calculate to Total Sum of Squares ($SS_{Total}$) and then partition into the two components: between and within. In addition, there are two different degrees of freedom: $df_{between}$ and $df_{within}$. As a result, the total degrees of freedom ($df_{Total}$) will also be partioned. Figure 10.1 displays how $SS_{Total}$ and $df_{Total}$ are partitioned and calculated. These calculations require several new notation symbols, which are defined in the figure. Although, our focus in using ANOVA will be on interpreting computer output (whew!), the calculation steps for ANOVA are presented on the following page.

Figure 10.1
*Partitioning of $SS_{Total}$ and $df_{Total}$*

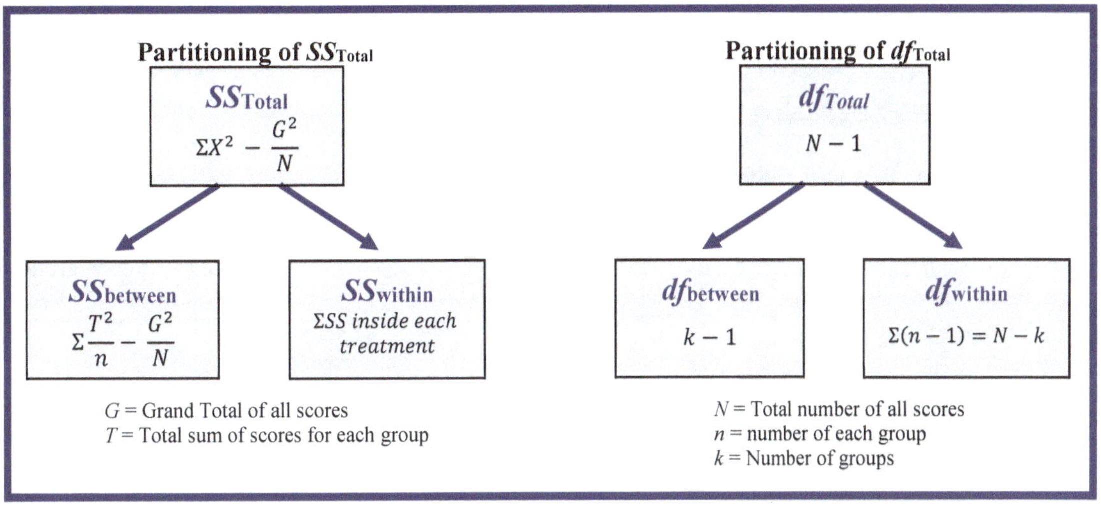


## 10.13 The *F* Distribution and Determining Significance

Because the *F*-ratio is computed so that the numerator and denominator are measuring the exact same variance when the treatment has no effect, the value will always be positive. Therefore, the *F* distribution is positively skewed, where the majority of *F*-ratios cluster around 1 (See Figure 10.2A). Since the *F*-ratio measures two variances, the shape of the *F* distribution is based upon degrees of freedoms for these two variances—between groups and within groups (individuals). Recall, that degrees of freedom for a single sample is $df = n$-1. In applying this to our example, we identify three education levels ($k$=3) with five in each group ($n$=5, $N$=15). The *df* for groups ($k$) is $df_{between} = k$-1 = 3-1 = 2. The *df* for individuals is $df_{within} = N$-$k$ = 15-3 = 12. When the treatment has had an effect, the $MS_{between}$ should be much larger than $MS_{within}$, therefore generating a large *F*-ratio. Similar to our previous test statistics, determining significance of a hand calculated *F* requires the identification of $F_{critical}$ through the *F* Distribution Table (Appendix F), which necessitates the knowledge of $df_{between}$ and $df_{within}$. Figure 10.2B presents an excerpt of this table, where the top columns are based upon $df_{between}$ ($k$-1) and the rows define the $df_{within}$ ($N$-$k$). Each cell provides critical values for α=.05 and **α=.01 (bold).** For our example that has *df* of (2, 12), the intersecting cell identifies $F_{critical}$ for .05 as 3.88 and $F_{critical}$ for .01 as 6.93. The example provided α=.05, so our $F_{critical}$=3.88.

Figure 10.2
*F Distribution and Table*

**A. *F* Distribution with Critical Values for *df*=2, 12**

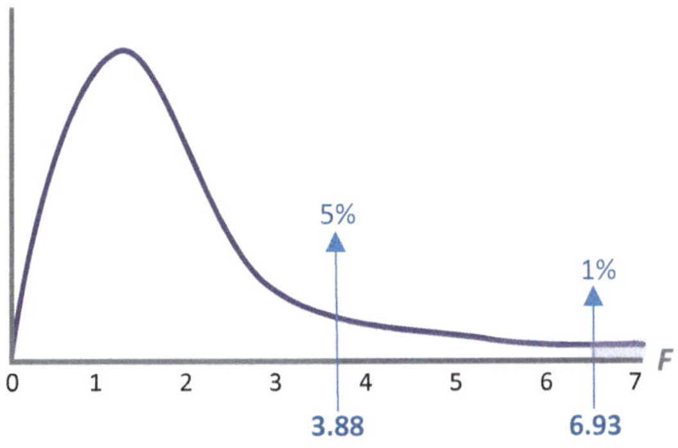


**B. Excerpt from *F* Distribution Table**

| $df_{within}$ ($N$-$k$) | $df_{between}$ ($k$-1) | | | |
|---|---|---|---|---|
| | 1 | 2 | 3 | 4 |
| 10 | 4.96<br>**10.04** | 4.10<br>**7.56** | 3.71<br>**6.55** | 3.48<br>**5.99** |
| 11 | 4.84<br>**9.65** | 3.98<br>**7.20** | 3.59<br>**6.22** | 3.36<br>**5.67** |
| 12 | 4.75<br>**9.33** | 3.88<br>**6.93** | 3.49<br>**5.95** | 3.26<br>**5.41** |
| 13 | 4.67<br>**9.07** | 3.80<br>**6.70** | 3.41<br>**5.74** | 3.18<br>**5.20** |
| 14 | 4.60<br>**8.86** | 3.74<br>**6.51** | 3.34<br>**5.56** | 3.11<br>**5.03** |

# Calculating the F-ratio (F-Bomb—Ugh!)

Recall that in our example, we are comparing three education levels (1=less than HS diploma, 2=HS diploma, 3=college degree) on optimism scores that range from 1 to 5. The table presents raw data for five individuals in each group. The calculation of the *F*-ratio requires extensive computations and formulas. Before any formulas are applied, eight basic calculations are required for Step 1.

**Step 1**

Calculations for **each group** include:

- *T* (the total sum of scores),
- *n* (the number of scores),
- *M* (the mean of scores), and
- *SS* (the sum of squares).

Calculations for the **entire data set** include:

- $\Sigma X^2$ is the sum of each score squared,
- Grand (*G*) total of all scores was calculated,
- Total sample size (*N*) and
- Number of groups (*k*).

| Education Level | | | |
|---|---|---|---|
| 1 | 2 | 3 | |
| <HS | HS | College | $\Sigma X^2$=153 $\Sigma X$= sum of each score squared<br>*G*=45 *G* = grand total of ALL score<br>*N*=15 *N* = total number of ALL scores<br>*k*=3 *k* = number of groups |
| 1 | 3 | 3 | |
| 2 | 2 | 5 | |
| 3 | 4 | 3 | |
| 2 | 3 | 5 | |
| 2 | 3 | 4 | |
| $T_1$=10 | $T_2$=15 | $T_3$=20 | *T* is the total sum of scores in each group |
| $n_1$=5 | $n_2$=5 | $n_3$=5 | *n* is the number of scores in each group |
| $M_1$=2 | $M_2$=3 | $M_3$=4 | *M* is the mean for each group |
| $SS_1$=2 | $SS_2$=2 | $SS_3$=4 | *SS* is the sum of squares for each group |

**Step 2:** Compute the sum of squares for all three parts: $SS_{Total}$, $SS_{between}$, **and** $SS_{within}$.

| $SS_{Total}$ | $SS_{between}$ | $SS_{within}$ |
|---|---|---|
| $SS_{Total} = \Sigma X^2 - \frac{G^2}{N}$<br>$= 153 - \frac{45^2}{15}$<br>$= 153 - \frac{2025}{15}$<br>$SS_{Total} = 153 - 135 = 18$ | $SS_{between} = \Sigma\frac{T^2}{n} - \frac{G^2}{N}$<br>$= \frac{T_1^2}{n_1} + \frac{T_2^2}{n_2} + \frac{T_3^2}{n_3} - \frac{G^2}{N}$<br>$= \frac{10^2}{5} + \frac{15^2}{5} + \frac{20^2}{5} - \frac{45^2}{15}$<br>$= \frac{100}{5} + \frac{225}{5} + \frac{400}{5} - \frac{2025}{15}$<br>$SS_{between} = 20 + 45 + 80 - 135 = 10$ | $SS_{within} = \Sigma SS_{within\ each\ treatment}$<br>$SS_{within} = 2 + 2 + 4 = 8$ |

**Step 3:** Compute ***MS*** **values and *F*-ratio.**

| $MS_{between}$ | $MS_{within}$ | *F*-ratio |
|---|---|---|
| $MS_{between} = \frac{SS_{between}}{df_{between}}$<br>$= \frac{10}{k-1}$<br>$MS_{between} = \frac{10}{3-1} = \frac{10}{2} = 5$ | $MS_{within} = \frac{SS_{within}}{df_{within}}$<br>$= \frac{8}{N-k}$<br>$MS_{within} = \frac{8}{15-3} = \frac{8}{12} = .667$ | $F = \frac{MS_{between}}{MS_{within}}$<br>$F = \frac{5}{.667} = 7.50$ |

**Assumptions.** ANOVA requires the fulfillment of three assumption—the same that were applied to a *t*-test of independent samples.

1. Independent observations
2. Normality of the populations from which our samples were selected.
3. Equal variances (homogeneity of variances) across population groups.

Normality is typically not a huge concern as long as sample sizes are fairly large. At a minimum, groups must have at least five individuals. The assumption of equal variances is an important one and will regularly be examined using the Levene's Test. Both SPSS and StatCrunch will generate the Levene's Test with just an additional click. Recall, that whenever using a statistical tests to examine assumptions, the result should NOT be significant—meaning the *p*-value should be greater than .05 to fulfill this assumption. The SPSS and StatCrunch Levene's results identify $p$=.397, which is greater than .05 and NOT significant. Therefore, we have fulfilled the assumption of equal variances.

**Test of Homogeneity of Variances**

optimism

| Levene Statistic | df1 | df2 | Sig. |
|---|---|---|---|
| 1.000 | 2 | 12 | .397 |

**Levene's Test for Homogeneity of Variance**

| Test Statistic | DF 1 | DF 2 | P-value |
|---|---|---|---|
| 1 | 2 | 12 | 0.3966 |

Typically we will examine the Levene's test first, to make sure that this assumption has been fulfilled and then proceed to examine the remainder of the output. When this assumption has been violated, such that $p$>.05, it likely due to groups having very different sizes and lack of normality. SPSS does provide some methods to deal with this assumption violation, when group size cannot be adjusted.

**Interpreting Computer Output.** Fortunately, we will continue to utilize computer output to determine significance, which will require the comparison of the computer-generated *p*-value to the predetermined alpha level. Whenever, $p$ is less than alpha, the results are significant, and we reject the null hypothesis. SPSS and StatCrunch generate identical output for our example, where $F$=7.5 and $p$=.008. The *p*-value is less than alpha of .05 and is therefore significant, so we reject the null.

## Example

The value of a college education has been called into question in light of its increasing cost. A group of researchers examined the how parent education level:

1=less than HS ($n$=5)
2= HS diploma ($n$=5);
3=college degree ($n$=5)

affects optimism among adults (age 20-65). Test at the .05 level.

**RQ:** Does parent education level affect optimism among US adults?

**Step 1: State Hypothesis**
**IV:** Level of education
**DV:** Optimism

**Alternative Hypothesis**
Parent education level will significantly affect optimism among US adults.

**Null Hypothesis**
Parent education level will significantly affect optimism among US adults.

**Hypothesis Notation:**
*H₁*: At least one $M$ will differ.
*Ho*: $\mu_1 = \mu_2 = \mu_1$

**Step 2: Establish Significance Criteria**
An alpha of .05 is applied.

**Step 3: Collect and Analyze Data**
**Equal Variances?**
Levene's Test is not significant (p=.397), so equal variances are assumed.

**ANOVA Results?**
Output indicates: $F$=7.5, $df$=2,12 and $p$=.008.

**Step 4: Evaluate Null and Draw Conclusion**
$p$=.008 is less than alpha of .05, therefore group means are significantly different

- Significance→Reject the Null→Restate Alternative
- Parent education level significantly effects optimism among US adults; $F(2,12)=7.5, p=.008$.

**SPSS**

**ANOVA**

optimism

| | Sum of Squares | df | Mean Square | F | Sig. |
|---|---|---|---|---|---|
| Between Groups | 10.000 | 2 | 5.000 | 7.500 | .008 |
| Within Groups | 8.000 | 12 | .667 | | |
| Total | 18.000 | 14 | | | |

**StatCrunch**
**ANOVA table**

| Source | DF | SS | MS | F-Stat | P-value |
|---|---|---|---|---|---|
| educ | 2 | 10 | 5 | 7.5 | 0.0077 |
| Error | 12 | 8 | 0.66666667 | | |
| Total | 14 | 18 | | | |

## 10.14 Effect Size

**Effect Size**

$$\eta^2 = \frac{SS_{between}}{SS_{Total}}$$

| $\eta^2$ | Size of Effect |
|---|---|
| < 0.09 | Small |
| 0.09 – 0.25 | Medium |
| > 0.25 | Large |

As previously noted, hypothesis testing only indicates the probability of finding significance out of error; it does not provide a measure of the size of the treatment effect. For ANOVA, the effect size of eta squared ($\eta^2$) is commonly reported. Eta squared is similar to $r^2$, and represents the percentage of variance explained by the independent variable. Calculation of $\eta^2$ requires two values presented in the ANOVA output: $SS_{between}$ and $SS_{Total}$. For our example, the output indicates that $SS_{between}$=10 and $SS_{Total}$=18 generating an $\eta^2$=10/18= .56, which indicates that parent education level accounts for 56% of the variability in adult optimism—a large effect.

## 10.15 Post Hoc tests

Since ANOVA compares all the group means simultaneously, our conclusion is limited to some difference across the groups. As a result, we are unable to determine WHICH groups are significantly different. Although, we could run a *t*-test of independent samples for each pair of groups, running multiple tests of significance increases our chance of eventually finding significance out of error (Type I error). Consequently, researchers have developed techniques that allow us to still make the paired comparisons, while minimizing Type I error. These techniques are called ***Post Hoc Tests***. As the name indicates, such tests are conducted after the initial ANOVA whenever there are three or more groups. Several post hoc tests are available—each with a unique method in minimizing Type I error. SPSS also provides post hoc tests when the assumption of equal variances has not been met. For the sake of simplicity we will focus on three post hoc tests. The first two assume equal variances--Tukey's HSD and Scheffé. The third is when the assumption of equal variances has been violated (Levene's Test is significant)—Tamhane's T2.

- ***Tukey's Honestly Significant Difference (HSD)*** is a commonly used post hoc test throughout social sciences. Tukey's HSD determines the minimum group difference that is necessary for significance. If a group difference exceeds this minimum standard, then the difference is considered significant. Tukey's HSD is the only post hoc test available in StatCrunch. SPSS results present each paired comparison with the mean difference, standard error, level of significance, and the 95% confidence interval. Notice the asterisk by the mean difference (-2.00000*) between group 1 and 3—this indicates a significant difference in addition to the *p*-value of .006. StatCrunch output differs a bit in that it only presents the confidence interval and *p*-value for each comparison. Again, we can see that the difference between group 1 and 3 is significant with *p*=.0058. Although confidence intervals are reported for post hoc test, often they are not reported.

**Multiple Comparisons**

Dependent Variable: optimism
Tukey HSD

| (I) educ | (J) educ | Mean Difference (I-J) | Std. Error | Sig. | 95% Confidence Interval Lower Bound | 95% Confidence Interval Upper Bound |
|---|---|---|---|---|---|---|
| 1.00 | 2.00 | -1.00000 | .51640 | .171 | -2.3777 | .3777 |
| | 3.00 | -2.00000* | .51640 | .006 | -3.3777 | -.6223 |
| 2.00 | 1.00 | 1.00000 | .51640 | .171 | -.3777 | 2.3777 |
| | 3.00 | -1.00000 | .51640 | .171 | -2.3777 | .3777 |
| 3.00 | 1.00 | 2.00000* | .51640 | .006 | .6223 | 3.3777 |
| | 2.00 | 1.00000 | .51640 | .171 | -.3777 | 2.3777 |

*. The mean difference is significant at the 0.05 level.

**Tukey HSD results (95% level)**

1 subtracted from

| | Difference | Lower | Upper | P-value |
|---|---|---|---|---|
| 2 | 1 | -0.37767887 | 2.3776789 | 0.1709 |
| 3 | 2 | 0.62232113 | 3.3776789 | 0.0058 |

2 subtracted from

| | Difference | Lower | Upper | P-value |
|---|---|---|---|---|
| 3 | 1 | -0.37767887 | 2.3776789 | 0.1709 |

- ***Scheffé Test*** is one of the most conservative post hoc tests for reducing the risk of a Type I error. Its cautious nature is based upon identifying a critical value using the degrees of freedom for between (groups), *k*-1, which results in a very low value. Significance is difficult to achieve with such a small *df*. The SPSS Scheffé results indicate the same pair as significant, however, the *p*-value is slightly larger, *p*=.008.

**Multiple Comparisons**

Dependent Variable: optimism
Scheffe

| (I) educ | (J) educ | Mean Difference (I-J) | Std. Error | Sig. | 95% Confidence Interval Lower Bound | 95% Confidence Interval Upper Bound |
|---|---|---|---|---|---|---|
| 1.00 | 2.00 | -1.00000 | .51640 | .196 | -2.4395 | .4395 |
| | 3.00 | -2.00000* | .51640 | .008 | -3.4395 | -.5605 |
| 2.00 | 1.00 | 1.00000 | .51640 | .196 | -.4395 | 2.4395 |
| | 3.00 | -1.00000 | .51640 | .196 | -2.4395 | .4395 |
| 3.00 | 1.00 | 2.00000* | .51640 | .008 | .5605 | 3.4395 |
| | 2.00 | 1.00000 | .51640 | .196 | -.4395 | 2.4395 |

*. The mean difference is significant at the 0.05 level.

- ***Tamhane's T2*** is used when equal variances have been violated likely due to unequal group sizes. Pairwise comparisons are conducted but applying a very conservative method. Output is similar to other post hoc tests.

## 10.16 Reporting the Results

When reporting the results of a ANOVA, you need include a concluding statement with results notation. The concluding statement should identify the sample, the variables, and the relationship studied. This statement is typically based upon the hypothesis generated. In addition, several results should be included:

- Group means, standard deviations, and size
- *F* with both degrees of freedom in parentheses
- Level of significance (*p*)
- Effect size ($\eta^2$)
- Post hoc results if significant. Indicate which groups are different from each other.

Since ANOVA is examining multiple groups, you may want to use a table to present group means and standard deviations. Again, both SPSS and StatCrunch generate these descriptive statistics.

> **Example**
>
> **Effect Size**
>
> Using $\eta^2$, we generate a very large effect size.
>
> $$\eta^2 = \frac{SS_{between}}{SS_{Total}} = \frac{10}{18} = .56$$
>
> **Post hoc**
>
> Tukey's HSD indicates that Group 1 (no diploma) have significant less optimism than Group 3 (college degree), *p*=.006.
>
> **Updated Results**
>
> Based upon our example, the following conclusion with results notation would be reported.
>
> - Parent education level significantly effects optimism among US adults; ***F*(2,12)=7.5, *p*=.008, $\eta^2$=.56.** Table 1 presents descriptive statistics for the three education groups. Tukey's HSD post hoc test indicates that adults with parents who have a college education have significantly higher optimism than adults whose parents do not have a HS diploma (*p*=.006).
>
> **Table 1**
>
> | | *n* | *M* | *SD* |
> |---|---|---|---|
> | **No HS Diploma** | 5 | 2.0 | 0.71 |
> | **HS Diploma** | 5 | 3.0 | 0.71 |
> | **College Degree** | 5 | 4.0 | 1.00 |

## 10.17 Module Summary

Analysis of Variance (ANOVA) is a hypothesis test that allows us to compare multiple group means.

- The alternative hypothesis would indicate that at least one mean will differ. While the null hypothesis indicates that the group means will not differ:

  $H_1$: At least one *M* will differ $\qquad$ $H_0$: $\mu_1 = \mu_2 = \mu_1$

- ANOVA test statistic is the *F*-ratio and focuses on variance, representing the differences across all the groups.
  - $F = \frac{\text{variance between group means}}{\text{variance expected due to chance}} = \frac{SS_{between}/df_{between}}{SS_{within}/df_{within}} = \frac{MS_{between}}{MS_{within}}$
- Since the *F*-ratio measures two variances, the *F* distribution is based upon degrees of freedoms for these two variances—between groups ($df_{between} = k-1$) within groups ($df_{within} = N-k$).
- The *F* distribution is positively skewed, with most values clustered around 1.
- A significant *F* will be larger than 1 with a *p*-value less than .05.
- ANOVA assumptions include:
  1. Independent observations
  2. Normality—usually not a big deal with large samples
  3. Equal variances (homogeneity of variances) across population groups.
     - Important! Use Levene's Test within ANOVA—should not be significant to fulfill assumption.
- The effect size for ANOVA is eta squared ($\eta^2$) and is evaluated the same as $r^2$.
- Post hoc tests are used to determine WHICH groups are significantly different. Tukey's HSD and Scheffé Test are commonly used.
- When writing results, you should include a concluding statement based upon your hypothesis as well as the following statistical results:
  - Group means, standard deviations, and size (possibly in a table)
  - *F* with both degrees of freedom in parentheses
  - Level of significance (*p*)
  - Effect size ($\eta^2$)
  - Post hoc results if significant. Indicate which groups are different from each other.

# Part 2: The Learning Guide

## Example

The value of a college education has been called into question in light of its increasing cost. A group of researchers examined the how parent education level—1=no HS diploma ($n$=5); 2= HS diploma ($n$=5); 3=college degree ($n$=5)—affects optimism among adults (age 20-65). Test at the .05 level.

**RQ:** Does parent education level affect optimism among US adults?

**Step 1: State the Hypotheses**

**IV:** Parent education level (no HS diploma, HS diploma, college degree)
**DV:** optimism

**Alternative Hypothesis:** Parent education level will significantly affect optimism among US adults.

**Null Hypothesis:** Parent education level will significantly affect optimism among US adults.

**Hypothesis Notation:** $H_1$: At least one $M$ will differ. $H_0$: $\mu_1 = \mu_2 = \mu_1$

### 10.21V ANOVA: Purpose and Hypothesis Notation

Analysis of Variance (ANOVA) is a hypothesis test that allows us to compare multiple group means.

- The alternative hypothesis would indicate that at least one mean will differ. While the null hypothesis indicates that the group means will not differ:

  $H_1$: At least one $M$ will differ $H_0$: $\mu_1 = \mu_2 = \mu_1$

- Predictions are no longer one-tailed or two-tailed, since we are only looking for a difference across multiple groups.

### 10.22V The Concepts behind Calculating ANOVA $F$-ratio

$F$-ratio is the test statistic for ANOVA. Since it is not focusing on a single difference, the equation is written in terms of variance, representing the differences across all the groups.

- The $F$-ratio numerator represents the variance (differences) across/between all group means, while the denominator is similar to standard error in that it is a measure of variability within each group.
  - $F = \frac{\text{variance between sample means}}{\text{variance expected due to chance}} = \frac{\text{treatment effect+differences due to chance}}{\text{differences due to chance}}$
  - When the treatment has had a large enough effect, $F$ should be large.

- The variances in $F$ are called mean squares (MS).

  $$F = \frac{\text{variance between group means}}{\text{variance expected due to chance}} = \frac{SS_{between}/df_{between}}{SS_{within}/df_{within}} = \frac{MS_{between}}{MS_{within}}$$

- The calculation of $F$ requires over 22 separate computations, depending upon the number of groups compared.

### 10.23V The $F$ Distribution and Determining Significance

The $F$ distribution is positively skewed, where the majority of $F$-ratios cluster around 1.

- Since the $F$-ratio measures two variances, the shape of the $F$ distribution is based upon degrees of freedoms for these two variances—between groups and within groups (individuals).
  - $df_{between} = k\text{-}1$
  - $df_{within} = N\text{-}k$

### Assumptions

1. Independent observations
2. Normality—usually not a big deal with large samples
3. Equal variances (homogeneity of variances) across population groups.
   - Important! Use Levene's Test within ANOVA—should not be significant to fulfill assumption.

**Test of Homogeneity of Variances**

optimism

| Levene Statistic | df1 | df2 | Sig. |
|---|---|---|---|
| 1.000 | 2 | 12 | .397 |

**Levene's Test for Homogeneity of Variance**

| Test Statistic | DF 1 | DF 2 | P-value |
|---|---|---|---|
| 1 | 2 | 12 | 0.3966 |

### Interpreting Computer Output

Compare the computer-generated $p$-value to the predetermined alpha level.

- Whenever, $p$ is less than alpha, the results are significant, and we reject the null hypothesis.

**SPSS**

**ANOVA**

optimism

| | Sum of Squares | df | Mean Square | F | Sig. |
|---|---|---|---|---|---|
| Between Groups | 10.000 | 2 | 5.000 | 7.500 | .008 |
| Within Groups | 8.000 | 12 | .667 | | |
| Total | 18.000 | 14 | | | |

**StatCrunch**

**ANOVA table**

| Source | DF | SS | MS | F-Stat | P-value |
|---|---|---|---|---|---|
| educ | 2 | 10 | 5 | 7.5 | 0.0077 |
| Error | 12 | 8 | 0.66666667 | | |
| Total | 14 | 18 | | | |

## Example

**Step 2: Establish Significance Criteria**

An alpha of .05 is applied.

**Step 3: Collect and Analyze Data**

**Equal Variances?**

Levene's Test is not significant (p=.397), so equal variances are assumed.

**ANOVA Results?**

Output indicates: $F$=7.5, $df$=2,12 and $p$=.008.

**Step 4: Evaluate Null and Draw Conclusion**

$p$=.008 is less than alpha of .05, therefore group means are significantly different

- Significance→Reject the Null→Restate Alternative
- Parent education level significantly effects optimism among US adults; ***F*(2,12)=7.5, *p*=.008.**

### 10.24V Effect Size

For ANOVA, the effect size of eta squared ($\eta^2$) is commonly reported.

- Eta squared is similar to $r^2$, and represents the percentage of variance explained by the independent variable.
- Calculation of $\eta^2$ requires two values presented in the ANOVA output: $SS_{\text{between}}$ and $SS_{\text{Total}}$.

**Effect Size**

$$\eta^2 = \frac{SS_{between}}{SS_{Total}}$$

| $\eta^2$ | Size of Effect |
|---|---|
| < 0.09 | Small |
| 0.09 – 0.25 | Medium |
| > 0.25 | Large |

### 10.25V Post Hoc Tests

Since ANOVA results only indicates that <u>some</u> difference is significant across the groups, a post hoc test is used to determine WHICH groups are significantly different.

- Each pair of groups are compared, however, most post hoc tests utilize conservative calculation methods to minimize Type I error. Two common post hoc tests are Tukey's HSD and Scheffé.
  - ***Tukey's Honestly Significant Difference (HSD)*** determines the minimum group difference that is necessary for significance. If a group difference exceeds this minimum standard, then the difference is considered significant.

- ***Scheffé Test*** is one of the most conservative post hoc tests for reducing the risk of a Type I error. Its cautious nature is based upon identifying a critical value using the degrees of freedom for between (groups), *k*-1, which results in a very low values.
- ***Tamhane's T2*** is used when equal variances have been violated likely due to unequal group sizes. Pairwise comparisons are still conducted but applying a very conservative method.

**Multiple Comparisons**

Dependent Variable: optimism
Tukey HSD

| (I) educ | (J) educ | Mean Difference (I-J) | Std. Error | Sig. | 95% Confidence Interval Lower Bound | Upper Bound |
|---|---|---|---|---|---|---|
| 1.00 | 2.00 | -1.00000 | .51640 | .171 | -2.3777 | .3777 |
| | 3.00 | -2.00000* | .51640 | .006 | -3.3777 | -.6223 |
| 2.00 | 1.00 | 1.00000 | .51640 | .171 | -.3777 | 2.3777 |
| | 3.00 | -1.00000 | .51640 | .171 | -2.3777 | .3777 |
| 3.00 | 1.00 | 2.00000* | .51640 | .006 | .6223 | 3.3777 |
| | 2.00 | 1.00000 | .51640 | .171 | -.3777 | 2.3777 |

*. The mean difference is significant at the 0.05 level.

**Tukey HSD results (95% level)**

1 subtracted from

| | Difference | Lower | Upper | P-value |
|---|---|---|---|---|
| 2 | 1 | -0.37767887 | 2.3776789 | 0.1709 |
| 3 | 2 | 0.62232113 | 3.3776789 | 0.0058 |

2 subtracted from

| | Difference | Lower | Upper | P-value |
|---|---|---|---|---|
| 3 | 1 | -0.37767887 | 2.3776789 | 0.1709 |

## 10.26V Reporting the Results

The concluding statement should identify the sample, the variables, and the relationship studied. This statement is typically based upon the hypothesis generated. In addition, several results should be included:

- Group means, standard deviations, and size
- *F* with both degrees of freedom in parentheses
- Level of significance (*p*)
- Effect size ($\eta^2$)
- Post hoc results if significant. Indicate which groups are different from each other.

# Example

### Effect Size

Using $\eta^2$, we generate a very large effect size.

$$\eta^2 = \frac{SS_{between}}{SS_{Total}} = \frac{10}{18} = .56$$

### Post hoc

Tukey's HSD indicates that Group 1 (no diploma) have significant less optimism than Group 3 (college degree), *p*=.006.

### Updated Results

Based upon our example, the following conclusion with results notation would be reported.

- Parent education level significantly effects optimism among US adults; ***F*(2,12)=7.5, *p*=.008, $\eta^2$=.56.** Table 1 presents descriptive statistics for the three education groups. Tukey's HSD post hoc test indicates that adults with parents who have a college education have significantly higher optimism than adults whose parents do not have a HS diploma (*p*=.006).

**Table 1**

| | *n* | *M* | *SD* |
|---|---|---|---|
| **No HS Diploma** | 5 | 2.0 | 0.71 |
| **HS Diploma** | 5 | 3.0 | 0.71 |
| **College Degree** | 5 | 4.0 | 1.00 |

## 10.27V A Complete Example

In Module 2, we were introduced to a study that asked 8th grades to identify their preferred technology device (1=basic phone, 2=smart phone, 3=tablet, 4= computer). In addition, technology use was measured as the sum score of five items that applied a 4-point scale so that scores range between 5 and 20. Data was slightly adjusted for this example in which we explore if technology use differs by preferred device. Use α=.05.

**Descriptives**

use

| | N | Mean | Std. Deviation | Std. Error | 95% Confidence Interval for Mean | | Minimum | Maximum |
|---|---|---|---|---|---|---|---|---|
| | | | | | Lower Bound | Upper Bound | | |
| 1.00 | 7 | 14.4286 | 3.25869 | 1.23167 | 11.4148 | 17.4424 | 10.00 | 19.00 |
| 2.00 | 25 | 13.6000 | 2.73861 | .54772 | 12.4696 | 14.7304 | 10.00 | 20.00 |
| 3.00 | 5 | 15.8000 | 2.77489 | 1.24097 | 12.3545 | 19.2455 | 13.00 | 20.00 |
| 4.00 | 7 | 18.1429 | 1.46385 | .55328 | 16.7890 | 19.4967 | 16.00 | 20.00 |
| Total | 44 | 14.7045 | 3.07714 | .46390 | 13.7690 | 15.6401 | 10.00 | 20.00 |

**Test of Homogeneity of Variances**

use

| Levene Statistic | df1 | df2 | Sig. |
|---|---|---|---|
| 1.363 | 3 | 40 | .268 |

**ANOVA**

use

| | Sum of Squares | df | Mean Square | F | Sig. |
|---|---|---|---|---|---|
| Between Groups | 119.788 | 3 | 39.929 | 5.558 | .003 |
| Within Groups | 287.371 | 40 | 7.184 | | |
| Total | 407.159 | 43 | | | |

**Multiple Comparisons**

Dependent Variable: use
Tukey HSD

| (I) device | (J) device | Mean Difference (I-J) | Std. Error | Sig. | 95% Confidence Interval | |
|---|---|---|---|---|---|---|
| | | | | | Lower Bound | Upper Bound |
| 1.00 | 2.00 | .82857 | 1.14617 | .887 | -2.2436 | 3.9008 |
| | 3.00 | -1.37143 | 1.56945 | .818 | -5.5782 | 2.8354 |
| | 4.00 | -3.71429 | 1.43271 | .061 | -7.5545 | .1260 |
| 2.00 | 1.00 | -.82857 | 1.14617 | .887 | -3.9008 | 2.2436 |
| | 3.00 | -2.20000 | 1.31310 | .350 | -5.7197 | 1.3197 |
| | 4.00 | -4.54286* | 1.14617 | .002 | -7.6151 | -1.4706 |
| 3.00 | 1.00 | 1.37143 | 1.56945 | .818 | -2.8354 | 5.5782 |
| | 2.00 | 2.20000 | 1.31310 | .350 | -1.3197 | 5.7197 |
| | 4.00 | -2.34286 | 1.56945 | .451 | -6.5497 | 1.8639 |
| 4.00 | 1.00 | 3.71429 | 1.43271 | .061 | -.1260 | 7.5545 |
| | 2.00 | 4.54286* | 1.14617 | .002 | 1.4706 | 7.6151 |
| | 3.00 | 2.34286 | 1.56945 | .451 | -1.8639 | 6.5497 |

*. The mean difference is significant at the 0.05 level.

**Step 1: Develop Hypotheses:**

a. Independent Variable = Scale: Categorical Quantitative

b. Dependent Variable = Scale: Categorical Quantitative

c. Alternative hypothesis in sentence form.

d. Null hypothesis in sentence form.

e. Write the alternative and null hypotheses using correct notation.

$H_1$: $H_0$:

**Step 2: Establish significance criteria**

f. α =

**Step 3: Calculate test statistic, effect size, and post hoc results**

g. Can you assume equal variances?

h. $F$ = Level of significance ($p$) =

i. Decision: reject null or fail to reject null

j. Calculate effect size =

k. Which groups are significantly different from each other?

**Step 4: Draw conclusion**

l. Write your conclusion in sentence form including appropriate results notation.

## 10.28V Additional Practice

In 2002, a group of researchers examined age differences in road rage among US drivers. They found that drivers under the age of 30 reported the most road rage (angry threatening driving). The results below are from 60 drivers from California in 2018 age is broken into three groups: 1= less than 30 years, 2=30-55 years, 3=greater than 55 years. Does road rage still differ by age category? Does the age category of less than 30 years still have the highest road rage? StatCrunch results are presented. Use α=.05.

**Analysis of Variance results:**
Responses: road rage
Factors: age

**Response statistics by factor**

| age | n | Mean | Std. Dev. | Std. Error |
|---|---|---|---|---|
| 1 | 20 | 2.275 | 0.69802353 | 0.15608281 |
| 2 | 20 | 1.51 | 0.81492654 | 0.18222311 |
| 3 | 20 | 0.825 | 0.50039458 | 0.11189163 |

**ANOVA table**

| Source | DF | SS | MS | F-Stat | P-value |
|---|---|---|---|---|---|
| age | 2 | 21.046333 | 10.523167 | 22.521702 | <0.0001 |
| Error | 57 | 26.633 | 0.46724561 | | |
| Total | 59 | 47.679333 | | | |

**Levene's Test for Homogeneity of Variance**

| Test Statistic | DF 1 | DF 2 | P-value |
|---|---|---|---|
| 3.355186 | 2 | 57 | 0.0519 |

**Tukey HSD results (95% level)**

1 subtracted from

| | Difference | Lower | Upper | P-value |
|---|---|---|---|---|
| 2 | -0.765 | -1.2851681 | -0.2448319 | 0.0023 |
| 3 | -1.45 | -1.9701681 | -0.9298319 | <0.0001 |

2 subtracted from

| | Difference | Lower | Upper | P-value |
|---|---|---|---|---|
| 3 | -0.685 | -1.2051681 | -0.1648319 | 0.0068 |

**Step 1: Develop Hypotheses:**

a. Independent Variable =
Scale: Categorical Quantitative

b. Dependent Variable =
Scale: Categorical Quantitative

c. Alternative hypothesis in sentence form.

d. Null hypothesis in sentence form.

e. Write the alternative and null hypotheses using correct notation.
$H_1$: $H_0$:

**Step 2: Establish significance criteria**

f. α =

**Step 3: Calculate test statistic, effect size, and post hoc results**

g. Can you assume equal variances?

h. $F$ = Level of significance ($p$) =

i. Decision: reject null or fail to reject null

j. Calculate effect size =

k. Which groups are significantly different from each other?

**Step 4: Draw conclusion**

l. Write your conclusion in sentence form including appropriate results notation.

Wells-Parker, E., Ceminsky, J., Hallberg, V., Snow, R.W., Dunaway, G., Guiling, S. Williams, M. & Anderson, B. (2002). An exploratory study of the relationship between road rage and crash experience in a representative sample of US drivers. *Accident Analysis & Prevention, 34*(3), 271-278.

## 10.29 Hands-on Activity: *F*-Ratio Applet

This activity utilizes an applet at http://digitalfirst.bfwpub.com/stats_applet/stats_applet_1_anova.html

The applet applies three groups, where individual scores can range from 0 to 10. In the applet, you may adjust two aspects: standard deviation and sample size. As you adjust these, the F-ratio and p-value will change at the bottom of the screen.

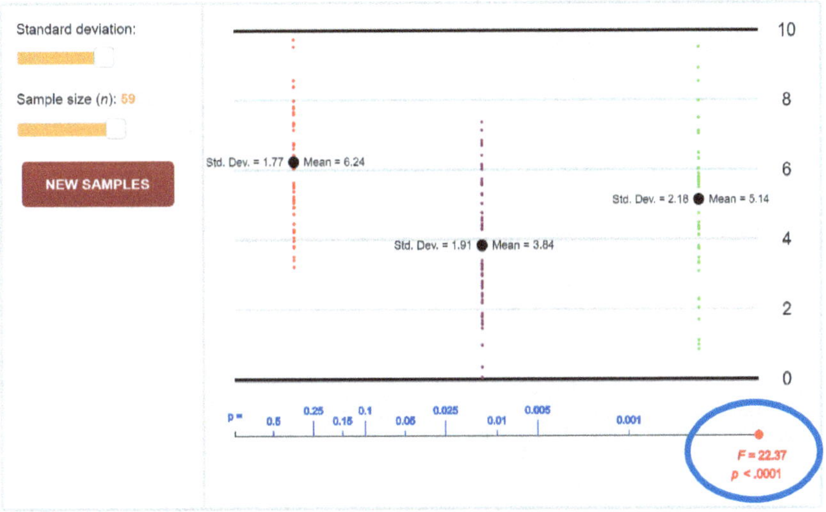


1. Increase the standard deviation (slide the bar to the right). Describe what happens to the groups. What happens to *F* and *p*?

2. Move the standard deviation back to its original starting point. Increase the sample (slide the bar to the right). Describe what happens to the groups. What happens to *F* and *p*?

3. Move the standard deviation to about the middle and do not change. Move the sample size to 15. Click the red "New Samples" button, for a total of five times. After each time, note the *F* and *p*-values. Why do the values change each time? How many times did you find significance?
   1. $F =$ $p =$
   2. $F =$ $p =$
   3. $F =$ $p =$
   4. $F =$ $p =$
   5. $F =$ $p =$

## 10.30V In the Literature

This excerpt presents a portion of the study results that examined GPA differences by test anxiety levels. ANOVA results are presented for two groups—female and male.

**Excerpt from:** Chapell, M. S., Blanding, S. B., Silverstein, M.E., Takahashi, M., Newman, B., Gubi, A., & McCann, N. (2005). Test anxiety and academic performance in undergraduate and graduate Students. *Journal of Educational Psychology, 97*(2), 268–274.

This study investigated the GPA differences by gender and test anxiety levels (low, moderate, and high) among 4,000 undergraduate students. Test anxiety was measured using the Test Anxiety Inventory (TAI, Spielberger, 1980), which is a self-report instrument that consists of 20 items or statements in which respondents are asked to report how often they experience anxiety symptoms before, during, and after taking tests. Each statement is followed by a 4-point Likert-type scale, where respondents indicate how often they have experienced the reaction to tests described in the statement, yielding a total test anxiety score ranging from a minimum of 20 to a maximum of 80 points. Based upon TAI scores, students were placed into three groups of text anxiety levels (low, moderate, and high). Table 1 presents descriptive statistics are presented by test anxious level and gender.

**Table 1.** Descriptive Statistics of GPA by Test Anxiety Groups and Gender

| | **Test Anxiety Group** | | | | | | | | |
|---|---|---|---|---|---|---|---|---|---|
| | **Low** | | | **Moderate** | | | **High** | | |
| | *M* | *SD* | *n* | *M* | *SD* | *n* | *M* | *SD* | *n* |
| Female | 3.35 | .38 | 353 | 3.20 | .45 | 1,041 | 3.12 | .52 | 274 |
| Male | 3.22 | .47 | 257 | 3.04 | .47 | 653 | 2.97 | .52 | 152 |

GPA significantly differed by test anxiety level among female students female students; $F(2, 1665) = 25.97$, $p = .0001$, $\eta^2 = .03$. Scheffé tests showed that the low-test anxious group had higher GPAs than the moderate and high-test-anxious groups ($p = .0001$), and that the moderate group had higher GPAs than the high-test-anxious group ($p = .05$). Male GPA also significantly differed by test anxiety levels; $F(2, 1058) = 16.80$, $p = .0001$, $\eta^2 = .031$. Scheffé tests confirmed that the low-test-anxious group had higher GPAs than the moderate and high-test-anxious groups, $p = .0001$, but there was no significant difference between the moderate- and high-test-anxious groups.

1. Write the two alternative hypotheses that are being examined with ANOVA.

2. Do you reject the null hypothesis for females? For males?

3. Based upon the group means for GPA, which gender consistently scores higher despite test anxiety level?

4. What percent of variance in GPA does text anxiety level account for among females? Among males?

5. What can you conclude about GPA and test anxiety levels among females and males?

## 10.31 Using the Computer

The following instructions will guide you in conducting ANOVA in SPSS and StatCrunch. A couple things to keep in mind. SPSS automatically calculates the Levene's Test, but you have to select a post hoc test. In contrast, for StatCrunch you must select both the post hoc test and Levene's test. StatCrunch only provides the post hoc test of Tukey's HSD. Both programs automatically provides the descriptive statistics for groups.

### SPSS

1. Enter data.
2. 🖱 the **`Analyze`** menu.
3. Select **`Compare Means`** and **`One-way ANOVA`**.
4. 🖱 the independent variable (group) and move to Factor:.
5. 🖱 the dependent variable and move to the Dependent List.
6. 🖱 **`Post Hoc`** and select the preferred post hoc test.
7. 🖱 **`Options`** and check Descriptive and Homogeneity of variance test. 🖱 **`Continue`**.
8. 🖱 **`OK`**.

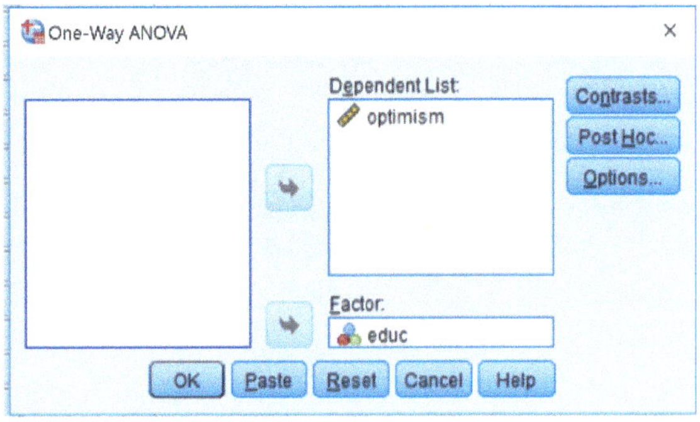


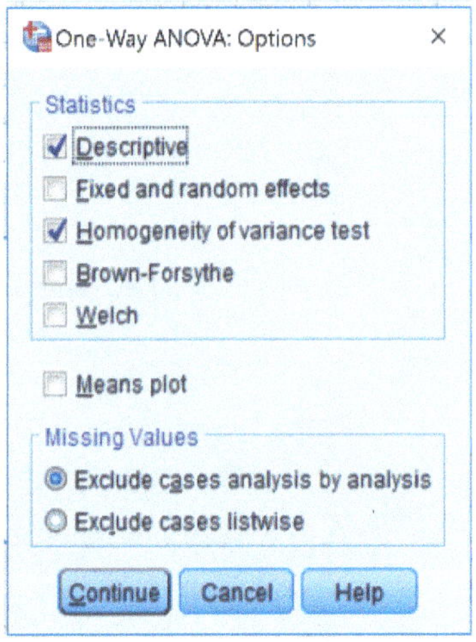


### StatCrunch

1. Enter data.
2. Within the data window, 🖱 the **Stat** menu, select **ANOVA**.
3. Within One Way ANOVA dialogue box, under **Compare:**
   - Values in single column.
4. Under **Responses in:**
   - Select dependent variable.
5. Under **Options:** check both:
   - **Computer Tukey HSD**
   - **Test of homogeneity of variance** (Levene's test)
6. 🖱 **Compute!**

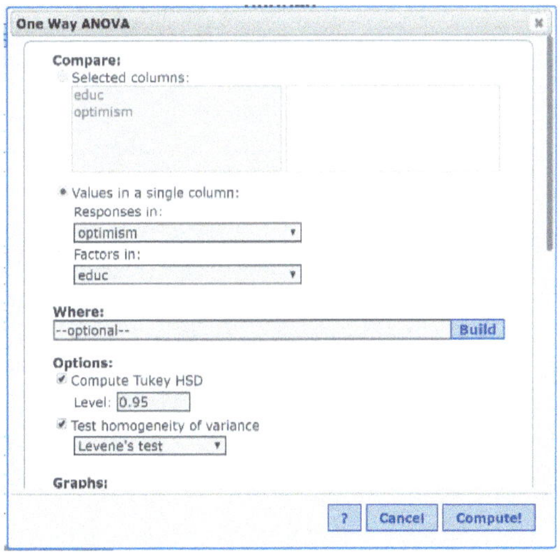

## 10.32 Exercises
### Reviewing the Concepts

1. How many groups may be compared with ANOVA?

2. Why does ANOVA's name and process focus on variance rather than difference?

3. Why is an *F*-ratio only positive?

4. The Levene's Test examines which ANOVA assumption? For this assumption to be fulfilled, should the Levene's test be significant?

5. Why are two degrees of freedom necessary for ANOVA? What does each one represent?

6. Why is a post hoc test necessary with a significant ANOVA?

7. The F-ratio represents the $MS_{\text{between}}/MS_{\text{within}}$. Explain the difference between "between" and "within"?

8. What effect size is calculated for ANOVA? What does is represent and how is it evaluated?

## Interpreting Results

9. In 2003, a study by Dietmar Heinke (http://www.dietmar-heinke.co.uk/files/one_way.pdf) examined the effects of alcohol on driving ability. Thirty-six individuals participated in the experiment in which they were randomly assignments to three conditions: 1) placebo (no alcohol), 2) low alcohol, and 3) high alcohol. Drinks tasted the same despite the differing levels of alcohol. Participants were weighed and given the appropriate amount of drinks. After 30 minutes of drinking, participants drove in a simulator for 10 minutes. The number of errors were recorded by the simulator. These results closely replicate Heinke's findings. Does alcohol level significantly effect the number of driving errors among adults? Use α=.01.

**Descriptives**

errors

| | N | Mean | Std. Deviation | Std. Error | 95% Confidence Interval for Mean Lower Bound | Upper Bound | Minimum | Maximum |
|---|---|---|---|---|---|---|---|---|
| 1.00 | 12 | 4.0000 | .95346 | .27524 | 3.3942 | 4.6058 | 3.00 | 6.00 |
| 2.00 | 12 | 4.9167 | .99620 | .28758 | 4.2837 | 5.5496 | 4.00 | 7.00 |
| 3.00 | 12 | 5.5833 | 1.08362 | .31282 | 4.8948 | 6.2718 | 4.00 | 7.00 |
| Total | 36 | 4.8333 | 1.18322 | .19720 | 4.4330 | 5.2337 | 3.00 | 7.00 |

**Test of Homogeneity of Variances**

errors

| Levene Statistic | df1 | df2 | Sig. |
|---|---|---|---|
| .409 | 2 | 33 | .668 |

**ANOVA**

errors

| | Sum of Squares | df | Mean Square | F | Sig. |
|---|---|---|---|---|---|
| Between Groups | 15.167 | 2 | 7.583 | 7.397 | .002 |
| Within Groups | 33.833 | 33 | 1.025 | | |
| Total | 49.000 | 35 | | | |

**Multiple Comparisons**

Dependent Variable: errors
Scheffe

| (I) alcohol | (J) alcohol | Mean Difference (I-J) | Std. Error | Sig. | 95% Confidence Interval Lower Bound | Upper Bound |
|---|---|---|---|---|---|---|
| 1.00 | 2.00 | -.91667 | .41337 | .101 | -1.9762 | .1429 |
| | 3.00 | -1.58333* | .41337 | .002 | -2.6429 | -.5238 |
| 2.00 | 1.00 | .91667 | .41337 | .101 | -.1429 | 1.9762 |
| | 3.00 | -.66667 | .41337 | .286 | -1.7262 | .3929 |
| 3.00 | 1.00 | 1.58333* | .41337 | .002 | .5238 | 2.6429 |
| | 2.00 | .66667 | .41337 | .286 | -.3929 | 1.7262 |

*. The mean difference is significant at the 0.05 level.

**Step 1: Develop Hypotheses:**

a. Independent Variable = Scale: Categorical Quantitative

b. Dependent Variable = Scale: Categorical Quantitative

c. Alternative hypothesis in sentence form.

d. Null hypothesis in sentence form.

e. Write the alternative and null hypotheses using correct notation.

$H_1$: $H_0$:

**Step 2: Establish significance criteria**

f. α =

**Step 3: Calculate test statistic, effect size, and post hoc results**

g. Can you assume equal variances?

h. $F$ = Level of significance ($p$) =

i. Decision: reject null or fail to reject null

j. Calculate effect size =

k. Which groups are significantly different?

**Step 4: Draw conclusion**

l. Write your conclusion in sentence form including appropriate results notation.

10. This study utilizes a data set based upon 4,833 responses to a 2017 Social Media Survey. The results below present age group differences in the daily amount of social media use (minutes). Five age groups were compared: 1) < 18, 2) 19-24, 3) 25-29, 4) 30-39, 5) 40+. Can we conclude that daily amount of social media use differs by age group? Test at α=.05.

**Descriptives**

time

| | N | Mean | Std. Deviation | Std. Error | 95% Confidence Interval for Mean Lower Bound | 95% Confidence Interval for Mean Upper Bound | Minimum | Maximum |
|---|---|---|---|---|---|---|---|---|
| 1.00 | 1531 | 139.6736 | 173.54970 | 4.43544 | 130.9734 | 148.3738 | .00 | 1000.00 |
| 2.00 | 1913 | 127.8600 | 172.28431 | 3.93902 | 120.1348 | 135.5852 | .00 | 1000.00 |
| 3.00 | 476 | 78.8571 | 96.69581 | 4.43205 | 70.1483 | 87.5660 | .00 | 1000.00 |
| 4.00 | 523 | 60.1530 | 99.32114 | 4.34301 | 51.6210 | 68.6849 | .00 | 1000.00 |
| 5.00 | 390 | 55.3821 | 114.21605 | 5.78355 | 44.0111 | 66.7530 | .00 | 1000.00 |
| Total | 4833 | 113.6006 | 159.10559 | 2.28864 | 109.1138 | 118.0873 | .00 | 1000.00 |

**Test of Homogeneity of Variances**

time

| Levene Statistic | df1 | df2 | Sig. |
|---|---|---|---|
| 46.888 | 4 | 4828 | .000 |

**ANOVA**

time

| | Sum of Squares | df | Mean Square | F | Sig |
|---|---|---|---|---|---|
| Between Groups | 4820225.019 | 4 | 1205056.255 | 49.515 | .000 |
| Within Groups | 117499870.9 | 4828 | 24337.173 | | |
| Total | 122320095.9 | 4832 | | | |

**Multiple Comparisons**

Dependent Variable: time
Dunnett T3

| (I) agecat2 | (J) agecat2 | Mean Difference (I-J) | Std. Error | Sig. | 95% Confidence Interval Lower Bound | 95% Confidence Interval Upper Bound |
|---|---|---|---|---|---|---|
| 1.00 | 2.00 | 11.81360 | 5.93203 | .379 | -4.8042 | 28.4313 |
| | 3.00 | 60.81646* | 6.27026 | .000 | 43.2366 | 78.3964 |
| | 4.00 | 79.52064* | 6.20764 | .000 | 62.1185 | 96.9228 |
| | 5.00 | 84.29155* | 7.29852 | .000 | 63.8386 | 104.7445 |
| 2.00 | 1.00 | -11.81360 | 5.93203 | .379 | -28.4313 | 4.8042 |
| | 3.00 | 49.00287* | 5.92949 | .000 | 32.3759 | 65.6298 |
| | 4.00 | 67.70705* | 5.86324 | .000 | 51.2685 | 84.1456 |
| | 5.00 | 72.47796* | 6.99753 | .000 | 52.8357 | 92.1202 |
| 3.00 | 1.00 | -60.81646* | 6.27026 | .000 | -78.3964 | -43.2366 |
| | 2.00 | -49.00287* | 5.92949 | .000 | -65.6298 | -32.3759 |
| | 4.00 | 18.70419* | 6.20522 | .026 | 1.2949 | 36.1134 |
| | 5.00 | 23.47509* | 7.28646 | .013 | 3.0193 | 43.9309 |
| 4.00 | 1.00 | -79.52064* | 6.20764 | .000 | -96.9228 | -62.1185 |
| | 2.00 | -67.70705* | 5.86324 | .000 | -84.1456 | -51.2685 |
| | 3.00 | -18.70419* | 6.20522 | .026 | -36.1134 | -1.2949 |
| | 5.00 | 4.77091 | 7.23265 | .999 | -15.5334 | 25.0752 |
| 5.00 | 1.00 | -84.29155* | 7.29852 | .000 | -104.7445 | -63.8386 |
| | 2.00 | -72.47796* | 6.99753 | .000 | -92.1202 | -52.8357 |
| | 3.00 | -23.47509* | 7.28646 | .013 | -43.9309 | -3.0193 |
| | 4.00 | -4.77091 | 7.23265 | .999 | -25.0752 | 15.5334 |

*. The mean difference is significant at the 0.05 level.

**Step 1: Develop Hypotheses:**

a. Independent Variable = Scale: Categorical Quantitative

b. Dependent Variable = Scale: Categorical Quantitative

c. Alternative hypothesis in sentence form.

d. Null hypothesis in sentence form.

e. Write the alternative and null hypotheses using correct notation.

$H_1$: $H_0$:

**Step 2: Establish significance criteria**

f. α =

**Step 3: Calculate test statistic, effect size, and post hoc results**

g. Can you assume equal variances?

h. $F$ = Level of significance ($p$) =

i. Decision: reject null or fail to reject null

j. Calculate effect size =

k. Which groups are significantly different?

**Step 4: Draw conclusion**

l. Write your conclusion in sentence form including appropriate results notation.

11. In this study, the authors do not present the full ANOVA results. Rather they indicate the $p$-values and use various symbols (ⴕ, §) to indicate which groups are different based upon the post hoc results.

**Excerpt from:** de Dios, M. A., Anderson, B. J., Herman, D. S., Hagerty, C. E., Caviness, C. M., Budney, A. J. & Stein, M, (2010) Marijuana use subtypes in a community sample of young adult women. *Women's Health Issues, 20*, 201-210.

This study examined how different levels of marijuana use affects other risk behaviors among 308 female marijuana (MRJ) users between the ages of 18 and 24 from the Southern New England region. The three groups were created using criteria from the Diagnostic and Statistical Manual of Mental Disorders (DSM-IV); 1) unaffected/mild use (37%); 2) moderate problem users (41.6%); and 3) severe problem users (21.4%). Participants complete a survey that measured a variety of substance behaviors. Table 1 presents some of the study results.

**Table 1.** Marijuana User Group Comparisons

| | 1<br>Mild User<br>($n$=114) | 2<br>Moderate<br>User ($n$=128) | 3<br>Severe User<br>($n$=68) | $p$ |
|---|---|---|---|---|
| # MRJ times/use per day§ | 1.5 (0.7) | 2.7 (1.8) | 3.8 (3.4) | .000 |
| Mean ($SD$) age of MRJ first useⴕ | 15.1 (2.4) | 14.9 (1.8) | 13.8 (2.1) | .027 |
| Mean ($SD$) days (past 90 days) of opioid useⴕ | 0.2 (0.9) | 0.5 (1.9) | 2.1 (7.1) | .002 |
| Mean ($SD$) days (past 90 days) of cocaine use | 0.3 (1.2) | 0.3 (1.0) | 0.6 (1.5) | .331 |

ⴕGroups 1 and 2 are significantly (Bonferroni corrected $p$<.017) different than group 3.

§ All pairwise comparisons between classes are significant (Bonferroni $p$<.017).

a. Based upon the number of participants and groups, what are the two degrees of freedom that would be reported with the ANOVA results?

b. Of the four ANOVA test report, which one is not significant? What does this result mean in terms of severity of marijuana use and this particular dependent variable?

c. Is the first hypothesis test in the table significant? If so, which groups are significantly different?

d. Which group started using marijuana at the youngest age? Which group uses marijuana and opioids more frequently?

12. In this study, the authors present the ANOVA and post hoc results in a table along with group means and standard deviations. Although group comparisons were made for all the unit tests throughout the course, this excerpt only presents results for a summative assessment and the final course grade.

**Excerpt from:** Ashby, J., Sadera, W.A., & McNary, S.W. (2011). *Comparing student success between developmental math courses offered online, blended, and face-to-face. Journal of Interactive Online Learning, 10*(3), 128-140.

This study compared student success in a community college Developmental Math course offered in three different learning environments—online, blended, and face-to-face (F2F)—out of concern that an online environment would not be as effective. At the end of the course, the 167 participants was collected the standardized Intermediate Algebra Competency Exam scores. Intermediate Algebra Competency Exam (IACE) is a 48 item summative assessment created by faculty in a Mid-Atlantic community college Math Department. In addition, final course grades were compared across the three groups. ANOVA was utilized with a post hoc test of Tukey's HSD. Results are presented in Table 1.

| | **F2F** ($n$=54) | **Blended (B)** ($n$=32) | **Online (O)** ($n$=48) | $F$**(2, 131)** | $p$ | **Pairwise** |
|---|---|---|---|---|---|---|
| IACE | 64.7 (16.0) | 65.8 (19.4) | 66.5 (19.1) | 0.13 | 0.878 | |
| Final Course Grade | 71.6 (13.3) | 73.1 (15.8) | 78.1 (10.1) | 3.37 | 0.038 | O > F2F |

a. Identify the independent variable.

b. Identify the two dependent variables.

c. Which group consistently scored the highest for the two dependent variables? Which group consistently scored the lowest?

d. Which dependent variable produced a significant group difference? Write out the statistical notation that supports that result.

e. For the significant result, which groups were significantly different?

f. What additional statistical result should be reported to support the treatment effect?

g. Based upon these results, what is your general conclusion regarding learning environment affecting student success?

## Conducting Analysis

13. The Rand Corporation (McEachin &Atteberry, 2017) has done a great deal of research on stopping the "summer slide"—the skills regression that typically occurs over the summer, especially among low socio-economic students. The data below presents an experiment in which three groups were compared at the beginning of the school year in late August. Scores represent percentile change (growth) in reading achievement. Group 1 participated in a year-round school, in which two week breaks are conducted throughout the year. Group 2 participated in a summer enrichment program over a 6-week period, that included 3-hour morning sessions, three days each week. Group 3 served as a control group—attending a 9-month school with no summer enrichment. All participants were of low SES, had finished first grade and were going into second. In addition, students had not experienced the treatments before. Use SPSS or StatCrunch to determine if summer programming affects reading growth. Use $\alpha$=.05.

**Step 1: Develop Hypotheses:**

a. Independent Variable =
   Scale: CategoricalQuantitative

b. Dependent Variable =
   Scale: CategoricalQuantitative

c. Alternative hypothesis in sentence form.

d. Null hypothesis in sentence form.

e. Write the alternative and null hypotheses using correct notation.
   $H_1$: $H_0$:

**Step 2: Establish significance criteria**

f. $\alpha$ =

**Step 3: Calculate test statistic, effect size, and post hoc results**

g. Can you assume equal variances?

h. $F$ = Level of significance ($p$) =

i. Decision: reject null or fail to reject null

j. Calculate effect size =

k. Which groups are significantly different?

l. Write your conclusion in sentence form including appropriate results notation.

| Group | Reading Growth |
|---|---|
| 1 | 2 |
| 1 | 4 |
| 1 | 6 |
| 1 | 7 |
| 1 | 3 |
| 1 | 1 |
| 1 | 0 |
| 1 | -1 |
| 1 | 3 |
| 1 | 6 |
| 1 | 8 |
| 1 | 4 |
| 1 | 9 |
| 1 | -2 |
| 1 | 6 |
| 2 | 2 |
| 2 | 4 |
| 2 | 5 |
| 2 | 6 |
| 2 | 3 |
| 2 | 2 |
| 2 | 0 |
| 2 | 4 |
| 2 | 1 |
| 2 | -1 |
| 2 | -2 |
| 2 | 3 |
| 2 | 2 |
| 2 | 4 |
| 2 | 2 |
| 3 | 0 |
| 3 | -3 |
| 3 | -5 |
| 3 | 2 |
| 3 | -9 |
| 3 | 0 |
| 3 | 1 |
| 3 | 3 |
| 3 | -10 |
| 3 | -4 |
| 3 | 0 |
| 3 | 2 |
| 3 | -6 |
| 3 | -2 |
| 3 | -6 |

McEachin, A. & Atteberry, A. (2017). The impact of summer learning loss on measures of school performance. *Education Finance and Policy, 12*(4), 468-491.

14. This study examine the recent social phenomenon of binge-watching (watching TV for more than two hours in one sitting) and how that differs by relationship status (1=seeing no one; 2=casually dating, 3=in a committed relationship—engaged, living together, or married). The data below is a random sample of 30 adults (age ranging 25-40 years) and represents the average number of times in a week (over 10 weeks) a person binged. Test at the .05 level.

| Status | Binge |
|---|---|
| 1 | 3.20 |
| 1 | 4.10 |
| 1 | 2.10 |
| 1 | 1.80 |
| 1 | 3.90 |
| 1 | 6.80 |
| 1 | 4.20 |
| 1 | 3.60 |
| 1 | 5.50 |
| 1 | 1.20 |
| 2 | 1.40 |
| 2 | .80 |
| 2 | 2.00 |
| 2 | 1.90 |
| 2 | 2.30 |
| 2 | .00 |
| 2 | 1.70 |
| 2 | 2.20 |
| 2 | .00 |
| 2 | 1.30 |
| 3 | 4.40 |
| 3 | 3.60 |
| 3 | 2.50 |
| 3 | 3.80 |
| 3 | 2.00 |
| 3 | 1.80 |
| 3 | 2.70 |
| 3 | 3.20 |
| 3 | 2.90 |
| 3 | 2.50 |

**Step 1: Develop Hypotheses:**

a. Independent Variable =
   Scale: Categorical          Quantitative

b. Dependent Variable =
   Scale: Categorical          Quantitative

c. Alternative hypothesis in sentence form.

d. Null hypothesis in sentence form.

e. Write the alternative and null hypotheses using correct notation.
   $H_1$:          $H_0$:

**Step 2: Establish significance criteria**

f. $\alpha$ =

**Step 3: Calculate test statistic, effect size, and post hoc results**

g. Can you assume equal variances?

h. $F$ =          Level of significance ($p$) =

i. Decision: reject null or fail to reject null

j. Calculate effect size =

k. Which groups are significantly different?

**Step 4: Draw conclusion**

l. Write your conclusion in sentence form including appropriate results notation.

# Module 11

## Correlation & Regression

### Learning Targets

After completing Module 11 you should be able to:

- Explain the difference between causality and correlation.
- Create a scatterplot to represent the relationship between two quantitative variables and examine its linearity.
- Use Pearson correlation coefficient to describe the direction and strength of a relationship.
- Calculate coefficient of determination ($r^2$) to describe amount of variance explained.
- Apply the process of hypothesis testing using Pearson correlation to determine statistical significance.
- Apply the process of hypothesis testing using regression to determine statistical significance.
- Interpret regression results to generate a regression equation.
- Use a regression equation to predict $Y$ when given $X$.
- Write appropriate correlation and regression conclusions with statistical results notation.

# Part 1: The Concepts

Up to this point, we have focused on examining causality by comparing groups. As such, the independent variable has always been categorical in order to create groups. Conclusions of causality require an independent variable that is manipulated to create a treatment group and a control group.

This module finally explains the process of examining a mutual relationship. Recall from Module 1, a mutual relationship is studied when both variables are quantitative. We aren't interested in showing that the independent variable causes a change in the dependent variable, rather we examine how one variable changes as the other changes. Let's take the simple relationship between the SAT and college freshman GPA, which has been used in college admissions for years. Because of the strong positive relationship between these two quantitative variables, colleges conclude that as SAT scores increase, so will one's college freshman GPA. Therefore, students with high SAT scores will likely be successful in college. Yet, colleges cannot conclude that high SAT scores CAUSE high GPAs, instead they realize that many variables contribute to obtaining a high SAT score (IQ, work ethic, achievement, coping skills, socio-economic status, etc.) and hence a high freshman GPA. Thus only an association, a relationship is assumed between these two quantitative variables.

## 11.11 Characteristics of Correlation: Direction, Form, Degree

Correlation measures the statistical relationship between two quantitative variables and therefore requires two scores for each individual. Typically these scores are referred to as *X* and *Y*. Since a mutual relationship is examined, it usually doesn't matter which variable is *X* (the independent variable) or *Y* (the dependent variable); however, if there is some chronological order where one variable occurs before the other, then the first occurring variable becomes *X*. In our first example, we will study the relationship between amount of sleep last night and one's enthusiasm for the day upon waking among college students. Figure 11.1 displays a table of scores for six individuals, where *X* is the number of hours of sleep and *Y* is their rating of "enthusiasm for the day". Obviously, in this scenario sleep occurs before waking up. Enthusiasm is measured on a 5-point scale in which 1 is absolute dread and 5 is complete excitement. These scores may also graphed in a scatterplot, in which each dot represents an individual. Person D slept for 6 hours and has an enthusiasm score of 3. The scatterplot displays patterns or trends in the relationship between these two variables. We can see a positive trend in that as sleep increases so does enthusiasm for the day. Correlation provides information on three characteristics: 1) direction, 2) form, and 3) degree.

**Figure 11.1**
*Table and scatterplot of Sleep (X) and Enthusiasm (Y)*

| Person | *X* | *Y* |
|---|---|---|
| A | 5 | 1 |
| B | 7 | 2 |
| C | 8 | 3 |
| D | 6 | 3 |
| E | 9 | 4 |
| F | 7 | 3 |

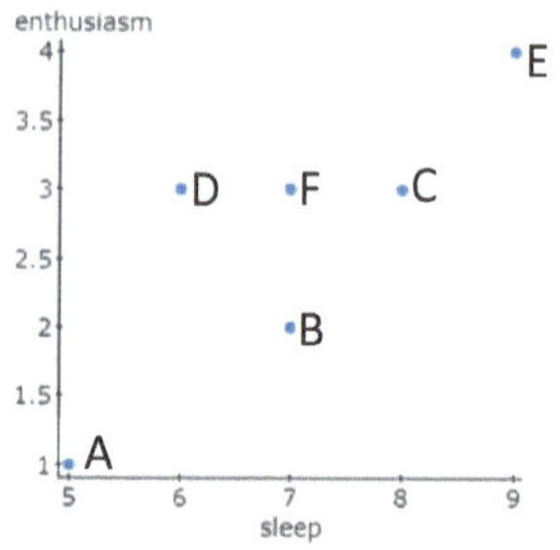


**Direction.** The ***direction*** of a relationship represents the direction of *Y* as *X* increases. Two directions are possible: positive and negative. A ***positive relationship*** is seen when *Y* increases as *X* increases, such that both variables are moving in the same direction. This is exemplified in our initial example where enthusiasm for the day increases as sleep increases (see Figure 11.2A). In contrast, if we were to examine the relationship of sleep with depression, where 1 is low depression and 5 is high depression, the scatterplot in Figure 11.2B reveals that depression decreases as sleep increases—a ***negative relationship***. A negative relationship is also referred to as an inverse relationship. When a statistic is used to represent a relationship, a positive value (+) will indicate a positive relationship, while a negative value (-) will represent a negative relationship.

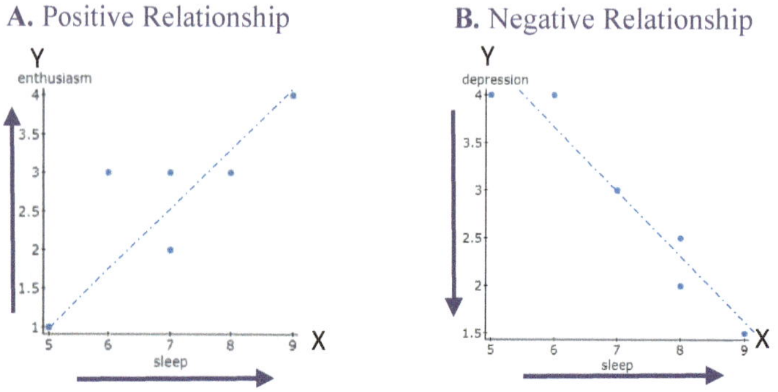


**Figure 11.2**
*Examples of Positive (A) and Negative (B) Relationships*

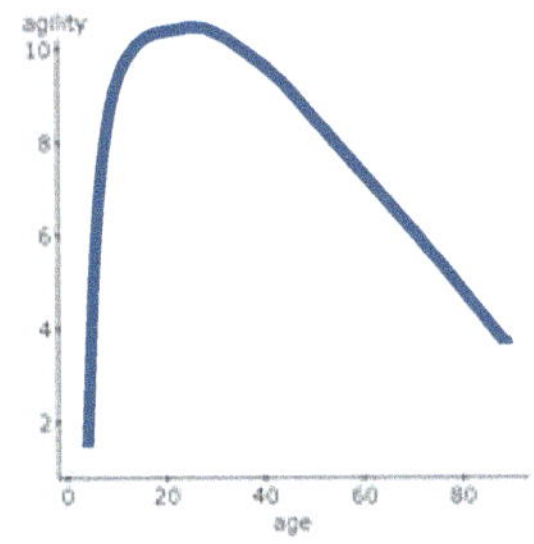


**Figure 11.3** *Example of a Curvilinear Relationship*

**Form.** ***Form*** is another characteristic represented by a relationship, especially in a scatterplot. The preceding examples both display ***linear form***, in that points fall close to a straight line. The statistical tests we will be using to examine relationship assume a linear relationship. Essentially, we need to make sure our data does not create a ***curvilinear form***, where data create a curved pattern. Figure 11.3 presents the curvilinear relationship between age across the lifespan with physical agility, measured on a 1-10 scale with 10 as high. This sad scatterplot indicates that from infancy into early adulthood physical agility increases at a very rapid pace, then plateaus for a few years and eventually starts decreasing.

**Degree.** The last characteristic is ***degree*** or ***strength*** of the relationship. This represents how well the data fit the form, or in our case for a linear relationship, a straight line. The degree of the relationship is measured with a numerical ***correlation coefficient*** ($r$) that ranges from -1 to +1. Keep in mind, sign or direction in front of the coefficient only represent direction. For strength, we only examine the value of the coefficient. A perfect correlation is 1.00 (positive or negative), while no correlation is 0. Figure 11.4 displays several positive relationships of various strength. When examining a scatterplot, I like to use the analogy of bread shapes/types for correlational strength. Figure 11.4A presents a correlation of zero (0), where data points are all of over the place creating more of a circle than a line. As you can see, a zero (0) correlation looks similar to a round loaf of sourdough bread. As data points start to get closer to a straight line, the strength of the correlation increases. In Figure 11.4B, data points are still a bit spread out but clustering around a line creating a moderate correlation ($r$ =.60) in the shape of an Italian loaf. Figure 11.4C shows a strong correlation ($r$ =.90) where data points are fairly close together creating a Baguette shape loaf. Finally 11.4D displays a perfect relationship ($r$ =1.0) in the form of a breadstick where all data points fall on a straight line. When evaluating the degree or strength of the correlation, only consider the numerical value and NOT the sign in front of it. The sign (+/-) is only an indicator of direction. Therefore, $r$ = -.90 is actually stronger than $r$ = .60.

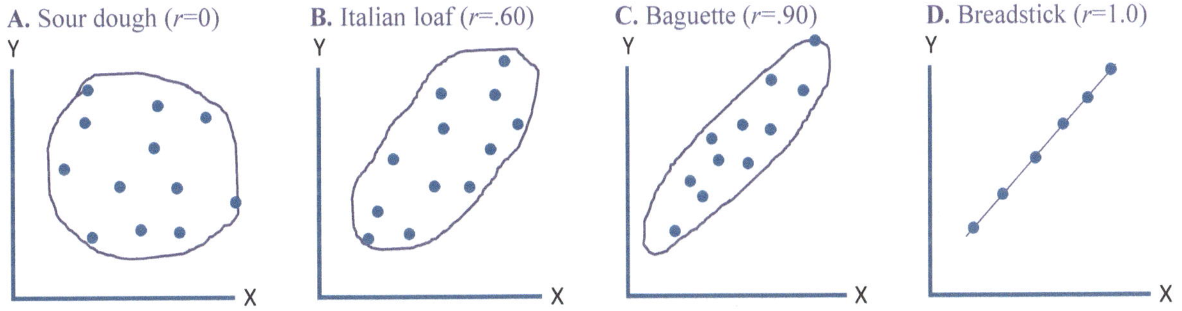


**Figure 11.4** *Strength by Shape*

## 11.12 Calculation and Interpretation of the Pearson Correlation Coefficient

The most common correlation coefficient is the ***Pearson correlation***, originally termed the Pearson product-moment correlation. The Pearson coefficient measures the degree and direction of a linear relationship between two quantitative variables. Represented by $r$, this correlation coefficient conceptually represents:

$$r = \frac{\text{degree to which X and Y vary together}}{\text{degree to which X and Y vary separately}} = \frac{\text{covariability of X and Y}}{\text{variability of X and Y separately}}$$

While we are used to calculating the variability of individual variables, as represented by the denominator, the numerator presents a new concept—the covariability of two variables. This covariability is the change in $Y$ as $X$ increases. In a perfect relationship, every time the value $X$ increases, the value of $Y$ increases (or decreases) by a consisten value. This means that the amount of covariability is identical to the amount of variability of $X$ and $Y$ separately, thus generating a perfect coefficient of 1.00 (or -1.00). When no relationship is present ($r$ = 0), the change in $X$ does not correspond to a predictable change in $Y$.

The calculation of covariability is done by computing the ***sum of products*** (***SP***) of deviations. Recall when calculating standard deviation for a single variable, we learned how to calculate the sum of squares (the sum of squared differences). The sum of products is similar in that we will compare each score to its variable mean ($X - M_X$); however, instead of squaring each difference, we will multiply each difference by its paired difference for $Y$ ($Y - M_Y$) where

$$SP = \Sigma(X - M_X)(Y - M_Y)$$

Let's go back to our example of sleep and enthusiasm in which we have expanded our data to include a sample of 10 individuals. Calculating the deviations and then products, we generate a sum of products (*SP*) of 14.

| | Scores | | Deviations | | Products |
|---|---|---|---|---|---|
| Person | *X* | *Y* | $X\text{-}M_X$ | $Y\text{-}M_Y$ | $(X - M_X)(Y - M_Y)$ |
| A | 5 | 1 | -2 | -2 | 4 |
| B | 7 | 2 | 0 | -1 | 0 |
| C | 8 | 3 | 1 | 0 | 0 |
| D | 6 | 3 | -1 | 0 | 0 |
| E | 9 | 4 | 2 | 1 | 2 |
| F | 7 | 3 | 0 | 0 | 0 |
| G | 10 | 4 | 3 | 1 | 3 |
| H | 6 | 3 | -1 | 0 | 0 |
| I | 4 | 2 | -3 | -1 | 3 |
| J | 8 | 5 | 1 | 2 | 2 |
| | $M_X$=7 | $M_Y$=3 | | | *SP*=14 |

**Steps to calculate Sum of Products**

1. Compute the mean for each set of scores.
2. Calculate the *X* deviation and the *Y* deviation for each individual.
3. Multiply each paired deviations to compute the product.
4. Sum the products.

The sum of products represents to the covariability of *X* and *Y*, the numerator for Pearson correlation. To calculate the denominator, the variability of *X* and *Y* separately, we will use the sum of squares for *X* ($SS_X$) and *Y* ($SS_Y$) multiply these and then take the square root ($\sqrt{SS_xSS_Y}$). This generates our final equation for Pearson *r*.

$$r = \frac{\text{covariability of } X \text{ and } Y}{\text{variability of } X \text{ and } Y \text{ separately}} = \frac{SP}{\sqrt{SS_xSS_Y}}$$

Continuing with our example, we calculate sum of squares for *X* and *Y*: $SS_X$=30 and $SS_Y$=12. Now we are ready to plug all our values into the equation, which generates a correlation coefficient of $r$ =.738. Our old friend Cohen also provides some guidance on how to evaluate the strength of Pearson correlation coefficients. He recommends that anything less than .30 is a weak relationship; between .30 and .49 is a moderate, between .50-.79 is strong, and .80 and above is very strong. Based upon $r$ =.738, the relationship between sleep and enthusiasm for the day is strong.

| | Scores | | Deviations | | Squared Deviations | |
|---|---|---|---|---|---|---|
| Person | *X* | *Y* | $X\text{-}M_X$ | $Y\text{-}M_Y$ | $(X - M_X)^2$ | $(Y - M_Y)^2$ |
| A | 5 | 1 | -2 | -2 | 4 | 4 |
| B | 7 | 2 | 0 | -1 | 0 | 1 |
| C | 8 | 3 | 1 | 0 | 1 | 0 |
| D | 6 | 3 | -1 | 0 | 1 | 0 |
| E | 9 | 4 | 2 | 1 | 4 | 1 |
| F | 7 | 3 | 0 | 0 | 0 | 0 |
| G | 10 | 4 | 3 | 1 | 9 | 1 |
| H | 6 | 3 | -1 | 0 | 1 | 0 |
| I | 4 | 2 | -3 | -1 | 9 | 1 |
| J | 8 | 5 | 1 | 2 | 1 | 4 |
| | $M_X$=7 | $M_Y$=3 | | | $SS_X$=30 | $SS_Y$=12 |

$$r = \frac{SP}{\sqrt{SS_xSS_Y}} = \frac{14}{\sqrt{30 * 12}} = \frac{14}{18.97} = .738$$

| *r* | **Strength** |
|---|---|
| <.30 | Weak |
| .30-.49 | Moderate |
| .50-.79 | Strong |
| >.80 | Very Strong |

Other considerations when interpreting a correlation coefficient is to remember that it is only representing a relationship and not causality. Second, the value of a correlation coefficient can be easily exaggerated when the range of scores is limited. For example, I once computed the Pearson correlation between two technology-related items that utilized a 4-point scale. One item measured the comfort of using a device, and the other item measured the frequency of using the device. The scatterplot in Figure 11.5 reveals the four single data points representing over 100 respondents. Essentially, everyone responded using a 3 or a 4 for both items, creating a perfect square and a correlation coefficient of zero ($r$ = 0). Another consideration is the impact of outliers. A single outlier can greatly increase the value of a correlation coefficient. As a result, a scatterplot should ALWAYS be created to examine the data in order to confirm linearity and evaluate for range limitations as well as outliers.

**Figure 11.5** *Scatterplot with Limited Range*

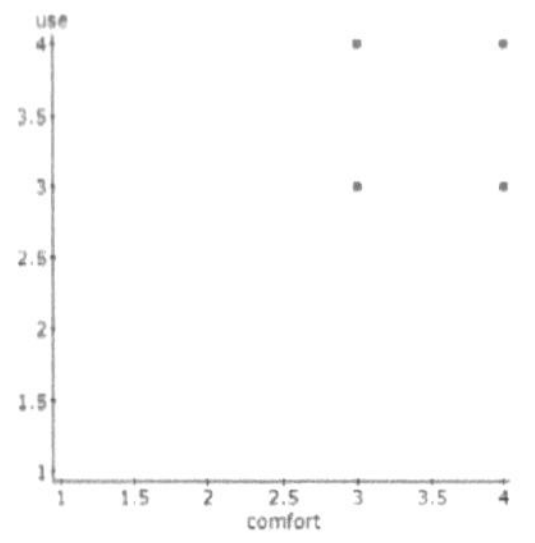

## 11.13 Coefficient of Determination ($r^2$)

Finally, since the correlation coefficient can range from 0 to 1 (positive or negative), you may be tempted to think of this value as a proportion and convert it to a percent, so that a correlation coefficient of .738 represents 73.8% accuracy in our ability to predict $Y$ from $X$. That is not the case! In order to determine this degree of accuracy, we must square $r$ ($r^2$). Recall in previous Modules, we used $r^2$ as an effect size, where it represented the percent of variance in dependent variable explained by the independent variable. We are going to use $r^2$ the same way; and yes, we even will refer to it as an effect size, even though we are not measuring cause and effect. The value $r^2$ is termed the ***coefficient of determination*** and represents the amount or percent of variance in $Y$ explained by $X$. In applying the correlation coefficient of sleep and enthusiasm ($r = +.738$), we compute $r^2$ as .54 or 54%. This means that the amount of sleep accounts for 54% of the variance in enthusiasm for the day.

## 11.14 Hypotheses Testing with Pearson Correlation

Thus far, we have only used Pearson correlation as a descriptive statistic—describing the direction and strength of a linear relationship. However, Pearson correlation is also used as an inferential statistic, where we can test the hypothesis about the relationship existing in the population. When predicting a general relationship, we develop a non-directional hypothesis and use a two-tailed test. Recall that the hypothesis notation should always be written in terms of the population. In previous Modules, our hypotheses have referred to the population mean ($\mu$), but this is no longer the case. The correlation in the population is represented by the Greek letter rho ($\rho$). Since we are predicting a general relationship between sleep and enthusiasm, the non-directional hypothesis notation is applied.

$$H_1: \rho \neq 0 \qquad H_0: \rho = 0$$

**Example**

**RQ:** Does the amount of sleep last night significantly relate to one's enthusiasm for the day among college students?

**Step 1: State Hypothesis**
IV ($X$): Amount of sleep
DV ($Y$): Enthusiasm for the day

**Alternative Hypothesis**
The amount of sleep last night significantly relate to one's enthusiasm for the day among college students.

**Null Hypothesis**
The amount of sleep last night does NOT significantly relate to one's enthusiasm for the day among college students.

**Hypothesis Notation:** $H_1: \rho \neq 0$ $H_0: \rho = 0$

When we have some notion of direction (positive or negative), a directional hypothesis is examined through a one-tailed test. For example, we may predict that a positive relationship between amount of sleep and enthusiasm, in which a directional hypothesis notation is applied to show that the relationship will be greater than zero.

$$H_1: \rho > 0 \qquad H_0: \rho \leq 0$$

Although we have learned how to calculate Pearson coefficient and could use a table of significant values for $r$ to determine $r_{critical}$, we will focus on interpreting computer output to determine statistical significance. As with most test statistics, the computer calculates the $p$-value or probability of obtaining a significant result out of error. Figure 11.6 presents the data set ($n$=10), scatterplot and SPSS output for Pearson Correlation.

**Figure 11.6** *Data, Scatterplot, and SPSS Output for Sleep and Enthusiasm*

| | Scores | |
|---|---|---|
| Person | $X$ | $Y$ |
| A | 5 | 1 |
| B | 7 | 2 |
| C | 8 | 3 |
| D | 6 | 3 |
| E | 9 | 4 |
| F | 7 | 3 |
| G | 10 | 4 |
| H | 6 | 3 |
| I | 4 | 2 |
| J | 8 | 5 |

SPSS

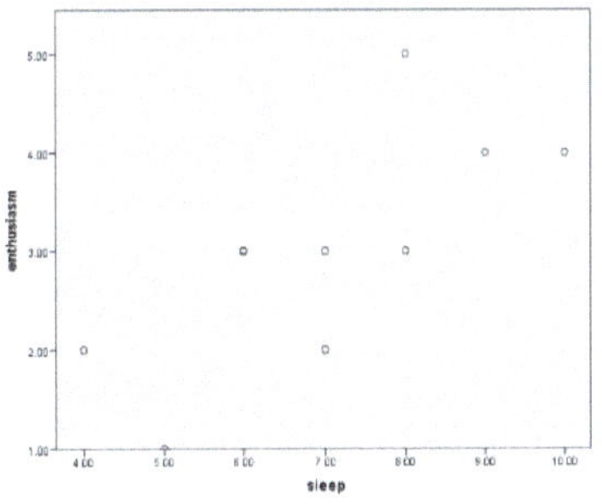


**Descriptive Statistics**

| | Mean | Std. Deviation | N |
|---|---|---|---|
| sleep | 7.0000 | 1.82574 | 10 |
| enthusiasm | 3.0000 | 1.15470 | 10 |

**Correlations**

| | | sleep | enthusiasm |
|---|---|---|---|
| sleep | Pearson Correlation | 1 | .738* |
| | Sig. (2-tailed) | | .015 |
| | N | 10 | 10 |
| enthusiasm | Pearson Correlation | .738* | 1 |
| | Sig. (2-tailed) | .015 | |
| | N | 10 | 10 |

*. Correlation is significant at the 0.05 level (2-tailed).

The correlation results indicate that the Pearson Correlation is $r$ =.738; the significance level ($p$-value) is for a two-tailed test and is .015; the sample size is $n$=10. Notice the asterisk (*) by the correlation coefficient, this indicates significance at $p$<.05. Since the actual $p$-value of .015 is reported, we really don't need the asterisk to realize that $p$ is less than an alpha of .05 and is significant. The correlation results are presented in a matrix, so you will see duplicate results.

## 11.15 Reporting the Results

When reporting the results of Pearson correlation, you need to include a concluding statement with results notation. This statement is usually based upon the hypothesis posed. In addition, several results should be included:

- Variable means and standard deviations;
- *r* with degrees of freedom in parentheses;
- Level of significance (*p*); and
- Number of tails.

Since the output did not provide degrees of freedom, you will need to calculate this ($df = n$-2). We subtract two because we need at least two data points to create a line, which generates a perfect correlation. Therefore, two data point are not free to vary, hence *n*-2.

> **Example**
>
> **Step 2: Establish Significance Criteria** α = .05
>
> **Step 3: Collect and Analyze Data**
> Output: *r*=.738 and *p*=.015.
>
> **Step 4: Evaluate Null and Draw Conclusion**
> *p*=.015 is less than alpha of .05.
> - Significance→Reject the Null→Restate Alternative
> - The amount of sleep last night **(*M*=7.00, *SD*=1.83)** significantly relates to one's enthusiasm **(*M*=3.00, *SD*=1.54)** for the day (upon waking up) among college students; ***r*(8)=.738, *p*=.015, two-tailed.**

## 11.16 Regression

In correlation, we examine how two variables relate to one another. A primary application of correlation is the ability to predict *Y* from the knowledge of *X* through the use of linear regression. Regression uses the correlation results to establish a ***regression line***, the best fitting line for the data points. The equation of this regression line is then used to predict *Y* from *X*.

**The Regression Line.** Figure 11.6 presents the scatterplot of our example of sleep and enthusiasm. Data points certainly do not fall on a perfectly straight line, however, the red line represents the best fitting line for the data in that the error between the actual data points and the predicted ones based upon the regression line is the least possible amount. Notice data point A is quite a distance from the regression line. This distance between the actual point and the predicted point is error, referred to as residual. The most common method for creating this best-fitting line is the Least-Squares method. Once this regression line has been established, an equation for the line is generated. If you recall basic algebra, the equation of a line is

$$Y = mX + b \text{ (old style)}$$

where $m$ = slope (rise/run), and $b$ is the $Y$-intercept or constant. For some reason statisticians felt the need to mix it up a bit and use different notation for the regression line, where

$$Y = bX + a \text{ (regression line)}$$

Now, the regression equation defines $b$=slope and $a$ as the $Y$-intercept or constant. To calculate the our regression equation by hand,

$$b = \frac{SP}{SS_X} \qquad a = M_Y - bM_X$$

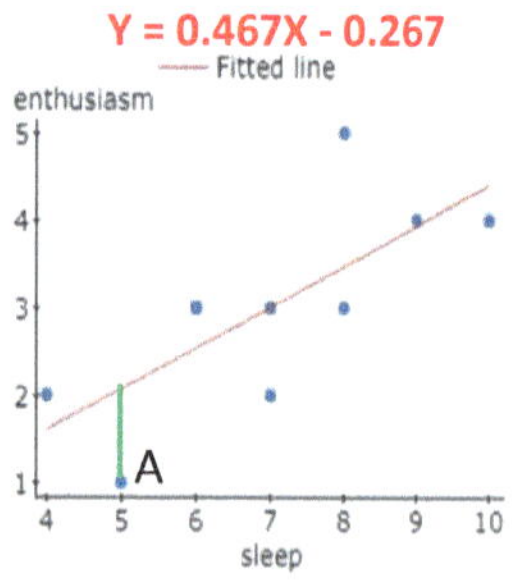


**Figure 11.6** *Scatterplot and Regression Equation of Sleep and Enthusiasm*

We first need to calculate the slope by using the sum of products ($SP$) and the sum of squares for $X$ ($SS_X$) that have already been calculated from Pearson Correlation. Next, we compute the constant or Y-intercept using the means for each variable ($M_X$, $M_Y$) and the slope. Using the previously calculated values—$SP$=14, $SS_X$=30, $M_X$=7, $M_Y$=3—we generate the following:

$$b = \frac{SP}{SS_X} = \frac{14}{30} = .467 \qquad a = M_Y - bM_X = 3 - .467(7) = -.267$$

The regression equation for predicting enthusiasm using sleep data is:

$$\mathbf{Y = 0.467X - 0.267.}$$

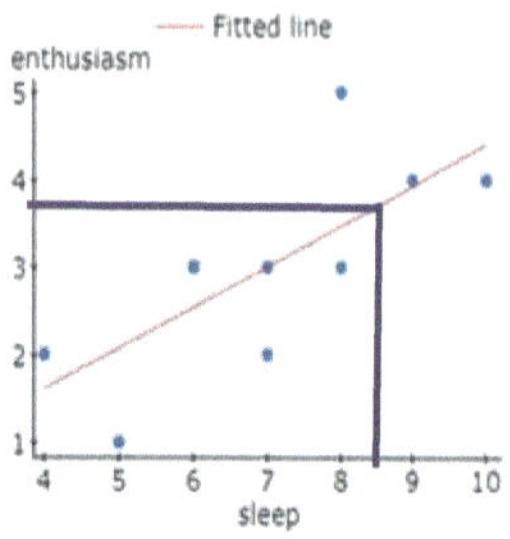


**Figure 11.7** *Scatterplot using Regression Line to Predict Y from X*

Using this equation, we can now predict someone's enthusiasm for the day based upon the sleep obtained the night before. For example, if Rashon scored slept 8.5 hours, we would predict his enthusiasm for the day to be a rating 3.70, moderate enthusiasm (Enthusiasm= .467*8.5 - .267= 3.70). Figure 11.7 shows how the regression line is used to predict the Enthusiasm rating from 8.5 hours of sleep. While this ability to predict is extremely helpful, we still don't know how accurate the prediction is or with what confidence.

**Hypothesis Testing with Regression.** Using regression as an inferential test allows us to examine the significance of the regression equation, specifically the slope ($b$) of the equation. Recall that slope is rise over run—meaning a consistent change in $Y$ occurs as $X$ changes. Essentially, we are predicting that $X$ will be a significant predictor of $Y$, such that the slope will not equal zero. To apply this to our sleep example, we state the alternative hypothesis as amount of sleep will significantly predict enthusiasm for the day. The hypothesis notation is written with the population slope ($B$) in mind.

$$H_1: B \neq 0 \qquad H_0: B = 0$$

The statistical test used to evaluate the regression equation, is ANOVA ($F$-ratio). The ANOVA results indicate the significance of the regression model to predict $Y$. Keep in mind, we are learning about simple regression in which one predictor variable is the model being examined. Multiple regression utilizes multiple predictors; therefore, ANOVA evaluates the model as a whole, and a $t$-test evaluates each predictor's ability. Our regression results will present both ANOVA and $t$-test results, which will be identical for a regression model with one predictor.

**Regression Equation by Hand**

$$b = \frac{SP}{SS_x}$$

$$a = M_Y - bM_X$$

# Example

**RQ:** Does the amount of sleep last night significantly predict to one's enthusiasm for the day (upon waking up) among college students?

**Step 1: State Hypothesis**
IV ($X$): Amount of sleep
DV ($Y$): Enthusiasm for the day

**Alternative Hypothesis**
The amount of sleep last night significantly predict to one's enthusiasm for the day (upon waking up) among college students.

**Null Hypothesis**
The amount of sleep last night does NOT significantly predict to one's enthusiasm for the day (upon waking up) among college students.

**Hypothesis Notation:**
$H_1: B \neq 0$
$H_0: B = 0$

**Interpreting the Output.** StatCrunch and SPSS regression output are presented below. One benefit of the StatCrunch output is that the regression equation is presented along with a scatterplot with the regression line (scatterplot shown in Figure 11.7). In contrast, you need to utilize SPSS output to piece together the regression equation. Output from both sources present a lot of information that we will review step-by-step with color coding.

- Correlation coefficient ($r$) is .738. Although regression doesn't specifically identify a $p$-value for the correlation coefficient, the $p$-value generated for the regression ANOVA and $t$-test are identical to the original $p$-value calculated for Pearson correlation: $p$=.015.
- $R^2$ is .54, which indicates that sleep accounts for 54% of the variance in enthusiasm for the day.
- ANOVA result is $F(1, 8)=9.56$, $p=.015$, which indicates that the regression model of sleep signficantly predicts enthusiasm.
- Regression coefficients used to create the regression equation.
  - **StatCrunch** identifies these as Parameter estimates. Under the column of Parameter are two rows: Intercept and Slope. Under the column of Estimates are the values associated with the Intercept (-.267) and Slope (.467). Intercept refers to the $Y$-intercept or constant in the regression equation.
  - SPSS presents these two values under the column heading of Unstandardized Coefficients (B). The first row is the constant or $Y$-intercept of -.267. The second row is the slope for the predictor (.467)
  - These two values contribute to the regression equation to create: $\boldsymbol{Y = .467X - .267}$

**StatCrunch**

**Simple linear regression results:**
Dependent Variable: enthusiasm
Independent Variable: sleep
enthusiasm = -0.26666667 + 0.46666667 sleep
Sample size: 10
R (correlation coefficient) = 0.73786479
R-sq = 0.54444444
Estimate of error standard deviation: 0.82663978

**Parameter estimates:**

| Parameter | Estimate | Std. Err. | Alternative | DF | T-Stat | P-value |
|---|---|---|---|---|---|---|
| Intercept | -0.26666667 | 1.0883218 | ≠ 0 | 8 | -0.24502556 | 0.8126 |
| Slope | 0.46666667 | 0.15092309 | ≠ 0 | 8 | 3.0920827 | 0.0148 |

**Analysis of variance table for regression model:**

| Source | DF | SS | MS | F-stat | P-value |
|---|---|---|---|---|---|
| Model | 1 | 6.5333333 | 6.5333333 | 9.5609756 | 0.0148 |
| Error | 8 | 5.4666667 | 0.68333333 | | |
| Total | 9 | 12 | | | |

**SPSS**

**Model Summary**

| Model | R | R Square | Adjusted R Square | Std. Error of the Estimate |
|---|---|---|---|---|
| 1 | .738[a] | .544 | .488 | .82664 |

a. Predictors: (Constant), sleep

**ANOVA[a]**

| Model | | Sum of Squares | df | Mean Square | F | Sig. |
|---|---|---|---|---|---|---|
| 1 | Regression | 6.533 | 1 | 6.533 | 9.561 | .015[b] |
| | Residual | 5.467 | 8 | .683 | | |
| | Total | 12.000 | 9 | | | |

a. Dependent Variable: enthusiasm
b. Predictors: (Constant), sleep

**Coefficients[a]**

| Model | | Unstandardized Coefficients B | Unstandardized Coefficients Std. Error | Standardized Coefficients Beta | t | Sig. |
|---|---|---|---|---|---|---|
| 1 | (Constant) | -.267 | 1.088 | | -.245 | .813 |
| | sleep | .467 | .151 | .738 | 3.092 | .015 |

a. Dependent Variable: enthusiasm

**Reporting the Results.** When reporting the results of simple regression, you need include a concluding statement with results notation. The concluding statement should identify the sample, the variables, and the relationship studied. This statement is usually based upon the hypothesis posed. In addition, several results should be included:

- Variable means and standard deviations;
- ANOVA results with degrees of freedom in parentheses and level of significance ($p$);
- $R^2$ as the percent of variance explained; and
- Regression equation.

> **Example**
>
> **Step 2: Establish Significance Criteria**
> $\alpha = .05$
>
> **Step 3: Collect and Analyze Data**
> Output: ANOVA results indicate that model is significant; $F(1, 8)=9.56$, $p=.015$. $R^2=.54$ meaning that sleep ($X$) explains 54% of variance in enthusiasm ($Y$). Regression coefficients generate a regression equation of: $Y = .467X - .267$
>
> **Step 4: Evaluate Null and Draw Conclusion**
> $p=.028$ is less than alpha of .05.
> - Significance→Reject the Null→Restate Alternative
> - The amount of sleep last night (***M*=7.00, *SD*=1.83**) significantly predicts one's enthusiasm for the day (***M*=3.00, *SD*=1.54**) among college students; ***F*(1, 8)=9.56, *p*=.015.** Amount of sleep ($X$) explains 54% of variance in enthusiasm ($Y$). The regression equation predicting enthusiasm is ***Y* = .467*X* - .267.**

## 11.17 Module Summary

- ***Correlation*** measures the statistical relationship between two quantitative variables and requires two scores ($X$ and $Y$) for each individual.
- Correlation provides information on three characteristics: 1) direction, 2) form, and 3) degree.
  1. The ***direction*** of a relationship represents the direction of $Y$ as $X$ increases. Two directions are possible.
     - A ***positive*** (+) ***relationship*** is seen when $Y$ increases as $X$ increases, such that both variables are moving in the same direction.
     - A ***negative*** (-) ***relationship*** or inverse relationship occurs when $Y$ decreases as $X$ increases.
     - The sign only indicates direction and NOT strength. For example, $r = -.9$ is stronger than $r = .7$
  2. ***Form*** is the shape created by the data points in a scatterplot.
     - ***Linear form*** is created when points fall close to a straight line. The statistical tests we will be using to examine relationship assume a linear relationship.
     - ***Curvilinear form*** is when data create a curved pattern.
  3. ***Degree*** or ***strength*** of the relationship represents how well the data fit the straight line.
     - Measured with a numerical correlation coefficient ($r$) that ranges from -1 to +1.
     - The closer data are to a line, the stronger the coefficient.

| *r* | **Strength** |
|---|---|
| <.30 | Weak |
| .30-.49 | Moderate |
| .50-.79 | Strong |
| >.80 | Very Strong |

- ***Pearson correlation* (*r*)** measures the degree and direction of a linear relationship between two quantitative variables.

$$r = \frac{\text{degree to which X and Y vary together}}{\text{degree to which X and Y vary separately}} = \frac{\text{covariability of X and Y}}{\text{variability of X and Y separately}} = \frac{SP}{\sqrt{SS_x SS_Y}}$$

  - The numerator is the covariability of $X$ and $Y$ and is computed as the ***sum of products* (*SP*)** of deviations.
    - $SP = \Sigma(X - M_X)(Y - M_Y)$
  - The denominator is the variability of $X$ and $Y$ separately ($\sqrt{SS_x SS_Y}$).
  - Cohen provide guidance on how to evaluation Pearson.
  - Other considerations when interpreting a correlation coefficient:
    - Represents a relationship and not causality.
    - Limited range of scores and outliers may exaggerate size of coefficient.
- ***Coefficient of determination* ($r^2$)** represents the amount or percent of variance in $Y$ explained by $X$.
- Pearson correlation may be used as an inferential statistic, where we test the hypothesis about the relationship existing in the population.
  - Correlation in the population is represented by the Greek letter rho ($\rho$).
  - Non-directional hypothesis (two-tailed) notation is: $H_1$: $\rho \neq 0$ $H_0$: $\rho = 0$
  - Directional hypothesis (one-tailed test) for positive: $H_1$: $\rho > 0$ $H_0$: $\rho \leq 0$
  - When the associated $p$-value is less than alpha, then the relationship is significant→reject the null.

- Results should include a concluding statement based upon the hypothesis and the following results: variable means and standard deviations; *r* with degrees of freedom in parentheses; level of significance (*p*); and number of tails.
    - Degrees of freedom for correlation is ($df = n$-2), since a line requires a minimum of two data points.
- ***Regression*** uses correlation to predict *Y* from the knowledge of *X*.
- *A **regression line*** and its corresponding equation are used to predict *Y* from *X*.
    - $Y = bX + a$
    - Where *b* is the slope (rise/run) and *a* is the *Y*-intercept (constant)
        - $b = \frac{SP}{SS_X}$ $a = M_Y - bM_X$
- Regression may be used as an inferential test, which allows us to examine the significance of the regression equation, specifically the slope (*b*) of the equation.
    - We are hypothesizing that *X* will be a significant predictor of *Y*, such that the slope will not equal zero.
    - Hypothesis notation is written with the population slope (*B*) in mind: $H_1$: $B \neq 0$ $H_0$: $B = 0$
- ANOVA (*F*-ratio) is used to evaluate the significance of the regression model to predict *Y*.
- The concluding statement is based upon the hypothesis posed and include results notation of: variable means and standard deviations; ANOVA results with degrees of freedom in parentheses and level of significance (*p*); $R^2$ as the percent of variance explained; and Regression equation.

## Part 2: The Learning Guide

Inferential statistics examines two relationships: causal and mutual.

- To study a causal relationship, we usually manipulate a categorical independent variable to create a treatment group and a control group.
- A mutual relationship is studied when both variables are quantitative. We are focused on how one variable changes as the other changes.

### Example

What is the relationship between amount of sleep last night ($X$) and one's enthusiasm for the day($Y$) among six college students?

| Person | $X$ | $Y$ |
|---|---|---|
| A | 5 | 1 |
| B | 7 | 2 |
| C | 8 | 3 |
| D | 6 | 3 |
| E | 9 | 4 |
| F | 7 | 3 |

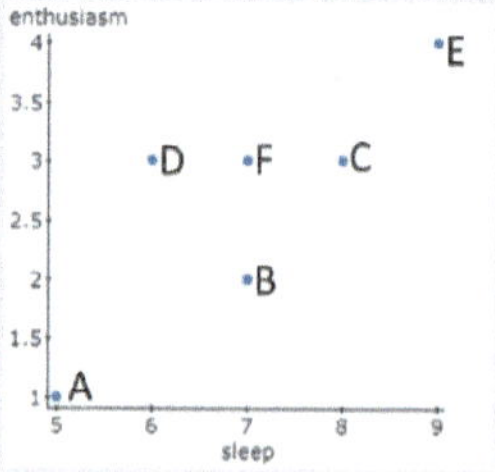


### 11.21V Characteristics of Correlation: Direction, Form, Degree

- Correlation measures the statistical relationship between two quantitative variables and therefore requires two scores for each individual, usually referred to as $X$ and $Y$.
- Correlation provides information on three characteristics: 1) direction, 2) form, and 3) degree.
  - The ***direction*** of a relationship represents the direction of $Y$ as $X$ increases. Two directions are possible.
    - A ***positive*** (+) ***relationship*** is seen when $Y$ increases as $X$ increases, such that both variables are moving in the same direction.
    - A ***negative*** (-) ***relationship*** or inverse relationship occurs when $Y$ decreases as $X$ increases.
    - The sign only indicates direction and is not an indicator or strength. For example, $r = -.9$ is stronger than $r = .7$.

**A.** Positive Relationship

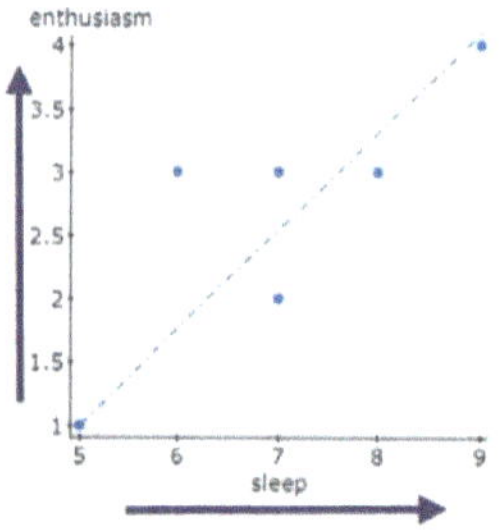


**B.** Negative Relationship

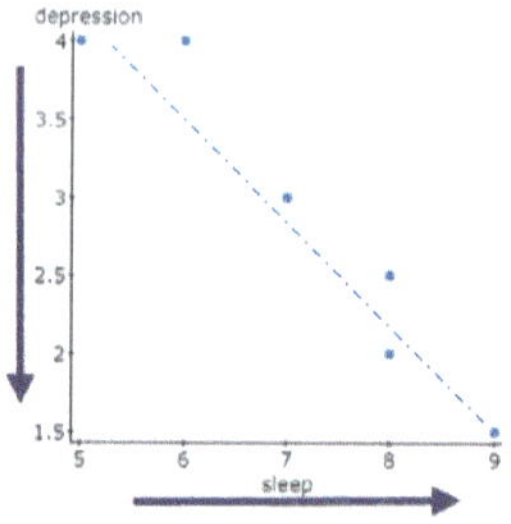


  - ***Form*** is the shape created by the data points in a scatterplot.
    - ***Linear form*** is created when points fall close to a straight line. The statistical tests we will be using to examine relationship assume a linear relationship.
    - ***Curvilinear form*** is when data create a curved pattern.
  - ***Degree or strength*** of the relationship represents how well the data fit the straight line.
    - Measured with a numerical correlation coefficient ($r$) that ranges from -1 to +1.
    - The closer data are to a line, the stronger the coefficient.

**A.** Sour dough ($r$=0)

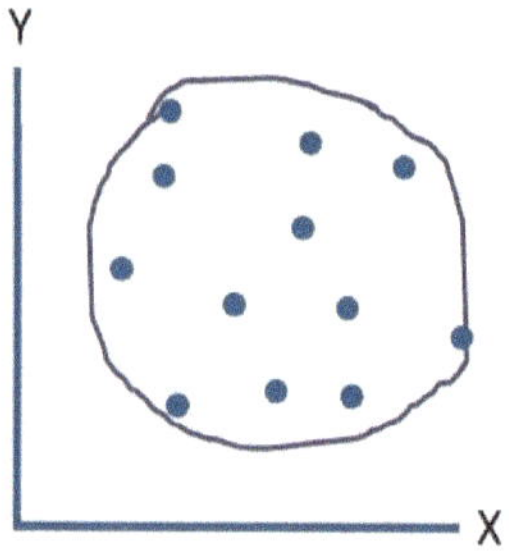


**B.** Italian loaf ($r$=.60)

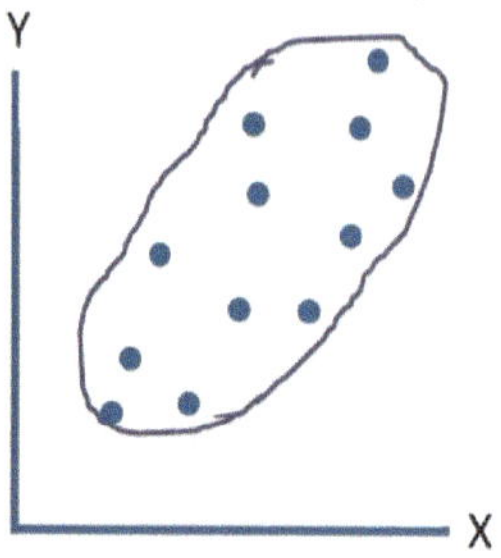


**C.** Baguette ($r$=.90)

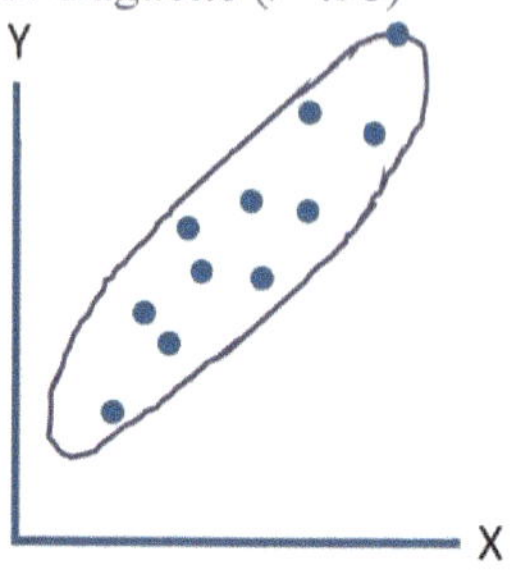


**D.** Breadstick ($r$=1.0)

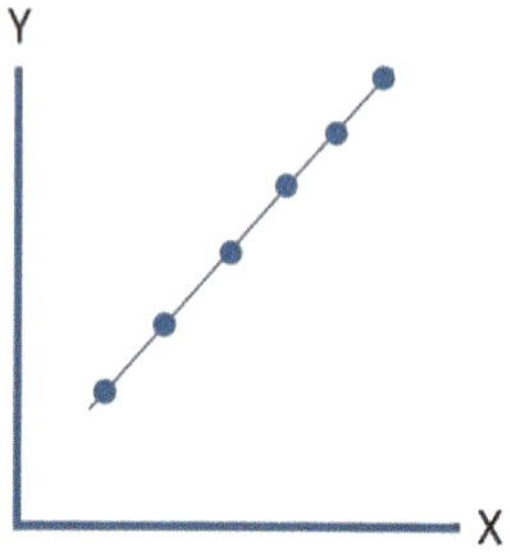

## 11.22V Calculation and Interpretation of the Pearson Correlation Coefficient

***Pearson correlation*** ($r$) measures the degree and direction of a linear relationship between two quantitative variables.

$$r = \frac{\text{degree to which X and Y vary together}}{\text{degree to which X and Y vary separately}} = \frac{\text{covariability of X and Y}}{\text{variability of X and Y separately}} = \frac{SP}{\sqrt{SS_x SS_Y}}$$

- The numerator for $r$ represents the covariability of two variables—the change in $Y$ as $X$ increases.
  - In a perfect relationship, every time the value $X$ increases, the value of $Y$ increases (or decreases) by a consistent value.
  - Covariability of $X$ and $Y$ is computed as the ***sum of products*** (***SP***) of deviations: $SP = \Sigma(X - M_X)(Y - M_Y)$

| | Scores | | Deviations | | Products |
|---|---|---|---|---|---|
| Person | $X$ | $Y$ | $X$-$M_X$ | $Y$-$M_Y$ | $(X - M_X)(Y - M_Y)$ |
| A | 5 | 1 | -2 | -2 | 4 |
| B | 7 | 2 | 0 | -1 | 0 |
| C | 8 | 3 | 1 | 0 | 0 |
| D | 6 | 3 | -1 | 0 | 0 |
| E | 9 | 4 | 2 | 1 | 2 |
| F | 7 | 3 | 0 | 0 | 0 |
| G | 10 | 4 | 3 | 1 | 3 |
| H | 6 | 3 | -1 | 0 | 0 |
| I | 4 | 2 | -3 | -1 | 3 |
| J | 8 | 5 | 1 | 2 | 2 |
| | $M_X$=7 | $M_Y$=3 | | | $SP$=14 |

**Steps to calculate Sum of Products**

1. Compute the mean for each set of scores.
2. Calculate the $X$ deviation and the $Y$ deviation for each individual.
3. Multiply each paired deviations to compute the product.
4. Sum the products.

- The denominator is the variability of $X$ and $Y$ separately, which requires use first to calculate the sum of squares for $X$ ($SS_X$) and $Y$ ($SS_Y$), multiply these, and then take the square root ($\sqrt{SS_x SS_Y}$).

- $r = \frac{SP}{\sqrt{SS_X SS_Y}} = \frac{14}{\sqrt{30*12}} = \frac{14}{18.97} = .738$

| | Scores | | Deviations | | Squared Deviations | |
|---|---|---|---|---|---|---|
| Person | $X$ | $Y$ | $X$-$M_X$ | $Y$-$M_Y$ | $(X - M_X)^2$ | $(Y - M_Y)^2$ |
| A | 5 | 1 | -2 | -2 | 4 | 4 |
| B | 7 | 2 | 0 | -1 | 0 | 1 |
| C | 8 | 3 | 1 | 0 | 1 | 0 |
| D | 6 | 3 | -1 | 0 | 1 | 0 |
| E | 9 | 4 | 2 | 1 | 4 | 1 |
| F | 7 | 3 | 0 | 0 | 0 | 0 |
| G | 10 | 4 | 3 | 1 | 9 | 1 |
| H | 6 | 3 | -1 | 0 | 1 | 0 |
| I | 4 | 2 | -3 | -1 | 9 | 1 |
| J | 8 | 5 | 1 | 2 | 1 | 4 |
| | $M_X$=7 | $M_Y$=3 | | | $SS_X$=30 | $SS_Y$=12 |

| $r$ | Strength |
|---|---|
| <.30 | Weak |
| .30-.49 | Moderate |
| .50-.79 | Strong |
| >.80 | Very Strong |

- Considerations when interpreting a correlation coefficient:
  - Represents a relationship and not causality.
  - The correlation coefficient can be easily exaggerated when the range of scores is limited.
  - Outlier can greatly increase the value of a correlation coefficient.

## 11.23V Coefficient of Determination ($r^2$)

- Correlation coefficient **does not** represent a proportion that can be converted to a percent.
- ***Coefficient of determination*** ($r^2$) represents the amount or percent of variance in $Y$ explained by $X$.

## 11.24V Hypotheses Testing with Pearson Correlation

- Pearson correlation can be a descriptive statistic to describe the direction and strength of a linear relationship.
- Also be used as an inferential statistic, where we can test the hypothesis about the relationship existing in the population.

### Hypothesis Notation.

- Correlation in the population is represented by the Greek letter rho (ρ).
- Non-directional hypothesis (two-tailed) notation is:
    - $H_1$: $\rho \neq 0$ $H_0$: $\rho = 0$
- Directional hypothesis (one-tailed test) for positive:
    - $H_1$: $\rho > 0$ $H_0$: $\rho \leq 0$

### Determining Significance.

- The *p*-value generated in the computer output must be less than alpha to indicate a significant relationship. Results below utilize the data set of $n$=10.

SPSS

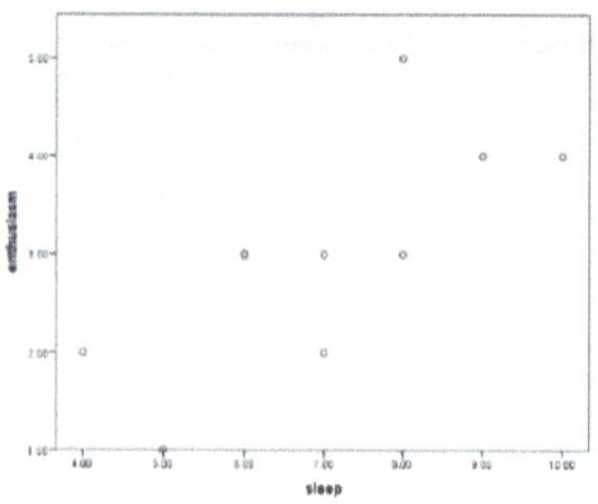


**Descriptive Statistics**

| | Mean | Std. Deviation | N |
|---|---|---|---|
| sleep | 7.0000 | 1.82574 | 10 |
| enthusiasm | 3.0000 | 1.15470 | 10 |

**Correlations**

| | | sleep | enthusiasm |
|---|---|---|---|
| sleep | Pearson Correlation | 1 | .738* |
| | Sig. (2-tailed) | | .015 |
| | N | 10 | 10 |
| enthusiasm | Pearson Correlation | .738* | 1 |
| | Sig. (2-tailed) | .015 | |
| | N | 10 | 10 |

*. Correlation is significant at the 0.05 level (2-tailed).

## 11.25V Reporting the Results

Concluding statement is based upon the hypothesis posed with the appropriate results notation:

- Variable means and standard deviations;
- *r* with degrees of freedom in parentheses;
- Level of significance (*p*); and
- Number of tails.

Degrees of freedom for correlation is ($df = n$-2), since a line requires a minimum of two data points.

**Example**

**RQ:** Does the amount of sleep last night significantly relate to one's enthusiasm for the day (upon waking up) among college students?

**Step 1: State Hypothesis**
IV (*X*): Amount of sleep
DV (*Y*): Enthusiasm for the day

**Alternative Hypothesis**
The amount of sleep last night significantly relate to one's enthusiasm for the day (upon waking up) among college students.

**Null Hypothesis**
The amount of sleep last night does NOT significantly relate to one's enthusiasm for the day (upon waking up) among college students.

**Hypothesis Notation:**
$H_1$: $\rho \neq 0$
$H_0$: $\rho = 0$

**Step 2: Establish Significance Criteria**
$\alpha$ = .05

**Step 3: Collect and Analyze Data**
Output: *r*=.738 and *p*=.015.

**Step 4: Evaluate Null and Draw Conclusion**
*p*=.028 is less than alpha of .05.

- Significance→Reject the Null→Restate Alternative
- The amount of sleep last night **(*M*=7.00, *SD*=1.83)** significantly relates to one's enthusiasm **(*M*=3.00, *SD*=1.54)** for the day (upon waking up) among college students; ***r*(8)=.738, *p*=.015, two-tailed.**

## 11.26V Regression

Regression uses correlation to <u>predict</u> *Y* from the knowledge of *X*.

### The Regression Line.

- Based upon the data points of *X* and *Y*, a ***regression line***, the best fitting line, is generated. The equation of this regression line is then used to predict *Y* from *X*.
- The Least-Squares method is the most common method of determining the regression line, in which distance (error/residual) between the actual point and the predicted point (the line) is the least amount for all the data points.
- In statistics, the equation for a regression line is: $\mathbf{Y = bX + a}$
    - Where *b* is the slope (rise/run) and *a* is the *Y*-intercept (constant)
        - $b = \frac{SP}{SS_X}$ $a = M_Y - bM_X$
- The regression equation for our sleep data is: $\mathbf{Y = 0.467X - 0.267}$.
- If Rashon scored slept 8.5 hours, we would predict his enthusiasm for the day to be a rating 3.70, moderate enthusiasm (Enthusiasm= .467*8.5 - .267= 3.70).

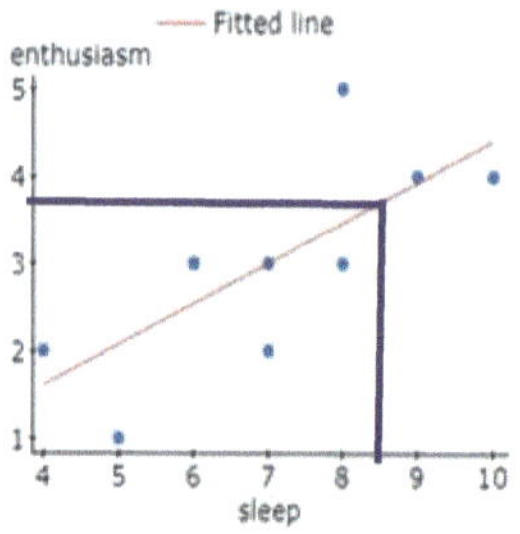

## Hypothesis Testing with Regression.

***Regression*** may be used as an inferential test to examine the significance of the regress ion equation, specifically the slope ($b$) of the equation.

- We are hypothesizing that $X$ will be a significant predictor of $Y$, such that the slope will not equal zero.
- Hypothesis notation is written with the population slope ($B$) in mind.
  - $H_1$: $B \neq 0$ $H_0$: $B = 0$
- ANOVA ($F$-ratio) is used to evaluate the significance of the regression model to predict $Y$.
- Regression output for both SPSS and StatCrunch presents a lot of results for interpretation.
- StatCrunch generates the actual regression equation, whereas with SPSS it will need to be pieced together
- Correlation coefficient ($r$) is .738. The ANOVA $p$-value may be used as the $p$-value for the correlation coefficient.
- $R^2$ is .54, which indicates that sleep accounts for 54% of the variance in enthusiasm for the day.
- ANOVA result is $F(1, 8)$=9.56, $p$=.015, which indicates that the regression model of sleep signficantly predicts enthusiasm.
- Regression coefficients used to create the regression equation.
  - **StatCrunch**: Under Parameter estimates are the Intercept ($Y$-Intercept) and Slope.
  - **SPSS:** Under Unstandardized Coefficients (B) are the constant or $Y$-intercept of -.267 and the slope for the predictor (.467)
  - These two values contribute to the regression equation to create: $Y = .467X - .267$

### Example

**RQ:** Does the amount of sleep last night significantly predict to one's enthusiasm for the day (upon waking up) among college students?

**Step 1: State Hypothesis**
IV ($X$): Amount of sleep
DV ($Y$): Enthusiasm for the day

**Alternative Hypothesis**
The amount of sleep last night significantly predict to one's enthusiasm for the day (upon waking up) among college students.

**Null Hypothesis**
The amount of sleep last night does NOT significantly predict to one's enthusiasm for the day (upon waking up) among college students.

**Hypothesis Notation:**
$H_1$: $B \neq 0$
$H_0$: $B = 0$

**StatCrunch**

**Simple linear regression results:**
Dependent Variable: enthusiasm
Independent Variable: sleep
enthusiasm = -0.26666667 + 0.46666667 sleep
Sample size: 10
R (correlation coefficient) = 0.73786479
R-sq = 0.54444444
Estimate of error standard deviation: 0.82663978

**Parameter estimates:**

| Parameter | Estimate | Std. Err. | Alternative | DF | T-Stat | P-value |
|---|---|---|---|---|---|---|
| Intercept | -0.26666667 | 1.0883218 | ≠ 0 | 8 | -0.24502556 | 0.8126 |
| Slope | 0.46666667 | 0.15092309 | ≠ 0 | 8 | 3.0920827 | 0.0148 |

**Analysis of variance table for regression model:**

| Source | DF | SS | MS | F-stat | P-value |
|---|---|---|---|---|---|
| Model | 1 | 6.5333333 | 6.5333333 | 9.5609756 | 0.0148 |
| Error | 8 | 5.4666667 | 0.68333333 | | |
| Total | 9 | 12 | | | |

**SPSS**

**Model Summary**

| Model | R | R Square | Adjusted R Square | Std. Error of the Estimate |
|---|---|---|---|---|
| 1 | .738[a] | .544 | .488 | .82664 |

a. Predictors: (Constant), sleep

**ANOVA[a]**

| Model | | Sum of Squares | df | Mean Square | F | Sig. |
|---|---|---|---|---|---|---|
| 1 | Regression | 6.533 | 1 | 6.533 | 9.561 | .015[b] |
| | Residual | 5.467 | 8 | .683 | | |
| | Total | 12.000 | 9 | | | |

a. Dependent Variable: enthusiasm
b. Predictors: (Constant), sleep

**Coefficients[a]**

| Model | | Unstandardized Coefficients | | Standardized Coefficients | t | Sig. |
|---|---|---|---|---|---|---|
| | | B | Std. Error | Beta | | |
| 1 | (Constant) | -.267 | 1.088 | | -.245 | .813 |
| | sleep | .467 | .151 | .738 | 3.092 | .015 |

a. Dependent Variable: enthusiasm

## Reporting Regression Results.

The concluding statement is based upon the hypothesis posed and include results notation of:

- Variable means and standard deviations;
- ANOVA results with degrees of freedom in parentheses and level of significance ($p$);
- $R^2$ as the percent of variance explained; and regression equation.

### Example

**Step 2: Establish Significance Criteria:** $\alpha$ = .05

**Step 3: Collect and Analyze Data**
Output: ANOVA results indicate that model is significant; $F(1, 8)$=9.56, $p$=.015. $R^2$=.54 meaning that sleep ($X$) explains 54% of variance in enthusiasm ($Y$). Regression coefficients generate a regression equation of: $Y = .467X - .267$

**Step 4: Evaluate Null and Draw Conclusion**

- $p$=.028 is less than alpha of .05. Significance→Reject the Null→Restate Alternative
- The amount of sleep last night **($M$=7.00, $SD$=1.83)** significantly predicts one's enthusiasm for the day **($M$=3.00, $SD$=1.54)** among college students; **$F(1, 8)$=9.56, $p$=.015.** Amount of sleep ($X$) explains **54% of variance** in enthusiasm ($Y$). The regression equation predicting enthusiasm is **$Y = .467X - .267$.**

## 11.27V Additional Practice

A 2012 College Board study (eric.ed.gov/?id=ED563202) indicates that SAT scores and college freshman GPA produce a large correlation coefficient of $r$ = .53. The scatterplot below presents a small data set ($n$=35) that recreates SAT's correlation with GPA among college students. Use the results to determine if SAT is a significant predictor of college freshman GPA. Apply α=.05.

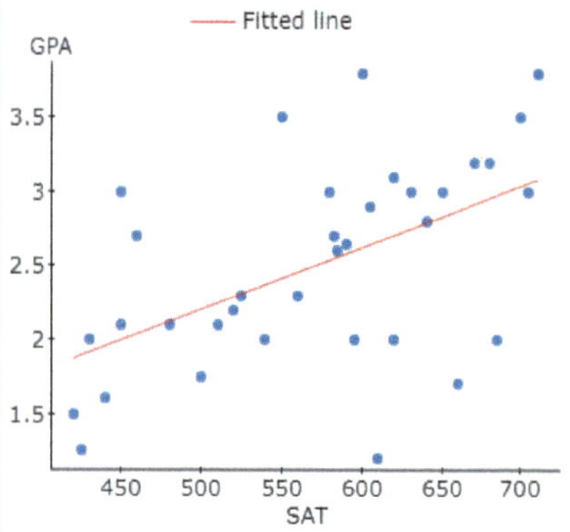


**Simple linear regression results:**
Dependent Variable: GPA
Independent Variable: SAT
GPA = 0.12315944 + 0.0041665542 SAT
Sample size: 35
R (correlation coefficient) = 0.52978298
R-sq = 0.28067
Estimate of error standard deviation: 0.59967403

**Parameter estimates:**

| Parameter | Estimate | Std. Err. | Alternative | DF | T-Stat | P-value |
|---|---|---|---|---|---|---|
| Intercept | 0.12315944 | 0.67048738 | ≠ 0 | 33 | 0.18368644 | 0.8554 |
| Slope | 0.0041665542 | 0.0011611442 | ≠ 0 | 33 | 3.5883177 | 0.0011 |

**Analysis of variance table for regression model:**

| Source | DF | SS | MS | F-stat | P-value |
|---|---|---|---|---|---|
| Model | 1 | 4.6303333 | 4.6303333 | 12.876024 | 0.0011 |
| Error | 33 | 11.867095 | 0.35960895 | | |
| Total | 34 | 16.497429 | | | |

**Step 1: Develop Hypotheses:**

a. Independent Variable = Scale: Categorical Quantitative

b. Dependent Variable = Scale: Categorical Quantitative

c. Alternative hypothesis in sentence form.

d. Null hypothesis in sentence form.

e. Write the alternative and null hypotheses using correct notation.

$H_1$: $H_0$:

**Step 2: Establish significance criteria**

f. α =

**Step 3: Calculate test statistic, $R^2$, and regression equation**

g. $F$ = Level of significance ($p$) =

h. Decision: reject null or fail to reject null

i. $R^2$ =

j. Regression Equation:

k. If Caty's SAT score is 507, what is her predicted freshman GPA?

**Step 4: Draw conclusion**

l. Write your conclusion in sentence form including appropriate results notation.

## 11.28 Hands-on Activities

1. Go to http://shiny.stat.tamu.edu:3838/eykolo/Correlation/ applet. Generate at least five different scatterplots using the same sample size (it doesn't matter—just choose one). For each scatter plot, do the following:
   - Do not show correlation until the scatterplot has been created.
   - Guess the correlation, write down your guess in the table below.
   - Check Yes for Show Correlation! Write down the actual *r*.
   - Under Add Outlier, check Yes. Add an extreme data point. What is the new correlation coefficient?

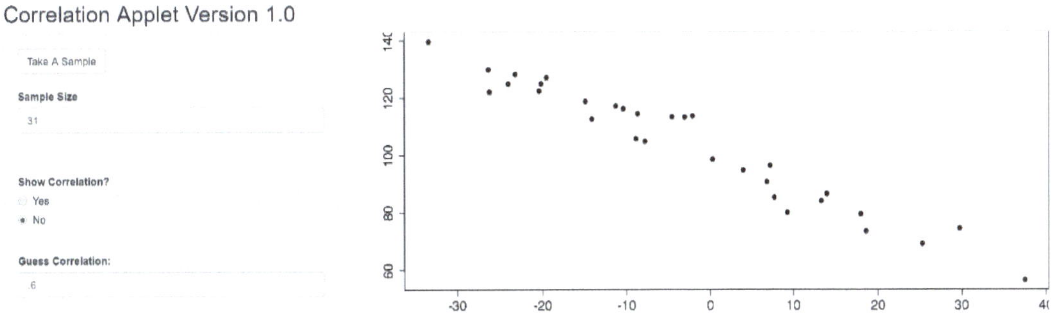


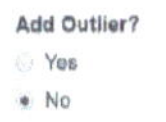


| | Guess *r* | Actual *r* | New *r* with Outlier |
|---|---|---|---|
| Sample 1 | | | |
| Sample 2 | | | |
| Sample 3 | | | |
| Sample 4 | | | |
| Sample 5 | | | |

a. What affect does adding the outlier have on the correlation coefficient?

2. View the TEDx Talk on ***The danger of mixing up causality and correlation*** by Ionica Smeets at:

   https://www.youtube.com/watch?v=8B271L3NtAw

   Based upon the video, complete the following questions.

   a. How can there be a correlation between ice cream sales and the number of drowning, yet ice cream sales not be the cause of drowning?

   b. What are the variables "behind" ice cream sales that could be the real cause of drownings?

   c. Why does society continue to mistakenly identify causes when the relationship is only correlational?

## 11.29V In the Literature

This research article does not present the ANOVA results for the regression model, but rather relies on the *t*-test result, which is fine since only a single predictor is being examined. Also, note that the authors do not present a correlation coefficient or $R^2$.

**Excerpt from:** Kalubula M., Liu Q., Song G.R., Li X.F. (2016) A district level linear regression analysis of malaria morbidity and associated control interventions in Lusaka Province. *Epidemiology: Open Access, 6*:238. doi:10.4172/2161-1165.1000238

Despite being a largely preventable and treatable disease, malaria is responsible for an estimated 50% of all infant mortality and 20% of all maternal mortality in Zambia and presents severe social and economic burdens on communities living in endemic areas. This study aimed at establishing the relationship between malaria morbidity and associated control interventions in Lusaka Province of Zambia using malaria surveillance data from 2009 to 2013 through the Zambian District Health Information System. Data on annual provincial and district population were collected from Central Statistics Office (CSO) of the Republic of Zambia. Lusaka district, the capital city, is the smallest in terms of surface area (360 square kilometres), but had the largest population of 2,046,272 in 2013. The dependent variable of malaria morbidity was measured as the number of malaria cases per thousand population. The independent variable of Insecticide Treated Nets (ITNs) was measured as the number used per thousand population. ITN coverage in Lusaka Province was low during the study period. In 2009, 275 ITNs were distributed per 1,000 populations, which went down to 247 in 2010 before further going down to 245 in 2011. There was however an increase in coverage during the year 2012 where 274 ITNs were distributed per 1,000 population. The year 2013 reported the highest coverage of 302 per 1,000 populations. Linear regression model was used to establish the association between malaria morbidity (dependent variable) and ITN coverage (independent variable) in Lusaka province from 2009 to 2013. The relationship of these two variables are presented in the scatter plot. The regression model shows relatively strong association between malaria morbidity and ITN coverage with *p*-value of 0.003.

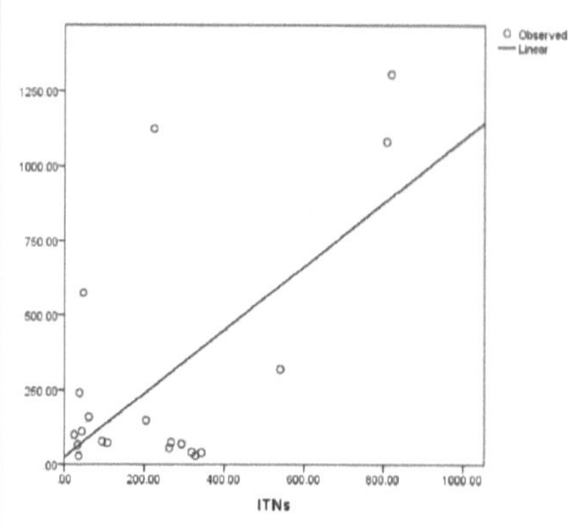

Figure 3: Association between malaria morbidity and ITNs.

**Table 1.** *Regression Coefficients of ITNs Predicting Malaria Morbidity*

| | *B* | *SE* | Beta | *t* | *p*-value |
|---|---|---|---|---|---|
| (Constant) | 25.82 | 104.38 | | 0.25 | 0.807 |
| ITN | 1.06 | 0.31 | 0.63 | 3.45 | 0.003 |

1. Write the alternative hypothesis being tested.

2. Write the hypotheses notation.

3. Based upon the results, what is your decision regarding the null hypothesis?

4. Write the regression equation.

5. Write the conclusion with results notation.

## 11.30 Using the Computer

The following instructions will guide you in conducting a scatterplot, Pearson correlation, and simple regression. SPSS and StatCrunch differ in how they generate these results (see Table below).

| | SPSS | StatCrunch |
|---|---|---|
| Scatterplot | Conducted separately through Chartbuilder. | May be conducted separately in Graphs or within Regression. In Regression, the regression line will be placed in the scatterplot |
| Pearson Correlation | Conducted separately through `Correlate` or within `Regression`. Both will generate related *p*-values. | Conducted separately within **Summary Statistics**, then **Correlation**. Also presented in **Regression**. |
| Regression | Conducted through `Regression`. Provides correlation matrix and descriptive statistics. Does not provide regression equation, must create using regression coefficients. | Conducted through **Regression**. Provides regression equation and scatterplot with regression line. |

### SPSS

Enter data. Make sure variables apply "scale" measurement.

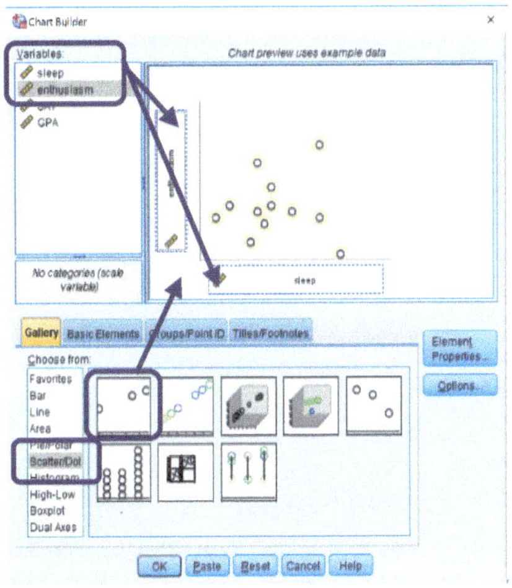


#### `Scatterplot`

1. 🖱 the `Graphs` menu, select `Chart Builder.`
2. Within the `Chart Builder` dialogue box, under Gallery, 🖱 ScatterDot.
3. 🖱 the first scatterplot and drag to the Chart Preview.
4. 🖱 on the independent variable and drag to the *X*-axis. 🖱 on the dependent variable and drag to the *Y*-axis.
5. 🖱 `OK.`

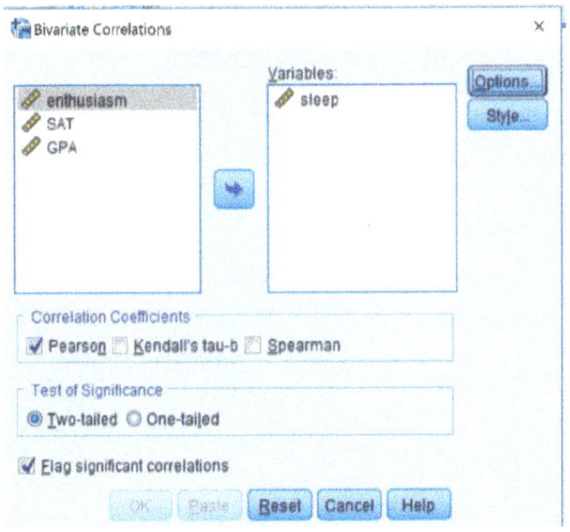


#### `Correlation`

1. 🖱 the `Analyze` menu, select `Correlate,` then `Bivariate.`
2. Within the `Bivariate Correlations` dialogue box, 🖱 (highlight) a variable, 🖱 the arrow to move it to the `Variables` box. Select all pertinent variables.
3. Select either Two-tailed or One-tailed.
4. 🖱 `Options`, you may want to select Means and Standard Deviations.
5. 🖱 `OK.`

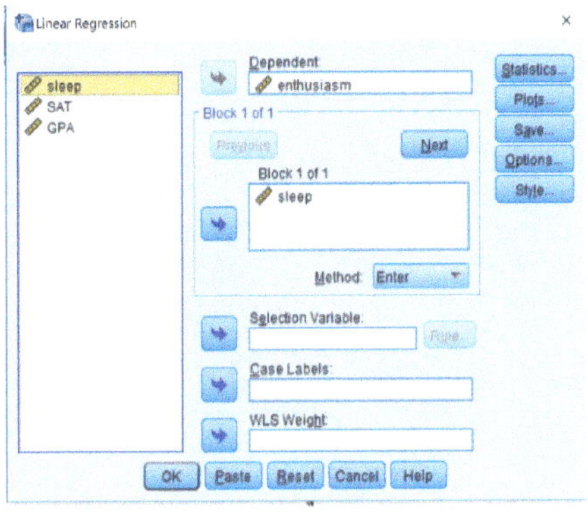


#### `Regression`

1. 🖱 the `Analyze` menu, select `Regression`, then `Linear.`
2. Within the Linear Regression dialogue box, 🖱 the dependent variable (*Y*) and move to Dependent
3. 🖱 the independent variable and move to Block 1 of 1.
4. 🖱 `Statistics` and add a check to `Descriptives`.
5. 🖱 `OK.`

## StatCrunch

### Scatterplot

1. 🖱 the **Graph** menu, select **Scatter Plot.**
2. Under X variable, select the independent variable.
3. Under Y variable, select the dependent variable.
4. 🖱 **Compute!**

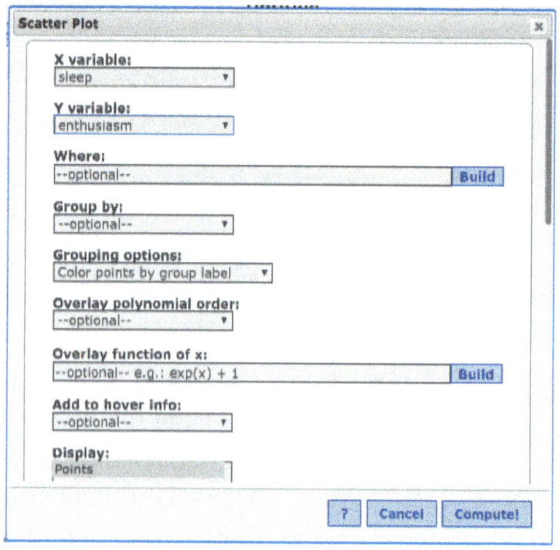


### Correlation

1. 🖱 the **Stat** menu, select **Summary Stats**, then **Correlation**.
2. Press the shift key and click all pertinent variables under Select Column(s): and move to empty white box.
3. Under **Display,** check Two-sided *p*-value.
4. 🖱 Compute!

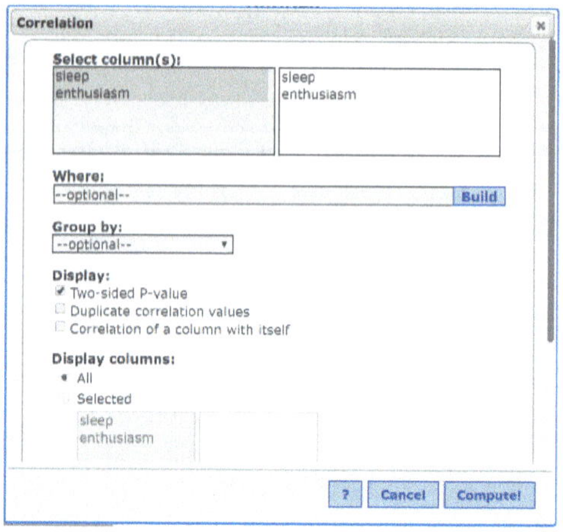


### Regression

1. 🖱 the **Stat** menu, select **Regression**, then **Simple Linear**.
2. Under X variable, select the independent variable.
3. Under Y variable, select the dependent variable.
4. 🖱 Compute!

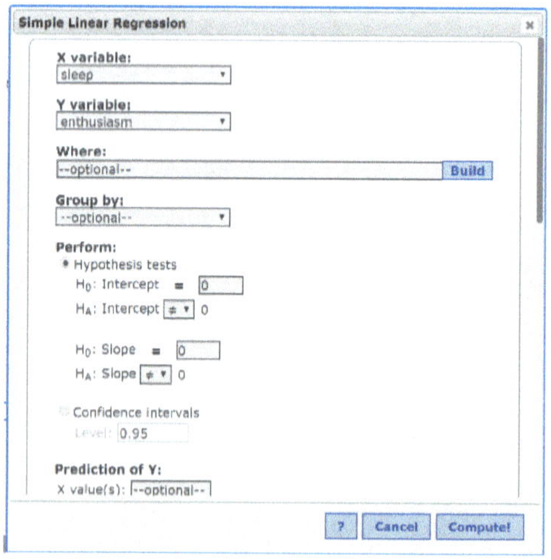

## 11.31 Exercises
### Reviewing the Concepts

1. Describe the difference between correlation and causality? Reflect on purpose and scale of variables.

2. Describe the difference in purpose between correlation and regression?

3. Why is a scatterplot always necessary when examining a mutual relationship?

4. Explain why the degrees of freedom for correlation is $n$-2.

5. What is the difference between $r$ and $r^2$? How are they evaluated differently?

6. How does hypothesis notation differ between correlation and regression?

7. You have been provided the regression equation of $Y = 3X + .5$. If $X$=2, what is $Y$?

8. What test statistic represents the significance of the regression model?

9. If $r^2$=.75, what is $r$?

10. Place the following correlation coefficients in order of strength (weakest to strongest): .85, -.24, -.78, .55

11. Reflect on the bread metaphor and order loaves from weakest to strongest correlation.

## Interpreting Results

12. In a previous example, we examined the ability of the SAT to predict college freshman GPA. Interestingly a 2016 study found that high school GPA actually has the strongest correlation with college freshman GPA ($r$=.58). Based upon this finding, the following results have replicated this relationship. Use these results to determine if HS GPA is also a significant predictor of college freshman GPA. Apply an alpha of .05.

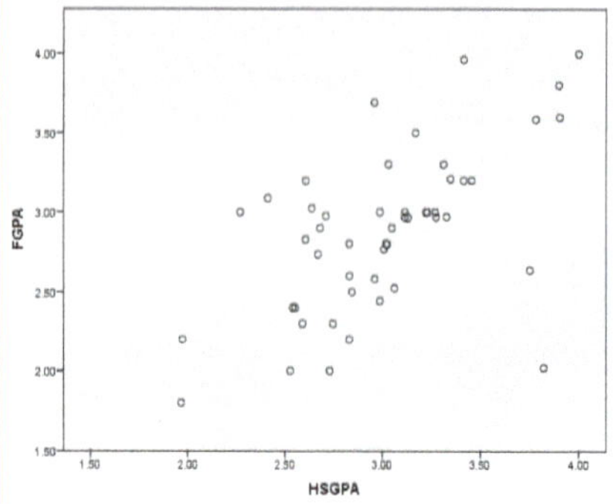


**Descriptive Statistics**

| | Mean | Std. Deviation | N |
|---|---|---|---|
| FGPA | 2.8787 | .50566 | 50 |
| HSGPA | 3.0123 | .46281 | 50 |

**Model Summary**

| Model | R | R Square | Adjusted R Square | Std. Error of the Estimate |
|---|---|---|---|---|
| 1 | .581[a] | .338 | .324 | .41581 |

a. Predictors: (Constant), HSGPA

**ANOVA[a]**

| Model | | Sum of Squares | df | Mean Square | F | Sig. |
|---|---|---|---|---|---|---|
| 1 | Regression | 4.229 | 1 | 4.229 | 24.462 | .000[b] |
| | Residual | 8.299 | 48 | .173 | | |
| | Total | 12.529 | 49 | | | |

a. Dependent Variable: FGPA

b. Predictors: (Constant), HSGPA

**Coefficients[a]**

| Model | | Unstandardized Coefficients | | Standardized Coefficients | | |
|---|---|---|---|---|---|---|
| | | B | Std. Error | Beta | t | Sig. |
| 1 | (Constant) | .966 | .391 | | 2.471 | .017 |
| | HSGPA | .635 | .128 | .581 | 4.946 | .000 |

a. Dependent Variable: FGPA

**Step 1: Develop Hypotheses:**

a. Independent Variable = Scale: Categorical Quantitative

b. Dependent Variable = Scale: Categorical Quantitative

c. Alternative hypothesis in sentence form.

d. Null hypothesis in sentence form.

e. Write the alternative and null hypotheses using correct notation.

$H_1$: $H_0$:

**Step 2: Establish significance criteria**

f. $\alpha$ =

**Step 3: Calculate test statistic, $R^2$, and regression equation**

g. $F$ = Level of significance ($p$) =

h. Decision: reject null or fail to reject null

i. $R^2$ =

j. Regression Equation:

k. If Sasha's GPA is 3.10, what is his predicted freshman GPA?

**Step 4: Draw conclusion**

l. Write your conclusion in sentence form including appropriate results notation.

Allen, J. & Mattern, K. (2016). ACT scores, high school GPA, and predictors of college success. *ACT College Readiness Benchmarks*. Found at: http://www.legis.nd.gov/files/committees/64-2014%20appendices/17_5083_03000appendixp.pdf

13. Psychologist Arthur Aron (2015) asserts that "The single biggest predictor of human happiness is the quality of [a person's] relationships." To test this, a researcher has asked 100 US adults (ranging in age from 25 to 50) to complete assessments on overall happiness (1-10) and relationship quality (1-5). Use the following StatCrunch output to determine if relationship quality is a significant predictor of happiness. Test at α=.05.

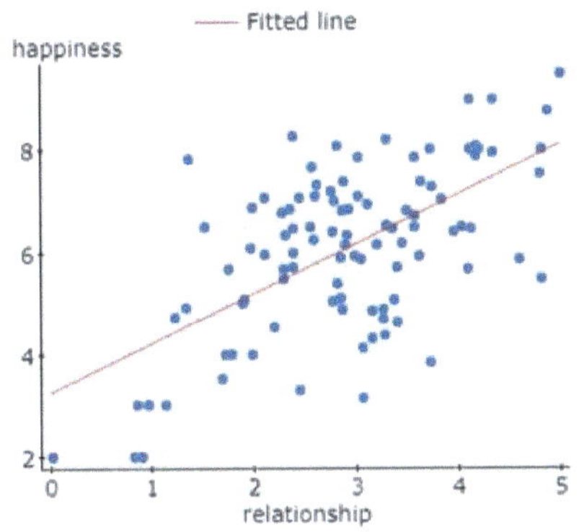


**Simple linear regression results:**
Dependent Variable: happiness
Independent Variable: relationship
happiness = 3.2433083 + 0.97500488 relationship
Sample size: 100
R (correlation coefficient) = 0.60660352
R-sq = 0.36796783
Estimate of error standard deviation: 1.3023232

**Parameter estimates:**

| Parameter | Estimate | Std. Err. | Alternative | DF | T-Stat | P-value |
|---|---|---|---|---|---|---|
| Intercept | 3.2433083 | 0.39791198 | ≠ 0 | 98 | 8.1508184 | <0.0001 |
| Slope | 0.97500488 | 0.12907984 | ≠ 0 | 98 | 7.5535025 | <0.0001 |

**Analysis of variance table for regression model:**

| Source | DF | SS | MS | F-stat | P-value |
|---|---|---|---|---|---|
| Model | 1 | 96.768565 | 96.768565 | 57.0554 | <0.0001 |
| Error | 98 | 166.21248 | 1.6960457 | | |
| Total | 99 | 262.98104 | | | |

**Step 1: Develop Hypotheses:**

a. Independent Variable = Scale: Categorical Quantitative

b. Dependent Variable = Scale: Categorical Quantitative

c. Alternative hypothesis in sentence form.

d. Null hypothesis in sentence form.

e. Write the alternative and null hypotheses using correct notation.

$H_1$: $H_0$:

**Step 2: Establish significance criteria**

f. α =

**Step 3: Calculate test statistic, $R^2$, and regression equation**

g. $F$ = Level of significance ($p$) =

h. Decision: reject null or fail to reject null

i. $R^2$ =

j. Regression Equation:

k. If Sam reports a relationship quality score of 3.8, what is her predicted happiness score?

**Step 4: Draw conclusion**

l. Write your conclusion in sentence form including appropriate results notation.

**Source:** http://www.thejournal.ie/psychologist-says-happiness-can-be-predicted-2315880-Sep2015/

14. In this excerpt, the authors examine the correlation of shopping orientation with two variables. They did not pursue a regression analysis.

**Excerpt from:** Büttner, O., Florack, A., Göritz, A.S. (2013). Shopping orientation and mindsets: How motivation influences consumer information processing during shopping. *Psychology and Marketing, 30*(9): 779–793.

This study examined the relationship between chronic shopping orientation and deliberating processing (thought about buying an item) and implementing processing (planning to buy the item) among 96 participants (48% women; $M_{age}$ = 22.7 years).

- Chronic shopping orientation was assessed by the 7-item Chronic Shopping Orientation (CSO) scale in which low levels indicating a chronic task-focused shopping orientation and high levels indicating a chronic experiential shopping orientation (1=*task-focused*, 7=*experiential*; $M$ = 3.52, $SD$ = 1.28). When shopping under a **task-focused orientation**, individuals seek to maximize their utilitarian shopping value by shopping efficiently. Consumer with an **experiential shopping orientation** may derive value from browsing through products and, hence, be more open to information that is irrelevant to his or her focal goal.
- After participants completed the CSO items, they read a shopping scenario. In detail, they were asked to imagine that they went on a shopping trip to purchase a pair of trousers. To increase immersion in the scenario, they were asked to write down a few sentences describing what this shopping trip would look like. Participants then indicated according to eight statements what they would think and how they would act during the shopping trip. Four items referred to evaluating trousers and making a decision about which pair to buy (**deliberative processing**) and four items referred to planning and carrying out the shopping trip (**implemental processing**).

The authors hypothesized that:

$H_1$: As shopping orientation increased (toward experiential) the more consumers would think about which product to buy (deliberative processing).

$H_2$: As shopping orientation increased (toward experiential) the less consumers would think about planning their shopping trip (implemental processing).

One-tailed tests were used for all directional hypotheses. Pearson correlation results indicate chronic shopping orientation was positively correlated with deliberative processing ($H_1$), $r$ =0.43, $p < 0.001$, and was negatively correlated with implemental processing ($H_2$), $r = -0.52$, $p < 0.001$.

a. Why did the authors use one-tailed tests?

b. What is the degrees of freedom for each result?

c. Examine result for $H_1$. What is the decision regarding the null? What is the direction of this relationship? Evaluate the strength of the correlation coefficient. How much variance does shopping orientation explain in deliberative processing?

d. Examine result for $H_2$. What is the decision regarding the null? What is the direction of this relationship? Evaluate the strength of the correlation coefficient. How much variance does shopping orientation explain in deliberative processing?

15. This excerpt presents a series of correlation coefficients within a table. While the independent variable is Teacher Comfort with Technology, three measures represent this variable (pre, post, and growth). Growth is calculated as post-pre. In addition, the dependent variables are also presented as pre, post, and growth. Table 1 presents correlations across these nine variables. Authors use asterisks to indicate significance at $p<.05$.

**Excerpt from:** Reinhart, R.V., Shaffer, S., Sondergeld, T. & Banister, S. (2015). Teacher Comfort Related to Current and Future Technology Use. In D. Rutledge & D. Slykhuis (Eds.), *Proceedings of SITE 2015--Society for Information Technology & Teacher Education International Conference* (pp. 1027-1030). Las Vegas: AACE. Retrieved May 3, 2018 from https://www.learntechlib.org/primary/p/150131/.

The purpose of this study was to examine the relationship of Teacher Comfort with technology (pre, post, growth) with Teacher Technology Use (pre, post, growth) and Facilitation of Student Use (pre, post, growth) as a result of a 1:1 student laptop pilot. The 1:1 laptop pilot was implemented in 2013-14 in a suburban northwest Ohio district in grades 5, 8, and 9. Approximately 45 teachers in grades 5, 8 and 9 participated in the pilot and taught approximately 875 students. Among the 45 teachers, only 34 completed both the pre and post surveys. The district is predominately white (85.35 %) with a high SES; the poverty ratio is 2.81% (Ohio Department of Education, 2013). Data was collected through the 1:1 Teacher Laptop Survey and was administered in September 2013 and again in March 2014. The study focused on the following three measurement points—pre, post, and growth (post-pre)—for each variable.

- **Frequency of Teacher Use** consisted of 12 items, and utilized a 5-point frequency scale where 0=never and 4=daily. Examples of teacher use items are: communicating with parents, students and other teachers; creating documents; classroom management; and presentations.
- **Facilitation of Student Use** measured student use such as: creating projects; completing homework; communicating with teachers and other students; and creating documents. This subscale utilized 17 items with the same 5-point frequency scale.
- **Teacher Comfort with Technology** consisted of 9 items and utilized a 4-point Likert scale. Teacher Comfort measured one's comfort and confidence in: learning new technologies, troubleshooting, showing students new technologies, using technology in one's teaching. Some items within this subscale were recoded to create unidirectional items.

Subscale scores were calculated as the means of the respective items. Pearson correlations of Teacher Technology Use and Facilitation of Student Use with Teacher Comfort are presented.

| | Teacher Comfort | | |
|---|---|---|---|
| | Pre | Post | Growth |
| Teacher Technology Use | | | |
| • Pre | .437* | .173 | - .142 |
| • Post | .158 | .665* | .468* |
| • Growth | -.286 | .371* | .583* |
| Facilitation of Student Use | | | |
| • Pre | .278 | .317 | .057 |
| • Post | .311 | .523* | -.119 |
| • Growth | .056 | .621* | -.173 |

Note: * $p<.05$

a. Among the dependent variables, which has the strongest relationship with:
   Pre Teacher Comfort?
   Post Teacher Comfort?
   Teacher Comfort Growth?

b. What is the correlation between Pre Teacher Comfort and Teacher Technology Growth? Is it significant? Explain the relationship.

c. A primary goal of the 1:1 laptop program is that teachers Facilitate Student Use at a high level. Examine the correlation coefficients of Facilitation for Post and Growth; which measure of Teacher Comfort has the strongest relationship? What conclusion can you infer from these results?

## Conducting Analysis

16. Loneliness is the perception of the quality of one's relationships. Recent studies have shown that loneliness is not only a predictor of depression, but also anxiety, stress, anger and health. This data set of 20 undergraduate college students presents scores for loneliness and depression. Loneliness was measured with a three-item Loneliness Scale, with scores ranging from 3 to 9, where 9 indicates extreme loneliness. Depression was measured using the Beck Depression Inventory, where scores range from 0-63. Scores 30 and above indicate severe depression. Use SPSS or StatCrunch to examine the ability of loneliness to predict depression. Test at $\alpha$=.05.

**Step 1: Develop Hypotheses:**

a. Independent Variable = Scale: Categorical Quantitative

b. Dependent Variable = Scale: Categorical Quantitative

c. Alternative hypothesis in sentence form.

| Loneliness | Depression |
|---|---|
| 3 | 13 |
| 4 | 10 |
| 5 | 12 |
| 6 | 8 |
| 5 | 20 |
| 6 | 4 |
| 7 | 20 |
| 8 | 11 |
| 9 | 32 |
| 6 | 4 |
| 7 | 16 |
| 4 | 9 |
| 5 | 12 |
| 3 | 4 |
| 7 | 24 |
| 8 | 9 |
| 3 | 4 |
| 4 | 7 |
| 5 | 11 |
| 7 | 18 |

d. Null hypothesis in sentence form.

e. Write the alternative and null hypotheses using correct notation.

$H_1$: $H_0$:

**Step 2: Establish significance criteria**

f. $\alpha$ =

**Step 3: Calculate test statistic, $R^2$, and regression equation**

g. $F$ = Level of significance ($p$) =

h. Decision: reject null or fail to reject null

i. $R^2$=

j. Regression Equation:

k. If Laila reports a loneliness score of 7.5, what is her predicted depression score?

**Step 4: Draw conclusion**

l. Write your conclusion in sentence form including appropriate results notation.

**Source:** Latson, J. (2018). A cure for disconnection. *Psychology Today, 51*(2), 42-51.

17. Several studies have verified that males with high levels of testosterone are at greater risk of sexually assaulting women. To explore the role of testosterone in sexual harassment, one researcher examines the relationship between male levels of testosterone and the likelihood to sexually harass women. Twenty college males, self-identified as heterosexual, completed the Likelihood to Sexually Harass (LHS) Scale, which is comprised of ten scenarios. Scores range from 10 to 50, with higher scores indicating a greater likelihood to sexually harass. After completion of the survey, participant saliva was collected to measure testosterone levels. The typical testosterone level 679 ng/dL. Does testosterone levels significantly predicts likelihood to sexually harass women among male college students? Use SPSS or StatCrunch to analyze the data below. Test at $\alpha$=.05.

**Step 1: Develop Hypotheses:**

a. Independent Variable = Scale: Categorical Quantitative

b. Dependent Variable = Scale: Categorical Quantitative

c. Alternative hypothesis in sentence form.

| Testosterone | LSH |
|---|---|
| 488 | 12 |
| 546 | 13 |
| 703 | 35 |
| 532 | 28 |
| 441 | 47 |
| 500 | 31 |
| 931 | 48 |
| 682 | 34 |
| 620 | 10 |
| 584 | 43 |
| 558 | 30 |
| 547 | 27 |
| 392 | 18 |
| 661 | 30 |
| 455 | 20 |
| 806 | 47 |
| 759 | 34 |
| 692 | 26 |
| 699 | 49 |
| 775 | 10 |

d. Null hypothesis in sentence form.

e. Write the alternative and null hypotheses using correct notation.
$H_1$: $H_0$:

**Step 2: Establish significance criteria**

f. $\alpha$ =

**Step 3: Calculate test statistic, $R^2$, and regression equation**

g. $F$ = Level of significance ($p$) =

h. Decision: reject null or fail to reject null

i. $R^2$=

j. Regression Equation:

**Step 4: Draw conclusion**

k. Write your conclusion in sentence form including appropriate results notation.

**Source:** Seltzer, L. F. (2018). Uncharted territory. *Psychology Today, 51*(2), 69-71.

Chi- 

# Module 12

## Chi-Square

### Learning Targets

After completing Module 12, you should be able to:

- Differentiate between parametric and non-parametric statistical tests.
- Apply the process of hypothesis testing to conduct a Chi-square Goodness of Fit and Chi-square Test of Independence.
- Interpret Chi-square results (SPSS/StatCrunch output) to determine statistical significance and draw appropriate conclusions.
- Utilize Chi-square results to calculate appropriate effect size.
- Write appropriate conclusions with statistical results notation.

# Part 1: The Concepts

Up to this point, the inferential tests we have utilized have had a quantitative dependent variable, where we have tested a hypothesis about the population parameters ($\mu$, $\mu_D$, $\rho$). Several assumptions regarding the dependent variable and its population parameters needed to be met, such as assumptions of normality and equality variances. Such tests are called ***parametric tests***, since population parameters need to full certain requirement so that we may then generalize our results to the population. However, in statistics we are not always concerned with a quantitative outcome, at times we are interested in exploring a categorical outcome. And at other times, our quantitative data just doesn't fulfill the parametric assumptions. Fortunately, researchers have developed multiple hypothesis tests that address these "other" options and are appropriately termed ***nonparametic tests***. This module will focus on two nonparametric tests, both of which utilize the test statistic of chi-square. Although both tests use sample data to examine a hypothesis about proportions or relationships that exist in the population, the hypotheses for nonparametric tests are not stated in terms of population parameters. In addition, non-parametric tests are not as sensitive in detecting a real difference or relationship than parametric tests. Therefore, whenever possible, a parametric test should always be the priority when possible.

A chi-square test seeks to examine the relationship between two categorical variables, Specifically, the test compares frequencies, not scores, across groups. Therefore each variable must be categorical with distinct, independent groups. The chi-square test compares two types of frequencies: ***observed ($f_o$)*** and ***expected ($f_e$)***. Expected frequencies are based upon theoretical or prior knowledge. The chi-square test examines the differences between the observed and expected frequencies, both of which are used in calculating chi-square ($\chi^2$). In this module, we will learn about two chi-square test: 1) Goodness of Fit, and 2) Test of Independence.

## Example

### Goodness of Fit

While eye color varies across the world, brown is the dominant color with nearly 70% having brown eyes. Blue is the next common with only 8%, followed by Hazel (5%), and the rare green (2%). But does the United States have similar distribution of eye color?

**RQ:** Do eye color proportions in the U.S. significantly differ from those in the world?

**Step 1: State Hypothesis**
IV: U.S. vs World
DV: eye color

**Alternative Hypothesis**
U.S. eye color proportions will significantly differ from those in the world.

**Null Hypothesis**
U.S. eye color proportions will NOT significantly differ from those in the world.

**Hypothesis Notation:**

***Ho:***

| Brown | Blue | Hazel | Green | Other |
|---|---|---|---|---|
| 70% | 8% | 5% | 2% | 15% |

## 12.11 Chi-Square Goodness of Fit

The most basic chi-square test is Goodness of Fit, in which the observed frequencies for each group in ONE categorical variables are analyzed against the expected frequencies for each group. The expected frequencies are based upon our knowledge of the population, hence we are comparing the sample proportions to the population proportions. This comparison of sample to population is conceptually similar to a *t*-test of single sample, in which the sample mean is compared to the population mean.

**Hypotheses.** When identifying expected frequencies, we may predict that frequencies/proportions will be equally distributed across the groups, and other times, we may predict varied group proportions. Either way, the alternative hypotheses predicts a difference between our sample (observed) proportions and the expected proportions. In contrast, the null hypothesis indicates no difference. When writing the hypothesis notation, only the null notation is written and is presented as a table of expected proportions across categories. For our example of eye color, the distribution of eye color across the world is quite varied with the majority (70%) having brown eyes. Suppose we were to randomly select 75 U.S. adults and document their eye color. The alternative hypothesis states that the U.S. population will significantly differ in eye color proportion from the world population. The null hypothesis then indicates that U.S. eye color proportions will NOT differ from the world proportions. The null hypothesis notation is presented as

$H_0$:

| | Brown | Blue | Hazel | Green | Other |
|---|---|---|---|---|---|
| World | 70% | 8% | 5% | 2% | 15% |

**The Chi-Square Statistic.** To determine how well our sample data ($f_o$) fit the hypothesized population ($f_e$), the chi-square statistic makes multiple comparisons between the observed and expected frequencies. The formula for chi-square is

$$\text{chi-square } (\chi^2) = \Sigma \frac{(f_o - f_e)^2}{f_e}$$

While the ***observed frequencies ($f_o$)*** are based upon the sample frequencies that fall into each category/group, expected frequencies must be calculated based upon predicted (observed proportions). Keep in mind, categories/groups must be distinctive and independent with no overlapping. To calculate the ***expected frequencies ($f_e$)*** for each group, we multiple the expected group proportion ($p$) by the total sample size ($n$).

If our U.S. population were to follow the world proportions, then 70% of the 75 U.S. individuals would have brown eyes (.70 * 75 = 52.5), generated an expected frequency of 52.5. Table 12.1 presents the observed frequencies for the U.S. sample and the calculations for the expected frequencies based upon the world proportions.

**Table 12.1** *Observed and Expected Frequencies for Eye Color*

| | Brown | Blue | Hazel | Green | Other | |
|---|---|---|---|---|---|---|
| U.S. (observed—$f_o$) | 31 | 24 | 9 | 8 | 3 | $n$=75 |
| | | | | | | |
| Expected calculation | .7(75) | .08(75) | .05(75) | .02(75) | .15(75) | |
| U.S. (expected—$f_e$) | 52.5 | 6 | 3.75 | 1.5 | 11.25 | |

Once expected frequencies are computed, then chi-square may be calculated using the following steps:

1. Calculate the difference between the observed and expected frequency for each category.
2. Square each difference.
3. Divide each squared difference by the respective expected frequency ($f_e$).
4. Lastly, sum the values from all the categories.

**Chi-Square**

$$\chi^2 = \sum \frac{(f_o - f_e)^2}{f_e}$$

Applying this process to our eye color example, we calculate a $\chi^2$ = 104.40 (see Table 12.2). As with our other test statistics, a table of significant values is available for chi-square (see Appendix G). The chi-square distribution is similar to the $F$ distribution in that it is positively skewed, since chi-square will always be positive as a result of squaring the difference (see Figure 12.1). Therefore, when there is a large difference between the observed and expected frequencies, chi-square will be large and lead to the rejection of the null hypothesis. However, when the difference between observed and expected frequencies is small, a small chi-square is likely generated; so we conclude that our sample "fits" the population and has similarly distributed proportions across the categories/groups. In this case, we fail to reject the null.

**Table 12.2** *Calculation of Chi-Square*

| | | 1 | 2 | 3 | |
|---|---|---|---|---|---|
| $f_o$ | $f_e$ | $f_o - f_e$ | $(f_o - f_e)^2$ | $(f_o - f_e)^2/f_e$ | |
| 31 | 52.5 | -21.50 | 462.25 | 8.80 | |
| 24 | 6.00 | 18.00 | 324.00 | 54.00 | |
| 9 | 3.75 | 5.25 | 27.56 | 7.35 | |
| 8 | 1.50 | 6.50 | 42.25 | 28.20 | |
| 3 | 11.25 | -8.25 | 68.10 | 6.05 | |
| | | | | Σ = 104.40 | 4 |

**Determining Significance.** Determining significance for chi-square is based upon degrees of freedom and the selected alpha level. Degrees of freedom is calculated as the number of categories ($C$) in the variable minus one ($df = C$ -1). Since the calculation of chi-square sums the differences from each category, we are much more likely to calculate a large chi-square with more categories. Our eye color example has five categories of color, which generates a degrees of freedom of 4 ($df$ = 5-1 = 4). Using the table excerpt of chi-square significant values in Figure 12.1 (Appendix G) and applying an alpha of .05 with $df$=4, we identify a critical chi-square of 9.49. The chi-square value ($\chi^2$=104.4) for the eye color study exceeds the critical value of 9.49; we have significance and reject the null.

**Figure 12.1** *Chi-Square Distribution and Table*

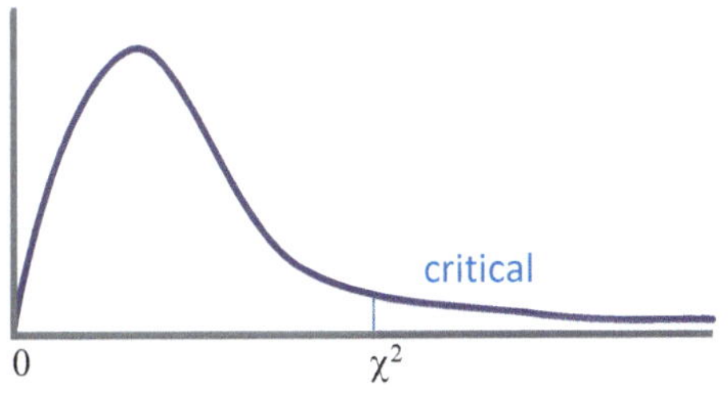


| *df* | Proportion in Critical Region | | | | |
|---|---|---|---|---|---|
| | 0.10 | 0.05 | 0.025 | 0.01 | 0.005 |
| 1 | 2.71 | 3.84 | 5.02 | 6.63 | 7.88 |
| 2 | 4.61 | 5.99 | 7.38 | 9.21 | 10.60 |
| 3 | 6.25 | 7.81 | 9.35 | 11.34 | 12.84 |
| 4 | 7.78 | 9.49 | 11.14 | 13.28 | 14.86 |
| 5 | 9.24 | 11.07 | 12.83 | 15.09 | 16.75 |
| 6 | 10.64 | 12.59 | 14.45 | 16.81 | 18.55 |

As in our previous modules, we will rely on computer output to determine significance. For both SPSS and StatCrunch, the observed and expected frequencies are presented along with the $\chi^2$=104.40, $df$=4, $p$<.0001. When $p$ is less than alpha, we have significance and reject the null.

**SPSS**

**eyecolor**

| | Observed N | Expected N | Residual |
|---|---|---|---|
| brown | 31 | 52.4 | -21.4 |
| blue | 24 | 6.0 | 18.0 |
| hazel | 9 | 3.8 | 5.2 |
| green | 8 | 1.5 | 6.5 |
| other | 3 | 11.3 | -8.3 |
| Total | 75 | | |

**Test Statistics**

| | eyecolor |
|---|---|
| Chi-Square | 104.322[a] |
| df | 4 |
| Asymp. Sig. | .000 |

a. 2 cells (40.0%) have expected frequencies less than 5. The minimum expected cell frequency is 1.5.

**StatCrunch**

**Chi-Square goodness-of-fit results:**
Observed: var1
Expected: var2

| N | DF | Chi-Square | P-value |
|---|---|---|---|
| 75 | 4 | 104.32246 | <0.0001 |

| Observed | Expected |
|---|---|
| 3 | 11.28 |
| 8 | 1.50 |
| 9 | 3.79 |
| 6 | 6.00 |
| 31 | 52.43 |

**Reporting the Results.** In addition to the concluding statement based upon the hypothesis, you also need to include the supporting statistics. The chi-square value is reported with degrees of freedom and sample size in parentheses, followed by the *p*-value. In addition, you may want to report the observed and expected frequencies for each category. For our example, we would state:

> U.S. eye color proportions significantly differ from world eye color proportions; $\chi^2$**(4, *n*=75) = 104.40, *p*<.0001.**

## 12.12 Chi-Square Test of Independence

Another common use of chi-square is the Test of Independence, where the relationship between two categorical variables is examined. Individuals are classified on two separate variables. For example, we may study the relationship between gender (female, male) and political affiliation (Democrat, Republican, Independent). Although we expect a fairly even distribution of males and females, political affiliation is another matter. The Pew Research found in 2018 that the general population reports 51.5% leaned toward the Democratic Party, while 41.5% leaned toward Republican. For our study, we randomly selected 200 U.S. adults to indicate their political leanings. Responses or observed frequencies by gender and political party are presented in Table 12.3. This ***two-way table*** is typical when reporting the intersecting frequencies of two categorical variables. The row variable is binary gender, and the column variable is political affiliation with three categories. The values are the counts or frequencies in each gender-by-political affiliation class. Table 12.3 indicates that the majority of females reported leanings toward the Democratic Party, whereas the majority of males reported Republican as their likely affiliation.

**Table 12.3**
*Observed Frequencies for Gender and Political Affiliation*

| | Democrat (1) | Republican (2) | Independent (3) | |
|---|---|---|---|---|
| Female (1) | 62 | 36 | 6 | 104 |
| Male (2) | 42 | 46 | 8 | 96 |
| Total | 104 | 82 | 14 | *n*=200 |

**Hypotheses.** As with Chi-square Goodness of Fit, we are interested in determining if the observed frequencies differ from the expected frequencies, or in this case proportions for all U.S. voters as reported by Pew Research. However, for the Test of Independence we are specifically interested in the relationship between the two studied variables. If there is a relationship between the two variables, then the observed proportions will differ from the expected proportions. In other words, the proportions of political affiliation will differ by gender. The use of the term "relationship" may get a bit confusing, since we have only associated it with a mutual relationship between two quantitative variables. But we can also apply the term between two categorical variables. As such, we can write our hypotheses two ways depending upon your emphasis and comfort: 1) relationship and 2) difference.

| | Alternative Hypothesis | Null Hypothesis |
|---|---|---|
| **Relationship** | Gender and political affiliation significantly <u>relate</u> among U.S. registered voters. | Gender and political affiliation do NOT significantly <u>relate</u> among U.S. registered voters. |
| **Difference** | Political affiliation significantly <u>differs</u> by gender among U.S. registered voters. | Political affiliation does NOT significantly <u>differ</u> by gender among U.S. registered voters. |

Essentially, the two null hypotheses have the same meaning and will use the same analysis for inferential testing. Personally, I am more comfortable focusing on the difference; however, I will vary the way in which I write the hypotheses for educational purposes. Since the chi-square distribution is positively skewed, hypotheses do not indicate a specific direction for the relationship or difference, hence the number of tails is not indicated.

### Example
#### Goodness of Fit

**Step 2: Establish Significance Criteria**
An alpha of .05 is applied.

**Step 3: Collect and Analyze Data**
Output: $\chi^2$=104.40, *df*=4, *p*<.0001.

**Step 4: Evaluate Null and Draw Conclusion**
*p*<.0001 is less than alpha of .05, therefore sample proportions (U.S.) are significantly different from the population proportions (world).

- Significance→Reject the Null→Restate Alternative
- U.S. eye color proportions significantly differ from world eye color proportions; $\chi^2$**(4, *n*=75) = 104.40, *p*<.0001.**

### Example
#### Test of Independence

In 2018, the Pew Research Center found that approximately 51.5% of registered voters affiliated with or leaned toward the Democratic Party. While 41.5% reported/leaned Republican, and 7% as Independent. Do the political affiliation proportions differ by gender?

**RQ:** Does political affiliation differ by gender among U.S. registered voters?

**Step 1: State Hypothesis**
IV: gender
DV: political affiliation

**Alternative Hypothesis**
Political affiliation will significantly differ by gender among U.S. registered voters.

**Null Hypothesis**
Political affiliation will NOT significantly differ by gender among U.S. registered voters.

**Expected frequency**

$$f_e = \frac{row\ total\ x\ column\ total}{table\ total\ (n)}$$

**Calculating Chi-Square.** To test the null hypothesis, we again compare the observed frequencies to the expected frequencies, the counts we would expect from the population, or the total sample. If the observed frequencies are greatly different from the expected frequencies, then chi-square will be rather large and indicate a significant difference. The method of calculating chi-square is same, so our next step is calculating the expected frequencies for each cell or class. Since we have two variables being examined, our calculations have "multiplied." Since expected frequencies are based upon the proportions for our total sample, we utilize the row and column totals to calculate the expected frequency for each cell. The Table 12.4 presents the column and row totals from our observed data. To compute the expected frequency ($f_e$) for each cell, we multiply the respective row and column totals and divide by the total sample size. Therefore the $f_e$ for female Republicans = 104*82/100 = 42.64.

**Table 12.4** *Calculation of Expected Frequencies for Each Cell*

| | Democrat | Republican | Independent | |
|---|---|---|---|---|
| **Female** | $\frac{104 * 104}{200} = 54.08$ | $\frac{104 * 82}{200} = 42.64$ | $\frac{104 * 14}{200} = 7.28$ | 104 |
| **Male** | $\frac{96 * 104}{200} = 49.92$ | $\frac{96 * 82}{200} = 39.36$ | $\frac{96 * 14}{200} = 6.72$ | 96 |
| **Total** | 104 | 82 | 14 | $n$=200 |

**Chi-Square**

$$\chi^2 = \sum \frac{(f_o - f_e)^2}{f_e}$$

Once expected frequencies are computed, we follow the same steps for calculating chi-square.

1. Calculate the difference between the observed and expected frequency for each category.
2. Square each difference.
3. Divide each squared difference by the respective expected frequency ($f_e$).
4. Lastly, sum the values from all the categories.

The table below presents the comparison of observed and expected frequencies for each cell leading to the calculation of chi-square ($\chi^2$ = 5.05).

**Table 12.5** *Calculation of Chi-Square*

| | | | 1 | 2 | 3 | |
|---|---|---|---|---|---|---|
| | $f_o$ | $f_e$ | $f_o - f_e$ | $(f_o - f_e)^2$ | $(f_o - f_e)^2/f_e$ | |
| Female Dem | 62 | 54.08 | 7.92 | 62.73 | 1.16 | |
| Female Rep | 36 | 42.68 | -6.68 | 44.62 | 1.05 | |
| Female Ind | 6 | 7.28 | 1.28 | 1.64 | 0.23 | |
| Male Dem | 42 | 49.92 | -7.92 | 62.73 | 1.26 | |
| Male Rep | 46 | 39.36 | 6.64 | 44.09 | 1.12 | |
| Male Ind | 8 | 6.72 | 1.28 | 1.63 | 0.24 | |
| | | | | | Σ = 5.05 | 4 |

***df* for Chi-Square Test of Independence**

$df = (R\text{-}1)(C\text{-}1)$

**Determining Significance.** Determining significance for Chi-square Test of Independence is identical to that of Goodness of Fit; the only difference is how degrees of freedom is calculated. Because the Test of Independence examines two variables, each with many categories that are presented in a two-way table as rows and columns, we use the number of rows to represent the number categories for one variable and the number columns to represent the categories of the second variable. Therefore, degrees of freedom is calculated as the number of rows ($R$) minus 1 ($R$-1) multiplied by the number of columns ($C$) minus 1 ($C$-1), which generates the equation of: $df = (R\text{-}1)(C\text{-}1)$. Considering our example of gender and political affiliation, $df$ = (2-1)(3-1) = 1*2 = 2. Applying the $df$ of 2 and $\alpha$=.05 to Figure 12.1, the table excerpt of chi-square significant values, we identify chi-square critical to be 5.99. In this case, the calculated $\chi^2$ of 5.05 does not exceed the $\chi^2_{critical}$ of 5.99; therefore we do not have significance and fail to reject the null.

Usually we will interpret computer output, where we just compare the computer-generated $p$-value to the predetermined alpha. Computer output identifies $p$=.0805, which is NOT less than an alpha of .05. therefore, we do not have significance and fail to reject the null. Both outputs provide the observed and expected frequencies.

SPSS

**gender * political Crosstabulation**

| | | | political | | | |
|---|---|---|---|---|---|---|
| | | | democrat | republican | independent | Total |
| gender | female | Count | 62 | 36 | 6 | 104 |
| | | Expected Count | 54.1 | 42.6 | 7.3 | 104.0 |
| | male | Count | 42 | 46 | 8 | 96 |
| | | Expected Count | 49.9 | 39.4 | 6.7 | 96.0 |
| Total | | Count | 104 | 82 | 14 | 200 |
| | | Expected Count | 104.0 | 82.0 | 14.0 | 200.0 |

**Chi-Square Tests**

| | Value | df | Asymptotic Significance (2-sided) |
|---|---|---|---|
| Pearson Chi-Square | 5.039[a] | 2 | .080 |
| Likelihood Ratio | 5.059 | 2 | .080 |
| Linear-by-Linear Association | 4.354 | 1 | .037 |
| N of Valid Cases | 200 | | |

a. 0 cells (0.0%) have expected count less than 5. The minimum expected count is 6.72.

**StatCrunch**

**Contingency table results:**
Rows: gender
Columns: None

**Cell format**
Count
(Expected count)

| | dem | rep | ind | Total |
|---|---|---|---|---|
| female | 62 | 36 | 6 | 104 |
| | (54.08) | (42.64) | (7.28) | |
| male | 42 | 46 | 8 | 96 |
| | (49.92) | (39.36) | (6.72) | |
| Total | 104 | 82 | 14 | 200 |

**Chi-Square test:**

| Statistic | DF | Value | P-value |
|---|---|---|---|
| Chi-square | 2 | 5.0394434 | 0.0805 |

## Example

### Test of Independence

**Step 2: Establish Significance Criteria:** An alpha of .05 is applied.

**Step 3: Collect and Analyze Data:** $\chi^2$=5.04, *df*=2, *p*=.0805.

**Step 4: Evaluate Null and Draw Conclusion**
*p*=.0805 is NOT less than alpha of .05, therefore political affiliation does not differ by gender.

- Significance→Fail to reject the Null→Restate Null
- Political affiliation does NOT significantly differ by gender among U.S. adults; **$\chi^2$(2, *n*=200) = 5.04, *p*=.0805.**

## 12.13 Effect Size

As usual, due to hypothesis testing limitations, reporting an effect size is always recommended. Two effect sizes are typical for chi-square: phi-coefficient ($\phi$) and Cramér's V. ***Phi-coefficient*** may only be used when a 2 x 2 matrix is created as a result of the two variables—meaning each variable may only have two categories. The phi-coefficient is a correlation that represents the strength of the relationship, rather than the significance. Phi is calculated as

$$\phi = \sqrt{\frac{\chi^2}{n}}$$

Note that the numerator is chi-square itself and does not need additional squaring. Since our example applies a 2 x 3, we are unable to use the phi-coefficient. Interpretation of phi follows the same standards as those applied to $r^2$ where less than .09 is a small effect, .09-.25 is a medium effect, and greater than .25 is a large effect.

The second effect size, ***Cramér's V*** allows us to go beyond a 2 x 2 matrix; now our variables may have more than two categories. Cramér's V is a modification of phi-coefficient. The calculation is very similar, however, $df^*$ is multiplied in the denominator. The asterisks indicate a special calculation of df. Recall that for Test of Independence, $df = (R\text{-}1)(C\text{-}1)$. For Cramér's V, we will still calculate the *df* for rows (*R*-1) and columns (*C*-1), but we will only <u>select the smaller of the two</u>. For our example of gender and political affiliation, the *df* for rows (gender) is $df = 2\text{-}1 = 1$. The *df* for columns (political affiliation) was $df = 3\text{-}1 = 2$. The *df* for rows is the smaller of the two, so this will be used in our calculation.

$$V = \sqrt{\frac{\chi^2}{n(df^*)}} = \sqrt{\frac{5.04}{200(1)}} = .16$$

### Effect Size

**Phi-Coefficient**

$$\phi = \sqrt{\frac{\chi^2}{n}}$$

| $r^2$ | Size |
|---|---|
| <.09 | Small |
| .09-.25 | Medium |
| <.25 | Large |

**Cramér's V**

$$V = \sqrt{\frac{\chi^2}{n(df^*)}}$$

| *df* | Small | Medium | Large |
|---|---|---|---|
| 1 | .10 | .30 | .50 |
| 2 | .07 | .21 | .35 |
| 3 | .06 | .17 | .29 |
| 4 | .05 | .15 | .25 |
| 5 | .05 | .13 | .22 |

Guidelines for interpreting Cramér's V were developed by Cohen and are based upon our special $df^*$. For our example, Cramér's V is calculated as .16, which is a medium effect. SPSS and StatCrunch provides the option of calculating these effect sizes.

**Symmetric Measures**

| | | Value | Approximate Significance |
|---|---|---|---|
| Nominal by Nominal | Phi | .159 | .080 |
| | Cramer's V | .159 | .080 |
| N of Valid Cases | | 200 | |

**Cramer's V test for association:**

| Measure | DF | Value | P-value |
|---|---|---|---|
| Cramer's V | 2 | 0.15874 | 0.0805 |

## 12.14 Assumptions

As always, several assumptions must be satisfied to use a Chi-Square Goodness of Fit or Test of Independence.

- **Independence of observations** is important with any test. For chi-square it means that an individual cannot fall into multiple categories or classes. Each category must be exclusive.
- **Size of expected frequencies.** Chi-square should not be conducted when the size of expected frequencies is less than 5. Such a violation distorts the chi-square value and often enlarges it. Since chi-square is very sensitive to small expected frequencies, large samples are recommended.

## 12.15 Reporting the Results

Results summary always begin with a concluding statement based upon the hypothesis. In addition, the following supporting statistics should be presented:

- Chi-square value with *df* and sample size in parentheses;
- *p*-value;
- Effect size; and
- Observed and expected frequencies (possibly in a table).

**Example**

**Test of Independence**

**Updated Results:**

Political affiliation does NOT significantly differ by gender among U.S. adults; $\chi^2(2, n=200) = 5.04$, $p=.0805$, Cramér's V=.16.

| | Observed *f* | Expected *f* |
|---|---|---|
| Female Democrat | 62 | 54.08 |
| Female Republican | 36 | 42.68 |
| Female Independent | 6 | 7.28 |
| Male Democrat | 42 | 49.92 |
| Male Republican | 46 | 39.36 |
| Male Independent | 8 | 6.72 |

## 12.16 Module Summary

- ***Parametric tests*** typically have:
  - a quantitative dependent variable;
  - a hypothesis about the population parameters ($\mu$, $\mu_D$, $\rho$).
  - several assumptions (normality, equality of variances) regarding the dependent variable and its population parameters that need to be met.
- ***Non-parametric tests*** are used when the quantitative dependent variable cannot fulfill the necessary assumption OR the dependent variable is categorical.
- ***Chi-Square tests*** are a non-parametric and compare observed and expected frequencies.

***Chi-square goodness of fit*** compares the observed frequencies in a sample to the expected/predicted frequencies in the population.

- Chi-square goodness of fit is similar to *t*-test of single sample, since sample statistic is being compared to the population norm.
- The alternative hypothesis predicts that sample proportions will differ from the expected proportions.
- Only hypothesis notation for the null is presented and is based upon as a table of expected proportions across categories.
- The chi-square statistic determines how well our sample data ($f_o$) fit the hypothesized population ($f_e$).
  - chi-square $(\chi^2) = \sum \frac{(f_o - f_e)^2}{f_e}$
    - ***Observed frequencies ($f_o$)*** are based upon the sample frequencies that fall into each category/group,
    - ***Expected frequencies ($f_e$)*** for each group are calculated by multiplying the expected group proportion (*p*) by the total sample size (*n*).
    - Once expected frequencies are computed, then chi-square may be calculated using the following steps:
      1. Calculate the difference $(f_o - f_e)$ between the observed and expected frequency for each category.
      2. Square each difference $(f_o - f_e)^2$.
      3. Divide each squared difference by the respective expected frequency $(f_o - f_e)^2/f_e$.
      4. Lastly, sum the values from all the categories.
- Determining significance for chi-square is based upon degrees of freedom and the selected alpha level.
- Degrees of freedom is calculated as the number of categories (*C*) in the variable minus one ($df = C - 1$).
- When using computer output, *p* must be less than alpha to be significant.
- Results should include: concluding statement based upon the hypothesis; chi-square value with degrees of freedom and sample size in parentheses; *p*-value; observed and expected frequencies for each category (optional).

***Chi-Square Test of Independence*** examines the relationship between two categorical variables.

- A ***two-way table*** is typical when reporting the intersecting frequencies of two categorical variables.
- Still examines the difference between observed frequencies and expected frequencies,
- Hypotheses may focus on relationship or difference:
  1. Chi-square **relationship** is not the same as a mutual relationship, where Y increases or decreases as X increases. Rather the emphasis is on changes across categories in that as X categorical membership changes, Y changes.
  2. Chi-square **difference** asserts that Y categorical membership will differ across X categorical membership.
  - An alternative hypothesis predicting a relationship is the same as predicting a difference.
  - Hypothesis notation is not developed for chi-square test of independence.
- Calculating chi-square follows the same equation and process as Goodness of Fit:

$$\text{chi-square } (\chi^2) = \sum \frac{(f_o - f_e)^2}{f_e}$$

  - Since expected frequencies are based upon the proportions for our total sample, we utilize the row and column totals to calculate the expected frequency for each cell.
- Determining significance for Chi-square Test of Independence is identical to that of Goodness of Fit; the only difference is how degrees of freedom is calculated.
  - Degrees of freedom is calculated as the number of rows (*R*) minus 1 (*R*-1) multiplied by the number of columns (*C*) minus 1 (*C*-1), which generates the equation of: $df = (R-1)(C-1)$.
  - Computer output presents chi-square, *p*-value, and observed and expected frequencies. Significance is determined by comparing the computer-generated *p*-value to the predetermined alpha.
- Two effect sizes are typical for chi-square: phi-coefficient (ϕ) and Cramér's V.
  - ***Phi-coefficient*** may only be used when a 2 x 2 matrix is created as a result of the two variables—meaning each variable may only have two categories.
    - The phi-coefficient is a correlation that represents the strength of the relationship, rather than the significance. Phi is calculated as

$$\phi = \sqrt{\frac{\chi^2}{n}}$$

| $r^2$ | Size |
|---|---|
| <.09 | Small |
| .09-.25 | Medium |
| <.25 | Large |

    - Interpretation of phi follows the same standards as those applied to $r^2$ where less than .09 is a small effect, .09-.25 is a medium effect, and greater than .25 is a large effect.
  - ***Cramér's V*** allows us to go beyond a 2 x 2 matrix. The calculation is very similar to Cramér's V, however, $df^*$ is multiplied in the denominator. The smaller *df* of rows or columns is used in the calculation.

$$V = \sqrt{\frac{\chi^2}{n(df^*)}}$$

| *df* | Small | Medium | Large |
|---|---|---|---|
| 1 | .10 | .30 | .50 |
| 2 | .07 | .21 | .35 |
| 3 | .06 | .17 | .29 |
| 4 | .05 | .15 | .25 |
| 5 | .05 | .13 | .22 |

- Several assumptions must be satisfied to use a Chi-Square Goodness of Fit or Test of Independence.
  - Independence of observations—an individual cannot fall into multiple categories or classes. Each category must be exclusive.
  - Size of expected frequencies should be 5 or greater. Large samples are recommended.
- Results summary always begins with a concluding statement based upon the hypothesis and includes supporting statistics: Chi-square value with *df* and sample size in parentheses; *p*-value; effect size; and observed and expected frequencies (possibly in a table).

# Part 2: The Learning Guide

***Parametric tests*** typically have:

- a quantitative dependent variable;
- a hypothesis about the population parameters ($\mu$, $\mu_D$, $\rho$).
- several assumptions (normality, equality of variances) regarding the dependent variable and its population parameters that need to be met.

***Nonparametric tests*** are used:

- when the quantitative dependent variable doesn't fulfill the necessary assumptions; OR
- the outcome is categorical.

A ***chi-square test*** examines the relationship between two categorical variables

- Compares the proportions across groups—proportions that are based upon frequencies—***observed*** $(f_o)$ and ***expected*** $(f_e)$ —not scores.

> **Examples**
>
> **Goodness of Fit RQ:** Do eye color proportions in the U.S. significantly differ from those in the world?
>
> **Test of Independence RQ:** Does political affiliation differ by gender among U.S. registered voters?

## 12.21V Chi-Square Goodness of Fit

- Chi-square test is Goodness of Fit compares the sample proportions across groups (based upon the observed frequencies for each group in ONE categorical variables) against the predicted proportions across groups (based upon the expected frequencies for each group).
  - Expected frequencies are based upon our knowledge of the population
  - Conceptually similar to a *t*-test of single sample, in which the sample mean is compared to the population mean
- ***Observed frequencies*** are just frequencies that fall into each category/group.
  - Categories cannot overlap—they must be distinctive and independent.
- ***Expected frequencies*** are the predict frequencies for each category/group.
  - At times, we predict that frequencies will be equally distributed across the groups.
  - Other times, we predict different group proportions based upon previous knowledge.

### Hypotheses

- The alternative hypothesis predicts that sample proportions will differ from the expected proportions.
- The null hypothesis indicates that the sample proportions will NOT differ from the expected proportions.
  - Only hypothesis notation for the null is presented and is based upon as a table of expected proportions across categories.
    - $H_O$:

| Brown | Blue | Hazel | Green | Other |
|---|---|---|---|---|
| 70% | 8% | 5% | 2% | 15% |

### The Chi-Square Statistic

- The chi-square statistic makes multiple comparisons between the observed and expected frequencies to determine how well our sample data $(f_o)$ fit the hypothesized population $(f_e)$.

$$\text{chi-square } (\chi^2) = \sum \frac{(f_o - f_e)^2}{f_e}$$

- ***Observed frequencies*** $(f_o)$ are based upon the sample frequencies that fall into each category/group,
- ***Expected frequencies*** $(f_e)$ for each group are calculated by multiplying the expected group proportion ($p$) by the total sample size ($n$).
- If our U.S. population were to follow the world proportions, then 70% of the 75 U.S. individuals would have brown eyes (.70 * 75 = 52.5).

> **Example**
>
> **Goodness of Fit**
>
> While eye color varies across the world, brown is the dominant color with nearly 70% having brown eyes. Blue is the next common with only 8%, followed by Hazel (5%), and the rare green (2%). But does the United States have similar distribution of eye color?
>
> **RQ:** Do eye color proportions in the U.S. significantly differ from those in the world?
>
> **Step 1: State Hypothesis**
> IV: U.S. vs World
> DV: eye color
>
> **Alternative Hypothesis**
> U.S. eye color proportions will significantly differ from those in the world.
>
> **Null Hypothesis**
> U.S. eye color proportions will NOT significantly differ from those in the world.
>
> **Hypothesis Notation:**

| Brown | Blue | Hazel | Green | Other |
|---|---|---|---|---|
| 70% | 8% | 5% | 2% | 15% |

| | Brown | Blue | Hazel | Green | Other |
|---|---|---|---|---|---|
| U.S. (observed—$f_o$) | 31 | 24 | 9 | 8 | 3 |
| | | | | | |
| Expected calculation | .7(75) | .08(75) | .05(75) | .02(75) | .15(75) |
| U.S. (expected—$f_e$) | 52.5 | 6 | 3.75 | 1.5 | 11.25 |

$n$=75

- Once expected frequencies are computed, then chi-square may be calculated using the following steps:
  1. Calculate the difference $(f_o - f_e)$ between the observed and expected frequency for each category.
  2. Square each difference $(f_o - f_e)^2$.
  3. Divide each squared difference by the respective expected frequency $(f_o - f_e)^2/f_e$.
  4. Lastly, sum the values from all the categories.

| | | 1 | 2 | 3 |
|---|---|---|---|---|
| $f_o$ | $f_e$ | $f_o - f_e$ | $(f_o - f_e)^2$ | $(f_o - f_e)^2/f_e$ |
| 31 | 52.5 | -21.50 | 462.25 | 8.80 |
| 24 | 6.00 | 18.00 | 324.00 | 54.00 |
| 9 | 3.75 | 5.25 | 27.56 | 7.35 |
| 8 | 1.50 | 6.50 | 42.25 | 28.20 |
| 3 | 11.25 | -8.25 | 68.10 | 6.05 |
| | | | | Σ = 104.40 |

4

## Determining Significance

- Determining significance for chi-square is based upon degrees of freedom and the selected alpha level.
- Degrees of freedom is calculated as the number of categories ($C$) in the variable minus one ($df = C - 1$).
- The chi-square distribution is similar to the $F$ distribution in that it is positively skewed, since chi-square will always be positive as a result of squaring the difference.
- When there is a large difference between the observed and expected frequencies, chi-square will be large and lead to the rejection of the null hypothesis.
- When using computer output, $p$ must be less than alpha to be significant.

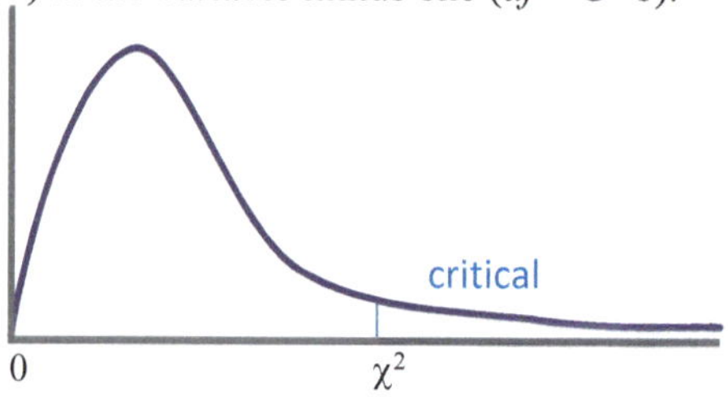


**SPSS**

**eyecolor**

| | Observed N | Expected N | Residual |
|---|---|---|---|
| brown | 31 | 52.4 | -21.4 |
| blue | 24 | 6.0 | 18.0 |
| hazel | 9 | 3.8 | 5.2 |
| green | 8 | 1.5 | 6.5 |
| other | 3 | 11.3 | -8.3 |
| Total | 75 | | |

**Test Statistics**

| | eyecolor |
|---|---|
| Chi-Square | 104.322[a] |
| df | 4 |
| Asymp. Sig. | .000 |

a. 2 cells (40.0%) have expected frequencies less than 5. The minimum expected cell frequency is 1.5.

**StatCrunch**

**Chi-Square goodness-of-fit results:**
Observed: var1
Expected: var2

| N | DF | Chi-Square | P-value |
|---|---|---|---|
| 75 | 4 | 104.32246 | <0.0001 |

| Observed | Expected |
|---|---|
| 3 | 11.28 |
| 8 | 1.50 |
| 9 | 3.79 |
| 6 | 6.00 |
| 31 | 52.43 |

## Reporting the Results

- Results should include:
  - concluding statement based upon the hypothesis;
  - chi-square value with degrees of freedom and sample size in parentheses;
  - $p$-value;
  - observed and expected frequencies for each category (optional).

### Example

**Goodness of Fit**

**Step 2: Establish Significance Criteria**
An alpha of .05 is applied.

**Step 3: Collect and Analyze Data**
Output: $\chi^2$=104.40, $df$=4, $p$<.0001.

**Step 4: Evaluate Null and Draw Conclusion**
$p$<.0001 is less than alpha of .05, therefore sample proportions (U.S.) are significantly different from the population proportions (world).

- Significance→Reject the Null→Restate Alternative
- U.S. eye color proportions significantly differ from world eye color proportions; **$\chi^2$(4, $n$=75) = 104.40, $p$<.0001.**

## 12.22V Chi-Square Test of Independence

- Examines the relationship between two categorical variables.
- Individuals are classified on two separate variables.
- A ***two-way table*** is typical when reporting the intersecting frequencies of two categorical variables.
- Still examine the difference between observed frequencies and expected frequencies,

### Hypotheses

- When there is a relationship between the two categorical variables, then the observed proportions will differ from the expected proportions.
- Hypotheses may focus on relationship or difference:
  - Chi-square **relationship** is not the same as a mutual relationship, where Y increases or decreases as X increases. Rather the emphasis is on changes across categories in that as X categorical membership changes, Y changes.
  - Chi-square **difference** asserts that Y categorical membership will differ across X categorical membership.
- Note that an alternative hypothesis predicting a relationship is the same as predicting a difference.
- Relationship or difference is an issue of preference.
- Chi-square distribution is positively skewed, hypotheses do not indicate a specific direction for the relationship or difference, hence the number of tails is not indicated.
- Hypothesis notation is not developed for chi-square test of independence.
- The null hypothesis is always the focus of inferential statistics.

> **Example**
>
> **Test of Independence**
>
> In 2018, the Pew Research Center found that approximately 51.5% of registered voters affiliated with or leaned toward the Democratic Party. While 41.5% reported/leaned Republican, and 7% as Independent. Do the political affiliation proportions differ by gender?
>
> **RQ:** Does political affiliation differ by gender among U.S. registered voters?
>
> **Step 1: State Hypothesis**
> IV: gender
> DV: political affiliation
>
> **Alternative Hypothesis**
> Political affiliation will significantly differ by gender among U.S. registered voters.
>
> **Null Hypothesis**
> Political affiliation will NOT significantly differ by gender among U.S. registered voters.

| | Alternative Hypothesis | Null Hypothesis |
|---|---|---|
| **Relationship** | Gender and political affiliation significantly <u>relate</u> among U.S. voters. | Gender and political affiliation do NOT significantly <u>relate</u> among U.S. voters. |
| **Difference** | Political affiliation significantly <u>differs</u> by gender among U.S. voters. | Political affiliation does NOT significantly <u>differ</u> by gender among U.S. voters. |

### Calculating Chi-Square

- The method of calculating chi-square is same.
- Since expected frequencies are based upon the proportions for our total sample, we utilize the row and column totals to calculate the expected frequency for each cell.
- The Table 12.4 presents the column and row totals from our observed data. To compute the expected frequency ($f_e$) for each cell, we multiply the respective row and column totals and divide by the total sample size. Therefore the $f_e$ for female Republicans = 104*82/100 = 42.64.

> **Chi-Square**
>
> $$\chi^2 = \Sigma \frac{(f_o - f_e)^2}{f_e}$$
>
> **Expected frequency**
>
> $$f_e = \frac{row\ total\ x\ column\ total}{table\ total\ (n)}$$

**Table 12.4**
*Calculation of Expected Frequencies for Each Cell*

| | Democrat | Republican | Independent | |
|---|---|---|---|---|
| **Female** | $\frac{104 * 104}{200} = 54.08$ | $\frac{104 * 82}{200} = 42.64$ | $\frac{104 * 14}{200} = 7.28$ | 104 |
| **Male** | $\frac{96 * 104}{200} = 49.92$ | $\frac{96 * 82}{200} = 39.36$ | $\frac{96 * 14}{200} = 6.72$ | 96 |
| **Total** | 104 | 82 | 14 | $n$=100 |

- Once expected frequencies are computed, we follow the same steps for calculating chi-square.
  1. Calculate the difference between the observed and expected frequency for each category.
  2. Square each difference.
  3. Divide each squared difference by the respective expected frequency ($f_e$).
  4. Lastly, sum the values from all the categories.
- Table 12.5 presents the comparison of observed and expected frequencies for each cell leading to the calculation of chi-square ($\chi^2 = 5.05$).

**Table 12.5**
*Calculation of Chi-Square*

| | | | 1 | 2 | 3 |
|---|---|---|---|---|---|
| | $f_o$ | $f_e$ | $f_o - f_e$ | $(f_o - f_e)^2$ | $(f_o - f_e)^2/f_e$ |
| Female Dem | 62 | 54.08 | 7.92 | 62.73 | 1.16 |
| Female Rep | 36 | 42.68 | -6.68 | 44.62 | 1.05 |
| Female Ind | 6 | 7.28 | 1.28 | 1.64 | 0.23 |
| Male Dem | 42 | 49.92 | -7.92 | 62.73 | 1.26 |
| Male Rep | 46 | 39.36 | 6.64 | 44.09 | 1.12 |
| Male Ind | 8 | 6.72 | 1.28 | 1.63 | 0.24 |
| | | | | | $\Sigma = 5.05$ 4 |

## Determining Significance

- Determining significance for Chi-square Test of Independence is identical to that of Goodness of Fit; the only difference is how degrees of freedom is calculated.
- Degrees of freedom is calculated as the number of rows ($R$) minus 1 ($R$-1) multiplied by the number of columns ($C$) minus 1 ($C$-1), which generates the equation of: $df = (R\text{-}1)(C\text{-}1)$.
  - Considering our example of gender and political affiliation, $df = (2\text{-}1)(3\text{-}1) = 1{*}2 = 2$.
- Computer output presents chi-square, $p$-value, and observed and expected frequencies. Significance is determined by comparing the computer-generated $p$-value to the predetermined alpha.
  - Computer output identifies $p$=.0805, which is NOT less than an alpha of .05. Therefore, we do not have significance and fail to reject the null.

**$df$ for Chi-Square Test of Independence**

$df = (R\text{-}1)(C\text{-}1)$

**StatCrunch**

**Contingency table results:**
Rows: gender
Columns: None

**Cell format**
Count
(Expected count)

| | dem | rep | ind | Total |
|---|---|---|---|---|
| female | 62<br>(54.08) | 36<br>(42.64) | 6<br>(7.28) | 104 |
| male | 42<br>(49.92) | 46<br>(39.36) | 8<br>(6.72) | 96 |
| Total | 104 | 82 | 14 | 200 |

**Chi-Square test:**

| Statistic | DF | Value | P-value |
|---|---|---|---|
| Chi-square | 2 | 5.0394434 | 0.0805 |

**SPSS**

**gender * political Crosstabulation**

| | | | political democrat | political republican | political independent | Total |
|---|---|---|---|---|---|---|
| gender | female | Count | 62 | 36 | 6 | 104 |
| | | Expected Count | 54.1 | 42.6 | 7.3 | 104.0 |
| | male | Count | 42 | 46 | 8 | 96 |
| | | Expected Count | 49.9 | 39.4 | 6.7 | 96.0 |
| Total | | Count | 104 | 82 | 14 | 200 |
| | | Expected Count | 104.0 | 82.0 | 14.0 | 200.0 |

**Chi-Square Tests**

| | Value | df | Asymptotic Significance (2-sided) |
|---|---|---|---|
| Pearson Chi-Square | 5.039[a] | 2 | .080 |
| Likelihood Ratio | 5.059 | 2 | .080 |
| Linear-by-Linear Association | 4.354 | 1 | .037 |
| N of Valid Cases | 200 | | |

a. 0 cells (0.0%) have expected count less than 5. The minimum expected count is 6.72.

# Example

## Test of Independence

**Step 2: Establish Significance Criteria:** An alpha of .05 is applied.

**Step 3: Collect and Analyze Data:** $\chi^2$=5.04, $df$=2, $p$=.0805.

**Step 4: Evaluate Null and Draw Conclusion**
$p$=.0805 is NOT less than alpha of .05, therefore political affiliation does not differ by gender.

- Significance→Fail to reject the Null→Restate Null
- Political affiliation does NOT significantly differ by gender among U.S. adults; **$\chi^2$(2, $n$=200) = 5.04, $p$=.0805.**

## 12.23V Effect Size

Two effect sizes are typical for chi-square: phi-coefficient (ϕ) and Cramér's V.

- ***Phi-coefficient*** may only be used when a 2 x 2 matrix is created as a result of the two variables—meaning each variable may only have two categories.
  - The phi-coefficient is a correlation that represents the strength of the relationship, rather than the significance. Phi is calculated as

$$\phi = \sqrt{\frac{\chi^2}{n}}$$

  - Interpretation of phi follows the same standards as those applied to $r^2$ where less than .09 is a small effect, .09-.25 is a medium effect, and greater than .25 is a large effect.

- ***Cramér's V*** allows us to go beyond a 2 x 2 matrix; now our variables may have more than two categories. The calculation is very similar to Cramér's V, however, $df^*$ is multiplied in the denominator. The smaller *df* of rows or columns is used in the calculation.
  - For our example of gender and political affiliation, the *df* for rows (gender) is *df* = 2-1 = 1. The *df* for columns (political affiliation) was *df* = 3-1 = 2. The *df* for rows is the smaller of the two, so this will be used in our calculation.

$$V = \sqrt{\frac{\chi^2}{n(df^*)}} = \sqrt{\frac{5.04}{200(1)}} = .16$$

**Effect Size**

**Phi-Coefficient**

$$\phi = \sqrt{\frac{\chi^2}{n}}$$

| $r^2$ | Size |
|---|---|
| <.09 | Small |
| .09-.25 | Medium |
| <.25 | Large |

**Cramér's V**

$$V = \sqrt{\frac{\chi^2}{n(df^*)}}$$

| *df* | Small | Medium | Large |
|---|---|---|---|
| 1 | .10 | .30 | .50 |
| 2 | .07 | .21 | .35 |
| 3 | .06 | .17 | .29 |
| 4 | .05 | .15 | .25 |
| 5 | .05 | .13 | .22 |

- Guidelines for interpreting Cramér's V were developed by Cohen and are based upon our special $df^*$. SPSS and StatCrunch provides the option of calculating these effect sizes.

**Symmetric Measures**

| | | Value | Approximate Significance |
|---|---|---|---|
| Nominal by Nominal | Phi | .159 | .080 |
| | Cramer's V | .159 | .080 |
| N of Valid Cases | | 200 | |

```
Cramer's V test for association:
 Measure DF Value P-value
Cramer's V  20.15874  0.0805
```

## 12.24V Assumptions

Several assumptions must be satisfied to use a Chi-Square Goodness of Fit or Test of Independence.

- **Independence of observations** is important with any test. For chi-square it means that an individual cannot fall into multiple categories or classes. Each category must be exclusive.
- **Size of expected frequencies.** Chi-square should not be conducted when the size of expected frequencies is less than 5. Such a violation distorts the chi-square value and often enlarges it. Since chi-square is very sensitive to small expected frequencies, large samples are recommended.

## 12.25V Reporting the Results

Results summary always begins with a concluding statement based upon the hypothesis and includes supporting statistics:

- Chi-square value with *df* and sample size in parentheses;
- *p*-value;
- Effect size; and
- Observed and expected frequencies (possibly in a table).

**Example**

**Test of Independence**

**Updated Results:**

Political affiliation does NOT significantly differ by gender among U.S. adults; **$\chi^2$(2, *n*=200) = 5.04, *p*=.0805, Cramér's V=.16.**

| | Observed *f* | Expected *f* |
|---|---|---|
| Female Democrat | 62 | 54.08 |
| Female Republican | 36 | 42.68 |
| Female Independent | 6 | 7.28 |
| Male Democrat | 42 | 49.92 |
| Male Republican | 46 | 39.36 |
| Male Independent | 8 | 6.72 |

## 12.26V A Complete Example: Goodness of Fit

In late 2017, the Gallop Poll surveyed 53,769 individuals from 55 countries on their happiness. Results for the US indicate that 64% are happy. Apparently in the same year, South Dakota (SD) was identified as the happiest state based upon the Gallup-Sharecare Well-being Index. A sociologist surveys 1,000 South Dakotans on their level of happiness to determine if South Dakota has significantly different happiness proportions than the US. Expected frequencies were calculated based upon the US norms. Does the state of South Dakota have significantly different happiness proportions than the USA? Test at the .05 level.

| | Happy | Neutral | Unhappy | Don't Know |
|---|---|---|---|---|
| USA | 64% | 20% | 14% | 2% |
| SD expected *f* | 640 | 200 | 140 | 20 |
| SD observed *f* | 702 | 193 | 90 | 15 |

**Test Statistics**

| | happy |
|---|---|
| Chi-Square | 25.358[a] |
| df | 3 |
| Asymp. Sig. | .000 |

a. 0 cells (0.0%) have expected frequencies less than 5. The minimum expected cell frequency is 20.0.

**Step 1: Develop Hypotheses:**

a. Independent Variable = Scale: Categorical Quantitative

b. Dependent Variable = Scale: Categorical Quantitative

c. Alternative hypothesis in sentence form.

d. Null hypothesis in sentence form.

e. Write null hypotheses notation. $H_0$:

**Step 2: Establish significance criteria**

f. $\alpha =$

**Step 3: Calculate test statistic and effect size.**

g. $\chi^2 =$ Level of significance ($p$) =

i. Decision: reject null or fail to reject null

j. Calculate effect size.

**Step 4: Draw conclusion**

k. Write your conclusion in sentence form including appropriate results notation.

Gallup International (2017). *Happiness, Hope, Economic Optimism: Gallup International's 41st Annual Global End of Year Survey.* http://www.gallup-international.com/wp-content/uploads/2017/12/2017_Happiness_Hope_Economic-Optimism.pdf

Mejia, Zameena (Feb 2018). The top 10 happiest and healthiest states in the US. *CNBC Make It.* https://www.cnbc.com/2018/02/23/the-top-10-happiest-and-healthiest-states-in-the-us.html

## A Complete Example: Test of Independence

A study by a food and beverage research group, Mintel (Turkey Hill, 2009), explored gender differences in ice cream flavor preferences. They found that men prefer plain flavors (vanilla, chocolate), while women prefer "fancier" flavors with chocolate or candy bits. A nutritionist randomly samples 100 college students to determine if ice cream preference (plain vs fancy flavor) differ by gender. Test at $\alpha$=.05.

```
Contingency table results:
Rows: gender
Columns: flavor

 Cell format
Count
(Expected count)

           plain   fancy  Total
female        8      48    56
         (24.08)(31.92)
male         35       9    44
         (18.92)(25.08)
Total        43      57   100

Chi-Square test:
 Statistic DF   Value    P-value
Chi-square  142.814224<0.0001

Cramer's V test for association:
 Measure DF  Value  P-value
Cramer's V  10.65433<0.0001
```

**Step 1: Develop Hypotheses:**

a. Independent Variable =

   Scale: Categorical          Quantitative

b. Dependent Variable =

   Scale: Categorical          Quantitative

c. Alternative hypothesis in sentence form.

d. Null hypothesis in sentence form.

**Step 2: Establish significance criteria**

e. $\alpha$ =

**Step 3: Calculate test statistic and effect size.**

f. $\chi^2$ =          Level of significance ($p$) =

g. Decision:     reject null          or          fail to reject null

h. Calculate effect size.

**Step 4: Draw conclusion**

i. Write your conclusion in sentence form including appropriate results notation.

Turkey Hill. (2009). Men and women agree to disagree on ice cream flavors. *Ice Cream Journal*. https://icecreamjournal.turkeyhill.com/index.php/2009/09/10/men-and-women-agree-to-disagree-on-ice-cream-flavors/

## 12.27 Hands-on Activity

Mars provides a pleasing proportion of their milk chocolate colored candies as follow:

| Color | % |
|---|---|
| Blue | 24 |
| Orange | 20 |
| Green | 16 |
| Yellow | 14 |
| Red | 13 |
| Brown | 13 |

http://www.mms.com/

This experiment seeks to determine if your package of M&M's fulfills these official proportions. You may purchase any size package you like, but it must be milk chocolate.

1. Count the total number of M&M's in your package. Based upon the total number, calculate the expected frequencies; document in the table below.
2. Separate M&M's by color, and count the number of candies in each color. Enter observed frequencies in the table below.

| Color | Observed | Expected | |
|---|---|---|---|
| | *f* | % | *f* |
| Blue | | 24 | |
| Orange | | 20 | |
| Green | | 16 | |
| Yellow | | 14 | |
| Red | | 13 | |
| Brown | | 13 | |

3. Use StatCrunch or SPSS to conduct Chi-square goodness of fit and complete the hypothesis testing process. Test at .05.

   a. Alternative hypothesis in sentence form.

   b. Null hypothesis in sentence form.

   c. Write null hypotheses notation. $H_0$:

**Step 2: Establish significance criteria**

d. $\alpha =$

**Step 3: Calculate test statistic and effect size.**

e. $\chi^2 =$ Level of significance ($p$) =

f. Decision: reject null or fail to reject null

g. Calculate effect size.

**Step 4: Draw conclusion**

h. Write your conclusion in sentence form including appropriate results notation.

## 12.28V In the Literature: Test of Independence

Chi-square test of independence is a common statistical technique in higher education, since the ultimate outcomes are student retention and graduation. This excerpt presents the results of a treatment (Freshmen Success Course) on retention and graduation.

**Excerpt from:** McGrath, S.M., & Burd, G.D. (2012). A success course for freshmen on academic probation: Persistence and graduation outcomes. *NACADA Journal, 32*(1), 43-52.

This quasi-experimental study examines the effects Freshman Success Course completion on 154 first-time full-time freshmen placed on academic probation after their first semester of college. A control group of 100 similar students was established. The Freshman Success Course curriculum consisted of five core areas: student development; test-taking and note-taking strategies; campus policies and procedures; exploration of different majors; and engagement with faculty members, advisors, and other student resources on campus. The researchers tested three hypotheses:

*H1.* Students who took the success course will **regain good standing** (cumulative GPA of 2.0 or higher) by the end of their freshman year at significantly higher rates than students who did not take the success course.

*H2.* Students who took the success course will **persist into their 2nd, 3rd, and 4th years** at significantly higher rates than those who did not take the course.

*H3.* Students who took the success course will **graduate** within 5 years of matriculation at significantly higher rates than those who did not take the course.

Chi-square test for independence results support all three hypotheses. Treatment participants had significantly higher success rates than the control group in all dependent variables (reinstatement to acceptable academic standing, persistence into the 2nd, 3rd, and 4th years of college, as well as graduation within 4 to 5 years of matriculation) (see Table 3).

**Table 3.** Results of hypotheses tests: descriptive, chi square, and φ coefficients

| Groups and Tests | Off Probation | Persist to 2nd Year | Persist to 3rd Year | Persist to 4th Year | Graduate |
|---|---|---|---|---|---|
| Comparison group | 9% | 22% | 9% | 6% | 2% |
| Treatment group | 49% | 60% | 47% | 41% | 25% |
| Chi square | 44.34* | 38.03* | 42.20* | 37.34* | 24.37* |
| Effect size, φ | 0.42 | 0.39 | 0.41 | 0.38 | 0.31 |

*Note.* * $p < .001$

1. Each hypothesis is examining the effect of the treatment of the Freshman Success Course, by comparing treatment and control group participants. What are the dependents variables for each hypothesis?

   *H1:*

   *H2:*

   *H3:*

2. On which dependent variable did the treatment have its greatest effect? What statistic did you use to examine this question? What is a likely explanation for this dependent variable having the greatest effect?

3. What effect size did the authors report? Why this effect size?

4. At what $p$-value are the chi-square results significant?

## 12.29 Using the Computer: Chi-Square Goodness of Fit

### SPSS

Two data entry methods are possible with Goodness of Fit in SPSS.

1. **Individual Participant Data.** Enter the category value for each participant. For the eye color example, if a person has blue eyes, one would receive a "2." Therefore, each of the 75 individuals would have an eye color value, ranging from 1 to 5.
2. **Frequencies in each category.** Enter the number of individuals in each category.

### Individual Participant Data

| | Category | $f_e$ |
|---|---|---|
| Brown | 1 | 52.5 |
| Blue | 2 | 6.0 |
| Hazel | 3 | 3.8 |
| Green | 4 | 1.5 |
| Other | 5 | 11.3 |

1. Enter raw categorical data in a column.
2. 🖱 **Analyze** menu, select **Nonparametric Tests, Legacy Dialogues,** then **Chi-square.**
3. Within the **Chi-square Test** dialogue box, select your variable, 🖱 the arrow to move to the Test Variable List box.
4. Under **Expected Values,**
   - 🖱 **All categories equal,** IF you expect an equal distribution of frequencies across the categories.
   - If you expect different frequencies, 🖱 **Values:** Indicate the expected frequency for each category group, in order from lowest to highest category value. For the eye color example, the brown category of 1 has an expected frequency of 52.5. After each expected frequency, 🖱 **Add,** until all expected frequencies have been entered.
5. 🖱 Options. Under **Statistics,** check **Descriptive.** 🖱 **Continue,** 🖱 **OK.**

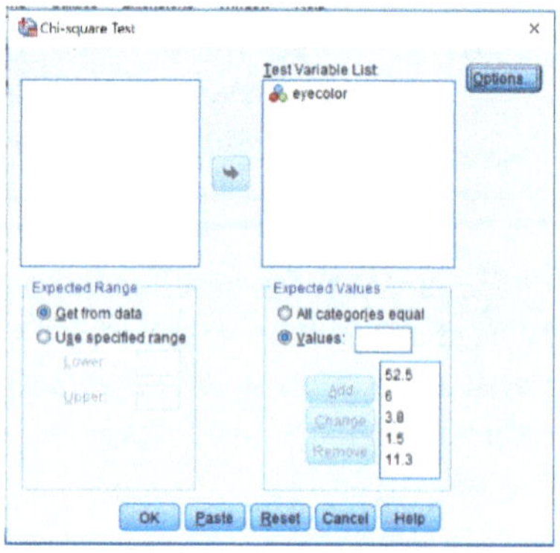


### Frequencies in Each Category

1. Enter the summary of observed frequencies. In the first column, enter the categorical value options in order from low to high. In a second column, enter the observed frequency summary for each category. For the eye color example, 31 individuals reported having brown (1) eyes.
2. Weight frequencies: 🖱 **Data** menu and select **Weight Cases.**
3. In the Weight Cases dialogue box, check **Weight cases by.** Click on frequency variable and move under **Frequency Variable:** 🖱 **OK.**
4. 🖱 **Analyze** menu, select **Nonparametric Tests, Legacy Dialogues,** then **Chi-square.**
5. Within **Chi-square Test** dialogue box, select the categorical variable, 🖱 the arrow to move to the Test Variable List box.
6. Under **Expected Values,**
   - 🖱 **All categories equal,** IF you expect an equal distribution of frequencies across the categories.
   - If you expect different frequencies, 🖱 **Values:** Indicate the expected frequency for each category group in order from lowest to highest category value. For the eye color example, the brown category of 1 has an expected frequency of 52.5. After each expected frequency, 🖱 **Add,** until all expected frequencies have been entered.
8. 🖱 Options and check **Descriptive** under **Statistics.** 🖱 **Continue,** 🖱 **OK.**

| | color | frequency |
|---|---|---|
| 1 | 1.00 | 31.00 |
| 2 | 2.00 | 24.00 |
| 3 | 3.00 | 9.00 |
| 4 | 4.00 | 8.00 |
| 5 | 5.00 | 3.00 |

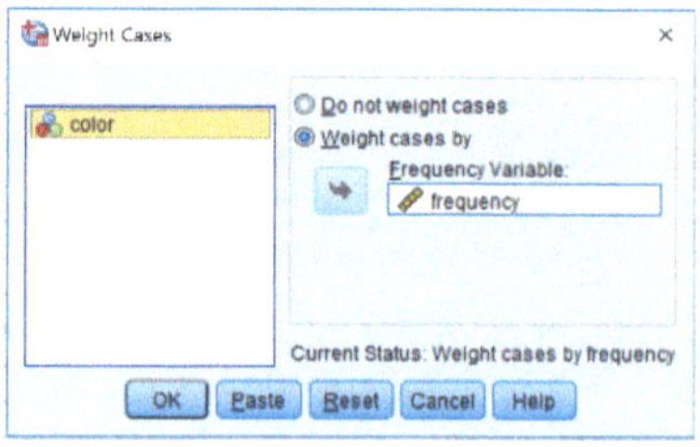


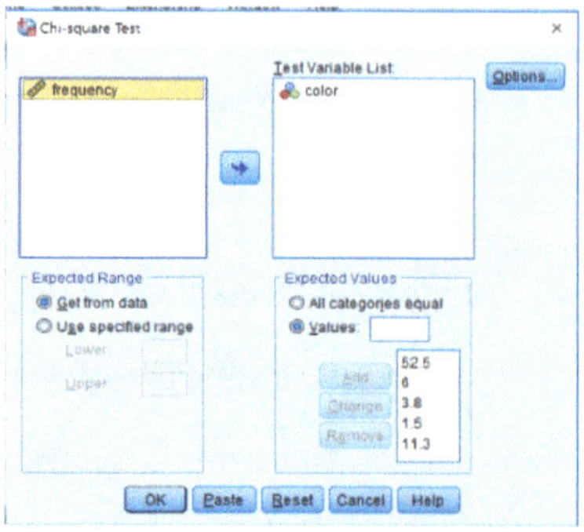

**StatCrunch**

1. Enter observed frequencies in one column and expected frequencies in another.
2. 🖱 the **Stat** menu, select **Goodness-of-Fit,** then **Chi-square Test.**
3. Under Observed, select the variable of observed frequencies.
4. Under Expected, if expected frequencies are unequal select variable of expected frequencies.
   - If expected frequencies are equally distributed, then check **All cells in equal proportion.** 🖱 **Compute!**

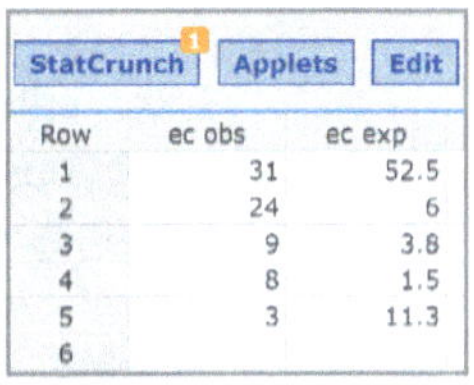


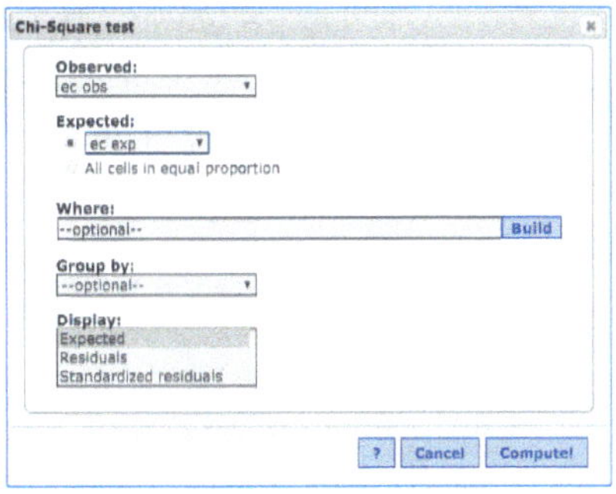


## 12.30 Using the Computer: Chi-Square Test of Independence

**SPSS**

1. Enter raw categorical data in each column.
2. 🖱 `Analyze` menu, select `Descriptive Statistics`, then `Crosstabs`.
3. Within the `Crosstabs` dialogue box, select one variable and move to Row(s); select the second categorical variable and move to Column(s).

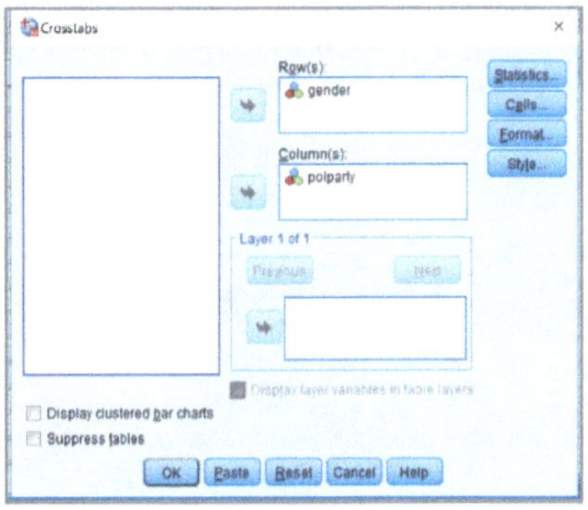


4. 🖱 `Statistics`, check `Chi-square`. Under `Nominal`, check **`Phi and Cramer's V`**. 🖱 `Continue`.
5. 🖱 `Cells`, under `Counts`, check `Observed` and `Expected`.
6. 🖱 `Continue`, 🖱 `OK`

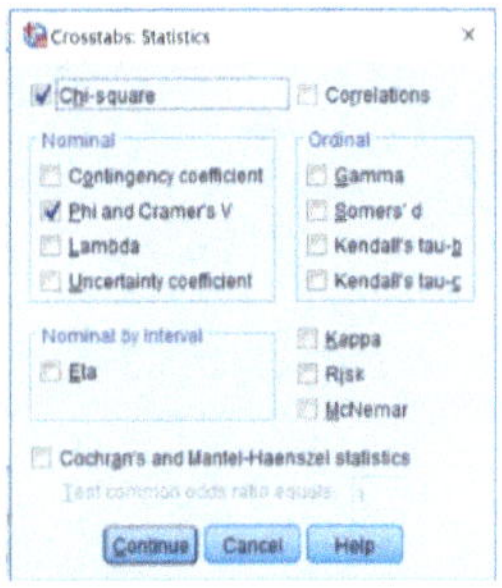


**StatCrunch** (with data)

1. Enter raw categorical data in each column.
2. 🖱 the **Stat** menu, select **Tables,** then **Contingency, with data.**
3. Under Row variable, select the categorical variable.
4. Under Column variable, select other categorical variable.
5. Under Display, select **Expected Count**.
6. Under Hypothesis tests:, select **Chi-Square test for independence,** then hold the Ctrl key and select **Cramer's V test for association**.
4. 🖱 **Compute!**

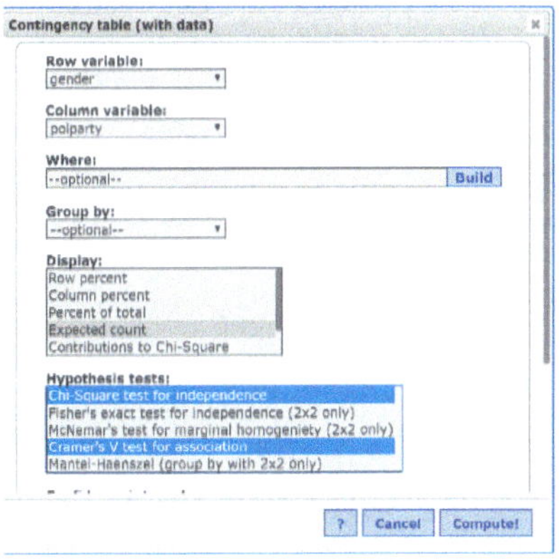

**Stat**Crunch (with summary)

| Row | gender | plain | fancy |
|---|---|---|---|
| 1 | female | 8 | 48 |
| 2 | male | 35 | 9 |
| 3 | | | |
| 4 | | | |

1. Enter summary of frequencies. In the first column, name the categories for the row variable. For this example, the categories are female and male for the variable of gender. Use the following columns to identify the frequencies for each category of the column variable. In this example, the column variable is ice cream preference with the two categories of plain and fancy. You can see 8 females prefer plain ice cream, whereas, 48 females prefer fancy ice cream.
2. the **Stat** menu, select **Tables,** then **Contingency, with summary.**
3. Under **Select column(s):**, hold the shift key and select/highlight each category of the column variable.
4. Under **Row label:**, select the row variable.
4. Under **Column label:**, type in a name for the column variable.
5. Under Display, select **Expected Count**.
6. Under Hypothesis tests:, select **Chi-Square test for independence**, then hold the Ctrl key and select **Cramer's V test for association**.
4. **Compute!**

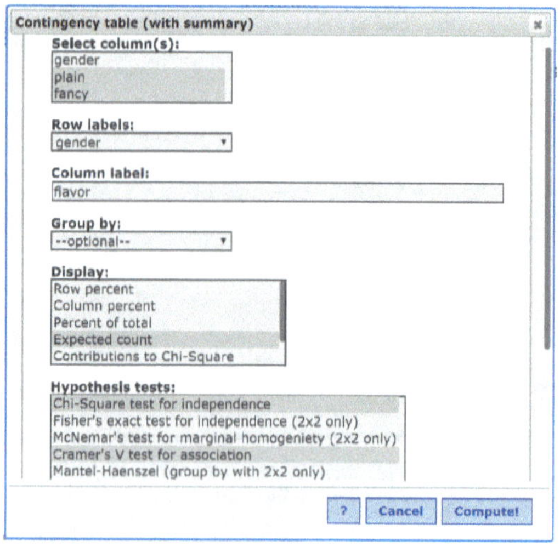

## 12.31 Exercises
### Reviewing the Concepts

1. Describe the differences between parametric and non-parametric tests. Reflect on the variables, the data, and the assumptions.

2. Chi-Square analyzes:
   a. frequencies
   b. means
   c. raw scores

3. Why is chi-square unable to fulfill the parametric assumption of normality?

4. Explain the difference between Chi-Square Goodness of Fit and Chi-Square Test of Independence.

5. How does degrees of freedom differ between Chi-Square Goodness of Fit and Chi-Square Test of Independence?

6. When does Cramer's V effect size need to be used?

## Interpreting Results

7. **Chi-square Goodness of Fit**

This study explores birth rate by season. For years, US data has shown that in the summer months are most popular for birth, indicating that conception often occurs when the cold weather begins in the fall. Miami-Dade County in Florida is curious to determine if their birthrates follow the typical US proportions, since Miami has such a warmer climate year round. In 2017, Dade County reported 31,797 live births. The table below presents the percent of births by season for the US and the number of births by season for Dade County. Chi-square goodness of fit was conducted to examine if Dade County's birth rate follows US seasonal proportions. An alpha of .05 was applied.

| | **Winter** (Dec-Feb) | **Spring** (March-May) | **Summer** (June-Aug) | **Fall** (Sept-Nov) |
|---|---|---|---|---|
| US | 23.5 | 24.5 | 26.5 | 25.5 |
| Dade Co. (observed) | 8,008 | 7,820 | 7,472 | 8,497 |
| Dade Co. (expected) | 7,472 | 7,790 | 8,426 | 8,108 |

**Test Statistics**

| | season |
|---|---|
| Chi-Square | 165.236a |
| df | 3 |
| Asymp. Sig. | .000 |

a. 0 cells (0.0%) have expected frequencies less than 5. The minimum expected cell frequency is 7472.2.

**Step 1: Develop Hypotheses:**

a. Independent Variable = Scale: Categorical Quantitative

b. Dependent Variable = Scale: Categorical Quantitative

c. Alternative hypothesis in sentence form.

d. Null hypothesis in sentence form.

e. Write null hypotheses notation. $H_0$:

**Step 2: Establish significance criteria**

f. $\alpha =$

**Step 3: Calculate test statistic and effect size.**

g. $\chi^2 =$ Level of significance ($p$) =

i. Decision: reject null or fail to reject null

j. Calculate effect size.

**Step 4: Draw conclusion**

k. Write your conclusion in sentence form including appropriate results notation.

8. **Chi-square Test of Independence**

Megert (2005) examined the relationship between method of qualifying for an honors scholarship and the retention of such scholarship. Students could qualify through multiple criterion: 1) high school GPA; 2) completing a high level math class in HS (i.e., trigonometry, pre-calculus, or calculus), referred to as HighMath; and 3) high school GPA and HighMath. Participants included 395 full-time junior college freshmen. Retention of the scholarship was determined after the first semester college GPA. Using Megert's data, we generated the following output to examine if there is a relationship between scholarship criterion met and scholarship retention? An alpha of .05 was applied.

| | **Retention of Scholarship** | | **Total** |
|---|---|---|---|
| **Qualified by:** | **Yes** | **No** | |
| GPA | 107 | 78 | 185 |
| HighMath | 13 | 24 | 37 |
| GPA & HighMath | 77 | 28 | 105 |

```
Contingency table results:
Rows: criterion
Columns: Scholarship Retention

  Cell format
Count
(Expected count)

               yes        no   Total
GPA            107        78   185
          (111.45)(73.55)
HM              13        24    37
           (22.29)(14.71)
HM GPA          77        28   105
           (63.26)(41.74)
Total          197       130   327

Chi-Square test:
 Statistic DF   Value    P-value
Chi-square   217.698038  0.0001

Cramer's V test for association:
 Measure DF  Value  P-value
Cramer's V   20.23264  0.0001
```

**Step 1: Develop Hypotheses:**

a. Independent Variable = Scale: Categorical Quantitative

b. Dependent Variable = Scale: Categorical Quantitative

c. Alternative hypothesis in sentence form.

d. Null hypothesis in sentence form.

**Step 2: Establish significance criteria**

e. $\alpha$ =

**Step 3: Calculate test statistic and effect size.**

f. $\chi^2$ = Level of significance ($p$) =

g. Decision: reject null or fail to reject null

h. Effect size=

**Step 4: Draw conclusion**

i. Write your conclusion in sentence form including appropriate results notation.

Megert, D. A. (2005). The relationship between high school math courses, high school GPA, and retention of honors scholarships. *NASFAA Journal of Student Financial Aid, 35*(2), 51-60.

9. Use the excerpt to complete the questions.

After determining that alcohol serves as the primary gateway drug to illicit drug use, this study utilized chi-square test of independence to present the relationship between alcohol use (yes/no) and use (yes/no) of ten other drugs.

**Excerpt from:** Kirby, T. & Barry, A.E. (2012). Alcohol as a gateway drug: A study of US 12th graders. *Journal of School Health, 82*(8), 371-379.

The Gateway Drug Theory suggests that licit drugs, such as tobacco and alcohol, serve as a "gateway" toward the use of other, illicit drugs. However, there remains some discrepancy regarding which drug—alcohol, tobacco, or even marijuana—serves as the initial "gateway" drug subsequently leading to the use of illicit drugs such as cocaine and heroin. The purpose of this investigation was to determine which drug (alcohol, tobacco, or marijuana) was the actual "gateway" drug leading to additional substance use among a nationally representative sample of high school seniors. This investigation conducted a secondary analysis of the 2008 Monitoring the Future 12th-grade data. Initiation into alcohol, tobacco, and other drug use was analyzed using a Guttman scale. Coefficients of reliability and scalability were calculated to evaluate scale fit. Subsequent cross tabulations and chi-square test for independence were conducted to better understand the relationship between the identified gateway drug and other substances' use. Results from the Guttman scale indicated that alcohol represented the "gateway" drug, leading to the use of tobacco, marijuana, and other illicit substances. Moreover, students who used alcohol exhibited a significantly greater likelihood of using both licit and illicit drugs. The findings from this investigation support that alcohol should receive primary attention in school-based substance abuse prevention programming, as the use of other substances could be impacted by delaying or preventing alcohol use. Therefore, it seems prudent for school and public health officials to focus prevention efforts, policies, and monies, on addressing adolescent alcohol use.

**Table 1.** Association between Drinking Status and Use of Other Licit and Illicit Substances ($N$=14,577)

| | $\chi^2$ | $p$ | Phi |
|---|---|---|---|
| Cigarettes | 2,221.9 | .001 | .439 |
| Marijuana | 2,331.4 | .001 | .452 |
| Other narcotics | 550.1 | .001 | .220 |
| Amphetamines | 356.1 | .001 | .176 |
| Tranquilizers | 338.5 | .001 | .172 |
| Sedatives | 286.4 | .001 | .158 |
| Other hallucinogens | 309.9 | .001 | .164 |
| Cocaine | 277.0 | .001 | .156 |
| LSD | 131.4 | .001 | .107 |
| Heroine | 30.1 | .001 | .051 |

a. Write the alternative hypothesis for cigarettes.

b. Was the null hypothesis rejected for cigarettes? Write the conclusion with results notation for cigarettes.

c. Which substance use shows the greatest relationship with drinking status? What statistics support this result?

d. What substance use shows the greatest effect size? Evaluate the effect size.

## Conducting Analysis

### Chi-Square Goodness of Fit

10. The rate of children being diagnosed with myopia (difficulty seeing faraway) is rising at alarming rates especially in highly developed countries, where technology use is the norm. Researchers have found that nearsightedness isn't just a function of genetics, but also lifestyle. In areas of the world where outdoor activity is highly valued and encouraged, children spend less time reading and on devices and have lower myopia rates (Dolgin, 2015). In 2004, The Brian Holden Vision Institute reported that 42% of 12-50 year-olds in the US have myopia. The following results represent a 2018 random sample of 1,000 individuals, age 12-50 from throughout the US, where 575 (54.5%) had myopia. Does the current rate of myopia significantly differ from that of 2004? Test at .05.

**Step 1: Develop Hypotheses:**

a. Independent Variable = Scale: Categorical Quantitative

b. Dependent Variable = Scale: Categorical Quantitative

c. Alternative hypothesis in sentence form.

d. Null hypothesis in sentence form.

e. Write null hypotheses notation. $H_0$:

**Step 2: Establish significance criteria**

f. $\alpha$ =

**Step 3: Calculate test statistic and effect size.**

g. $\chi^2$ = Level of significance ($p$) =

i. Decision: reject null or fail to reject null

j. Calculate effect size.

**Step 4: Draw conclusion**

k. Write your conclusion in sentence form including appropriate results notation.

Dolgin, E. (March 2015). The myopia boom. *Nature, 519*, 276-278. https://www.nature.com/news/the-myopia-boom-1.17120

**Chi-square Test of Independence**

11. Cardiologists Friedman and Rosenman (1976) began researching personality in their heart patients after it was pointed out by an upholsterer that their waiting room chairs experienced very unusual wear—essentially their patients had difficulty sitting still, usually sat at the edge of the seat, wore out the arms of the chairs, and leaped up frequently. Their ground-breaking research established the personality Types of A (competitive, impatient, aggressive) and B (patient, relaxed, easy-going) as well as the relationship between personality and heart disease. They found that Type A personalities were much more likely to develop heart disease. Approximately 70% of heart disease patients were of Type A personality. You have randomly sampled 250 adults (age 40-60) and documented personality type and presence of heart disease. You seek to determine if this data supports Friedman and Rosenman's relationship between personality type and presence of heart disease. The observed frequencies are as follows. Test at .05.

| | Type A | Type B |
|---|---|---|
| Heart Disease | 110 | 29 |
| No Heart Disease | 39 | 72 |

**Step 1: Develop Hypotheses:**

a. Independent Variable = Scale: Categorical Quantitative

b. Dependent Variable = Scale: Categorical Quantitative

c. Alternative hypothesis in sentence form.

d. Null hypothesis in sentence form.

**Step 2: Establish significance criteria**

e. $\alpha$ =

**Step 3: Calculate test statistic and effect size.**

f. $\chi^2$ = Level of significance ($p$) =

g. Decision: reject null or fail to reject null

h. Calculate effect size.

**Step 4: Draw conclusion**

i. Write your conclusion in sentence form including appropriate results notation.

McLeod, S. (2017) Type A personality. *Simply Psychology*. https://www.simplypsychology.org/personality-a.html

# Module 13

## All Together Now!

### Learning Targets

After completing Module 13, you should be able to:

- Differentiate the various statistical techniques by purpose.
- Identify the appropriate statistical test to use based upon variable type and scale.
- Differentiate the various effect sizes and apply the appropriate evaluation criteria.

# The Concepts & Learning Guide

This final module provides an overview of all the statistical techniques we have learned as well as guidance on how to determine the appropriate descriptive and inferential statistics to use. Since much of the content is in outline form, Part 1 (The Concepts) and Part 2 (The Learning Guide) are combined. I have underlined key points, which would be comparable to bullet points in the Learning Guide.

## 13.11V Overview of Statistical Tests

We have learned a total of nine inferential techniques in Baby Stats! Although our first hypothesis test used *z*, I am not including it in this review since it is rarely used. Keep in mind, it was a great starting point in learning about hypothesis testing. The following tests are organized by the relationship being examined: causal, mutual, and proportion. In describing each statistical test, I have identified: 1) the type and scale of variables; 2) the effect sizes; 3) hypothesis notation, and 4) appropriate descriptive statistics typically presented with results.

### Causal Relationship Tests

Studying causation requires the comparison of groups, which are based upon an independent variable that is categorical. This categorical variable may be a treatment where a treatment group is being compared to a control group, or may be based upon some grouping characteristic such as gender or ethnicity. The dependent variable or outcome is quantitative, since groups means are usually compared.

***t*-Test Single Sample (*t*)** compares a sample mean to a population mean/norm and uses the sample standard deviation to estimate standard error.

IV = categorical (sample vs norm)
DV = quantitative
Effect size = Cohen's *d*
Hypothesis Notation (with 50 as population norm)
Two-tailed $H_1: \mu \neq 50$ $H_0: \mu = 50$
One-tailed $H_1: \mu > 50$ $H_0: \mu \leq 50$
Descriptive statistics = sample *M*, *SD*, *n*; population mean.

***t*-Test Independent Samples (*t*)** compares two group means. Groups are completely independent and separate.

IV = categorical (group 1 vs group 2))
DV= quantitative
Effect size = Cohen's *d* or $r^2$
Hypothesis Notation
Two-tailed $H_1: \mu_1 - \mu_2 \neq 0$ $H_0: \mu_1 - \mu_2 = 0$
One-tailed $H_1: \mu_1 - \mu_2 > 0$ $H_0: \mu_1 - \mu_2 \leq 0$
Descriptive statistics = group *M*s, *SD*s, and *n*.

***t*-Test Related Samples (*t*)** compares related scores. Typically, pre and post scores are compared for a single group, in that the scores will likely change from pre to post as a result of a treatment. Pre and Post means are NOT compared! Rather the difference between each pair of scores is calculated, and the mean of differences is evaluated.

IV = categorical (pre vs post)
DV = quantitative
Effect size = Cohen's *d* or $r^2$
Hypothesis Notation
Two-tailed $H_1: \mu_D \neq 0$ $H_0: \mu_D = 0$
One-tailed $H_1: \mu_D > 0$ $H_0: \mu_D \leq 0$
Descriptive statistics= pre and post *M*s and *n*, mean and *SD* of differences.

**ANOVA (*F*)** compares three or more independent group means. Post hoc tests (i.e., Tukey's HSD, Scheffé, Tamhane's T2) are required to determine which groups are significantly different.

IV = categorical (3+ groups)
DV = quantitative
Effect size = eta squared ($\eta^2$)
Hypothesis Notation $H_1$: At least one $\mu$ will differ $H_0: \mu_1 = \mu_2 = \mu_3$
Descriptive statistics = group *M*s, *SD*s, and *n*.

### Mutual Relationship Tests

The examination of a mutual relationship requires both variables to be quantitative since we are studying how one variable ($Y$) changes as the other ($X$) increases.

**Correlation ($r$)** examines the relationship between two quantitative variables. The correlation coefficient represents the strength and direction of the relationship

IV = quantitative
DV = quantitative
Effect size = $r^2$
Hypothesis Notation

| | | |
|---|---|---|
| Two-tailed | $H_1$: $\rho \neq 0$ | $H_0$: $\rho = 0$ |
| One-tailed | $H_1$: $\rho > 0$ | $H_0$: $\rho \leq 0$ |

Descriptive statistics = *M*s, *SD*s, and *n*.

**Regression ($F$, regression equation)** examines the degree to which one variable ($X$) predicts another variable ($Y$). The regression equation ($Y = bX + a$) is used to predict $Y$ based upon knowledge of $X$. The ANOVA ($F$) result represents the significance of the regression model.

IV ($X$) = quantitative
DV ($Y$) =quantitative
Effect size = $R^2$
Hypothesis Notation $H_1$: $B \neq 0$ $H_0$: $B = 0$
Descriptive statistics = group *M*s, *SD*s, and *n*.

### Proportion Relationship/Difference Tests

Proportional tests compares the observed frequency of individuals in categories/groups to the expected frequencies. Expected frequencies are based upon previous knowledge (population norms), equal distribution, or proportional distribution.

**Chi-Square Goodness of Fit ($\chi^2$)** compares the observed frequencies of a sample to the expected frequencies based upon population proportions for some categorical variable.

IV = categorical (sample vs norm)
DV = categorical
Effect size = Phi coefficient ($\phi$) or Cramer's V
Hypothesis Notation (null)—table of expected frequencies by category
Descriptive statistics = observed and expected frequencies for each category

**Chi-Square Test of Independence ($\chi^2$)** examines the relationship or difference between two categorical variables. Observed frequencies for each cell (intersecting category) are compared to the expected frequencies.

IV = categorical
DV = categorical
Effect size = Phi coefficient ($\phi$) or Cramer's V
Descriptive statistics = observed and expected frequencies for each category

## 13.12V Determining the Appropriate Statistical Test

The identification of variables, both type and scale, as well as the focus of research (causal, mutual, proportions) is crucial in determining the appropriate inferential test you need to use. Once variables have been identified, The Table of Statistical Tests (Figure 13.1) may guide you in the decision-making process. This table includes four cells, however, only three are utilized. **Cell 1** presents tests that have a categorical IV and DV and include our two Chi-Square tests. **Cell 2** focuses on group differences for the most part, where the IV is categorical and the DV is quantitative. Tests in Cell 2 includes the various *t*-tests and ANOVA. Finally, **Cell 3** focuses on a mutual relationship where both the IV and DV are quantitative. The two options include Pearson correlation when relationship is the emphasis and regression when prediction is the goal.

Use of the table requires analysis of your research question or scenario to determine the IV and DV and their corresponding measurement scales. We will use the following questions to guide us in the process:

1. Who are we studying?
2. What are we studying?
3. Is there a key word?
4. What is the scale of each variable?
5. Which is the outcome variable (DV) that will likely change as a result of the IV?
6. Which variable is having an impact on the DV or chronologically occurs before the DV?

**Table 13.1**
*Table of Statistical Tests*

| | | Independent Variable | |
|---|---|---|---|
| | | **Categorical** | **Quantitative** |
| **Dependent Variable** | **Categorical** | Chi-Square Goodness of Fit<br>Chi-Square Test of Independence<br>**1** | |
| | **Quantitative** | *t*-Test (2)<br>Single Sample (sample vs norm)<br>Independent Samples (2 groups)<br>Related Samples (pre/post)<br>ANOVA (3+)<br>**2** | Pearson Correlation (relate)<br>Regression (predict)<br>**3** |

**Research Scenario 1.** Let's apply this process to several research scenarios. For example in Research Scenario 1, these questions help use determine the following:

1. Who are we studying? Freshmen and sophomore students—this helps us eliminate this as a variable.
2. What are we studying? Service learning participation and Student Sense of Belongingness
3. Is there a key word? Effect—this tells us that the IV will be categorical.
4. What is the scale of each variable? Service learning participation is categorical and SSB is quantitative.
5. Which is the outcome variable (DV) that will likely change as a result of the IV? SSB
6. Which variable is having an impact on the DV or chronologically occurs before the DV? Service learning

A college dean of students examines the effect of service learning participation (yes/no) on Student Sense of Belongingness among Freshmen and Sophomore students. Student Sense of Belongingness (SSB) is measured on a 100 point scale.

Now that we have identified our variable, we are ready to use the Table of Statistical Tests. The categorical IV and the quantitative DV places us in **Cell 2**. Since the IV creates two separate groups (participants vs non-participants), we would use a *t*-test of independent samples.

**Research Scenario 2.** In Research Scenario 2, these questions help use determine the following:

1. Who are we studying? College seniors
2. What are we studying? Amount of weekly exercise and amount of alcohol consumed
3. Is there a key word? Relate—this tells us that both variables will the same the scale
4. What is the scale of each variable? Both variables indicate "amount" and are quantitative.
5. Which is the outcome variable (DV) that will likely change as a result of the IV? Alcohol
6. Which variable is having an impact on the DV or chronologically occurs before the DV? Exercise

Does the amount of weekly exercise significantly relate to the amount of alcohol consumed among college seniors?

Having identified our variable, we are ready to use the Table of Statistical Tests. The quantitative IV and DV places us in **Cell 3**. Since the keyword is relate, we would use Pearson Correlation.

**Research Scenario 3.** In Research Scenario 3, these questions help use determine the following:

1. Who are we studying? College juniors and seniors
2. What are we studying? Level of college satisfaction and major
3. Is there a key word? Differ—at least one variable will be categorical
4. What is the scale of each variable? Both variables are categorical.
5. Which is the outcome variable (DV) that will likely change as a result of the IV? Level of Satisfaction
6. Which variable is having an impact on the DV or chronologically occurs before the DV? Major

Does level of college satisfaction (low, medium, high) significantly differ by major among college juniors and seniors?

Now that we have identified our variables, we are ready to use the Table of Statistical Tests. The catgorical IV and DV places us in **Cell 1**. Since the question examines two distinct categorical variables, we will use Chi-square test of independence.

## 13.13V Effect Sizes

The focus of hypothesis testing is to disprove or reject the null hypothesis by determining that there is a significant effect or relationship in the sample and therefore the population. Significance is established when the probability (*p*) of finding of significance due to error is extremely low, typically less than 5%, or whatever the alpha level is set (.05 or .01). Although finding significance allows us to generalize our results to the population, the test statistic and *p*-value are not indicative of the size of the effect. Therefore, the research community highly recommends the reporting of effect size in addition to the inferential results. Throughout this course, we have learned about many different effect sizes. Table 13.2 presents the corresponding effect size options for each statistical test and the appropriate criteria for evaluation. Cohen's *d* and $r^2$ are the two most common; however, keep in mind the calculation of these may vary from test to test. In addition, the evaluation of effect sizes is different for each effect size. When multiple effect size options are possible, examine what descriptive statistics are available for the easiest calculation.

**Table 13.2** *Effect Sizes and Evaluation Criteria by Test*

| | Effect Size | | Evaluation: Small | Medium | Large |
|---|---|---|---|---|---|
| *t*-test Single Sample | Cohen's $d = \frac{M-\mu}{SD}$ | | .01-.19 | .20-.79 | .80+ |
| | $r^2 = \frac{t^2}{t^2+df}$ | | .01-.08 | .09-.25 | .26+ |
| *t*-test Independent Samples | Cohen's $d = \frac{M_1 - M_2}{\sqrt{s_p^2}}$ | | .01-.19 | .20-.79 | .80+ |
| | $r^2 = \frac{t^2}{t^2+df}$ | | .01-.08 | .09-.25 | .26+ |
| *t*-Test Related Samples | Cohen's $d = \frac{M_D}{SD}$ | | .01-.19 | .20-.79 | .80+ |
| | $r^2 = \frac{t^2}{t^2+df}$ | | .01-.08 | .09-.25 | .26+ |
| ANOVA | $\eta^2 = \frac{SS_{between}}{SS_{total}}$ | | .01-.08 | .09-.25 | .26+ |
| Correlation | $r$ | | .01-.29 | .30-.49 | .50+ |
| | $r^2$ | | .01-.08 | .09-.25 | .26+ |
| Regression | $R^2$ | | .01-.08 | .09-.25 | .26+ |
| Chi-Square | Phi $\phi = \sqrt{\frac{\chi^2}{n}}$ | | .01-.08 | .09-.25 | .26+ |
| | Cramer's $V = \sqrt{\frac{\chi^2}{n(df^*)}}$ | 1 | .01-.10 | .11-.49 | .50+ |
| | | 2 | .01-.07 | .08-.34 | .35+ |
| | | 3 | .01-.06 | .07-.28 | .29+ |
| | | 4 | .01-.05 | .06-.24 | .25+ |
| | | 5 | .01-.05 | .06-.21 | .22+ |

## 13.14V The Power of Statistics

In this course, we have learned about many basic statistical methods—methods that describe a set of data or even allow us to draw inferences from our sample results to a population. These statistical results may guide our decision-making from simple purchases to large-scale program implementation. However, the basic principal in using data for such purposes is that the data itself is accurate and has been correctly analyzed. Unfortunately, we have learned that researchers and media outlets may exaggerate results or even falsify conclusions for the sake of supporting an agenda or having a sensational headline. As potential researchers and avid consumers of statistics for your daily life or employer, we are obligated to critically evaluate statistical results to ensure the most informed decisions are made and resources are effectively used. Essentially, use statistics for good!!!!! The following questions may guide you in this evaluation:

- Who is the messenger of the statistical results and what possible agenda are they trying to support?
- Did the researchers use an adequate sample size and appropriate target population based upon their generalizations?
- Did the researchers use appropriate statistical methods? Were assumptions fulfilled?
- Are the descriptive and inferential results reported appropriately and accurately? Are effect sizes or confidence intervals reported?
- Do the results support the conclusions?

## 13.15 Additional Practice

Identify the variables by type and scale to determine the appropriate statistical method.

1. Does kindergarten reading preparedness (measured on a 20-point scale) differ by socio-economic status (low, middle, high) among preschoolers?
   a. Independent variable = Scale: Categorical Quantitative
   b. Dependent variable = Scale: Categorical Quantitative
   c. Statistical test =

2. Do GRE (Graduate Record Exam) scores significantly predict first semester GPA of graduate school?
   a. Independent variable = Scale: Categorical Quantitative
   b. Dependent variable = Scale: Categorical Quantitative
   c. Statistical test =

3. Does a workshop on positive thinking significant increase self-esteem scores among middle school students? (Self-esteem was measured before and after the workshop).
   a. Independent variable = Scale: Categorical Quantitative
   b. Dependent variable = Scale: Categorical Quantitative
   c. Statistical test =

4. Does learning style type differ by hand preference among high school students?
   a. Independent variable = Scale: Categorical Quantitative
   b. Dependent variable = Scale: Categorical Quantitative
   c. Statistical test =

5. Does foot size significantly relate to IQ among adults?
   a. Independent variable = Scale: Categorical Quantitative
   b. Dependent variable = Scale: Categorical Quantitative
   c. Statistical test =

6. Does the number of driving violations differ by gender among young adults (age 16-25)?

   a. Independent variable = Scale: Categorical Quantitative

   b. Dependent variable = Scale: Categorical Quantitative

   c. Statistical test =

7. Does the annual amount of minutes of daylight for the state of New Mexico significantly differ from the US norm?

   a. Independent variable = Scale: Categorical Quantitative

   b. Dependent variable = Scale: Categorical Quantitative

   c. Statistical test =

## 13.16 Activity

View John Oliver's video from Last Week Tonight on *Scientific Studies*. He provides many examples of how media twists research results for the sake of headlines. https://youtu.be/0Rnq1NpHdmw

1. Based upon Oliver's video, are there additional questions that should guide you in evaluating research?

2. Are there any hot topics in your field of study in which research is sensationalized and being pushed on you or the public?

3. How can you be a more critical consumer in your job (current or future) or everyday life?

## 13.17 Exercises

1. What does a *p*-value represent?

2. Why should an effect size be reported with inferential results?

3. Which effect sizes use the following evaluation guidelines?

| Small | Medium | Large |
|---|---|---|
| .01-.08 | .09-.25 | .26+ |

4. Cohen's *d* may be calculated three different ways depending on the statistical test. How do these differ and why?

Identify the variables by type and scale to determine the appropriate statistical method.

5. Does degree of ethical behavior (measured through a 100 point test) differ by political affiliation (democrat, republican, independent)?

   a. Independent variable = Scale: Categorical Quantitative

   b. Dependent variable = Scale: Categorical Quantitative

   c. Statistical test =

6. Does participation in service-learning (yes/no) significantly relate to 2nd-year retention among freshmen college students?

   a. Independent variable = Scale: Categorical Quantitative

   b. Dependent variable = Scale: Categorical Quantitative

   c. Statistical test =

7. Does yoga participation significantly increase flexibility among adults 65 years and older? Participant flexibility was measured before and after one month of yoga (4 days/week).

   a. Independent variable = Scale: Categorical Quantitative

   b. Dependent variable = Scale: Categorical Quantitative

   c. Statistical test =

8. Does total lung capacity (volume of air in lungs at maximum inflation) significantly predict to time to complete running one mile among college distance athletes?

   a. Independent variable = Scale: Categorical Quantitative

   b. Dependent variable = Scale: Categorical Quantitative

   c. Statistical test =

# APPENDIX A
# The *z* Distribution

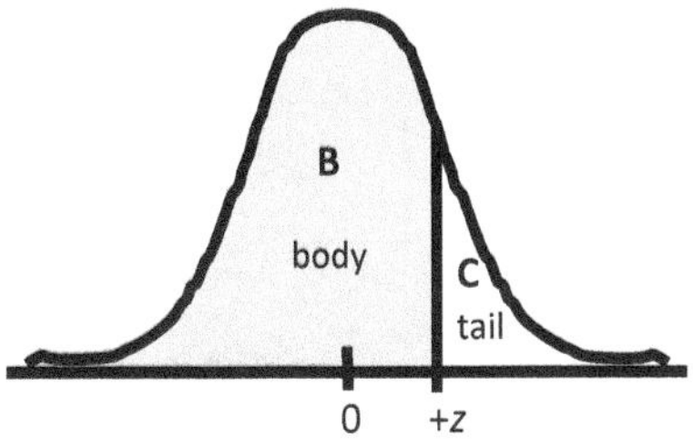


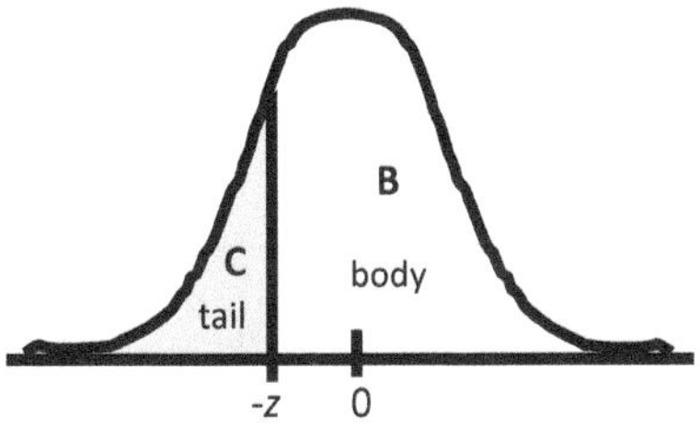


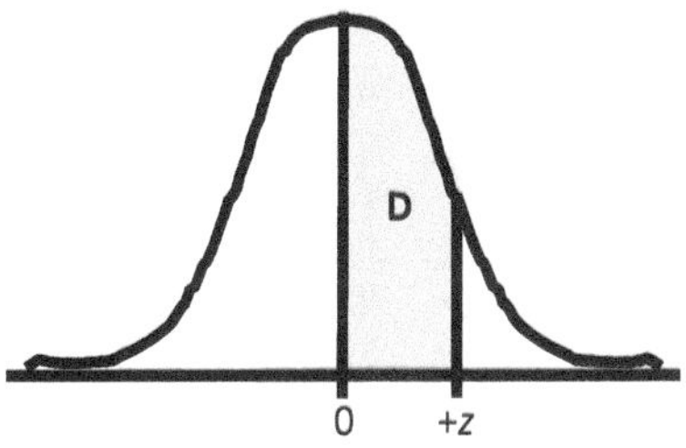


| (A) *z* | (B) Proportion in body | (C) Proportion in tail | (D) Proportion between *M* and *z* | (A) *z* | (B) Proportion in body | (C) Proportion in tail | (D) Proportion between *M* and *z* |
|---|---|---|---|---|---|---|---|
| 0.00 | .5000 | .5000 | .0000 | 0.25 | .5987 | .4013 | .0987 |
| 0.01 | .5040 | .4960 | .0040 | 0.26 | .6026 | .3974 | .1026 |
| 0.02 | .5080 | .4920 | .0080 | 0.27 | .6064 | .3936 | .1064 |
| 0.03 | .5120 | .4880 | .0120 | 0.28 | .6103 | .3897 | .1103 |
| 0.04 | .5160 | .4840 | .0160 | 0.29 | .6141 | .3859 | .1141 |
| 0.05 | .5199 | .4801 | .0199 | 0.30 | .6179 | .3821 | .1179 |
| 0.06 | .5239 | .4761 | .0239 | 0.31 | .6217 | .3783 | .1217 |
| 0.07 | .5279 | .4721 | .0279 | 0.32 | .6255 | .3745 | .1255 |
| 0.08 | .5319 | .4681 | .0319 | 0.33 | .6293 | .3707 | .1293 |
| 0.09 | .5359 | .4641 | .0359 | 0.34 | .6331 | .3669 | .1331 |
| 0.10 | .5398 | .4602 | .0398 | 0.35 | .6368 | .3632 | .1368 |
| 0.11 | .5438 | .4562 | .0438 | 0.36 | .6406 | .3594 | .1406 |
| 0.12 | .5478 | .4522 | .0478 | 0.37 | .6443 | .3557 | .1443 |
| 0.13 | .5517 | .4483 | .0517 | 0.38 | .6480 | .3520 | .1480 |
| 0.14 | .5557 | .4443 | .0557 | 0.39 | .6517 | .3483 | .1517 |
| 0.15 | .5596 | .4404 | .0596 | 0.40 | .6554 | .3446 | .1554 |
| 0.16 | .5636 | .4364 | .0636 | 0.41 | .6591 | .3409 | .1591 |
| 0.17 | .5675 | .4325 | .0675 | 0.42 | .6628 | .3372 | .1628 |
| 0.18 | .5714 | .4286 | .0714 | 0.43 | .6664 | .3336 | .1664 |
| 0.19 | .5753 | .4247 | .0753 | 0.44 | .6700 | .3300 | .1700 |
| 0.20 | .5793 | .4207 | .0793 | 0.45 | .6736 | .3264 | .1736 |
| 0.21 | .5832 | .4168 | .0832 | 0.46 | .6772 | .3228 | .1772 |
| 0.22 | .5871 | .4129 | .0871 | 0.47 | .6808 | .3192 | .1808 |
| 0.23 | .5910 | .4090 | .0910 | 0.48 | .6844 | .3156 | .1844 |
| 0.24 | .5948 | .4052 | .0948 | 0.49 | .6879 | .3121 | .1879 |

| (A)<br>*z* | (B)<br>Proportion in body | (C)<br>Proportion in tail | (D)<br>Proportion between *M* and *z* | (A)<br>*z* | (B)<br>Proportion in body | (C)<br>Proportion in tail | (D)<br>Proportion between *M* and *z* |
|---|---|---|---|---|---|---|---|
| 0.50 | .6915 | .3085 | .1915 | 1.00 | .8413 | .1587 | .3413 |
| 0.51 | .6950 | .3050 | .1950 | 1.01 | .8438 | .1562 | .3438 |
| 0.52 | .6985 | .3015 | .1985 | 1.02 | .8461 | .1539 | .3461 |
| 0.53 | .7019 | .2981 | .2019 | 1.03 | .8485 | .1515 | .3485 |
| 0.54 | .7054 | .2946 | .2054 | 1.04 | .8508 | .1492 | .3508 |
| 0.55 | .7088 | .2912 | .2088 | 1.05 | .8531 | .1469 | .3531 |
| 0.56 | .7123 | .2877 | .2123 | 1.06 | .8554 | .1446 | .3554 |
| 0.57 | .7157 | .2843 | .2157 | 1.07 | .8577 | .1423 | .3577 |
| 0.58 | .7190 | .2810 | .2190 | 1.08 | .8599 | .1401 | .3599 |
| 0.59 | .7224 | .2776 | .2224 | 1.09 | .8621 | .1379 | .3621 |
| 0.60 | .7257 | .2743 | .2257 | 1.10 | .8643 | .1357 | .3643 |
| 0.61 | .7291 | .2709 | .2291 | 1.11 | .8665 | .1335 | .3665 |
| 0.62 | .7324 | .2676 | .2324 | 1.12 | .8686 | .1314 | .3686 |
| 0.63 | .7357 | .2643 | .2357 | 1.13 | .8708 | .1292 | .3708 |
| 0.64 | .7389 | .2611 | .2389 | 1.14 | .8729 | .1271 | .3729 |
| 0.65 | .7422 | .2578 | .2422 | 1.15 | .8749 | .1251 | .3749 |
| 0.66 | .7454 | .2546 | .2454 | 1.16 | .8770 | .1230 | .3770 |
| 0.67 | .7486 | .2514 | .2486 | 1.17 | .8790 | .1210 | .3790 |
| 0.68 | .7517 | .2483 | .2517 | 1.18 | .8810 | .1190 | .3810 |
| 0.69 | .7549 | .2451 | .2549 | 1.19 | .8830 | .1170 | .3830 |
| 0.70 | .7580 | .2420 | .2580 | 1.20 | .8849 | .1151 | .3849 |
| 0.71 | .7611 | .2389 | .2611 | 1.21 | .8869 | .1131 | .3869 |
| 0.72 | .7642 | .2358 | .2642 | 1.22 | .8888 | .1112 | .8888 |
| 0.73 | .7673 | .2327 | .2673 | 1.23 | .8907 | .1093 | .3907 |
| 0.74 | .7701 | .2296 | .2701 | 1.24 | .8925 | .1075 | .3925 |
| 0.75 | .7734 | .2266 | .2734 | 1.25 | .8944 | .1056 | .3944 |
| 0.76 | .7764 | .2236 | .2764 | 1.26 | .8962 | .1038 | .3962 |
| 0.77 | .7794 | .2206 | .2794 | 1.27 | .8980 | .1020 | .3980 |
| 0.78 | .7823 | .2177 | .2823 | 1.28 | .8997 | .1003 | .3997 |
| 0.79 | .7852 | .2148 | .2852 | 1.29 | .9015 | .0985 | .4015 |
| 0.80 | .7881 | .2119 | .2881 | 1.30 | .9032 | .0968 | .4032 |
| 0.81 | .7910 | .2090 | .2910 | 1.31 | .9049 | .0951 | .4049 |
| 0.82 | .7939 | .2061 | .2939 | 1.32 | .9066 | .0934 | .4066 |
| 0.83 | .7967 | .2033 | .2967 | 1.33 | .9082 | .0918 | .4082 |
| 0.84 | .7995 | .2005 | .2995 | 1.34 | .9099 | .0901 | .4099 |
| 0.85 | .8023 | .1977 | .3023 | 1.35 | .9115 | .0885 | .4115 |
| 0.86 | .8051 | .1949 | .3051 | 1.36 | .9131 | .0869 | .4131 |
| 0.87 | .8078 | .1922 | .3078 | 1.37 | .9147 | .0853 | .4147 |
| 0.88 | .8106 | .1894 | .3106 | 1.38 | .9162 | .0838 | .4162 |
| 0.89 | .8133 | .1867 | .3133 | 1.39 | .9177 | .0823 | .4177 |
| 0.90 | .8159 | .1841 | .3159 | 1.40 | .9192 | .0808 | .4192 |
| 0.91 | .8186 | .1814 | .3186 | 1.41 | .9207 | .0793 | .4207 |
| 0.92 | .8212 | .1788 | .3212 | 1.42 | .9222 | .0778 | .4222 |
| 0.93 | .8238 | .1762 | .3238 | 1.43 | .9236 | .0764 | .4236 |
| 0.94 | .8264 | .1736 | .3264 | 1.44 | .9251 | .0749 | .4251 |
| 0.95 | .8289 | .1711 | .3289 | 1.45 | .9265 | .0735 | .4265 |
| 0.96 | .8315 | .1685 | .3315 | 1.46 | .9279 | .0721 | .4279 |
| 0.97 | .8340 | .1660 | .3340 | 1.47 | .9292 | .0708 | .4292 |
| 0.98 | .8365 | .1635 | .3365 | 1.48 | .9306 | .0694 | .4306 |
| 0.99 | .8389 | .1611 | .3389 | 1.49 | .9319 | .0681 | .4319 |

| (A) z | (B) Proportion in body | (C) Proportion in tail | (D) Proportion between *M* and *z* | (A) z | (B) Proportion in body | (C) Proportion in tail | (D) Proportion between *M* and *z* |
|---|---|---|---|---|---|---|---|
| 1.50 | .9332 | .0668 | .4332 | 2.00 | .9772 | .0228 | .4772 |
| 1.51 | .9345 | .0655 | .4345 | 2.01 | .9778 | .0222 | .4778 |
| 1.52 | .9357 | .0643 | .4357 | 2.02 | .9783 | .0217 | .4783 |
| 1.53 | .9370 | .0630 | .4370 | 2.03 | .9788 | .0212 | .4788 |
| 1.54 | .9382 | .0618 | .4382 | 2.04 | .9793 | .0207 | .4793 |
| 1.55 | .9394 | .0606 | .4394 | 2.05 | .9798 | .0202 | .4798 |
| 1.56 | .9406 | .0594 | .4406 | 2.06 | .9803 | .0197 | .4803 |
| 1.57 | .9418 | .0582 | .4418 | 2.07 | .9808 | .0192 | .4808 |
| 1.58 | .9429 | .0571 | .4429 | 2.08 | .9812 | .0188 | .4812 |
| 1.59 | .9441 | .0559 | .4441 | 2.09 | .9817 | .0183 | .4817 |
| 1.60 | .9452 | .0548 | .4452 | 2.10 | .9821 | .0179 | .4821 |
| 1.61 | .9463 | .0537 | .4463 | 2.11 | .9826 | .0174 | .4826 |
| 1.62 | .9474 | .0526 | .4474 | 2.12 | .9830 | .0170 | .4830 |
| 1.63 | .9484 | .0516 | .4484 | 2.13 | .9834 | .0166 | .4834 |
| 1.64 | .9495 | .0505 | .4495 | 2.14 | .9838 | .0162 | .4838 |
| 1.65 | .9509 | .0495 | .4509 | 2.15 | .9842 | .0158 | .4842 |
| 1.66 | .9515 | .0485 | .4515 | 2.16 | .9846 | .0154 | .4846 |
| 1.67 | .9525 | .0475 | .4525 | 2.17 | .9850 | .0150 | .4850 |
| 1.68 | .9535 | .0465 | .4535 | 2.18 | .9854 | .0146 | .4854 |
| 1.69 | .9545 | .0455 | .4545 | 2.19 | .9857 | .0143 | .4857 |
| 1.70 | .9554 | .0446 | .4554 | 2.20 | .9861 | .0139 | .4861 |
| 1.71 | .9564 | .0436 | .4564 | 2.21 | .9864 | .0136 | .4864 |
| 1.72 | .9573 | .0427 | .4573 | 2.22 | .9868 | .0132 | .4868 |
| 1.73 | .9582 | .0418 | .4582 | 2.23 | .9871 | .0129 | .4871 |
| 1.74 | .9591 | .0409 | .4591 | 2.24 | .9875 | .0125 | .4875 |
| 1.75 | .9599 | .0401 | .4599 | 2.25 | .9878 | .0122 | .4878 |
| 1.76 | .9608 | .0392 | .4608 | 2.26 | .9881 | .0119 | .4881 |
| 1.77 | .9616 | .0384 | .4616 | 2.27 | .9884 | .0116 | .4884 |
| 1.78 | .9625 | .0375 | .4625 | 2.28 | .9887 | .0113 | .4887 |
| 1.79 | .9633 | .0367 | .4633 | 2.29 | .9890 | .0110 | .4890 |
| 1.80 | .9641 | .0359 | .4641 | 2.30 | .9893 | .0107 | .4893 |
| 1.81 | .9649 | .0351 | .4649 | 2.31 | .9896 | .0104 | .4896 |
| 1.82 | .9656 | .0344 | .4656 | 2.32 | .9898 | .0102 | .4898 |
| 1.83 | .9664 | .0336 | .4664 | 2.33 | .9901 | .0099 | .4901 |
| 1.84 | .9671 | .0329 | .4671 | 2.34 | .9904 | .0096 | .4904 |
| 1.85 | .9678 | .0322 | .4678 | 2.35 | .9906 | .0094 | .4906 |
| 1.86 | .9686 | .0314 | .4686 | 2.36 | .9909 | .0091 | .4909 |
| 1.87 | .9693 | .0307 | .4693 | 2.37 | .9911 | .0089 | .4911 |
| 1.88 | .9699 | .0301 | .4699 | 2.38 | .9913 | .0087 | .4913 |
| 1.89 | .9706 | .0294 | .4706 | 2.39 | .9916 | .0084 | .4916 |
| 1.90 | .9713 | .0287 | .4713 | 2.40 | .9918 | .0082 | .4918 |
| 1.91 | .9719 | .0281 | .4719 | 2.41 | .9920 | .0080 | .4920 |
| 1.92 | .9726 | .0274 | .4726 | 2.42 | .9922 | .0078 | .4922 |
| 1.93 | .9732 | .0268 | .4732 | 2.43 | .9925 | .0075 | .4925 |
| 1.94 | .9738 | .0262 | .4738 | 2.44 | .9927 | .0073 | .4927 |
| 1.95 | .9744 | .0256 | .4744 | 2.45 | .9929 | .0071 | .4929 |
| 1.96 | .9750 | .0250 | .4750 | 2.46 | .9931 | .0069 | .4931 |
| 1.97 | .9756 | .0244 | .4756 | 2.47 | .9932 | .0068 | .4932 |
| 1.98 | .9761 | .0239 | .4761 | 2.48 | .9934 | .0066 | .4934 |
| 1.99 | .9767 | .0233 | .4767 | 2.49 | .9936 | .0064 | .4936 |

| (A) <br> $z$ | (B) <br> Proportion in body | (C) <br> Proportion in tail | (D) <br> Proportion between $M$ and $z$ |
|---|---|---|---|
| 2.50 | .9938 | .0062 | .4938 |
| 2.51 | .9940 | .0060 | .4940 |
| 2.52 | .9941 | .0059 | .4941 |
| 2.53 | .9943 | .0057 | .4943 |
| 2.54 | .9945 | .0055 | .4945 |
| 2.55 | .9946 | .0054 | .4946 |
| 2.56 | .9948 | .0052 | .4948 |
| 2.57 | .9949 | .0051 | .4949 |
| 2.58 | .9951 | .0049 | .4951 |
| 2.59 | .9952 | .0048 | .4952 |
| 2.60 | .9953 | .0047 | .4953 |
| 2.61 | .9955 | .0045 | .4955 |
| 2.62 | .9956 | .0044 | .4956 |
| 2.63 | .9957 | .0043 | .4957 |
| 2.64 | .9959 | .0041 | .4959 |
| 2.65 | .9960 | .0040 | .4960 |
| 2.66 | .9961 | .0039 | .4961 |
| 2.67 | .9962 | .0038 | .4962 |
| 2.68 | .9963 | .0037 | .4963 |
| 2.69 | .9964 | .0036 | .4964 |
| 2.70 | .9965 | .0035 | .4965 |
| 2.71 | .9966 | .0034 | .4966 |
| 2.72 | .9967 | .0033 | .4967 |
| 2.73 | .9968 | .0032 | .4968 |
| 2.74 | .9969 | .0031 | .4969 |
| 2.75 | .9970 | .0030 | .4970 |
| 2.76 | .9971 | .0029 | .4971 |
| 2.77 | .9972 | .0028 | .4972 |
| 2.78 | .9973 | .0027 | .4973 |
| 2.79 | .9974 | .0026 | .4974 |
| 2.80 | .9974 | .0026 | .4974 |
| 2.81 | .9975 | .0025 | .4975 |
| 2.82 | .9976 | .0024 | .4976 |
| 2.83 | .9977 | .0023 | .4977 |
| 2.84 | .9977 | .0023 | .4977 |
| 2.85 | .9978 | .0022 | .4978 |
| 2.86 | .9979 | .0021 | .4979 |
| 2.87 | .9979 | .0021 | .4979 |
| 2.88 | .9980 | .0020 | .4980 |
| 2.89 | .9981 | .0019 | .4981 |
| 2.90 | .9981 | .0019 | .4981 |
| 2.91 | .9982 | .0018 | .4982 |
| 2.92 | .9982 | .0018 | .4982 |
| 2.93 | .9983 | .0017 | .4983 |
| 2.94 | .9984 | .0016 | .4984 |

| (A) <br> $z$ | (B) <br> Proportion in body | (C) <br> Proportion in tail | (D) <br> Proportion between $M$ and $z$ |
|---|---|---|---|
| 2.95 | .9984 | .0016 | .4984 |
| 2.96 | .9985 | .0015 | .4985 |
| 2.97 | .9985 | .0015 | .4985 |
| 2.98 | .9986 | .0014 | .4986 |
| 2.99 | .9986 | .0014 | .4986 |
| 3.00 | .9987 | .0013 | .4987 |
| 3.01 | .9987 | .0013 | .4987 |
| 3.02 | .9987 | .0113 | .4987 |
| 3.03 | .9988 | .0012 | .4988 |
| 3.04 | .9988 | .0012 | .4988 |
| 3.05 | .9989 | .0011 | .4989 |
| 3.06 | .9989 | .0011 | .4989 |
| 3.07 | .9989 | .0011 | .4989 |
| 3.08 | .9990 | .0010 | .4990 |
| 3.09 | .9990 | .0010 | .4990 |
| 3.10 | .9990 | .0010 | .4990 |
| 3.11 | .9991 | .0009 | .4991 |
| 3.12 | .9991 | .0009 | .4991 |
| 3.13 | .9991 | .0009 | .4991 |
| 3.14 | .9992 | .0008 | .4992 |
| 3.15 | .9992 | .0008 | .4992 |
| 3.16 | .9992 | .0008 | .4992 |
| 3.17 | .9992 | .0008 | .4992 |
| 3.18 | .9993 | .0007 | .4993 |
| 3.19 | .9993 | .0007 | .4993 |
| 3.20 | .9993 | .0007 | .4993 |
| 3.21 | .9993 | .0007 | .4993 |
| 3.22 | .9994 | .0006 | .4994 |
| 3.23 | .9994 | .0006 | .4994 |
| 3.24 | .9994 | .0006 | .4994 |
| 3.30 | .9995 | .0005 | .4995 |
| 3.40 | .9997 | .0003 | .4997 |
| 3.50 | .9998 | .0002 | .4998 |
| 3.60 | .9998 | .0002 | .4998 |
| 3.70 | .9999 | .0001 | .4999 |
| 3.80 | .99993 | .00007 | .49993 |
| 3.90 | .99995 | .00005 | .49995 |
| 4.00 | .99997 | .00003 | .49997 |

# APPENDIX B

# Power Table for *z*-test

| *z* | α=.05 | | α=.01 | |
|---|---|---|---|---|
| | **2-tail** | **1-tail** | **2-tail** | **1-tail** |
| 1.0 | 0.170 | 0.260 | 0.058 | 0.092 |
| 1.1 | 0.196 | 0.293 | 0.070 | 0.110 |
| 1.2 | 0.224 | 0.328 | 0.085 | 0.130 |
| 1.3 | 0.255 | 0.365 | 0.101 | 0.152 |
| 1.4 | 0.288 | 0.403 | 0.120 | 0.177 |
| 1.5 | 0.323 | 0.442 | 0.141 | 0.204 |
| 1.6 | 0.360 | 0.482 | 0.165 | 0.234 |
| 1.7 | 0.398 | 0.522 | 0.191 | 0.266 |
| 1.8 | 0.437 | 0.562 | 0.219 | 0.299 |
| 1.9 | 0.476 | 0.601 | 0.250 | 0.335 |
| 2.0 | 0.516 | 0.639 | 0.282 | 0.372 |
| 2.1 | 0.556 | 0.639 | 0.282 | 0.372 |
| 2.2 | 0.595 | 0.711 | 0.354 | 0.450 |
| 2.3 | 0.633 | 0.744 | 0.391 | 0.489 |
| 2.4 | 0.670 | 0.775 | 0.430 | 0.529 |
| 2.5 | 0.705 | 0.804 | 0.470 | 0.569 |
| 2.6 | 0.739 | 0.830 | 0.510 | 0.608 |
| 2.7 | 0.770 | 0.854 | 0.549 | 0.646 |
| 2.8 | 0.800 | 0.876 | 0.589 | 0.682 |
| 2.9 | 0.826 | 0.895 | 0.627 | 0.717 |
| 3.0 | 0.851 | 0.912 | 0.664 | 0.750 |
| 3.1 | 0.873 | 0.927 | 0.700 | 0.780 |
| 3.2 | 0.893 | 0.940 | 0.734 | 0.809 |
| 3.3 | 0.910 | 0.951 | 0.766 | 0.835 |
| 3.4 | 0.925 | 0.960 | 0.795 | 0.859 |
| 3.5 | 0.938 | 0.968 | 0.822 | 0.880 |
| 3.6 | 0.950 | 0.975 | 0.847 | 0.899 |
| 3.7 | 0.959 | 0.980 | 0.870 | 0.915 |
| 3.8 | 0.967 | 0.984 | 0.890 | 0.930 |
| 3.9 | 0.974 | 0.988 | 0.907 | 0.942 |
| 4.0 | 0.979 | 0.991 | 0.923 | 0.953 |

# APPENDIX C

# The *t* Distribution

| | PROPORTION IN ONE TAIL | | | | | |
|---|---|---|---|---|---|---|
| | 0.25 | 0.10 | 0.05 | 0.025 | 0.01 | 0.005 |
| | PROPORTION IN TWO TAILS | | | | | |
| *df* | 0.50 | 0.20 | 0.10 | 0.05 | 0.02 | 0.01 |
| 1 | 1.000 | 3.078 | 6.314 | 12.706 | 31.821 | 63.657 |
| 2 | 0.816 | 1.886 | 2.920 | 4.303 | 6.965 | 9.925 |
| 3 | 0.765 | 1.638 | 2.353 | 3.182 | 4.541 | 5.841 |
| 4 | 0.741 | 1.533 | 2.132 | 2.776 | 3.747 | 4.604 |
| 5 | 0.727 | 1.476 | 2.015 | 2.571 | 3.365 | 4.032 |
| 6 | 0.718 | 1.440 | 1.943 | 2.447 | 3.143 | 3.707 |
| 7 | 0.711 | 1.415 | 1.895 | 2.365 | 2.998 | 3.499 |
| 8 | 0.706 | 1.397 | 1.860 | 2.306 | 2.896 | 3.355 |
| 9 | 0.703 | 1.383 | 1.833 | 2.262 | 2.821 | 3.250 |
| 10 | 0.700 | 1.372 | 1.812 | 2.228 | 2.764 | 3.169 |
| 11 | 0.697 | 1.363 | 1.796 | 2.201 | 2.718 | 3.106 |
| 12 | 0.695 | 1.356 | 1.782 | 2.179 | 2.681 | 3.055 |
| 13 | 0.694 | 1.350 | 1.771 | 2.160 | 2.650 | 3.012 |
| 14 | 0.692 | 1.345 | 1.761 | 2.145 | 2.624 | 2.977 |
| 15 | 0.691 | 1.341 | 1.753 | 2.131 | 2.602 | 2.947 |
| 16 | 0.690 | 1.337 | 1.746 | 2.120 | 2.583 | 2.921 |
| 17 | 0.689 | 1.333 | 1.740 | 2.110 | 2.567 | 2.898 |
| 18 | 0.688 | 1.330 | 1.734 | 2.101 | 2.552 | 2.878 |
| 19 | 0.688 | 1.328 | 1.729 | 2.093 | 2.539 | 2.861 |
| 20 | 0.687 | 1.325 | 1.725 | 2.086 | 2.528 | 2.845 |
| 21 | 0.686 | 1.323 | 1.721 | 2.080 | 2.518 | 2.831 |
| 22 | 0.686 | 1.321 | 1.717 | 2.074 | 2.508 | 2.819 |
| 23 | 0.685 | 1.319 | 1.714 | 2.069 | 2.500 | 2.807 |
| 24 | 0.685 | 1.318 | 1.711 | 2.064 | 2.492 | 2.797 |
| 25 | 0.684 | 1.316 | 1.708 | 2.060 | 2.485 | 2.787 |
| 26 | 0.684 | 1.315 | 1.706 | 2.056 | 2.479 | 2.779 |
| 27 | 0.684 | 1.314 | 1.703 | 2.052 | 2.473 | 2.771 |
| 28 | 0.683 | 1.313 | 1.701 | 2.048 | 2.467 | 2.763 |
| 29 | 0.683 | 1.311 | 1.699 | 2.045 | 2.462 | 2.756 |
| 30 | 0.683 | 1.310 | 1.697 | 2.042 | 2.457 | 2.750 |
| 40 | 0.681 | 1.303 | 1.684 | 2.021 | 2.423 | 2.704 |
| 60 | 0.679 | 1.296 | 1671 | 2.000 | 2.390 | 2.660 |
| 120 | 0.677 | 1.289 | 1.658 | 1.980 | 2.358 | 2.617 |
| ∞ | 0.674 | 1.282 | 1.645 | 1.960 | 2.326 | 2.576 |

# APPENDIX D1

# Power: *t* Single & t Related

**Two-tailed Test, α=.05**

| n | Cohen's *d* | | | | | | | | | | | | | | | | | | | |
|---|---|---|---|---|---|---|---|---|---|---|---|---|---|---|---|---|---|---|---|---|
| | .20 | .25 | .30 | .35 | .40 | .45 | .50 | .55 | .60 | .65 | .70 | .75 | .80 | .90 | 1.00 | 1.10 | 1.20 | 1.30 | 1.40 | 1.50 |
| 3 | .05 | .05 | .05 | .05 | .05 | .05 | .06 | .06 | .06 | .06 | .06 | .06 | .06 | .07 | .08 | .08 | .09 | .10 | .11 | .13 |
| 4 | .05 | .05 | .06 | .06 | .06 | .07 | .07 | .08 | .08 | .09 | .10 | .10 | .11 | .14 | .17 | .21 | .25 | .31 | .37 | .44 |
| 5 | .06 | .06 | .06 | .07 | .08 | .09 | .10 | .11 | .12 | .13 | .15 | .17 | .19 | .25 | .31 | .39 | .47 | .55 | .63 | .70 |
| 6 | .06 | .07 | .07 | .08 | .09 | .11 | .12 | .14 | .17 | .19 | .22 | .25 | .29 | .37 | .46 | .55 | .64 | .72 | .79 | .84 |
| 7 | .06 | .07 | .08 | .10 | .11 | .13 | .16 | .18 | .21 | .25 | .29 | .33 | .38 | .48 | .58 | .67 | .75 | .82 | .87 | .91 |
| 8 | .07 | .08 | .09 | .11 | .13 | .16 | .19 | .23 | .27 | .31 | .36 | .41 | .46 | .57 | .67 | .76 | .83 | .88 | .92 | .95 |
| 9 | .07 | .09 | .10 | .13 | .15 | .19 | .22 | .27 | .31 | .37 | .42 | .48 | .54 | .65 | .75 | .83 | .88 | .93 | .95 | .97 |
| 10 | .08 | .09 | .12 | .14 | .18 | .21 | .26 | .31 | .36 | .42 | .48 | .54 | .60 | .71 | .80 | .87 | .92 | .95 | .97 | .98 |
| 11 | .08 | .10 | .13 | .16 | .20 | .24 | .29 | .35 | .41 | .47 | .54 | .60 | .66 | .77 | .85 | .91 | .94 | .97 | .98 | .99 |
| 12 | .09 | .11 | .14 | .17 | .22 | .27 | .33 | .39 | .45 | .52 | .59 | .65 | .71 | .81 | .88 | .93 | .96 | .98 | .99 | .99 |
| 13 | .09 | .12 | .15 | .19 | .24 | .30 | .36 | .42 | .49 | .56 | .63 | .70 | .75 | .85 | .91 | .95 | .97 | .99 | .99 | |
| 14 | .10 | .13 | .16 | .21 | .26 | .32 | .39 | .46 | .53 | .61 | .67 | .74 | .79 | .88 | .93 | .96 | .98 | .99 | | |
| 15 | .10 | .13 | .17 | .22 | .28 | .35 | .42 | .49 | .57 | .64 | .71 | .77 | .82 | .90 | .95 | .97 | .99 | .99 | | |
| 16 | .11 | .14 | .19 | .24 | .30 | .37 | .45 | .53 | .60 | .68 | .74 | .80 | .85 | .92 | .96 | .98 | .99 | | | |
| 17 | .11 | .15 | .20 | .26 | .32 | .40 | .48 | .56 | .64 | .71 | .77 | .83 | .87 | .93 | .97 | .99 | .99 | | | |
| 18 | .12 | .16 | .21 | .27 | .34 | .42 | .50 | .59 | .67 | .74 | .80 | .85 | .89 | .95 | .98 | .99 | | | | |
| 19 | .12 | .17 | .22 | .29 | .36 | .45 | .53 | .62 | .69 | .76 | .82 | .87 | .91 | .96 | .98 | .99 | | | | |
| 20 | .13 | .17 | .23 | .30 | .38 | .47 | .56 | .64 | .72 | .79 | .84 | .89 | .92 | .97 | .99 | .99 | | | | |
| 21 | .13 | .18 | .24 | .32 | .40 | .49 | .58 | .67 | .74 | .81 | .86 | .90 | .94 | .97 | .99 | | | | | |
| 22 | .14 | .19 | .26 | .33 | .42 | .51 | .60 | .69 | .76 | .83 | .88 | .92 | .95 | .98 | .99 | | | | | |
| 23 | .14 | .20 | .27 | .35 | .44 | .53 | .63 | .71 | .78 | .85 | .89 | .93 | .95 | .98 | .99 | | | | | |
| 24 | .15 | .21 | .28 | .36 | .46 | .55 | .65 | .73 | .80 | .86 | .91 | .94 | .96 | .99 | | | | | | |
| 30 | .18 | .25 | .35 | .45 | .56 | .66 | .75 | .83 | .89 | .93 | .96 | .98 | .99 | | | | | | | |
| 40 | .23 | .33 | .45 | .58 | .69 | .79 | .87 | .92 | .96 | .98 | .99 | | | | | | | | | |
| 50 | .28 | .41 | .54 | .68 | .79 | .88 | .93 | .97 | .98 | .99 | | | | | | | | | | |
| 60 | .33 | .47 | .63 | .76 | .86 | .93 | .97 | .99 | .99 | | | | | | | | | | | |
| 70 | .37 | .54 | .70 | .82 | .91 | .96 | .98 | .99 | | | | | | | | | | | | |
| 80 | .42 | .60 | .75 | .87 | .94 | .98 | .99 | | | | | | | | | | | | | |
| 90 | .46 | .65 | .80 | .91 | .96 | .99 | | | | | | | | | | | | | | |
| 100 | .51 | .70 | .84 | .93 | .98 | .99 | | | | | | | | | | | | | | |

**One-tailed Test, α=.05**

| n | Cohen's *d* | | | | | | | | | | | | | | | | | | | |
|---|---|---|---|---|---|---|---|---|---|---|---|---|---|---|---|---|---|---|---|---|
| | .20 | .25 | .30 | .35 | .40 | .45 | .50 | .55 | .60 | .65 | .70 | .75 | .80 | .90 | 1.00 | 1.10 | 1.20 | 1.30 | 1.40 | 1.50 |
| 3 | .06 | .07 | .07 | .07 | .08 | .08 | .09 | .09 | .10 | .11 | .11 | .12 | .13 | .15 | .18 | .21 | .24 | .29 | .33 | .39 |
| 4 | .07 | .08 | .09 | .10 | .11 | .12 | .13 | .15 | .17 | .18 | .21 | .23 | .25 | .31 | .37 | .44 | .52 | .59 | .66 | .72 |
| 5 | .08 | .10 | .11 | .12 | .14 | .16 | .18 | .21 | .24 | .27 | .30 | .34 | .37 | .46 | .54 | .62 | .69 | .76 | .81 | .86 |
| 6 | .09 | .11 | .13 | .15 | .17 | .20 | .23 | .27 | .30 | .34 | .39 | .43 | .48 | .57 | .66 | .74 | .80 | .85 | .89 | .92 |
| 7 | .10 | .12 | .15 | .17 | .21 | .24 | .28 | .32 | .37 | .42 | .47 | .52 | .57 | .66 | .75 | .81 | .87 | .91 | .94 | .96 |
| 8 | .11 | .14 | .17 | .20 | .24 | .28 | .32 | .37 | .42 | .48 | .53 | .59 | .64 | .73 | .81 | .87 | .91 | .94 | .96 | .97 |
| 9 | .12 | .15 | .18 | .22 | .26 | .31 | .36 | .42 | .48 | .53 | .59 | .65 | .70 | .79 | .86 | .91 | .94 | .96 | .98 | .99 |
| 10 | .13 | .16 | .20 | .24 | .29 | .35 | .40 | .46 | .52 | .59 | .64 | .70 | .75 | .83 | .89 | .93 | .96 | .98 | .99 | .99 |
| 11 | .14 | .17 | .22 | .26 | .32 | .38 | .44 | .50 | .57 | .63 | .69 | .74 | .79 | .87 | .92 | .95 | .97 | .98 | .99 | .99 |
| 12 | .15 | .19 | .23 | .29 | .34 | .41 | .48 | .54 | .61 | .67 | .73 | .78 | .82 | .89 | .94 | .97 | .98 | .99 | .99 | |
| 13 | .15 | .20 | .25 | .31 | .37 | .44 | .51 | .58 | .65 | .71 | .76 | .81 | .85 | .92 | .95 | .98 | .99 | .99 | | |
| 14 | .16 | .21 | .26 | .33 | .39 | .47 | .54 | .61 | .68 | .74 | .79 | .84 | .88 | .93 | .96 | .98 | .99 | | | |
| 15 | .17 | .22 | .28 | .35 | .42 | .49 | .57 | .64 | .71 | .77 | .82 | .86 | .90 | .95 | .97 | .99 | .99 | | | |
| 16 | .18 | .23 | .29 | .36 | .44 | .52 | .60 | .67 | .74 | .79 | .84 | .88 | .92 | .96 | .98 | .99 | | | | |
| 17 | .19 | .24 | .31 | .38 | .46 | .54 | .62 | .70 | .76 | .82 | .86 | .90 | .93 | .97 | .98 | .99 | | | | |
| 18 | .19 | .25 | .32 | .40 | .48 | .57 | .65 | .72 | .78 | .84 | .88 | .92 | .94 | .97 | .99 | | | | | |
| 19 | .20 | .26 | .34 | .42 | .50 | .59 | .67 | .74 | .81 | .86 | .90 | .93 | .95 | .98 | .99 | | | | | |
| 20 | .21 | .27 | .35 | .44 | .52 | .61 | .69 | .76 | .82 | .87 | .91 | .94 | .96 | .98 | .99 | | | | | |
| 21 | .21 | .28 | .37 | .45 | .54 | .63 | .71 | .78 | .84 | .89 | .92 | .95 | .97 | .99 | | | | | | |
| 22 | .22 | .29 | .38 | .47 | .56 | .65 | .73 | .80 | .86 | .90 | .93 | .96 | .97 | .99 | | | | | | |
| 23 | .23 | .30 | .39 | .48 | .58 | .67 | .75 | .82 | .87 | .91 | .94 | .96 | .98 | .99 | | | | | | |
| 24 | .24 | .31 | .40 | .50 | .60 | .69 | .77 | .83 | .88 | .92 | .95 | .97 | .98 | .99 | | | | | | |
| 30 | .28 | .37 | .48 | .59 | .69 | .77 | .85 | .90 | .94 | .96 | .98 | .99 | .99 | | | | | | | |
| 40 | .34 | .46 | .58 | .70 | .80 | .87 | .93 | .96 | .98 | .99 | | | | | | | | | | |
| 50 | .40 | .54 | .67 | .79 | .87 | .93 | .97 | .98 | .99 | | | | | | | | | | | |
| 60 | .45 | .60 | .74 | .85 | .92 | .96 | .98 | .99 | | | | | | | | | | | | |
| 70 | .50 | .66 | .80 | .89 | .95 | .98 | .99 | | | | | | | | | | | | | |
| 80 | .55 | .72 | .84 | .93 | .97 | .99 | | | | | | | | | | | | | | |
| 90 | .59 | .76 | .88 | .95 | .98 | .99 | | | | | | | | | | | | | | |
| 100 | .63 | .80 | .91 | .97 | .99 | | | | | | | | | | | | | | | |

# APPENDIX D2

# Power: *t* Independent

| Two-Sample Two-tailed Test $\alpha$ =.05 | | | | | | | | | | | | | | | |
|---|---|---|---|---|---|---|---|---|---|---|---|---|---|---|---|
| **Cohen's *d*** | | | | | | | | | | | | | | | |
| *n* | 0.10 | 0.20 | 0.30 | 0.40 | 0.50 | 0.60 | 0.70 | 0.80 | 0.90 | 1.00 | 1.10 | 1.20 | 1.30 | 1.40 | 1.50 |
| 2 | 0.05 | 0.05 | 0.05 | 0.06 | 0.06 | 0.07 | 0.07 | 0.08 | 0.09 | 0.10 | 0.10 | 0.11 | 0.13 | 0.14 | 0.15 |
| 3 | 0.05 | 0.05 | 0.06 | 0.07 | 0.08 | 0.09 | 0.10 | 0.12 | 0.14 | 0.16 | 0.18 | 0.21 | 0.23 | 0.26 | 0.29 |
| 4 | 0.05 | 0.06 | 0.07 | 0.08 | 0.09 | 0.11 | 0.13 | 0.16 | 0.19 | 0.22 | 0.26 | 0.30 | 0.34 | 0.38 | 0.43 |
| 5 | 0.05 | 0.06 | 0.07 | 0.09 | 0.11 | 0.13 | 0.16 | 0.20 | 0.24 | 0.29 | 0.33 | 0.39 | 0.44 | 0.49 | 0.55 |
| 6 | 0.05 | 0.06 | 0.08 | 0.10 | 0.12 | 0.16 | 0.20 | 0.24 | 0.29 | 0.35 | 0.41 | 0.47 | 0.53 | 0.59 | 0.65 |
| 7 | 0.05 | 0.06 | 0.08 | 0.11 | 0.14 | 0.18 | 0.23 | 0.28 | 0.34 | 0.41 | 0.47 | 0.54 | 0.61 | 0.67 | 0.73 |
| 8 | 0.05 | 0.07 | 0.09 | 0.12 | 0.15 | 0.20 | 0.26 | 0.32 | 0.39 | 0.46 | 0.54 | 0.61 | 0.68 | 0.74 | 0.80 |
| 9 | 0.05 | 0.07 | 0.09 | 0.13 | 0.17 | 0.22 | 0.29 | 0.36 | 0.43 | 0.51 | 0.59 | 0.67 | 0.74 | 0.80 | 0.85 |
| 10 | 0.06 | 0.07 | 0.10 | 0.14 | 0.19 | 0.25 | 0.32 | 0.40 | 0.48 | 0.56 | 0.64 | 0.72 | 0.78 | 0.84 | 0.89 |
| 11 | 0.06 | 0.07 | 0.10 | 0.15 | 0.20 | 0.27 | 0.35 | 0.43 | 0.52 | 0.61 | 0.69 | 0.76 | 0.83 | 0.88 | 0.92 |
| 12 | 0.06 | 0.08 | 0.11 | 0.16 | 0.22 | 0.29 | 0.37 | 0.47 | 0.56 | 0.65 | 0.73 | 0.80 | 0.86 | 0.91 | 0.94 |
| 13 | 0.06 | 0.08 | 0.11 | 0.16 | 0.23 | 0.31 | 0.40 | 0.50 | 0.60 | 0.69 | 0.77 | 0.84 | 0.89 | 0.93 | 0.96 |
| 14 | 0.06 | 0.08 | 0.12 | 0.17 | 0.25 | 0.33 | 0.43 | 0.53 | 0.63 | 0.72 | 0.80 | 0.86 | 0.91 | 0.95 | 0.97 |
| 15 | 0.06 | 0.08 | 0.12 | 0.18 | 0.26 | 0.35 | 0.46 | 0.56 | 0.66 | 0.75 | 0.83 | 0.89 | 0.93 | 0.96 | 0.98 |
| 16 | 0.06 | 0.09 | 0.13 | 0.19 | 0.28 | 0.38 | 0.48 | 0.59 | 0.69 | 0.78 | 0.85 | 0.91 | 0.94 | 0.97 | 0.98 |
| 17 | 0.06 | 0.09 | 0.14 | 0.20 | 0.29 | 0.40 | 0.51 | 0.62 | 0.72 | 0.81 | 0.87 | 0.92 | 0.96 | 0.98 | 0.99 |
| 18 | 0.06 | 0.09 | 0.14 | 0.21 | 0.31 | 0.42 | 0.53 | 0.65 | 0.75 | 0.83 | 0.89 | 0.94 | 0.97 | 0.98 | 0.99 |
| 19 | 0.06 | 0.09 | 0.15 | 0.22 | 0.32 | 0.44 | 0.56 | 0.67 | 0.77 | 0.85 | 0.91 | 0.95 | 0.97 | 0.99 | 0.99 |
| 20 | 0.06 | 0.09 | 0.15 | 0.23 | 0.34 | 0.46 | 0.58 | 0.69 | 0.79 | 0.87 | 0.92 | 0.96 | 0.98 | 0.99 | 1.00 |
| 21 | 0.06 | 0.10 | 0.16 | 0.24 | 0.35 | 0.48 | 0.60 | 0.72 | 0.81 | 0.89 | 0.94 | 0.97 | 0.98 | 0.99 | 1.00 |
| 22 | 0.06 | 0.10 | 0.16 | 0.25 | 0.37 | 0.49 | 0.62 | 0.74 | 0.83 | 0.90 | 0.95 | 0.97 | 0.99 | 0.99 | 1.00 |
| 23 | 0.06 | 0.10 | 0.17 | 0.26 | 0.38 | 0.51 | 0.64 | 0.76 | 0.85 | 0.91 | 0.95 | 0.98 | 0.99 | 1.00 | 1.00 |
| 24 | 0.06 | 0.10 | 0.17 | 0.27 | 0.40 | 0.53 | 0.66 | 0.77 | 0.86 | 0.92 | 0.96 | 0.98 | 0.99 | 1.00 | 1.00 |
| 25 | 0.06 | 0.11 | 0.18 | 0.28 | 0.41 | 0.55 | 0.68 | 0.79 | 0.88 | 0.93 | 0.97 | 0.99 | 0.99 | 1.00 | 1.00 |
| 26 | 0.06 | 0.11 | 0.19 | 0.29 | 0.42 | 0.56 | 0.70 | 0.81 | 0.89 | 0.94 | 0.97 | 0.99 | 1.00 | 1.00 | 1.00 |
| 27 | 0.07 | 0.11 | 0.19 | 0.30 | 0.44 | 0.58 | 0.71 | 0.82 | 0.90 | 0.95 | 0.98 | 0.99 | 1.00 | 1.00 | 1.00 |
| 28 | 0.07 | 0.11 | 0.20 | 0.31 | 0.45 | 0.60 | 0.73 | 0.84 | 0.91 | 0.96 | 0.98 | 0.99 | 1.00 | 1.00 | 1.00 |
| 29 | 0.07 | 0.12 | 0.20 | 0.32 | 0.46 | 0.61 | 0.75 | 0.85 | 0.92 | 0.96 | 0.98 | 0.99 | 1.00 | 1.00 | 1.00 |
| 30 | 0.07 | 0.12 | 0.21 | 0.33 | 0.48 | 0.63 | 0.76 | 0.86 | 0.93 | 0.97 | 0.99 | 1.00 | 1.00 | 1.00 | 1.00 |

# APPENDIX E

# The *F* Distribution

Light face type are significant values for α=.05
**Bold face type** are significant values for α=.01

| *df*within (*N-k*) | *df*between (*k*-1) | | | | | | | | | | | | | | |
|---|---|---|---|---|---|---|---|---|---|---|---|---|---|---|---|
| | 1 | 2 | 3 | 4 | 5 | 6 | 7 | 8 | 9 | 10 | 11 | 12 | 14 | 16 | 20 |
| 1 | 161 | 200 | 216 | 225 | 230 | 234 | 237 | 239 | 241 | 242 | 243 | 244 | 245 | 246 | 248 |
| | **4052** | **4999** | **5403** | **5625** | **5764** | **5859** | **5928** | **5981** | **6022** | **6056** | **6082** | **6106** | **6142** | **6169** | **6208** |
| 2 | 18.51 | 19.00 | 19.16 | 19.25 | 19.30 | 19.33 | 19.36 | 19.37 | 19.38 | 19.39 | 19.40 | 19.41 | 19.42 | 19.43 | 19.44 |
| | **98.49** | **99.00** | **99.17** | **99.25** | **99.30** | **99.33** | **99.34** | **99.36** | **99.38** | **99.40** | **99.41** | **99.42** | **99.43** | **99.44** | **99.45** |
| 3 | 10.13 | 9.55 | 9.28 | 9.12 | 9.01 | 8.94 | 8.88 | 8.84 | 8.81 | 8.78 | 8.76 | 8.74 | 8.71 | 8.69 | 8.66 |
| | **34.12** | **30.82** | **29.46** | **28.71** | **28.24** | **27.91** | **27.67** | **27.49** | **27.34** | **27.23** | **27.13** | **27.05** | **26.92** | **26.83** | **26.69** |
| 4 | 7.71 | 6.94 | 6.59 | 6.39 | 6.26 | 6.16 | 6.09 | 6.04 | 6.00 | 5.96 | 5.93 | 5.91 | 5.87 | 5.84 | 5.80 |
| | **21.20** | **18.00** | **16.69** | **15.98** | **15.52** | **15.21** | **14.98** | **14.80** | **14.66** | **14.54** | **14.45** | **14.37** | **14.24** | **14.15** | **14.02** |
| 5 | 6.61 | 5.79 | 5.41 | 5.19 | 5.05 | 4.95 | 4.88 | 4.82 | 4.78 | 4.74 | 4.70 | 4.68 | 4.64 | 4.60 | 4.56 |
| | **16.26** | **13.27** | **12.06** | **11.39** | **10.97** | **10.67** | **10.45** | **10.27** | **10.15** | **10.05** | **9.96** | **9.89** | **9.77** | **9.68** | **9.55** |
| 6 | 5.99 | 5.14 | 4.76 | 4.53 | 4.39 | 4.28 | 4.21 | 4.15 | 4.10 | 4.06 | 4.03 | 4.00 | 3.96 | 3.92 | 3.87 |
| | **13.74** | **10.92** | **9.78** | **9.15** | **8.75** | **8.47** | **8.26** | **8.10** | **7.98** | **7.87** | **7.79** | **7.72** | **7.60** | **7.52** | **7.39** |
| 7 | 5.59 | 4.47 | 4.35 | 4.12 | 3.97 | 3.87 | 3.79 | 3.73 | 3.68 | 3.63 | 3.60 | 3.57 | 3.52 | 3.49 | 3.44 |
| | **12.25** | **9.55** | **8.45** | **7.85** | **7.46** | **7.19** | **7.00** | **6.84** | **6.71** | **6.62** | **6.54** | **6.47** | **6.35** | **6.27** | **6.15** |
| 8 | 5.32 | 4.46 | 4.07 | 3.84 | 3.69 | 3.58 | 3.50 | 3.44 | 3.39 | 3.34 | 3.31 | 3.28 | 3.23 | 3.20 | 3.15 |
| | **11.26** | **8.65** | **7.59** | **7.01** | **6.63** | **6.37** | **6.19** | **6.03** | **5.91** | **5.82** | **5.74** | **5.67** | **5.56** | **5.48** | **5.36** |
| 9 | 5.12 | 4.26 | 3.86 | 3.63 | 3.48 | 3.37 | 3.29 | 3.23 | 3.18 | 3.13 | 3.10 | 3.07 | 3.02 | 2.98 | 2.93 |
| | **10.56** | **8.02** | **6.99** | **6.42** | **6.06** | **5.80** | **5.62** | **5.47** | **5.35** | **5.26** | **5.18** | **5.11** | **5.00** | **4.92** | **4.80** |
| 10 | 4.96 | 4.10 | 3.71 | 3.48 | 3.33 | 3.22 | 3.14 | 3.07 | 3.02 | 2.97 | 2.94 | 2.91 | 2.86 | 2.82 | 2.77 |
| | **10.04** | **7.56** | **6.55** | **5.99** | **5.64** | **5.39** | **5.21** | **5.06** | **4.95** | **4.85** | **4.78** | **4.71** | **4.60** | **4.52** | **4.41** |
| 11 | 4.84 | 3.98 | 3.59 | 3.36 | 3.20 | 3.09 | 3.01 | 2.95 | 2.90 | 2.86 | 2.82 | 2.79 | 2.74 | 2.70 | 2.65 |
| | **9.65** | **7.20** | **6.22** | **5.67** | **5.32** | **5.07** | **4.88** | **4.74** | **4.63** | **4.54** | **4.46** | **4.40** | **4.29** | **4.21** | **4.10** |
| 12 | 4.75 | 3.88 | 3.49 | 3.26 | 3.11 | 3.00 | 2.92 | 2.85 | 2.80 | 2.76 | 2.72 | 2.69 | 2.64 | 2.60 | 2.54 |
| | **9.33** | **6.93** | **5.95** | **5.41** | **5.06** | **4.82** | **4.65** | **4.50** | **4.39** | **4.30** | **4.22** | **4.16** | **4.05** | **3.98** | **3.86** |
| 13 | 4.67 | 3.80 | 3.41 | 3.18 | 3.02 | 2.92 | 2.84 | 2.77 | 2.72 | 2.67 | 2.63 | 2.60 | 2.55 | 2.51 | 2.46 |
| | **9.07** | **6.70** | **5.74** | **5.20** | **4.86** | **4.62** | **4.44** | **4.30** | **4.19** | **4.10** | **4.02** | **3.96** | **3.85** | **3.78** | **3.67** |
| 14 | 4.60 | 3.74 | 3.34 | 3.11 | 2.96 | 2.85 | 2.77 | 2.70 | 2.65 | 2.60 | 2.56 | 2.53 | 2.48 | 2.44 | 2.39 |
| | **8.86** | **6.51** | **5.56** | **5.03** | **4.69** | **4.46** | **4.28** | **4.14** | **4.03** | **3.94** | **3.86** | **3.80** | **3.70** | **3.62** | **3.51** |
| 15 | 4.54 | 3.68 | 3.29 | 3.06 | 2.90 | 2.79 | 2.70 | 2.64 | 2.59 | 2.55 | 2.51 | 2.48 | 2.43 | 2.39 | 2.33 |
| | **8.68** | **6.36** | **5.42** | **4.89** | **4.56** | **4.32** | **4.14** | **4.00** | **3.89** | **3.80** | **3.73** | **3.67** | **3.56** | **3.48** | **3.36** |
| 16 | 4.49 | 3.63 | 3.24 | 3.01 | 2.85 | 2.74 | 2.66 | 2.59 | 2.54 | 2.49 | 2.45 | 2.42 | 2.37 | 2.33 | 2.28 |
| | **8.53** | **6.23** | **5.29** | **4.77** | **4.44** | **4.20** | **4.03** | **3.89** | **3.78** | **3.69** | **3.61** | **3.55** | **3.45** | **3.37** | **3.25** |
| 17 | 4.45 | 3.59 | 3.20 | 2.96 | 2.81 | 2.70 | 2.62 | 2.55 | 2.50 | 2.45 | 2.41 | 2.38 | 2.33 | 2.29 | 2.23 |
| | **8.40** | **6.11** | **5.18** | **4.67** | **4.34** | **4.10** | **3.93** | **3.79** | **3.68** | **3.59** | **3.52** | **3.45** | **3.35** | **3.27** | **3.16** |
| 18 | 4.41 | 3.55 | 3.16 | 2.93 | 2.77 | 2.66 | 2.58 | 2.51 | 2.46 | 2.41 | 2.37 | 2.34 | 2.29 | 2.25 | 2.19 |
| | **8.28** | **6.01** | **5.09** | **4.58** | **4.25** | **4.01** | **3.85** | **3.71** | **3.60** | **351** | **3.44** | **3.37** | **3.27** | **3.19** | **3.07** |
| 19 | 4.38 | 3.52 | 3.13 | 2.90 | 2.74 | 2.63 | 2.55 | 2.48 | 2.43 | 2.38 | 2.34 | 2.31 | 2.26 | 2.21 | 2.15 |
| | **8.18** | **5.93** | **5.01** | **4.50** | **4.17** | **3.94** | **3.77** | **3.63** | **3.52** | **3.43** | **3.36** | **3.30** | **3.19** | **3.12** | **3.00** |
| 20 | 4.35 | 3.49 | 3.10 | 2.87 | 2.71 | 2.60 | 2.52 | 2.45 | 2.40 | 2.35 | 2.31 | 2.28 | 2.23 | 2.18 | 2.12 |
| | **8.10** | **5.85** | **4.94** | **4.43** | **4.10** | **3.87** | **3.71** | **3.56** | **3.45** | **3.37** | **3.30** | **3.23** | **3.13** | **3.05** | **2.94** |
| 21 | 4.32 | 3.47 | 3.07 | 2.84 | 2.68 | 2.57 | 2.49 | 2.42 | 2.37 | 2.32 | 2.28 | 2.25 | 2.20 | 2.15 | 2.09 |
| | **8.02** | **5.78** | **4.87** | **4.37** | **4.04** | **3.81** | **3.65** | **3.51** | **3.40** | **3.31** | **3.24** | **3.17** | **3.07** | **2.99** | **2.88** |
| 22 | 4.30 | 3.44 | 3.05 | 2.82 | 2.66 | 2.55 | 2.47 | 2.40 | 2.35 | 2.30 | 2.26 | 2.23 | 2.18 | 2.13 | 2.07 |
| | **7.94** | **5.72** | **4.82** | **4.31** | **3.99** | **3.76** | **3.59** | **3.45** | **3.35** | **3.26** | **3.18** | **3.12** | **3.02** | **2.94** | **2.83** |
| 23 | 4.28 | 3.42 | 3.03 | 2.80 | 2.64 | 2.53 | 2.45 | 2.38 | 2.32 | 2.28 | 2.24 | 2.20 | 2.14 | 2.10 | 2.04 |
| | **7.88** | **5.66** | **4.76** | **4.26** | **3.94** | **3.71** | **3.54** | **3.41** | **3.30** | **3.21** | **3.14** | **3.07** | **2.97** | **2.89** | **2.78** |
| 24 | 4.26 | 3.40 | 3.01 | 2.78 | 2.62 | 2.51 | 2.43 | 2.36 | 2.30 | 2.26 | 2.22 | 2.18 | 2.13 | 2.09 | 2.02 |
| | **7.82** | **5.61** | **4.72** | **4.22** | **3.90** | **3.67** | **3.50** | **3.36** | **3.25** | **3.17** | **3.09** | **3.03** | **2.93** | **2.85** | **2.74** |
| 25 | 4.24 | 3.38 | 2.99 | 2.76 | 2.60 | 2.49 | 2.41 | 2.34 | 2.28 | 2.24 | 2.20 | 2.16 | 2.11 | 2.06 | 2.00 |
| | **7.77** | **5.57** | **4.68** | **4.18** | **3.86** | **3.63** | **3.46** | **3.32** | **3.21** | **3.13** | **3.05** | **2.99** | **2.89** | **2.81** | **2.70** |

| $df_{within}$ (N-k) | $df_{between}$ (k-1) 1 | 2 | 3 | 4 | 5 | 6 | 7 | 8 | 9 | 10 | 11 | 12 | 14 | 16 | 20 |
|---|---|---|---|---|---|---|---|---|---|---|---|---|---|---|---|
| 26 | 4.22 | 3.37 | 2.98 | 2.74 | 2.59 | 2.47 | 2.39 | 2.32 | 2.27 | 2.22 | 2.18 | 2.15 | 2.10 | 2.05 | 1.99 |
| | **7.72** | **5.53** | **4.64** | **4.14** | **3.82** | **3.59** | **3.42** | **3.29** | **3.17** | **3.09** | **3.02** | **2.96** | **2.86** | **2.77** | **2.66** |
| 27 | 4.21 | 3.35 | 2.96 | 2.73 | 2.57 | 2.46 | 2.37 | 2.30 | 2.25 | 2.20 | 2.16 | 2.13 | 2.08 | 2.03 | 1.97 |
| | **7.68** | **5.49** | **4.60** | **4.11** | **3.79** | **3.56** | **3.39** | **3.26** | **3.14** | **3.06** | **2.98** | **2.93** | **2.83** | **2.74** | **2.63** |
| 28 | 4.20 | 3.34 | 2.95 | 2.71 | 2.56 | 2.44 | 2.36 | 2.29 | 2.24 | 2.19 | 2.15 | 2.12 | 2.06 | 2.02 | 1.96 |
| | **7.64** | **5.45** | **4.57** | **4.07** | **3.76** | **3.53** | **3.36** | **3.23** | **3.11** | **3.03** | **2.95** | **2.90** | **2.80** | **2.71** | **2.60** |
| 29 | 4.18 | 3.33 | 2.93 | 2.70 | 2.54 | 2.43 | 2.35 | 2.28 | 2.22 | 2.18 | 2.14 | 2.10 | 2.05 | 2.00 | 1.94 |
| | **7.60** | **5.42** | **4.54** | **4.04** | **3.73** | **3.50** | **3.33** | **3.20** | **3.08** | **3.00** | **2.92** | **2.87** | **2.77** | **2.68** | **2.57** |
| 30 | 4.17 | 3.32 | 2.92 | 2.69 | 2.53 | 2.42 | 2.34 | 2.27 | 2.21 | 2.16 | 2.12 | 2.09 | 2.04 | 1.99 | 1.93 |
| | **7.56** | **5.39** | **4.51** | **4.02** | **3.70** | **3.47** | **3.30** | **3.17** | **3.06** | **2.98** | **2.90** | **2.84** | **2.74** | **2.66** | **2.55** |
| 32 | 4.15 | 3.30 | 2.90 | 2.67 | 2.51 | 2.40 | 2.32 | 2.25 | 2.19 | 2.14 | 2.10 | 2.07 | 2.02 | 1.97 | 1.91 |
| | **7.50** | **5.34** | **4.46** | **3.97** | **3.66** | **3.42** | **3.25** | **3.12** | **3.01** | **2.94** | **2.86** | **2.80** | **2.70** | **2.62** | **2.51** |
| 34 | 4.13 | 3.28 | 2.88 | 2.65 | 2.49 | 2.38 | 2.30 | 2.23 | 2.17 | 2.12 | 2.08 | 2.05 | 2.00 | 1.95 | 1.89 |
| | **7.44** | **5.29** | **4.42** | **3.93** | **3.61** | **3.38** | **3.21** | **3.08** | **2.97** | **2.89** | **2.82** | **2.76** | **2.66** | **2.58** | **2.47** |
| 36 | 4.11 | 3.26 | 2.86 | 2.63 | 2.48 | 2.36 | 2.28 | 2.21 | 2.15 | 2.10 | 2.06 | 2.03 | 1.98 | 1.93 | 1.87 |
| | **7.39** | **5.25** | **4.38** | **3.89** | **3.58** | **3.35** | **3.18** | **3.04** | **2.94** | **2.86** | **2.78** | **2.72** | **2.62** | **2.54** | **2.43** |
| 38 | 4.10 | 3.25 | 2.85 | 2.62 | 2.46 | 2.35 | 2.26 | 2.19 | 2.14 | 2.09 | 2.05 | 2.02 | 1.96 | 1.92 | 1.85 |
| | **7.35** | **5.21** | **4.34** | **3.86** | **3.54** | **3.32** | **3.15** | **3.02** | **2.91** | **2.82** | **2.75** | **2.69** | **2.59** | **2.51** | **2.40** |
| 40 | 4.08 | 3.23 | 2.84 | 2.61 | 2.45 | 2.34 | 2.25 | 2.18 | 2.12 | 2.07 | 2.04 | 2.00 | 1.95 | 1.90 | 1.84 |
| | **7.31** | **5.18** | **4.31** | **3.83** | **3.51** | **3.29** | **3.12** | **2.99** | **2.88** | **2.80** | **2.73** | **2.66** | **2.56** | **2.49** | **2.37** |
| 42 | 4.07 | 3.22 | 2.83 | 2.59 | 2.44 | 2.32 | 2.24 | 2.17 | 2.11 | 2.06 | 2.02 | 1.99 | 1.94 | 1.89 | 1.82 |
| | **7.27** | **5.15** | **4.29** | **3.80** | **3.49** | **3.26** | **3.10** | **2.96** | **2.86** | **2.77** | **2.70** | **2.64** | **2.54** | **2.46** | **2.35** |
| 44 | 4.06 | 3.21 | 2.82 | 2.58 | 2.43 | 2.31 | 2.23 | 2.16 | 2.10 | 2.05 | 2.01 | 1.98 | 1.92 | 1.88 | 1.81 |
| | **7.24** | **5.12** | **4.26** | **3.78** | **3.46** | **3.24** | **3.07** | **2.94** | **2.84** | **2.75** | **2.68** | **2.62** | **2.52** | **2.44** | **2.32** |
| 46 | 4.05 | 3.20 | 2.81 | 2.57 | 2.42 | 2.30 | 2.22 | 2.14 | 2.09 | 2.04 | 2.00 | 1.97 | 1.91 | 1.87 | 1.80 |
| | **7.21** | **5.10** | **4.24** | **3.76** | **3.44** | **3.22** | **3.05** | **2.92** | **2.82** | **2.73** | **2.66** | **2.60** | **2.50** | **2.42** | **2.30** |
| 48 | 4.04 | 3.19 | 2.80 | 2.56 | 2.41 | 2.30 | 2.21 | 2.14 | 2.08 | 2.03 | 1.99 | 1.96 | 1.90 | 1.86 | 1.79 |
| | **7.19** | **5.08** | **4.22** | **3.74** | **3.42** | **3.20** | **3.04** | **2.90** | **2.80** | **2.71** | **2.64** | **2.58** | **2.48** | **2.40** | **2.28** |
| 50 | 4.03 | 3.18 | 2.79 | 2.56 | 2.40 | 2.29 | 2.20 | 2.13 | 2.07 | 2.02 | 1.98 | 1.95 | 1.90 | 1.85 | 1.78 |
| | **7.17** | **5.06** | **4.20** | **3.72** | **3.41** | **3.18** | **3.02** | **2.88** | **2.78** | **2.70** | **2.62** | **2.56** | **2.46** | **2.39** | **2.26** |
| 55 | 4.02 | 3.17 | 2.78 | 2.54 | 2.38 | 2.27 | 2.18 | 2.11 | 2.05 | 2.00 | 1.97 | 1.93 | 1.88 | 1.83 | 1.76 |
| | **7.12** | **5.01** | **4.16** | **3.68** | **3.37** | **3.15** | **2.98** | **2.85** | **2.75** | **2.66** | **2.59** | **2.53** | **2.43** | **2.35** | **2.23** |
| 60 | 4.00 | 3.15 | 2.76 | 2.52 | 2.37 | 2.25 | 2.17 | 2.10 | 2.04 | 1.99 | 1.95 | 1.92 | 1.86 | 1.81 | 1.75 |
| | **7.08** | **4.98** | **4.13** | **3.65** | **3.34** | **3.12** | **2.95** | **2.82** | **2.72** | **2.63** | **2.56** | **2.50** | **2.40** | **2.32** | **2.20** |
| 65 | 3.99 | 3.14 | 2.75 | 2.51 | 2.36 | 2.24 | 2.15 | 2.08 | 2.02 | 1.98 | 1.94 | 1.90 | 1.85 | 1.80 | 1.73 |
| | **7.04** | **4.95** | **4.10** | **3.62** | **3.31** | **3.09** | **2.93** | **2.79** | **2.70** | **2.61** | **2.54** | **2.47** | **2.37** | **2.30** | **2.18** |
| 70 | 3.98 | 3.13 | 2.74 | 2.50 | 2.35 | 2.23 | 2.14 | 2.07 | 2.01 | 1.97 | 1.93 | 1.89 | 1.84 | 1.79 | 1.72 |
| | **7.01** | **4.92** | **4.08** | **3.60** | **3.29** | **3.07** | **2.91** | **2.77** | **2.67** | **2.59** | **2.51** | **2.45** | **2.35** | **2.28** | **2.15** |
| 80 | 3.96 | 3.11 | 2.72 | 2.48 | 2.33 | 2.21 | 2.12 | 2.05 | 1.99 | 1.95 | 1.91 | 1.88 | 1.82 | 1.77 | 1.70 |
| | **6.96** | **4.88** | **4.04** | **3.56** | **3.25** | **3.04** | **2.87** | **2.74** | **2.64** | **2.55** | **2.48** | **2.41** | **2.32** | **2.24** | **2.11** |
| 100 | 3.94 | 3.09 | 2.70 | 2.46 | 2.30 | 2.19 | 2.10 | 2.03 | 1.97 | 1.92 | 1.88 | 1.85 | 1.79 | 1.75 | 1.68 |
| | **6.90** | **4.82** | **3.98** | **3.51** | **3.20** | **2.99** | **2.82** | **2.69** | **2.59** | **2.51** | **2.43** | **2.36** | **2.26** | **2.19** | **2.06** |
| 125 | 3.92 | 3.07 | 2.68 | 2.44 | 2.29 | 2.17 | 2.08 | 2.01 | 1.95 | 1.90 | 1.86 | 1.83 | 1.77 | 1.72 | 1.65 |
| | **6.84** | **4.78** | **3.94** | **3.47** | **3.17** | **2.95** | **2.79** | **2.65** | **2.56** | **2.47** | **2.40** | **2.33** | **2.23** | **2.15** | **2.03** |
| 150 | 3.91 | 3.06 | 2.67 | 2.43 | 2.27 | 2.16 | 2.07 | 2.00 | 1.94 | 1.89 | 1.85 | 1.82 | 1.76 | 1.71 | 1.64 |
| | **6.81** | **4.75** | **3.91** | **3.44** | **3.14** | **2.92** | **2.76** | **2.62** | **2.53** | **2.44** | **2.37** | **2.30** | **2.20** | **2.12** | **2.00** |
| 200 | 3.89 | 3.04 | 2.65 | 2.41 | 2.26 | 2.14 | 2.05 | 1.98 | 1.92 | 1.87 | 1.83 | 1.80 | 1.74 | 1.69 | 1.62 |
| | **6.76** | **4.71** | **3.88** | **3.41** | **3.11** | **2.90** | **2.73** | **2.60** | **2.50** | **2.41** | **2.34** | **2.28** | **2.17** | **2.09** | **1.97** |
| 400 | 3.86 | 3.02 | 2.62 | 2.39 | 2.23 | 2.12 | 2.03 | 1.96 | 1.90 | 1.85 | 1.81 | 1.78 | 1.72 | 1.67 | 1.60 |
| | **6.70** | **4.66** | **3.83** | **3.36** | **3.06** | **2.85** | **2.69** | **2.55** | **2.46** | **2.37** | **2.29** | **2.23** | **2.12** | **2.04** | **1.92** |
| 1000 | 3.85 | 3.00 | 2.61 | 2.38 | 2.22 | 2.10 | 2.02 | 1.95 | 1.89 | 1.84 | 1.80 | 1.76 | 1.70 | 1.65 | 1.58 |
| | **6.66** | **4.62** | **3.80** | **3.34** | **3.04** | **2.82** | **2.66** | **2.53** | **2.43** | **2.34** | **2.26** | **2.20** | **2.09** | **2.01** | **1.89** |
| ∞ | 3.84 | 2.99 | 2.60 | 2.37 | 2.21 | 2.09 | 2.01 | 1.94 | 1.88 | 1.83 | 1.79 | 1.75 | 1.69 | 1.64 | 1.57 |
| | **6.64** | **4.60** | **3.78** | **3.32** | **3.02** | **2.80** | **2.64** | **2.51** | **2.41** | **2.32** | **2.24** | **2.18** | **2.07** | **1.99** | **1.87** |

# APPENDIX F
# Pearson Correlation

| | LEVEL OF SIGNIFICANCE FOR ONE-TAILED TEST | | | |
|---|---|---|---|---|
| | .05 | .025 | .01 | .005 |
| | LEVEL OF SIGNIFICANCE FOR TWO-TAILED TEST | | | |
| *df* = *n* - 2 | .10 | .05 | .02 | .01 |
| 1 | .988 | .997 | .9995 | .9999 |
| 2 | .900 | .950 | .980 | .990 |
| 3 | .805 | .878 | .934 | .959 |
| 4 | .729 | .811 | .882 | .917 |
| 5 | .669 | .754 | .833 | .874 |
| 6 | .622 | .707 | .789 | .834 |
| 7 | .582 | .666 | .750 | .798 |
| 8 | .549 | .632 | .716 | .765 |
| 9 | .521 | .602 | .685 | .735 |
| 10 | .497 | .576 | .658 | .708 |
| 11 | .476 | .553 | .634 | .684 |
| 12 | .458 | .532 | .612 | .661 |
| 13 | .441 | .514 | .592 | .641 |
| 14 | .426 | .497 | .574 | .623 |
| 15 | .412 | .482 | .558 | .606 |
| 16 | .400 | .468 | .542 | .590 |
| 17 | .389 | .456 | .528 | .575 |
| 18 | .378 | .444 | .516 | .561 |
| 19 | .369 | .433 | .503 | .549 |
| 20 | .360 | .423 | .492 | .537 |
| 21 | .352 | .413 | .482 | .526 |
| 22 | .344 | .404 | .472 | .515 |
| 23 | .337 | .396 | .462 | .505 |
| 24 | .330 | .388 | .453 | .496 |
| 25 | .323 | .381 | .445 | .487 |
| 26 | .317 | .374 | .437 | .479 |
| 27 | .311 | .367 | .430 | .471 |
| 28 | .306 | .361 | .423 | .463 |
| 29 | .301 | .355 | .416 | .456 |
| 30 | .296 | .349 | .409 | .449 |
| 35 | .275 | .325 | .381 | .418 |
| 40 | .257 | .304 | .358 | .393 |
| 45 | .243 | .288 | .338 | .372 |
| 50 | .231 | .273 | .322 | .354 |
| 60 | .211 | .250 | .295 | .325 |
| 70 | .195 | .232 | .274 | .302 |
| 80 | .183 | .217 | .256 | .283 |
| 90 | .173 | .205 | .242 | .267 |
| 100 | .164 | .195 | .230 | .254 |

# Appendix G
# Chi-Square Distribution

| | Proportion in Critical Region | | | | |
|---|---|---|---|---|---|
| *df* = *C* - 1 | 0.10 | 0.05 | 0.025 | 0.01 | 0.005 |
| 1 | 2.71 | 3.84 | 5.02 | 6.63 | 7.88 |
| 2 | 4.61 | 5.99 | 7.38 | 9.21 | 10.60 |
| 3 | 6.25 | 7.81 | 9.35 | 11.34 | 12.84 |
| 4 | 7.78 | 9.49 | 11.14 | 13.28 | 14.86 |
| 5 | 9.24 | 11.07 | 12.83 | 15.09 | 16.75 |
| 6 | 10.64 | 12.59 | 14.45 | 16.81 | 18.55 |
| 7 | 12.02 | 14.07 | 16.01 | 18.48 | 20.28 |
| 8 | 13.36 | 15.51 | 17.53 | 20.09 | 21.96 |
| 9 | 14.68 | 16.92 | 19.02 | 21.67 | 23.59 |
| 10 | 15.99 | 18.31 | 20.48 | 23.21 | 25.19 |
| 11 | 17.28 | 19.68 | 21.92 | 24.72 | 26.76 |
| 12 | 18.55 | 21.03 | 23.34 | 26.22 | 28.30 |
| 13 | 19.81 | 22.36 | 24.74 | 27.69 | 29.82 |
| 14 | 21.06 | 23.68 | 26.12 | 29.14 | 31.32 |
| 15 | 22.31 | 25.00 | 27.49 | 30.58 | 32.80 |
| 16 | 23.54 | 26.30 | 28.85 | 32.00 | 34.27 |
| 17 | 24.77 | 27.59 | 30.19 | 33.41 | 35.72 |
| 18 | 25.99 | 28.87 | 31.53 | 34.81 | 37.16 |
| 19 | 27.20 | 30.14 | 32.85 | 36.19 | 38.58 |
| 20 | 28.41 | 31.41 | 34.17 | 37.57 | 40.00 |
| 21 | 29.62 | 32.67 | 35.48 | 38.93 | 41.40 |
| 22 | 30.81 | 33.92 | 36.78 | 40.29 | 42.80 |
| 23 | 32.01 | 35.17 | 38.08 | 41.64 | 44.18 |
| 24 | 33.20 | 36.42 | 39.36 | 42.98 | 45.56 |
| 25 | 34.38 | 37.65 | 40.65 | 44.31 | 46.93 |
| 26 | 35.56 | 38.89 | 41.92 | 45.64 | 48.29 |
| 27 | 36.74 | 40.11 | 43.19 | 46.96 | 49.64 |
| 28 | 37.92 | 41.34 | 44.46 | 48.28 | 50.99 |
| 29 | 39.09 | 42.56 | 45.72 | 49.59 | 52.34 |
| 30 | 40.26 | 43.77 | 46.98 | 50.89 | 53.67 |
| 40 | 51.81 | 55.76 | 59.34 | 63.69 | 66.77 |
| 50 | 63.17 | 67.50 | 71.42 | 76.15 | 79.49 |
| 60 | 74.40 | 79.08 | 83.30 | 88.38 | 91.95 |
| 70 | 85.53 | 90.53 | 95.02 | 100.42 | 104.22 |
| 80 | 96.58 | 101.88 | 106.63 | 112.33 | 116.32 |
| 90 | 107.56 | 113.14 | 118.14 | 124.12 | 128.30 |
| 100 | 118.50 | 124.34 | 129.56 | 135.81 | 140.17 |

# Appendix H

# Answer Key

## Module 1

### *1.26V Examples*

1. IV-SAT scores; DV-GPA; design-correlational
2. IV-diet of oat bran; DV-cholesterol; design-experimental
3. IV-major; DV-amount of extracurricular activity; design-causal-comparative
4. IV-type of reading instruction; DV-reading achievement; design-quasi-experimental

### *1.27V Additional Practice*

1. IV-gender; DV-writing ability; design-causal comparative
2. IV-physical flexibility; DV-body mass; design-correlational
3. IV-laptop program; DV-reading achievement; design; quasi-experimental
4. IV-extended student orientation program; DV-student satisfaction; design-experimental
5. IV-political affiliation; DV-# of volunteer hours; design-causal-comparative

### *1.29 Exercises*

#### Reviewing Concepts

1. Since Dr. Burn's sample consists of freshmen at two small Midwest liberal arts colleges that are predominantly White; he can only generalize his results to students from similar colleges.
2. Random sampling helps ensure that the sample represents the population so that you can be more confident in generalizing the results to the population.
3. Descriptive statistics use numbers, tables, and graphs to summarize and describe the sample. Inferential statistics utilize sample data to study a relationship and generalize the results to the population.
4. No. Political affiliation is a categorical variable where the numbers only represent a category and have no numerical value.
5. Experimental research uses random assignment of individuals to groups, whereas quasi-experimental does not.

#### Applying Concepts

1a. IV-drug treatment (alirocumab); DV-LDL (bad) cholesterol
1b. IV-instructional format (flipped vs traditional); DV-English course grades
1c. IV-gender; DV-math achievement
1d. IV-minutes of exercise per week; DV-BMI

2. IV-bachelor's degree (yes/no); DV-income; design-causal-comparative
3. IV-number of hours of work per week; DV-GPA; design-correlational
4. IV-teaching method; DV-critical thinking skills; design-experimental
5. IV-norm vs Our University; DV-amount of alcohol use; design-causal-comparative
6. IV-gamblers vs non-gamblers; DV-optimism; design-causal-comparative
7. IV-method of financial aid training; DV-amount of loan debt; design-quasi-experimental

# Module 2

## 2.26V Examples

1.

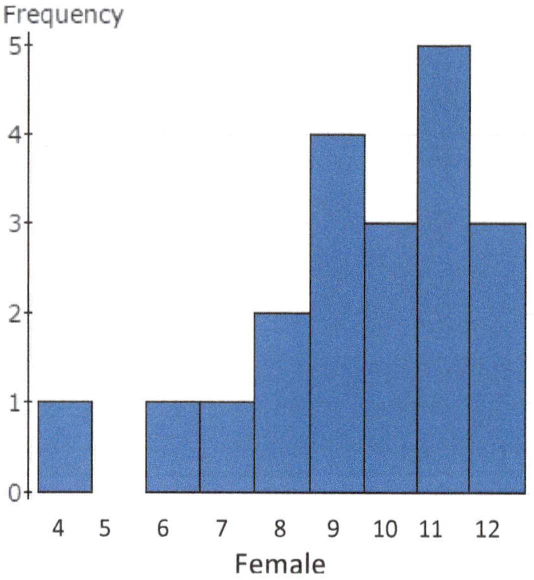


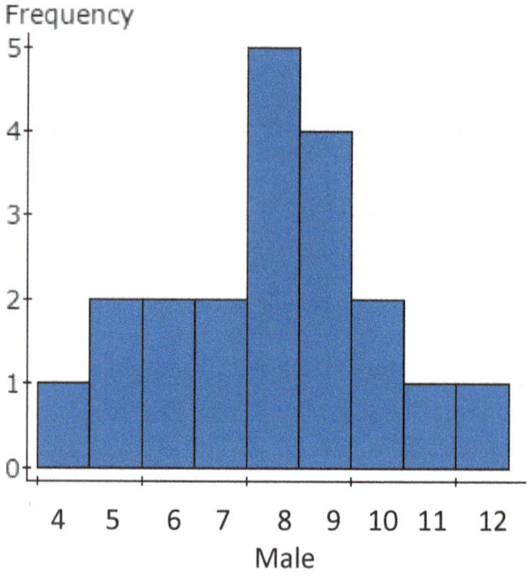


The sample females and males do seem to be fairly close to Robert's norm. Females are clustered around 10, while males are clustered around 8.

2. Three interval widths may be used to obtain 8-12 intervals:
    - Interval width =5; # of intervals=10; Starting interval =50; Approximate shape=slightly negatively skewed
    - Interval width =4; # of intervals=12; Starting interval =52; Approximate shape=slightly negatively skewed
    - Interval width =6; # of intervals=8; Starting interval =54; Approximate shape=slightly negatively skewed

## 2.27V Additional Practice

1. Pie chart is great at showing the <u>proportion</u> of the when Americans drink coffee, especially since the amounts are portions of a whole. A bar graph could also be used.

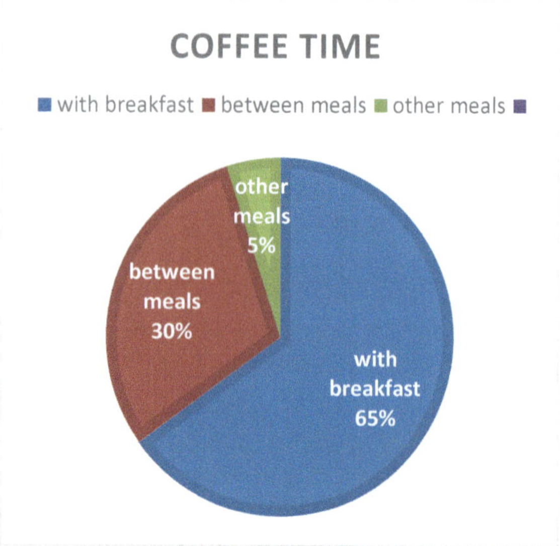


2.

| # Cups | *f* |
|---|---|
| 0 | 2 |
| 1 | 2 |
| 2 | 6 |
| 3 | 5 |
| 4 | 8 |
| 5 | 4 |
| 6 | 4 |
| 7 | 1 |
| 8 | 1 |
| 10 | 2 |

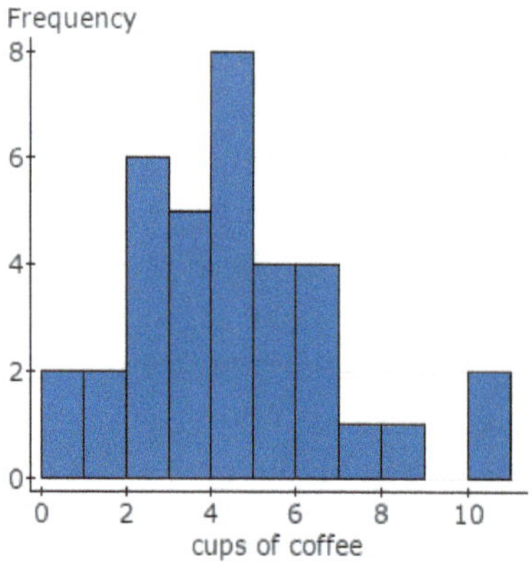

a. somewhat normal
b. College student definitely drink more than 3.1 cups per day.

3. Interval width =25; # of intervals=9; Starting interval =0-24; Approximate shape=normal

## 2.29V In the Literature

1. 12
2. No, male and female values are pretty close.
3. Household income less than $40,000 has the most credit card debt.
4. Household income over $80,000 has the least credit card debt.
5. Results are generalizable to upper class college students.

## 2.32 Exercises

### Reviewing the Concepts

1. The touching bars show the continuity of the scores.
2. Percentage gives a quick picture of the proportion of the group.
3. Pie chart is used to show how a total sample is divided across categories.
4. Grouped frequency distribution is used when the range of scores exceeds 20 and the sample size is greater than 20.
5. A normal distribution will have a symmetrical bell-shaped curve. A positively skewed distribution will have extreme scores (the tail) on the high end of the distribution and the curve on the low end. A negatively skewed distribution will have extreme scores (the tail) on the low end of the distribution and the curve on the high end.
6. Most consumers do not realize that reading a statistical graph requires accurately interpreting several aspects of the graph. The eye is so easily tricked; especially when being told an inaccurate conclusion.

### Interpreting Results

8a. Instagram
8b. Both Pinterest and Instagram saw 13% growth.
8c. Instagram
8d. To be close to 71.
8e. 2014 Facebook uses range between 68.1% and 73.9%

9a. Figure 1 should include the average income of a high school graduate over time.
9b. Obviously if a college graduate is unemployed for a year or more, lifetime income will decrease.

10a.StatCrunch histograms are presented in Example 1 of 2.26V. SPSS histogram is as follows.

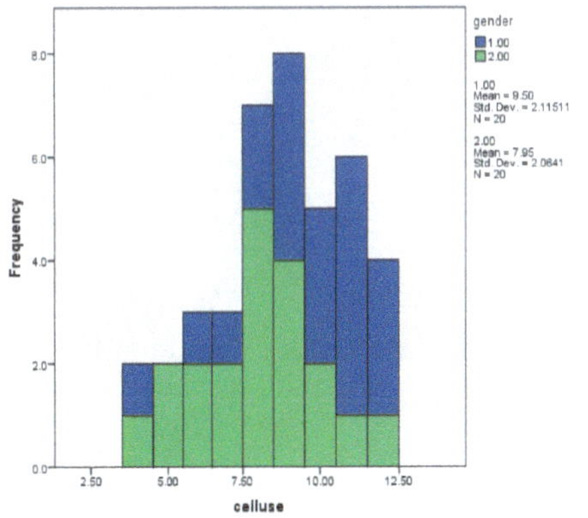


10b.The pie chart below is not very effective. It would be best to indicate that gender was equally represented.

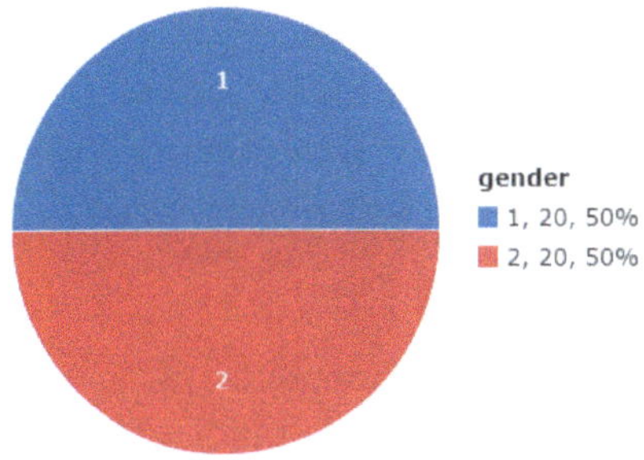

10c.A pie chart for a quantitative variable like hours of cell phone use is not very helpful since there are so many pieces of pie.

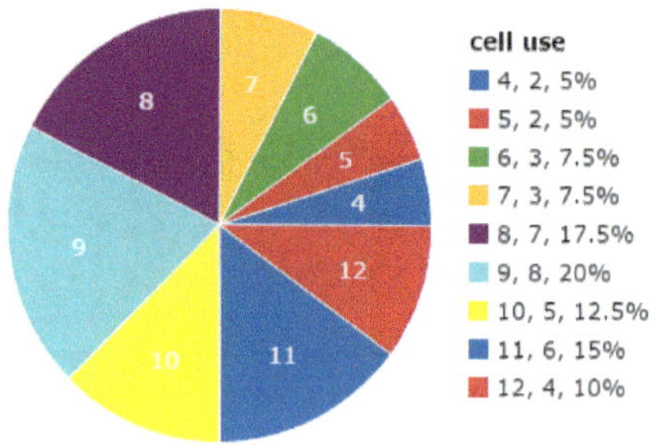


11a. Both StatCrunch and SPSS created histograms with a width of 25 for 9 intervals. However, these values may be different depending upon the defaults within your program.
11b. Hopefully, it is the same.
11c. As long as the generated histograms utilize 8-12 intervals, they are fairly accurate. But be careful, SPSS and StatCrunch will not always generate a histogram with 8-12 intervals. You may need to tell the program the desired width.

# Module 3

### *3.26 Examples*

1a. $M$ = 5.0; Median = 5; Mode = 5; Range = 4; $df$ = 13; $SD$ = 1.03
1b. Normal
1c. 92% (based on percentage of four or more drinks)

2a.

| | Honors Only | College Courses |
|---|---|---|
| Mean | 621.75 | 666.75 |
| Median | 610 | 663 |
| Range | 250 | 240 |
| *SD* | 70.08 | 68.72 |

2b. College Courses
2c. College Courses

3a. 68%
3b. 95%

### *3.27V Additional Practice*

1a. $M$ = 8; Median = 9; Mode = 9; Range = 8; $df$ = 14; $SD$ = 3.14
1b. Slight negative skew

### *3.29V In the Literature*

1. Females
2. **Males Higher** – Games, YouTube, Other Apps
   **Females Higher** – Calls, Texts, Email, Banking, Pictures, Calendar, Clock, Facebook, Twitter, Pinterest, Instagram, Internet, Amazon, CouponApps, Google Maps
   **About the Same** – Books, Bible, Pandora, iPod, iTunes

2a. 12
2b. No
3. Texting and Emails – Women
   Texting and Emails – Men

4. Pinterest is 24.9 range difference
5. Women texting – SD is large because scores are spread
6. Coupon Apps; negatively skewed
7. Yes

### 3.32 Exercises

1. For fairly normal distributions, the mean is the best measure to report. If the distribution is skewed, use the median and when reporting categorical variables, use the mode.

2a. Negative skew

2b. Positive skew

2c. Normal

3. Since the range only relies upon the two extremes scores of distribution it often doesn't provide an accurate description of the distribution spread. The standard deviation uses the mean as a reference point or standard to calculate the distance between each score and the mean.

4a. *SD*= 3.35

4b. *SD* = 2.53; Having more scores closer to the mean decreases the size of the standard deviation.

5a. 68%

5b. 95%

5c. Between 55 and 145

6a. Bonds – He had the highest mean

6b. Ruth, because he had the lowest mean

6c. Bonds

6d. Ruth had the greatest variability. Aaron had the least. Aaron was the most consistent because he had the smallest amount of variability. In addition, Aaron hit at least 10 homeruns each season, while there was at least one season in which Ruth didn't hit a homerun.

7a. Group 1 had greater tech use based upon the mean since the distribution was close to normal.

7b. The SD for both groups was very similar, meaning the data points were spread out across the range in the same way.

8a. Highest Scottish Pessimism score: Low SES; Highest English Pessimism score: Low SES

8b. Highest Scottish Optimism score: High SES; Highest English Optimism score: High SES

8c. There is a relationship between SES and Pessimism, but not for SES and Optimism

8d. The Scottish sample

9a.

| | *M* | Median | SD |
|---|---|---|---|
| Starting Price | 64.19 | 52.80 | 25.61 |
| City MPG | 18.40 | 19.50 | 3.31 |
| Highway MPG | 27.40 | 28.50 | 11.68 |

9b. Median; Prices range widely (*SD*= 25.1) and the higher extremes skew the mean.

9c. Mean; *SD* is small and mean and median are very close.

9d. The BMW 4-Series has the highest average MPG.

10a. Mean = 3.8 Range = 10
Median = 3 Degrees of freedom = 34
Mode = 2 Standard deviation = 2.6

10b. Close to normal curve (slightly positive skew)

10c. Comparable – within a cup

11a.

| | Females | Males |
|---|---|---|
| *N* | 20 | 20 |
| *M* | 9.5 | 7.95 |
| Median | 10 | 8 |
| Mode | 11 | 8 |
| SD | 2.11 | 2.06 |
| Range | 8 | 8 |

11b. Females

11c. Yes

# Module 4

### *4.26V Examples* *(Note: percentile rank has been rounded to a whole number)*

1. $z = 0.58$; Percentile Rank = 72
2. $z = -1.52$; Percentile Rank = 6
3. $z = 2.36$; Percentile Rank = 99
4. $p = 0.0091$
5. $z = -0.76$; Percentile Rank = 22
6. 143.54

### *4.27V Additional Practice*

1. $z$ (Brad) = 0.50; Percentile Rank = 69
   $z$ (Belle) = 2.00; Percentile Rank = 98
   The standard deviation for Women's heights is less than the standard deviation for Men's heights, making the Women's distribution skinnier.
2. $z = -1.43$; Percentile Rank = 8
3. $z$ (men's) = 1.00; Percentile Rank = 84
   $z$ (women's) = 2.57; Percentile Rank = 99

### *4.30 Exercises*

1. $p = 1/52 = .019$
2. The mean is the reference point
3. Percentile rank reflects the percent of values in the population or sample that falls *below* the raw score. The percentage correct on a test is the number correct divided by the total number of questions.
4. Since the graph is symmetric, showing negative $z$-scores would be repetitive.

5a. $z = -0.62$; Percentile Rank = 27
5b. $z = 0.36$; Percentile Rank = 64
5c. 586
5d. 23
5e. $p = 0.8790$

6a. $z = -0.80$; Percentile Rank = 0.2119
6b. 5.48%
6c. Between 5 and 10 lbs.
6d. 9.1 lbs.
6e. Student responses will vary

# Module 5

## 5.24V A Complete Example

1. $\sigma_M = 1$; $z = 2.00$; probability below = 0.9772; probability above = 0.0228
2. $\sigma_M = 0.5$; $z = -1.00$; probability below = 0.1587; probability above = 0.8413

## 5.25V Additional Practice

1a. $\sigma_M = 2$; $z = 1.50$; probability below = 0.9332; probability above = 0.02282

1b. $\sigma_M = 1.0$; $z = 1.00$; probability higher = 0.1587; 99% of sample falls between: 16.42 & 21.58

## 5.27V In the Literature

1. Greatest Difference: Science is one of my favorite subjects. The percentage of males who agree that one of their favorite subjects was science is a little over 13% higher than the percentage of females who felt the same way. With the SE for each group being slightly higher than 1%, the percentage of males with this opinion seems to be clearly higher than the percentage of females.
2. Smallest Difference was for "Like Mathematics" since responses to the 4-point Likert scale were more consistent.
3. Students' opinion on Science is more varied than their opinion on Mathematics.

## 5.28 Exercises

1. One cannot compare a sample (a group) to a population of individuals.
2. The mean stays the same because the distribution of sample means still includes the same individuals. The standard deviation changes because it is dependent on the sample size (n).

3. Standard Error is the standard amount of difference between the *M* (mean of the sample means) and $\mu$ of the original population

3a. Divide the standard deviation by the square root of the sample size (n)

3b. It decreases

4. Less error and the better the distribution is approximately normal

5a. Expected value = 80; Standard error = 2

5b. Expected value = 80; Standard error = 1

6a. Approximately zero

6b. Below: 0.1587; Higher: 0.8413

6c. Higher: zero; Between: 49.5 and 50.5

7a. 20

7b. 3

7c. Highest: Japan; Lowest: Spain

7d. The sample size is larger for international than any individual country

7e. Standard deviation is likely larger for the U.S. than Estonia

# Module 6

## 6.32V A Complete Example

**Step 1: Develop Hypotheses:**

a. Independent Variable = technology and gaming access Scale: Categorical
b. Dependent Variable = time spent playing videos Scale: Quantitative
c. One-tailed
d. Alternative hypothesis: The average time spent playing videos by all kids (age 8-18 years) is greater than 13.2 hours.
e. Null hypothesis: The average time spent playing videos by all kids (age 8-18 years) is equal to 13.2 hours.
f. Hypotheses notation. $H_1$: $\mu > 13.2$ $H_0$: $\mu = 13.2$

**Step 2: Establish significance criteria**

g. $\alpha = 0.05$

**Step 3: Calculate test statistic, effect size, confidence interval, and power**

h. $z_{calculated} = 1.76$ Level of significance ($p$) = 0.0396
i. Decision: reject null
j. Effect size = $d$ = 0.176
k. 95% confidence interval [12.93, 18.07]

**Step 4: Draw conclusion**

l. Conclusion: The increase in technology and gaming access ($n$=100, $M$=15.5) does significantly increase children's time spent playing videos when compared to 2007 ($\mu$=13.2, $\sigma$=13.1); $z$=1.76, $p$=.0396, one-tailed, Cohen's $d$=.18.

## 6.33V Additional Practice

### 1. Roberts (2014) Study

**Step 1: Develop Hypotheses:**

a. Independent Variable = major Scale: Categorical
b. Dependent Variable = minutes of cell phone use Scale: Quantitative
c. Two-tailed
d. Alternative hypothesis: The average levels of cell phone use for students majoring in technology related fields will differ from the norm (528 minutes).
e. Null hypothesis: The average levels of cell phone use for students majoring in technology related fields will not differ from the norm (528 minutes).
f. Hypotheses notation. $H_1$: $\mu \neq 528$ $H_0$: $\mu = 528$

**Step 2: Establish significance criteria**

g. $\alpha = 0.05$

**Step 3: Calculate test statistic, effect size, confidence interval, and power**

h. $z_{calculated} = 0.74$ Level of significance ($p$) = 0.4609
i. Decision: fail to reject null
j. Effect size = $d$ = 0.104
k. 95% confidence interval [463.33, 670.67]

**Step 4: Draw conclusion**

l. Conclusion: The average cell phone use for students majoring in technology fields ($n$=50, $M$=567) does not significantly differ from the cell phone use for college students in general ($\mu$=528, $\sigma$=374); $z$=0.74, $p$=.4609, two-tailed, Cohen's $d$=.104.

### 2. SAT Math Scores

**Step 1: Develop Hypotheses:**

a. Independent Variable = curriculum Scale: Categorical

b. Dependent Variable = SAT math scores Scale: Quantitative

c. One-tailed

d. Alternative hypothesis: The average SAT math score for students who have taken the new math curriculum will be higher than the norm (514 points).

e. Null hypothesis: The average SAT math score for students who have taken the new math curriculum will be not differ from the norm (514 points).

f. Hypotheses notation. $H_1$: $\mu > 514$ $H_0$: $\mu \leq 514$

**Step 2: Establish significance criteria**

g. $\alpha = 0.05$

**Step 3: Calculate test statistic, effect size, confidence interval, and power**

h. $z_{calculated} = 1.92$ Level of significance ($p$) = 0.0276

i. Decision: reject null

j. Effect size = $d$ = 0.136

k. 95% confidence interval [513.65, 546.35]

l. power=.601

**Step 4: Draw conclusion**

m. Conclusion: The average SAT math score for students who have taken the new math curriculum ($n$=200, $M$=530) is significantly higher than the average score for all students ($\mu$=514, $\sigma$=118); $z$=1.92, $p$=.0276, Cohen's $d$=.14, one-tailed.

## *6.37 Exercises*

### Reviewing the Concepts

1. To "prove" the alternative hypothesis, one would need all the information about the population (need 100% proof, which is impossible)
2. Directional hypothesis: examines a change in a specific direction. Non-directional hypothesis: just examines some relationship, effect, or difference—it isn't specific
3. Hypotheses are predictions about the population
4. An alpha level of .01 is more conservative since the critical region is smaller.
5. When a decision is made to support (not prove) the alternative hypothesis, one can conclude that the treatment did have an effect on the sample and therefore would likely occur in the population
6. Yes. Yes. The $p$-value in both cases is less than the significance criteria.
7. The $p$-value is probability of finding significance out of error
8. Type 1: Null hypothesis is rejected out of error
   Type 2: Fail to reject a false null
   Type 1 is more serious because when significant results are found, leaders are quick to act to implement change.
9. Tests of significance do not provide information regarding the size of a treatment effect; thus, it is informative to report the effect size. Confidence intervals estimate the treatment effect in the population.
10. Effect size is a measure of the size or magnitude of the treatment effect. A confidence interval estimates the population parameter (after treatment effect)
11. As power increases so does the chance of a Type II error.

### 12. Mozart Effect

**Step 1: Develop Hypotheses:**

a. Independent Variable = listening to Mozart Scale: Categorical
b. Dependent Variable = visual-spatial processing Scale: Quantitative
c. Two-tailed
d. Alternative hypothesis: Listening to Mozart will have a significant impact on average visual-spatial processing for college students.
e. Null hypothesis: Listening to Mozart will NOT have a significant impact on average visual-spatial processing for college students.
f. Hypotheses notation. $H_1: \mu \neq 10$ $H_0: \mu = 10$

**Step 2: Establish significance criteria**

g. $\alpha = 0.01$

**Step 3: Calculate test statistic, effect size, confidence interval, and power**

h. $z_{calculated} = 1.83$ Level of significance ($p$) = 0.0679
i. Decision: fail to reject null
j. Effect size = $d$ = 0.333
k. 99% confidence interval [9.59, 12.41]

**Step 4: Draw conclusion**

l. Conclusion: Listening to Mozart ($n$=30, $M$=11) does NOT significantly impact the average visual-spatial processing for college students ($\mu$=10, $\sigma$=3); $z$=1.83, $p$=.0679, two-tailed, Cohen's $d$=.33.

### 13. Women Basketball Height

**Step 1: Develop Hypotheses:**

a. Independent Variable = professional basketball Scale: Categorical
b. Dependent Variable = upper arm length Scale: Quantitative
c. One-tailed
d. Alternative hypothesis: Females in the WNBA have significantly longer upper arms than the norm of U.S. females over 20 years old ($\mu$=35.8).
e. Null hypothesis: Females in the WNBA do NOT have significantly longer upper arms than the norm of U.S. females over 20 years old ($\mu$=35.8).
f. Hypotheses notation. $H_1: \mu > 35.8$ $H_0: \mu \leq 35.8$

**Step 2: Establish significance criteria**

g. $\alpha = 0.05$

**Step 3: Calculate test statistic, effect size, confidence interval, and power**

h. $z_{calculated} = 8.09$ Level of significance ($p$) = <0.0001
i. Decision: reject null
j. Effect size = $d$ = 1.81
k. 95% confidence interval [38.68, 40.52]
l. power=1

**Step 4: Draw conclusion**

m. Conclusion: Females in the WNBA ($n$=20, $M$=39.6) do have a significantly longer average upper arm length when compared to U.S. females over 20 years old ($\mu$=35.8, $\sigma$=2.1); $z$=8.09, $p$=<0.0001, one-tailed, Cohen's $d$= 1.81.

## *Conducting the Analysis*

### 14. 2009 Census

**Step 1: Develop Hypotheses:**

a. Independent Variable = location — Scale: Categorical
b. Dependent Variable = commute times — Scale: Quantitative
c. One-tailed
d. Alternative hypothesis: NYC residents have significantly longer commute times than the U.S. norm ($\mu$=25.1).
e. Null hypothesis: NYC residents do NOT have significantly longer commute times than the U.S. norm ($\mu$=25.1).
f. Hypotheses notation. $H_1$: $\mu$ >25.1 $H_0$: $\mu \leq 25.1$

**Step 2: Establish significance criteria**

g. $\alpha$ = 0.01

**Step 3: Calculate test statistic, effect size, confidence interval, and power**

h. $z_{calculated}$ = 53.67 — Level of significance (*p*) = <0.0001
i. Decision: reject null
j. Effect size = *d* = 5.37
k. 99% confidence interval [79.27, 84.73]

**Step 4: Draw conclusion**

l. Conclusion: NYC residents (*n*=100, *M*=82) do have a significantly longer commute times than the U.S. norm ($\mu$=25.1, $\sigma$=10.6); *z*=53.67, *p*=<0.0001, one-tailed, Cohen's *d* = 5.37.

### 14. Only Child

**Step 1: Develop Hypotheses:**

a. Independent Variable = # of siblings — Scale: Categorical
b. Dependent Variable = vocabulary skills — Scale: Quantitative
c. One-tailed
d. Alternative hypothesis: Children from one child families have significantly greater vocabulary skills than the norm ($\mu$=60).
e. Null hypothesis: Children from one child families do NOT have significantly greater vocabulary skills than the norm ($\mu$=60).
f. Hypotheses notation. $H_1$: $\mu$ >60 $H_0$: $\mu \leq 60$

**Step 2: Establish significance criteria**

g. $\alpha$ = 0.05

**Step 3: Calculate test statistic, effect size, confidence interval, and power**

h. $z_{calculated}$ = 1.39 — Level of significance (*p*) = .0823
i. Decision: fail to reject null
j. Effect size = *d* = .44
k. 95% confidence interval [58.2, 70.6]

**Step 4: Draw conclusion**

l. Conclusion: Children from one child families (*n*=10, *M*=64.4) do NOT have a significantly greater vocabulary skills than the norm ($\mu$=60, $\sigma$=10); *z*=1.39, *p*=0.0823, one-tailed, Cohen's *d*=.44.

# Module 7

## *7.26V Additional Practice*

### 1. Google Work Place

**Step 1: Develop Hypotheses:**

a. Independent Variable = work environment Scale: Categorical
b. Dependent Variable = sense of well-being Scale: Quantitative
c. Two-tailed
d. Alternative hypothesis: A supportive environment significantly impacts a sense of well-being ($\mu$=50) among its employees.
e. Null hypothesis: A supportive environment does NOT significantly impact a sense of well-being ($\mu$=50) among its employees.
f. Hypotheses notation. $H_1: \mu \neq 50$ $H_0: \mu = 50$

**Step 2: Establish significance criteria**

g. $\alpha = 0.05$

**Step 3: Calculate test statistic, effect size, confidence interval, and power**

h. $t = 3.66$ Level of significance ($p$) = .003
i. Decision: reject null
j. Effect size = $d$ = .98
k. 95% CI of Difference [2.98, 11.59]

**Step 4: Draw conclusion**

l. Conclusion: Google employees, who work in a supportive work environment ($M$ = 57.286, $SD$ = 7.457) do have a significantly different sense of well-being than the norm ($\mu$=50); $t(13) = 3.66$, $p$=.003, two-tailed, Cohen's $d$=.98, 95% CI of Difference [2.98, 11.59].

### 2. Spiritual Conviction

**Step 1: Develop Hypotheses:**

a. Independent Variable = spiritual conviction Scale: Categorical
b. Dependent Variable = purpose/meaning in life Scale: Quantitative
c. One-tailed
d. Alternative hypothesis: College students who have reported strong spiritual convictions report more meaning and purpose in life than the norm ($\mu$ = 109).
e. Null hypothesis: College students who have reported strong spiritual convictions will NOT report more meaning and purpose in life than the norm ($\mu$ = 109).
f. Hypotheses notation. $H_1: \mu > 109$ $H_0: \mu \leq 109$

**Step 2: Establish significance criteria**

g. $\alpha = 0.05$

**Step 3: Calculate test statistic, effect size, confidence interval, and power**

h. $t = .719$ Level of significance ($p$) = .2403
i. Decision: fail to reject null
j. Effect size = $d$ = .16, low.
k. 95% confidence interval [105.47, 116.23]

**Step 4: Draw conclusion**

l. Conclusion: College students who have reported strong spiritual convictions ($M$ = 105.9, $SD$ = 25.12) do not experience significantly more meaning and purpose in life than the norm ($\mu$=109); $t(20) = -0.55$, $p$=.7063, one-tailed, Cohen's $d$=-0.123

### 7.28V In the Literature

1. Summarize pattern of results; *p*=.02
2. Determine whether an inference is supported by information.
   Explain how changes might affect a solution.
   Identify additional information.
   Provide relevant alternative interpretations.

3a. Reject the null

3b. Students majoring in agricultural education (*M* = 16.42, *SD* = 4.15) scored significantly different overall on the CAT than the norm ($\mu$=19.04); $t(74) = -5.48$, *p*=<0.01, two-tailed, Cohen's *d*=0.51.

4. A *t*-test is much more common. A z-test isn't even available in SPSS.
5. Identify additional information; large.
6. No. Students scored lower on all (five of which were significantly lower) but two skill areas. Also, these students scored significantly lower than the national norm on the CAT total score.

### 7.31 Exercises

### Reviewing Concepts

1. The population standard deviation is not known for a *t*-test, therefore is estimated using the sample standard deviation.
2. The population standard deviation is not known.
3. Greater than 120.
4. At $\alpha$=.05, yes since .0134 is less than .05.
   At $\alpha$=.01, no since .0134 is greater than than .01.
5. $t_{critical}$ = - 2.65. No, you do not have significance since $t_{calculated}$=3.29 (positive). Since we are predicting that the sample will be less than the norm, the $t_{calculated}$ fall beyond the tcritical of -2.65.
6. As the confidence increases from 95% to 99%, the interval width increases so we can be more accurate.
7. A *t* test only provides an indication of "significance"—the likelihood of obtaining the result out of error or chance. The test is a function of the sample size. The effect size is not a function of the sample size and provides an indication of the size of the treatment effect.

### Interpreting Results

**8. 4th Grade Reading**

**Step 1: Develop Hypotheses:**

a. Independent Variable = special course on reading/test-taking — Scale: Categorical
b. Dependent Variable = statewide 4th grade reading exam — Scale: Quantitative
c. Two-tailed
d. Alternative hypothesis: Students who receive a semester course on test taking skills and reading strategies score significantly different from the population norm ($\mu$=71) on the statewide 4th grade reading exam.
e. Null hypothesis: Students who receive a semester course on test taking skills and reading strategies do NOT score significantly different from the population norm ($\mu$=71) on the statewide 4th grade reading exam.
f. Hypotheses notation. $H_1: \mu \neq 71$ $H_0: \mu = 71$

**Step 2: Establish significance criteria**

g. $\alpha = 0.05$

**Step 3: Calculate test statistic, effect size, confidence interval, and power**

h. $t = 2.188$ — Level of significance (*p*) = .034
i. Decision: reject null
j. Effect size = *d* = .3125
k. 95% confidence interval difference [0.16, 3.76]

**Step 4: Draw conclusion**

l. Conclusion: Students who receive a semester course on test taking skills and reading strategies ($M$ = 73, $SD$ = 6.27) do score significantly different from the population norm ($\mu$ =71) on the statewide 4th grade reading exam; $t(48) = 2.19$, $p$=.034, two-tailed, Cohen's $d$=0.31, 95% CI difference [0.16, 3.76].

## 9. Sleep among College Students

**Step 1: Develop Hypotheses:**

a. Independent Variable = undergraduate college attendance — Scale: Categorical
b. Dependent Variable = amount of sleep — Scale: Quantitative
c. One-tailed
d. Alternative hypothesis: College students report significantly less sleep than the recommended 7 hours per night.
e. Null hypothesis: College students do NOT report significantly less sleep than the recommended 7 hours per night.
f. Hypotheses notation. $H_1$: $\mu < 7$ $H_0$: $\mu \geq 7$

**Step 2: Establish significance criteria**

g. $\alpha = 0.05$

**Step 3: Calculate test statistic, effect size, confidence interval, and power**

h. $t = -6.8$ Level of significance ($p$) = <.0001
i. Decision: reject null
j. Effect size = $d$ = -.68
k. 95% confidence interval [5.9, 6.4]

**Step 4: Draw conclusion**

m. Conclusion: College students at this university ($M$ = 6.15, $SD$ = 1.25) report significantly less sleep than the recommend amount ($\mu$=7); $t(99) = -6.8$, $p$=<0.0001, one-tailed, Cohen's $d$=-0.68, 95% CI [5.9, 6.4].

## 10. Eating and Temperature

**Step 1: Develop Hypotheses:**

a. Independent Variable = temp (50° vs norm of 72°) — Scale: Categorical
b. Dependent Variable = amount of food per day — Scale: Quantitative
c. One-tailed
d. Alternative hypothesis: A decrease in temperature to 50° significantly increases the amount of food that rats eat per day when compared to the norm at 72° ($\mu$ =21).
e. Null hypothesis: A decrease in temperature significantly will NOT increases the amount of food that rats eat per day when compared to the norm ($\mu$ =21).
f. Hypotheses notation. $H_1$: $\mu > 21$ $H_0$: $\mu \leq 21$

**Step 2: Establish significance criteria**

g. $\alpha = 0.01$

**Step 3: Calculate test statistic, effect size, confidence interval, and power**

h. $t = 11.02$ Level of significance ($p$) = <.0001
i. Decision: reject null
j. Effect size = $d$ = 2.46
k. 99% confidence interval difference [5.26, 8.94]
l. Power=1, therefore we are confident in generalizing to the population.

**Step 4: Draw conclusion**

m. Conclusion: Decreasing the temperature to 50° significantly increases the amount of food that rats eat per day ($M$ = 28.1, $SD$ = 2.88) when compared to the norm at 72° ($\mu$ =21); $t(19) = 11.02$, $p$<.0001, one-tailed, Cohen's $d$=2.46, 99% CI difference [5.26, 8.94].

### 11. Overestimation of Ability

11a. Incompetent individuals (*M* = 66) will overestimate their ability to recognize what is funny when compared with their more competent peers ($\mu$ = 50).

11b. $H_1$: $\mu > 50$

11c. 50

11d. Incompetent individuals (*M* = 66) significantly overestimate their ability to recognize what is funny when compared with their more competent peers ($\mu$ = 50); $t(64) = 7.02$, $p<.0001$, one-tailed.

11e. Effect size cannot be calculated since standard deviation is not provided.

## *Conducting Analysis*

### 12. Gambling and Optimisim

SPSS Output

**One-Sample Statistics**

| | N | Mean | Std. Deviation | Std. Error Mean |
|---|---|---|---|---|
| Optimism | 21 | 5.7619 | 1.44585 | .31551 |

**One-Sample Test**

| | Test Value = 5 | | | | | |
|---|---|---|---|---|---|---|
| | | | | | 99% Confidence Interval of the Difference | |
| | t | df | Sig. (2-tailed) | Mean Difference | Lower | Upper |
| Optimism | 2.415 | 20 | .025 | .76190 | -.1358 | 1.6596 |

**Step 1: Develop Hypotheses:**

a. Independent Variable = Gambling at least once/month vs norm — Scale: Categorical

b. Dependent Variable = positive thinking — Scale: Quantitative

c. One-tailed

d. Alternative hypothesis: Gamblers have significantly higher levels of positive thinking or optimism than the norm ($\mu$ = 5).

e. Null hypothesis: Gamblers do NOT have significantly higher levels of positive thinking or optimism than the norm ($\mu$ = 5).

f. Hypotheses notation. $H_1$: $\mu > 5$ $H_0$: $\mu \leq 5$

**Step 2: Establish significance criteria**

g. $\alpha = 0.01$

**Step 3: Calculate test statistic, effect size, confidence interval, and power**

h. $t = 2.415$ Level of significance ($p$) = .0125

i. Decision: fail to reject null

j. Effect size = $d$ = .527

k. 99% confidence interval difference [-0.15, 1.66]

l. Power=.467, which does not meet the recommended power of .80. Therefore, our ability to generalize the results to the population is weak.

**Step 4: Draw conclusion**

m. Conclusion: Gamblers (*M* = 5.76, *SD* = 1.45) do not have significantly higher levels of positive thinking or optimism than the norm ($\mu$ =5); $t(20) = 2.42$, $p$=.013, one-tailed, Cohen's $d$=0.53, 99% CI difference [-0.15, 1.66].

### 13. Phone Donations

**StatCrunch Output**

**One sample T hypothesis test:**
μ : Mean of variable
$H_0 : \mu = 25$
$H_A : \mu > 25$

| Variable | Sample Mean | Std. Err. | DF | T-Stat | P-value |
|---|---|---|---|---|---|
| donation$ | 40 | 7.5645371 | 9 | 1.9829369 | 0.0393 |

**95% confidence interval results:**

| Variable | Sample Mean | Std. Err. | DF | L. Limit | U. Limit |
|---|---|---|---|---|---|
| donation$ | 40 | 7.5645371 | 9 | 22.887828 | 57.112172 |

**Step 1: Develop Hypotheses:**

a. Independent Variable = contact method (phone vs norm) Scale: Categorical
b. Dependent Variable = donation amount Scale: Quantitative
c. One-tailed
d. Alternative hypothesis: Phone contributions significantly exceed the norm donation amount of $25.
e. Null hypothesis: Phone contributions do NOT significantly exceed the norm donation amount of $25.
f. Hypotheses notation. $H_1: \mu > 25$ $H_0: \mu \leq 25$

**Step 2: Establish significance criteria**

g. $\alpha = 0.05$

**Step 3: Calculate test statistic, effect size, confidence interval, and power**

h. $t = 1.98$ Level of significance ($p$) = .0393
i. Decision: reject null
j. Effect size = $d$ = .627
k. 95% confidence interval [22.89, 57.11]
l. Using Power Table in Appendix D1 for a one-tailed test, $\alpha$=.05, $n$=10, and $d$=.60, Power=.52, which does not meet the .80 recommendation.

**Step 4: Draw conclusion**

m. Conclusion: Phone techniques ($M$ = 40, $SD$ = 23.92) do significantly exceed the norm donation amount (μ =25); $t(9) = 1.98$, $p$=.0395, one-tailed, Cohen's $d$=0.627, 95% CI [22.89, 57.11].

# Module 8

## *8.26V Additional Practice*

### 1. Swim Training

**Step 1: Develop Hypotheses:**

a. Independent Variable = Type of off-season swim training Scale: Categorical
b. Dependent Variable = race time of 100 m Scale: Quantitative
c. two-tailed
d. Alternative hypothesis: Type of off-season swim training (interval sprints vs distance) will significantly impact 100m freestyle race times.
e. Null hypothesis: Type of off-season swim training (interval sprints vs distance) will Not significantly impact 100m freestyle race times.
f. Hypotheses notation. $H_1: \mu_{sprint} - \mu_{ddistance} \neq 0$ $H_0: \mu_{sprint} - \mu_{ddistance} = 0$

**Step 2: Establish significance criteria**

g. $\alpha = 0.05$

**Step 3: Calculate test statistic, effect size, confidence interval, and power**

h. $t = -2.104$ Level of significance ($p$) = .069
i. Decision: fail to reject null
j. Effect size = $r^2$= .356
k. 95% confidence interval difference [-1.97, 0.09]

**Step 4: Draw conclusion**

l. Conclusion: Type of off-season swim training (interval sprints vs distance) does not significantly impact 100m freestyle race times; $t(8)$=-2.104, $p$=.069, two-tailed, $r^2$= .356.

## 2. Roberts Cell Phone Study

**Step 1: Develop Hypotheses:**

a. Independent Variable = gender Scale: Categorical
b. Dependent Variable = number of texts per week Scale: Quantitative
c. one-tailed
d. Alternative hypothesis: High school females text significantly more per week than males.
e. Null hypothesis: High school females do NOT text significantly more per week than males.
f. Hypotheses notation. $H_1: \mu_{females} - \mu_{males} > 0$ $H_0: \mu_{females} - \mu_{males} \leq 0$

**Step 2: Establish significance criteria**

g. $\alpha = 0.05$

**Step 3: Calculate test statistic, effect size, confidence interval, and power**

h. $t = 2.84$ Level of significance ($p$) = .0036
i. Decision: reject null
j. Effect size = $d$ =.90
k. Power = .99, which indicates strong confidence in generalizing to the population.

**Step 4: Draw conclusion**

l. Conclusion: High school females text significantly more per week than males; $t(38)=2.84$, $p$=.0036, one-tailed, Cohen's $d$=.90.

## *8.28 In the Literature*

1. Personality types (A and B)
2. Reaction time, number of errors, and memory
3. Personaliity Type A individuals will perform faster on the Test of Reaction Speed than those with Type B personality.
   Personaliity Type A individuals will have more errors on the Peeron Test of Accuracy than those with Type B personality.
   Personaliity Type A individuals will remember less on the Verbal Memory Test than those with Type B personality.—This hypothesis is tricky since the authors aren't specific about memory.

4a. Type A took less time, so they were faster. The result is not significant ($p$=.068).
4b. Type A recorded more errors. The result is significant ($p$=.01).
4c. Type A remembered more words. The result is significant ($p$=.001).
5. Results are mixed. Although Type A individuals were faster, this was not significant. And although Type A had more errors on the Peeron Test, they were able to remember more words on the Verbal Memory Test.

## *8.31 Exercises*

### Reviewing the Concepts

1. Single Sample t compares a sample mean to a population mean. Independent Sample t compares two sample means.
2. Pooled variance takes into account different group sizes by giving greater weight to the larger group.
3. If a Levene's test is significant ($p$<.05), then we CANNOT assume equal variances.
4. The group difference in the population.
5. Cohen's $d$ is the size of the effect based upon some standard deviation. $R^2$ represents the proportion of variance explained by the treatment. They are evaluated differently. An $r^2$ of .25 is a large effect, whereas Cohen's $d$ must be at least .8 to be considered large.
6. Minimum sample size is 64, or 32 per group.

| $r^2$ | Cohen's $d$ | Size of Effect |
|---|---|---|
| < 0.09 | < 0.2 | Small |
| 0.09 – 0.25 | 0.2 – 0.8 | Medium |
| > 0.25 | > 0.8 | Large |

## Interpreting the Results

### 7. Partner Violence

**Step 1: Develop Hypotheses:**

a. Independent Variable = Being in an abusive relationship Scale: Categorical
b. Dependent Variable = self-esteem Scale: Quantitative
c. one-tailed
d. Alternative hypothesis: College females in an abusive relationship have significantly lower self-esteem than non-abused college women.
e. Null hypothesis: College females in an abusive relationship do NOT have significantly lower self-esteem than non-abused college women.
f. Hypotheses notation. $H_1$: $\mu_{\text{abused}} - \mu_{\text{not abused}} < 0$ $H_0$: $\mu_{\text{abused}} - \mu_{\text{not abused}} \geq 0$

**Step 2: Establish significance criteria**

g. $\alpha = 0.01$

**Step 3: Calculate test statistic, effect size, confidence interval, and power**

h. $t$ = -3.147 Level of significance ($p$) = .0035 (divided in half since 1-tailed)
i. Decision: reject null
j. Effect size = $r^2$ =.89
k. 99% confidence interval difference [-9.46, -1.79]
l. Power = .87, which indicates strong confidence in generalizing to the population.

**Step 4: Draw conclusion**

m. Conclusion: High school females text significantly more per week than males; $t(38)=2.84$, $p=.0036$, one-tailed, Cohen's $d=.89$, 99% CI difference [-9.46, -1.79].

### 8. Problematic Internet Use

**Step 1: Develop Hypotheses:**

a. Independent Variable = Computer ownership Scale: Categorical
b. Dependent Variable = Problematic internet use Scale: Quantitative
c. two-tailed
d. Alternative hypothesis: Computer ownership significantly effects problematic internet use scores among college students.
e. Null hypothesis: Computer ownership does NOT significantly effects problematic internet use scores among college students.
f. Hypotheses notation. $H_1$: $\mu_{\text{comp}} - \mu_{\text{no comp}} \neq 0$ $H_0$: $\mu_{\text{comp}} - \mu_{\text{no comp}} = 0$

**Step 2: Establish significance criteria**

g. $\alpha = 0.05$

**Step 3: Calculate test statistic, effect size, confidence interval, and power**

h. $t$ = -.72 Level of significance ($p$) = .47
i. Decision: fail to reject null
j. 95% CI [-12.65, 5.59]

**Step 4: Draw conclusion**

l. Conclusion: Computer ownership does NOT significantly effects problematic internet use scores among college students.; $t(390)=-.72$, $p=.47$, two-tailed.

### 9. Women of Color

a. Items 2, 4, 5, and 6 were all significant. White women scored higher for all items except item 4.
b. Positive $t$ indicates White women scored higher; negative $t$ indicates non-White women scored higher.
c. $p=.0000$ should never be report, rather use $p<.0001$ since there is always some error.
d. $r^2=.043$, which is a small effect.
e. Items 1, 3, 7, and 8.
f. Women of color perceive that their race has limited their opportunities and that they receive less support from men and women when compared to White women.

### 10. Cell Phone Use

a. Texting-females, email-females, pictures-females, games-males, calendar-females, clock-females, Facebook-females, Pinterest-females, Instagram-females
b. No, most researchers will just use asterisks.
c. Among the significant results, all **bold** effect sizes are medium except for Pinterest use, which is large.
d. Using the online effect size calculator, Cohen's *d*=.384, which is a medium effect.
e. Females having higher cell phone use for most activities, except games, books, YouTube, Pandora, and other apps.

## Conducting the Analysis

### 11. Summer Reading Program

**StatCrunch Output**
**Two-tailed T hypothesis test:**
$\mu_1$ : Mean of var2 where var1=1
$\mu_2$ : Mean of var2 where var1=2
$\mu_1 - \mu_2$ : Difference between two means
$H_0 : \mu_1 - \mu_2 = 0$
$H_A : \mu_1 - \mu_2 > 0$
(without pooled variances)

**Hypothesis test results:**

| Difference | Sample Diff. | Std. Err. | DF | T-Stat | P-value |
|---|---|---|---|---|---|
| $\mu_1 - \mu_2$ | 10.566667 | 7.8053462 | 23 | 1.353773 | 0.0945 |

**95% confidence interval results:**

| Difference | Sample Diff. | Std. Err. | DF | L. Limit | U. Limit |
|---|---|---|---|---|---|
| $\mu_1 - \mu_2$ | 10.566667 | 7.8053462 | 23 | -5.5799222 | 26.713256 |

**Step 1: Develop Hypotheses:**

a. Independent Variable = Summer reading program — Scale: Categorical
b. Dependent Variable = oral reading fluency (DIBELS) — Scale: Quantitative
c. one-tailed
d. Alternative hypothesis: The summer library reading program significantly increase oral reading fluency (words correct) among third grade students.
e. Null hypothesis: The summer library reading program does not significantly increase oral reading fluency (words correct) among third grade students.
f. Hypotheses notation. $H_1$: $\mu_{RP} - \mu_{no\ RP} > 0$ $H_0$: $\mu_{RP} - \mu_{no\ RP} \leq 0$

**Step 2: Establish significance criteria**

g. $\alpha = 0.05$

**Step 3: Calculate test statistic, effect size, confidence interval, and power**

h. $t = 1.35$ Level of significance ($p$) = .0945
i. Decision: fail to reject null
j. Effect size = $r^2$ =.07
k. 95% confidence interval [-5.58, 26.71]
l. Minimum sample size = 50 or 25 per group.

**Step 4: Draw conclusion**

m. Conclusion: The summer library reading program does not significantly increase oral reading fluency (words correct) among third grade students; $t(23)$= 1.35, $p$=.09, one-tailed, $r^2$=07.

### 12. Child-rearing

**SPSS Output**

**Independent Samples Test**

| | | Levene's Test for Equality of Variances | | t-test for Equality of Means | | | | | 95% Confidence Interval of the Difference | |
|---|---|---|---|---|---|---|---|---|---|---|
| | | F | Sig. | t | df | Sig. (2-tailed) | Mean Difference | Std. Error Difference | Lower | Upper |
| control | Equal variances assumed | .002 | .962 | 2.266 | 14 | .040 | 8.12500 | 3.58537 | .43514 | 15.81486 |
| | Equal variances not assumed | | | 2.266 | 13.845 | .040 | 8.12500 | 3.58537 | .42706 | 15.82294 |

**Step 1: Develop Hypotheses:**

a. Independent Variable = Parental culture (Chinese/US) Scale: Categorical

b. Dependent Variable = Parental control Scale: Quantitative

c. two-tailed

d. Alternative hypothesis: Parental culture (Chinese/US) will significantly affect parental control.

e. Null hypothesis: Parental culture (Chinese/US) will NOT significantly affect parental control.

f. Hypotheses notation. $H_1$: $\mu_{CH} - \mu_{US} \neq 0$ $H_0$: $\mu_{CH} - \mu_{US} = 0$

**Step 2: Establish significance criteria**

g. $\alpha = 0.05$

**Step 3: Calculate test statistic, effect size, confidence interval, and power**

h. $t = 2.27$ Level of significance ($p$) = .040

i. Decision: reject null

j. Effect size = $r^2$ =.27

k. 95% confidence interval difference [0.44, 15.81]

l. Power=.11

**Step 4: Draw conclusion**

m. Conclusion: Parental culture (Chinese/US) does significantly affect parental control; $t(14)$= 2.26, $p$=.04, two-tailed, $r^2$=27.

# Module 9

## *9.26V Additional Practice*

### 1. Twin Study

**Step 1: Develop Hypotheses:**

a. Independent Variable = Twin environment Scale: Categorical

b. Dependent Variable = IQ Scale: Quantitative

c. Two-tailed

d. Alternative hypothesis: Twins raised apart will have significantly different IQ.

e. Null hypothesis: Twins raised apart will NOT have significantly different IQ.

f. Hypotheses notation. $H_1$: $\mu_D \neq 0$ $H_0$: $\mu_D = 0$

**Step 2: Establish significance criteria**

g. $\alpha = 0.05$

**Step 3: Calculate test statistic, effect size, confidence interval, and power**

h. $t = -.248$ Level of significance ($p$) = .81

i. Decision: fail to reject null

j. $n$=33

**Step 4: Draw conclusion**

k. Conclusion: Twins raised apart do NOT have significantly different IQ ($M_D$= -.60, $s_D$=7.66); $t(9)$= -.248, $p$=.81, two-tailed.

### 2. Cognitive Behavioral Therapy

**Step 1: Develop Hypotheses:**

a. Independent Variable = CBT treatment Scale: Categorical

b. Dependent Variable = Self-esteem Scale: Quantitative

c. One-tailed

d. Alternative hypothesis: CBT treatment will significantly increase self-esteem among mildly depressed HS students.

e. Null hypothesis: CBT treatment will NOT significantly increase self-esteem among mildly depressed HS students.

f. Hypotheses notation. $H_1: \mu_D > 0$ $H_0: \mu_D \leq 0$

**Step 2: Establish significance criteria**

g. $\alpha = 0.05$

**Step 3: Calculate test statistic, effect size, confidence interval, and power**

h. $t = 2.76$ Level of significance ($p$) = .028

i. Decision: reject null

j. Calculate effect size = .98

k. Determine the 95% confidence interval: 95% CI Difference [.20, 2.55]

l. What is the power of this study? .794

**Step 4: Draw conclusion**

k. Conclusion: CBT treatment will significantly increase self-esteem among mildly depressed high school students ($M_D$=1.37, $s_D$=1.41); $t(7)$= 2.76, $p$=.028, one-tailed, Cohen's $d$=.98.

## *9.27 Hands-on Activity*

**Step 1: Develop Hypotheses:**

a. Independent Variable = prediction vs actual Scale: Categorical

b. Dependent Variable = Taste ability Scale: Quantitative

c. Two-tailed

d. Alternative hypothesis: One's prediction of taste accuracy will significantly differ from one's actual ability to taste the difference between Coke and Pepsi.

e. Null hypothesis: One's prediction of taste accuracy will NOT significantly differ from one's actual ability to taste the difference between Coke and Pepsi.

f. Hypotheses notation. $H_1: \mu_D \neq 0$ $H_0: \mu_D = 0$

**Step 2: Establish significance criteria**

g. $\alpha = 0.05$

Remaining answers depend upon your data.

## *9.28V In the Literature*

1. Message—Positive comparison
2. Gang—Positve
3. There is never 0% chance of error, so researchers should report $p$<.0001.
4. Perception differences in the population will range between 3.37 and 5.66 with 95% confidence.
5. Perceptions of safety differ by graffiti type.

## *9.30 Exercises*

### Reviewing the Concepts

1. $t$-test of Single Sample compares a sample mean to a population mean. $t$-test of Independent Samples compares two group means. $t$-test of Related Samples compares related (usually pre and post) scores.
2. $\mu_D$ represents the mean of differences in the population
3. No, pre and post SCORES are compared to calculate the mean of differences.

4. Trauma-related Knowledge

**Step 1: Develop Hypotheses:**

a. Independent Variable =Trauma-informed Care Training Scale: Categorical
b. Dependent Variable = Trauma-related Knowledge Scale: Quantitative
c. Two-tailed
d. Alternative hypothesis: Trauma-informed Care Training will significantly affect Trauma-related Knowledge among middle school staff.
e. Null hypothesis: Trauma-informed Care Training will NOT significantly affect Trauma-related Knowledge among middle school staff.
f. Hypotheses notation. $H_1$: $\mu_D \neq 0$ $H_0$: $\mu_D = 0$

**Step 2: Establish significance criteria**

g. $\alpha = 0.05$

**Step 3: Calculate test statistic, effect size, confidence interval, and power**

h. $t = 15.13$ Level of significance ($p$) <.0001
i. Decision: reject null
j. Cohen's $d = M_D/s_D$ = .44063/.67784 =.65
k. Determine the 95% confidence interval: 95% CI Difference [.38, 50]
l. Using the Power Table in Appendix D1, Power = .99

**Step 4: Draw conclusion**

m. Conclusion: Trauma-informed Care Training significantly affects Trauma-related Knowledge among middle school staff; $t(541)$= 15.13, $p$<.0001, two-tailed, Cohen's $d$=.65.

5. Empathic Concern

**Step 1: Develop Hypotheses:**

a. Independent Variable =Trauma-informed Care Training Scale: Categorical
b. Dependent Variable = Empathic Concern Scale: Quantitative
c. Two-tailed
d. Alternative hypothesis: Trauma-informed Care Training will significantly affect Empathic Concern among middle school staff.
e. Null hypothesis: Trauma-informed Care Training will NOT significantly affect Empathic Concern among middle school staff.
f. Hypotheses notation. $H_1$: $\mu_D = 0$ $H_0$: $\mu_D \neq 0$

**Step 2: Establish significance criteria**

g. $\alpha = 0.05$

**Step 3: Calculate test statistic, effect size, confidence interval, and power**

h. $t = 3.12$ Level of significance ($p$) =.002
i. Decision: reject null
j. Cohen's $d$ = .14
k. Determine the 95% confidence interval: 95% CI Difference [.015, 064]

**Step 4: Draw conclusion**

l. Conclusion: Trauma-informed Care Training significantly affects Empathic Concern among middle school staff; $t(529)$= 3.12, $p$=.002, two-tailed, Cohen's $d$=.13.

6a. No, the difference between each pair of scores is calculated.
6b. The three-week goal-setting treatment will NOT significantly increase Reading Series scores among 3rd grade students. Fail to reject the null.
6c. The pretreatment values are actually higher than the post treatment scores; so there was a decrease not an increase.
6d. Critical thinking/Problem solving and Language Arts are both statistically significant. Effect size or confidence interval would provide a better indication of the treatment effect on the population.
6e. No, in general a sample should be at least 30. The sample size calculator indicates that 26 would suffice.

7a. To provide the readers with a general idea of the pre and post scores.
7b. IV=30 minute educational STD session; DV1=STD knowledge; DV2=Safe sex and STD attitudes
7c. STD knowledge significantly increased; $t(131) = -13.53$, $p < .0001$.
7d. Probably not, since attitudes did not increase with knowledge.
7e. Effect size or confidence intervals.

## Conducting Analysis

### 8. Mindfulness

**Paired Samples Statistics**

| | | Mean | N | Std. Deviation | Std. Error Mean |
|---|---|---|---|---|---|
| Pair 1 | post | 99.3824 | 34 | 5.99502 | 1.02814 |
| | pre | 95.3529 | 34 | 7.34798 | 1.26017 |

**Paired Samples Test**

| | | Paired Differences | | | | | t | df | Sig. (2-tailed) |
|---|---|---|---|---|---|---|---|---|---|
| | | | | | 95% Confidence Interval of the Difference | | | | |
| | | Mean | Std. Deviation | Std. Error Mean | Lower | Upper | | | |
| Pair 1 | post - pre | 4.02941 | 4.12300 | .70709 | 2.59083 | 5.46799 | 5.699 | 33 | .000 |

**Step 1: Develop Hypotheses:**

a. Independent Variable =5 week Mindfulness Meditation — Scale: Categorical
b. Dependent Variable = Social skills — Scale: Quantitative
c. One-tailed
d. Alternative hypothesis: The 5 week Mindfulness Meditation intervention significantly increases social skills among adolescents with learning disabilities.
e. Null hypothesis: The 5 week Mindfulness Meditation intervention does NOT significantly increase social skills among adolescents with learning disabilities.
f. Hypotheses notation. $H_1: \mu_D > 0$ $H_0: \mu_D \leq 0$

**Step 2: Establish significance criteria**

g. $\alpha = 0.05$

**Step 3: Calculate test statistic, effect size, confidence interval, and power**

h. $t = 5.79$ Level of significance ($p$) <.0001
i. Decision: reject null
j. Calculate effect size = .98
k. Determine the 95% confidence interval: 95% CI Difference [2.59, 5.47]
l. What is the power of this study? 1.0

**Step 4: Draw conclusion**

m. Conclusion: The 5 week Mindfulness Meditation intervention significantly increases social skills among adolescents with learning disabilities.; $t(33)= 5.79$, $p<.0001$, one-tailed, Cohen's $d=.98$.

### 9. Grit

**Paired T hypothesis test:**

$\mu_D = \mu_1 - \mu_2$ : Mean of the difference between post and pre

$H_0 : \mu_D = 0$

$H_A : \mu_D \neq 0$

and pre

**Hypothesis test results:**

| Difference | Mean | Std. Err. | DF | T-Stat | P-value |
|---|---|---|---|---|---|
| post - pre | 0.45 | 0.065494074 | 19 | 6.8708507 | <0.0001 |

**Paired T confidence interval:**

$\mu_D = \mu_1 - \mu_2$ : Mean of the difference between post

**95% confidence interval results:**

| Difference | Mean | Std. Err. | DF | L. Limit | U. Limit |
|---|---|---|---|---|---|
| post - pre | 0.45 | 0.065494074 | 19 | 0.31291933 | 0.58708067 |

**Step 1: Develop Hypotheses:**

a. Independent Variable = 9-week Grit course — Scale: Categorical
b. Dependent Variable = Grit scale scores — Scale: Quantitative
c. One-tailed
d. Alternative hypothesis: The 9-week Grit course significantly impacts grit scores among high school students.
e. Null hypothesis: The 9-week Grit course does NOT significantly impact grit scores among high school students.
f. Hypotheses notation. $H_1$: $\mu_D = 0$  $H_0$: $\mu_D \neq 0$

**Step 2: Establish significance criteria**

g. $\alpha = 0.05$

**Step 3: Calculate test statistic, effect size, confidence interval, and power**

h. $t = 6.87$  Level of significance ($p$) <.0001
i. Decision: reject null
j. Calculate effect size = $r^2$=.713
k. Determine the 95% confidence interval: 95% CI Difference [.313, .587]
l. What is the power of this study? .86

**Step 4: Draw conclusion**

m. Conclusion: The 9-week Grit course significantly impacts grit scores among high school students; $t(19)= 6.87$, $p<.0001$, two-tailed, $r^2$=.713.

# Module 10

## *10.27V Full Example*

**Step 1: Develop Hypotheses:**

a. Independent Variable = Preferred device — Scale: Categorical
b. Dependent Variable = Technology use — Scale: Quantitative
c. Alternative hypothesis: Technology use will significantly differ by preferred device among 8th graders.
d. Null hypothesis: Technology use will NOT significantly differ by preferred device among 8th graders.
e. Hypotheses notation. $H_1$: At least $\mu$ will differ  $H_0$: $\mu_1 = \mu_2 = \mu_3 = \mu_4$

**Step 2: Establish significance criteria**

f. $\alpha = 0.05$

**Step 3: Calculate test statistic, effect size, confidence interval, and power**

g. Equal variances? Yes, Levene's test was not significant ($p$=.268)
h. $F = 5.56$  Level of significance ($p$) =.003
i. Decision: reject null
j. Calculate effect size = $\eta^2$= .29
k. Significant group differences? Smart phone and computer groups are significantly different.

**Step 4: Draw conclusion**

l. Conclusion: Technology use will significantly differ by preferred device among 8th graders; $F(3, 40)$= 5.56, $p$=.003, $\eta^2$=.29. Preferred technology device had a large effect on technology use. Tukey's HSD post hoc test revealed that the Computer group had significantly more technology use than the Smartphone group ($p$=.002).

### *10.28V Additional Practice*

**Step 1: Develop Hypotheses:**

a. Independent Variable = Age group Scale: Categorical
b. Dependent Variable = Road rage Scale: Quantitative
c. Alternative hypothesis: Road rage will significantly differ by age category among 2018 Californian drivers.
d. Null hypothesis: Road rage will NOT significantly differ by age category among 2018 Californian drivers.
e. Hypotheses notation. $H_1$: At least μ will differ $H_0$: $\mu_1 = \mu_2 = \mu_3$

**Step 2: Establish significance criteria**

f. $\alpha = 0.05$

**Step 3: Calculate test statistic, effect size, confidence interval, and power**

g. Equal variances? Yes, Levene's test was not significant ($p$=.0519)
h. $F$ = 22.52 Level of significance ($p$) <.0001
i. Decision: reject null
j. Calculate effect size = $\eta^2$= .44
k. Significant group differences? All age groups are significantly different from each other in road rage, with the youngest group (<30 years) having the highest road rage.

**Step 4: Draw conclusion**

l. Conclusion: Road rage does significantly differ by age category among 2018 Californian drivers; $F(2, 57)$= 22.52, $p$<.0001, $\eta^2$=.44. Age category has a large effect on road rage. Tukey's HSD post hoc test indicates that all age groups are significantly different from each other in road rage, with the youngest group (<30 years) having the highest road rage.

### *10.30V In the Literature*

1. a. Test anxiety level will significantly effect GPA among female college students.
   b. Test anxiety level will significantly effect GPA among male college students.
2. Females? yes
   Males? Yes
3. Females reported higher GPA than males among all test anxiety groups.
4. Females? 3%
   Males? 3.1%
5. Having low test anxiety will result in higher GPAs for both females and males.

### *10.32V Exercises*

### Reviewing the Concepts

1. Two or more.
2. Since multiple groups are being compared, several differences are being calculated. In order to determine how the treatment effect (group differences) as a whole, variance (all the differences) is the focus.
3. The F distribution is positively skewed since no treatment effect generates an $F$ of zero. As the effect increases, F can only increase in the positive direction.
4. For this assumption to be fulfilled, should the Levene's test be significant?
   Levene's Test examines equal variances and should NOT be significant in order to support the assumption.
5. Since two variances (between and within) are calculated, we need a $df$ for each variance—$df_{between}$ and $df_{within}$. $df_{between}$ represents the groups ($k$-1), while $df_{within}$ represents the individuals in the groups ($N$-$k$).
6. ANOVA only determines is a significant difference is present. Post hoc test is need to identify WHICH groups are different.
7. Between represents "between groups", whereas within represents "within groups."

8. Eta squared ($\eta^2$) is the ANOVA effect size and is comparable to $r^2$ where a small effect is <.09, a medium effect is between .09 and .25, and a large effect is <.25. We can interpret $\eta^2$ as the percent of variance in the DV explained by the IV (treatment).

## Interpreting the Results

### 9. Alcohol and Driving

**Step 1: Develop Hypotheses:**

a. Independent Variable = Alcohol amount level Scale: Categorical
b. Dependent Variable = Driving errors Scale: Quantitative
c. Alternative hypothesis: Alcohol level significantly affects the number of driving errors among adults.
d. Null hypothesis: Alcohol level will NOT significantly affect the number of driving errors among adults..
e. Hypotheses notation. $H_1$: At least $\mu$ will differ $H_0$: $\mu_1 = \mu_2 = \mu_3$

**Step 2: Establish significance criteria**

f. $\alpha = 0.01$

**Step 3: Calculate test statistic, effect size, confidence interval, and power**

g. Equal variances? Yes, Levene's test was not significant ($p$=.668)
h. $F$ = 7.40 Level of significance ($p$) = .002
i. Decision: reject null
j. Calculate effect size = $\eta^2$= .31
k. Significant group differences? The high alcohol group has significantly more errors than the control group ($p$=.002)

**Step 4: Draw conclusion**

l. Conclusion: Alcohol level significantly affects the number of driving errors among adults--$F(2,33)$= 7.40, $p$=.002, $\eta^2$=.31. ($p$=.002)—representing a large effect on driving ability. The high alcohol group had significantly more errors than the control group ($p$=.002).

### 10. Social Media Use

**Step 1: Develop Hypotheses:**

a. Independent Variable = Age group Scale: Categorical
b. Dependent Variable = Daily social media use (minutes) Scale: Quantitative
c. Alternative hypothesis: Daily amount of social media use differs by age group.
d. Null hypothesis: Daily amount of social media use will NOT differ by age group.
e. Hypotheses notation. $H_1$: At least $\mu$ will differ $H_0$: $\mu_1 = \mu_2 = \mu_3 = \mu_4 = \mu_5$

**Step 2: Establish significance criteria**

f. $\alpha = 0.05$

**Step 3: Calculate test statistic, effect size, confidence interval, and power**

g. Equal variances? No, Levene's test is significant ($p$<.0001). Tamhane's T2 was used to address this violation
h. $F$ = 49.52 Level of significance ($p$) <.0001
i. Decision: reject null
j. Calculate effect size = $\eta^2$= .039
k. Significant group differences? The two youngest groups are significantly different from the three older groups.

**Step 4: Draw conclusion**

l. Conclusion: Daily amount of social media use differs by age group; $F(4,4828)$= 49.52, $p$=.002, $\eta^2$=.039. ($p$<.0001). However, age only accounts for 3.9% of the variance in amount of social media use, which is a small effect. The two youngest groups (<18 and 19-24 years) reported significantly higher social media use than the three older groups (25-29, 30-39, and 40+ years).

### 11. Marijuana Use

a. $df_{between} = k\text{-}1 = 3\text{-}1 = 2$. $df_{within} = N\text{-}k = 310 - 3 = 307$. (2, 307)

b. M day (past 90) of cocaine use. Although severe MRJ users are using cocaine more than the other users, it is not significant.

c. Yes ($p<.0001$). All pairs are significantly different, with the daily use increasing with severity of use.

d. The severe group.

### 12. F2F, Blended, Online Learning Environments

a. Learning environment (F2F, blended, online)

b. IACE test score and final course grade

c. Highest--online group. Lowest—F2F.

d. Final course grade, $F(2, 131) = 3.37$, $p=.038$.

e. The online group scored significantly higher than the F2F group.

f. Effect size should be reported.

g. Students in the online environment performed just as well or better than F2F or blended students.

## Conducting the Analysis

### 13. Summer Slide

**Analysis of Variance results:**
Responses: reading
Factors: group

**Response statistics by factor**

| group | n | Mean | Std. Dev. | Std. Error |
|---|---|---|---|---|
| 1 | 15 | 3.7333333 | 3.3051187 | 0.85337798 |
| 2 | 15 | 2.3333333 | 2.1930627 | 0.56624634 |
| 3 | 15 | -1.8666667 | 3.204164 | 0.82731158 |

**ANOVA table**

| Source | DF | SS | MS | F-Stat | P-value |
|---|---|---|---|---|---|
| group | 2 | 254.8 | 127.4 | 14.7 | <0.0001 |
| Error | 42 | 364 | 8.6666667 | | |
| Total | 44 | 618.8 | | | |

**Levene's Test for Homogeneity of Variance**

| Test Statistic | DF 1 | DF 2 | P-value |
|---|---|---|---|
| 2.5049959 | 2 | 42 | 0.0938 |

**Tukey HSD results (95% level)**

1 subtracted from

| | Difference | Lower | Upper | P-value |
|---|---|---|---|---|
| 2 | -1.4 | -4.0116273 | 1.2116273 | 0.4018 |
| 3 | -5.6 | -8.2116273 | -2.9883727 | <0.0001 |

2 subtracted from

| | Difference | Lower | Upper | P-value |
|---|---|---|---|---|
| 3 | -4.2 | -6.8116273 | -1.5883727 | 0.001 |

**Step 1: Develop Hypotheses:**

a. Independent Variable = summer program  Scale: Categorical

b. Dependent Variable = Reading growth  Scale: Quantitative

c. Alternative hypothesis: Summer programming significantly affects reading growth among 2nd grade students.

d. Null hypothesis: Summer programming does NOT significantly affect reading growth among 2nd grade students.

e. Hypotheses notation. $H_1$: At least $\mu$ will differ  $H_0: \mu_1 = \mu_2 = \mu_3$

**Step 2: Establish significance criteria**

f. $\alpha = 0.05$

**Step 3: Calculate test statistic, effect size, confidence interval, and power**

g. Equal variances? Yes, Levene's test was not significant ($p=.0938$)

h. $F = 14.70$  Level of significance ($p$) $<.0001$

i. Decision: reject null

j. Calculate effect size = $\eta^2 = .41$

k. Significant group differences? The control group had significantly lower reading growth than both summer program groups.

**Step 4: Draw conclusion**

l. Conclusion: Summer programming significantly affects reading growth among 2nd grade students; $F(2,42) = 14.70$, $p<.0001$, $\eta^2=.41$. Summer programming had a large effect on reading growth, as both groups with program reported significant growth, whereas the control group with no programming actually lost ground in reading achievement. Use $\alpha=.05$.

### 14. Binge-watching

**Descriptives**

binge

| | N | Mean | Std. Deviation | Std. Error | 95% Confidence Interval for Mean Lower Bound | 95% Confidence Interval for Mean Upper Bound | Minimum | Maximum |
|---|---|---|---|---|---|---|---|---|
| 1.00 | 10 | 3.6400 | 1.69784 | .53690 | 2.4254 | 4.8546 | 1.20 | 6.80 |
| 2.00 | 10 | 1.3600 | .84485 | .26717 | .7556 | 1.9644 | .00 | 2.30 |
| 3.00 | 10 | 2.9400 | .81677 | .25828 | 2.3557 | 3.5243 | 1.80 | 4.40 |
| Total | 30 | 2.6467 | 1.50464 | .27471 | 2.0848 | 3.2085 | .00 | 6.80 |

**Test of Homogeneity of Variances**

binge

| Levene Statistic | df1 | df2 | Sig. |
|---|---|---|---|
| 2.360 | 2 | 27 | .114 |

**ANOVA**

binge

| | Sum of Squares | df | Mean Square | F | Sig. |
|---|---|---|---|---|---|
| Between Groups | 27.283 | 2 | 13.641 | 9.599 | .001 |
| Within Groups | 38.372 | 27 | 1.421 | | |
| Total | 65.655 | 29 | | | |

**Multiple Comparisons**

Dependent Variable: binge
Scheffe

| (I) relationship | (J) relationship | Mean Difference (I-J) | Std. Error | Sig. | 95% Confidence Interval Lower Bound | 95% Confidence Interval Upper Bound |
|---|---|---|---|---|---|---|
| 1.00 | 2.00 | 2.28000* | .53314 | .001 | .8992 | 3.6608 |
| | 3.00 | .70000 | .53314 | .434 | -.6808 | 2.0808 |
| 2.00 | 1.00 | -2.28000* | .53314 | .001 | -3.6608 | -.8992 |
| | 3.00 | -1.58000* | .53314 | .022 | -2.9608 | -.1992 |
| 3.00 | 1.00 | -.70000 | .53314 | .434 | -2.0808 | .6808 |
| | 2.00 | 1.58000* | .53314 | .022 | .1992 | 2.9608 |

*. The mean difference is significant at the 0.05 level.

**Step 1: Develop Hypotheses:**

a. Independent Variable = Relationship status Scale: Categorical
b. Dependent Variable = Binge-watching frequency Scale: Quantitative
c. Alternative hypothesis: Freq. of binge-watching differs by relationship status among adults (25-40 yrs).
d. Null hypothesis: Freq. of binge-watching will NOT differ by relationship status among adults (25-40 yrs).
e. Hypotheses notation. $H_1$: At least μ will differ $H_0: \mu_1 = \mu_2 = \mu_3$

**Step 2: Establish significance criteria**

f. α = 0.05

**Step 3: Calculate test statistic, effect size, confidence interval, and power**

g. Equal variances? Yes, Levene's test is not significant ($p$=.114).
h. $F$ = 9.60 Level of significance ($p$) = .001
i. Decision: reject null
j. Calculate effect size = $\eta^2$= .42
k. Group differences? Group 2 (casually dating) had sig. lower freq. in binge-watching than the other two groups.

**Step 4: Draw conclusion**

l. Conclusion: Frequency of binge-watching differs by relationship status among adults (25-40 years).; $F(2, 27)$= 9.60, $p$=.001, $\eta^2$=.42. Relationship status is a large effect on binge-watching. Group 2 (casually dating) had significantly lower frequency in binge-watching than the other two groups.

# Module 11

## *11.27V Additional Practice*

**Step 1: Develop Hypotheses:**

a. Independent Variable = SAT Scale: Quantitative
b. Dependent Variable = College Freshman GPA Scale: Quantitative
c. Alternative hypothesis: SAT is a significant predictor of college freshman GPA.
d. Null hypothesis: SAT is a NOT significant predictor of college freshman GPA.
e. Hypothesis notation. $H_1: B \neq 0$ $H_0: B = 0$

**Step 2: Establish significance criteria**

f. α = .05

**Step 3: Calculate test statistic, $R^2$, and regression equation**

g. $F$ = 12.88 Level of significance ($p$) = .0011
h. Decision: reject null
i. $R^2$ = .28
j. Regression Equation: Y = .0042X + .123
k. If $X$=507, $Y$=2.25

**Step 4: Draw conclusion**

l. Conclusion: SAT is a significant predictor of college freshman GPA; *F*(1, 33)=12.87, *p*=.0011. SAT accounts for 28.1% of the variance in college freshman GPA with a regression equation of Y = .0042X + .123.

### *11.29V In the Literature*

1. Insecticide Treated Nets (ITNs) will significantly predict malaria morbidity in the Zambia Lusaka Province.
2. Write the hypotheses notation. $H_1$: $B \neq 0$ $H_0$: $B = 0$
3. Reject the null.
4. Y = 1.064X + 25.82
5. Insecticide Treated Nets (ITNs) significantly predict malaria morbidity in the Zambia Lusaka Province; *t*=3.45, *p*=.003. This relationship generated a regression equation of Y = 1.064X + 25.82.

### *11.31 Exercises*

### Reviewing the Concepts

1. Causality manipulates groups to show that a treatment has caused a change in the dependent variable. Correlation examines the mutual relationship between two quantitative variables. We are examining how *Y* changes as *X* changes.
2. Correlation examines the relationship between two quantitative variables. Regression examines the ability of one quantitative variable to predict another quantitative variable.
3. A scatterplot must be reviewed to ensure a linear relationship.
4. A line requires two data points.
5. The correlation coefficient is *r* and represents the direction and degree of the relationship. The coefficient of determination is *r* squared ($r^2$) and represents the amount of variance in *Y* explained by *X*. $r^2$ can be used as an effect size.
6. Hypothesis notation for correlation uses rho ($\rho$), where as the hypothesis notation for regression focuses on the slope (B)?
7. *Y*=6.5
8. What test statistic represents the significance of the regression model? ANOVA represents the significance of the regression model; however for simple regression, t-test results may also be used to represent the significance of the single predictor.
9. *r* = .867
10. Weakest to strongest: -.24, .55, -.78, .85
11. Weakest to strongest: sourdough, Italian, baguette, bread stick

### Interpreting Results

**12. HS GPA**

**Step 1: Develop Hypotheses:**

a. Independent Variable = HS GPA Scale: Quantitative
b. Dependent Variable = College Freshman GPA Scale: Quantitative
c. Alternative hypothesis: HS GPA is a significant predictor of college freshman GPA.
d. Null hypothesis: HS GPA is a NOT significant predictor of college freshman GPA.
e. Hypothesis notation. $H_1$: $B \neq 0$ $H_0$: $B = 0$

**Step 2: Establish significance criteria**

f. $\alpha$ = .05

**Step 3: Calculate test statistic, $R^2$, and regression equation**

g. *F* = 24.46 Level of significance (*p*) <.0001
h. Decision: reject null
i. $R^2$ = .338

j. Regression Equation: $Y = .635X + .966$
k. If $X$=3.10, $Y$=2.93

**Step 4: Draw conclusion**

l. Conclusion: HS GPA ($M$=3.01, $SD$=.46) is a significant predictor of college freshman GPA ($M$=2.88, $SD$=.51); $F(1, 48)=24.46$, $p<.0001$. HS GPA accounts for 33.8% of the variance in college freshman GPA with a regression equation of $Y = .635X + .966$.

### 13. Relationship Quality and Happiness

**Step 1: Develop Hypotheses:**

a. Independent Variable = Relationship quality  Scale: Quantitative
b. Dependent Variable = Happiness  Scale: Quantitative
c. Alternative hypothesis: Relationship quality is a significant predictor of happiness among US adults.
d. Null hypothesis: Relationship quality is NOT a significant predictor of happiness among US adults.
e. Hypothesis notation.  $H_1: B \neq 0$  $H_0: B = 0$

**Step 2: Establish significance criteria**

f. $\alpha = .05$

**Step 3: Calculate test statistic, $R^2$, and regression equation**

g. $F = 57.06$  Level of significance ($p$) <.0001
h. Decision: reject null
i. $R^2 = .37$
j. Regression Equation: $Y = .98X + .3.24$
k. If $X$=3.8, $Y$=6.96

**Step 4: Draw conclusion**

l. Conclusion: Relationship quality is a significant predictor of happiness among US adults; $F(1, 98)=57.06$, $p<.0001$. Relationship quality accounts for 37% of the variance in happiness with a regression equation of $Y = .98X + .3.24$.

### 14. Shopping Orientation and Mindset

a. Hypotheses were directional.
b. Since the sample size is 96, $df$=96-2=94.
c. Reject the null; positive; $r$=.43, which is medium strength.
d. Reject the null; negative; $r$= -.52, which is large strength.

### 15. Teacher Comfort with Technology

a. Pre Teacher Comfort? Pre Teacher Tech Use; Post Teacher Comfort? Post Teacher Tech Use; Teacher Comfort Growth? Teacher Tech Use Growth
b. $r$ = -.286, it is not significant. The relationship is negative, which means that as Pre Teacher Comfort increased, Teacher Tech Use Growth decreased.
c. Teacher Comfort Post had the strongest relationship with both. Both correlations were significant. As Teacher Comfort Post increased, Facilitation of Student Use Post and Growth significantly increased.

## Conducting the Analysis

### 16. Loneliness and Depression

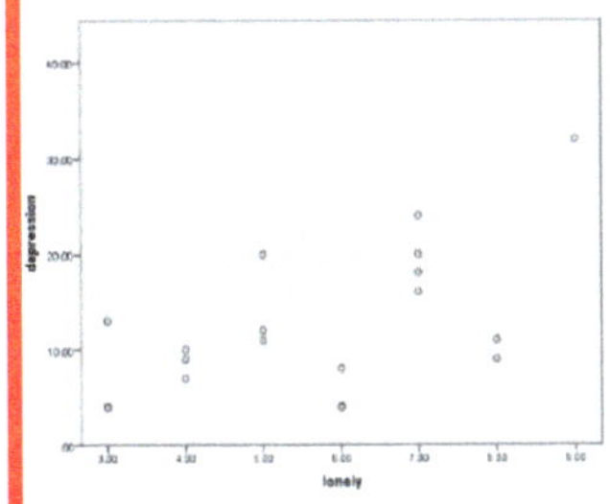

**Descriptive Statistics**

| | Mean | Std. Deviation | N |
|---|---|---|---|
| depression | 12.4000 | 7.40839 | 20 |
| lonely | 5.6000 | 1.78885 | 20 |

**Coefficients[a]**

| Model | | Unstandardized Coefficients B | Unstandardized Coefficients Std. Error | Standardized Coefficients Beta | t | Sig. |
|---|---|---|---|---|---|---|
| 1 | (Constant) | -.789 | 4.709 | | -.168 | .869 |
| | lonely | 2.355 | .803 | .569 | 2.933 | .009 |

a. Dependent Variable: depression

**Model Summary**

| Model | R | R Square | Adjusted R Square | Std. Error of the Estimate |
|---|---|---|---|---|
| 1 | .569[a] | .323 | .286 | 6.26066 |

a. Predictors: (Constant), lonely

**ANOVA[a]**

| Model | | Sum of Squares | df | Mean Square | F | Sig. |
|---|---|---|---|---|---|---|
| 1 | Regression | 337.274 | 1 | 337.274 | 8.605 | .009[b] |
| | Residual | 705.526 | 18 | 39.196 | | |
| | Total | 1042.800 | 19 | | | |

a. Dependent Variable: depression
b. Predictors: (Constant), lonely

**Step 1: Develop Hypotheses:**

a. Independent Variable = Loneliness Scale: Quantitative
b. Dependent Variable = Depression Scale: Quantitative
c. Alternative hypothesis: Loneliness will significantly predict depression among college students.
d. Null hypothesis: Loneliness will NOT significantly predict depression among college students.
e. Hypothesis notation. $H_1$: $B \neq 0$ $H_0$: $B = 0$

**Step 2: Establish significance criteria**

f. $\alpha = .05$

**Step 3: Calculate test statistic, $R^2$, and regression equation**

g. $F = 8.61$ Level of significance ($p$) =.009
h. Decision: reject null
i. $R^2 = .323$
j. Regression Equation: $Y = 2.36X - .789$
k. If $X$=7.5, $Y$=16.91

**Step 4: Draw conclusion**

l. Conclusion: Loneliness will significantly predict depression among college students; $F(1, 8)=8.61$, $p$=.009 Loneliness accounts for 32.3% of the variance in depression with a regression equation of $Y = 2.36X - .789$.

### 17. Testosterone and Sexual Harassment

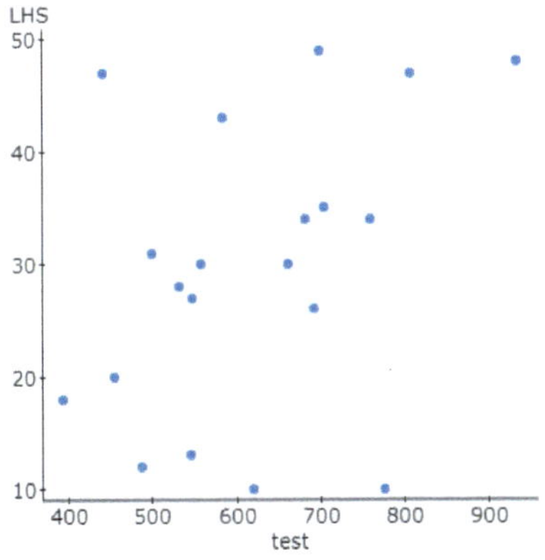


**Simple linear regression results:**

Dependent Variable: LHS
Independent Variable: test
LHS = 7.8125559 + 0.035223416 test
Sample size: 20
R (correlation coefficient) = 0.37791067
R-sq = 0.14281648
Estimate of error standard deviation: 12.291984

**Parameter estimates:**

| Parameter | Estimate | Std. Err. | Alternative | DF | T-Stat | P-value |
|---|---|---|---|---|---|---|
| Intercept | 7.8125559 | 12.877815 | ≠ 0 | 18 | 0.60666782 | 0.5516 |
| Slope | 0.035223416 | 0.020339626 | ≠ 0 | 18 | 1.7317632 | 0.1004 |

**Analysis of variance table for regression model:**

| Source | DF | SS | MS | F-stat | P-value |
|---|---|---|---|---|---|
| Model | 1 | 453.12812 | 453.12812 | 2.9990037 | 0.1004 |
| Error | 18 | 2719.6719 | 151.09288 | | |
| Total | 19 | 3172.8 | | | |

**Step 1: Develop Hypotheses:**

a. Independent Variable = Testosterone Scale: Quantitative
b. Dependent Variable = Likelihood to sexually harass Scale: Quantitative
c. Alternative hypothesis: Testosterone levels significantly predicts male likelihood to sexually harass women among male college students.
d. Null hypothesis: Testosterone levels does NOT significantly predict male likelihood to sexually harass women among male college students.
e. Hypothesis notation. $H_1: B \neq 0$ $H_0: B = 0$

**Step 2: Establish significance criteria**

f. $\alpha = .05$

**Step 3: Calculate test statistic, $R^2$, and regression equation**

g. $F = 3.00$ Level of significance ($p$) =.1004
h. Decision: fail to reject null
i. $R^2 = .143$
j. Regression Equation: $Y = .0352X + 7.81$

**Step 4: Draw conclusion**

k. Conclusion: Testosterone levels does NOT significantly predict male likelihood to sexually harass women among male college students; $F(1, 18)=3.00$, $p=.1004$. Testosterone only accounts for 14.3% of the variance in likelihood to sexually harass.

# Module 12

## 12.26 Full Example: Goodness of Fit

**Step 1: Develop Hypotheses:**

a. Independent Variable = SD vs USA, Categorical
b. Dependent Variable = levels of happiness, Categorical
c. Alternative hypothesis: The state of South Dakota will have significantly different happiness proportions than the USA.
d. Null hypothesis: The state of South Dakota will NOT have significantly different happiness proportions than the USA.
e. Write null hypotheses notation. $H_0$

| | Happy | Neutral | Unhappy | Don't Know |
|---|---|---|---|---|
| SD expected $f$ | 640 | 200 | 140 | 20 |

**Step 2: Establish significance criteria**

f. $\alpha = .05$

**Step 3: Calculate test statistic and effect size.**

g. $\chi^2 = 25.36$, $p < .0001$
i. Decision: reject null
j. Phi coefficient = .159

**Step 4: Draw conclusion**

k. The state of South Dakota will have significantly different happiness proportions than the USA; $\chi^2(3, n=1{,}000)=25.36$, p<.0001, $\phi = .159$.

## Full Example: Test of Independence

**Step 1: Develop Hypotheses:**

a. Independent Variable = gender, Categorical
b. Dependent Variable = ice cream flavor preference, Categorical
c. Alternative hypothesis: Ice cream preference (plain vs fancy flavor) will differ by gender among college students.
d. Null hypothesis: Ice cream preference (plain vs fancy flavor) will NOT differ by gender among college students.

**Step 2: Establish significance criteria**

e. $\alpha$ = .05

**Step 3: Calculate test statistic and effect size.**

f. $\chi^2$ = 42.81, $p$<.0001

g. Decision: reject null

h. Cramer's V=.65

**Step 4: Draw conclusion**

i. Ice cream preference (plain vs fancy flavor) will differ by gender among college students; $\chi^2$(1, $n$=1,00)=42.81, p<.0001, Cramer's V = .65.

## 12.27 Hands-on Activity

3. a. Alternative hypothesis: My sample M&M's will significantly differ from official proportions of color.
   b. Null hypothesis: My sample M&M's will significantly NOT differ from official proportions of color.
   d. $\alpha$ = .05

   Remaining answers differ by individual sample

## 12.28 In the Literature

1. H1: Regain good standing (get off probation)
   H2: Persist into 2nd, 3rd, and 4th years
   H3: Graduate within 5 years of matriculation
2. Getting off probation; effect size is .42. Getting off probation is achieved much faster than persistence to another year or graduation.
3. Phi coefficient since each analysis was a 2 x 2 (two categories for each variable).
4. $p$<.001

## 12.31 Exercises

1. Parametric tests typically have a quantitative variable so it may fulfill several assumptions about the population (normality and equal variances). The hypothesis is about the population parameters. Non-parametric tests are used when the quantitative dependent variable cannot fulfill the necessary assumptions for parametric test of the DV is categorical.
2. Chi-Square analyzes **frequencies.**
3. Chi-square has a DV variable that is categorical and therefore cannot be normally distributed.
4. Chi-Square Goodness of Fit compares the observed frequencies in a sample to the expected/predicted frequencies in the population. Chi-Square Test of Independence examines the relationship between two categorical variables.
5. **Chi-Square Goodness of Fit:** the number of categories ($C$) in the variable minus one ($df = C$ -1).
   **Chi-Square Test of Independence:** the number of rows ($R$) minus 1 ($R$-1) multiplied by the number of columns ($C$) minus 1 ($C$-1), which generates the equation of: $df = (R\text{-}1)(C\text{-}1)$.
6. Cramer's V must be used when the number of categories of at least of one the variables exceeds two.

### Interpreting the Results

#### 7. Chi-square Goodness of Fit: Birth rates by season

a. Independent Variable = birth rates for Dade County vs US, Categorical

b. Dependent Variable = season, Categorical

c. Alternative hypothesis: Dade County's birth rates will significantly differ from the US seasonal proportions.

d. Null hypothesis: Dade County's birth rates will NOT significantly differ from the US seasonal proportions.

e. Write null hypotheses notation. *$H_0$:*

| | Winter | Spring | Summer | Fall |
|---|---|---|---|---|
| Dade expected *f* | 7,472 | 7,790 | 8,426 | 8,108 |

**Step 2: Establish significance criteria**

f. $\alpha = .05$

**Step 3: Calculate test statistic and effect size.**

g. $\chi^2$ =165.33, *p* <.0001

i. Decision: reject null

j. Phi coefficient = 07.

**Step 4: Draw conclusion**

k. Dade County's birth rates significantly differ from the US seasonal proportions; $\chi^2$(3, *n*= 31,797)=165.33, *p*<.0001, Phi coefficient = 07

### 8. Chi-square Test of Independence: Criterion for Scholarship

**Step 1: Develop Hypotheses:**

a. Independent Variable = Scholarship criterion met, Categorical

b. Dependent Variable = Scholarship retention, Categorical

c. Alternative hypothesis: Scholarship criterion met and scholarship retention are significantly related among junior college freshmen.

d. Null hypothesis: Scholarship criterion met and scholarship retention are significantly related among junior college freshmen.

**Step 2: Establish significance criteria**

e. $\alpha = .05$

**Step 3: Calculate test statistic and effect size.**

f. $\chi^2$ =17.70 , *p*<.0001

g. Decision: reject null

h. Cramer's V=.23

**Step 4: Draw conclusion**

i. Scholarship criterion met and scholarship retention are significantly related among junior college freshmen.; $\chi^2$(2, *n*=327)=17.70, p<.0001, Cramer's V = 23. Students who qualified with both GPA and HighMath were more likely to retain their scholarship.

### 9. Alcohol as Gateway

a. Write the alternative hypothesis for cigarettes. Alcohol use and cigarette use are significantly related among 12th grade students.

b. Yes. Alcohol use and cigarette use are significantly related among 12th grade students; $\chi^2$(1, *n*=327)=2,221.9, *p*<.001, Phi = .439.

c. Marijuana; $\chi^2$(1, *n*=327)=2,221.9, *p*<.001.

d. Marijuana. Effect size of .452 is large.

## Conducting Analysis

### 10. Chi-Square Goodness of Fit: Myopia

**Test Statistics**

| | myopia |
|---|---|
| Chi-Square | 64.142[a] |
| df | 1 |
| Asymp. Sig. | .000 |

**Step 1: Develop Hypotheses:**

a. Independent Variable = 2004 vs 2018, Categorical

b. Dependent Variable = having myopia, Categorical

c. Alternative hypothesis: 2018 rates of having myopia will significantly differ from 2004.

d. Null hypothesis: 2018 rates of having myopia will NOT significantly differ from 2004.

e. Write null hypotheses notation. *$H_0$*

| | Myopic | |
|---|---|---|
| | **yes** | **no** |
| 2018 expected *f* | 575 | 425 |

**Step 2: Establish significance criteria**

f. $\alpha = .05$

**Step 3: Calculate test statistic and effect size.**

g. $\chi^2 = 64.14$, $p < .0001$

i. Decision: reject null

j. Phi coefficient = 07.

**Step 4: Draw conclusion**

k. 2018 rates of having myopia will significantly differ from 2004; $\chi^2(1, n = 1{,}000) = 64.14$, $p < .0001$, $\phi = 07$

## 11. Chi-Square Test of Independence: Personality & Heart

**heartdisease * personality Crosstabulation**

| | | | personality | | |
|---|---|---|---|---|---|
| | | | Type A | Type B | Total |
| heartdisease | yes | Count | 110 | 29 | 139 |
| | | Expected Count | 82.8 | 56.2 | 139.0 |
| | no | Count | 39 | 72 | 111 |
| | | Expected Count | 66.2 | 44.8 | 111.0 |
| Total | | Count | 149 | 101 | 250 |
| | | Expected Count | 149.0 | 101.0 | 250.0 |

**Chi-Square Tests**

| | Value | df | Asymptotic Significance (2-sided) |
|---|---|---|---|
| Pearson Chi-Square | 49.626[a] | 1 | .000 |
| Continuity Correction[b] | 47.815 | 1 | .000 |
| Likelihood Ratio | 51.007 | 1 | .000 |
| Fisher's Exact Test | | | |
| Linear-by-Linear Association | 49.427 | 1 | .000 |
| N of Valid Cases | 250 | | |

a. 0 cells (0.0%) have expected count less than 5. The minimum exp

b. Computed only for a 2x2 table

**Symmetric Measures**

| | | Value | Approximate Significance |
|---|---|---|---|
| Nominal by Nominal | Phi | .446 | .000 |
| | Cramer's V | .446 | .000 |
| N of Valid Cases | | 250 | |

**Step 1: Develop Hypotheses:**

a. Independent Variable = Personality type, Categorical

b. Dependent Variable = Heart disease, Categorical

c. Alternative hypothesis: Personality type and the presence of heart disease are significantly related among adults (40 -60 years old).

d. Null hypothesis: Personality type and the presence of heart disease are NOT significantly related among adults (40 -60 years old).

**Step 2: Establish significance criteria**

e. $\alpha = .05$

**Step 3: Calculate test statistic and effect size.**

f. $\chi^2 = 49.63$, $p < .0001$

g. Decision: reject null

h. phi =.446

**Step 4: Draw conclusion**

i. Personality type and the presence of heart disease are significantly related among adults (40 - 60 years old); $\chi^2(1, n = 250) = 49.63$, $p < .0001$, $\phi = .446$. Those with Type A personality are more likely to have heart disease.

# Module 13

## 13.14 Additional Practice

1. a) IV = SES, categorical; b) DV = kindergarten reading preparedness, quant; c) Test = ANOVA, 3 groups
2. a) IV = GRE, quant; b) DV = first semester GPA of grad school; c) Test = regression
3 a) IV = positive thinking workshop, categorical; b) DV = self-esteem, quant; c) Test = *t*-test of related samples
4. a) IV = hand preference, categorical; b) DV = learning style type, categorical; c) Test = Chi-Square test of independence
5. a) IV = foot size, quant; b) DV = IQ, quant; c) Test = Pearson correlation
6. a) IV = gender, categorical; b) DV = number of driving violations, quant; c) Test = *t*-test of independent samples
7. a) IV = New Mexico vs US norm, categorical; b) DV = Amount of daylight, quant; c) Test = *t*-test of single samples

## 13.14 Exercises

1. The *p*-value represents the probability of finding significance due to error.
2. Inferential results do not indicate the size or magnitude of the effect.
3. $r^2$, $\eta^2$, Phi $\phi$
4. Cohen's *d* represents the mean differences (or mean difference) divided by a form of standard deviation. For single sample, *d* is the difference between the sample and pop means divided by the sample SD. For Independent samples, *d* is the difference between the two group means divided by pooled variance. For related samples, the mean of differences is divided by the *SD* of differences.
5. a) IV = political affiliation, categorical; b) DV = ethical behavior, quant; c) Test = ANOVA, 3 groups
6. a) IV = service-learning, categorical; b) DV = retention, categorical; c) Test = Chi-square test of independence
7. a) IV = yoga participation, categorical; b) DV = flexibility, quant; c) Test = *t* test of related samples
8. a) IV = lung capacity, quant; b) Test = *t* test of related samples; c) Test = regression (predict)